CHARLES BROCKDEN BROWN

THE OXFORD HANDBOOK OF

CHARLES BROCKDEN BROWN

Edited by

PHILIP BARNARD, HILARY EMMETT,

and

STEPHEN SHAPIRO

OXFORD

UNIVERSITY PRESS

OXFORD
UNIVERSITY PRESS

Oxford University Press is a department of the University of Oxford. It furthers
the University's objective of excellence in research, scholarship, and education
by publishing worldwide. Oxford is a registered trade mark of Oxford University
Press in the UK and certain other countries.

Published in the United States of America by Oxford University Press
198 Madison Avenue, New York, NY 10016, United States of America.

Library of Congress Cataloging-in-Publication Data
Names: Barnard, Philip, 1951– editor. | Emmett, Hilary, editor. |
Shapiro, Stephen, 1964– editor.
Title: The Oxford handbook of Charles Brockden Brown / edited by
Philip Barnard, Hilary Emmett, and Stephen Shapiro.
Description: New York, NY : Oxford University Press, [2019] | Includes
bibliographical references and index.
Identifiers: LCCN 2018036742| ISBN 9780199860067 (hardback) |
ISBN 9780190942267 (ebook) | ISBN 9780199983278 (online component)
Subjects: LCSH: Brown, Charles Brockden, 1771–1810—Criticism and interpretation.
Classification: LCC PS1137 .O94 2019 | DDC 813/.2—dc23 LC record
available at https://lccn.loc.gov/2018036742

1 3 5 7 9 8 6 4 2
Printed by Sheridan Books, Inc., United States of America

Acknowledgments

As editors of a long-delayed collection, we owe our thanks first and most emphatically to this volume's many contributors, who have stuck by the project over its lifetime and have helped us bring it to completion through thick and thin. In a large sense, this collection is the work of the entire Brown studies community, which in addition to the contributors listed here, and in overlapping fashion, includes the Charles Brockden Brown Society, the volume editors of the ongoing Bucknell University Press *Collected Writings of Charles Brockden Brown*, and colleagues past and present who have shaped the collective project of advancing commentary on this key author of the Revolutionary period.

We are likewise grateful for support from the English Department at the University of Kansas and the School of Art, Media, and American Studies at the University of East Anglia. Hilary Emmett received initial support from the Menzies Centre for Australian Studies at King's College, London. She thanks also, with love, David, Charlie, Leo, and Clancy. Personal thanks and Woldwinite relations of reason and desire link Philip to Cheryl Lester and Julia Barnard, and Stephen to Anne Schwan. Finally, the editors and staff, past and present, at Oxford University Press have been generous with their help and attention to the preparation and design of the volume.

CONTENTS

PART III. THE HISTORY-FICTION NEXUS

PART IV. WRITINGS IN OTHER GENRES

PART V. POLITICS AND THE WORLD-SYSTEM

ABBREVIATIONS

Note: Since variable, non-standardized spellings were acceptable during Brown's literary career, we have not generally used "[sic]" to mark such spellings in citations from Brown's prose. However, we have used it to indicate accurate transcriptions in certain instances, e.g., the title of Brown's pamphlet *Monroe's Embassy*, and in citations from the prose of others.

Novels and Related Works by Brown

AL   *Alcuin*
          Brown, Charles Brockden. *Alcuin; A Dialogue with Memoirs of Stephen Calvert*. Vol. 6 of *The Novels and Related Works of Charles Brockden Brown*. Sydney J. Krause and S. W. Reid, eds. Kent, Ohio: Kent State University Press, 1987.

AM   *Arthur Mervyn*
          Brown, Charles Brockden. *Arthur Mervyn; or, Memoirs of the Year 1793, First and Second Parts*. Vol. 3 of *The Novels and Related Works of Charles Brockden Brown*. Sydney J. Krause and S. W. Reid, eds. Kent, Ohio: Kent State University Press, 1980.

CH   *Clara Howard*
          Brown, Charles Brockden. *Clara Howard; in a Series of Letters with Jane Talbot, a Novel*. Vol. 5 of *The Novels and Related Works of Charles Brockden Brown*. Sydney J. Krause and S. W. Reid, eds. Kent, Ohio: Kent State University Press, 1986.

EH   *Edgar Huntly*
          Brown, Charles Brockden. *Edgar Huntly; or, Memoirs of a Sleep-Walker*. Vol. 4 of *The Novels and Related Works of Charles Brockden Brown*. Sydney J. Krause and S. W. Reid, eds. Kent, Ohio: Kent State University Press, 1984.

JT   *Jane Talbot*
          Brown, Charles Brockden. *Clara Howard; In a Series of Letters with Jane Talbot, A Novel*. Vol. 5 of *The Novels and Related Works of Charles Brockden Brown*. Sydney J. Krause and S. W. Reid, eds. Kent, Ohio: Kent State University Press, 1986.

MC   *Memoirs of Carwin*
                    Brown, Charles Brockden. *Wieland; or, The Transformation, an American Tale, with Memoirs of Carwin the Biloquist.* Vol. 1 of *The Novels and Related Works of Charles Brockden Brown.* Sydney J. Krause and S. W. Reid, eds. Kent, Ohio: Kent State University Press, 1977.

O   *Ormond*
                    Brown, Charles Brockden. *Ormond; or, The Secret Witness.* Vol. 2 of *The Novels and Related Works of Charles Brockden Brown.* Sydney J. Krause and S. W. Reid, eds. Kent, Ohio: Kent State University Press, 1982.

SC   *Stephen Calvert*
                    Brown, Charles Brockden. *Alcuin; A Dialogue with Memoirs of Stephen Calvert.* Vol. 6 of *The Novels and Related Works of Charles Brockden Brown.* Sydney J. Krause and S. W. Reid, eds. Kent, Ohio: Kent State University Press, 1987.

W   *Wieland*
                    Brown, Charles Brockden. *Wieland; or, The Transformation, an American Tale with Memoirs of Carwin the Biloquist.* Vol. 1 of *The Novels and Related Works of Charles Brockden Brown.* Sydney J. Krause and S. W. Reid, eds. Kent, Ohio: Kent State University Press, 1977.

Letters by Brown

Letters   *Letters and Early Epistolary Writings*
                    Brown, Charles Brockden. *Letters and Early Epistolary Writings.* Vol. 1 of *Collected Writings of Charles Brockden Brown.* Philip Barnard, Elizabeth Hewitt, and Mark Kamrath, eds. Lewisburg, Pa.: Bucknell University Press, 2013.

Pamphlets by Brown

AC   *Address to the Congress*
                    Brown, Charles Brockden. *An Address to the Congress of the United States, on the Utility and Justice of Restrictions upon Foreign Commerce, etc.* Philadelphia: C. & A. Conrad, 1809.

AG   *Address to the Government*
                    Brown, Charles Brockden. *An Address to the Government of the United States, on the Cession of Louisiana to the French, etc.* Philadelphia: John Conrad, 1803.

ME   *Monroe's Embassy*
                    Brown, Charles Brockden. *Monroe's Embassy, or, The Conduct of the Government, in Relation to Our Claims to the Navigation of the Missisippi* [sic], *etc.* Philadelphia: John Conrad, 1803.

Other Works by Brown

Annals   "Annals of Europe and America"
              Brown, Charles Brockden. "Annals of Europe and America," Vols. 1–5,
              *The American Register; or, General Repository of History, Politics, and
              Science*. Philadelphia: C. & A. Conrad, January 1807–January 1810.

Difference   "The Difference between History and Romance"
              Brown, Charles Brockden. "The Difference between History and Romance."
              The Monthly Magazine, and American Review 2.4 (April 1800): 251–253.

Rhapsodist   "The Rhapsodist"
              Brown, Charles Brockden. "The Rhapsodist." *The Columbian Magazine,
              or, Monthly Miscellany* 3.8 (August 1789): 464–467; 3.9 (September 1789):
              537–541; 3.10 (October 1789): 587–601; 3.11 (November 1789): 661–665.

Walstein   "Walstein's School of History"
              Brown, Charles Brockden. "Walstein's School of History. From the German
              of Krants of Gotha." *The Monthly Magazine, and American Review* 1.5
              (August 1799): 335–338; 1.6 (September–December 1799): 407–411.

Books by Others

Allen   *The Life of Charles Brockden Brown*
              Allen, Paul. *The Life of Charles Brockden Brown* [c. 1811–1814].
              Charles E. Bennett, ed. Delmar, N.Y.: Scholar's Facsimiles & Reprints, 1975.

Dunlap 1815   *The Life of Charles Brockden Brown*
              Dunlap, William. *The Life of Charles Brockden Brown: Together with
              Selections from the Rarest of His Printed Works, from His Original Letters,
              and from His Manuscripts before Unpublished*, 2 vols. Philadelphia:
              James P. Parke, 1815.

Dunlap 1930   *Diary of William Dunlap*
              Dunlap, William. *Diary of William Dunlap (1766–1839): The Memoirs
              of a Dramatist, Theatrical Manager, Painter, Critic, Novelist, and
              Historian*, 3 vols. Dorothy C. Barck, ed. New York: New York Historical
              Society, 1930.

Smith   *The Diary of Elihu Hubbard Smith*
              Smith, Elihu Hubbard. *The Diary of Elihu Hubbard Smith*. James E. Cronin,
              ed. Philadelphia: American Philosophical Society, 1973.

Periodicals

AR   *American Register*
              *The American Register; or, General Repository of History, Politics, and
              Science*. Philadelphia: C. & A. Conrad, January 1807–January 1810.

CM   *Columbian Magazine*
            The Columbian Magazine, or, Monthly Miscellany. Philadelphia:
            W. Young, September 1786–February 1790.

LM   *Literary Magazine*
            The Literary Magazine, and American Register. Vols. I–VIII. Philadelphia:
            C. & A. Conrad, October 1803–December 1807.

MM   *Monthly Magazine*
            The Monthly Magazine, and American Review. Vols. I–III. New York:
            T. & J. Swords, April 1799–December 1800.

PF   *Port Folio*
            The Port Folio. Philadelphia: H. Maxwell, January 1801–December 1827.

WM   *Weekly Magazine*
            *The Weekly Magazine of Original Essays, Fugitive Pieces, and Interesting
            Intelligence.* Philadelphia: J. Watters, February 1798–May 1799.

Contributors

Philip Barnard is Professor Emeritus of English at the University of Kansas. He is textual editor of the Charles Brockden Brown Electronic Archive and Scholarly Edition (brockdenbrown.cah.ucf.edu) and the Bucknell *Collected Writings of Charles Brockden Brown* edition, as well as a volume coeditor (with Mark L. Kamrath and Elizabeth Hewitt) on Vol. 1, *Letters and Early Epistolary Writings* (2013). With Kamrath and Stephen Shapiro, he edited *Revising Charles Brockden Brown: Culture, Politics, and Sexuality in the Early Republic* (2004); with Shapiro, he edited Brown's four canonical romances and Mary Wollstonecraft's *A Vindication of the Rights of Woman* (2006–2013), translated and edited François Guéry and Didier Deleule's *The Productive Body* (1972/2014), and authored *Pentecostal Modernism: Lovecraft, Los Angeles, and World-Systems Culture* (2017). With Cheryl Lester, he translated and edited Philipe Lacoue-Labarthe and Jean-Luc Nancy's *The Literary Absolute: The Theory of Literature in German Romanticism* (1978/1988).

Robert Battistini is Associate Professor of English at Centenary University in New Jersey. He is coeditor of *The Literary Magazine and Other Writings, 1801–1807*, Vol. 3 of the *Collected Writings of Charles Brockden Brown* series, and has written on Brown's *Historical Sketches*.

Sarah Boyd is a Teaching Assistant Professor in the Department of English and Comparative Literature at the University of North Carolina at Chapel Hill. Her research and writing concentrates on nineteenth-century US literature and culture. Her dissertation explores the queer masculine poetics of white American manhood in the early fiction of *The Atlantic Monthly*.

Martin Brückner is Professor in the English Department and Co-director of the Center for Material Culture Studies at the University of Delaware. He is author of *The Social Life of Maps in America, 1750–1860*; *The Geographic Revolution in Early America*, which was awarded the Louis Gottschalk Prize in Eighteenth-Century Studies; and the online exhibition catalog *Common Destinations: Maps in the American Experience* (commondestinations.winterthur.org). He is editor of two volumes, *Early American Cartographies* and *American Literary Geographies: Spatial Practice and Cultural Production, 1500–1900* (together with Hsuan L. Hsu). His published essays have appeared in the journals *American Art, American Quarterly, American Literary History, English Literary History, Winterthur Portfolio*, and numerous essay collections.

Michelle Burnham is Professor of English at Santa Clara University. She has written and edited several books and numerous articles on early American literature, which engage in literary recovery and pursue new models for American literary and cultural history. Her newest book is *Transoceanic America: Risk, Writing, and Revolution in the Global Pacific.*

Michael A. Cody is Professor of English at East Tennessee State University, where he teaches American and American Indian literatures. He is coeditor of *The Literary Magazine and Other Writings, 1801–1807*, Vol. 3 of the *Collected Writings of Charles Brockden Brown* series. Cody is author of *Charles Brockden Brown and the* Literary Magazine: *Cultural Journalism in the Early American Republic* (2004), the first attempt at an in-depth study of the *Literary Magazine, and American Register* (1803–1807). His published essays have studied Brown's "Somnambulism: A Fragment" and Brown's literary connections to the work of Nathaniel Hawthorne.

Michael C. Cohen is Associate Professor of English at the University of California, Los Angeles. He is the author of *The Social Lives of Poems in Nineteenth-Century America* (2015), and coeditor (with Alexandra Socarides) of *Poems*, Vol. 7 of the Bucknell *Collected Writings of Charles Brockden Brown* edition (2019).

Andy Doolen is Professor of English at the University of Kentucky. He is the author of *Territories of Empire: U.S. Writing from the Louisiana Purchase to Mexican Independence* (2014) and *Fugitive Empire: Locating Early American Imperialism* (2005). His essays and reviews have appeared in many journals and collections, including *American Literature, American Literary History, Studies in American Fiction, The Cambridge History of American Women's Literature*, and *Mapping Region in Early American Writing.*

Michael J. Drexler is Professor of English at Bucknell University. He is coeditor (with Elizabeth Maddock Dillon) of *The Haitian Revolution and the Early United States* (2016). He and Ed White published their monograph, *The Traumatic Colonel: The Founding Fathers, Slavery, and the Phantasmatic Aaron Burr*, in 2014. He and White also collaborated on the essay collection *Beyond Douglass: New Perspectives on Early African American Literature* (2008). His essays have appeared in *American Literary History, Early American Literature, Atlantic Studies*, and several edited collections.

Scott Ellis is a Professor of English at Southern Connecticut State University, where he teaches early and contemporary American literature and culture. He has published several essays on early American literature and pedagogy, including "Charles Brockden Brown's *Ormond*, Property Exchange, and the Literary Marketplace in the Early American Republic" (*Studies in the Novel*), " 'Reviewers Reviewed': John Davis and the Early American Literary Field" (*Early American Literature*), "Science and Technology in Hawthorne's Short Fiction" (*Nathaniel Hawthorne in the College Classroom*), "Early American Print Culture in a Digital Age: Pedagogical Possibilities" (*Pedagogy*), and "The Medium, the Message, and Digital Pedagogy in an Early American Literature Course" (*Teaching American Literature*).

Hilary Emmett is Senior Lecturer in American Studies at the University of East Anglia, where she teaches American literature in its transnational contexts, with a particular focus on transpacific approaches. She has published essays on comparative Australian and American literature in *Journal of American Studies* and *Australasian Journal of American Studies* as well as in several edited collections. She is coeditor (with Matthew Pethers and Leonard von Morzé) of *The Monthly Magazine and Other Writings 1789–1802*, Vol. 2 of the *Collected Writings of Charles Brockden Brown* series.

Duncan Faherty is Associate Professor of English and American Studies at Queens College and the Graduate Center, CUNY. He is also a core faculty member of the Committee on Globalization and Social Change. At the Graduate Center, he is also the Director of the Early Research Initiative. He is a coeditor of the journal *Studies in American Fiction* and, along with Ed White, codirector of the Just Teach One digital humanities project housed at the American Antiquarian Society. He is the author of *Remodeling the Nation: The Architecture of American Identity, 1776–1858*, and his work has also appeared in *American Literature, American Quarterly, Early American Literature*, and *Reviews in American History*. He is currently at work on a book, tentatively titled *Incipient Fevers: The Haitian Revolution and the Early Republic of Letters*, which explores the impact of the Haitian revolution on and in early American print culture.

Fritz Fleischmann is Professor of English at Babson College. He is the author, editor, or coeditor of six books and the author or coauthor of numerous scholarly articles about American literature and culture, entrepreneurship, college management, and organic farming. His publications about Charles Brockden Brown go back to 1982; his dissertation, *"A Right View of the Subject": Feminism in the Works of Charles Brockden Brown and John Neal*, was published in 1983. The founding chair of the editorial board for the Charles Brockden Brown Electronic Archive and Scholarly Edition and the initiator of the Charles Brockden Brown Society, he also served as a consulting editor for *Letters and Early Epistolary Writings* (2013), Vol. 1 of the Bucknell *Collected Writings* edition.

Anthony Galluzzo earned his Ph.D. in English Literature at the University of California, Los Angeles. He specializes in radical transatlantic English-language literary cultures of the late eighteenth and nineteenth centuries. He has taught at the United States Military Academy at West Point, Colby College, and New York University.

Elizabeth Hewitt is an Associate Professor in the Department of English at Ohio State University. She is the author of *Correspondence and American Literature, 1770–1865* (2005) and a coeditor of the *Letters and Early Epistolary Writings* volume of the *Collected Writings of Charles Brockden Brown* series (2013).

Elizabeth Jane Wall Hinds is Professor of English at the State University of New York, Brockport. She is the author of *Private Property: Charles Brockden Brown and the Gendered Economics of Virtue* and editor of *The Multiple Worlds of Pynchon's Mason & Dixon: Eighteenth-Century Contexts, Postmodern Observations*, along with other works on Brown, Pynchon, the eighteenth century, and critical animal studies.

Mark L. Kamrath is Professor of English at the University of Central Florida. He is general editor of the Charles Brockden Brown Electronic Archive and Scholarly Edition and codirector of the UCF Center for Humanities and Digital Research. He teaches American literature to 1865, the American novel to the Civil War, Native American literature, and courses in bibliography and research as well as digital humanities. He coedited *Letters and Early Epistolary Writings*, Vol. 1 of the *Collected Writings of Charles Brockden Brown* (2013), and has developed with Philip Barnard and others an XML-based archive of all of Brown's writings that incorporates TEI (Text Encoding Initiative) standards. He is a member of the Steering Committee for the Florida Digital Humanities Consortium. He is currently coediting a volume of Brown's political pamphlets and doing research on the body, nature, and natural rights.

Christopher Looby is Professor of English at the University of California, Los Angeles. He is the author of *Voicing America: Language, Literary Form, and the Origins of the United States* (1996), and edited *The Complete Civil War Journals and Selected Letters of Thomas Wentworth Higginson* (2000), as well as Robert Montgomery Bird's *Sheppard Lee, Written by Himself* (2008). With Cindy Weinstein, he coedited *American Literature's Aesthetic Dimensions* (2012). He is the general editor of *Q19: The Queer American Nineteenth Century*, a series of editions of queer literary recoveries. He has recently published essays on queer temporality in Herman Melville's *Billy Budd* and on the serialization of George Lippard's *The Quaker City* and has essays forthcoming on the strange temporalities of Robert Beverley Tucker's Confederate novel *The Partisan Leader*, as well as on sex and marble statues.

Robert Miles is Professor of English at the University of Victoria. His publications include *Gothic Writing 1750–1820: A Genealogy* (1993), *Ann Radcliffe: The Great Enchantress* (1995), and *Romantic Misfits* (2008).

Nicholas E. Miller is Assistant Professor of English at Valdosta State University, where he teaches multicultural American literature, gender and sexuality studies, and comics studies. He is the author of " 'In Utter Fearlessness of the Reigning Disease': Imagined Immunities and the Outbreak Narratives of Charles Brockden Brown," published in *Literature and Medicine* (2017), and "Asexuality and Its Discontents: Making the 'Invisible Orientation' Visible in Comics," published in *Inks: The Journal of the Comics Studies Society* (2017). He is a former executive board member of the Charles Brockden Brown Society and a founding member of the Comics Studies Society.

Leonard von Morzé is Associate Professor of English at the University of Massachusetts, Boston. He is the editor of *Cities and the Circulation of Culture in the Atlantic World: From the Early Modern to Modernism* (2017) and coeditor of *The Monthly Magazine and Other Writings, 1789–1802* (in progress), Vol. 2 of the Bucknell *Collected Writings of Charles Brockden Brown* edition. He has published two essays on Brown's *Ormond*.

Hannah Lauren Murray is Teaching Fellow in Early American Studies at King's College, London. Her book project *Inexplicable Voices: Liminal Whiteness in*

Early U.S. Fiction examines marginal and precarious whiteness in the work of Charles Brockden Brown, Robert Montgomery Bird, Edgar Allan Poe, Nathaniel Hawthorne, and Herman Melville. Her work has appeared in *The Irish Journal of Gothic and Horror Studies* and *Journal of American Studies*, and she sits on the Steering Committee for the British Association of Nineteenth-Century Americanists (BrANCA).

Stephen Rachman is Associate Professor in the Department of English, former director of the American Studies Program, and codirector of the Digital Humanities Literary Cognition Laboratory at Michigan State University. He is the editor of *The Hasheesh Eater* by Fitz-Hugh Ludlow. He is a coauthor of the award-winning *Cholera, Chloroform, and the Science of Medicine: A Life of John Snow* and coeditor of *The American Face of Edgar Allan Poe*. He has written numerous articles on Poe, literature and medicine, cities, popular culture, and an award-winning website on Sunday-school books for the Library of Congress American Memory Project. He is a past president of the Poe Studies Association and is currently completing a study of Poe titled "The Jingle Man: Edgar Allan Poe and the Problems of Culture."

Siân Silyn Roberts is Associate Professor of English at Queens College, CUNY. She is the author of *Gothic Subjects: The Transformation of Individualism in American Fiction, 1790–1861* (2014), and editor of the Broadview edition of *Edgar Huntly* (2018). She is a contributor to *The Haitian Revolution and the Early United States* (2016), edited by Elizabeth Maddock Dillon and Michael Drexler, and *Transnational Gothic: Literary and Social Exchanges in the Long Nineteenth Century* (2013), edited by Monika Elbert and Bridget M. Marshall.

Oliver Scheiding is Professor of American Literature and Early American Studies in the Obama Institute for Transnational American Studies at the University of Mainz, Germany. His research focuses on literary markets, periodical studies, and the socio-materiality of literature. He is the author of *Worlding America: A Transnational Anthology of Short Narratives before 1800* (2015), which documents the traffic of short forms of narration in the early Americas, and published the monograph *The Early American Novel* (2003). He also coedited *A Peculiar Mixture: German-Language Cultures and Identities in Eighteenth-Century North America* (2013). He edits the journal *Amerikastudien—American Studies* on behalf of the German Association of American Studies. Currently, he is working on a manuscript tentatively titled "Transnational Periodicals: Materiality, Networks, and Agency."

Stephen Shapiro teaches in the Department of English and Comparative Literary Studies at the University of Warwick. He is a volume editor (with Mark L. Kamrath and Maureen Tuthill) of *Political Pamphlets*, Vol. 4 of the ongoing Brown Electronic Archive (brockdenbrown.cah.ucf.edu) and the *Collected Writings of Charles Brockden Brown* edition. He is the author of *The Culture and Commerce of the Early American Novel: Reading the Atlantic World-System* (2008). With Philip Barnard and Kamrath, he edited *Revising Charles Brockden Brown: Culture, Politics, and Sexuality in the Early Republic* (2004); with Barnard, he edited Brown's four canonical romances and

Mary Wollstonecraft's *A Vindication of the Rights of Woman* (2006–2013), translated and edited François Guéry and Didier Deleule's *The Productive Body* (1972/2014), and authored *Pentecostal Modernism: Lovecraft, Los Angeles, and World-Systems Culture* (2017).

Scott Slawinski is Associate Professor in the Department of English at Western Michigan University, where he teaches classes in American literature from the colonial period through the early twentieth century, and is currently serving as Director of Graduate Studies. He is the author of a book on Brown's editorship of the *Monthly Magazine* and has edited the collected works of Sukey Vickery, titled *Emily Hamilton and Other Writings*. His research interests include gender studies, history of the book, the American and British novel, and modernist poetry. Currently, he is working on a biography and introduction to the works of Gothic novelist Sally Sayward Barrell Keating Wood and, with Karen Weyler, is editing for publication two of Wood's novels, *Dorval* and *Amelia*.

Jordan Alexander Stein teaches in the English department at Fordham University and is coeditor of *Early African American Print Culture* (2012).

Abigail Smith Stocker teaches creative writing and art history at Eastern High School in Louisville, Kentucky. Her research interests include Kentucky history at the turn of the nineteenth century and its transatlantic ties. In 2016, she published an article in a festschrift for Professor Janet Todd in the journal *Women's Writing* about the influence of Mary Wollstonecraft's life and death on early American culture. Currently, she is editing her novel-length historical fiction about Madison, Indiana, set in 1882.

Ezra Tawil is Professor of English at the University of Rochester. He is the author of *Literature, American Style: The Originality of Imitation in the Early Republic* (2018) and *The Making of Racial Sentiment: Slavery and the Birth of the Frontier Romance* (2006) and the editor of *The Cambridge Companion to Slavery in American Literature* (2016) and James Fenimore Cooper's *The Deerslayer* (2013).

Bryan Waterman is Global Network Associate Professor of Literature at New York University and Vice Provost for Undergraduate Academic Development at New York University, Abu Dhabi. A past president of the Charles Brockden Brown Society, he is editor of the Norton Critical Edition of Brown's *Wieland* and *Memoirs of Carwin the Biloquist* (2011) and author of *Republic of Intellect: The Friendly Club of New York City and the Making of American Literature* (2007). His writing on Brown has appeared in *Early American Literature*, *The William and Mary Quarterly*, and *The Cambridge History of the American Novel*.

Lisa West is Associate Professor of English at Drake University, where she teaches American literature before 1900 and nature writing. Her work on Charles Brocken Brown reflects her broader interests in early American fictionality, the hybridity of early American genres, writing of or in relationships, and the social and environmental construction of place. Her essay "'I May Be a Stranger to the Grounds of Your Belief':

Constructing Sense of Place in *Wieland*" was published in *Early American Literature*. Other work on James Fenimore Cooper, Susan Fenimore Cooper, Catharine Maria Sedgwick, and Susannah Rowson appears in *Legacy*, *Literature in the Early American Republic*, and other period journals and collections. She is currently working on a book-length project on domestic violence, which will include a chapter on Brown.

Gretchen J. Woertendyke is Associate Professor of English and the Assistant Director of Global Studies at the University of South Carolina. Her first book, *Hemispheric Regionalism: Romance and the Geography of Genre* (2016), looked at the influence of the Haitian Revolution and Cuban Annexation on the romance genre in eighteenth- and nineteenth-century America. In addition to her work on Charles Brockden Brown, she has published essays on secret histories, slave narratives, and sensational fiction. An essay, "Romance," is forthcoming in the *Oxford Encyclopedia of Literary Theory*, and an essay "Regionalism" is forthcoming in *American Literature in Transition*, Vol. 2, (1820–1860). Her current book project is titled *A History of Secrecy in the United States*.

THE OXFORD HANDBOOK OF

CHARLES BROCKDEN BROWN

INTRODUCTION

PHILIP BARNARD, HILARY EMMETT, AND STEPHEN SHAPIRO

THE *Oxford Handbook of Charles Brockden Brown* seeks to introduce readers to Brown's work across his life and across the multiple genres in which he wrote. We hope to give those who have never encountered Brown a foundation for approaching and better understanding his writing, its historical context and intellectual concerns, and the critical approaches that have been used to consider it. To readers somewhat familiar with Brown, the *Oxford Handbook* seeks to cast a light for further exploration across his extensive and varied corpus of writings. Its chapters seek to build on readers' initial encounter with Brown by showing other avenues into his work, from the relatively well-known long fictions to the lesser-known journalism, poetry, short fictions, and political writings. In the following chapters, you will find discussions of the manifold aspects of Brown's life and creative production that should both inform and encourage the next steps toward more independent study.

Since his own lifetime (1771–1810), Brown has always had a somewhat paradoxical status within American literary and cultural history. He figures in literary and cultural studies as a canonical figure well known to those versed in literary history and commonly included in university-level curricula, yet likewise as a writer not generally known to the wider public to the same degree as more iconic names such as Edgar Allan Poe, Herman Melville, William Faulkner, and so on. At no point has Brown ever really been a forgotten figure. Even when his long fictions were least known, such as, for instance, at the end of the nineteenth century, they were nevertheless still printed in collected editions and available to interested readers. Indeed, when the first generation of American studies scholars began assembling materials for the literary study of the pre-1830s years, Brown's work was always included, often given more notice than any other creative writer before Washington Irving and James Fenimore Cooper. Yet on the other hand, Brown has not had the wider public status or consecration that might be expected for someone who has been continually known as a writer of high repute.

In the nearly forty years since the first scholarly editions of Brown's novels were published, his work has provided seemingly inexhaustible fuel for energizing and, at times, catalyzing, the evolution of early American literary studies. From early work on Brown that meditated on his "firstness"—whether this was to debate his position as the first professional American novelist or to stage his so-called paternity of a uniquely American literary aesthetic—through his centrality to the New Americanist project of scholars throughout the 1980s and onward who sought to unsettle ideas of America's exceptionalism in the world by revealing the nation's transnational connections and intranational conflicts, to Brown's place in contemporary scholarship in burgeoning fields such as environmental and medical humanities, his corpus has yielded reliably rich results for scholars.

The *Oxford Handbook* surveys the recent state of Brown studies and provides resources for those interested in Brown in several ways. First, students of Brown have benefited from an expanded knowledge of Brown's biography and contexts within the early American republic (loosely defined as the national period up to the 1820s). Partly due to the conventions of nineteenth-century biography, a few clichéd or stereotypical representations of Brown were repeated as fact and cast a long shadow on later commentary. Somewhat due to the emerging stereotype of the literary figure as a Romantic misfit, Brown was initially and firmly presented as a melancholic and fragile recluse, despite contemporary accounts of his being a convivial, sociable conversationalist and a respected editor. While Brown was active in realms of literary production and editing, as well as contributing in later years to the work of his brothers' mercantile enterprises, the prior lack of attention to the day-by-day interactions with Philadelphia's literary and social spheres left many readers dependent on descriptions by tourists, who were inclined to present somewhat melodramatic portraits of the author, not least since the convention of a travel narrative required strong statements, broad strokes, and memorable characterizations.

In a similar way, and increasingly in recent decades, Brown's reception by scholars has also provided ways to both understand him as a writer and see the ways in which past characterizations have prejudged or (mis)shaped his legacy. In this respect, the *Oxford Handbook* provides some new insights into and perspectives on Brown's life and social environment, based on information and methodological tools that were not available to previous generations of readers.

Second, in keeping with Brown scholarship's developments in the twenty-first century, the *Oxford Handbook* expands the spectrum of consideration of Brown. Whereas scholarship throughout the twentieth century focused primarily on Brown's long fictions, the *Oxford Handbook* takes all of Brown's writing as a coherent corpus worthy of serious consideration. The previous focus on the four best-known long fictions (*Wieland, Ormond, Edgar Huntly*, and *Arthur Mervyn*, all from the 1798–1800 moment) is put to the side as the following chapters explore the breadth of Brown's work, as well as the changing shape of his career, a career that if anything increased in productivity in the last years of his life, before his untimely death from tuberculosis in 1810. His poetry, later writing, and journalism are considered in their relations to the better-known fiction and as notable and foundational works in their own right. Brown, as biographical subject and creator, is considered in these chapters from a variety of perspectives, many of them moving forward in substantial ways from the assumptions that governed earlier discussions.

The *Oxford Handbook* also places Brown in greater conversation with international or transnational frameworks than has previously been the case. Not only was Brown deeply informed about and fascinated with world events, but his writing can be usefully considered as belonging to contexts in which the United States is not primary. Scholarship on postcolonialism, world literature, and other transnational perspectives increasingly finds reason to be interested in Brown. In this light, the later work on history writing and international history has become more prominent.

If in the 1970s and 1980s Brown's canonical status seemed to remain under advisement, in 2019 it is well established and deeply rooted, in large part because of the tenacity with which his work has gripped scholars throughout the varied "turns" that have shaped early American studies: the transnational, spatial, archival, aesthetic, and affective. This *Handbook* thus takes stock of the significant role played by Brown in shaping scholarly understanding of the early republic and also tracks the ways in which his writing has remained central to how scholars define their own literary-historical moments.

It is our hope that in surveying the recent and current state of Charles Brockden Brown studies and providing a resource for scholars new to his writing, the *Handbook* will enable and underpin future advances in work on Brown and his milieu. The *Handbook* is the first collection of its kind in Charles Brockden Brown studies. Two earlier essay collections on Brown—Bernard Rosenthal's *Critical Essays on Charles Brockden Brown* (1981) and Philip Barnard, Mark Kamrath, and Stephen Shapiro's *Revising Charles Brockden Brown: Culture, Politics and Sexuality in the Early Republic* (2004)—both staged a series of vital interventions into Brown scholarship by demonstrating his relevance to understandings of topics from historicism to transnationalism and sexuality in the early republic, but both collections required familiarity with Brown's work and key theoretical and methodological approaches in the field of American literary studies.

This *Handbook* takes up and extends these questions but initially aims to familiarize the reader with Brown's complex literary persona and milieu(s). It provides a first section on Brown's biography that utilizes recently available archival resources and correspondence to update familiar narratives about Brown's life and career. It provides chapter-length considerations of the long fictions with which Brown has traditionally been associated but also provides detailed considerations of his production in other genres (e.g., letters, poetry, political pamphlets) and from a number of thematic and methodological or interpretative perspectives.

Finally, it is notable that the *Handbook* has come into being alongside the long-running Charles Brockden Brown Electronic Archive and Scholarly Edition project (2007–present), which identifies, edits, and makes available in digital form Brown's complete known corpus of writings (http://brockdenbrown.cah.ucf.edu), as well as providing the basis for an ongoing seven-volume Bucknell University Press edition of Brown's nonnovelistic writings. In serendipitous ways, these projects have operated in tandem; the electronic archive provides a powerful tool for accessing reliable texts of all of Brown's work, much of it available for the first time, and thereby enriches and extends Brown scholarship in significant ways. Many of the editorial contributors to the electronic archive and the Bucknell edition have provided chapters for this book, so that the *Handbook* seeks to provide the first knowing look onto the expanded horizon of Brown's work as a whole. This *Handbook*, therefore, for the first time in Brown studies aims, if not to destabilize the primacy of the novels, then to ensure that critical work on Brown's best-known writings is considered inseparably from his vast epistolary, poetic, essayistic, philosophical, and political oeuvre.

PART I

BIOGRAPHY

CHAPTER 1

··

EARLY YEARS, 1771–1795

··

LISA WEST

CHARLES Brockden Brown was born in Philadelphia on January 17, 1771.[1] At the time, Philadelphia was not only the most populous city in colonial America but also a global center of commerce and the site of important political gatherings leading up to the American Revolution. Brown was five years old when independence was declared at the Pennsylvania State House, less than a mile from his home at 117 South Second Street. The era's social, economic, and political upheaval influenced Brown's early life in many ways; while there was volatility, there was also enthusiasm for long-lasting positive change and the promise of Enlightenment and Revolutionary ideals.

Through the year 1795, when Brown experienced a rift within his Philadelphia social network and turned his attention more fully to the New York intellectual scene, Brown's biography can be divided into five sections. First, his Quaker lineage, which stretches back to the origins of the religion in mid-seventeenth-century England, is significant. Brown received a solid grounding in concepts such as "the inner light," or direct communication with God, and Philadelphia's Quaker culture contributed to his lifelong pursuit of articulating moral dilemmas and understanding virtue. The first section of this chapter includes discussion of the unlawful arrest and exile of Brown's father, an event that has reached iconic status in Brown's biography. The second section reviews Brown's youth, adolescence, and classical education under Robert Proud at the Friends Latin School, where Brown continued until the age of sixteen. The third section discusses biographers' second-most-cited aspect of Brown's youth: his vexed years as a lawyer's apprentice. Brown read law for six years in the office of Alexander Wilcocks, a period during which he avoided taking the bar, devoted himself to literary and philosophical clubs, and circulated written texts in a variety of forms. His intense friendships with William Wood Wilkins and Joseph Bringhurst, Jr., played a large role in this stage of development. The fourth section also focuses on the years 1787–1793, addressing Brown's larger Philadelphia social circle, his early published material, and his unpublished epistolary narratives. The final section focuses on the years 1793–1795, in which Brown continued his literary experiments and widened the emotional and intellectual distance from his Quaker Philadelphia youth.

I. Quaker Roots and
Arrest of Elijah Brown

According to Peter Kafer, the Brown family's Quaker patriarch was Richard Browne, not William Browne, as the family's personal history erroneously reported (Kafer 18). This Richard Browne, of Sywell, Northamptonshire, and his wife, Mary, were Baptists, then Puritans, before becoming Quakers. Richard died in 1662, the same year that Parliament passed the Quaker Act, which not only made it illegal for Quakers to worship in a group but also criminalized their credo of refusing to swear oaths. Ensuing years would see additional anti-Quaker legislation.[2] James Browne, born in 1656, was the fourth son of Richard and Mary, and he grew up amid this widespread persecution of Quakers in England. The Quakers' faith must have seemed positively anarchical to their contemporaries. Other English dissenters, such as the Puritans (Calvinists), already deviated dramatically from the Church of England and attempted to dismantle church hierarchies, eliminate the ritual elements of worship, and foster a return to the Bible as the ultimate religious authority. The Quakers took these reforms to further extremes, dispensing with the sacraments of baptism and communion and eliminating all clerical titles. In essence, the Quakers, or Friends, as they called themselves, affirmed that each individual, male or female, could have a personal, mystic, unmediated relationship with God, independent of a church and its customs.

According to the Quaker Records in the library of the Pennsylvania Historical Society, James Browne sailed from England in 1677 and helped to lay out the town of Burlington, New Jersey, in fellowship with other Quakers (Clark 13). William Penn had played a role in this first wave of Quaker emigration, but it wasn't until 1681 that he acquired the colony of Pennsylvania as repayment of a debt Charles II owed to Penn's father.[3] The terms of Penn's charter would have long-standing impact on the Brown clan; by guaranteeing the toleration of Quakers, Penn's colony proved to be a place where Quaker culture—and Quaker families—could thrive.

In 1702, James and his brother William Browne moved to the Quaker settlement of Nottingham on the Pennsylvania–Maryland border, where they retained five of thirty-seven original township lots (Kafer 18, 20). In this rural borderland community, they became a prominent religious family, in conjunction with the Churchmans, with whom they often intermarried (19). The Quakers did not have ministers per se, but they applied this term—or the less frequently used term *seer*—to those they thought especially graced with the inner light who were therefore well qualified to testify to others (22–23); Charles Brockden Brown was descended from a long line of such individuals. James Browne's son William was born in 1682 (Warfel 15), and William in turn fathered a son, James, who was born in Nottingham. James Brown (later generations of Browns dropped the *e* from their surname) had five children, including Elijah (b. 1740), the father of Charles Brockden Brown (16). The isolated farming community of Nottingham, fifty miles outside Philadelphia, was the ideal place to promote the Quaker practice of finding the inner light, or hearing the voice of God within. But while the fellowship of like-minded Quakers in Nottingham surely advanced the spiritual knowledge of its inhabitants, the town's limited opportunities and homogeneity must have stifled those with more worldly ambitions. Elijah moved to Philadelphia in 1757 (16).

On July 9, 1761, Elijah Brown married fellow Quaker Mary Armitt at the Arch Street Meeting House in Philadelphia. By all accounts, this was an upwardly mobile match for Elijah (Kafer 30). In addition to having as fine a Quaker pedigree as the Browns—the Armitts numbered among Penn's original followers and had helped to lay out the city of Philadelphia—they were also quite wealthy (Clark 14). Mary Armitt's late father, Joseph, had left a considerable estate to his widow, Elizabeth, which included slaves, several properties, and a three-story brick house on Second Street (Kafer 30). Elizabeth's people, the Lisles, had also been well-to-do, and Elizabeth Armitt's name appears frequently in Philadelphia land records for the purchase and sale of real estate (Warfel 16). That the couple named their fourth son Charles Brockden, after a prosperous merchant–lawyer relation of Mary's (and the first recorder of Philadelphia), suggests that Elijah Brown, like the Armitts, was interested in redrawing the boundaries of Quaker worldliness.[4]

The anti-Quaker feeling that led to the arrest, imprisonment, and banishment of Charles Brockden Brown's father, Elijah, in 1777, has roots in the history of Quaker relations with the colonial government of America. As pacifists, Quakers object to bearing arms, and they also take seriously the biblical injunction against swearing oaths. Hence, Quakers often found themselves at odds with colonial authorities for refusing military service in defense of their fledgling settlements or for declining to swear loyalty to the British crown. These tensions came to a head during the French and Indian War (1754–1763). Quakers dominated the Pennsylvania Assembly at the time, and a political rift developed between those Quakers who objected to allocating tax money for military defense and those willing to compromise their strict principles. Ultimately, the pacifist Quakers conceded to pressure to resign their posts in 1756 (Moses 17; Kafer 26–28). This concession marks the decline of Quaker political involvement in the colony, although "Quakers dominated the mercantile life of Philadelphia" (Moses 18). Quaker relations with Native Americans also angered Pennsylvania frontiersmen, who resented attempts to integrate Indians into colonial society. In what became known as the Paxton Riots of 1763–1764, a Scots-Irish vigilante group murdered twenty Indians and marched on Philadelphia, threatening both Indians and Quakers (Kafer 32). Further adding to mistrust of Quakers in the 1770s was the transatlantic nature of the religion; there were strong ties between members of the Philadelphia and London Yearly Meetings (Moses 17).

Charles Brockden Brown was six years old in 1777, when his father was unlawfully arrested and banished with other members of his community. A few weeks before the arrests, the Continental Congress had gained possession of papers that suggested that the Quakers were involved in treasonous activity and in league with the British cause. Although the papers were later revealed to be forgeries, high-profile Quakers, Anglican Tories, and other suspects were rounded up and jailed in the first week of September. All those willing to give a loyalty oath to the United States were awarded parole; all of the Quakers refused this option on principle. No charges were brought against the prisoners, nor did they receive a hearing or trial. In spite of the outcry raised by Philadelphia's considerable Quaker community, the Pennsylvania Assembly sanctioned the injustice by passing a special act that suspended habeas corpus for the twenty remaining prisoners. The party was banished to Winchester, Virginia, where they remained from September 29, 1777, to April of the following year. Only constant pressure on the Supreme Executive Council of Pennsylvania, as well as publicity about the deaths of two of the exiles by disease, led to the prisoners' release some eight months after their incarceration.[5] That a merchant like Elijah who had signed a community protest declaration in response to the Stamp Act in 1765 (Clark 14; Kafer 30) could be arrested in 1777 for suspicion of treason indicates the way Quaker principles of hard work and political neutrality could be misinterpreted during the period's turbulence.

II. Youth, Adolescence, and Education

Six of Elijah and Mary Brown's children survived to adulthood: Joseph (b. 1764), James (b. 1766), Armitt (b. 1768), Charles (b. 1771), Elizabeth (b. 1775), and Elijah, Jr. (b. 1776) (Letters 920). While Charles's brothers probably attended the Quaker grammar school, entering commerce as soon as they were able, he was the only sibling to continue on to the prestigious Friends Latin School (Kafer 46). It is likely that the family planned for him to become more highly educated, and eventually an attorney, so that he could help manage the litigation that accompanied their mercantile projects (Letters 842). Brown's first biographer, Paul Allen, characterizes Charles as book-oriented and studious from earliest childhood:

> The parents relate, that when an infant, in their absence from home, he required nothing but a book to divert him, and that on their return he would be found musing over the page with all the gravity of a student. On his return from school they would find him at the hour of dinner in the parlour, where, having slipped off his shoes, he was mounted on a table, and deeply engaged in the consultation of a map suspended on the side of the wall.   (Allen 10)

The intellectual, emotional, and religious atmosphere of the Brown household depended heavily on Quaker culture, which integrated home, community, and learning, stressing moral behavior, piety, plain living, and tolerance (Moses 18). Children were required to attend meetings from a young age. Daily and weekly meetings encouraged both men and women to speak, or testify, about personal experiences. Monthly meetings handled organizational and membership issues—including discipline (Kafer 22). Elijah Brown was disowned in 1768, a year after the Townsend duties were passed, for failing to make good on business debt (30–31), but even after this formal discipline, the Browns moved in Quaker circles, attended Quaker meetings, and were educated in Quaker schools with the city's leading Quaker families.

Early biographers stress the instability of Elijah Brown's financial status. It is true that Elijah was disowned by the Meeting in 1768 and imprisoned for debt in 1784, his personal finances reflecting the unpredictability of mercantile life. However, the family could turn to the Armitt real estate holdings (and their more stable financial status) during difficult financial times, and Elijah became a real estate conveyancer and land broker when trade failed (Shapiro 164–165). While Elijah's finances did fluctuate, the family never was destitute and might best be described as of the "middling orders" (Watts 27).

Despite financial fluctuations, there is much evidence to suggest that the Brown home was rich in intellectual inquiry. Elijah maintained a "lively correspondence" with friends and relatives in England and recorded extracts from international newspapers in his journal (Watts 28). Elijah's journal postdates the period of Charles's youth, but his enthusiastic reception of William Godwin and Mary Wollstonecraft reveals that he was curious about current intellectual trends and progressive in his thought. Charles's biographer Harry Warfel notes the "fat calfskin volumes by travelers and merchant explorers" that peopled the shelves in the Browns' parlor and asserts that the globe and the atlas were put to regular use (Warfel 23). Beyond the requirements of their Quaker milieu, Brown's family seems to have delighted in knowledge for its own sake as well as for pious or moral reasons.

At the Friends Latin School, Brown was trained in the rudiments of Latin and Greek, as well as in mathematics, geography, rhetoric, and the Bible. Many of Brown's biographers have theorized that it was his schoolmaster, Robert Proud, who inspired and fostered young Brown's philomathic tendencies. Indeed, Proud—who had emigrated from England in 1759—was a distinguished scholar, notable for penning the prodigious volume *The History of Pennsylvania* in 1797. Though a Quaker, Proud was well versed in both the classics and the sciences, and David Lee Clark believes "it was precisely [Proud's] catholicity of interests and tastes that had the most abiding influence upon Brockden Brown's ideals" (Clark 21). Allen asserts that Proud was more than simply a tutor, and he relates a story according to which the instructor, having noticed Brown's tendency to study in excess of what his frail health could support, advised daily exercise to the boy as a way of bolstering his physique. Brown became so enamored of this pedestrian activity that long, solitary walks grew to be a lifelong habit (Allen 11).

During these school years (1781–1786), Brown began writing poetry, a practice that he continued throughout his life. Some of these poems may have been connected to pedagogical exercises; all attest to his growing familiarity with classical models and popular eighteenth-century poetic forms, including epigram, mock heroic poem, Hudibrastic satire, sonnet, and locodescriptive verse. These early poems existed in a manuscript culture, shared in letters, written inside a book (for one poem), copied into commonplace books, and, we can assume, read aloud and shared among family and friends.[6] While little of this early material was published in print, motifs and images recur in his later writing.

Brown's earliest surviving poem, "On Some of His School Fellows" (1786), mocks his fellow students and shows powers of observation and humor. "To Miss D.P." and "To Estrina," both written for Dolley Payne (the future Dolley Madison), show conventions of love and unrequited love. Poetic allusions and imitations range from Alexander Pope to John Milton, Edward Young (*Night-Thoughts*), James Thomson (*The Seasons*), Virgil, and hymnist Isaac Watts.[7] "The Rising Glory of America," whose subject matter and title anticipate poems of the early national period, was written when Brown was sixteen years old and follows the neoclassical transformation of classical pastoral poetry by writers such as Pope. Written in heroic couplets, the poem follows the trope of *translatio studii*, or the westward transfer (and progress) of culture from classical civilizations to Britain and now America. "In Praise of Schuylkill," also composed in the late 1780s, extols the local landscape. Brown's now-lost journal also indicated ambitious plans for epic poems on Columbus, Pizarro, and Cortez (Allen 11). Brown's education and early writing reveal a broad experience with literary genres, both classical and modern. His interest in poetry, rhetorical technique, and geography would continue throughout his life.

III. Law Apprenticeship, Club Membership, Friendship, and Letters

In 1787, Brown began an apprenticeship at the law office of Alexander Wilcocks. Quaker families typically did not send their children to university, preferring instead to complete their earlier "guarded" Quaker education with apprenticeship "for specific training in a trade or profession" (Moses 19). Wilcocks, an Anglican, supporter of the American Revolution and member of the American Philosophical Society, was a prominent lawyer; it is a testament to Brown's talent and family status that he secured such a prestigious (and likely expensive) apprenticeship (Moses 19). While law might seem a logical choice for a bookish young man, it also fit family needs. Brown's two eldest brothers began a mercantile firm in the 1780s; Brown likely was expected to help resolve the litigious situations that frequently arose (Letters 823; Warfel 29).

During this apprenticeship (1787–1793), Brown existed in a constant whirlwind of intellectual activity. In addition to his rigorous studies, he found time to teach himself French and, with his friends, invent a unique style of shorthand. He organized club meetings with like-minded intellectuals and composed essays that he debated with his peers. From 1789 to 1791, when Wilcocks was appointed city recorder of Philadelphia, Brown served as a copyist, and we can imagine the deadening influence of this task on a man of Brown's vision. No one could describe the mundane aspects of law better than Brown himself, in this oft-noted passage from *Ormond* (1799):

> He was perpetually encumbered with the rubbish of law, and waded with laborious steps through its endless tautologies, its impertinent circuities, its lying assertions, and hateful artifices. Nothing occurred to relieve or diversify the scene. It was one tedious round of scrawling and jargon; a tissue made up of the shreds and remnants

of barbarous antiquity, polluted with the rust of ages, and patched by the stupidity of modern workmen, into new deformity.   (O 20)

Despite similar rhetorical denunciations in other writings, such as his mock criticisms of lawyers and legal practice in letters to friends, Brown did seem to appreciate the moral questions and social concerns undergirding his field of study.[8] While Brown spent the day in legal writing, he spent evenings writing in his journal, transcribing letters, narrating "household incidents," engaging in self-reflection, and writing lines of poetry (Allen 12–13, 16).

In the early days of his law apprenticeship, Brown honed his knowledge by participating in a legal society with other students (Watts 32). The club, which met once a week, argued a previously determined case or question, and the president's duty was to sit as judge for the moot court and record his decision. During Brown's term as president of the society, he became expert at affecting the dry, disembodied voice of legal discourse, though he switched easily from this mode of writing to his journal and what early biographer Allen deemed "a poetical effusion as much distinguished by its wild and excentric brilliance as the other composition was for its plain sobriety and gravity of style" (Allen 15). Born within a year of Romantic poets William Wordsworth and Samuel Taylor Coleridge, like them, he favored meditations on the workings of the mind over more practical writing, and like them, he was motivated to salvage the imagination from the materialism of modern life.

Far more to Brown's taste than the legal society, to be sure, was the Belles Lettres Society, which he formed in conjunction with eight friends in 1787. The club, including classmates from the Latin School as well as some non-Quakers, was primarily a literary society, though, in keeping with the period, Brown understood literature, or belles-lettres, to include science and reflections on the connectedness of different branches of knowledge, as he commented in the opening address (Watts 29). The young men debated philosophical and moral questions, and they shared original essays, poetry, and fiction. The Belles Lettres Society was active for several years, and it evolved into the Society for the Attainment of Useful Knowledge in the early 1790s. This Philadelphia club, like the better-known Friendly Club of New York, provided both an intellectual and a social support system. Bryan Waterman has argued that salons such as these united the eighteenth-century ideal of diplomatic, "friendly" conversation to the Enlightenment preoccupation with scientific discovery: "The relationship between the intense emotion of romantic friendship and Enlightenment modes of intellectual inquiry justified rituals of conversation, familiar correspondence, and club life itself" (Waterman 32).

One topic that engrossed the club members was the question of suicide. William Wood Wilkins, a fellow law apprentice, delivered an address, "Is Suicide Justified?" before the Society for the Attainment of Useful Knowledge in 1792, generating multiple responses from the members as they took various positions on what was generally considered a crime or an immoral act. Brown's letters to Joseph Bringhurst, Jr., in 1792 can be seen as part of that larger discussion (Letters 832–833). Brown, like Wilkins, takes an anti-Christian position that suicide can be justified on moral grounds.[9] In these letters, Brown overtly addresses moral and religious positions; he considers the "utility" of believing the soul is infinite; he evokes sympathy in asking a reader to consider the emotional position of a possible Self-Destroyer; he uses legal terminology of "crime" and "motive"; he writes of real or imagined personal experience. This multidimensional performance shows how Brown uses a variety of rhetorical registers to address the topic at hand. Throughout these performances, he adheres to the stance that such arguments are themselves speculative— and limited. In the last of a trio of letters to Bringhurst in October–November 1792, he writes: "I still continue to think that whether Suicide be justifiable or not, is a question of importance only to those who are incited to commit it," adding, "I have stated it as unquestionably certain that no one destroys himself in consequence of the mere conviction of the moral justifiableness of his conduct" (Letters 151–152).

Even within the literary club, Wilkins, Bringhurst, and Brown formed an intimate trio.[10] Bringhurst, four years older than Brown, was a Quaker, a schoolmate, and a founding member of the Belles Lettres Society; he was training in the medical field. Wilkins, one or two years younger than Brown, moved to Philadelphia in 1788 to study law with attorney John Todd; he and Brown shared lodgings in 1791–1792. The letters show the intensity of their triangulated emotional, intellectual, and aspirational relationship. The future novelist fretted over whether Wilkins returned the intensity of his love and whether Bringhurst and Wilkins enjoyed a closer bond with each other than either one did with Brown. Comments within letters indicate they regularly shared letters among the threesome—yet also at times took umbrage at the sharing of certain information, such as personal criticism. They discussed their reading passionately; Brown was particularly effusive about Jean-Jacques Rousseau and Samuel Richardson. They debated social and moral questions, with Brown often agonizing with Wilkins over the law in theory and practice.[11] Biographers have tended to consider Brown's 1790–1793 letters windows into his deepest self,[12] but recent scholarship points to the 1790–1793 letters as more consciously constructed than autobiographical. Elizabeth Hewitt notes how, despite the emotional intensity, Brown offers very little "biographical or psychological information"; the letters are crafted to *produce* emotional response (and thus create or foster affective connection) rather than articulate genuine emotion (Hewitt 90–91). They therefore are more indicative of "epistolary performance" than autobiographical truth (Barnard 521).

One regular performance is that of the culture of eighteenth-century sensibility. When Brown writes to Bringhurst on May 6, 1792, "O My friend! Can I stay the torment of my emotions? Can I stifle the burst of tenderness or check the tears of rapture, with which my heart was agitated and my eyes suffused, on the perusal of thy letter?" (Letters 39), he invokes the rhetoric and role of an ideal friend and "man of feeling,"[13] using stylized language that asserts affective connection and sympathy. Using this manner of address, he was "drawing on well-established eighteenth-century arguments and themes such as associated sentiment (the idea that emotions are communicated from one individual to another and may be used to encourage constructive, progressive behavior)" (Barnard and Shapiro xv), derived from discussions of sympathy in Adam Smith's *The Theory of Moral Sentiments* and similar texts. In a Smithian vein, Brown continually links friendship to virtue due to the power of the sympathetic connection. In a letter written soon after October 1792 to Wilkins, then his closest friend, Brown writes of the romantic power of such connection: "[F]riendship is, perhaps more pure but certainly not less violent than love. Between friends there must exist a perfect and intire Similarity of dispositions." He continues to link idealized friendship to a "fiction of Romance," or "magnetical influence." In such an ideal state, "Their bodies may be removed to a distance from each other but the union of their souls can never be dissolved" (Letters 158).[14]

In addition to producing emotion, performing sensibility, and discussing moral questions, there is another function of these letters that only recently has received scholarly attention. Brown's letters from this period are full of fictional fragments, comments on the nature of fiction, and transitions into and out of the imagination.[15] The letters of 1792–1793, therefore, can be considered a "laboratory for the development of Brown's early ideas and techniques concerning fiction writing" (Letters 833). Brown slips effortlessly into fanciful narratives about trips abroad which he never took and experiences he never had, including a doomed early marriage that was purely fictional or an imagined residence in a Rousseauvian Swiss village where he serves as preceptor to a young girl. He speaks in a variety of personae, for example, as a law student in England whose will decrees that his books be burned and the ashes inserted into his cranial cavity after his death. These letters frequently employ dramatic language and invented dialogue. Rousseau and Richardson are his most obvious touchstones in these experiments, but he also draws heavily on Pope, William Shakespeare, French Enlightenment writers, Johann Wolfgang von Goethe, and other influences. Some of these experiments end with a shift in tone as Brown overtly asks for the approval or critique of his reader; at other times, the fiction is sustained throughout the letter or even across multiple letters. The dead wife motif, for instance, is referred to at least three times in surviving letters. Sometimes Brown connects these moments to altered states of consciousness, like dreams or visions. Because he so often laces his personal letters to Wilkins and Bringhurst with these fictional episodes, created personae, or maudlin performances of feeling, they are best treated as a training ground for his narrative voice as opposed to reliable autobiographical documents.

Some of these ventures into fiction present sketches or plans for longer works. For example, within a letter dated July 29 and August 1, 1793, Brown tells the story of "Jackie Cooke," an Irish debtor who drinks heavily and physically abuses his wife (Letters 250–254). Instead of being grateful for her neighbors' kind intervention, the wife is mortified at exposure: "Their offers were received with a sullen kind of gratitude and unwilling condescension" (252). The bleak tale raises questions of benevolence and beneficence, which Brown regularly distinguishes in his letters as the difference between wishing well and doing well; it experiments with the narrative position of an observer rather than an active participant; and it illustrates female subordination and the dangers of "custom" over reason in shaping female behavior, because the mother's unreasonable dislike of help comes from socially ingrained views of decorum.

In a long letter to Bringhurst from May 1792, Brown presents a more fully realized narrative sketch, the "Story of Julius" (Letters 85–98). Julius dies of heartbreak and torment in trying to reconcile his mother's dying wishes for his marriage with his own romantic desire. His "virtuous" struggle has implications for others' happiness, since all three younger female characters (both potential lovers and a sister) reject the mother's dictates, pursuing their own interpretations of virtuous behavior. While the *Werther*-derived plot shows the influence of Brown's reading during this time, the complex frame of this tale shows broader awareness of the possible connections between fiction writing and letter writing or of narrative and epistolary writing in general.[16] Brown creates a fictitious framework in which he alleges to Bringhurst that this "sketch" is part of an existing longer narrative that he wrote for another (fictitious) correspondent, Henrietta, and never got back. In yet another layer of this inside joke, Henrietta, the fictitious correspondent, is herself a character within a text Brown was revising during this time. Brown comments to Bringhurst near the end of the letter that he felt a deep sympathetic connection with Julius as he wrote, even conflating himself with his character. This admiration for the powers of fiction and sympathy alike can be seen in Brown's stunning rebuttal to Bringhurst's more orthodox Christianity, in his letter of December 21, 1792, which asserts that Richardson's *Sir Charles Grandison* (1753) presents a better model of narrating virtue than New Testament stories of Jesus (Letters 207). In these and other letters, moral issues often discussed by the club members (virtue, friendship, sympathy) extended to specifically literary questions. Brown clearly was thinking about connections between conjectural history, fiction, and virtue that he would work out more systematically in later writings.

IV. Brown's Larger Philadelphia Circle, Earliest Publications, and Epistolary Narratives

Brown's 1787–1793 Philadelphia circle included women as well as men. Bryan Waterman and Frederika Teute both write of the larger mixed-company circles that extended the connections of the New York Friendly Club. "[M]ixed-sex social settings…took up significant amounts of club members' time, energy, and theoretical consideration" (Waterman 131). These activities could include walks, dinner parties, and group readings of recently published material. Teute stresses the role of conversation and face-to-face encounters in these gatherings, which extended the goals of the club to facilitate a "republic of intellect." "In their exchanges of ideas and sentiments, these women and men performed an Enlightenment ideal of sensibility as they shaped their relationships with each other in a discourse of reason and affective ties" (Teute 150–151). Similar mixed-company gatherings also existed within Brown's Philadelphia circle, although the circle was shaped in part by shared Quaker values. As in New York, friends often gathered at the homes of married friends, and sisters (and their friends) often were present at other home gatherings or outings (Waterman 132; Teute 159). One such outing was a 1795 visit to the Eckstein Gallery in Philadelphia, where Bringhurst and Brown viewed sculpture and painting with female Quaker associates Louisa Biddle, Mary Attmore, Ruth Paxson, Ann Thompson, and another friend whose "Aurelia" pseudonym remains unidentified.[17] The importance of mixed-sex conversation is consistent with the message of Mary Wollstonecraft in her

1792 *A Vindication of the Rights of Woman.* Even before 1792, Brown's writing often refers to "custom" (not nature) as responsible for gender roles. His Quaker upbringing ascribed the same spiritual authority to women and men, and even these early writings situate women as rational equals to men.

As indicated earlier, some of Brown's early poems were addressed to women. Like his letters to male friends, these poems use effusive language, reflect poetic models, comment on the nature of affection and imagination, and, at times, reflect larger social issues. He wrote "To Miss D.P." and "To Estrina" for Dolley Payne, the former when he was enamored of her and the latter as a farewell poem in 1789, before her 1790 marriage to John Todd, to whom Wilkins was apprenticed for his law education. Todd died in the yellow fever epidemic of 1793, and the widow Dolley married James Madison a year later. While both of these poems rely heavily on conventional imagery and poetic language of love, the vision of domestic bliss in "To Estrina" advocates intellectual as well as emotional affinity: "We should have liv'd the happiest pair on earth / Form'd for each other, nature gave us birth; / And minds, and manners, taste & fortune strove / alike in each to warm with mutual Love" (lines 41–44).[18] Alas, instead, the narrator has to envision her connected to one "Whose soul alike unmov'd by joys, or woes, / One dull unvarying temper only knows; / And when nor taste, nor genius, save in dress / And in mechanic arts have deign'd to bless" (lines 79–82).[19] "To D.F." was written for Deborah Ferris, a member of Brown's Philadelphia circle (and sister of friend and Belles Lettres Society member John Ferris), who was courted by both Brown and Bringhurst. The poem was written by Brown inside the front cover of Ferris's copy of Samuel Johnson's didactic treatise on happiness, *Rasselas*; the location provides yet another example of the intersection of reading, writing, social issues, and poetry of this time.

It was not a large leap for men to move from intellectual exchange in literary clubs or mixed-sex circles to writing for a more public audience. Brown, Bringhurst, and Wilkins all published poetry or essays in Philadelphia periodicals during this time. When Elihu Hubbard Smith traveled to Philadelphia in 1790 to study medicine with Benjamin Rush, making the acquaintance of Brown, Bringhurst, and others, one such publication venture resulted. In 1791, Smith, adopting the persona "Ella," began a poetic exchange (of primarily sonnets) in the *Gazette of the United States* that has become known as the "Ella-Birtha-Henry" correspondence. Bringhurst, writing as "Birtha," and later Brown, writing as "Henry," responded to "Ella" in print (Bennett). This poetic exchange imitated the briefly popular writings of the Della Cruscans in England, a literary circle of male and female poets who wrote stylized verse with pseudonyms that was published for a broader audience but mimicked intimate poetic correspondence (Waterman 44). Brown ultimately provided four of the thirty-five letters in what was then the longest literary correspondence in periodicals in America. The literary names used in this exchange were also repeated as pseudonyms in letters between the friends, blurring the boundaries of public and private conversation.

Although there is no doubt that Brown's vision was shaped by intimate dialogues with his peers, the narrator of his first significant prose publication is presented as a solitary rambler or "Rhapsodist." From August to November 1789, Brown published four essays in *The Universal Asylum, and Columbian Magazine*, signed in succession with the letters of his surname (B, R, O, W). Brown's model in these short pieces is, on the one hand, the periodical essay format perfected by Joseph Addison and Richard Steele in the *Tatler* and *Spectator*; yet, on the other, the series' satirical presentation of a self-defeating narrator also reveals the influence of Sterneian comic sentiment and the *Sturm und Drang* of Goethe. Instead of a disembodied observer or "spectator," Brown's rhapsodist is a solipsist, whose reflections never burst the bounds of a self-reflexive intellect. He decries sociable circles, intellectual effort, or communal grasp for knowledge. Friendship and romance are deemed "irksome" (Rhapsodist 537). "Love and friendship, and all the social passions, are excluded from his bosom" (538). He is "an enemy to conversation" who loves, instead, to "converse with beings of his own creation" (537). Self-focused, his observations focus on his processes of perception, the "devious wanderings of a quick but thoughtful mind" (467). Yet, despite these potentially antisocial attributes, he insists that he writes like a common man. The phrasing "A rhapsodist is one who delivers the sentiments suggested by the moment in artless and unpremeditated language" (467) anticipates, albeit with some irony, Wordsworth's manifesto in the preface to the 1800 *Lyrical Ballads*. The third and fourth installments combine a fictitious personal history of the narrator—a history that professes early communion with nature along the "solitary banks of the Ohio" (589)—with the elaborate hoax of a (fictitious) intercepted letter, which questions the veracity of the narrator's tale and is excerpted into the essay. Amid the jokes about self-representation in "The Rhapsodist," there are serious reflections on the nature of the imagination, as when the essay considers that "The enthusiasm of religion is little different from that of poetry, and these are with great difficulty distinguished from a sublime and rational philosophy. They flow in separate channels, but it is most probable that they are derived from the self same fountain" (539). This interconnectedness of forms of knowledge remains a determining feature of Brown's mind.

The manuscript "Henrietta Letters," a designation coined by later scholars, is an epistolary fiction consisting of seventeen letters between "Henrietta" (also referred to as "Harriet") and "C.B.B." While the "Henrietta Letters" themselves are not in the body of Brown's correspondence, they are frequently referred to within the letters, for example, in the long letter than contains "The Story of Julius" (Letters 89–90); as a result, some early biographers assumed Henrietta was a real person rather than a textual creation (e.g., Clark 54). The narrative was written in 1790 (before the death of John Davidson, to whom the final letter is addressed), then copied and revised, with changes from content of the 1790–1792 Bringhurst-Wilkins letters, with the surviving manuscript dated to 1792.[20] The final letter in the series is written to "J_____ D _____," or John Davidson, providing an example of the way Brown blurred "the lines between the letters' invented and non-invented elements" (Barnard 523). The postscript to this letter leaves the amorous, Rousseauvian world of Henrietta and C.B.B. and refers to issues more closely associated with the friends' participation in literary clubs.

The theme and style of the "Henrietta Letters" reflect Brown's deep interest in Rousseau at this time, and the romantic-sensual-intellectual correspondence refers to the lover-tutor trope in Rousseau's *La nouvelle Héloise* (which Brown first read in 1788) as well as aspects of Richardson's *Clarissa*. Brown's text, however, revises Rousseau's views on women, especially insofar as it affirms their capacity to be educated as independent individuals rather than merely companions to men. Henrietta asks, "Why should Women be outstripped by men in literary pursuits? For is not female curiousity insatiable, and what other passion is requisate, to render learned labour successfull?" (Letters 688). The C.B.B. character, by contrast, engages in more stylized, emotional language than Henrietta and even includes voyeuristic fantasies of seeing her in various stages of undress. In Henrietta, Brown presents the voice of a woman with both sensual *and* intellectual desires. While she scolds C.B.B. for sharing his most explicit desires—a representational joke, since she has to evoke them to rebuke them—she seeks to tone down his passions rather than quench them completely, making them more productive of virtue but no less strong. In Letter X, she defends passionate love or "amorous" feelings as "enobling," "proof not of the weakness or depravity, but of the purity of the heart, and loftiness of the understanding of him, who is influenced by it" (699).

What are now called the "Godolphin" fragment and the "Ellendale" fragment are additional epistolary fictional experiments in the early Brown archive, both dated 1793. The Godolphin fragment is a one-sided correspondence (with moments of reported dialogue with a third party, William Conswould) from "R.H." to "Susan." The first several pages discuss a global "chain of Causes" (Letters 780) and present a global picture of civilization linking science, geology, and poetry to its sense of history. The Ellendale fragment opens with an address to "W.C.," presumably the same William Conswould mentioned in the Godolphin text. The date line identifies the place of composition as "Ellendale," a fictitious estate on the Schuylkill near Philadelphia (Letters 807 n. 3). The fictional correspondence, like Brown's actual letters, refers to "Conversations" previously held by the writer and the recipient, seeming to continue discussions on the Intellect, the Poet, Christianity, and other topics that were held face-to-face as well as in writing. What is perhaps most interesting about these fragments is that the places and characters overlap with those in other Brown fictional fragments from the early to mid-1790s: "The Story of Julius," the "Medwaye" fragment, the "Harry Wallace" fragment, and the "Adini" fragment. "None of these fragments align precisely, but this re-cycling of fictional names, locales, and motifs suggests that they were loosely associated as several outlines or experiments toward a larger fictional project that never took shape" (Letters 807 n. 3). The connections across texts, a dominant trait of the varied 1792–1794 writings, challenge simple generic categorization during these early years. They also point to Brown's literary ambition and experimentation, as well as to his circulation of materials with peers.

While it may seem that the years 1787 to 1793 are shaped by a tension between law and literature, it may be more productive to consider the way Brown's reading, writing, and conversing all intersect. His rhetorical effusions of emotion explored social character more than they exposed personal intimacy; his interest in speculative narrative was connected to the study of legal and moral dilemmas; his imaginative locales were not solipsistic spaces but playfully shared with his friends.

V. 1793–1795: Changes

In 1793, the Reign of Terror began in France; a yellow fever epidemic claimed the lives of several thousand people in Philadelphia, throwing the city into a panic; and Brown read William Godwin's *Enquiry Concerning Political Justice* (1793), the treatise that would shift his attention from Rousseau and writers of the French Enlightenment to the Godwin circle and their brand of sociopolitical, cultural, and religious critique. In 1792, Wilkins moved to New Jersey to study for the bar and launched his own law practice the following year; other colleagues were likewise moving on to their careers. Letters from Brown to family and friends comment on his anxieties over parental approval (suggesting he feared conflict over leaving the law permanently) and his uncertainty for his future (e.g., Letters 243–245).

Brown spent May–August 1793 with Elihu Hubbard Smith in Connecticut, where he met Richard Alsop, Theodore Dwight, and other "Hartford Wits," a circle of established New England poets. He reveled in the Connecticut landscape, claiming in a July 1793 letter to Bringhurst that it was superior to Rousseauvian fantasies of "social and studious retirement" (Letters 240). He also appreciated the usefulness of these new connections, and how these connections, as well as the place, could help him pursue his plans to be a writer. Brown's professional life, however, stagnated on his return to Philadelphia in the fall. Records suggest he may have taught at the Friends Grammar School in Philadelphia for at least part of 1793–1794 (Letters 467 n. 2). Aside from this possible post, Brown avoided paid employment.

William Dunlap, a playwright and friend Brown met through Smith, stayed with Brown in Philadelphia to attend, as a delegate, the first American Convention for Promoting Abolition of Slavery in January 1794 (Letters 264 n. 10). Letters suggest that Brown visited New York City regularly in 1794, including attending, in April, a performance of Dunlap's tragedy *The Fatal Deception* (268 n. 1, 288 n. 1). While his friendships with Smith and Dunlap were growing stronger, there were still ties in Philadelphia. Brown included his longest-surviving poem, "Devotion: An Epistle," in an October 4, 1794, letter to Deborah Ferris.[21] The poem opens with an evocation of the emotional triangle that had developed between Brown, Bringhurst, and Ferris, unfolding into an "early-romantic intellectual autobiography presented to an inspiring muse who is romantically attracted not to the poet, but to another friend" (284). The letter did not achieve its goals in at least one sense, for Ferris and Bringhurst became engaged in March 1795, although they did not marry until 1799.

Wilkins died in early 1795, and, in an April 19, 1795, letter to his brother James, Brown connected that deep sorrow to his failure to attempt the bar: "It is his death that hath prevented me from fulfilling your expectations" (Letters 291). Even at that date, Brown suggested deferral rather than irrevocable rejection of the law. Brown spent the summer of 1795 in New York and Perth Amboy, the New Jersey country home of Dunlap. By this time, Bringhurst and Ferris were commenting in their letters to each other about Brown, or "Romeo," as they termed him, and his relationship (presumably a poetic exchange) with Ruth Paxson, or "Stella," the wife of Timothy Paxson.[22] Ferris's letters are sharply critical not only of Ruth Paxson's behavior but also of her general character. Bringhurst and Ferris attempted to intervene in Brown's friendship with Ruth Paxson through a variety of means, involving other members of their social circle. An October 1795 letter from Brown to Bringhurst, remarkable for its personal content and lack of exaggerated emotion, reveals Brown's hurt and anger. The letter begins and ends with reproaches about Bringhurst's intervention with his friendship and threat to hurt Ruth Paxson's reputation.[23] The rest of the long letter is Brown's most cogent rejection of orthodox Christianity during these years, particularly its socially prescribed sense of decorum. "I listen with respect to your advice on the subject of Christianity, but, my friend, we are far from well understanding each other on this subject" (297). From this polite expression of a possible misunderstanding, or human failing in friendship's union of souls, he takes a more doctrinaire position that responds both to Bringhurst's personal meddling with Brown's friendships and to his intellectual orientation: "I once thought, as, possibly, you now think that religious beliefs were desirable, even if it were erroneous. I am now of a different opinion, and believe that utility must always be coincident to truth" (302).

With such an emotional, intellectual, and religious break with his Quaker Philadelphia circle, Brown was ready to move on. In the fall of 1795, he shifted his affiliation from Quaker views of religious tolerance to the more radical (even atheistic) views of Godwin, from the apprenticeship world of Philadelphia to the intellectual circles of New York City, from the circulation of writing within a relatively closed circle to more public ventures.

NOTES

1. I would like to thank Drake University's Office of the Provost for support in completing this project. Philip Barnard provided essential direction toward recent resources. I am indebted to Lana Finley for an earlier draft of this material, particularly her research on Quakerism and Elijah Brown.
2. Parliament did pass a law in 1695 that allowed Quakers to provide an affirmation instead of an oath under certain circumstances, but the law was intended to make it easier to litigate against Quakers rather than provide alternative legal procedures for their defense.
3. Penn sailed for the colonies on the ship *Welcome* in 1682.
4. Steven Watts and Stephen Shapiro both place the Brown family history within a larger American story of how early religious or idealized colonial ventures became enmeshed in the political and economic systems of the long eighteenth century (Watts xviii; Shapiro 4).
5. For more on Elijah Brown's arrest, see Moses 20–21 and Kafer 1–14, 29–32. Kafer contends that Brown was not a typical prisoner, less respected and less religiously motivated than his fellow exiles.
6. "Historical Essay," cited from the electronic files (no pagination) for the forthcoming *Poems*, Vol. 7 of *Collected Writings of Charles Brockden Brown*, ed. Michael Cohen and Alexandra Socarides.
7. Ibid.
8. Biographers often stress a tension between his intended profession and literary aspirations; see Watts 27–48 and Ferguson 129–134.

9. That Bringhurst adopts a more orthodox Christian position is evident from comments within a May 1792 letter, such as Brown's question, "Dost thou wish me to become a convert to your doctrine? Implicitly to believe in my own Immortality?" (Letters 39).

10. Another close friend and classmate, John Davidson, died in 1790.

11. Ferguson argues that Brown was increasingly disheartened by the "inability of the law to control or even to define behavior" (Ferguson 139).

12. For example, Watts sees them as symptomatic of "severe emotional turmoil" (Watts 36) or unhealthy "internal fragmentation" (41). Caleb Crain describes Brown as "adolescent" and sees in the letters patterns of "imposture" or deception due to unstable self-image (Crain 55).

13. The "man of feeling" was a literary type popularized by Laurence Sterne's *A Sentimental Journey through France and Italy* (1768) and Henry Mackenzie's *The Man of Feeling* (1771).

14. On the homosocial structure of the friendship network in these letters, see Crain 66–69.

15. In fact, "Imaginative scenes and dialogues recur in seventeen of the forty-five letters from 1792–1793" ("Historical Essay," Letters 833).

16. Hewitt argues such conflations challenge the boundaries of letter writing and fiction writing (96–97; see also her chapter 14 in this volume).

17. Bringhurst to Deborah Ferris, April 3, 1785 (ms. in Charles Brockden Brown Papers, 1792–1821, Bowdoin College Library).

18. Cited from the electronic files (no pagination) for the forthcoming *Poems*, Vol. 7 of *Collected Writings of Charles Brockden Brown*, ed. Michael Cohen and Alexandra Socarides.

19. The descriptions of Estrina's future spouse, like the one here, resemble Brown's other written comments on Todd. For more on the Dolley Payne–Todd–Madison connection, see Letters 26 n. 2.

20. The "Henrietta Letters" provide an example of the "blending of fictional and ordinary correspondence during the 1792–1794 period" (Letters 751 n. 41). For a general discussion, see "Historical Essay" (Letters 838–840).

21. This blank-verse poem, like some of the other love poetry, has a life beyond its initial intention. Brown likely sent the same poem to Elizabeth Linn during their courtship, and "Devotion: An Epistle—To Calista" was revised, depersonalized, and published in the *American Register* in 1808.

22. For a summary of the Brown–Bringhurst–Ferris correspondence and the Paxson issue, see Letters 305–310.

23. In a subsequent letter, Brown directly refers to Ruth Paxson's "sencibility to reputation," as well as the harm Bringhurst's continued intervention could bring to her and her marriage (Letters 314).

Works Cited

Barnard, Philip. "The Letters of Charles Brockden Brown: Epistolary Performance and New Paths for Scholarship." In Celeste-Marie Bernier, Judie Neman, and Matthew Pethers, eds., *The Edinburgh Companion to Nineteenth-Century American Letters and Letter-Writing*, 511–524. Edinburgh: Edinburgh University Press, 2016.

Barnard, Philip, and Stephen Shapiro. "Introduction." In Charles Brockden Brown, *Ormond: Or the Secret Witness, with Related Texts*, ix–liv. Indianapolis: Hackett, 2009.

Bennett, Charles E. "A Poetical Correspondence among Elihu Hubbard Smith, Joseph Bringhurst, Jr., and Charles Brockden Brown in *The Gazette of the United States*." *Early American Literature* 12.3 (1977): 277–285.

Bringhurst, Joseph, Jr. "Correspondence, Other, 1795–1821." In *Charles Brockden Brown Papers, 1792–1821.* George Mitchell Department of Special Collections and Archives, Bowdoin College Library, Brunswick, Maine, no date.

Brown, Charles Brockden. *Poems*, Vol. 7 of *Collected Writings of Charles Brockden Brown.* Michael Cohen and Alexandra Socarides, eds. Lewisburg, Pa.: Bucknell University Press, forthcoming 2018.

Brown, Charles Brockden. "The Rhapsodist." CM 3.8–3.11 (August–November 1789): 464–467, 537–541, 587–601, 661–665.

Clark, David Lee. *Charles Brockden Brown: Pioneer Voice of America.* Durham, N.C.: Duke University Press, 1952.

Crain, Caleb. *American Sympathy: Men, Friendship, and Literature in the New Nation.* New Haven, Conn.: Yale University Press, 2008.

Ferguson, Robert. *Law and Letters in American Culture.* Cambridge, Mass.: Harvard University Press, 1984.

Hewitt, Elizabeth. "The Authentic Fictional Letters of Charles Brockden Brown." In Theresa Strouth Gaul and Sharon M. Harris, eds., *Letters and Cultural Transformations in the United States, 1760–1860*, 79–98. Burlington, Vt.: Ashgate, 2009.

Kafer, Peter. *Charles Brockden Brown's Revolution and the Birth of American Gothic.* Philadelphia: University of Pennsylvania Press, 2004.

Moses, Richard P. "The Quakerism of Charles Brockden Brown." *Quaker History* 75.1 (Spring 1986): 12–25.

Shapiro, Stephen. *The Culture and Commerce of the Early American Novel: Reading the Atlantic World-System.* University Park: Pennsylvania State University Press, 2008.

Teute, Frederika J. "'A Republic of Intellect': Conversation and Criticism among the Sexes in 1790s New York." In Philip Barnard, Mark L. Kamrath, and Stephen Shapiro, eds., *Revising Charles Brockden Brown: Culture, Politics, and Sexuality in the Early Republic*, 149–181. Knoxville: University of Tennessee Press, 2004.

Warfel, Harry R. *Charles Brockden Brown, American Gothic Novelist.* Gainesville: University of Florida Press, 1949.

Waterman, Bryan. *Republic of Intellect: The Friendly Club of New York and the Making of American Literature.* Baltimore: Johns Hopkins University Press, 2007.

Watts, Steven. *The Romance of Real Life: Charles Brockden Brown and the Origins of American Culture.* Baltimore: Johns Hopkins University Press, 1994.

CHAPTER 2

....

LATER YEARS, 1795–1810

....

BRYAN WATERMAN

THE summer of 1795 marked the start of a significant transition in Charles Brockden Brown's life, from a primary intellectual orientation toward his former Friends Latin School classmates in Philadelphia to a network of associates in New York who gathered in and around a group called the Friendly Club. This transition eased other passages in Brown's life: away from Quaker practice and Christian belief and toward freethinking; away from the sentimentalism of Rousseau and toward the radical sensibility of William Godwin and Mary Wollstonecraft; away from legal study and toward professional writing and editing; and away from the polite regulation of mixed-sex sociability and toward increasingly unconventional views on friendship between men and women that would find expression in some of his earliest published writing. These shifts would characterize Brown's primary literary output and his social life for half a decade. Several of the friendships would endure even after he returned to Philadelphia permanently in 1800, as would Brown's fascination with the ideas that animated them.

Multiple crises spurred Brown's move to New York in the summer of 1795. In April, he lost his friend William Wood Wilkins, who a few years earlier had been his most intimate companion but whose friendship had waned as Wilkins's legal career, which took him away from the city for a time, eclipsed his sociability. Brown, already disenchanted with the idea of his own legal career, now blamed his decision to abandon it altogether on his friend's death. Suffering through "a disease, called by some Nosographers, the *dumps*" (Letters 290–291),[1] he found other friendships growing strained. Most notably, his friends Joseph Bringhurst and Deborah Ferris, who had begun to form their own romantic attachment, were pressuring Brown to curb his apparently clandestine poetic exchanges with a mutual married friend, Ruth Paxson.[2] When Brown left Philadelphia in July, Bringhurst and Ferris rejoiced that "his correspondence" with Paxson would "be entirely at an end,"[3] and by summer's end, Bringhurst could report that Brown's New York friends had convinced him the behavior had been in error.[4] But such hopes for Brown's reform would not be long-lived. Bringhurst must not have realized fully that Brown's New York friends harbored deistic beliefs and progressive views on gender relations.[5] While these new friends also prodded Brown to reform specific aspects of his behavior, they provided him with intellectual freedom and solidarity during the years in which his writing career began to mature (Teute; Waterman 2007; Kaplan).

Brown had met some of these associates during a trip to New York and Connecticut in 1793, when he had traveled to visit Elihu Hubbard Smith, whose friendship he had gained while Smith was a medical student in Philadelphia in 1790–1791.[6] After Smith moved to New York in the fall of 1793, he activated a network of associates who had been educated at Yale or else were married into prominent Connecticut and Long Island merchant families with Yale ties. Smith himself had finished Yale at age fifteen, the school's youngest graduate to that date. He studied further with Timothy Dwight at the private, coeducational Greenfield Hill Academy before moving to Philadelphia to study medicine with Benjamin Rush. In Philadelphia, Smith had joined Brown and Bringhurst in a poetic correspondence in the city's magazines and newspapers (Bennett). Shortly after Brown's first visit to Connecticut, Smith had published *American Poems, Selected and Original*, a volume collecting and canonizing major poetry of the post-Revolutionary era. Brown may have contributed to the editorial process, but the volume includes none of his early poems. Still, his friendship with Smith opened him to a broader field of early American publishing than he had participated in to that point.

Other New York friendships solidified as Brown visited Smith in New York. William Dunlap, whose work had been featured in Smith's *American Poems*, was the son of a former British officer and Loyalist merchant. Leaving home, he joined the revolutionary cause and became an itinerant portrait painter, whose sitters included George Washington. In 1784, Dunlap's father sent him to study painting with Benjamin West in London; instead, he spent most of his time in theaters. Returning to New York City three years later, he launched a career as a playwright and cultivated intellectual interests by joining New York's Philological Society (whose members included Noah Webster) and, later, the Friendly Club. Following his father's death in 1791, Dunlap left the family business to pursue his work as a playwright. In 1796, he would purchase a quarter interest in the Old American Company, a professional acting troupe, and in 1798, he would help to open the Park Theater, which would become the city's principal playhouse for a generation.

Other new friends included William Johnson, a young lawyer and Yale graduate who lived with Smith and also participated in the Friendly Club. Two years older than Smith, Johnson had been two years behind him at Yale. Though he did not publish literary work under his own name, he became an important figure in American legal publishing. He also (like Smith, Brown, and Dunlap) kept a regular diary he shared with friends, especially after periods of separation, and he was an avid consumer of fiction whose tastes matched Brown's, Smith's, and Dunlap's.[7] Johnson would assist Brown in multiple literary and commercial projects in coming years.

Many of Brown's New York friends later achieved prominence: Smith, along with two latecomers to the club, Edward Miller and Samuel Latham Mitchill, founded the *Medical Repository*; Mitchill, a Columbia science professor who like Edward Miller was a club associate for years before beginning to attend regularly in 1798, was eventually elected to both the US Congress and the US Senate; James Kent, law professor at Columbia, became a state judge, a state chancellor, and a nationally prominent legal writer; and

Dunlap was already an active playwright, painter, and theater manager and later in life wrote histories of American theater and other arts. The group's merchants, Dunlap's brothers-in-law George and William Woolsey, belonged to important mercantile networks and were descended from, married into, and progenitors of New England clerical dynasties.[8] The Reverend Samuel Miller, Edward's brother and another latecomer to the club, would write a substantial intellectual history of the eighteenth century that gave many of these friends, including Brown, pride of place (Waterman 2007 231–242).

These friends provided the intellectual context for Brown's most significant works, including an orientation toward the British writers—William Godwin, Thomas Holcroft, Robert Bage, Mary Wollstonecraft, Mary Hays, Erasmus Darwin—whose thought would most influence his (see chapter 17 in this volume). They also provided Brown with models of industrious authorship and publishing and pushed him to make good on his literary ambitions. In the fall of 1795, after his first extended stay among these New York friends, Brown returned to Philadelphia, renewed in his determination to write fiction. He wrote Dunlap about progress on a novel that would be "equal in extent" to Godwin's *Caleb Williams*, which would "render my system of morality perfect in all its parts" and "produce something valuable for its utility."[9] The note illuminates Brown's conception of fiction at this crucial juncture, when Godwin provided him with not only a formal model for philosophical fiction but also a utilitarian rationale for critiquing institutional—especially religious—impediments to truth seeking. Over the next few years, as Brown experimented with fictional forms, including periodical essays and philosophical dialogues, and attempted to start several novels before drafting the now-lost *Sky-Walk* in 1797, he would test Godwin's ideas by having his characters adhere to or depart from basic principles. And to the end of his career, he explored, in terms resembling Godwin's, the relationship between narrative history and romance (Emerson).

Brown's letters to Bringhurst in the fall of 1795 reveal not only his irritation at Bringhurst's meddling in his friendship with Ruth Paxson but also his determination to challenge conventional Christian morality. Doubting Christ's divinity, Brown felt "the acceptance of his doctrines, moral and metaphysical, must depend on their intrinsic evidence" to be regarded as true and useful. He rendered anathema the idea that people should adopt Christian precepts out of a fear of eternal punishment. Such ideas had been percolating for some time. Three years earlier, he had similarly provoked Bringhurst by suggesting that Samuel Richardson's novel *Sir Charles Grandison* might be a more useful "picture of moral perfection" than the New Testament.[10] Parting ways intellectually with Bringhurst, Brown announced that his present thinking was governed by a new "Oracle," Godwin's massive philosophical treatise *Enquiry concerning Political Justice*, which had been published two years earlier.[11]

Smith, in an unsent letter, would later narrate this momentous turn in Brown's intellectual history. "Now & then a ray of truth broke in, but with an influence too feeble to dissipate the phantoms, which error had conjured up around you," Smith wrote of his friend's romantic past. Then "*Godwin came and all was light!*"[12] Smith shared Brown's enthusiasm. A month after making a birthday resolve to "keep my eye, & my heart, fixed on the majestic, simple, sublime, & venerable temple of Truth,"[13] Smith received an update from Brown on his novel in progress, which he expected would be controversial: "What different sentiments will it excite! And how much rancor, & misrepresentation must he encounter! And not he alone, but all those who are united to him by the ties of friendship & bonds of resembling opinions." The novel Brown was composing may have been an early attempt at *Arthur Mervyn*, as many critics assume, though it may also have been a continuation of a series of stories he had worked on for years, in which he reimagined the Christian story in a contemporary setting on a farm outside Philadelphia. Smith thought the book would generate enough public opposition to put their philosophy to the test: "Storms & tempests hover over our heads, ready to burst, or are gathering in slow & sullen vengeance, to break, & overwhelm us with destruction. But I trust that we shall put forth the conductors of virtue, & turn aside, or disarm the lightnings of superstitious fury."[14]

For Smith, the resistance he and Brown had both received from conservative friends offered the first sign of these looming storms. Brown ended his summer 1795 trip with a stay at Dunlap's country home in Perth Amboy, New Jersey, a visit that seems to have been a catalyzing moment for Brown, Smith, and Dunlap. Brown came away determined to confront Bringhurst and to take up novel writing in earnest. Smith, similarly resolved to write and publish, worried that "the unavoidable disclosure of my peculiar sentiments" would wound his parents and perhaps even lead to blasphemy prosecution in his home state of Connecticut, something the friends explicitly discussed in Perth Amboy.[15] Dunlap, echoing Brown, followed up these conversations by writing to Godwin and Holcroft about his desire to embody their principles in his plays. "Your political justice is my Gospel," he wrote to Godwin in October 1795. "I read in it daily, I weigh its arguments and trace its doctrines to all their consequences. To aid the progress of these truths, I conceive to be a duty incumbent on me both by writing and acting" (Green 441–443).

The enthusiasm these friends showed for Godwin stemmed from more than admiration of style and resulted in more than mere imitation. Gathering information about Godwin's circle by piecemeal, intuiting connections between favorite authors, they identified almost spiritually with what they took these writers to represent: a belief in the progress of knowledge (and with it, the possibility of human perfectibility) through a free and friendly exchange of ideas; a rationalist approach to morality that eschewed motives such as fear of divine punishment or hope for eternal reward in the afterlife; a confidence that truth telling—unrelenting sincerity and frankness—would have tangible positive effect on society; and a utilitarian commitment to community good rather than personal profit. Their reading of Holcroft, Wollstonecraft, Elizabeth Inchbald, and Hays especially fostered their interest in women's education and the possibilities of mixed-sex friendship and conversation. When they learned that Godwin and Wollstonecraft had become a couple, they were ecstatic. "Miss Wollstonecraft is now the wife of Mr. Godwin," Smith wrote to his Connecticut friend Idea Strong in October 1797. "[And] as he is a man independent in his circumstances, we may expect that she will have ample leisure for the cultivation of those sciences in which she so much delights, & for gratifying her friends by successive & interesting publications." Just a few weeks later, papers arrived with the news of Wollstonecraft's death in childbirth.

"The loss of 50,000 french & as many Austrians, on the Rhine or in Italy, would have affected me less," Smith wrote in his journal.[16]

From summer 1796 through the following March, Brown spent much of his time in New York reading and writing, often in the company of friends. In Smith and Dunlap in particular, Brown found monitors who held him to his own ideals. Whereas his early friendships were sometimes articulated in a highly sentimental, Rousseauistic vein, the defining characteristic of his friendships in New York was a frank mutual assessment of successes and especially failures. The early friendships had been founded on a principle of likeness. "Between friends there must exist a perfect and entire Similarity of dispositions," he had written to his early friend Wilkins. "Not only the same excellences but the same defects must be common to both. Soul must be knit unto Soul."[17] By contrast, Brown's new friends both pointed out and complemented his strengths and weaknesses. "No two men were ever more sincerely attached to each other than Charles Brockden Brown and Elihu Hubbard Smith; yet in many particulars no two men were ever more different," Dunlap wrote years later in his biography of Brown, emphasizing their ability to maintain intimacy in spite of limited personal similarities.[18]

Friendly Club members believed that such differences offered opportunities to confront error and receive correction. Godwin himself put it this way in a letter to Dunlap in 1796: "The consent of a judicious & unprejudiced neighbour, confirms me in my sentiment, & gives me satisfaction in my conduct."[19] This idea could best be implemented in a social circle like theirs. "[U]nreserved communication in a smaller circle, and especially among persons who are already awakened to the pursuit of truth, is of unquestionable advantage" to society's improvement, Godwin wrote in *Political Justice*. "[C]andid and unreserved communication" allowed such friends "to compare their ideas, to suggest their doubts, to remove their difficulties, and to cultivate a collected and striking manner of delivering their sentiments" before "go[ing] forth to the world." In this ideal scenario, "Every man will be eager to tell and to hear what the interest of all requires them to know. The bolts and fortifications of the temple of truth will be removed.... Knowledge will be accessible to all" (Godwin 1793, 1: 212, 214–215).

Such a thought animated Brown's friends. Smith echoes Godwin's intellectual utopianism in a description of the Friendly Club he sent to a British magazine editor in early 1798, volunteering his friends' services as American correspondents:

> There exists in this city, a small association of men, who are connected by mutual esteem, & habits of unrestricted communication. They are of different professions & occupations; of various religious & moral opinions; & tho' they coincide in the great outlines of political faith, they estimate very variously many of the political transactions of the men who have, from time to time directed the councils of the nation. This diversity of sentiment, however, as it has never affected their friendship, has made them more active in investigation; & tho' they may have formed different judgments concerning facts, has led them to a general concurrence in the facts themselves.[20]

This concurrence enacts what Godwin called a removal of difficulties; it stems from what he elsewhere in *Political Justice* called the "intercourse of mind with mind" in conversation, "one or the other party always yielding to have his ideas guided by the other" (Godwin 1793, 2: 379). This model of communication—what Smith, referring to Holcroft's *Anna St. Ives*, called "severe truth"—was not just the club's raison d'être (Smith 44). It also provided an ideal social environment for emerging writers, who served not just as trial audiences for one another's work but as collaborators in a larger intellectual project.

Though Brown had attended the Friendly Club intermittently as a visitor during previous visits to New York, the winter of 1796–1797 saw him admitted as a full member. He attended just more than a dozen club meetings at friends' homes on Saturday evenings between September and March. During the months of Brown's greatest activity, club members started publishing the *Medical Repository*, the first American medical journal; staged Smith's slight opera and two plays by Dunlap; and, with their larger, mixed-sex circle, read several novels, including work by Bage, Hays, Friedrich Schiller, Inchbald, and Cajetan Tschink. Brown and Smith both contemplated dramatic adaptations of Bage's novel *Hermsprong*. The group also consumed new medical literature by Erasmus Darwin, whose *Zoonomia* club members would issue in an American edition and Brown would cite in *Wieland*. Although Brown apparently did not join them, perhaps for financial reasons, nearly all other Friendly Club members participated in the abolitionist Manumission Society.[21]

Brown left New York rather suddenly in March 1797, apparently having had a temporary falling out with Dunlap. The move was "fortunate," Smith thought, and even though Brown "went away, apparently, not with the best spirits," Smith hoped he might establish connections with Vermont editor Joseph Dennie to find an outlet for the myriad projects he had started but had not yet seen to completion. "I fear he will effect but little, in Phila.," Smith wrote (Smith 300). But his worries turned out to have been ill founded. Back in Philadelphia, Brown set about the most industrious period of his career. That summer, he completed substantial portions of *Alcuin*, a fictionalized philosophical dialogue on women's rights, which Smith read to male and female friends in New York before he set about publishing it there. By January 1798, Brown had finished writing his first novel, *Sky-Walk* (Dunlap 1930, 1: 201).

Brown's banner year would be 1798, though it also included a number of personal tragedies. Working with Philadelphia magazine editor James Watters, whose publishing office was located in close proximity to the Brown family's home, Brown began to serialize several periodical sketches and novels, including "The Man at Home," "A Series of Original Letters," a version of *Alcuin* titled "The Rights of Women," a chapter of *Sky-Walk*, and early chapters of *Arthur Mervyn*. Brown and Ruth Paxson, who also became a *Weekly Magazine* contributor, dug out their scandalous poetic correspondence of 1795 and submitted it to Watters as well.[22] In March, Brown wrote to Smith that he was "assiduously writing novels & in love."[23] That romance, with a young woman named Susan Potts, would dissolve under family pressure, the first of his disappointments that year. "Brown tells me the manner in which his mother breaks off his connection with Miss Potts," Dunlap wrote in his diary in September 1798, although the relationship languished for more than two more years (Dunlap 1930, 1: 343).[24] Having resumed his friendship with Dunlap, apologizing for his behavior the previous winter, Brown returned to New York in July with *Wieland* mostly completed. *Sky-Walk*, at press with Watters in Philadelphia, would go missing when the printer died of yellow fever there that summer. In New York, Smith died in a yellow fever outbreak in mid-September, just as copies of *Wieland* were coming from the press. Brown, who believed himself also infected, recovered.

Smith's death devastated the club and the larger circle but didn't slow Brown's productivity. He had already drafted portions of *Wieland*'s sequel, *Memoirs of Carwin the Biloquist*, that fall. He completed *Ormond* in the last few weeks of the year. His friends began to work on proposals for a new magazine he would edit. Within months, Brown had become an American of some "intellectual renown," at least in New York and Philadelphia. Traveler John Davis described meeting Brown in "a dismal room in a dismal street" in New York around this time, "quite in the costume of an author, embodying virtue in a new novel, and making his pen fly before him" (Davis 1: 157). Brown noted in a February 1799 letter to a brother that "to be the writer of Wieland and Ormond is a greater recommendation" in society "than ever I imagined it would be" and that he spent most nights "conversing with male or female friends."[25] But not all his early readers were equally warm to his fiction. Margaret Bayard, a young New Yorker who would soon become fast friends with Brown's New York circle, was more than favorably impressed by Brown's conversation when she first met him in October 1798 in the wake of Smith's death. But she was less than enthusiastic about his new novel. "Weiland [sic] has met with a bad reception in [New] Brunswick," she reported to her future sister-in-law, Mary Ann Smith, in October 1798, "& I have not heard of one who was pleased with it. I cannot deny that it is a display of genious & strong nervous language, but I regret having read it. Do not even look into it, Mary, for from the first to the last page the gloomiest terror is prevalent. It has several nights disturbed my repose & I fear its bad effects are not yet erased from my mind. I asked him, what could have given rise to such dreadful images & found the book had been written, while he was in the midst of the yellow fever & his mind under the influence of misery & terror which it produced."[26] Later, complaining to her fiancé, Samuel Harrison Smith, that Brown's books gave her nightmares, she said she had politely declined to read *Edgar Huntly* and only took up *Arthur Mervyn* with caution.[27]

Other female readers seemingly agreed. In an undated letter written around the turn of the nineteenth century, Margaretta Akerly, another New Yorker, wrote to her sister, Catharine Mitchill, about the "curious...taste" of a mutual acquaintance, "the Charming Mrs. Higinson," who "must be a little nervous, for I heard her say, that reading Brown's Ormond made her unwell for near a week."[28] Mrs. Higinson's reaction would seem to confirm the opinion of a Philadelphia reviewer a few years later, who wrote that Brown was "unpopular with the female world, on account of his terrific subject."[29] But Akerly herself suggests some disdain for Higinson's nervousness, and Bayard noted in another letter a female acquaintance who found Brown's Gothic novels perfectly "adapted to her taste."[30] When Davis reencountered Brown in Philadelphia later in his travels, he found him "ingratiating himself into the favor of the ladies by writing a new novel." Whether women readers enjoyed Brown's novels in large numbers is difficult to know, but Davis clearly imagined they did (Davis 2: 20).

Brown's Gothic mode didn't settle well with some male readers, either. Federalist jurist Kent, Brown's Friendly Club associate, expressed some objections to *Wieland* when it was published in the fall of 1798, based on its dark tone and indebtedness to Godwin. Though initially receptive to Godwin, Kent had been put off by his posthumous biography of Wollstonecraft, which revealed her suicide attempts and unconventional sexual behavior, and in the wake of the French Revolution, he had adopted the conservative line that "projectors" or "speculators" like Godwin were laying out plans beyond the capacity of ordinary "men as they are."[31] Responding to Kent's criticism, William Johnson, who had helped Brown earlier that year decide on a "suitable catastrophe" for *Wieland*,[32] defended Brown in terms that help explain both Brown's agenda for his fiction and some readers' reluctance to embrace it. According to Johnson—perhaps disingenuously, considering that Brown was just then completing his draft of *Ormond*—Brown planned to *avoid*, in future publications,

> the development, or discussion of any principles, which will shock even your prejudices, on certain subjects.—But if I understand you, it is wrong to call your opinion a prejudice.—To us it must be a salutary principle of conduct, however we may, at times, regard with indulgence or approbation, ingenious speculations, on the consequences which should flow from a different state of things. The major propositions of Mr. G[odwin] and Mr. B[rown] are hypothetical, and the inferences are correctly made;—yet they afford not a rule of conduct for the beings who now walk the earth.—But enough.[33]

Johnson's explanation highlights the degree to which Brown imagined a philosophical-moral program for his fiction, one that seems to have united with its "doleful tone" in falling afoul of readers like Kent. Some of Brown's peers simply objected to his writing fiction at all. His Philadelphia friend Thomas Cope thought Brown "would please one better if instead of employing himself in producing mere works of fancy he would apply the rare talents of which he is undoubtedly possessed to the promotion of science & the pursuit of useful & practical philosophy" (Cope 43; November 16, 1800).

Brown indicated repeatedly, though, that his fiction aimed precisely for such promotions and pursuits.[34] Shortly after Smith's death, Brown aimed to supplement his literary career with an editorial one on the same set of principles. The *Monthly Magazine, and American Review*, starting in the spring of 1799, would expand his friends' field for practical observation and commentary on scientific as well as literary topics. Equally important, Brown hoped it would prove "very profitable" in financial terms as well.[35] Friendly Club member Samuel Miller, writing to the Massachusetts minister Jedidiah Morse to solicit subscribers, described the magazine as a group endeavor: "There is a Society or club of about 10 gentlemen," he wrote, "who meet once a week, to consult about the Magazine, & concert plans to make up its contents & to promote its interests."[36] Maria Templeton, part of the club's extended social circle, who would a decade later marry William Johnson, wrote to Bayard about the magazine's collaborative nature: "He will be aided by Dr. & Mr. Miller, Dr. Mitchell, Mr. W. Johnson, Mr. Dunlap, & Mr. [Samuel M.] Hopkins."[37] William Johnson wrote to a friend in Albany: "It is proposed by several Gentlemen to patronize, & aid the publication of a periodical work in this City.—Proposals have been circulated, and a considerable number of subscribers obtained.—The plan of the work would assign it a higher rank, among periodical works, than that of a magazine, though it bears that simple & vulgar appellation.—"[38] The *Monthly Magazine* began publication in April 1799 and continued through the end of the following year. Biographers have sometimes complained that Brown's friends failed him in producing content, but the period's conventions of anonymous or nearly anonymous publication make it difficult to know with any certainty which friends contributed and how regularly. Certainly, Bayard's accounts of the club's mixed-sex social circle in New York indicate that multiple members contributed and also actively solicited content from others, including her.[39]

The *Monthly Magazine* mirrored attempts within the club to transcend political differences. In its inaugural issue, Brown, as editor, announced: "There already exists a sufficient number of vehicles of political discussion and political information, and it is presumed that readers in general will be best pleased with a performance limited to scientific and literary topics."[40] A later piece, framed as a conversation between two *Monthly Magazine* readers, decried the general audience's quickness to assign political implications to virtually any contribution. "These things being considered," one participant concludes, seeming to state a position on behalf of the editors, "I cannot help thinking that the Magazine had better be free from theological and political polemics. I am willing to give up my share of them from this prudential consideration."[41]

Politics and religion, in the aftermath of the French Revolution and the lead-up to the presidential contest between John Adams and Thomas Jefferson, had become explosive topics, and the Friendly Club's members and extended circles were made up of people on all sides. Johnson and Kent were Federalists, as were the Woolsey brothers, allied with their brother-in-law Timothy Dwight in Connecticut. Smith had been a Federalist and a friend of Timothy Dwight and his brother, Theodore, but differed with them on religion. Mitchill and the Millers were Democrats. Dunlap remained quiet about politics but chafed at the staunch Federalism of his Woolsey and Dwight brothers-in-law and was an admirer of Jefferson throughout his life.[42] In the larger social circle, their friend Maria Nicholson belonged to a prominent New York Democratic-Republican family. Bayard was engaged to Samuel Harrison Smith, an aspiring Philadelphia journalist who would soon be tapped to edit Jefferson's *National Intelligencer*. Bayard, who wrote to her fiancé frequently about her evenings spent in conversation with Brown and friends, said she believed their views resembled his.[43] The range of views members held, then, which they had hoped would aid them in their search for truth, certainly had the potential to create friction in the political turmoil surrounding Jefferson's election.

The *Monthly Magazine*'s short life cycle coincided with one aspect of this political ferment that Brown found particularly intriguing: the rise of the New England clergy's campaign against the Bavarian Illuminati and other rumored Jacobin conspiracies to overthrow governments in Europe and America (Stauffer). The club's reaction to this transatlantic campaign was multifaceted and shifted in real time as accounts of the conspiracy circulated through the mid-Atlantic and the northeast. Elihu Smith seemed, before his death, to find the conspiracy theories fascinating but far-fetched (Smith 412). Dunlap rejected them as religious fanaticism and began to draft a never-completed novel, *The Anti-Jacobin*, in which he parodied his brother-in-law, Timothy Dwight (Dunlap 1930, 152–172, 322, 345). Brown's fictional appropriation of the Illuminati scare (particularly in *Memoirs of Carwin*) doesn't so much indicate his endorsement or denial of the rumors as it reveals his fascination with the anxieties about publicity and public authority that they evoked (Waterman 2007, chap. 2), and though the *Monthly Magazine* praises Morse for exposing legitimate "villainy," it warns against full-blown hysteria (Clark 153). The club's clearest public resistance to the Illuminati scare—and perhaps the source of political tension that eventually disbanded the club—came from the Reverend Samuel Miller, who criticized Morse's "indiscreet and excessive zeal" in the February 10, 1801, edition of the *American Citizen* under the pseudonym Candour. In response, the Reverend William Linn, who three years later would become Brown's father-in-law, wrote to Morse: "Mr. Miller['s]…piece is not such as your friends here approved…but he would do it his own way, & proved what I have often found, that it is in vain to remonstrate with a *Democrat*."[44] When Miller called on Brown to contribute to the second volume of his *Brief Retrospect of the Eighteenth Century* a few years later, Brown referred to this ongoing controversy; Miller had commented in that letter, dated December 1800, that he would "rather have Mr. Jefferson the President of the United States, than [Charles C. Pinckney] an aristocratic Christian."[45] Miller's and Mitchill's enthusiasm over Jefferson's ascension to the presidency—and Mitchill's career, launched in 1801, as a Democratic-Republican member of Congress—was probably received coolly by the club's Federalists. Most nineteenth-century accounts of the club credit political partisanship for its ultimate collapse.

By August 1800, Brown had begun to contemplate a return to Philadelphia if the *Monthly Magazine* didn't soon prove profitable (Cope 55). His New York publisher, the French émigré Hocquet Caritat, had traveled to London hoping to negotiate an edition of Brown's novels there.[46] *Arthur Mervyn*'s second part was set for publication that fall in New York, but Brown wasn't hopeful about its profitability, either. He had spent the spring and summer working on new novels, *Clara Howard* and *Jane Talbot*, in which he planned to abandon "gloomy representations" (Cope 43) and substitute "moral causes and daily incidents in place of the prodigious and singular" (Letters 462–464). If writing and editing could not earn him a living, however, he would be forced to join his brothers' mercantile firm. The prospect of moving back to Philadelphia was not inviting. "All the inanimate objects of this city," Brown wrote to his former teacher Robert Proud in September, "are uniform, monotonous, and dull. I have been surprised at the little power they have over my imagination." In spite of friends like the Paxsons and the Copes, he still lamented the loss of New York's "[s]ocial and intellectual pleasures," which to him were "every thing" (Letters 455–456).

In November, however, Brown met up in Philadelphia with Elizabeth Linn, the oldest daughter of the New York Dutch Reformed minister William Linn. The encounter would help him determine to abandon the magazine and stay in Philadelphia. Brown had been introduced to Elizabeth Linn earlier in the year in New York. They may even have met as early as the fall of 1796, when Elihu Smith noted in his diary that he had accompanied "the Misses Linn" home from an evening spent at Edward and Samuel

Miller's lodgings in New York. (Brown, who had spent the day with Smith, may have been there, too.) The Linns were only marginally connected to the Friendly Club's larger circle. Smith noted that though the Linn sisters apparently knew who he was when he met them in 1796, he had "not [been] at all acquainted" with them previously (Smith 226). He may not have been inclined to know them better; a few months earlier, he had "looked over a miserable sermon of Dr. Linn's," and a few days before that, at Dunlap's home, he had read a manuscript play that Elizabeth's brother, John Blair Linn, had submitted to Dunlap's theater company, which he thought was "not altogether deficient in marks of talent, [but] is eminently wanting in dramatic propriety."[47] When Brown met the Linn sisters again in early 1800 through New York friends, Elizabeth identified herself as a reader of his work (Letters 518). After they encountered each other again in Philadelphia, where John Blair Linn had settled in the ministry, the relationship intensified rapidly over the space of a few months.

As biographers have noted, the courtship changed Brown's career permanently. If nothing else, Brown's financial pressures were magnified by the prospect of marriage and family, and his determination to stay in Philadelphia meant not only joining his brothers in business but eventually taking up some anonymous political writing on topics related to commercial regulations. But his association with the Linn family also seems to have required some intellectual gymnastics, including what appear to be sly semidisavowals of positions his fiction had seemed to put forward, especially on matters of religion.

If William Linn's religious devotion and Federalist partisanship were at odds with Brown's Godwinian tendencies, the Linn family's literary sensibilities must have been attractive to him (Sprague; Anderson; Leary). Brown had favorably reviewed William Linn's oration on the death of Washington in the March 1800 *Monthly Magazine*.[48] He published commentary on John Blair Linn's work in the April and December 1800 issues, and he found the Linn sisters, during his courtship of Elizabeth, to be worthy interlocutors and correspondents.[49] In Brown's *American Review*, his brief continuation of the review portion of the *Monthly Magazine*, he offered a lengthy and even-handed review of John Blair Linn's long poem *The Power of Genius*.[50] When Brown began the monthly *Literary Magazine, and American Register* in 1803, Linn frequently contributed pieces signed "I.O."[51] Brown also published work by his soon-to-be sister-in-law Susan, who would in the 1820s herself turn novelist.[52] And shortly following his and Elizabeth's marriage in late 1804, Brown contributed a life sketch to a posthumous edition of another long poem by her brother, who had died in August that year.[53] The cumulative effect seems to be courtship by editorial promotion, but it also indicates the degree to which literary activity characterized the Linn family environment.

Brown and Linn's protracted courtship stretched from December 1800 to November 1804, though they seem to have reached an understanding about an engagement by April 1801. When their romance began, Brown was thirty years old; Linn was five years younger. Linn spent these years in Philadelphia and New York, and while Brown traveled to New York on occasion to see her, he maintained his Philadelphia residency, as Cope had predicted he would, for the rest of his life. These four years saw Brown undertake a number of new publishing projects: two novels, *Clara Howard* and *Jane Talbot*, both published in 1801; *The American Review, and Literary Journal*, which ran through 1802; and the early years of the *Literary Magazine, and American Register*, which ran from 1803 to 1807. Brown also published two anonymous political pamphlets, *Address to the Government* and *Monroe's Embassy* (both 1803; see chapter 12 in this volume), which critiqued Jeffersonian policy without necessarily advocating for Federalist alternatives, and a translation, with copious commentary in the notes, of the comte de Volney's *View of the Soil and Climate of the United States* (1804). Though the early courtship seems to have been dominated by Elizabeth's concerns about Brown's lingering feelings for Susan Potts[54] and her initial sense that Brown might engage in "imposture" and "duplicity,"[55] the evidence of their correspondence—or Brown's side of it, at least (her letters are not extant)—suggests that the largest obstacles were financial. Brown spent at least half of the four-year engagement working for his brothers. But he continued to hope that writing and editing might provide a living for him and his eventual family. Friends attempted to bring him business. Cope, for instance, secured for Brown a job writing a history of slavery, which Brown never completed, and Benjamin Rush hoped he would write a history of prison reform, a subject he felt "would glow under the eloquent strokes of his masterly pen" (Letters 637 n. 1).

Brown's parents and the Linn family may have objected to the engagement, though evidence is hard to come by. Linn's status as a non-Quaker may have troubled the Browns, though their older sons had also married outside the fellowship. They refused to attend the wedding, which was officiated by William Linn and resulted in Brown's expulsion from the Society of Friends.[56] William Linn, for his part, may have shared the sense of some that Brown's politics were too democratic; he may also have been exposed to rumors about Brown's early apostasy from Christian belief and preference for Godwin's system, which by this point had been associated in the Federalist imagination with Jefferson's politics.[57]

The Linns' feelings about their daughter's engagement to Brown may not be discernible from available evidence, but an episode in *Jane Talbot*, which Brown apparently had completed during the earliest months of his relationship with Linn (and then temporarily resolved not to publish), seems at least suggestive. The central dilemma is classic Brown: Jane Talbot is a married older woman whose husband passes away during the course of the story; Henry Colden is attracted to Jane but has already committed to another. In the novel, the moral monitoring comes from Jane's surrogate mother, Mrs. Fielder, who opposes Henry's attempt to marry Jane (now widowed). Henry's early letters, shown to her by one of his childhood friends, reveal him to have been a Godwinian: a "scoffer at promises," a "despiser of revelation," an "opponent of marriage." The novel never disproves her account of Henry's beliefs, and in the end, Henry undergoes a public conversion to Christianity that puts his sentiments in harmony with Jane's. But it seems significant, given fundamental narrative patterns in Brown's fiction, that this characterization of Godwinism comes from Mrs. Fielder, the novel's voice of false delicacy and rigid conservatism and the source of Jane's and Henry's misery. By contrast, throughout the novel, Jane repeatedly affirms that Henry's skepticism helps her refine her own faith. In the end, the epistolary form holds subversive potential, keeping alive Brown's tendency to frame his reading audience as jury, since we know less about Henry's actual beliefs than about others' views of him and his own self-interested epistolary performance.

It is tempting to read this episode in Brown's final novel as part of a campaign to protect his reputation from the same kinds of accusations Henry Colden faces. In May 1800, during the same months he may already have been writing *Clara Howard* and *Jane Talbot*—and well into the transatlantic anti-Jacobin backlash against Godwin and Wollstonecraft—Brown told his friend Bayard that he still believed Godwin's to be "the most perfect" philosophical system he had encountered: "But said he, were I to marry, I should wish for my wife to be a Christian, with this system engrafted on her. For religion would afford that sanction & authority which would enforce obedience, & those motives which encourage to perseverance."[58] If Henry's concession at the novel's end indeed mirrors the author's own compromises, however, Brown's reputation was already fixed as a radical. Almost a year after *Jane Talbot* was published, for instance, Federalist scion Thomas Boylston Adams could still describe Brown, in a letter to his brother John Quincy Adams, as "a small, sly Deist, a disguised, but determined Jacobin, a sort of Sammy Harison [*sic*] Smith in 'shape and size the same'."[59]

If Brown ever abandoned his confidence in Godwin's philosophy, he never made that disavowal publicly.[60] He did, though, in launching the *Literary Magazine* in late 1803, publicly affirm his support for—though not necessarily his faith in—Christianity. Following an extended fantasy scenario in which he imagines his readers' curiosity about his identity and sentiments ("In politics, for example, he may be a malcontent; in religion a heretic"), he offers, in characteristically cagey language, some assurances that he is "without equivocation or reserve, the ardent friend and willing champion of the Christian religion. Christian piety he reveres as the highest excellence of human beings, and the amplest reward he can seek, for his labour, is the consciousness of having, in some degree however inconsiderable, contributed to recommend the practice of religious duties." Like most of Brown's periodical work, the *Literary Magazine* had very little explicit commentary on religion or partisan politics. The editorial, then, which also includes Brown's often cited assertion that he "should enjoy a larger share of my own respect, at the present moment, if nothing had ever flowed from my pen, the production of which could be traced to me," seems to announce more than it actually does (Dunlap 1815 2:60). Brown doesn't express regret here for anything he has written, only that he is so readily known as the author.

And yet authorship remained a defining identity—and aspiration—throughout Brown's final decade. "[A]uthorship, as a mere trade," he wrote in the fall of 1803, "seems to be held in very little estimation":

> While the *poor author*, that is to say, the author by trade, is regarded with indifference or contempt, the *author*, that is, the man who devotes to composition the leisure secured to him by hereditary influence, or by a lucrative profession or office, obtains from mankind an higher, and more lasting, and more genuine reverence

than any other class of mortals. As there is nothing I should more fervently deprecate than to be enrolled in the former class, so there is nothing to which I more ardently aspire, than to be numbered among the latter.[61]

Writing as a man of leisure would never be Brown's lot, but his late work, much of it unpublished until after his death, belies the notion that his nineteenth-century career was merely that of an editorial hack. The old biographical commonplace that Brown abandoned fiction writing after 1801 turns out to be highly inaccurate. His *Historical Sketches*, probably composed in 1805–1806 and posthumously published in Dunlap's *Life*, make up an unfinished work of historical fiction—or fictional history—of nearly 115,000 words, longer than any of Brown's novels (if *Arthur Mervyn*'s volumes are taken separately). A series of fragments that treat nearly eighteen centuries in the history of a single family, the *Sketches* are part imitation and part parody of historical chronicles, part commentary on various modes of political and ecclesiastical organization, and part metafictional commentary on the relationship between narrative strategy, historical discourse, and social institutions such as family, church, and state. A few portions of this work made their way into Brown's *Literary Magazine*, but the whole suggests an ongoing concern with the same intellectual problems that had preoccupied him since the early 1790s (Barnard).

When the *Literary Magazine* folded in 1807, Brown conceived a new editorial project within months: *The American Register; or, General Repository of History, Politics, and Science*, which over two years would come to include thousands of pages of news, government reports, literary notices, and biographical and historical sketches, including his last significant publication, the "Annals of Europe and America," a history of the United States as part of global economic and political systems. When he died of tuberculosis in early 1810, Brown left behind a young family and unpublished projects of vast scope: *A System of General Geography*, for which he had published proposals and completed a partial draft, and large fragments of fictionalized chronicles of imaginary families and societies, through which he contemplates patterns in the ebb and flow of religious and governmental authority across time and space. Like Godwin, who eventually became a reader of Brown in a felicitous feedback loop of Atlantic literary exchange, Brown remained to the end convinced of the utility of fiction as a vehicle for philosophical engagements with history (Verhoeven; Apap).

Profitability was another matter. As Brown approached death, his friend Cope sketched an outline of Brown's life and family circumstances in a lengthy diary entry. At his death, Brown was receiving a salary of $1,500 a year to edit the *Register*. He had failed to lay by any savings, however, and had "lived in abundance," which led Cope to fear "he will leave his family very destitute." In the diary entry, Cope complained in detail about Brown's early and enduring enchantment with "the poisonous writings of the celebrated Godwin," a long source of contention between them (Cope 248–249). Less than ten days later, returning home from Brown's funeral, Cope revisited the theme, adding that even if Brown did "advocate the wild & mischievous doctrines of Godwin, his goodness of heart was ever a bar to his putting them into practice." But Cope would have the final word: "He died on the 21st in a happy frame of mind & obtained in his last moments that satisfactory evidence of the truth of religion, of which he had so often & so long doubted" (Cope 250). Cope attested to Brown's Christian death in a published obituary as well, providing "consolation, to his distant friends, to know that he died in the enjoyment of his mental faculties, a Christian, full of the hope of immortality, at peace with himself and with all mankind." In case that hadn't fully settled old scores, Cope provided additional posthumous apology for errors in Brown's thinking: "if, in early life, he indulged in speculative theories and opinions, it was to be ascribed to a versatile exuberance of a brilliant imagination—the unwearied inquisitiveness of a rich and active mind—and to that never failing propensity to scrutiny and investigation, consequent to a disposition to admit nothing on trust, when in search of truth."[62]

Dunlap's account of Brown's deathbed was more ambiguous than Cope's. Though he reported, on Elizabeth's testimony, that Brown had "bowed with submission to the Divine will," his friend's final moments, as Dunlap narrates them, are full of mystery and aesthetic pleasure, a scene closer to something from Brown's own fiction than to Christian funerary cliché: "sitting up in the bed, he fixed his eyes on the sky, and desired not to be spoken to until he first spoke. In this position and with a serene countenance, he continued some minutes and then said to his wife, 'when I desired you not to speak to me, I had the most transporting and sublime feelings I had ever experienced. I wanted to enjoy them, and know how long they would last'" (Dunlap 1815, 2:88–89).

Notes

1. "Wilkins' life was, indeed, the pledge of my Success in the legal profession," he wrote to his brother James on April 19 (Letters 290–291).
2. Bringhurst to Ferris, July 12, 1795 (Letters 306–307).
3. Ferris to Bringhurst, July 9, 1795 (Letters 306).
4. Bringhurst to Ferris, September 3, 1795 (Letters 309).
5. If Bringhurst sought an ally in William Dunlap, as his September 3 letter suggests, it might be worth noting that Dunlap's views on gender weren't quite as progressive as his friends'.
6. Though the New York friends were apparently more intellectually congenial for Brown in the mid-1790s, the friendship networks did overlap. Smith had befriended Bringhurst around the same time he met Brown. The three collaborated on poetry. Smith continued to write to Bringhurst, adopting Quaker pronouns as a cosmopolitan gesture. He eagerly befriended Timothy and Ruth Paxson and compared Brown's Philadelphia circle favorably with his impression of New York's Quakers. See Smith to William Johnson, January 4, 1796 (Smith 118).
7. On Johnson see Langbein, esp. 578–584.
8. On the mercantile culture to which many Friendly Club members belonged, see Shapiro 153–162. On the ecclesiastical and mercantile dynasty to which the Woolseys belonged and into which Dunlap was also married, see Clapham 201–207.
9. Brown to Dunlap, September 1795 (Letters 293).
10. Brown to Bringhurst, October 24, 1795 (Letters 298); Brown to Bringhurst, December 21, 1792 (Letters 206–207).
11. Brown to Bringhurst, October 24 and October 30, 1795 (Letters 297–303, 314–315).

12. Smith to Brown, May 27, 1796 (Smith 171). This draft of Smith's letter, though frequently cited by Brown's biographers, was never sent. See Smith's subsequent entry for July 3, 1796 (Smith 184).

13. Smith 43 (September 4, 1795). A year later, in a similar birthday resolution, Smith abandoned his practice of daily prayers as "inconsistent with the notions I entertain of the structure & constitution of the Universe" (213).

14. Smith 74 (October 17, 1795).

15. Smith 45 (September 5, 1795), 48 (September 7, 1795). Godwin came to Brown from multiple directions. The friends had read *Caleb Williams* prior to that Perth Amboy trip, but Brown's father had transcribed long extracts from *Political Justice* into his commonplace book even earlier (Kafer 66). The group's correspondence suggests that Brown embraced the book earlier and more readily than Smith. Smith wrote in the fall of 1795, shortly after Brown returned to Philadelphia, that before he had opened *Political Justice*, friends had told him Godwin's principles resembled his own (Smith 46; September 6, 1795). See also Smith to Theodore Dwight, November 22, 1795 (Smith 262). This letter, which ran for forty manuscript pages and included a defense of Godwin, played a key role in Smith's conflicts with his Connecticut friends. See Waterman 2007, chap. 2.

16. Smith 386 (November 5, 1797). Dunlap was less impressed than Smith was by Wollstonecraft: "[I]t appears to me that this woman had no clear Idea of the basis of morality," he wrote on July 12, before he had finished reading her *Vindication of the Rights of Woman*. "[T]here is much good sense in her volume, but much error, a bad style & strong indications of vanity" (Dunlap 1930 1: 101). For more detail on individual Friendly Club members' reception of these writers see Waterman 2007, 281 n. 30.

17. Brown to Wilkins, after October 1792 (Letters 158). Hewitt argues that this "Romance" of "Similarity" depends on imagination, which makes the blurring of fact and fiction in Brown's early letters particularly apt (Hewitt 79–98, esp. 92).

18. Dunlap 1815 1: 56.

19. Godwin to Dunlap, letter of January 1796 (Godwin 2011, 79).

20. Smith to John Aiken, April 14, 1798 (Smith 438). The letter was published in the July 1798 *Monthly Magazine, and British Register*.

21. The Manumission Society's minutes for January 17, 1797, New-York Historical Society (hereafter N-YHS), in Smith's handwriting, note the result of elections, with Friendly Club members taking a number of offices. See Waterman 2007, 267 n. 72.

22. See "To Stella—No. I. To Henry—No. 2," WM (June 16, 1798), 221; "To Stella—No. III. To Henry—No. IV. To Stella. –No. 5," WM (June 30, 1798), 285.

23. Smith's paraphrase as reported in Dunlap 1930, 236 (March 29, 1798).

24. Earlier that summer, Brown had shown Smith letters from his brothers that revealed what Smith called the "unjustifiable means which have been employed to separate him & Miss P" (Smith 455; July 10, 1798). Smith and Dunlap had met Potts earlier that year and were inclined in her favor (Letters 406–407 n. 1; for the prolonged nature of this breakup, see Letters 478 n. 1).

25. Brown to James Brown, February 15, 1799 (Letters 453–455).

26. Bayard to Mary Ann Smith, October 22, 1798, Margaret Bayard Smith Papers, Library of Congress. Hereafter MBSP.

27. Bayard to Samuel Harrison Smith, March 11, 1800, MBSP. Brown told Bayard he hoped his fiction would strengthen her mind "by immuring it to such scenes & images." See Waterman 2007, 289 n. 137.

28. Akerly to Catherine Akerly Mitchill, undated, filed under "Misc. Akerly," N-YHS. Catherine Akerly Cock married Brown's Friendly Club colleague Samuel Latham Mitchill in June 1799.

29. "For the Repository," *Philadelphia Repository and Weekly Register* 5.9 (March 2, 1805): 71.

30. Bayard to Samuel Harrison Smith, March 17, 1799, MBSP.

31. For Kent's evolving response to Godwin, see Waterman 2007, 281 n. 30, 289 n. 140.

32. Smith, *Diary*, 458 (29 July 1798).

33. Johnson to James Kent, December 8, 1798 [copy], James Kent Papers, Vol. 2, Library of Congress. In a later letter, Johnson promises to send Kent a copy of *Ormond* when it's printed. Johnson to Kent, January 4, 1799, quoted in Krause 241. For more on Kent's reaction to Brown's fiction, see Waterman 2011, 51–66, esp. 63.

34. See, for just one example, his preface to *Arthur Mervyn*, in which he frames himself as a "moral observer" who aims to "methodize his own reflections" on "instructive and remarkable events" related to Philadelphia's 1793 fever epidemic (AM 3). For a more detailed treatment of Brown's novels as vehicles of late-Enlightenment empiricism, see Waterman 2011.

35. Brown to Armitt Brown, December 20, 1798 (Letters 442–443); see also Brown to Armitt Brown, late December 1798 (Letters 449).

36. Miller to Jedidiah Morse, April 3, 1799, Samuel Miller Papers, Princeton University Library, filed inaccurately (Box 2, Folder 1) as a letter to the "American Monthly Magazine." Miller's other correspondents regarding the *Monthly Magazine* included Louis Duby, a Swiss minister who had formerly resided in New York. See Duby to Miller, July 13, [1799], Samuel Miller Papers. Duby writes that he'll contact friends in London to get "Ecclesiastical and litterary news, that could be good entertainment for the intended club and the ground and the beginning of a good American Review."

37. Templeton to Bayard, December [1799], MBSP, misdated as December 1800.

38. Letter from W[illiam] J[ohnson] to "My dear friend" [probably William Beers], January 14, 1799, N-YHS.

39. Bayard to Samuel Harrison Smith, May 23, 1800, MBSP.

40. MM, April 1799 (quoted in Clark 131–132).

41. Philomuthos, "Dialogues of the Living II," MM 2.2 (February 1800): 96.

42. For Dunlap's meeting with "the great man," Jefferson, in 1806, see Dunlap 1930, 2: 388 ff. (February 20, 1806).

43. She wrote: "tho' we often differ'd in opinion—I have remarked in [Brown's] opinions on most subjects, a strong resemblance to yours." Bayard to Samuel Harrison Smith, February 20, 1800, MBSP. The physical resemblance between Brown and Smith was remarked on by Thomas Boylston Adams and by Dunlap, who met Smith in 1806. But, he wrote to his wife, "Brown has the air of a philosopher while S. looks like a Monkey turned Barber." Dunlap to Elizabeth Dunlap, February 13, 1806 (Dunlap 1930, 2: 384).

44. Linn to Jedidiah Morse, February 25, 1801, N-YHS.

45. Brown to Miller, March 16, 1803 (Letters 603–605; see also 606 n. 7 for more details on this controversy).

46. Caritat's trip would result in Minerva's editions of *Ormond* (1800), *Wieland* (1803), *Arthur Mervyn* (1803), *Edgar Huntly* (1803), *Jane Talbot* (1804), and *Clara Howard* (1807).

47. Smith 138 (March 14, 1796), 134 (February 28, 1796). According to Dunlap, when he finally brought John Blair Linn's play to the stage in 1797, he and Brown had edited it heavily (Letters 522 n. 3). See also Dunlap 1930, 1: 305.

48. [Brown], "ART. XXII. A Funeral Eulogy, occasioned by Death of General Washington. Delivered February 22, 1800, before New-York State Society of Cincinnati," MM (March 1800): 222–224.

49. MM (April 1800): 309; (December 1800): 472. For Brown's friendship and correspondence with Elizabeth's sisters, see esp. Brown to Mary Linn, January 9, 1802 (Letters 574–575); Brown to Rebecca Linn, August 13, 1802 (Letters 584–585); Brown to Susan Linn, [after August] 1806 (Letters 651–652). See also the friendly letter to John Blair Linn, July 8, 1802 (Letters 579–580), in which Brown discusses publication of Linn's poetry, pays respectful attention to Mrs. Linn, and conveys news about William Linn's pending move to Albany, all signs of Brown's secured intimacy with the full family by the second summer of his engagement to Elizabeth.

50. "ARTICLE XII." *American Review, and Literary Journal* (1801): 201.

51. Leary, "John Blair Linn."

52. N.N. [Susan Linn], "A Description of Youth," LM 2.8 (May 1804): 117–118.

53. See Brown to William Linn, December 8, 1804 (Letters 626–627).

54. He tells her that he and Potts failed because their "minds [were] unakin" (Letters 476).

55. Brown to Elizabeth Linn, [February 24 or March 3, 1801?] (Letters 485).

56. Letters 628 n. 1. Brown subsequently petitioned to be readmitted to the Philadelphia Meeting's membership rolls. His request was granted. He was buried in a Friends cemetery.

57. One of the first Federalists to link Godwin to Jefferson was Elihu Smith's friend Theodore Dwight, to whom Smith had defended Godwin as early as 1795. See Pollin. For Brown's association with James Ogilvie, whose links to Godwin became a matter of public controversy in 1801, see Letters 669 n. 4.

58. Bayard to Samuel Harrison Smith, May 20, 1800, MBSP.

59. Thomas Boylston Adams to John Quincy Adams, November 30, 1802, Adams Papers, Massachusetts Historical Society.

60. References to Godwin in Brown's magazines include positive and more mixed reviews of later works, not all of which can be traced definitively to Brown. See "Remarks on Godwin's 'St. Leon,'" MM 2.6 (June 1800): 404–407; "Godwin and Malthus," LM 2.11 (August 1804): 361–369; the mostly positive "On Fleetwood, Godwin's Last Novel," LM 4.22 (July 1805): 60–66; and pieces that debated Godwin's defense of classical education: "On Classical Learning," LM 3.19 (April 1805): 256–258; "On the Anti-Christian Tendency of Classical Learning," LM 4.23 (August 1805): 137–141; and "Classical Learning No Anti-Christian Tendency," LM 4.24 (September 1805): 185–191.

61. "Authorship," LM 1.1 (October 1803): 8–9.

62. *Poulson's Daily American Advertiser* (February 27, 1810): 3.

Works Cited

Anderson, Philip J. "William Linn, 1752–1808: American Revolutionary & Anti-Jeffersonian." *Journal of Presbyterian History* 55.4 (Winter 1977): 381–394.

Apap, Christopher. "Irresponsible Acts: The Transatlantic Dialogues of William Godwin and Charles Brockden Brown." In Jennifer Phegley et al., eds., *Transatlantic Sensations*, 21–40. Farnham, UK: Ashgate, 2012.

Barnard, Philip. "Culture and Authority in Brown's *Historical Sketches*." In Philip Barnard, Mark L. Kamrath, and Stephen Shapiro, eds., *Revising Charles Brockden Brown: Culture, Politics, and Sexuality in the Early Republic*, 310–331. Knoxville: University of Tennessee Press, 2004.

Bennett, Charles E. "A Poetical Correspondence among Elihu Hubbard Smith, Joseph Bringhurst, Jr., and Charles Brockden Brown in *The Gazette of the United States*." *Early American Literature* 12.3 (1977): 277–285.

Clapham, Georgiana M. "Colonial Neighbors." *New England Magazine* 9.2 (October 1893): 201–207.

Clark, David Lee. *Charles Brockden Brown: Pioneer Voice of America*. Durham, N.C.: Duke University Press, 1952.

Cope, Thomas Pym. *Philadelphia Merchant: The Diary of Thomas P. Cope, 1800–1851*. South Bend, Ind.: Gateway Editions, 1978.

Davis, John. *Travels of John Davis in the United States of America from 1798 to 1802*, 2 vols., John Vance Cheney, ed. Boston: printed privately, 1910.

Emerson, Amanda. "The Early American Novel: Charles Brockden Brown's Fictitious Historiography." *NOVEL: A Forum on Fiction* 1.2 (2006): 125–150.

Godwin, William. *Enquiry concerning Political Justice*. London: G. G. J. and J. Robinson, 1793.

Godwin, William. *The Letters of William Godwin*, Vol. 1: 1778–1797. Pamela Clemit, ed. Oxford: Oxford University Press, 2011.

Green, David Bonnell. "Letters of William Godwin and Thomas Holcroft to William Dunlap." *Notes and Queries* 3.10 (1950): 441–443.

Hewitt, Beth. "The Authentic Fictional Letters of Charles Brockden Brown." In Theresa Strouth Gaul and Sharon M. Harris, eds., *Letters of Cultural Transformation in the United States, 1760–1860*, 79–98. Burlington, Vt.: Ashgate, 2009.

Kafer, Peter. *Charles Brockden Brown's Revolution and the Birth of American Gothic*. Philadelphia: University of Pennsylvania Press, 2004.

Kaplan, Catherine O'Donnell. *Men of Letters in the Early Republic: Cultivating Forums of Citizenship*. Chapel Hill: University of North Carolina Press, 2008.

Krause, Sidney J. "*Ormond*: How Rapidly and How Well 'Composed, Arranged, and Delivered.'" *Early American Literature* 13.3 (Winter 1978–1979): 238–249.

Langbein, John H. "Chancellor Kent and the History of Legal Literature," *Columbia Law Review* 93 (1993): 547–594.

Leary, Lewis. "John Blair Linn, 1777–1805." *William and Mary Quarterly* 4.2 (April 1947): 148–176.

Pollin, Burton R. "Godwin's Letter to Ogilvie, Friend of Jefferson, and the Federalist Propaganda," *Journal of the History of Ideas* 28.3 (July 1967): 432–444.

Shapiro, Stephen. *The Culture and Commerce of the Early American Novel: Reading the Atlantic World-System*. University Park: Pennsylvania State University Press, 2008.

Sprague, William Buell. "William Linn." In *Annals of the American Pulpit*, 9: 75–79. New York: R. Carter, 1857.

Stauffer, Vernon. *New England and the Bavarian Illuminati*. New York: Columbia University Press, 1918.

Teute, Frederika J. "'A Republic of Intellect': Conversation and Criticism among the Sexes in 1790s New York." In Philip Barnard, Mark L. Kamrath, and Stephen Shapiro, eds., *Revising Charles Brockden Brown: Culture, Politics, and Sexuality in the Early Republic*, 149–181. Knoxville: University of Tennessee Press, 2004.

Verhoeven, Wil. "'This Blissful Period of Intellectual Liberty': Transatlantic Radicalism and Enlightened Conservatism in Brown's Early Writings." In Philip Barnard, Mark L. Kamrath, and Stephen Shapiro, eds., *Revising Charles Brockden Brown: Culture, Politics, and Sexuality in the Early Republic*, 7–40. Knoxville: University of Tennessee Press, 2004.

Waterman, Bryan. "Charles Brockden Brown and the Novels of the Early Republic." In Leonard Cassuto et al., eds., *The Cambridge History of the American Novel*, 51–66. New York: Cambridge University Press, 2011.

Waterman, Bryan. *Republic of Intellect: The Friendly Club of New York City and the Making of American Literature*. Baltimore: Johns Hopkins University Press, 2007.

PART II

ROMANCES

CHAPTER 3

WIELAND; OR, THE TRANSFORMATION OF AMERICAN LITERARY HISTORY

DUNCAN FAHERTY

IN his landmark 1926 introduction to the first modern edition of *Wieland; or, The Transformation, An American Tale* (1798), Fred Lewis Pattee anointed Charles Brockden Brown the unquestionable "Father of American literature" (Pattee ix). Declaring Brown "a literary genius in a land barren of literary men," Pattee categorizes *Wieland* as the pinnacle of cultural achievement in the early republic (Pattee ix). Such primogenital assertions maintained a critical currency for much of the twentieth century, as a range of influential studies of the development of American literature echoed Pattee's approbations. Still, even as *Wieland* was routinely indexed as the first major US novel, it seldom received sustained attention prior to the Brown renaissance that began in the 1970s and 1980s.[1] In many ways, the fate of *Wieland* mirrored the field of early American literary studies itself: critics signaled its existence on evolutionary timelines but did so primarily to chart a larger developmental trajectory centered on mid-to-late-nineteenth-century authors. Plotting a Whiggish figuration of literary history, many of these canon-defining studies codified early American literature as unsophisticated and imitative. Instead of attending to the multivalent contours of the early American novel, they subsumed the intricacies of these texts in favor of narratives of progressive cultural cohesion. *Wieland* occupied the earliest point on this evolutionary timeline of American novels, a categorization that ultimately supported the commonplace idea that Brown's novel was a foundational text even if it was more noteworthy for heralding what would follow rather than for its discrete merits.

The explosion of the field of early American literary studies since the 1980s removed *Wieland* from its pedestal, and it now ranks (in all probability) as the most frequently taught novel of the early republic.[2] Such an assertion is difficult to prove, but there are more editions of *Wieland* by major publishers currently available than any other early

American text. Additionally, Brown is (arguably) the only early American novelist included in the prestigious Library of America series.[3] While few contemporary critics would cite Pattee's patriarchal canonization as a rationale for teaching *Wieland*, many still echo his claims of "firstness" by adjudicating it as the cornerstone of the American literary tradition. While early Americanists are less preoccupied with circumscribed notions of national origin and prescriptive canonical genealogies, the axiomatic figuration of *Wieland* as the first important American novel lingers because of how the field (and the syllabus) needs an origin story. The issue of national cohesion was far from settled during Brown's lifetime, yet *Wieland* remains anachronistically positioned as the originator of the trope of the American novel as chiefly concerned with delimiting national experience. While this residual sense of primacy has abated in the early twenty-first century, it continues to shape pedagogical presentations of the novel in large part because of how classroom editions often classify and market *Wieland* as an urtext. Even as modern editors have sought to reconcile the narratological, temporal, and geographic complexities of the novel to an ever-expanding series of contexts, many of them still represent the novel as foundational for subsequent domestic traditions. The long-standing critical economy that maintains *Wieland* as a quintessential wellspring for the development of the American novel has shifted its definition of what makes Brown's text an important pivot, yet the overall centrality of the novel has never really been dislodged.

This fluid primogenital taxonomy remains prevalent because of how the field has fixated on *Wieland* as emblematic of the post-Revolutionary cultural firmament. This is particularly true in terms of pedagogical praxis, which is often predicated (to one degree or another) on promoting the particularity of American literature as distinct from other national traditions. In their 1977 introduction to the Kent State edition of *Wieland*, Sydney Krause and S. W. Reid cast Brown as "America's first professional man of letters" and identify *Wieland*'s use of "the gothic sublime" as deeply influential on a range of nineteenth-century British and American authors (W xii, xxiv). In his introduction to the popular 1991 Penguin edition, Jay Fliegelman argues that *Wieland* "inaugurated the Gothic preoccupation with the psychological and historical meaning of America," a trope he underscores as central to American literary culture (Fliegelman vii). Accounting for the recovery of domestic novels published prior to *Wieland* (many of which exceeded it in popularity), Emory Elliott's Oxford World Classics edition acknowledges Brown's literary predecessors while recasting Brown as "a 'pioneer voice' who advanced the form of the novel in America" (Elliott xvi). Most recently, in his introduction to the Norton Critical Edition of *Wieland*, Bryan Waterman rechristens the primordial canonicity of the novel by arguing that "it was, as critics have often pointed out, the birth of the American Gothic novel" (Waterman 2011, vii).[4] The only editors who dissent from this tradition are Philip Barnard and Stephen Shapiro, who argue in their Hackett edition that "making Americanness or American identity the primary perspective from which to understand the novel fundamentally mistakes Brown's purpose" (Barnard and Shapiro x). Thus, as it currently stands, the majority of the classroom editions of the novel introduce *Wieland* as the veritable catalyst in the rise of literary and cultural nationalism in the early United States.

Since Pattee's recovery of the novel for classroom use, most editors of *Wieland* have included Brown's abortive prequel, *Memoirs of Carwin the Biloquist*, within their editions. Brown's optimism about the potential success of *Wieland* led him to announce his plans for this sequel in an "Advertisement" accompanying the first book publication of *Wieland*.[5] For much of the twentieth century, *Memoirs* received limited critical attention and (presumably) was seldom taught in tandem with Brown's completed novel. Despite its fragmentary state, Brown's sketch of Carwin has increasingly served as a kind of codex for many critics seeking to unravel his motivations for unsettling the titular Wieland family in the novel. While Carwin remains a shadowy figure in *Wieland*, *Memoirs* sketches his background in a way that magnifies the underlying circum-Atlantic themes of Brown's novel. The reconfiguration of *Memoirs* as a keystone to unraveling Carwin's mysterious behavior has increasingly served as a means of widening the geographic scope of critical treatments of *Wieland*. This capacious turn toward routes instead of roots aligns with larger field concerns about moving beyond the closed confines of the developing republic to consider the multivalent meanings of its cultural production. The influence of readings attending to *Memoirs* on the collective critical sense of *Wieland* will be examined in more detail here, but this trend stems, in part, from the way the plethora of classroom editions of *Wieland* has empowered this unfolding.

While *Wieland* certainly ranks among the most noteworthy domestic novels of the early post-Revolutionary period, it would be a mistake to imagine Brown's intent as mapping the conditions of possibility for national development within the closed ambit of US borders. Brown's expansive sense of cultural production was decidedly more porous than his novel is often retroactively cast as being. The convention that *Wieland* explores a unique national identity in the wake of the struggle for independence retains its saliency because of a number of critical commonplaces surrounding the novel (many of which are glossed in the introductions to popular classroom editions). Brown's decision to send Vice President Thomas Jefferson a copy of the novel demonstrates for many critics that he intended the novel to perform what Jane Tompkins labeled a kind of cultural work aimed at influencing "public policy" (Tompkins 43). The two subtitles of the novel—"The Transformation" and "An American Tale"—are also often didactically interpreted as signaling Brown's investment in charting the complex unfolding of the nascent republic after the break from colonial rule. The rejoinder offered by one of the novel's characters about the absurdity of making "the picture of a single family a model from which to sketch the condition of a nation" is regularly understood as a poetic sleight of hand meant to camouflage Brown's actual construction of a synecdochical connection between family and emerging nation (W 30). Finally, the novel's exploration of the ambiguous power of ungrounded voices, of the failures of reason to account for the irrational, are routinely understood as providing a direct commentary on the logocentric nature of the US political system. The readings that first posited these observations about *Wieland* are decidedly more nuanced than their commonplace redactions, yet the conjoined weight of these abstractions perpetuates the figuration of *Wieland* as intimately linked to questions of nation formation and community consolidation after the Revolution.

The critical and, more important, pedagogical traditions that figure *Wieland* as rooted in questions about US identity evince the ways in which the novel interrogates issues of historical legacies and inheritance. Still, disentangling the novel's own pronounced concern with genealogy and legacy from a desire to fashion a national literary tradition attendant to the political shifts occurring in the 1790s remains necessary to understanding the novel's import. Given the unsettled nature of the post-Revolutionary landscape, readings preoccupied with the inevitability of isolated nation-centered development fail to account for how such purely domestic concerns would have been foreign to Brown's experiences. The intricacy of the plot demands a consideration of its expansive network of influences to fully understand the motivations and actions of Brown's characters. He accentuates the geographical scope of eighteenth-century genealogies by opening the narrative with a detailed consideration of the variegated route that initially led the Wieland patriarch to Pennsylvania. Brown's signposts—which make manifest the myriad tangible historical and cultural contexts that shaped the experiences of the elder Wieland— accentuate that the horizons of the novel exceed the constraints of any restrictive notion of political borders. As such, Brown's consideration of the formation of a North American ethnoscape after the Revolution systematically reveals its intimate ligatures to larger notions of fluidity and cultural influence.

The novel opens with a concise history of the elder Wieland. This biography immerses the characters (and the overall plot of the novel) in wide-ranging networks of association. The elder Wieland, father of the novel's two protagonists, is the son of a nobleman from Saxony who is disowned by his aristocratic relatives after he marries the daughter of a Hamburg merchant. After the untimely death of his parents, the elder Wieland resides in his maternal grandfather's household until he is apprenticed at the age of seven into "mercantile servitude" with a London trader (W 7). His accidental discovery of some sectarian Huguenot writings breaks this morose existence, and he rapidly becomes an ardent believer in the unorthodox doctrines of the Camisards.[6] After completing the terms of his apprenticeship, the elder Wieland (financially unable to establish himself as a trader in Europe) immigrates to North America intending to disseminate "the truths of the gospel" to Native Americans (W 10). After his "resolution" is shaken by "a nearer survey of savage manners," he abandons his missionary work and purchases land on the banks of the Schuylkill River just outside Philadelphia (W 10). Over the next fourteen years, supported by "the service of African slaves," he converts his meager holdings into a self-sustaining plantation (W 10). Eventually, he marries, fathers two children (Theodore and Clara), and builds a domed temple adjacent to his house in which to hold his private daily devotions. He then dies after suffering a mysterious accident, likened to spontaneous combustion, during one of his midnight prayer sessions in the temple. The remainder of the narrative explores events concerning his children, who attempt to dwell in their father's house after his passing. Much of the initial action of the novel takes place in the temple, which the children have remodeled into a kind of summer retreat suitable for their own secular interests.

Even a cursory consideration of this prehistory manifests the impossibility of disentangling the Wieland family from a wide range of circum-Atlantic influences and networks—from colonization and conversion, to religious dissent and persecution, to global systems of capital predicated on the exploitation of unfree labor (through both systems of indenture and enslavement). Disconnected from hereditary wealth by his desire for a companionate marriage, Wieland Sr. possesses unrealistic expectations about North America prior to his immigration. The realities of frontier life convince him of the need to recalibrate his thinking. Forced to abandon his poorly conceived conversion mission, he remains guilt-ridden because of his failure to fulfill this imagined divine injunction. Altering course from his religious zeal, he takes advantage of inexpensive land and enslaved labor to forge an estate for himself. Wieland Sr.'s narrative, in a microcosm, weaves together a multihued tapestry of North American immigration and settlement histories, replete with a firm sense of the need to readjust a premeditated course of action after experiencing the realities of settler colonialism. The multivalent legacies that Wieland Sr. bequeaths to his children are complex not just for their ambiguities but also for how they continue to tether them to larger fluid and wide-ranging networks of association. Moreover, Brown's setting of the novel between "the conclusion of the French and the beginning of the revolutionary war" further undermines efforts to comprehend the text as primarily worried over the narrow formation of republican society and government (W 3). Readings that gloss over details of chronology anachronistically promote the concept of nation and national identity to a moment when it had yet to be called into being. Indeed, Brown's decision to ground the plot's prehistory in questions of empire, transnational capital, and mobility destabilizes readings that suggest that the concept of an isolated nation forms *Wieland*'s objective correlative.

While the majority of the narrative events that unfold in the novel occur within the relative remove of the Wieland family estate, Mettingen, outside Philadelphia, this geographic placement does not render the text territorially claustrophobic. The critical tendency to figure the novel's concerns as intrinsically protonational often forecloses on the possibility that readers perceive a more complex world in *Wieland*. Brown cogently imbricates the extended family network of Theodore and Clara—as well as that of the mysterious Carwin—in circum-Atlantic economic and epistolary circuits. This arrangement challenges a sustained reading of their isolation as totalizing or of the community of the novel as simply parochial. Instead of presenting the Wielands as hidebound, Brown's novel imagines the function of regional influences as an index of the effects of larger and more pervasive historical forces. Critics too often elide Brown's careful figuration of a rural Pennsylvania environment during the late 1760s; they do so in order to suggest that it metonymically represents the post-Revolutionary United States. This tradition mutes Brown's substantial use of references to European cultural and religious traditions, as well as his figuration of the particular local concerns of the area in which the novel unfolds. Considered in this regard, the novel's subtitle "An American Tale" does not refer to a tradition (or a nation) that has yet to manifest itself but is a nominative means of underscoring that North America contains many composite, uneven histories of settlement. Wieland Sr.'s unique experiences hardly represent the antecedents of the entire republic, and to figure them as such requires a rather imaginative leap.

The plot of *Wieland* draws inspiration from an actual 1781 familicide that occurred in upstate New York. According to contemporary periodical accounts, a religious fanatic named James Yates murdered his wife and four children and defended his actions by claiming that God commanded him to sacrifice his family. While only small notices of the brutal murder originally appeared, several Philadelphia and New York journals reprinted an account of the event fourteen years later, in 1796.[7] An avid reader of these journals, Brown borrowed details from these reports in outlining *Wieland*. While this evocation adds a patina of realism to Brown's novel, his plot does not strictly adhere to the details of the Yates murders but, rather, simply deploys them as a starting point. Ostensibly an epistolary novel, the entire narrative largely consists of a single letter written by Clara Wieland as a retrospective account of the recent family disaster. After detailing her father's history, Clara records how she and her brother, Theodore, were raised by their aunt alongside Catherine and Henry Pleyel (neighboring children who become intimately connected to the Wielands). After reaching maturity, Theodore marries Catherine, and they have four young children. Clara and Henry live nearby, and the two pairs of siblings form a kind of insulated community at Mettingen (with some unspoken sense that Henry and Clara will eventually wed). Their bucolic enclave becomes unsettled when they begin to hear mysterious unembodied voices that initially offer strange yet harmless commands. These weird voices trouble the Enlightenment-driven rationalist ideologies of the group and eventually lead them to question their sensory impressions and their commitment to reason as an organizing principle. They concurrently discover a mysterious stranger, Carwin, who has recently arrived in the area (and exhibits no signs of leaving), which further complicates their isolation. Carwin secretly possesses the ability to mimic and ventriloquize other people's voices—Brown coins the term *biloquism* to describe this kind of projected double speaking—and his presence particularly unnerves Clara.

A series of convoluted misunderstandings ensues, culminating in Clara's discovery of Carwin hiding in her bedroom closet. Before confessing his identity, Carwin uses his facility for biloquism to threaten Clara with rape and murder. Clara eventually confronts Carwin, only to learn very little about his motivations or history. Later, an eavesdropping Henry half overhears Carwin attempting to seduce a servant and mistakenly believes that Clara has entered into an illicit affair with Carwin. Outraged, Henry attempts to sever any connection with his childhood friend and his presumptive fiancée. As various members of the group continue to hear mysterious voices, they become individually and collectively anxious; eventually, their apprehension causes the close-knit kinship network to splinter. Theodore believes he hears "divine" voices urging him to sacrifice his family, and he brutally murders his wife and children. Clara discovers a disheveled Theodore and attempts to reason with him; still believing he follows God's commands, Theodore attempts to murder her. Carwin suddenly appears and rescues Clara by projecting his voice and ordering Theodore to stop. Carwin's mimicry echoes the voice Theodore claims to have heard, yet it remains uncertain if he has induced Theodore to commit these crimes or if Theodore has simply gone insane. This ambiguity regarding the impetus for Theodore's actions underscores the novel's concerns with the question of human agency. The novel concludes with Theodore's suicide and Clara's removal to France. While time has distanced her from the horrors she witnessed, Clara's final meditations on the fragility of human reason and morality do not suggest that she has developed any real clarity about the terrors that destroyed her family. Instead, the novel culminates in her attempt to moralize about the need for individuals to resist the seductions of "double-tongued deceiver[s]" by stead-fastly maintaining a disciplined commitment to sincerity in their social relations (W 244).

The warning against "double-tongued" insincerity circles back to a quatrain originally printed on the title page, in essence bookending the novel with moral injunctions about the dangers of disingenuous speech. This titular quatrain foreshadows Clara's imperatives about sincerity and social relations:

> From Virtue's blissful paths away
> The double-tongued are sure to stray;
> Good is a forth-right journey still,
> And mazy paths but lead to ill.

Privileging a forthright commitment to plain speech, the poem defines virtue as self-generated by placing emphasis on the danger facing a speaker who detaches her use of language from her genuine intentions. The individual who strays from virtue's path, the poem argues, bears responsibility for her own predicament. The quatrain does not model any form of resistance or clearly signal a method by which to avoid the delusory effects of being seduced by unrighteous speech. Given the ambiguity concerning the source of the voices that enjoin Theodore to murder his family—are they self-induced, or are they a result of Carwin's impostures?—the ethical imperative of Brown's moral suggests the need for a constant vigilance without offering any viable way to measure someone else's sincerity. Placing an emphasis on self-regulation, the quatrain affirms Clara's conclud-ing observation that "the errors of the sufferers" are what allow artifice to take hold and engender "catastrophe" (W 244).

The ways in which *Wieland* foregrounds questions of agency and self-regulation have long been central to readings of the novel that understand it as interrogating the viability of cultural stability in the early republic. Drawing metaphorical connections between the family and the young nation, these readings presume that Brown intended the text to func-tion as a form of political allegory. Larzer Ziff's foundational work on *Wieland* provides an exemplar of this strand of criticism, as he argues that the novel shifts from tracing the "brave new world" of the "American landscape" into suggesting how the prospects for boundless prosperity are complicated by the limits of "science and culture" to explain irrationality (Ziff 55, 56). Edwin Sill Fussell interprets the novel as a meditation on the violence of the Revolutionary War, figuring the Wieland family as the "young nation" seduced into unnecessary violence (Fussell 183). Historian Steven Watts reads *Wieland* as both an autobiographical reflection of Brown's own complicated relationship to his family and a meditation on "the larger struggle in post-Revolutionary America with the disturbing consequences of a late eighteenth-century 'revolt against patriarchal authority"' (Watts 83). Shirley Samuels positions *Wieland* against the backdrop of ongoing domestic debates about education, gender, and institutions in order to suggest that "in its consid-eration of these debates, the novel sometimes appears as an allegory of America and the dangers democracy poses" (Samuels 45). Christopher Looby intriguingly asserts that

Brown's "fetishization of voice" in *Wieland* serves to register "the weakness and inadequacy of a nation embodied in print," so much so that the novel finally demonstrates how Brown was a "complex counter-revolutionary writer" (Looby 5, 202). For Elizabeth Hinds, Brown's portrait of the Wieland family offers an extended critique of an aristocratic class, haunted by its own incestuous past, which has no generative connection to the "exploding free market, complete with all the risks of exchange, surrounding Brown at the end of the 1790s" (Hinds 108). More recently, Elizabeth Barnes argues that *Wieland* replicates how "the father-son relation symbolized political conflict" for early republican readers and as such suggests that the novel interrogates the cyclical nature of revolutionary violence and the meaning of such uncertain legacies for the emerging nation (Barnes 53). The critical school that reads the novel as nation-centered tends chiefly to focus attention on *Wieland* and seldom attends to *Memoirs* as a potential companion or complementary piece.

Another set of critical readings of *Wieland* interprets Brown's possible political intent against more immediate (either temporally or geographically) dimensions. These interpretations tend to avoid the tendency toward what Ed White has termed "nation fixation" (almost always routed through a figuration of family as nation) and focus their critical gaze on a different scale of region, event, or mobility rather than on a presumptive national history (White 44). Many of these readings explore how the combined weight of the invectives against imposture and deception in *Wieland* suggest a certain kind of xenophobia, a thematic reflection of late-eighteenth century anxieties about the dangers of foreign infiltration. Frank Shuffelton, for example, argues that while the novel expresses a great deal of anxiety about the validity of "private judgment," it really displays how Brown was opposed to legislative attempts to "coerce judgment and to define the public sphere by an act of the state" (Shuffelton 109). In Paul Downes's accounting, Brown's recursive use of obfuscation exemplifies how democracy relies on "the multiplication of secrets," a trope that allows Brown to symbolically wrestle with the question of authenticity in the early republic (Downes 142). In proposing that "theorizing the alien and his relationship to American identity is elemental to much of Brown's fiction," Jared Gardner registers how Brown's attentiveness to "lineage and inheritance" manifests itself as a means of exploring questions about foreign and domestic subjects (Gardner 63–64).

Gardner's observation suggests that Brown registered concerns about late-eighteenth-century large-scale global sociopolitical change. The seemingly interconnected and cyclical nature of circum-Atlantic revolutions—from the French (1789–1798) to the Haitian (1791–1804) to the United Irishmen Rebellion (1798)—sparked domestic anxieties in the United States about global radicalism, many of which percolate across Brown's novel. In particular, there was a great deal of suspicion concerning French, "French negro," and Irish immigrants and travelers in the late eighteenth century. These concerns helped spark the passage of the Alien and Sedition Acts and contributed to attempts by many elites to cultivate a countersubversive fervor among the public. The Alien and Sedition Acts authorized the arrest and deportation of foreigners who were even suspected of "treasonable or secret machinations against the government" of the United States.[8] The legislation simultaneously afforded the executive branch unprecedented powers in terms of regulating speech, making it illegal to write, print, publish, or utter any "any false, scandalous and malicious writing or writings against the government of the United States."[9] While few individuals were persecuted under these acts, their passage fueled a climate of paranoia concerning the supposed machinations of clandestine plotters and subversive organizations.

The prevalent suspicions about mysterious plans to unsettle domestic harmony have obvious resonances with the plot of *Wieland*, which a number of critics have seized upon in historicist contextualizations of the novel. One popular manifestation of these fears about foreign threats to domestic stability galvanized around the Illuminati, a secret society believed to be intent on a worldwide overthrow of church and state power in favor of clandestine rule. In the late 1790s, concerns arose that the Illuminati had deployed foreign agents in the United States to, as minister Jedidiah Morse wrote in 1798, "prepare the way among us, for the spread of those disorganizing opinions," which had been disrupting cultural order across the circum-Atlantic basin (Morse 399). In short order, reports like Morse's spread like wildfire from pulpits and soapboxes across the early republic and contributed to the vitriolic party tensions of the era. The global specter of the Illuminati scare illustrates how these partisan divisions always contained deeply transatlantic dimensions, as Federalist elites attempted to castigate their Democratic-Republican opponents by linking them to francophone and Illuminati interests. References to a secret society abound in *Memoirs* and recurrently suggest that Carwin may have had some connection to an Illuminati-type organization. These obscured hints about Carwin's potential associations have caused many critics to foreground his ambiguous motivations as a means of intertextually reading Brown's novel. Robert Levine interprets *Wieland* as a "political allegory of seduction," as Brown treats the "tension between innate and external influences" as a means of examining the "psychosocial pressures giving rise to conspiratorial fears" (Levine 29–30). Charles Bradshaw argues that Brown "was intrigued by the epistemological questions conspiratorial discourse generated" and crafted *Wieland* as "a narrative investigation of the concept of causality" which had been disrupted by fears of clandestine machinations (Bradshaw 369, 370). Bryan Waterman maintains that while Brown does not directly comment on "the actual Illuminati conspiracy" in *Wieland*, he does examine how "shrewd narrators" moved to "capitalize on fears of conspiracy by claiming secret knowledge" (Waterman 2007, 83). These readings, which link the unexplainable machinations of Carwin to issues of domestic or foreign intrigue and entanglement, highlight how *Wieland* indexes fears about secrecy and concerns about unregulated personal sovereignty and mobility.

An emergent trend of criticism figures Carwin as a palimpsest, imagining him as overwritten with the potential signifiers of an unending series of potentially subversive and countersubversive behaviors. Carwin's uncertain ancestry, his mysterious appearance and abilities, and his vague rationale for being in the vicinity of Mettingen covertly link him to many of the concerns that the Alien and Sedition Acts were intended to address. Moreover, his studied attempt to disquiet the elite preserve of the Wielands' extended social network embodies the very fears that the Alien and Sedition Acts were meant to stoke on the one hand and alleviate on the other. Carwin potentially represents an interloper bent on promoting an expansive conception of democracy and a radical reconfiguration of capital and property. Considered in this light, the protean Carwin potentially represents the central tenets of any number of global revolutionary practices. Intriguingly, this emergent focus on Carwin as a harbinger of circum-Atlantic intrigue likely mirrors the ways in which many nineteenth-century continental European readers initially encountered him. Both the 1808 French and the 1818 and 1830 Spanish "translations" of *Wieland* take liberties with the novel by veering off into new directions and subplots utterly foreign to the original plot of Brown's novel. In extending the novel's action in ways that center around Carwin as a transnational adventurer, these new versions of or additions to the novel animate Carwin as an important node in any number of global conspiracies and thus rescript the novel in such a way as to make explicit, and even spectacular, what Brown had initially presented as submerged hints concerning global revolutionary networks and conspiracies.[10]

Hsuan L. Hsu asserts that considering the *Memoirs of Carwin* alongside the novel allows one to better comprehend how "the spatial regime of expansion" saturating the novel manifests Brown's ambivalence about "the United States's imperialistic self-projection across and beyond foreign territories" (Hsu 137). David Kazanjian argues that scholars have labored, by reading *Wieland* and *Memoirs*, to position Brown as a foundational figure in "the 'natural' emergence of American literature, a narrative that replaces the violent history of white settler colonialism with an aesthetic call to incorporate scenes of 'wild' America into tales of white colonial life" (Kazanjian 140). Stephen Shapiro reads *Memoirs* in conjunction with *Wieland* to decode Brown's interest in dissecting how "universalizing claims" about a neutral public sphere in fact disguise "covert institutionality to structure class and gender violence within the publicized amity of pluralist concerns" (Shapiro 229). In Shapiro's recounting, Carwin "registers the pain" of his "hidden" struggle "to mask the disability of his background and conform" to the elitist "behavioral manners" of Mettingen (Shapiro 241). Ed White provocatively maintains that the novel's "spatial geography" manifests struggle between "rural subaltern" and urban center, suggesting that Brown was "groping" with fears about serial backcountry uprisings and the "geographical and class particularities" that actually define "the emergence of the American novel" (White 44). Laura Doyle offers a counter geography to White's by overwriting any differences between Euro-American texts and contexts and pinpointing universal characteristics to suggest that Carwin is "above all American in that he is a cultural chameleon, an uprooted individual who adopts native manners as an instrument, paradoxically, of mobility" (Doyle 243). Doyle magnifies the scale of *Wieland* away from the more nuanced regional concerns that White framed to position Brown as "the carrier of the Anglo-Saxon literary lineage his characters enact" (Doyle 253).

That White, Shapiro, and Doyle deploy *Wieland* and *Memoirs* as an axial force by which to reorient the geographic scale of early American literary studies testifies to the enduring ways in which Brown's novel has persistently functioned as a kind of sextant for early

Americanists. While White calls for an inward turn that would account for the long-neglected importance of the era's complex racial, ethnic, political, and class-inflected regional dimensions, Doyle offers an enlarged transatlantic lens that dissolves the separation between "English" and "American" in favor of an Anglo-Saxon novel conterminously developing on both sides of the Atlantic. Shapiro envisions the text as an emblematic instantiation of a world-literature system debating the viability of a Woldwinite project intent on using rational sentiment to counter the antiprogressive ideologies of elite privilege and the emerging market society. Such a sustained and variegated critical interest in Brown's novel renders the evolving debates about its long primogenital critical history somewhat irrelevant, since it hardly matters what novel was first published in the United States or was the republic's first Gothic novel or was the first novel published by a professional American writer. *Wieland* is certainly not the first, conceivably not the second, and only possibly the third. Without question, Brown's novel probes issues of agency, sincerity, democracy, and social formation, even as he critiques the limitations of an Enlightenment faith in rationality. All of these issues animated social development on all levels of spatial geography—from world-systems to regionalism to transatlanticism—and as such it would be a mistake to quarantine the novel from being conjoined to all these scales and dimensions. The novel's importance for our collective understanding of the development of American literary history does not reside in its claims to firstness; rather, the critical history of the novel demonstrates how it has routinely served as a crucial compass for larger arguments about the development of cultural production in the early republic.

Perhaps *Wieland*'s enduring contribution to our understanding of the development of American literature and culture remains Brown's insistence on the fallibility of isolationist narratives to register accurate genealogies or histories. The global and regional dimensions of the novel become even more apparent when considered alongside its aborted prequel, *Memoirs*; this later text overtly registers both the domestic and foreign mobility of its titular character to suggest that Mettingen's imagined "remove" from external influences sits upon a gossamer foundation. The novel's engagement with the confluence of revolutionary and religious energies of the period suggests the ways in which they might contribute to the collapse of the operant and emergent social orders. In addition, the novel explores how these concerns about destabilization dovetail with anxieties about the collapse of the family and an overall paranoia about the sudden obsolescence of intellectual and social traditions that had governed cultural organization for centuries. The sudden injection of disembodied voices, without reliable histories, obligations, or trajectories, threatened to foster an unending revolution and detach a structured community from its governing principles. Yet the semi-incestuous claustrophobia of the Wieland family members derives not from their national location but rather from a fragile fantasy of secure removal that renders them susceptible to external and internal deceptions. The limitations of their fantasies of hereditary seclusion arise because of their utopian nature; they are indeed sustainable in no real place. Again and again, at almost every turn in *Wieland*, Brown emphasizes the implausibility of total isolation. Removal, even as a momentary fantasy, cannot be preserved, since even the most isolated spaces in the circum-Atlantic world eventually exhibit the ways in which they remain tethered to larger fluctuations and epistemes.

NOTES

1. For an account of the shifting critical and pedagogical attention afforded Brown, see Waterman 2005.
2. The only other possible rival for *Wieland* in terms of teaching popularity would be Susanna Rowson's *Charlotte Temple* (1791), which until recently was included in the *Norton Anthology of American Literature*.
3. The only other "early" American novelist to appear in the Library of America is James Fenimore Cooper. The earliest text of Cooper's republished there is *The Pioneers* (1823), which first appeared more than two decades after the publication of Brown's last novel. Moreover, as if to signal Brown's anomalous status in the catalog, his work is indexed under the category "Fantasy, Science Fiction, & Horror," as opposed to appearing under either the "19th-Century Novels" or the "Early American History & Founding Fathers" heading. Given that William Bartram's *Travels and Other Writings* and the volume on *American Poetry: The Seventeenth and Eighteenth Centuries* both appear under the subject heading "Early American History & Founding Fathers," it is curious that Brown's novels are not also grouped there. The taxonomy may be a manifestation of the legacy I have just been describing: Brown's work is important to note but difficult to catalog within the kinds of Whiggish narratives about progressive development. See https://www.loa.org/books/topics/14-fantasy-science-fiction-horror.
4. The shift from Pattee to Waterman, from first novel to first Gothic novel, exhibits the trajectory of how critics have wanted to continue to claim firstness despite the discovery of compromising evidence.
5. Brown began work on *Memoirs* in 1798 before abandoning the project for several years. He returned to work on it in 1803 and serially published portions in the *Literary Magazine* over the next two years. As an index of the post-Pattee critical tendency to highlight this text, one can also note that it is included in the current ninth edition of the *Norton Anthology of American Literature*, the most widely used anthology in US college classrooms.
6. The Camisards were an eighteenth-century French Protestant sect that believed in ecstatic divine inspiration. In the early 1700s, they launched an insurgency against the French monarchy in response to decades of anti-Protestant persecution.
7. For more information on *Wieland* and the Yates family murders, see Williams.
8. An Act concerning Aliens; see http://memory.loc.gov/cgi-bin/ampage?collId=llsl&fileName=001/llsl001.db&recNum=693.
9. An Act for the Punishment of Certain Crimes against the United States (Sedition Act), Sec. 2; see http://memory.loc.gov/cgi-bin/ampage?collId=llsl&fileName=001/llsl001.db&recNum=719.
10. Gaspard Jean Eusèbe Pigault-Maubaillarcq translated Brown's novel in 1808 as *La famille Wieland, ou les prodiges* (Calais: Moreaux, 1808). This translation and stylized new narrative served as the basis for Don Luis Monfort's Spanish translations, *La familia de Vieland ó los prodigos* (Valencia: Estévan, 1818) and its prequel, *Carvino, ó el hombre prodigioso* (Valencia: Cabrerizo, 1830). For a discussion of the French translations, see Charras.

Works Cited

Barnard, Philip, and Stephen Shapiro. "Introduction." In Charles Brockden Brown, *Wieland; or The Transformation. An American Tale, with Related Texts*, ix–xlvi. Indianapolis: Hackett, 2009.

Barnes, Elizabeth. "Loving with a Vengeance: *Wieland*, Familicide and the Crisis of Masculinity in the Early Nation." In Milette Shamir and Jennifer Travis, eds., *Boys Don't Cry? Rethinking Narratives of Masculinity and Emotion in the U.S.*, 44–63. New York: Columbia University Press, 2002.

Bradshaw, Charles C. "The New England Illuminati: Conspiracy and Causality in Charles Brockden Brown's *Wieland.*" *New England Quarterly* 76.3 (2003): 356–377.

Charras, Françoise. "Variations et anamorphoses sure le mode gothique: Les traductions en français de *Wieland* au XIXe siècle." *Profils Américains* 11 (1999): 191–212.

Downes, Paul. *Democracy, Revolution, and Monarchism in Early American Literature*. Cambridge: Cambridge University Press, 2002.

Doyle, Laura. *Freedom's Empire: Race and the Rise of the Novel in Atlantic Modernity, 1640–1940*. Durham, N.C.: Duke University Press, 2008.

Elliott, Emory. "Introduction." In Charles Brockden Brown, *Wieland; or, The Transformation and Memoirs of Carwin the Biloquist*, vii–xxx. New York: Oxford University Press, 1994.

Fliegelman, Jay. "Introduction." In Charles Brockden Brown, *Wieland and Memoirs of Carwin the Biloquist*, vii–xlii. New York: Penguin, 1991.

Fussell, Edwin Sill. "*Wieland*: A Literary and Historical Reading." *Early American Literature* 18.2 (1983): 171–186.

Gardner, Jared. *Master Plots: Race and the Founding of an American Literature, 1787–1845*. Baltimore: Johns Hopkins University Press, 1998.

Hinds, Elizabeth Jane Wall. *Private Property: Charles Brockden Brown's Gendered Economics of Virtue*. Newark: University of Delaware Press, 1997.

Hsu, Hsuan L. "Democratic Expansionism in 'Memoirs of Carwin.'" *Early American Literature* 35.2 (2000): 137–156.

Kazanjian, David. *The Colonizing Trick: National Culture and Imperial Citizenship in Early America*. Minneapolis: University of Minnesota Press, 2003.

Levine, Robert S. *Conspiracy and Romance: Studies in Brockden Brown, Cooper, Hawthorne, and Melville*. New York: Cambridge University Press, 1989.

Looby, Christopher. *Voicing America: Language, Literary Form, and the Origins of the United States*. Chicago: University of Chicago Press, 1996.

Morse, Jedidiah. "A Sermon, Delivered at the New North Church Boston." In Jonathan M. Yeager, ed., *Early Evangelicalism: A Reader*, 396–400. New York: Oxford University Press, 2013.

Pattee, Fred Lewis. "Introduction." In Charles Brockden Brown, *Wieland, or The Transformation together with Memoirs of Carwin the Biloquist*, ix–xlvi. New York: Harcourt, Brace, 1926.

Samuels, Shirley. *Romances of the Republic: Women, the Family, and Violence in the Literature of the Early American Nation*. New York: Oxford University Press, 1996.

Shapiro, Stephen. *The Culture and Commerce of the Early American Novel: Reading the Atlantic World-System*. University Park: Pennsylvania State University Press, 2008.

Shuffelton, Frank. "Juries of the Common Reader: Crime and Judgment in the Novels of Charles Brockden Brown." In Philip Barnard, Mark L. Kamrath, and Stephen Shapiro, eds., *Revising Charles Brockden Brown: Culture, Politics, and Sexuality in the Early Republic*, 88–117. Knoxville: University of Tennessee Press, 2004.

Tompkins, Jane. *Sensational Designs: The Cultural Work of American Fiction 1790–1860*. New York: Oxford University Press, 1995.

Waterman, Bryan. "Charles Brockden Brown, Revised and Expanded." *Early American Literature* 40.1 (2005): 173–191.

Waterman, Bryan. "Preface." In Charles Brockden Brown, *Wieland and Memoirs of Carwin the Biloquist*, vii–x. New York: W. W. Norton, 2011.

Waterman, Bryan. *Republic of Intellect: The Friendly Club of New York City and the Making of American Literature*. Baltimore: Johns Hopkins University Press, 2007.

Watts, Steven. *The Romance of Real Life: Charles Brockden Brown and the Origins of American Culture*. Baltimore: Johns Hopkins University Press, 1994.

White, Ed. "Carwin the Peasant Rebel." In Philip Barnard, Mark L. Kamrath, and Stephen Shapiro, eds., *Revising Charles Brockden Brown: Culture, Politics, and Sexuality in the Early Republic*, 41–59. Knoxville: University of Tennessee Press, 2004.

Williams, Daniel E. "Writing under the Influence: An Examination of *Wieland*'s 'Well Authenticated Facts' and the Depiction of Murderous Fathers in Post-Revolutionary Print Culture." *Eighteenth-Century Fiction* 15.3–4 (2003): 643–668.

Ziff, Larzer. "A Reading of *Wieland*." *Publications of the Modern Language Association* 77.1 (1962): 51–57.

CHAPTER 4

ORMOND; OR, THE SECRET WITNESS

NICHOLAS E. MILLER

In his "Historical Essay" accompanying the bicentennial edition of *Ormond; or, The Secret Witness* (1982), Russel Nye famously referred to Charles Brockden Brown's *Ormond* as "a brilliantly bungled book," even though "flawed as it is, the novel remains an intriguing, intricate, and thematically rich performance" (Nye 307). Nye's claims reflect much of the early scholarship on *Ormond*, a critical landscape in which scholars were predominantly concerned with the frenzied pace of Brown's writing habits, the structural implausibilities of the novel, and its flawed narrative elements. These "tantalizing failures," as Kenneth Bernard called them, have similarly concretized the status of *Ormond* as the (perceived) least of Brown's four Gothic novels (Bernard 1008). Scholarly writings on *Ormond* consistently opened with apologies for (or at least acknowledgments of) the novel's supposed failures, until a critical shift took place in the 1990s in response to New Criticism and its approaches to American literature.[1] In 1973, for example, Sydney Krause remarked that "*Ormond* would seem the least gothicized, being somewhat heavy on rhetoric, the least dazzling as well" (Krause 1973, 570). That same year, Carl Nelson commented that "Charles Brockden Brown suffers badly because of the obvious thematic inconsistencies of his fiction. Faced with the structural shambles of his work, commentators on his novels adopt apologetics if they move beyond description of his often indecipherable plots" (Nelson 163). One year later, Paul Rodgers, Jr., wrote that *Ormond* was "a text thick-sown with promising formal and thematic initiatives, no one of which held Brown's attention long enough to organize the book" (Rodgers 5). To justify writing about *Ormond*, it seemed, required scholars to hastily and contritely apologize for the novel before attempting to redeem it. *Ormond* therefore reflects a problem rooted in early American studies more broadly: the need to apologize for a "literature" that has been seen as derivative and flawed.

For early critics, one justification for publishing on *Ormond* was that it provided insight into Brown and his writing habits. As scholars made the case for early American literature, they often turned to Brown as the "father" of said literature, while also acknowledging his authorial shortcomings. As Duncan Faherty also notes in this volume (chapter 3) in relation to *Wieland*, his experimental fiction was a precursor to later (implicitly better) fictions and part of a literary timeline that represented the chaos and uncertainty of post-Revolutionary America. Critics were quick to turn from the faults of *Ormond* to biographical anecdotes about how those faults came to be; they argued that Brown was a hurried "genius"—one who lacked formal writing habits—who somehow still managed to tap into a fraught cultural and historical moment. Rodgers, for example, writes that "Brown's difficulties originated not in aesthetic blindness or naiveté, but in his work habits and attitudes toward composition. He was ever a hasty, headlong, compulsive writer" (5).[2] Krause similarly wrote that Brown "was known for the frenzied pace at which he turned out copy during the brief period of his novel writing—especially in the legendary case of *Ormond*, which went to press with only a portion of the work completed" (1978, 238). Most scholars emphasize that Brown wrote *Ormond* in less than a six-week span, although he also drew material from other stories he had written.[3] An emphasis on Brown's haste also gave scholars—eager to point out the achievements in *Ormond*—an opportunity to do so within the context of Brown's life and literary aspirations. Krause, for example, writes that while "it has been somewhat easier to point out defects than to notice Brown's accomplishments," we should also note that "Brown's powers of invention seem to have been quite equal to the pressures of improvisation." (1978, 244). This pattern of scholarship holds up (this chapter being no exception) over the long history of *Ormond* criticism, as scholars simultaneously apologize for the novel's flaws only to push back against critiques of Brown's structure and form as somehow missing the point. The inability of scholars to reconcile the novel's formal inconsistencies with its thematic breadth and the rich potential of the novel remains one of *Ormond*'s most appealing attributes.

Apologetic readings likely made *Ormond* the only one of Brown's Gothic novels not to get a classroom edition of the Kent State bicentennial editions. It is also the only one of Brown's Gothic novels not included in the Library of America collection.[4] In 1937, Ernest Marchand noted that "of the four best novels of Brown...*Ormond* is the only one not readily available in recent years" (Marchand v). Although *Ormond* currently exists in two classroom editions—from Broadview Press (1999) and Hackett (2009)—it remains the least studied of Brown's Gothic novels, generating fewer hits in the scholarly archive than *Wieland*, *Edgar Huntly*, and *Arthur Mervyn*.[5] It is worth noting, however, that *Ormond* was not always considered Brown's "lesser" novel. As Paul Witherington notes, "*Ormond*, regarded by many early critics as one of [Brown's] best novels, has fallen into neglect" (Witherington 111). While Witherington resists calling for a "revival" of *Ormond*, he does point to its early popularity. Mary Chapman makes a similar claim, emphasizing the novel's popularity abroad, especially among the Woldwinite circle: "Although Brown's second novel has the distinction of having been the first American novel to be reprinted in England, and was praised by Romantic writers such as Percy Shelley, it was not as popular among Brown's American contemporaries...and in twentieth-century scholarship it has suffered from critical neglect" (Chapman 22).

That the plot of *Ormond* is notoriously difficult to summarize surely contributes to this tendency to apologize for the novel's perceived flaws. Chapman, however, offers a helpful overview when she argues that "*Ormond* tells the story of the young chaste Constantia Dudley's attempts to support herself and her family and to preserve her republican virtue, in a community threatened by a yellow fever epidemic, rising tides of immigrant refugees from political crises around the world, and confidence games associated with emergent market capitalism" (22). Framed as a "biographical sketch" of Constantia by her friend Sophia Courtland for what may be a prospective husband (the mysterious I. E. Rosenberg), *Ormond* opens by detailing a conspiracy enacted against Constantia's father. Swindled by a young man named Craig, Constantia's father loses his business, his home, his wife, and eventually his eyesight. In an attempt to preserve some privacy and pass his days unknown, Dudley removes his family to Philadelphia, where they are beset by a yellow fever epidemic that threatens the entire city. Constantia becomes not only the caretaker of her father during this period but also the public face of her household. In this capacity, she encounters two captivating individuals, Ormond and Martinette. Ormond, an "international man of mystery," is described by Philip Barnard and Stephen Shapiro as a figure who "seems to belong to an international secret society that seeks to distribute enlightenment values through opaque means that are as oppressive as the forces they seek to dismantle" (Barnard and Shapiro 2009, 3). Martinette, who is less explicitly depicted as an Illuminati figure, is radical in her own right. A cross-dressing freedom fighter, Martinette first appeals to Constantia as a potential "double" or kindred figure, before upsetting Constantia with her rejection of domestic ideals. Both Ormond and Martinette offer freethinking, cosmopolitan contrasts to the virtuous republicanism of Constantia. Constantia's admiration for Ormond, however, is interrupted when she is reunited with her long-lost childhood friend, Sophia (who, at this point, also reveals herself as the narrator). Constantia's passion for Sophia not only opens up the possibility of same-sex desire in *Ormond* but also frustrates the character of Ormond. Having murdered Constantia's father and jealous of Sophia, Ormond traps Constantia in a deserted farmhouse near the end of the novel and threatens to rape her for refusing to join him in his political and sexual machinations. Although readers do not see the act, Sophia arrives at the farmhouse and reports that Constantia has killed Ormond with a penknife. The novel closes with a subdued Constantia leaving for England with Sophia, who closes her letter to Rosenberg with an assurance that this story satisfactorily depicts Constantia's merits.

Yet the novel's merits—not Constantia's—have drawn the most attention from scholars, a criticism that Brown likely foresaw. Through the narrator, Sophia, Brown refers to *Ormond* as having "little of that merit which flows from unity of design" and instead emphasizes that Sophia's letters to Rosenberg should be read as a "biographical sketch...not as a poetical taste would prescribe" (O 3). Yet rather than offering a sketch of the narrator's friend, Constantia, the novel offers nearly a dozen character sketches, many of which are marked by shifting identities or personas. Norman Grabo has written on the doubling and mirroring of multiple characters in the novel as well as the fluidity of identity in *Ormond*, noting that "Constantia Dudley in *Ormond* bears an uncanny resemblance to her friend Sophia, and both look a lot like Ursula Monrose, otherwise known as Martinette, who of course resembles her brother Ormond" (Grabo ix). Other scholars, such as Bill Christopherson, have recognized how the struggles that accompany writing about the novel have only highlighted the difficulty in pinning down characters and their roles: "From the first, *Ormond* has been a Rorschach blot for critics. Its structure and characterization have been alternatively lauded and damned. Its literary mode has yet to be agreed upon. Its theme has long been moot. As of 1974, the novel's protagonist was still in question" (Christopherson 56). Indeed, the character of Constantia seems the most likely protagonist, as the titular character, Ormond, doesn't appear until one-third of the way through the novel, and the narrator, Sophia, doesn't make herself known until much later. And it was Constantia, not Ormond, who struck a chord with later writers such as Percy Shelley. Reeves Davies notes, "*Ormond* was memorable to Shelley because of its heroine, Constantia, whose name became his nickname for Jane (Claire) Clairmont, and appears in the titles of two lyrics of 1817, 'To Constantia,' and 'To Constantia, Singing'" (Davies 134). Thomas Peacock also spoke of Shelley's enthusiasm for *Ormond*, noting that "the heroine of this novel, Constantia Dudley, held one of the highest places, if not the very highest place, in Shelley's idealities of female character" (Peacock 77). That critics have often failed to identify the protagonist of the novel speaks to both the instability of identity and the gender politics at play in *Ormond*.

The complex gender politics of the novel and its emphasis on gender performativity gave rise to new approaches to *Ormond* in the 1990s that largely eclipsed earlier critiques dominated by its formal flaws.[6] In 1998, for example, Heather Smyth brought cross-dressing to the forefront of scholarship on *Ormond*, arguing that while cross-dressing permitted a certain blurring of gender and class, it ultimately did not endorse change to the point of gender transformation.[7] Julia Stern, meanwhile, emphasized the importance of Brown writing in the persona of a woman, "strategically assuming the female voice in several of his major novels, and particularly, in *Ormond*, he imagines a polity beset by epidemic disease, where brotherhood, masculinity, and affect itself are perilous liabilities" (Stern 183). Referring to this "rare moment" of a male writer writing in female voice, Stern sees this "transvestite" technique as a form of secret witnessing and—perhaps more important—as a form of "perceptual and emotional infection" (186). Chapman makes a similar argument, noting that "*Ormond* itself is a cross-dressed text written by a male author in the persona of a female narrator writing, among other topics, about the benefits and risks of private women's attempts to participate in public life" (Chapman 10). More recently, Paul Lewis has interrogated gender and sexuality in the content of *Ormond*, reading the text as an exploration of "female bodily strength and martial prowess" in the face of "the excesses of patriarchal surveillance and domination" (Lewis 39). In the same issue of *Early American Literature*, Kristin M. Comment argues that *Ormond* "tests the limits of female homoeroticism as a corollary to female independence," as lesbian possibility in the novel explores patriarchal efforts to regulate female intimacy (Comment 59). Interest in same-sex desire in the novel remains powerful, emphasized as well in the most recent edition of the text: "*Ormond*'s treatment of female relations and erotic contexts has become foregrounded as readers have increasingly noted the erotic charge that binds the novel's women, and debated the ways in which the novel seems to reflect on (proto)-lesbian desire" (Barnard and Shapiro 2009, xlvi). As scholars have repeatedly noted, Brown's *Ormond* offers a Butlerian take on gender, in which "the constructed status of gender is theorized as radically independent of sex" and "gender itself becomes a free-floating artifice" that subverts sexual distinctions (Butler 9).

Recent scholarship has thus tended to focus on the value of *Ormond* as an experimental and radical novel, one capable of destabilizing definitions of gender and genre. Barnard and Shapiro go so far as to argue that *Ormond* "is perhaps the most self-consciously radical fiction written in the United States before *Moby-Dick* or the later phase of modernism" (2009, xi). This vision of *Ormond* as a radical fiction resonates with recent critical work that often falls under the umbrella of posthumanism, particularly in what I argue is an American Gothic move toward *indistinction*, a move predicated on the radicalism of early American politics.[8] *Ormond* stands out as exemplary of the "revolutionary Gothic" genre, a mode of Gothic writing deeply influenced by (and often responding directly to) Edmund Burke's writings on liberty and revolution. As Ronald Paulson notes, Burke's rhetoric suggested a potentially dangerous relationship between liberty and violence: "Burke would have agreed that what the Revolution was all about, in its social dimension at least, was *difference*. Once it had achieved its first aim of 'liberty,' its second aim (perhaps a consequence of the first) was to bring about the 'equality' of undifferentiation, which he predicted would produce uncurbable violence" (Paulson 235–236).[9] Unlike Paulson, however, who uses the language of undifferentiation to describe cycles of retaliation in the Revolutionary Gothic, I turn to the language of indistinction to highlight how the novel engages with both Burkean fears of undifferentiation and the Gothic promise of taxonomic indistinction as a form of freedom. Indistinction helps to account for how American Gothic fiction challenges the bounded liberal self both politically and biologically. These challenges to stable categories are mirrored in the formal construction of *Ormond* itself.

None of Brown's novels is as heavily invested in exploring indistinction as *Ormond*. Unlike the European Gothic tradition, where Gothic horror often emerges from the violation of class boundaries, here Brown crafts an American Gothic in which we also see presumed biological boundaries transgressed. Brown imagines the move from a European Gothic to an American Gothic not merely as a geographical shift from European castles to the American wilderness—as indicated in his prefatory "To the Public" in *Edgar Huntly*—but also as an ontological shift: the American Gothic becomes a radical form that enables both political and biological indistinction.[10] In *Ormond*, we see an initial narrative of deception in which class and economic boundaries are violated in the fall of Stephen Dudley, but that narrative quickly evolves—due to the introduction of contagion (yellow fever) and conspiracy (Ormond and the fear of Illuminati-like subversion)—in ways that also render race and class boundaries indistinct and permeable. By the end of the novel, even the distinction between life and death is challenged through threats of necrophilia, as Ormond promises to rape Constantia dead or alive.

Understanding how indistinction functions in *Ormond*, however, also requires us to step back and examine the historical context of its origin, the political stakes of the moment, and Brown's investment in contagion, conspiracy, and crisis. Each of these concepts has been examined before in the text, but I want to emphasize that that each of them has both a political and a biological valence. To do this, I recognize *Ormond*, to some extent, as an outbreak narrative. Some critics have demonstrated a growing interest in the formative yellow fever chapters of *Ormond*, but few scholars have succeeded in bringing the text into a larger conversation with *Arthur Mervyn*.[11] Yet scholars have become increasingly interested in the intersections between literature and medicine, and *contagion* has become something of a recent critical buzzword. In the case of *Ormond*, it serves metaphorically as a mode of "othering" through narratives of quarantine and containment, it exposes fears of racial and cultural mixture, and it demonstrates the susceptibility of the body politic to revolutionary ideas. This contagionist reading of *Ormond* is essential because it highlights how indistinction functions similarly to miasma in the text: the characters are like the yellow fever in that they remain hazy, mistlike, and unseen throughout the text.[12] The narrative of transmission, in fact, relies on their indistinction (or miasmatic quality) to infect others, transgress boundaries, and create connections between the biological and the political. Peta Mitchell, in her synoptic account of contagion as metaphor, argues for a reassessment of miasmatic narratives: "Rethinking air in the context of contagion, then, requires that we consider ourselves to be part of a broader network that links the natural world with the social, the economic, the geographical and the cultural" (Mitchell 57). Such a network allows characters and narratives to become mutable, opens up the possibility for conspiracy, and permits Brown to call his own story into question repeatedly. Being attentive to conspiracy and contagion in *Ormond* builds a foundation for thinking about the novel as formally and thematically transgressive. Being either politically or biologically transmissive (contagious) is always a transgressive act in a period of revolution.

It is important to note, therefore, the influence of context—specifically, the yellow fever epidemic of 1798—on *Ormond*. In that year, Brown lost his close friend Elihu Hubbard Smith to yellow fever in New York and departed the pestilential city to take up residence with playwright William Dunlap in New Jersey. Shortly thereafter, he started crafting *Ormond* in earnest, drawing from some of his earlier writings and finishing the novel in a matter of weeks. *Ormond* was the first of his published novels to return to the Philadelphia he knew in 1793, a community threatened by disease but also by collapsing political hierarchies and social orders. Written against the backdrop of revolutions in both France and Saint-Domingue, *Ormond* became a sprawling narrative of conspiracy and contagion, an experiment in deconstructing the bonds that hold us together as a society. As disease, immigration, and revolution threatened the capital of the young republic, the perceived immunities and increased mobility of foreign agents in Philadelphia led to fears of a nation susceptible to both political and biological contagion. The contagionist rhetoric of the novel makes it one of the most remarkable examples in early American literature of the fluidity of gender and genre, the individual, and its relationship to the nation and other communities.[13]

Ormond, like *Arthur Mervyn*, opens as a narrative of yellow fever—the same fever that had recently claimed Smith's life. Commentators such as Christopherson and Peter Kafer have both argued that yellow fever operates in this novel as something more than a biological evil but as a political pestilence as well.[14] Such readings highlight the ways in which *Ormond* explores the transmission of both bodies and ideas in a post-revolutionary society. The notion of contagion being both physical and ideational is perhaps best described by Priscilla Wald, whose research also provides an enlightening approach to thinking about outbreak narratives. Her description of the politics of contagion offers a particularly useful framework for thinking about *Ormond* as a text that is invested in both political and biological boundary crossings. Wald writes:

> The word *contagion* means literally "to touch together," and one of its earliest usages in the fourteenth century referred to the circulation of ideas and attitudes. Revolutionary ideas were contagious, as were heretical beliefs and practices. The circulation of disease and the circulation of ideas were material and experiential, even if not visible. Both...demonstrated the simultaneous fragility and tenacity of social bonds.   (Wald 12–13)

The fragility of bonds and boundaries is central to *Ormond*, and Wald's description of contagion opens up important readings of contagion and conspiracy as transgressive themes. As Brown's novel of *conspiracy* (the etymology of which is "to breathe together") is permeated by narratives of *contagion* ("to touch together"), the distinction between political and biological identities becomes blurred. Here, Mitchell's emphasis on the airborne nature of contagion as a metaphor seems important: the "breathing together" of conspiratorial politics mirrors the miasmatic yellow fever that permeates Philadelphia. The language of contagion and conspiracy enables narratives of indistinction and destabilizes the bounded self, allows Constantia to inhabit traditionally male roles as she cares for her father, allows Martinette to cross-dress and experience new forms of social mobility, and allows Ormond to witness (secretly) the private life of the Dudley family while in blackface. The boundaries that structure individual and societal identities are rendered indistinct in a revolutionary world struggling with radical politics and pestilential disease.

The novel opens with the fall of the Dudley family, as Stephen Dudley—Constantia's father—finds himself swindled by a deceptive business partner and his forgeries. The narrative of their fall is framed in the language of contagion, demonstrating that contagion, for Brown, is indeed an "evil, physical and political" (O 35). The yellow fever has yet to be introduced, but the social pestilence of forgery eventually infects the entire Dudley household. Stephen Dudley falls prey to a deep melancholy, an "infection" his wife soon catches as well. This change in social and economic status leads to actual physical ailments, as Dudley's body is described as no longer "exempt from infirmity" (18). Shortly thereafter, Brown again entangles physical disease with social transgression as he tells us that Stephen Dudley begins to display "symptoms of...depravity," his body infected by both biological and moral contagion (27). The fall of the Dudley family—what Barnard and

Shapiro refer to as a "social death"—eventually leads them into contact with the actual yellow fever, as their poverty and Stephen Dudley's pride force them to relocate from Baltimore to Philadelphia, which will become their "theatre of suffering" (Barnard and Shapiro 2009, xxv; O 61). The outbreak of yellow fever and their impoverished status make it impossible for them to leave the city. While trapped in Philadelphia, Stephen Dudley loses his wife and his vision, leaving him entirely dependent on his daughter, Constantia. At this point, Constantia becomes the de facto protagonist of the novel, and *Ormond* becomes the story of a chaste republican woman confined by both disease and her economic situation. Her story is one of perpetual contact and contagion; she finds herself threatened by both pestilence and the conspiratorial narratives of those she encounters. As Chapman notes, initially, "the permeability of boundaries" presented in the novel fuels the Gothic horror of *Ormond*, and eventually, Constantia's body is "threatened by rape, seduction, or contagion; the household is wracked by deceptive strangers, counterfeit cheques, [and] masquerading visitors" (24–25).

Enabling these contagious narratives is the state of crisis gripping Philadelphia in the 1790s. In addition to the yellow fever crisis, as Barnard and Shapiro note, "throughout the 1790s, and above all during the 1793–1794 period of extreme political and social crisis,... French exiles arrived in U.S. port cities and had an immediate impact on American culture" (Barnard and Shapiro 2009, xxxix). Refugees served as an immediate reminder of transnational political concerns as France found itself at war on multiple fronts and Washington strove to maintain neutrality on behalf of the United States. Tensions mounted as Edmond Charles Genêt, the new French minister, embarked on a tour from Charleston to Philadelphia, encouraging a war with England. Additionally, as thousands fled slave rebellions in Saint-Domingue, the United States was forced to confront the reality of revolution in the Caribbean and the fear of similar rebellions on US soil. Domestic concerns about the influence of French culture arose as well. Barnard and Shapiro note that "it was the French immigrants' potential for introducing a new set of 'irregular' cultural ideals, as well as their ability to circulate these practices through the lower strata of the city outside the control of the standing political and social order, that made them so threatening" (2009, xli). As Brown composed *Ormond* in 1798, these fears of political and cultural contagion heightened, stoked by the XYZ Affair and the Quasi-War with France, fears of secret societies with the publication of John Robinson's *Proofs of a Conspiracy*, and the signing of the Alien and Sedition Acts by John Adams in response to fears about not only foreign bodies but also dangerous writings.

In *Ormond*, Constantia comes into contact with both the yellow fever and these conspiratorial narratives through her encounters with Ormond and Martinette. Her first encounters with the yellow fever immediately draw attention to the social consequences of the plague. Upon the death of a close friend, Constantia finds herself walking alone through the streets of Philadelphia, where she notes "the symptoms of terror with which all ranks appeared to be seized... there were few passengers whose countenances did not betray alarm" (O 35). That Brown chooses to refer to the symptoms of yellow fever as a "terror" clearly evokes US fears of "the Terror" that took hold of France shortly after the first yellow fever outbreak struck Philadelphia. This connection was not lost on Brown, who later uses Martinette—herself an exiled French revolutionary—to explicitly refer to the "sanguinary tyranny of Robespierre" as she narrates her own history of violence to a frightened Constantia (206). Through characters such as Martinette (and Ormond), Brown uses the yellow fever outbreak to represent more than the physical presence of disease; epidemics also mark the arrival and ongoing presence of foreign bodies and ideas, allowing Brown to explore both the exigency and the danger of bodies in contact in the early Atlantic world in the 1790s. What makes these foreign characters dangerous is their ability to transgress social, moral, and biological boundaries and pass unseen through the social and political landscape of the young republic. This perfect storm of epidemic and revolution allows for new cultural forms and mobilities to take hold, and *Ormond* itself represents a new novelistic form capable of circulating these radical ideas and possibilities to an early American audience. If Brown believes that novels are capable of bringing about social reform, as his admiration of William Godwin might suggest, it is also reasonable to think that social reform might also require a re-formed (or formless) novel that challenges the conventions and generic distinctions that critics have demanded of him. The novel's most basic formal complexity, for example, is the unreliable narrative given by Sophia, whose impartiality and reactionary, counterrevolutionary partisanship are evident throughout. Indeed, the thoroughgoing irony of the novel's narrative form prompts the reader to confront a certain indistinction between the novel's "radical" content on the one hand and its unreliable and reactionary narrator on the other.

What also makes characters such as Martinette and Ormond potentially radical is their perceived immunity to both physical and political contagion. Wald uses the term "imagined immunities" to think about community formation through narratives of immunity to disease, and I find that term useful here.[15] Constantia, for example, wonders how Martinette survived alone in the streets during the epidemic and is shocked by the Frenchwoman's response: "Hast thou forgotten that there were at that time, at least ten thousand French in this city, fugitives from Marat and from St. Domingo? That they lived in utter fearlessness of the reigning disease: sung and loitered in the public walks, and prattled at their doors, with all their customary unconcern?" (O 209). As Robert Levine notes, "Constantia is surprised to learn that [Martinette] had found immediate refuge with her compatriots, 'fugitives from Marat and from St. Domingo,' who somewhat threateningly form a secretive subcommunity within Philadelphia" (Levine 51). Foreign exiles and revolutionaries are feared for their ability to form subcommunities and for their perceived immunities—a claim also leveled against the black carters and nurses in *Arthur Mervyn*. That foreign bodies could move freely through the nation's capital, immune to disease and violence, threatened to undermine established social and cultural hierarchies in the young nation, especially among a populace that feared the influx of refugees fleeing the violence in Saint-Domingue. Martinette's "customary unconcern" provides mobility across racial, political, pestilential, and moral boundaries. In the eyes of many, political exiles and black slaves had infiltrated the city and were spreading ideas that were dangerous to the United States, particularly stories of rebellion coming out of Saint-Domingue—again highlighting how narratives of contagion and conspiracy become intertwined in *Ormond*.

This intersection is most pronounced during moments of crisis in the novel. One useful example is Constantia attempting to nurse her neighbor, Mary Whiston, who is dying of the yellow fever. In addition to diagnosing her friend, Constantia also finds herself trying to diagnose the spaces and environments around her. What she sees is a contaminated space that is nevertheless vulnerable to the "malignant vapour" arising from a corpse outside the building (O 49). The fever, then, becomes its own secret witness, a foreign body that has permeated the domestic space of her friend's home. The belief that the fever is airborne leads Constantia to recognize the vulnerability of that space to outside influences, a microcosmic view that extends to a young nation being infiltrated by radical figures. Later in the novel, these types of physical and spatial violations return to Constantia in the form of Ormond, who traps her in another room in the presence of another corpse. His attempt to contaminate her mind with revolutionary ideas fails, and he turns instead to compromising her physical and emotional well-being. With both Mary and Ormond, Constantia is faced with a crisis from which she may not escape inviolate. In the first scenario, she is rescued by the benevolent efforts of black carters; in the latter, we are left unsure if she ever recovers from the violations of Ormond. This juxtaposition matters, because the carters are themselves indistinct figures, nameless men who appear out of nowhere to make the corpse of Mary Whiston disappear while Constantia is absent. The carters, in fact, represent what Michael J. Drexler and Ed White have referred to as "fantasy Others" who obscure (or render indistinct) the "unspeakable, namely, that the omnipresent but overlooked black (slave, servant, underclass) is the final arbiter of the republican subject's coherence" (Drexler and White 74). As indistinct, miasmatic figures, the black carters in *Ormond* represent the liberatory possibilities of contagion, in contrast to the oppressive possibilities of a figure like Ormond.[16]

By using these various acts of secret witnessing, Brown introduces us to multiple narratives of indistinction: the characters are rendered indistinct through doubling and performativity of race, class, and gender; the narrative is rendered indistinct through the late revelation of the narrator in a way that calls into question the motives of the novel; and the political systems of the Atlantic world are rendered indistinct as both physical contagion and revolutionary ideals alter what it means to belong to a nation or community. As scholars have noted, *Ormond* is a novel that eschews what is often seen as supernatural in his other Gothic fictions. Instead, Brown relies on narratives of indistinction to produce a radically experimental text in which all of the boundaries that order society are destabilized. This is most clearly seen in the character of Martinette, who at one point is seen as a helpless Frenchman's daughter (Ursula Monrose) and is later identified as Ormond's sister. Like so many characters in *Ormond*, Martinette is not what she appears. She is, for example, seen by Baxter as a Frenchwoman unable to speak English and by Constantia as a well-traveled American. In her own narrative, she identifies as a cross-dressing revolutionary who comes from France, but she is actually an orphan born of Greek and Ragusan parents. In many ways, Martinette represents US fears about the consequences of living in a truly egalitarian society—one not restricted by gender roles, religious beliefs, legal categories, or racial/ethnic identities. She represents revolutionary ideals taken to their logical extreme—an indictment, perhaps, of the violence of the French and Haitian revolutions—and the dangers of educated women who are susceptible to a "contagion of example" in a period of revolutionary ideas and energies (O 207). Yet Brown stops short of condemning Martinette; she remains a character full of promise as well as danger.

Threats of contagion and conspiracy are not restricted to women, however, and it is Martinette's brother, Ormond, who takes fears of indistinction to a more dangerous crisis point. As Levine has argued, "during the 1790s the fever was regularly portrayed as a duplicitous form of foreign infiltration and subversion," and the comparisons between the conspiratorial Ormond and the contagious yellow fever are striking (Levine 34). Like the unseen miasma of the yellow fever, Ormond infiltrates enclosed spaces, shows no regard for rank or race or class, and brings death to those he encounters.[17] Ormond is also a well-traveled soldier, like his sister, and is even more insistent about circulating his revolutionary ideals, especially to Constantia. He is suspected to be a member of an internationalist Illuminati-like conspiratorial society.[18] More important, it is clear that Ormond demonstrates a complete disregard for established societal codes. Like Martinette, his disregard is made possible by his ability to assume multiple identities. Whereas Martinette is fluent in multiple languages and can cross-dress in order to fight for her revolutionary ideals, Ormond does more than simply pass as an ordinary American citizen. Instead, he chooses to spy on Constantia by using blackface to impersonate a servant—a violation not only of class boundaries but also of racial boundaries, thus jeopardizing one of the important organizing hierarchies of early American society. Whereas Levine notes that "Brown's villains raise dark questions indeed about the futurity of a republic wherein 'emigrants' can theatrically fabricate identities as 'Americans,' all the while cloaking their origins, politics, and agendas," Ormond goes so far as to fabricate an identity as a noncitizen, one invisible to society; he mirrors the black carters discussed earlier (Levine 16). In this disguise, Ormond is able to transgress racial and moral boundaries, traveling unseen into the domestic space of a virtuous republican woman. Ormond becomes a spectral reminder of the perceived historical dangers of this moment: as Constantia finds herself surrounded by the malignant, unseen plague, she is also subject to the unseen presence of Ormond and his foreign ideas. Confined, Constantia finds herself susceptible to the conspiratorial plans of Ormond. Even after she escapes the farmhouse and the nation, the lingering—perhaps even miasmatic—effects of her encounter with Ormond remain.

Constantia's escape ultimately requires her to leave America, once again connecting her and the novel to a larger Atlantic world. If, as Barnard and Shapiro argue, "*Ormond* is the product of a tremendously cosmopolitan horizon," it is a biopolitical horizon in which narratives of political and biological indistinction redefine what it means to be part of a free society—a society subject to inevitable contact with the bodies and politics of (and bodies *as* politics in) a larger Atlantic world (Barnard and Shapiro 2009, xix).

This horizon, in addition to being a reflection on the historical and political questions of the moment, also influences the radically indistinct form of the novel. The biopolitical backdrop to *Ormond* turns this text from an aesthetic failure into one that ambitiously stitches together narratives of conspiracy and contagion, thus demonstrating the dangers of indistinction in a society where freedom and mobility are sought and outside influences are capable of circulating through communities as easily as pestilent diseases.

NOTES

1. In addition to general shifts away from New Criticism in literary studies, it is important to note the impact of Sydney Krause's Kent State editions of Brown's novels and the impact of New Historicism more broadly. For detailed examinations of Brown scholarship since the 1980s, see Kamrath; Barnard, Kamrath, and Shapiro; and Waterman.

2. It is worth noting that not all scholars accepted these claims about Brown and his haste or resistance to revision. James R. Russo notes that Rodgers's "arguments do not bear close scrutiny" and that Brown's "contradictions, inconsistencies, and downright unbelievable absurdities" are part of the "secrecy and deception" that "are at the very heart of *Ormond*" (Russo 206–207).

3. Scholars have identified moments in *Ormond* when Brown repurposed old material or unfinished stories and novels. Most notably, Brown incorporated material from his earlier periodical essay "The Man at Home" (WM, February–March 1798) into Baxter's tale in chapter 7. See the Kent State edition's "Textual Essay," 347–348.

4. See Charles Brockden Brown, *Three Gothic Novels* (New York: Library of America, 1998).

5. See, for example, the secondary bibliography in the online Charles Brockden Brown Electronic Archive and Scholarly Edition.

6. The turn to gender as a dominant focus of *Ormond* criticism may be a relatively recent development, but gender studies approaches to the novel were present as early as 1966, when Donald Ringe characterized *Ormond* as a "strongly feminist book" (34).

7. See Smyth for a detailed argument on cross-dressing.

8. In contemporary scholarship, indistinction typically represents an effort to deemphasize our historical reliance on distinctions between human life and animal life. In this chapter, I argue that a different set of challenges to the human that exist in the Revolutionary and post-Revolutionary Atlantic, where emergent democracies and protoevolutionary thought force a recalibration of the political and biological distinctions that previously defined bodies and bodies politic. *Ormond* exemplifies, in both its form and its content, this instability in what Donna Haraway has called "the Great Divides of animal/human, nature/culture, organic/technical, and wild/domestic" (Haraway 15).

9. In referring to *undifferentiation*, Paulson is drawing on an already-established aesthetic language used in describing the grotesque. For this chapter, however, I have chosen to use *indistinction* (although the two terms are similar) because that word is part of a contemporary critical discourse in posthumanism that includes Giorgio Agamben, Gilles Deleuze, Jacques Derrida, and Donna Haraway, among others.

10. In *Edgar Huntly*, for example, Brown embeds a European Gothic narrative within his American tale, allowing readers to consider the Gothic as a transatlantic mode that travels with Clithero from England to America. By depicting Clithero as a shapeshifting, lycanthropic figure upon his arrival in America, Brown represents this move not merely as a

geographical shift but as a transition from a Gothic fiction that disrupts rank and class distinctions (Clithero's narrative) to a Gothic fiction that enables biological indistinction (Edgar's narrative)—thereby redeeming America from European suspicions of degeneracy. On lycanthropy in *Edgar Huntly*, see Barnard and Shapiro 2006, xxxix–xlii.

11. Reading *Ormond* as an outbreak narrative provides an opportunity to bring *Ormond* and *Arthur Mervyn* together in future conversations. See Siân Silyn Roberts's argument for reconceptualizing Gothic fiction in *Arthur Mervyn*, for example, which may have broader implications for how we approach narratives of contagion in *Ormond* as well.

12. Emily Waples similarly argues that Brown's work with the yellow fever mobilized a "miasmatic imagination" that shaped American Gothic fiction and its fears of the "invisible agents" that haunt the American cultural imagination (Waples 15).

13. This reading of *Ormond* as an outbreak narrative partly follows my own (Miller). In this chapter, I am less interested in the operations of contagion and immunity than in indistinction as a necessary third term for thinking about the operations of contagion in *Ormond* and the novel's formal qualities.

14. Kafer emphasizes, for example, that beyond being politically topical, the novel is also geographically topical. *Ormond* is a novel about the Philadelphia of 1793. "In *Ormond*, Philadelphia is a cruel, heartless place, and not because of yellow fever. The contagion merely serves to reveal the plague of what's already there, or more to the point, what's not really there" (Kafer 160). Christopherson makes a similar argument about how yellow fever operates in the text: "*Ormond* opens, then, with the suggestion that evil, alive in society at large, is dormant in even the virtuous breast. The incursion of yellow fever into such a world seems almost poetically justified" (Christopherson 61–63).

15. Wald argues that "outbreak narratives actually make the act of imagining the community a central (rather than obscured) feature of its preservation." She sees the nation as an "immunological ecosystem" in which immunities create a (fragile) communal interdependence that, to some extent, helps us to imagine communities biologically (Wald 53).

16. It is worth noting how the black figures in *Ormond* are themselves miasmatic representations of the yellow fever. As Drexler and White note, "the black subject operates on three levels simultaneously: as an impure presence, as the identifier of structural impurity in the republican schema, and as the agent for cleansing those impurities" (74).

17. Sophia outlines the many deaths at his hands in her brief history of his life. In the novel, we see him indirectly responsible for the death of Helena, directly responsible for the deaths of Stephen Dudley and Craig, and threatening to kill Constantia.

18. The Bavarian Illuminati was an Enlightenment-era fraternal lodge and secret society founded in 1776. The term became associated with atheism and freethinking and with principles of deism and republicanism. The Illuminati were demonized by reactionary publicists and became the subject of a widespread and exaggerated partisan legend in which they were responsible for the French Revolution and Reign of Terror.

WORKS CITED

Barnard, Philip, Mark L. Kamrath, and Stephen Shapiro, eds. *Revising Charles Brockden Brown: Culture, Politics, and Sexuality in the Early Republic*. Knoxville: University of Tennessee Press, 2004.

Barnard, Philip, and Stephen Shapiro. "Introduction." In Charles Brockden Brown, *Edgar Huntly; or, Memoirs of a Sleep-Walker, with Related Texts*, ix–xlii. Indianapolis: Hackett, 2006.

Barnard, Philip, and Stephen Shapiro."Introduction." In Charles Brockden Brown, *Ormond; or, The Secret Witness, with Related Texts*, ix–lii. Indianapolis: Hackett, 2009.

Bernard, Kenneth. "The Novels of Charles Brockden Brown: Studies in Meaning." Ph.D. dissertation, Columbia University, 1962.

Butler, Judith. *Gender Trouble: Feminism and the Subversion of Identity*. New York and London: Routledge, 2006.

Chapman, Mary. "Introduction." In Charles Brockden Brown, *Ormond; or, The Secret Witness*, Mary Chapman, ed., 9–31. Peterborough, Ont.: Broadview Press, 1999.

Christopherson, Bill. *The Apparition in the Glass: Charles Brockden Brown's American Gothic*. Athens: University of Georgia Press, 1993.

Comment, Kristin M. "Charles Brockden Brown's *Ormond* and Lesbian Possibility in the Early Republic." *Early American Literature* 40.1 (2005): 57–78.

Davies, Reeves. "Charles Brockden Brown's *Ormond*: A Possible Influence upon Shelley's Conduct." *Philological Quarterly* 43.1 (1964): 133–137.

Drexler, Michael J., and Ed White. *The Traumatic Colonel: The Founding Fathers, Slavery, and the Phantasmatic Aaron Burr*. New York: New York University Press, 2014.

Grabo, Norman S. *The Coincidental Art of Charles Brockden Brown*. Chapel Hill: University of North Carolina Press, 1981.

Haraway, Donna. *When Species Meet*. Minneapolis: University of Minnesota Press, 2008.

Kafer, Peter. *Charles Brockden Brown's Revolution and the Birth of the American Gothic*. Philadelphia: University of Pennsylvania Press, 2004.

Kamrath, Mark L. "Charles Brockden Brown and Contemporary Theory: A Review of Recent Critical Trends in Brown Scholarship." *Profils Américains* 11 (1999): 213–245.

Krause, Sydney J. "*Ormond*: How Rapidly and How Well 'Composed, Arranged and Delivered.'" *Early American Literature* 13.3 (1978): 238–249.

Krause, Sydney. "*Ormond*: Seduction in a New Key." *American Literature* 44.4 (1973): 570–584.

Levine, Robert S. *Conspiracy and Romance: Studies in Brockden Brown, Cooper, Hawthorne, and Melville*. Cambridge: Cambridge University Press, 2009.

Lewis, Paul. "Attaining Masculinity: Charles Brockden Brown and Woman Warriors of the 1790s." *Early American Literature* 40.1 (2005): 37–55.

Marchand, Ernest. "Introduction." In Charles Brockden Brown, *Ormond*, Ernest Marchand, ed., ix–xliv. New York: American Book Company, 1937.

Miller, Nicholas E. " 'In Utter Fearlessness of the Reigning Disease': Imagined Immunities and the Outbreak Narratives of Charles Brockden Brown." *Literature and Medicine* 35.1 (2017): 144–166.

Mitchell, Peta. *Contagious Metaphor*. London: Bloomsbury, 2014.

Nelson, Carl. "A Just Reading of Charles Brockden Brown's *Ormond*." *Early American Literature* 8.2 (1973): 163–178.

Nye, Russel B. "Historical Essay." In Charles Brockden Brown, *Ormond; or, The Secret Witness*, Sydney J. Krause, S. W. Reid, and Russel B. Nye, eds., 295–341. Kent, Ohio: Kent State University Press, 1982.

Paulson, Ronald. *Representations of Revolution (1789–1820)*. New Haven, Conn.: Yale University Press, 1983.

Peacock, Thomas Love. *The Works of Thomas Love Peacock*, Vol. 8. H. F. B. Brett-Smith and C. E. Jones, eds. London: Constable, 1934.

Ringe, Donald A. *Charles Brockden Brown: Revised Edition*. Boston: Twayne, 1991.

Rodgers, Paul C., Jr. "Brown's *Ormond*: The Fruits of Improvisation." *American Quarterly* 26.1 (1974): 4–22.

Russo, James R. "The Tangled Web of Deception and Imposture in Charles Brockden Brown's *Ormond.*" *Early American Literature* 14.2 (1979): 205–227.

Silyn Roberts, Siân. "Gothic Enlightenment: Contagion and Community in Charles Brockden Brown's *Arthur Mervyn.*" *Early American Literature* 44.2 (2009): 307–332.

Smyth, Heather. "Imperfect Disclosures: Cross-Dressing and Containment in Charles Brockden Brown's *Ormond.*" In Merril D. Smith, ed., *Sex and Sexuality in Early America*, 24–61. New York: New York University Press, 1998.

Stern, Julia A. "The State of 'Women' in *Ormond*; or, Patricide in the New Nation." In Philip Barnard, Mark Kamrath, and Stephen Shapiro, eds., *Revising Charles Brockden Brown: Culture, Politics, and Sexuality in the Early Republic*, 182–215. Knoxville: University of Tennessee Press, 2004.

Wald, Priscilla. *Contagious: Cultures, Carriers, and the Outbreak Narrative.* Durham, N.C.: Duke University Press, 2008.

Waples, Emily. "'Invisible Agents': The American Gothic and the Miasmatic Imagination." *Gothic Studies* 17.1 (2015): 13–27.

Waterman, Bryan. "Introduction: Reading Early America with Charles Brockden Brown." *Early American Literature* 44.2 (2009): 235–242.

Witherington, Paul. "Charles Brockden Brown's *Ormond*: The American Artist and His Masquerades." *Studies in American Fiction* 4.1 (1976): 111–119.

CHAPTER 5

....

ARTHUR MERVYN; OR, MEMOIRS OF THE YEAR 1793

....

MICHAEL J. DREXLER

IN the very broadest terms, Charles Brockden Brown's *Arthur Mervyn; or, Memoirs of the Year 1793* is a tale of upward mobility and social aspiration at a time of economic uncertainty and corruption, political instability stoked by fear of foreigners, and political revolution emblematized by deadly plague weighted with symbolism. The novel was published in three phases between the fall of 1798 and the fall of 1800. The first nine chapters were released serially, in June–August 1798, in the Brown-edited *Monthly Magazine*. The whole of its "First Part" was published in the summer of 1799, with the "Second Part" appearing in full in the fall of 1800. Arguably the most ambitious element of Brown's burst of Gothic writing at the turn of the century, *Arthur Mervyn* challenges readers with a complex formal structure, multiple plot lines and entanglements, and a surprising number of characters whose surnames begin with *W* or who look alike. For their effort, readers get much in return: crime, sex, a plague, violence, corruption, and even romance. There's foreign intrigue, a radical crypto-Jewish Madonna, gravediggers, and gold-diggers. Despite the novel's challenges, readers may also marvel at how energetically Brown worked through his own era's struggles to comprehend revolution, racism, and gender anxiety.

The novel's setting is also vast. From rural Chester County, Pennsylvania, to the streets of Philadelphia, from Charleston, South Carolina, to Baltimore, and from France to England and revolutionary Saint-Domingue (soon to become Haiti), the geography of *Arthur Mervyn* is global. And yet, despite this rich tapestry, the novel is replete with Gothic tropes of claustrophobia. Arthur will be trapped in closets, cellars, and mysterious attic nooks. He will face obstacles that threaten to circumscribe his freedom: rural obscurity, criminal activity, premature marriage, live burial. Yet not all circumstances that circumscribe are so unpleasant: the novel begins in medias res with a scene of domesticity around a hearth, where the eponymous hero shares his history with a kindly couple, who have opened their home to him.

Just two weeks have passed since Arthur, a farm boy not yet twenty years old, has arrived on the Stevenses' doorstep in Philadelphia sorely weakened and disoriented from a bout of the "reigning malady," the deadly yellow fever. Fortunately for Arthur, his benevolent host is a doctor and his wife an able nurse. Once restored to health, Arthur is invited to tell his story. The matter is pressing. A reliable friend has warned the doctor that Arthur must not be trusted; he is a known associate of a criminal on the lam, the notorious Thomas Welbeck, a suspect in financial and other capital crimes. Arthur must clear his name. To do so, he will explain what he knows of Welbeck's misdeeds, including forgery, seduction, and murder. He will confess to having helped dispose of a victim's corpse and having aided Welbeck's flight from his pursuers. He will exculpate himself with acts of benevolence, including a return to the city to save a young merchant from the spreading fever and an errand southward to provide restitution to those who fell prey to Welbeck's schemes. By the end of the novel, Arthur will have assuaged the doctor's concerns about his sincerity, relocated to the city, and begun an apprenticeship in medicine as Stevens's protégé. It's a most improbable rise from rags to riches abetted, not insignificantly, by the power of telling a good story.

Much of the novel is narrated retrospectively. Dr. Stevens looks back on the yellow fever epidemic, he explains, "merely to compose a narrative of some incidents with which my situation made me acquainted" (AM 5). Arthur's history begins in the second chapter and opens with recollections of childhood. As is consistent with Brown's writing generally, *Arthur Mervyn* also contains its share of other characters' backstories. The layers of mediation can be difficult to follow, but this layering can be read as an experiment in realism. For as new characters enter the plot, Brown develops them with attention to their own idiosyncratic life stories, and each of these are deeply embedded in historical events that would have resonated with contemporary readers: the French and Haitian revolutions, epidemics of yellow fever that hit Philadelphia especially hard in 1793, and financial and sexual scandals that filled the local newspapers. Exposition is thus always ongoing in Brown's universe.

Formally, the novel consists of three distinct scenes of storytelling divided between the two separate volumes in which it appeared in book form. In addition to the hearth scene that concludes the First Part, a second at the opening of the Second Part has Arthur bringing his hosts up to date since lingering at the rural Hadwin farm and making his second and third trips back to Philadelphia. In this second scene, Arthur must once again overcome Dr. Stevens's suspicions and prove his good-heartedness. Toward the end of the Second Part, a third scene introduces a surprising formal shift into the present; Arthur narrates the last several chapters without mediation. Having been tasked to take over from Dr. Stevens and complete writing his story for himself, Arthur seemingly steps away from his manuscript and narrates the remainder in an anticipatory mode. That is, the story is still unfolding as the novel concludes. At this point, Arthur has risen from a poor country bumpkin to an aspiring physician and is on the cusp of marriage to a wealthy Jewish divorcée, Achsa Fielding, only lately arrived from England. The novel ends as Arthur awaits a response to his marriage proposal.

The shift to unmediated first-person narration has suggested to critics that Brown wished to wash away suspicions about Arthur's character. Nevertheless, critical appraisal of the novel began with competing claims about Arthur's veracity. Were readers to have confidence in Dr. Stevens's judgment? Or were we, along with the naive or perhaps idealistic doctor, dupes of a master deceiver? These questions were bound up with critics' desire to justify Brown's status as a major figure in American literary history. Because Brown traded in scandal, sexual intrigue, and other narrative elements associated with Gothic fiction, twentieth-century critics had to defend his artistry and contest the widely held position that authentically "American" literature only came to be written following James Fenimore Cooper in 1820s.[1]

Perhaps inspired by the bicentennial of US independence, critical interest in early American writers bloomed in the 1970s. Thus, scholars returned to Brown at the height of New Criticism, which privileged close reading to elucidate artists' mastery of craftsmanship associated with irony, paradox, and formal integrity or completeness. In *Arthur Mervyn*, critics rediscovered a text that met these criteria, and this is evident in the titles of journal articles from that time. A few examples are Patrick Brancaccio's "Studied Ambiguity: *Arthur Mervyn* and the Problem of the Unreliable Narrator," Carl Nelson's "A Method for Madness: The Symbolic Patterns in *Arthur Mervyn*," and Emory Elliott's "Narrative Unity and Moral Resolution in *Arthur Mervyn*." As these titles indicate, scholars worried over Arthur's character, some advocating that the hero was naive yet benevolent and others convinced of the character's duplicity. In one particularly ingenious article, James Russo argues that Arthur is an imposter "who finds the guise of a country bumpkin well adapted to his necessity" (387). According to Russo, Arthur is really the missing heir to the Clavering estate that at the beginning of the novel has been rented out to Welbeck. Pretending to have witnessed the young Clavering's death, "Arthur" is free to marry whom he chooses; Clavering's parents had rejected his mistress and thus prompted the youth to elope to Europe. Despite Russo's creative rereading, most critics tended to argue that Arthur ought to be believed.

The success of efforts to raise Brown's reputation may be judged by the more frequent reprinting of his oeuvre, including the MLA-certified "Bicentennial Edition" of novels and related works published by Kent State University Press in 1977–1987. Comprehensively framed by historical and textual essays, this series' scholarly edition of *Arthur Mervyn* encouraged robust historicist work on the novel in the following decade. Robert Levine, Shirley Samuels, and George Spangler were among those who argued that the novel was enmeshed in the fears and anxieties of the post-Revolutionary era, including the changing role of women, revolutions abroad, insurrections at home, and development of national character. A third phase gradually challenged this ethnonationalist approach by placing the novel in wider discursive networks of the Atlantic world. In place of concerns for the formation of national identity, scholars pointed to political economy, philosophical touchstones such as John Locke and Adam Smith, medical speculations about racial difference, and the rise of a transatlantic bourgeoisie.[2]

Noteworthy in this vein is the Hackett edition of the novel published in 2008. Editors Philip Barnard and Stephen Shapiro place Brown in an intellectual circle that includes William Godwin, Mary Wollstonecraft, and novelist Thomas Holcroft. They argue that Brown aimed to exemplify enlightened Woldwinite principles, including the emphasis on freedom from tyranny and egalitarianism between men and women. Readers of the Hackett edition can track Brown's commitment to these principles in the editors' footnotes. They will find an exhaustive but prescriptively focused elaboration of Brown's motives laid bare in allusions to the Woldwinites and their writing as well as in denotative interpretations of nominal details and relevant historical contexts. As with Brown's self-evaluation, Barnard and Shapiro aim to mediate, or reconcile, a gap of understanding between audience and object. In particular, they contest what was once a common understanding about Brown's politics, that is, the idea that as Brown matured, his views became more politically conservative, or consistent with the Federalists, who had been tossed from power with the election of Thomas Jefferson in 1801. By yoking Brown to the Woldwinites, Barnard and Shapiro argue for Brown's democratic bona fides. Barnard and Shapiro extend Brown's progressive political affiliations to thematic analysis of the text; this, too, is consistent with Brown's aspirant-class position. In addition to Brown's self-proclaimed motive, Barnard and Shapiro extend Brown's politics to a critique of the credit-based market economy, which, unlike the rational discussion of enlightened professionals, relied on rumor and was subject to manipulation and the uncertainties of fate. The villains in the novel are thus speculators and the bankers who invest in their schemes.

Another angle has scholars returning to Brown's biography and to formal and aesthetic considerations, though now informed by the histories of affect and ideas as well as events.[3] Peter Kafer's biography of Brown, published in 2004, emphasized the trauma Brown experienced when his father was rounded up by loyalist-hunting revolutionaries in 1777. Bryan Waterman examines Brown's circle of male associates who came to call themselves the Friendly Club. Members came from several professions—doctors, lawyers, and artists—with the common thread being that all were dedicated writers. The club's central figure was New York physician Elihu Hubbard Smith. Smith contracted the yellow fever and succumbed to it in 1798, a devastating blow to Brown, who may also have caught the fever but survived. *Arthur Mervyn* was the first novel Brown began writing after Smith's death. Indeed, the yellow fever figures prominently in the novel as both metaphor and catalyzing tragedy.

I. The Reigning Malady

Yellow fever epidemics struck US coastal cities periodically during the summer months. The rich escaped to more temperate retreats, abandoning the cities to the sick and the poor. The number of deaths is staggering. In Philadelphia, the fever of 1793 killed approximately five thousand people, or 10 percent of the population. As the deaths mounted, physicians and government officials scurried to identify the fever's origin, how it spread, and how it could be cured or controlled. Physicians and natural scientists were divided about the origins and pathways of the fever. Some believed that it was local in origin, while others contended that it originated in the Caribbean and got to Philadelphia via stale air in the holds of merchant ships. Contrary to the contagionists, who believed the fever spread through contact with poisonous miasma, others, including Benjamin Rush—so-called first doctor of the republic—contended that healthy diets and cleanliness could protect against infection, a theory that Dr. Stevens espouses in Brown's novel. We now know that yellow fever is transmitted by infected mosquitoes, but in 1793, Rush's views were progressive, on the cusp of scientifically reasoned argument. Rush also believed that patients could be cured by extreme bleedings, possibly causing more harm than good; his pathological work surpassed his palliative care. Nevertheless, Rush worked to dispel vernacular speculation that an unusual number of pigeons had brought the disease to the city or that wearing a mask dipped in garlic could prevent it.

Rumors led to other faulty conclusions. People of African descent were mistakenly believed by some to be immune to the disease and were consequently exploited to nurse the ill, drive hearses, and dig graves. Prominent black freemen petitioned for unpaid wages, while the press heaped scorn upon them for stealing from the dead or charging exorbitant sums for manual labor. Most notable were accusations from one of the city's most prolific publishers, Mathew Carey, and a counterpamphlet written by Absalom Jones and Richard Allen, founders of the African Methodist Episcopal Church, titled "A Narrative of the Proceedings of the Black People during the Late Awful Calamity in Philadelphia." Jones and Allen lashed out at Carey, who fled the city and "left [the blacks] to struggle with their arduous and hazardous task." They also charged Carey with appropriating controversy to make money: "We believe he has made more money by the sale of his 'scraps' than a dozen of the greatest extortionists among the black nurses," they wrote. As this dispute illustrates, the yellow fever yoked disease and race in powerful and unfortunate ways. Indeed, the rhetoric of contagion metastasized into politics as well. Fear of a spreading disease of uncertain origin encouraged those who felt America had been infected by foreign ideas, especially those connected to revolutionary events in the Caribbean basin and, by association, the French Revolution.

Partisans noted that Philadelphia, New York, Baltimore, Charleston, and New Orleans had opened their doors to refugees from the violent slave revolt on the French island Saint- Domingue (to become the independent black republic of Haiti in 1805). Refugee plantation owners, the *grands blancs*, fled north and were often accompanied by their "loyal" slaves. By the thousands, these émigrés brought a foreign Creole culture that, because it was also French, implied dangerous ideas associated with Jacobinism, the radical ideology that stoked the Terror of 1793. Americans worried that slaves from the Caribbean had imbibed revolutionary aspirations and might spread these among the domestic slave population. These fears were realized in August 1800, when Gabriel Prosser, known as Gabriel, hatched his plans to lead one thousand slaves to assault Richmond under the banner of "Liberty or Death," a slogan of both American and French revolutionaries. Gabriel's plot was quashed before it materialized, but at trial, the scope of his revolt was recorded: Gabriel planned to capture Governor James Monroe and kill all white people, excepting only Quakers, Methodists, French expatriates, and those who were known to support emancipation. Thus, miasma, insurrectionary violence, and racial animus converged in the yellow fever, which thus served as a multivalent sign of often contradictory symbolic values.

Brown included all of this in his novel. He played on metaphoric fantasies that cast the yellow fever as an ominous sign that the new republic, only a decade old, had gone astray. The pathologies of the nation could be traced to economic and social ties to the Caribbean, the slave trade, the entanglements of the European wars, the spread of dangerous and radical ideas from France and Ireland, or, paradoxically, the nation's embrace of monarchist refugees. But despite leveraging these anxieties to heighten the drama of his story, Brown seems to deny an analogous extension of the fever's meaning in his preface, where he explains that his motive has been to "snatch some [remarkable and instructive instances] from oblivion" to inspire both emulation and sympathy for those who have fallen ill (AM 3). Compared to hyperbolic conspiracy theorists such as Carey, Brown was remarkably moderate. Indeed, he argues for the rational use of fiction.

II. MEDIATION, DIFFERENCE, AND INCOMPREHENSION

Brown imagines that fiction can mediate, or mitigate, the gap between readers and sufferers.[4] He aims to activate his audience by both moving them and inspiring them to become agents of benevolence and thus not to inspire or encourage their most outrageous fears. Though a seemingly modest goal, formally, Brown's impulse is utopic: to reduce the gap between an author's desire for X and the actions of his readers, that is, to eliminate the problem of mediation. Of course, to eliminate such a gap would require that readers first pay for the book. That is, Brown does stand to gain if his benevolent project is successful. We may forgive such commercialism, recalling that Brown was among the first American writers to aim to make a living by writing fiction. The novel provides at least one overt expression of this desire. In one of his retreats from Philadelphia, Arthur decides to translate a book he had taken from Welbeck's library. When he reaches a passage that details the author's efforts to secure his money from bandits, Arthur finds that the pages are curiously pasted together and, once he has separated them, finds banknotes of considerable value deposited between them.

Discovery of the Lodi treasure that Welbeck had previously embezzled from his mistress, Clemenza Lodi, drives much of the Second Part of the novel, wherein Arthur determines to return the ill-gotten gains to the rightful beneficiaries. This includes money found on the body of the murdered Amos Watson. Indeed, much of what Arthur uses to clear his name for the second time with the increasingly skeptical Dr. Stevens consists of the story of his good deeds. He finds Clemenza, stillborn babe in her lap, at a reputed bordello and vows to use the Lodi fortune for her benefit. Though confronted in the brothel by the mistress of the house and grazed by a bullet for failing to heed a warning to leave, he also meets the woman to whom he will later become engaged, the mysterious wandering Jew, Achsa Fielding. Finding her amenable to protecting Clemenza, Arthur removes both to the care of the matronly Mrs. Wentworth, at whose home Arthur will court Fielding in the novel's final pages. This crafting of a female circle of friends and his welcome among them are another sign of Arthur's transformation from rural youth to bourgeois adult and may stand in for the Wollstonecraft-Godwin circle Brown so much admired. It seems important, at the least, to recognize that Brown places Arthur in contact with a rich diversity of women characters who vary in their conscious awareness of the era's gendered inequalities.

Mrs. Wentworth, though a minor character, is in the end crucial to bringing the strands of the novel together. For one thing, she has rented out the home of Mr. and Mrs. Clavering, parents of a young man whom Arthur met in Chester County before the events of the novel commence. Recognizing the similar physiognomy Arthur and Clavering share, she is further tested when Arthur reveals to her that young Clavering had died in his presence. This is important news not only for the tragedy of the young man's demise but also because his elopement from Philadelphia had led his parents to seek him out in Europe and thus make the estate available. Thomas Welbeck and the youthful Clemenza Lodi have rented the property. The wayward male characters, Welbeck, Clavering, and Arthur, bemuse and unsettle Mrs. Wentworth, while the co-location of the women under her roof at the end of the novel resolves much of that tension. Among the women taken under her wing are Clemenza, Eliza Hadwin—another youthful character Arthur had briefly considered for marriage—and Achsa Fielding. It is also Mrs. Wentworth who asks Arthur to complete his story in writing, a task still evolving as the novel comes to a close.

In addition to Clemenza, who represents foreign innocence, Eliza, who represents simple rural domesticity, and Achsa Fielding, who, previously married and nomadic, represents foreign experience, are a few mother-surrogates. Arthur leaves for Philadelphia in the first instance because he cannot stomach the usurpation of his dead mother's place by Betty, a former maid for the Mervyn family, now married to Arthur's father. She may also be a prostitute, depending on whom one chooses to believe. Mrs. Stevens nurses Arthur to health from the fever. But most surprising, Arthur develops his admiration for Achsa Fielding by designating her as his *Mamma*. Like the sexually unobtainable Madonna, Achsa is unavailable to fulfill Arthur's romantic desire until he successfully transitions from worshipping her to loving her. Though Brown wrote a century before Sigmund Freud, the dynamics of childhood development, jealousy, desire, and rivalry had been mined for millennia. Freud, of course, relied on Sophocles, who wrote plays during the fourth century BCE, to expound the Oedipus complex. Freud also got inspiration from the works of E. T. A. Hoffmann, a Prussian contemporary of Brown's most famous for his novella *The Nutcracker and the Mouse King* and for "The Sandman," a story Freud used to explain the psychoanalytic definition of the uncanny. One may consider how Freud's theories might have changed had his model been Brown's uncanny universe.

Four other mothers make more minor contributions to the plot. Notably, two of these mothers have dead babies, and the other two have sickly ones. Arthur's mother has lost several children to an inherited disease that Arthur assumes will end his life, too, around the time he turns twenty. Mrs. Stevens allows her husband to jeopardize their child's life by inviting Arthur into their home while he is suffering from the yellow fever. Clemenza's child dies in her arms and, in an important and often overlooked scene, Arthur, hiding in a closet, overhears a conversation between Mr. and Mrs. Thetford, whose infant has just died. Thetford has come home with a foundling and presents it to his wife as a replacement. I will address the theme of surrogacy at the end of this essay, but suffice it to say here that the idea of originals and reproductions may be observed throughout the novel. When Dr. Stevens takes on Arthur as a physician's apprentice, Arthur may be seen as a surrogate for the Stevenses' infant, whom we met in the first chapter.

Much as Brown represented a variety of women characters in his novel, he also created a tapestry of black people that features a diversity of types. Though modern eyes may identify the portrayal of black characters as stereotypically racist, there is a similar structural logic to Brown's choices for the positionality of his women. Characters appear as analogues to subservience, violence, civic belonging, and revolutionary incomprehensibility. This last position is most pronounced in scenes about Arthur's last do-good mission before he can turn to more domestic concerns. As Arthur assumes the first-person narration of his life history (no longer mediated by Dr. Stevens's retelling), he determines he must repair the damage that Welbeck and his fraudulent schemes have wrought. He decides to restore Amos Watson's loot to his widow and other monies to the defrauded investor, Mrs. Maurice. In this capacity, Arthur takes a stagecoach to Baltimore, in which there features an often cited encounter with a Frenchman, his monkey, and two enslaved women.

The stagecoach scene is important for many reasons, as it ties together the novel's thematic interests in natural science, race, gender relations, and Atlantic commerce. The Frenchman, we learn, is an émigré from Saint-Domingue. Arthur observes his upbraiding of the monkey, named Dominique, a possible allusion to François-Dominique Toussaint Louverture, the black general most associated with the Haitian Revolution, still ongoing through the time of publication of *Arthur Mervyn* in 1800.[5] Coming in the section after Arthur has taken control of his story, speaking directly to his readers, the stagecoach is the vehicle that takes Arthur southward to Baltimore, the novel's only venture into slaveholding territory. The scene is a critical episode in Arthur's development and so is included here in full:

I mounted the stage-coach at daybreak the next day, in company with a sallow Frenchman from St. Domingo, his fiddle-case, an ape, and two female blacks. The Frenchman, after passing the suburbs, took out his violin and amused himself with humming to his own *tweedle-tweedle*. The monkey now and then mounched an apple, which was given to him from a basket by the blacks, who gazed with stupid wonder, and an exclamatory *La! La!* upon the passing scenery; or chattered to each other in a sort of open-mouthed, half-articulate, monotonous, and sing-song jargon.

> The man looked seldom either on this side or that; and spoke only to rebuke the
> frolicks of the monkey, with a Tenez! Dominique! Prenez garde! Diable noir!
>
> As to me, my thought was busy in a thousand ways. I sometimes gazed at the faces
> of my *four* companions, and endeavoured to discern the differences and samenesses
> between them. I took an exact account of the features, proportions, looks, and ges-
> tures of the monkey, the Congolese, and the Creole-Gaul. I compared them together,
> and examined them apart. I looked at them in a thousand different points of view,
> and pursued, untired and unsatiated, those trains of reflections which began at each
> change of tone, feature, and attitude.   (AM 370)

This curious group of four may suggest the eighteenth-century naturalist's fascination
with gradations of humanness. Arthur aims to categorize his four companions, including
the Frenchman, the ape, and the "Congolese," in a set of sameness and difference. The
inclusion of the ape rings with the stereotype of Africans and apes in the period's racial
discourse. And yet nowhere does Arthur explicitly draw this conclusion. In fact, the odd
doubling of the Congolese women (why are there two?) suggests that a meaningful
dialogue takes place between them, one from which Arthur is excluded by ignorance.
He hears the *tweedle-tweedle* of the Frenchman's violin, hears the monkey satisfying his
appetite by chomping the apples, but struggles to interpret the "open-mouthed, half-
articulate, monotonous, and sing-song jargon" of the blacks, "who gazed with stupid
wonder, and an exclamatory *La! La!* upon the passing scenery." Does Arthur master the
scene as the categorizing-obsessed Carl Linnaeus or the count de Buffon might? Note
that the result of Arthur's speculation is an "untired and unsatiated" appetite for these
reflections—and not action. Stuck within his thoughts, Arthur is more like the apple-
munching monkey than a protégé of Buffon. As with the monkey, the Congolese women
have provided Mervyn with much food for thought. And in this state of passive reflection, Arthur discovers that he is the one entrapped in "crude and inadequate" thoughts:

> I marked the country as it successively arose before me, and found endless employ-
> ment in examining the shape and substance of the fence, the barn, and the cottage,
> the aspect of earth and of heaven. How great are the pleasures of health and of men-
> tal activity.
>
> My chief occupation, however, related to the scenes into which I was about to
> enter. My imaginations were, of course, crude and inadequate; and I found an
> uncommon gratification in comparing realities, as they successively occurred, with
> the pictures which my wayward fancy had depicted.   (AM 370–371)

The Frenchman is a slaveholder from Saint-Domingue and most likely a refugee from
revolutionary violence. While home burns, he tweedles away on his fiddle, pleasing only
himself. His exasperated rebuke of the monkey is toothless: "Hold on! Dominique!
Watch out! Black devil!" The monkey, Dominique (i.e., of the Lord), frolics without
restraint. The two Congolese women pay no regard to the Frenchman but cater to the
monkey's appetite and look out the window at the passing scenery. Arthur tells us that
he finds the black women's speech disgusting. He intuits their stupid wonder, but what
might they really be thinking as they look out the window of the stagecoach? All we
know for sure is that Arthur resists approaching that question as he is overwhelmed by

what he, himself, sees outside the coach. The second half of the stagecoach episode is an inverse reflection of the first; it is now Arthur who appraises the landscape. He describes his own thoughts as "crude and inadequate," and he hesitates to share his dreams or the content of thoughts "suggested by the condition of the country through which I passed."

In the first part of the scene, the Frenchman dominates the monkey while tweedling along blithely as his Saint-Dominguan servants look with confusion on what surrounds them. Arthur shifts and arranges these moving parts. We are treated to this elaborate exercise in comparison and counting as Arthur describes his four companions. Critics hone in on the racist joke that includes the monkey in this series but miss the truly significant fact that the position of the Congolese women requires doubling. The monkey in the scene doubles Arthur doing his elaborate calculus without end, while the women actually talk to each other. In the second part, however, Arthur has nothing left to say. He withholds his knowledge from us as his "crude and inadequate" thoughts begin to congeal into knowledge. This knowledge is the truth that the resistant monkey is but an incomplete and inadequate screen that has prevented him from properly appraising the Congolese women. Arthur's disdainful commentary on how the black women responded to the passing scenery seems now, in retrospect, to describe his own incomprehension. Likewise, if understood as Freudian projection, we might learn what is happening outside the stagecoach from what is going on within. It is, after all, a stage from which the actors watch another scene played out through the window. The Frenchman makes no further impression here. His abuse of the monkey has been displaced by the scenery outside; this ought to raise our suspicion that something other than Arthur's dream is being withheld. On its way to Baltimore, the stage is, of course, entering the slaveholding south. Might scenes of slavery be witnessed, perhaps even episodes of disciplinary violence along the road? Might the women slaves' "stupid wonder," along with their seemingly incomprehensible exclamations, be expressions of dismay, grief, or horror? For Arthur, the slaves' liberty to speak without the master's intervention is actually the message, and not the sing-song chatter that he dismisses as nonsense. What Arthur misses is the irony, as both inside the stagecoach and outside on the stage of history is the specter of Haiti.

This encounter with an incomprehensible revolutionary agency joins with other types who appear on rare, but significant, occasions. One is an obsequious servant glimpsed briefly as a reflection in a mirror, interrupting Arthur's appraisal of himself dressed in rich clothing and inviting him to supper (AM 51). Carroll Smith-Rosenberg insightfully linked this first mirror scene with another episode amid the disease-infested apartments of the city. As Arthur searches for yet another character with a *W* surname, Wallace, he enters a room that contains a dead body and, on turning to leave, sees a tawny ruffian of monstrous proportions, who knocks him on the head with a club (AM 148).[6] This ghastly figure seems torn from the pages of Carey's pamphlet condemning black people for stealing from the dead, taking advantage of white people's misfortune. An unconscious Arthur is saved from premature burial by the Quaker Medlicote and his black steward Austin (whose name appears in italics in the text; AM 161), the first black character to be granted a proper name. Thus are both sides of the debate about the actions of black people during the fever represented. Black servants/slaves are also represented dually. Two black women collect Arthur's lost belongings from the street, bringing them ultimately to Mrs. Wentworth's, where Arthur will retrieve them (AM 66). But later, in Baltimore, Arthur is mistreated by two male slaves as he tries to gain an audience with Mrs. Maurice to return her money (379). These servants are vicious in the same ways that Mrs. Maurice is venal. By contrast, Arthur also first glimpses Mrs. Watson as she plays with a light-skinned black girl in a scene of domestic felicity.

If we return to consider the tawny ruffian in relation to the stagecoach Haitians, yet another doubling is apparent. While the ruffian knocks Arthur unconscious, the Haitian women spark conscious awareness of the limitations of his knowledge. Moreover, the ruffian's assault is individualized and isolated. It is also destined to fail, because racist ideology will always be prepared to account for sporadic outbursts of violence. On the other hand, the action of the free blacks in Philadelphia and the Haitian uprising are resolutely communal in form. While both are progressive responses to the horrors of the slavocracy, the Haitians are the only truly revolutionary agents. Here is confirmation of Michel-Rolph Trouillot's assertion that the Haitian revolution, as a radical emancipatory project, was unthinkable to its contemporaries. While this is certainly true in the scheme of "silencing the past," it may also be equally true that the revolution's incomprehensibility was a great source of its revolutionary agency (Trouillot and Carby).

What the panoply of black and women characters demonstrates is that Brown peopled his novel with structurally significant contraries, oppositions, complements, and doubles. If it seems odd to argue that Brown's timely and historically rich narrative may best be approached formally, consider Roland Barthes's famous argument that "a little formalism turns one away from History, but that a lot brings one back to it" (Barthes x). Such seems a productive gambit with this novel, as its framing and generic playfulness might be appraised not only as a great challenge but also as an opening for critical engagement. Jennifer Fleissner reminds us, "Such struggles require literary analysis for their detection, the lesson that texts—even texts as reassuringly familiar as novels—are not contourless containers of information or 'content,' but full-fledged miniature worlds, shaped by implicit choices about the most fundamental things: what a person is, what counts as making meaning, how to think about space and time. Here we remember what might be a much more lasting lesson of *The Political Unconscious* and its precursors in novel theory: the living struggles we unearth by taking seriously questions of form" (Fleissner 188). I will suggest that formal analysis of *Arthur Mervyn* yields a new context, itself deeply historical, that of the conditions of production under which it became a thing in the world.

III. FORM AND GENRE

A formal analysis might begin by relating *Arthur Mervyn* to Brown's other novels, especially the quartet of titles published in a frenzied period between August 1798 and the fall of 1800. While there are numerous similarities in style and structure among these

Gothic novels, it bears noting that Brown invests each with protagonists who wish to escape the drudgery of work. Edgar Huntly begins his story believing that an unexpected bounty has rescued his fiancée from poverty and enabled the couple to plan their marriage. Unfortunately, his hopes and fortune are blasted when their claims to the money are challenged. This crisis triggers Huntley's sleepwalking, mobility without consciousness, an apt metaphor for tedious and repetitive mechanical labor. Theodore Wieland has time for leisure because servants work his property. He also discovers that he has inherited a German estate but rejects assuming the property because it would take him away from his already rich and luxurious life; later, he will try to murder his whole family. Stephen Dudley, in *Ormond; or, The Secret Witness*, does all he can to avoid following his father into the apothecary business. He had wanted to become an artist, but circumstances compel him to take over the practice after his father's death. Years later and planning to retire, Dudley discovers that his seemingly reliable apprentice has embezzled his nest egg. On top of that, he goes blind. Now his daughter, Constantia, must bear the burden of wage earning.

Noting that within Brown's works characters are similarly situated regarding hard labor, we might think of this aversion in another way. If Brown's characters seek instant gratification, how might the subgenres of the novel form that he deploys in his complex, at times formally unstable works reflect or enable the quick fulfillment of a character's immediate desires? Consider how many fairy-tale elements appear in the early part of *Arthur Mervyn*, for example. Arthur was his mother's favorite child, but, like her and all his siblings, he is cursed. His mother and his five siblings have all died, and he is certain that he will also die in short order on the cusp of adulthood. He finds it unbearable to live under his father's roof, because an evil stepmother has usurped the place of his dead mother. Arthur gathers his earthly possessions into a bundle; they include three shirts, three pairs of socks, three quarters, and a talismanic portrait of a deceased friend, which he will soon lose. Arthur leaves for the city and crosses a bridge but finds he is unable to return. He loses his bundle but is saved from despair by a dapper young man in whom he sees his own likeness. He is taken on a wild journey through the mazes of the city but is betrayed by his guide and finds himself locked in a bedroom where a married couple sleeps. The wife has just miscarried, but her husband has "found" a replacement baby to console her. Like a shoemaker and his wife, the couple will awake to find Arthur's shoes, which he leaves behind to crawl out a window and make his escape. He wanders the city until he arrives at a castlelike mansion. He is hired by the master and taken into his home. A richly made set of clothing transforms the youth into a festooned prince. He fantasizes that he will marry the master's daughter and inherit the estate. Under the logic of the fairy tale, Arthur imagines shortcuts cuts between unpleasant circumstance and fulfillment, and this pattern repeats throughout the novel.

What else is common to these cycles of unpleasantness and desire? Allow me to propose a basic formula that integrates what we have already noted about Arthur's encounters with women and black people. First, something familiar is perceived as less so. For instance, Arthur's father turns him out of his home after the death of his mother has already altered it irreparably. In Philadelphia, Arthur meets Wallace, a young adult like himself but fully acclimated to city life. And yet this surrogate peer, like the distorted paternal relationship, goes awry. Indeed, Wallace abandons Arthur in another unfamiliar domestic space. The same may be said for Thomas Welbeck, who appears to be a bene-factor but ultimately does not have Arthur's best interests at heart. Next, the experience of estrangement, or the uncanny, brings Arthur into conflict with otherness, often in the guise of women or black characters. Recall that Arthur must leave home because he rejects his father's new wife. The search for Wallace will lead Arthur to a deserted house, where he will be knocked unconscious by the tawny ruffian. Welbeck's financial interests unravel because the ship in which he has invested is impounded when a British naval vessel discovers two Saint-Dominguan soldiers on board. But likewise, other char-acters can end up solving Arthur's dilemma, too. Arthur's father disowns his son because Arthur rejects his new stepmother; but Achsa Fielding (his new Mamma) is more viable first as mother and then as spouse. The black servant Austin helps Arthur after he is victimized by the ruffian. Arthur's mission southward is temporarily destabilized by the Creole black slaves on the stagecoach, but the encounter speeds Arthur toward restoring the money appropriated from Welbeck's failed commercial scheme. The promise of marriage and sex completes the cycle. Clemenza Lodi will become his princess, if only in fantasy. Eliza Hadwin will reconnect Arthur to rural life, until he decides he has become her superior. And finally, Achsa Fielding, who joins the foreignness of Clemenza to knowledge and experience beyond Eliza's capacity and as well via the racialized other-ness of her Jewish background, appears as the ultimate fulfillment of Arthur's dreams. Savvy readers will recognize that Brown closes the novel *before* Arthur and Achsa's wed-ding. Thus, even as Brown experiments with other subgenres of fiction, the cycle of wish, obstacle, and short-lived fulfillment appears again. Readers may want to consider other subgenres that Brown may be said to experiment with in *Arthur Mervyn*, even as the fairy tale remains the kernel of each restyling, much as Freud argued that dream work distorts the latent content of a dream into its manifest signification. Perhaps this is the novelist's insight, gained as he explores a variety of generic strategies from the eighteenth-century Bildungsroman (the development of a character from ingenue to enlightenment), to the picaresque tales of the itinerant hero, to the tidy conclusions of comedic romance.

The final element of consistency in *Arthur Mervyn* is that the cycle from sameness through difference and to resolution leads always to a new round of storytelling. The one who narrates, then, is the final arbiter of where one story ends and the next begins. Here is the quintessential insight: telling a good story may be even more remunerative than less scrupulous modes of securing wealth and also a more honorable way to avoid mind-numbing physical labor. In this sense, the New Critical questioning of Arthur's sincerity is irrelevant; it does not matter whether Arthur's story is true. It works! Brown is at pains to eliminate the possibility that Arthur should simply have to work hard and, viewing this result as its own reward, postpone the question of class elevation. If you can tell a good story, you can have it all now.

To conclude, let me suggest a less venal motive. Recall that Brown's circle—his Friendly Club—included other artists, such as playwright William Dunlap, but also lawyers and, most notably, physicians such as Elihu Hubbard Smith. In the preface to

Arthur Mervyn, Brown imagines a higher purpose for the novelist's art, what he would call the moral observer or, elsewhere, the moral painter. Physicians and political economists, he writes, have already taken their swipe at reflecting on the yellow fever. Like them, Brown imagines that the moral observer has much to contribute, though his narrative be "humble." Aiming to "methodize his own reflections," Brown claims that the moral observer plays an equally important role in drawing lasting value from the periodic catastrophe of fever season. "Men only require to be made acquainted with distress for their compassion and their charity to be awakened," he writes, adding that one who can do so "in lively colours," or with skill, "performs an eminent service to the sufferers, by calling forth benevolence in those who are able to afford relief" (AM 3). Is this not a bid for equal standing among the professional classes with whom Brown most wished to associate? We may no longer grant novelists these rights or rightful emoluments, yet this only underscores how the origins of professional authorship were bound to the conditions under which it developed.

NOTES

1. A rather late example of this perspective is Jeffrey Rubin-Dorsky's "The Early American Novel". He concludes that an argument can be made for the existence of an early American novel, though unless it accounts for the contradictions, inconsistencies, and instabilities in the genre as American writers adapted it, it is falsifying the achievement" (Rubin-Dorsky 25).
2. See Baker; Goudie; McAuley; Ostrowsky; Shapiro; Silyn Roberts; Smith-Rosenberg; Traister.
3. See Waterman; Cahill.
4. Mary Kathleen Eyring situates Brown's aim to use *Arthur Mervyn* for the social good within the context of charitable activity during the post-Revolutionary era. See esp. Eyring 19–64.
5. Louverture became general-in-chief of the quasi-independent French colony after delegates of the Constitutional Convention in Paris declared a universal emancipation in 1794. Louverture would be deposed with the arrival of Napoleon's forces, who aimed to reinstate slavery in 1802. The Haitian Revolution ended when Louverture's successor, Jean-Jacques Dessalines, repelled Napoleon's invasion and declared Haitian independence in 1804.
6. For contrary readings that emphasize Arthur's assumption of racial superiority, see Smith-Rosenberg; Goudie.

WORKS CITED

Baker, Jennifer J. *Securing the Commonwealth Debt, Speculation, and Writing in the Making of Early America*. Baltimore: Johns Hopkins University Press, 2010.

Barnard, Philip, and Stephen Shapiro. "Introduction." In Charles Brockden Brown, *Arthur Mervyn or, Memoirs of the Year 1793, with Related Texts*, ix–xliv. Indianapolis: Hackett, 2008.

Barthes, Roland. *Mythologies*. New York: Farrar, Straus and Giroux, 1972.

Brancaccio, Patrick. "Studied Ambiguities: Arthur Mervyn and the Problem of the Unreliable Narrator." *American Literature: A Journal of Literary History, Criticism, and Bibliography* 42.1 (1970): 18–27.

Cahill, Edward. *Liberty of the Imagination: Aesthetic Theory, Literary Form, and Politics in the Early United States*. Philadelphia: University of Pennsylvania Press, 2012.

Elliot, Emory. "Narrative Unity and Moral Resolution in Arthur Mervyn." In *Critical Essays on Charles Brockden Brown*, edited by Bernard Rosenthal, 142–63. Boston: Hall, 1981.

Eyring, Mary Kathleen. *Captains of Charity: The Writing and Wages of Postrevolutionary Atlantic Benevolence*. Lebanon: University of New Hampshire Press, 2017.

Fleissner, Jennifer L. "After the New Americanists: The Progress of Romance and the Romance of Progress in American Literary Studies." In Robert S. Levine and Caroline F. Levander Malden, eds., *A Companion to American Literary Study*, 173–190. New York: Wiley-Blackwell, 2011.

Goudie, Sean X. *Creole America: The West Indies and the Formation of Literature and Culture in the New Republic*. Philadelphia: University of Pennsylvania Press, 2006.

Jones, Absalom, and Richard Allen. *A Narrative of the Proceedings of the Black People during the Late Awful Calamity in Philadelphia in the Year 1793; And a Refutation of Some Censures Thrown upon Them in Some Late Publications*. Philadelphia: Richard Allen and Absalom Jones, 1794.

Kafer, Peter. *Charles Brockden Brown's Revolution and the Birth of American Gothic*. Philadelphia: University of Pennsylvania Press, 2004.

McAuley, Louis Kirk. "'Periodical Visitations': Yellow Fever as Yellow Journalism in Charles Brockden Brown's *Arthur Mervyn*." *Eighteenth-Century Fiction* 19.3 (2007): 307–340.

Nelson, Jr. Carl W. "A Method for Madness: The Symbolic Patterns in *Arthur Mervyn*." *West Virginia University Philological Papers* 22 (1975): 29–50.

Ostrowsky, Carl R. "'Fated to Perish by Consumption': The Political Economy of *Arthur Mervyn*." *Studies in American Fiction* 32.1 (2004): 3–20.

Rubin-Dorsky, "The Early American Novel." In Emory Elliott, ed., *The Columbia History of the American Novel*, 6–25. New York: Columbia University Press, 1991.

Russo, James, "The Chimeras of the Brain": Clara's Narrative in *Wieland*. *Early American Literature* 16.1 (1981): 60–88.

Shapiro, Stephen. *Culture and Commerce of the Early American Novel: Reading the Atlantic World-System*. University Park: Pennsylvania State University Press, 2009.

Silyn Roberts, Sian. "Gothic Enlightenment: Contagion and Community in Charles Brockden Brown's *Arthur Mervyn*." *Early American Literature* 44.2 (2009): 307–332.

Smith-Rosenberg, Carroll. *This Violent Empire: The Birth of an American National Identity*. Chapel Hill: University of North Carolina Press, 2012.

Traister, Bruce. "Libertinism and Authorship in America's Early Republic." *American Literature* 72.1 (2000): 1–30.

Trouillot, Michel-Rolph, and Hazel V. Carby. *Silencing the Past: Power and the Production of History*. Boston: Beacon Press, 2015.

Waterman, Bryan. *Republic of Intellect: The Friendly Club of New York City and the Making of American Literature*. Baltimore: Johns Hopkins University Press, 2011.

CHAPTER 6

....

ON FELONS AND
FALLACIES:
EDGAR HUNTLY

....

HILARY EMMETT

> History and romance are terms that have never been very clearly distin-
> guished from one another. It should seem that one dealt in fiction, and
> the other in truth; that one is a picture of the *probable* and certain, and the
> other a tissue of untruths; that one describes what *might* have happened,
> and what has *actually* happened, and the other what never had existence.
>
> Charles Brockden Brown,
> "The Difference between History and Romance" (251, italics in original)

THE breakdown of parallel structure in the opening lines of "The Difference between
History and Romance" suggests that the overwhelming of form by content that afflicts
so many of Charles Brockden Brown's protagonists seems here to have overtaken the
author himself, resulting in a moment at which the constitutive overlap between
historical and fictional narratives is not merely stated but performed. Brown's chiasmic
movement from romance to history to history to romance renders the distinction
unclear to the reader expecting an orderly, binary list and thus foregrounds Brown's
identification of both the fictionality of history (what's probable or possible but not necessarily certain) and the necessary historicity of fiction. It is this latter concern that I take
up here in order speculatively to extend Brown's engagement with contemporary questions of empire and colonial expansion to include the hitherto unexplored "antipodean"
context of Britain's 1788 establishment of a new colony at Port Jackson. Many commentators on the novel have placed the turbulent action of *Edgar Huntly* (1799) in the summer of 1787, and, in its engagement with questions of irrational and destructive
behaviour and how to expunge such elements from the body politic (or incorporate
them into it), the novel can be seen to reflect the debates taking place in Philadelphia as

the articles of the US Constitution were formulated and adopted (Grabo xviii; Marshall 107–108). Indeed, the number of potentially punning references to Edgar's bodily constitution are among the many clues that have led critics to designate *Edgar Huntly* as an allegory of national becoming (Gardner; Murison; Rowe), and it is widely accepted that Brown, as a Woldwinite novelist, intended to stage an intervention into affairs of state (he famously sent a copy of his first novel, *Wieland*, to then-Vice President Thomas Jefferson).

But 1787 also saw the commencement of another political venture. On May 13, just one day before the Constitutional Convention opened in Philadelphia, the First Fleet set sail from Portsmouth with a view to establishing the first European colony on the continent of New Holland (Australia). This chapter therefore builds on existing scholarship on *Edgar Huntly* as a novel that both explores the violence of colonial encounter in America and engages transatlantic questions regarding British imperial rule, by reading it within the context of the establishment of the British penal colony at Botany Bay. Taking as a point of departure Paul Giles's proposition of an antipodean America whereby America and Australia entered in the late eighteenth century into a triangulated relationship with Britain (as the old colony and the new vis-à-vis their imperial forebear), I posit *Edgar Huntly* as a novel that is highly aware of the expansion of the business of empire building occurring in the 1780s. Most significantly for the emerging field of antipodean or trans-Pacific American studies, I argue not only that Brown's foregrounding of violence between indigenous and settler communities contests the doctrine of *terra nullius* (uninhabited land) on which Australia was founded but also that his representation of Arthur Wiatte and Clithero Edny as Irish convicts equally stages a critique of transportation. For the Woldwinite Brown, a venture such as Botany Bay, which relies for its success on the willingness of convicted felons to begin the world anew, can only be doomed to failure. Ultimately, the Lockean logic of property that drove the dispossession of indigenous peoples in both the United States and Australia also works against the convict: the dispossessed white man with no propertied stake in society is as large a threat to a nascent nation as the so-called savage. Brown's tale, then, may be read not simply as national but as *trans*national allegory. In considering the dilemmas of settler colonialism in a comparative context, this chapter bears out Lorenzo Verancini's contention that settler colonialism is an inherently transnational phenomenon that national, imperial, and even postcolonial interpretative categories have failed to explain adequately (Verancini 2).

I. Thinking Globally, Writing Locally

As putatively the first professional American novelist, Brown both participated in and critiqued the colonial myth-making on which the new nation was founded. He admits as much in his often-cited preface to *Edgar Huntly*, in which he lays out his blueprint for the role of fiction in the new republic, a blueprint further developed in his manifesto on the difference between history and fiction in two contemporaneous essays. As Robert Miles unpacks at greater length in chapter 26 of this volume, Brown aligns himself in this preface with the Gothic tradition, but it is one that he self-consciously modernizes and Americanizes. The "castles and chimeras" of the European tradition are translated into frontier violence; "exploded manners" (EH 3) become the subjectivity-shattering confrontation with a "colonial mirror" that "reflect[ed] back onto the colonists the barbarity of their own social relations" (Taussig 164). As Justine Murison has argued, this preface

> has become a talisman in American studies scholarship, repeatedly invoked for its power to express the cultural nationalism of post-Revolutionary America....This iconic passage has allowed scholars to read *Edgar Huntly* as a national allegory in which Edgar's armed conflict with the Lenni Lenape Indians and his seemingly passive sleepwalking participate in the construction of a particularly violent and imperial American identity during the early national period.   (Murison 243)

Similarly, John Carlos Rowe has proposed that Brown's novels function as "microcosms of the ideology of the new nation" in the way his novels appear to justify the violence necessary to its founding. But where Murison and others tend to read Brown's engagement with colonial practice as uneasy and at times explicitly critical (Krause; Luck), for Rowe, Brown is deeply implicated in the US's bloody colonial becoming, in that by telling stories about conquered peoples (and violence against them) he contributes to an imperialist agenda that allowed the new nation to emerge "from its own anti-colonial struggle against Great Britain...by justifying its own colonization of the lands and peoples of North America, as well as people violently imported from Africa to support the southern slave economy." Brown's own vexed relationship with questions of literary authority was not simply a mirror held up to the early republic's volatile politics but in fact served to implicate fiction writing as a ballast for the new nation's colonialist aims (Rowe 28).

Alongside critical accounts of Brown as predominantly engaged in national myth-making run readings of *Huntly* as an explicitly transatlantic novel, in particular as a response to, and extension of, William Godwin's 1794 Gothic narrative of pursuit and surveillance (and the implication of legal institutions in both), *Caleb Williams* (Marshall). Moreover, very recent work by Ezra Tawil has argued that these two aspects are inextricably entangled in the way that "eighteenth-century arguments for American literary nationalism were quite explicitly shaped by the European culture of the aesthetic" (Tawil 122). Brown's work more broadly has been the subject of extensive treatment in Stephen Shapiro's *Culture and Commerce of the Early American Novel*, in which he argues that early American novels such as Brown's "arose as a local response to a global reconfiguration in the Atlantic political economy in the wake of the French revolution, brought about as a result of the long confrontation between Great Britain and France for imperial control of global resources" (Shapiro 2008). For Shapiro, the narrative of *Edgar Huntly* critiques the kind of "sentimental-liberal assumptions of laissez faire commerce exemplified by

Adam Smith's *Wealth of Nations*" (Barnard and Shapiro xxxi). Brown, he suggests, seems to see this newly emerging economic philosophy as leading to inevitable "conflict between nations in ways that simply re-create early modern cycles of vengeance in a new, commercial mode... International free trade, as an index to the rising middle class, does lead to benevolence, but introduces a new, modern feeling of revenge in entrepreneurial competition that generates new forms of global antagonism, which, in turn spark local emergencies" (Barnard and Shapiro xxxi). Shapiro's reading thus takes *Huntly* out of a simply *colonial* context and allows us to situate the novel within a much broader *imperial* context—a context that turns out to have an even wider ambit than his transatlantic focus allows.

In the substantial study that maps the contours of what he posits as antipodean American literature, Giles marks the concurrence of the Constitutional Convention with the embarkation of the First Fleet (Giles 45). To this coincidence, he adds the publication of Benjamin Franklin's satirical "On Sending Felons to America," in all probability written in response to the launch of those eleven ships. Giles uses this confluence to offer a reading of Franklin as a satirist, who, like Jonathan Swift (a fellow traveler in the realm of critique of British colonial power) mobilized a "logic of inversion" to diminish Britain's grand narrative of colonial expansion (49). For Giles, Franklin's satires of the 1770s "feed imaginatively off the idea of a parallel universe, which becomes a strategy for mirroring and displacing both the literal and metaphorical cartographies of the world" (52). Satirical essays such as "On Sending Felons to America" (1787) and earlier pieces on this topic, 1751's "On Transported Felons" and its companion piece "Rattlesnakes for Felons," reveal the, at best, self-defeating and, at worst, vicious nature of Britain's policies of transportation as a means of populating its colonies. In "Rattlesnakes," convicts are likened explicitly to the serpents given by the biblical archetype of the bad parent who offers them to children in place of fish, the emptying of gaols onto American soil is the equivalent of emptying a chamber pot onto the dining table (Franklin's outraged tone here reminds one of Swift's frenzied "Celia, Celia, Celia shits!") (Franklin 358). In the 1787 essay, the implications of this practice for soon-to-be Australia are made explicit: the United States will return its transported felons to Britain, all the better for the speedy population of its "promising new colony at Botany Bay" (Franklin 1144). To draw out the consciousness of Botany Bay and its status as an alternative America in the early republican period is, Giles argues, to recontextualize the United States "as one node in a triangle comprising Britain and Australasia [and] thus to restore to the American situation a sense of its fraught postcolonial condition" (Giles 52). Following Giles, we can read mentions of Botany Bay and New Holland by Franklin and, later, Brown as moments that rupture what Michael Warner has termed the "sweeping amnesia about colonialism" that characterized US national culture in the 1790s and beyond (Warner 63).

Like Franklin, Brown also wrote explicitly about the new colony, and in direct comparison to the United States. As Giles has highlighted, the first edition of Brown's *Address to the Government of the United States, on the Cession of Louisiana to the French* (1803) devoted a significant section to the European contest over dominion of "the new world in the eastern hemisphere" (Giles 107; AG 28). Presenting New Holland as a foil for and lesson to the American republic in the *Address*, Brown also reprinted in the *Literary Magazine* a piece titled "Thoughts on the Probable Duration of the American Republic," originally published in the London *Monthly Magazine* the previous year. This piece celebrates the new age of empire forged by "commerce and the arts of peace" but warns that the double threat of annihilation by rival European powers in combination with civil strife "between the eastern and western territories" of the United States may well give New Holland the advantage in a contest between New World empires (Anonymous 215). The "Thoughts" conclude: "very little doubt can be entertained of its becoming a more powerful empire than the United States, and in a more rapid progression" (217). Indeed, New Holland inhabits a small but insistently utopian space in many of Brown's lesser-known writings (Hsu 37–45; Giles 93–114). In the fragmentary "Signior Adini," reproduced in the Paul Allen version of the *Life*, New Holland appears as an "antipodal," topsy-turvy space in the tradition of Richard Brome's 1640 play, *The Antipodes*, or Swift's better-known *Gulliver's Travels*. But inverting, in turn, Swift's Lilliput, Adini's antipodes are populated by intellectual giants, and the inhabitants of New Holland make mental "pigmies" of the men of Europe (Allen 381). In 1793's "Godolphin" fragment, the inhabitants of New Holland are similarly celebrated, though in this case for their existence in something approaching an originary "pristine" state (Letters 272).

The antipodal reference with which readers of Brown may be most familiar occurs in *Memoirs of Carwin the Biloquist*. In this narrative, Carwin stumbles across a map marking out an archipelago situated "where the transverse parallels of the southern tropic and the 150th degree east longitude intersect each other" (MC 299)—coordinates that actually designate a position in north Queensland, not far from the town of Rockhampton. Due to the secrecy with which this map has been guarded by his sinister mentor Ludloe, Carwin comes to believe that it is on these islands that the wealth and arcane knowledge of the Illuminati-like secret society to which Ludloe claims to belong is located. This reference thus appears to bear out Hsu's claim that "Brown's views concerning US expansionism are mediated by a utopian fascination with Australia" (Hsu 41). And yet, given the unscrupulousness of Ludloe's dealings with Carwin—deceit, threats, blackmail, and finally, *Caleb Williams*-like pursuit across the globe—it is clear that this community, should it even exist, would be characterized by extortion and exploitation. In this light, I read *Huntly* as rather more cautious (and cautionary) than utopian in its consideration of New Holland. Brown's attachment to unpacking the motives and causes for human behavior via novelistic thought experiments allows us to consider the implication of the United States in injurious colonial practices as similarly admonitory for the founders of the colony at Botany Bay. By reading *Edgar Huntly* in the light of both Franklinian satire and Brown's own later flirtation with New Holland as America's surrogate self, we can thus identify a moment of resistance to the cultural amnesia suffered by both nations. Considering Brown's New World Gothic in relation to issues of Native American and Aboriginal Australian dispossession as well as convict transportation reveals the presence of Australia as the dark doppelgänger of the United States from the very moment of the new colony's conception—one of the many mirrorings and specular double displacements that Brown's novel presents.

II. "The Perils of the Western Wilderness": *Edgar Huntly* and Colonial Conquest

In his foundational essay on *Edgar Huntly*, Sydney Krause suggests that *Huntly*'s subtext is Brown's desire to inspire in his contemporaries "dark thoughts about the whites' past treatment of Native Americans" (Krause 473). Central to his argument is the contention that the Elm that is the site of both Waldegrave's untimely end and Clithero's somnambulant grief indexes the Treaty Elm that marked the legendary spot where, in 1682, William Penn purportedly entered into a treaty with the Lenape population, thus founding Pennsylvania. Krause goes on to illustrate how largely the Elm (the capitalization is Brown's) loomed in the cultural life of Philadelphians. As Barnard and Shapiro note, by the time *Huntly* was published, "the Treaty Elm was still a tourist attraction...and featured in many well-known images, from fabric and plates to Benjamin West's 1771 historical painting *Penn's Treaty with the Indians*" (Barnard and Shapiro xx). On the basis of the contemporary cultural resonance of the Elm, along with the location of the novel's action "on the upper branches of the Delaware," a zone constituting "the heart" of the area contested by the infamous "Walking Purchase" (Luck 272), *Edgar Huntly* has been convincingly read as a response to the abrogation of Penn's famous Treaty with the Lenni Lenape by his sons.[1] On this reading, the obscurity surrounding the Elm and the events that take place under it signify the "darkened enterprise" of the unjust disposal of land—Krause's term here evoking the "darker purpose" of Lear, the bloody results of whose own parceling up of land are matched and even exceeded in Brown's tale (Krause 470). Further, Edgar's capacities as a prodigious walker (from the outset of the novel, he is "one who walks with speed...regardless of impediments or crosspaths"; EH 6, 16) develop into somnambulism following his encounter with the maniac Clithero, leading him in turn to graphic feats of Indian killing. This culmination of walking in violence thus situates his day tripping in Indian territory on a continuum with his subsequent violent acts of settler reprisal. Excursion and exploration become indistinguishable from extermination.

Of his perambulations in the wilds surrounding Norwalk, Edgar says:

> Perhaps no one was more acquainted with this wilderness than I, but my knowledge was extremely imperfect. I had traversed parts of it, at an early age, in pursuit of berries and nuts, or led by a roaming disposition. Afterwards, the sphere of my rambles was enlarged and their purpose changed. When Sarsefield came among us, I became his favourite scholar and the companion of all of his pedestrian excursions. He was fond of penetrating into these recesses, partly from the love of picturesque

scenes, partly to investigate its botanical and mineral productions, and, partly to carry on more effectually that species of instruction which he had adopted with regard to me, and which chiefly consisted in moralizing narratives or synthetical reasonings.... Every new excursion indeed added somewhat to my knowledge. New tracks were pursued, new prospects detected, and new summits were gained, though they always terminated in the prospect of limits that could not be overleaped.   (EH 97)

Edgar's encounter with the wilderness here is attached firmly to Enlightenment ideas of education both scientific and sentimental. Under Sarsefield's tutelage, Edgar learns to taxonomize "botanical and mineral productions" as well as to refine his own moral sensibility through encounters with the picturesque and sublime outlooks their "rambles" provide.[2] Yet both his inquiries and his physical incursion into the landscape always terminate in "the prospect of limits that could not be overleaped." Such prospects can be read in keeping with Enlightenment philosophy as the limits of human comprehension made manifest by an initial encounter with the sublime—before the mind reconciles the grandeur of nature as "might without dominion," for example (Kant S28)—but which, in ultimately being overcome ("new prospects detected and new summits gained"), in fact reveal the sublimity of the human mind. Yet the idea of the "limit that could not be overleaped" can also be read more specifically to refer to a particular limit case supplied by the natural world—Clithero's underground cavern—and to what is signified by Edgar's achievement of it.

Of all the seemingly unassailable summits Edgar has attained, none has "led [him] wider from [his] customary paths than that which had taken place when in pursuit of Clithero" (EH 97). Clithero's cave, to which all of Edgar's perambulations—waking or sleeping—eventually lead, is initially a cause for eager anticipation regarding new exploratory conquest of the natural world. But where Edgar rhapsodizes that access to the cave might lead into "spaces hitherto unvisited, and to summits from which wider landscapes might be seen" (98)—and in literal terms it does—the cave ultimately does not lead to further enlightenment but becomes a space of savagery. In "overleaping" the chasm that prevents trespass and gaining entry to the cave, Edgar similarly overleaps the limits that preserve his humanity. In a series of scenes that scarcely require repeating, so central are they to his bizarre history and to critical accounts of it, Edgar returns to the cavern while suffering from a somnambulant episode. His subsequent journey from Norwalk back to Solebury sees him embroiled in escalating acts of barbarism, from the slaughter and consumption of a panther (the scene in which Edgar devours its "warm blood and reeking fibres" [167] is one of the most grotesque in the novel) to the gradual picking off (by hatchet and musket) of five Lenni Lenape who have returned to the area to effect reprisal killings in response to the violent dispersal of their communities by settlers.

For readers like Rowe, Brown's rendition of Edgar's violent conflict with the Lenni Lenape is part of a wider phenomenon whereby the appropriation of indigenous peoples' homelands and the decimation of their populations were brought about by the manipulation of "stories and cultural practices" (Rowe 43). On this reading, Brown's acts of storytelling about this wilderness and its inhabitants further the enterprise of Manifest Destiny in that every eruption of violence into the narrative that subsequently results in the reassertion of civilizing control is a subtle justification of "more tangible acts of colonial and early republican violence against Native Americans, aliens and women" (Rowe 47). Yet Edgar's repeated return to the cave and its environs can also be read as a repetition compulsion, a "re-walking" of the purchase (as Chad Luck puts it) that brings to light the violent dispossession inextricable from eighteenth-century land surveying, Romantic adventure, and Enlightenment natural philosophy. In this light, the novel demonstrates an awareness of the ways in which land symbolically appropriated by exploration is concretely annexed through bloodshed; acts of discovery forge paths not only to enlightenment but also to madness and colonial violence.

Moreover, the weak rationalizations Edgar offers for his murderous assaults on the Indians he encounters and his insistence on his own "mildness" and "antipathy" to violence despite all evidence to the contrary (indeed, he kills with "precision and, at times, glee" [Marshall 117]) further adumbrate the aura of unreliability that has hovered over his testimony ever since he drew attention to his own authorial credibility at the outset of the novel (EH 5). The untrustworthiness of the isolated narrator's perspective is thematized throughout Brown's novelistic oeuvre; in *Huntly*, with its one-sided epistolary form and overlapping concerns with madness, trauma, mistaken identity, and self-deception, this idea is somewhat relentlessly overdetermined. Such uncertainty sows seeds of doubt regarding a variety of issues, but most important for a reading concerned with Brown's take on frontier conflict, it undermines Edgar's claims that his violence against the Lenni Lenape is justified due to their (circumstantial and unsubstantiated) murder of Waldegrave. As Bridget Marshall argues, "Huntly believes that telling his story in a confessional letter to Mary will exonerate his guilt in four murders. But the lack of narrative closure, the absence of a response from Mary, and the ultimately unresolved questions about what happened to [Waldegrave], indicate that his case is not closed" (Marshall 117). The lingering sense of doubt regarding the justification for Edgar's actions, the novel's narrative remainder, underscores the way in which he duplicates and imitates the indigenous "savagery" that he initially deplored. The "perils" of an encounter with the "western wilderness" alluded to in Brown's preface are less incidents of "Indian hostility" than the effects of encounter on the settler himself. Not only does every act of violence do damage to the perpetrator virtually equal to that meted out to the victim, the novel seems to be saying, but the barbarity imputed to Native American peoples by contemporary commentators is similarly constitutive of the white settler.

III. "THIS WHISPERING IN THE BOTTOM OF OUR HEARTS": THE FANTASY OF *TERRA NULLIUS*

In writing the character of Edgar in this way, Brown enters into a broader Romantic conversation regarding the corrupting potentialities of colonization in its myriad forms—whether based on slavery, transportation, or even indentured labor. He was keenly aware of the scope of British colonialism and its attendant commercial enterprises, and, as Eric Goldman has argued convincingly vis-à-vis its representation of Edgar's mentor, Sarsefield, "the novel expresses America's struggle with its prospective imperial identity in an international, global context of European imperialism" (Goldman 558). Sarsefield's possession of a British army rifle ("the legacy of an English officer who died in Bengal" [EH 187]) makes clear that his service to the East India Company in India over the course of the Seven Years War was military. A "blatant symbol of British Imperialism" (Goldman 565), this gun is then deployed by Edgar in his massacre of American "Indians," yoking together by violence the nascent American and established British empires. Moreover, we know from Brown's 1803 correspondence with Samuel Miller that India and New Holland occupied contiguous space in Brown's mind. Noting that he "cannot imagine any obstacle" to the "universal conquest of India" by the British, he goes on immediately to propose that the "colonization of New Holland" will be of equal magnitude on the stage of world history (Letters 612).

In these final sections, therefore, I look at *Edgar Huntly* as a critique of two of the central philosophical underpinnings of British colonial ventures in both America and Australia: the principles of *vacuum domicilium* and *terra nullius*, which justified the dispossession of indigenous peoples, and the notion of labor as inherently redemptive, which underpinned the practice of convict transportation. This dual critique demonstrates Brown's awareness of how, in Warner's words, "the British American colonies [and the nation that evolved from them] were part of a larger British culture of colonialism, and how that larger project informs creole culture in America despite the differences between American emigrants, creoles, and British colonials elsewhere" (Warner 57). That the American colonies were simultaneously models for and to be perfected in the colony at Botany Bay has been illustrated by Deirdre Coleman's thorough account of the Romantic underpinnings of the venture to New Holland, which identifies both J. Hector St. John de Crèvecoeur's "pleasing scenes of farming" and Samuel Taylor Coleridge's ill-fated schemes to found a "high-soul'd Pantisocracy" on the banks of the Susquehanna as the rubrics for this settlement. Crucially, however, the new colony would have the distinction of being founded without reliance on slave labor. Quoting Godwin, Coleman notes that, for many Romantic observers, the practice of transportation that in the case of America was experienced as "banishment joined with slavery" would, in the New World, allow for the "rebirth" of convicts as free people. For Godwin, she argues, the loss of the American colonies was in fact a great gift to the British, who could now set about reforming old practices (Coleman 3–4). Although he is quick to note that banishment as a mode of punishment has yet to be enacted successfully, Godwin offers qualified support for colonization of "country *yet unsettled*" as an eligible mode of punishment: "the labour by which the undisciplined mind is best weaned from the vicious habits of a corrupt society is the labour, not which is prescribed by the mandate of a superior, but which is imposed by the necessity of subsistence" (Godwin 679–680).

There are, of course, a number of problems with this Romantic and romanticized notion of colonization founded on transported labor. In the case of the colony at Botany Bay, the first is immediately obvious: as all contemporary commentators observed, neither Botany Bay nor Port Jackson was "unsettled." Both were already inhabited by distinct groups of Aboriginal people, the Dharawal in the case of the former, the Gadigal in the latter. Indeed, Lieutenant Watkin Tench, a British marine officer of the First Fleet and one of the first to publish an account of the new colony, is at pains in his *Narrative of the Expedition to Botany Bay* (1789) to insist on the presence of "Indian" communities and their largely peaceful overtures toward the colonists (Flannery 40–43, 57–59).[3] Similarly, Governor Arthur Phillip's account of the voyage to Botany Bay, published in the same year, describes several interviews and skirmishes with the indigenous population. Yet despite the existence of this evidence to the contrary, by the middle of the nineteenth century, the concept of Australia as *terra nullius* (literally, land belonging to no one, or nobody's land) had come to undergird all decisions regarding sovereignty over the colonies' soil and inhabitants. This designation came about in part because the question of whether country was settled or unsettled did not depend on literal habitation but rather on a Lockean notion of ownership as determined by having tilled or cultivated the land in some way rather than simply having occupied it.

Terra nullius, like its American cousin *vacuum domicilium*, was not a literal descriptor of land belonging to no one but a designation of land that had not been put to a use identifiable and acceptable to the European settlers and, in being so, created as property.[4] It became the philosophical and, ultimately, juridical screen for what was in reality a series of violent displacements and dispossessions of Australian Aboriginal peoples. The centrality of this Lockean logic to Australian colonial law is exemplified in an 1842 speech given by parliamentarian and barrister Richard Windeyer. Windeyer had taken part in five-night public debate over the "Rights of the Aborigines in Australia." Following the culmination of proceedings, the *Sydney Morning Herald* reported: "we believe it to be the unanimous opinion of the members, that the speech of Mr Windeyer, for the negative, was the most argumentative and logical. . . . He distinctly proved . . . that the Blacks have no right to the soil of Australia for want of settled occupancy and cultivation" (September 12, 1842). Windeyer nevertheless concluded his "argumentative and logical" oration with a call to conscience: "How is it that our minds are not satisfied? . . . What means this whispering in the bottom of our hearts?" (Reynolds 1998, 21).

Windeyer's words attest to the constant threat of the return of the repressed reality on which settler societies are founded. This social imaginary—in which foundational violence is disavowed or rationalized—is held in common with a number of settler societies, including America (Verancini 79–80). Because the maintenance of such a fantasy requires the ongoing disavowal of such violence and of continuous Aboriginal and Torres Strait Islander presence on the land, the legal fiction that the land colonized by British settlers had not been "owned" by its original inhabitants became inextricably harnessed to historiographical, literary, and artistic fictions that its settlement had been inevitable, justified, and even largely peaceable.[5] Published only a decade after the colonization of New Holland and set in the very year of the establishment of the colony at Botany Bay, *Edgar Huntly* insists on the bloody nature of frontier conflicts and introduces an element of doubt into rationalizations of such violence. Its narrative reveals that the violence of settlement was not an occasional accident of settlement or a misguided attempt at "civilizing" barbarous races but was deeply strategic in the sense that it had involved consciously undertaken self-deceptions, ignored "whispers" of conscience, throughout its history. Thus, while Rowe and others are right to note that Brown's representation of the Lenni Lenape conforms to the trope of the vanishing Indian (Rowe n. 355), the graphic violence of their clashes with Edgar and other white settlers inscribes an irrefutable trace on the landscape. When read in the context of antipodean colonization, then, Brown's concern with indigenous dispossession and the effects of reprisal violence (violence that very clearly brutalizes both victim and perpetrator) functions as a warning of the dangers inherent in founding a society over the uneasy and unquiet remains of another.

IV. LOCKEAN ILLOGICALITIES: THE CASE OF TRANSPORTATION

But if the fantasy of *terra nullius* is predicated on a Lockean logic of property creation via labor and cultivation, the majority of the laborers who arrived in New Holland in 1788 were unable to enjoy such fruits. As transported felons, convicts were, like slaves, "civilly dead." Expelled from "the domain of rights," in the argot of the colony, convicts were explicitly referred to as "objects" (Brittan 1158). In fact, the first civil case to be tried in New South Wales, that of Henry and Susannah Kable, pertained to whether convicts could own private property. Alice Brittan has written convincingly about the object status of convicts (and about the status of convicts' objects) in relation to David Malouf's 1993 historical fiction about early settler society, *Remembering Babylon*. Citing Paula Byrne's study of New South Wales criminal law and the way it shaped colonial subjects, Brittan draws particular attention to the status of the personal property box—the "locked box"—in convict life. Such boxes, used to store personal items in households with motley residents, were "more important than friendship or household relations" (Byrne, cited in Brittan 1164). In a world in which the possession of personal property was one of the only things separating the settlers (convict or otherwise) from the perceived savagery of Aboriginal peoples, the locked box must have had a kind of apotropaic power, warding off the barrage of challenges to psychic integrity occasioned by the convict experience. Subject to punitive labor conditions and to constant confrontation with an inhospitable terrain and understandably resentful indigenous population, relegated to at best uncertain and at worst dehumanizing legal status, to be a convict was to be a subject under siege.

As in many Gothic fictions, the locked box as signifier of the intact mind is a trope central to *Edgar Huntly* (Verhoeven). The pair of mirrored scenes in which violations of personal property lead to the radical destabilization of characters' psychic integrity constitute the turning point of the novel. In the first, Edgar aggressively pursues intelligence regarding Clithero's motivations; drawing on his own skills as a "mechanist" of objects combining "the properties of secrecy, security and strength, in the highest possible degree," he trips the lock of Clithero's locked trunk (EH 116). When this fails to yield the information he desires, he returns to the Elm to retrieve the object whose moonlit burial first alerted him to Clithero's secret. This box he violently destroys in order to retrieve the manuscript within (120). In the second scene, Edgar returns to his rooms to discover that his own property has been similarly violated. A packet of letters has disappeared from its resting place in a cabinet constructed with a "mechanical genius" identical to that evinced by Clithero. As Edgar reels from this loss, a second divestment takes place with the arrival of Weymouth and his claim on the money with which Edgar and Mary Waldegrave had hoped to furnish their life together. The loss of personal property is thus the catalyst for the descent of both men into extreme violence (Hinds 1995, 54). To violate individuals' private property is to undermine their right to hold property and therefore to place them on par with the savage or less than human other. The parallels that emerge between Clithero, Edgar, and the Delaware in the second half of the novel are thus revealed as the consequences of the two modes of dispossession on which a penal colony like Botany Bay, for all its Romantic promise, was predicated. Dispossessed of their land, indigenous peoples in both the United States and Australia were driven to acts of violent reprisal. Dispossessed of their labor and its fruits—the capacity to own property—convicts, Brown seems to be saying, will be driven to the same extreme.

We might see this critique of transportation as evidence of Brown's reading Godwin against Franklin. *Huntly* offers an account of the effects of transportation that is suspended somewhere between their contrary positions on the subject. Indeed, the two felons of Brown's novel—Wiatte and Clithero—both seem to have walked off the pages of Franklin's satire and onto the pages of the novel. "On Transported Felons" begins with a graphic tale of mutiny on a convict transport followed immediately by an account of a convict servant who "went into his Master's house with an ax in his Hand determined to kill his Mistress; but changing his purpose on seeing, as he expressed it, how damned innocent she look'd" (Franklin 357–358). These two brief anecdotes are arguably reproduced and given substance in the backstories of Brown's ill-fated characters. Euphemia Lorimer's vicious brother, Arthur Wiatte, is fatefully assumed to have been killed taking part in a mutiny en route to America, while Clithero's manic desire to preserve his mistress's innocence drives his torturous, murderous logic.[6] But where Franklin's satirical writings on transportation both before and after the Revolutionary War leave no option open for transportation's rehabilitative effects (as evidenced by his recurring motif of the parent nation utterly unconcerned with the well-being of its colonies), Brown's novel offers a meditation on the possibility of restoration through sympathy and benevolence.

Edgar's repeated recourse to the lexicon of Enlightenment benevolence (EH 25, 31–32, 106) demonstrates Brown's familiarity with Woldwinite thinking regarding principles of self-improvement brought about by benign example (Barnard and Shapiro xv; Godwin 388, 646). Edgar has benefited from the benevolent example of his uncle (EH 25) and in turn seeks "to emulate a father's clemency" and thus restore Clithero to "purity and peace" (33). Similarly, Clithero presents himself as the ideal Godwinian felon eager to situate himself in a "new world…beyond the reach of human tribunals" (88–89). As Coleman has noted of Godwin and his contemporaries, "the belief that 'new situations make new minds' was a persistent one, as applicable to sites of repatriation or banishment as to carefully selected spots, such as [Coleridge and Robert Southey's proposed Pantisocracy on] the banks of the Susquehanna" (Coleman 4). According to Godwin, the greatest impediment to the rehabilitation of criminals via such relocation was their relentless pursuit by the odium of European government and its representatives; transportation or "banishment" had the potential to rehabilitate provided deportees were sufficiently provisioned for the establishment of new settlements and then left to their own devices. In his description of the ideal operations of transportation, convicts would not simply be redeemed and refined by their work but would find themselves in the position to found a new Rome, whose "settlement by Romulus and his vagabonds is a happy image of this [rehabilitation via subsistence labor]" (Godwin 680). That the founding of Rome through virtuous industry was not simply a rhetorical flourish mobilized by social reformers but a tangible model for the colony at Botany Bay is evidenced by the Territorial Seal of New South Wales, issued in August 1790 and described in the Royal Warrant as follows: "Convicts landed at Botany Bay; their fetters taken off and received by Industry, sitting on a bale of goods with her attributes, the distaff, beehive, pick axe, and spade, pointing to an oxen [sic] ploughing, the rising habitations, and a church on a hill at a distance, with a fort for their defence. Motto: Sic fortis etruria crevit; with this inscription round the circumference, Sigillum Nov. Camb. Aust."[7] The seal's motto—"So, I think, this is how brave Etruria grew"—explicitly indexes the humble Etruscan genesis of the Eternal City and speaks to Britain's hopes for its new venture, despite or, as the seal implies, because of its felonious origins.

Critics of the colony were quick to note the irony at work in this vision of salvific labor. In 1795, Coleridge spoke witheringly of those politicians "who having starved the wretch into Vice send him to the barren shores of New Holland to be starved back again into Virtue. It must surely charm the eye of humanity to behold Men reclaimed from stealing by being banished to a Coast, where there is nothing to steal" (Coleridge 68–69). More recently, Toby Benis has pointed out that the image of the fort on the colonial seal contains within it as much the inference of penal discipline as it does defense against potentially hostile indigenous peoples (Benis 287). What I want to draw out here, however, is a third irony, which brings together these questions of theft, protection, and punishment, in that for transported felons, labor is hardly redemptive if it does not lead to the ownership of land or the accumulation of property, both of which were vexed concepts in the new colony. The necessity of fortification in the New World reveals the sleight of hand necessary to the sustenance of the doctrines of *terra nullius* and *vacuum domicilium*, as previously noted. But equally, ownership of any material possession is compromised when you yourself are deemed an object under the law. There is thus little incentive in this scenario to move beyond a state of nature and begin the world anew. Coleridge's critique of transportation—that its efficacy is lodged in the fact that in the antipodes there is nothing to steal—both hits the nail on the head and misses the point entirely. Rehabilitation and the opportunity for theft are contingent on each other not simply through the operation of negation—the possibility of theft must first be available for you to eschew acting on it—but more fundamentally because, in a penal colony (as well as in a slave-owning society) and on the frontier, one's humanity is dependent on the ability to own and protect one's property. Only a subject can lay claim to an object, and, as both the fort on the seal and Edgar's and Clithero's complex machinations to protect their belongings imply, this subjectivity is precarious.

The quotation with which this chapter began suggests that Brown saw his novels as thought experiments in locating the reasons for the successes and failures of human enterprise. *Edgar Huntly* is one such experiment that interrogates the Lockean logic of subjectivity as predicated on the right to earn and own property via its collapse in the face of the dilemmas confronting the new American (and, by extension, Australian) nation. By reading *Huntly* next to Franklin's satirical writings on transportation and by contextualizing the motif of the locked box within the legal history of transportation and the vexed concept of convict property, Clithero's final breakdown and ultimate irredeemability are revealed to be the result of Edgar's violation of his private property. In Brown's novel, therefore, transportation is a failure not simply for the reasons Franklin cites—that felons will be felons—but, more important, is due to the inherent flaw in its Lockean logic: labor cannot be redemptive if you have no opportunity to capitalize it.

Brown's meditation on history and romance concludes with the expansive declamation, "How wide, then, if romance be the narrative of mere probabilities, is the empire of romance? This empire is absolute and undivided over the motives and tendencies of human actions" (Difference 253). If *Edgar Huntly*, in its exploration of the motives and tendencies of human action under the strain of psychological and social upheaval, is thus a citadel in the empire of romance, it is equally a romance of empire and one that offered a prescient warning to Britain on the occasion of its newest colonial venture.

NOTES

1. In 1737, John and Thomas Penn revealed the existence of a deed of sale for a tract of land that they claimed had been brokered between their father and the Lenape some fifty years earlier. This tract was defined as the amount of land that could be covered by a man walking at a regular pace, along a particular route, in a day and a half—under normal circumstances not more than twenty-five miles. Not only were the Lenape railroaded into ratifying a document of extremely dubious and almost certainly fraudulent provenance, but agents of the Penn brothers surreptitiously cleared a path in advance and then hired three trained athletes, along with a support team, in order to cover almost seventy miles in the allotted time. As a result of the Walking Purchase, the Delawares were defrauded of around twelve hundred square miles of tribal territory—an area the size of Yosemite National Park.

2. Barnard and Shapiro note the irony of the association of the wilderness with Enlightenment principles here, given that Norwalk will soon become the site of such savagery and irrationality (n. 67–68). What's at stake in this irony is, of course, that classifying the wilderness and lauding its effects on sensibility have shown themselves to be if not the necessary precursor to laying claim to the land through violence, then certainly the inevitable attendant of such claims. On *Edgar Huntly*, the sublime, and the American picturesque, see Berthold.

3. Tench's use of *Indians* as a generic term for indigenes here illustrates the extent to which understanding of the new colony was filtered through the lens of colonial experiences in the Americas. Equally interesting is to consider the ways Tench's *Narrative*, published in New York by T & J Swords in 1789, might inform or inflect writing about America's own frontier encounters.

4. For an account of the development and accuracy of the term *terra nullius* in Australian legal history, see Attwood.

5. Henry Reynolds's *The Other Side of the Frontier* (1981) was the first study to contest the narrative that the conquest of Australia had been peaceful. For an overview of the "history wars" subsequently fought over such questions, see Macintyre and Clark.

6. See Juliet Shields's account of the "Irish uncanny" in early American Gothic fiction.

7. http://www.environment.nsw.gov.au/Heritage/research/heraldry/firstseal.htm, accessed August 3, 2017.

WORKS CITED

Anonymous. "Thoughts on the Probable Duration of the American Republic." LM 2.9 (June 1804): 215–220.

Attwood, Bain. "Law, History and Power: The British Treatment of Aboriginal Rights in Land in New South Wales." *Journal of Imperial and Commonwealth History* 42.1 (2014): 171–192.

Barnard, Philip, and Stephen Shapiro. "Introduction." In Charles Brockden Brown, *Edgar Huntly; or, Memoirs of a Sleep-walker, with Related Texts*, ix–xlii. Indianapolis: Hackett, 2006.

Benis, Toby R. "Transportation and the Reform of Narrative." *Criticism* 45.3 (2003): 285–299.

Berthold, Dennis. "Charles Brockden Brown, *Edgar Huntly*, and the Origins of the American Picturesque." *William and Mary Quarterly* 41.1 (1984): 62–84.

Brittan, Alice. "B-b-british Objects: Possession, Naming, and Translation in David Malouf's *Remembering Babylon*." *Publications of the Modern Language Association* 117.5 (2002): 1158–1171.

Coleman, Deirdre. *Romantic Colonisation and British Anti-Slavery*. Cambridge: Cambridge University Press, 2005.

Coleridge, Samuel Taylor. *Collected Works*, Vol. 1, *Lectures, 1795: On Politics and Religion*. Lewis Patton and Peter Mann, eds. London, Routledge & Kegan Paul, 1971.

Flannery, Tim, ed. *Watkin Tench's 1788*. Melbourne: Text Publishing, 2009.

Franklin, Benjamin. *Writings*. New York: Library of America, 1987.

Gardner, Jared. "Alien Nation: Edgar Huntly's Savage Awakening." *American Literature* 66.3 (1994): 429–461.

Giles, Paul. *Antipodean America: Australasia and the Constitution of U.S. Literature*. Oxford and New York: Oxford University Press, 2013.

Godwin, William. *Enquiry concerning Political Justice and Its Influence on Modern Morals and Happiness* (1798). London: Penguin, 1978.

Goldman, Eric. "The 'Black Hole of Calcutta' in Charles Brockden Brown's America: American Exceptionalism and India in *Edgar Huntly*." *Early American Literature* 43.3 (2008): 557–579.

Grabo, Norman. "Introduction." In Charles Brockden Brown, *Edgar Huntly or, Memoirs of a Sleepwalker*, vii–xxiv. London: Penguin, 1988.

Hinds, Janie. "Charles Brockden Brown's Revenge Tragedy: *Edgar Huntly* and the Uses of Property." *Early American Literature* 30 (1995): 51–70.

Hinds, Janie. "Deb's Dogs: Animals, Indians, and Postcolonial Desire in Charles Brockden Brown's *Edgar Huntly.*" *Early American Literature* 39.2 (2004): 323–354.

Hsu, Hsuan. *Geography and the Production of Space in Nineteenth-Century American Literature.* Cambridge: Cambridge University Press, 2010.

Kant, Immanuel. *The Critique of Judgement* (1790). James Creed Meredith trans. Oxford: Oxford University Press, 1911.

Krause, Sydney J. "Penn's Elm and Edgar Huntly: Dark 'Instructions to the Heart'." *American Literature* 66.3 (1994): 463–484.

Luck, Chad. "Re-walking the Purchase: *Edgar Huntly*, David Hume, and the Origins of Ownership." *Early American Literature* 44.2 (2009): 271–306.

Marshall, Bridget M. *The Transatlantic Gothic Novel and the Law 1790–1860.* Farnham, UK: Ashgate, 2010.

Macintyre Stuart and Anna Clark. *The History Wars.* Melbourne: Melbourne University Press, 2004.

Murison, Justine S. "The Tyranny of Sleep: Somnambulism, Moral Citizenship, and Charles Brockden Brown's *Edgar Huntly.*" *Early American Literature* 44.2 (2009): 243–270.

Reynolds, Henry. *This Whispering in Our Hearts.* St Leonards: Allen & Unwin, 1998.

Reynolds, Henry. *The Other Side of the Frontier: Aboriginal Resistance to the European Invasion of Australia.* Sydney: University of New South Wales Press, 2006.

Rowe, John Carlos. *Literary Culture and U.S. Imperialism from the Revolution to World War II.* Oxford: Oxford University Press, 2000.

Shapiro, Stephen. *The Culture and Commerce of the Early American Novel: Reading the Atlantic World-System.* University Park: Pennsylvania State University Press, 2008.

Shields, Juliet. *Nation and Migration: The Making of British Atlantic Literature, 1765–1835.* New York: Oxford University Press, 2016.

Taussig, Michael. "Culture of Terror—Space of Death: Roger Casement's Putomayo Report and the Explanation of Torture." In Nicholas B. Dirks, ed., *Colonialism and Culture*, 135–174. Ann Arbor: University of Michigan Press, 1992.

Tawil, Ezra. *Literature, American Style: The Originality of Imitation in the Early Republic.* Philadelphia: University of Pennsylvania Press, 2018.

Verancini, Lorenzo. *Settler Colonialism.* London: Palgrave Macmillan, 2010.

Verhoeven, W. M. "Opening the Text: The Locked-Trunk Motif in Late Eighteenth-Century British and American Gothic Fiction." In Valeria Tinkler-Villani, Peter Davidson, and Jane Stevenson, eds., *Exhibited by Candlelight: Sources and Developments in the Gothic Tradition*, 205–220. Amsterdam: Rodopi, 1995.

Warner, Michael. "What's Colonial about Colonial America?" In Robert Blair St. George, ed., *Possible Pasts: Becoming Colonial in Early America*, 49–70. Ithaca, N.Y.: Cornell University Press, 2000.

CHAPTER 7

··

STEPHEN CALVERT'S
UNFINISHED BUSINESS

··

CHRISTOPHER LOOBY

WHEN Charles Brockden Brown left *Memoirs of Stephen Calvert* unfinished in June 1800, he left readers a great deal of room for speculation and candidly invited readers to imagine what might have ensued from the many tangled plots he had set in motion. Although *Calvert*'s fragmentary state has led to its critical neglect, it is in some ways the most daring and adventurous of Brown's writings, and the absence of its projected continuation ought to be understood as a meaningful feature of the text rather than as a mere defect. What does it mean for the narrator (Stephen himself) to tell us that his tale is absolutely incomparable ("There is, indeed, little danger that the story of any other human being will resemble mine. My fate is marked by uncommon hues: neither imagination nor memory can supply you with a parallel"),[1] tease us with repeated suggestions that it will comprise an "endless series of disasters and calamities" (SC 176), and then not only withhold the details that would justify these dire foreshadowings but also challenge us, on the last page, to imagine what he has plainly told us was unparalleled and unimaginable?

Like all of Brown's plots, that of *Calvert* is difficult to summarize briefly. For present purposes, the essential elements are as follows. The tale is told by Stephen himself in retrospect, from his self-imposed exile on the wilderness shore of Lake Michigan, where he has retreated in order to distance himself from "the footsteps and society of men," that is, "the world, [which he] found...too abundant in temptation and calamity... safely to remain in it" (71). Promising to tell us what led to this drastic removal, which evidently involved some very bad action on his own part, he begins with his family history and tells us how circumstances brought him as an infant to America with his parents while his twin brother, Felix, was temporarily left behind in England with his wet nurse. Stephen's father, a Protestant convert, was in flight from his malicious father, a Catholic noble who was plotting an insurrection against the king in which he expected his son to play a central role (a part that the son's converted conscience would, of course, not allow).[2] Events in England delayed the arrival of Felix, and eventually, in fact, he was lost, and his fate then remained for a time unknown. Stephen's father died in

Philadelphia, his mother was left to raise him on her own, and as the story proper proceeds, he is a young man who is prone to "lawless and wild enthusiasm" (112), who is "young, romantic, and without experience" (157), and who is reputed by his friends to be "capricious, fickle, and prejudiced" (172). These qualities lead him into terrible trouble, chiefly involving his fluctuating attachments to two women, his very homely but deeply virtuous cousin, Louisa Calvert, and a strikingly beautiful and intriguingly mysterious stranger, Clelia Neville. Although we begin to learn what transpires between these characters, we never get most of the tale and never learn what happened to lead Stephen into exile.

Scholars have usually classified *Calvert* as a Bildungsroman, a tale of a young man's balked moral development, while they often debate whether it can be considered complete or successful. In perhaps the first serious and detailed critical study, W. B. Berthoff described it aptly as a "sketch of a romantic egoist" (Berthoff 424) but also deemed it a "general failure" (423). Two important early articles shared an interest in Stephen as an embodiment of aesthetic imagination. Maurice J. Bennett argued that *Calvert* was "a pioneering American effort in the portrait-of-an-artist novel" (Bennett 495), not because Stephen was actually an artist but because his alienation could be traced to his "devotion to novel reading" (496), and this made Brown's novel an examination of "the relation of aesthetic experience to America" that asked "a sociohistorical question as to whether or not the imagination and its products can be usefully assimilated into American society at all" (495).[3] Robert A. Ferguson gave this theme a specific biographical dimension, since Brown himself was trained as a lawyer and experienced a profound conflict between his literary vocation and the more practical requirements of the legal profession. Stephen's fluctuating attractions to Louisa and Clelia symbolize, for Ferguson, Brown's suspension between the opposing worlds of duty and pleasure, social responsibility and sensual exploration; thus, Stephen "moves within a prism of shame and remorse formed out of his inability to reconcile the external requirements of social obligation and the private dictates of the creative imagination" (Ferguson 144).

More recently, critical attention has tended to focus on questions of gender and sexuality. Scott Slawinski, in his study of Brown's editorship of the *Monthly Magazine, and American Review*, where he serialized *Calvert*, argues that the novel participates in Brown's general project of rehabilitating the figure of the bachelor—who more often was understood at this time to represent social irresponsibility—by showing that bachelors actually could be decent, responsible, conforming members of society. Brian C. Neff, on the other hand, contends that *Calvert* is an experiment in articulating a new nonconformist style of masculinity that would be nonpatriarchal and "based not just on reason, but sympathy and affect" (Neff 63). Stephen Shapiro, in an article chiefly about *Edgar Huntly* (as well as in scattered observations elsewhere), has proposed that *Calvert* takes part in an imaginative effort to project, in coded terms, a "preemergent homoerotic culture" that is "forging means of subaltern expression within socially hostile circumstances" (Shapiro 2004, 224) and that the eighteenth-century novel is one of the specific institutions where such veiled intimations of emergent patterns of feeling and being can be articulated without necessarily being recognized by punitive authorities (223).

Interpretations of *Calvert* would all benefit from taking into account the material circumstances of its production and publication. Robert D. Arner, in his "Historical Essay" in the Kent State bicentennial volume that includes *Calvert*, has built a persuasive case that Brown apparently began work on this tale in late August or early September 1798, when his first novel, *Wieland*, was in press (Arner 298). Very soon, however, Brown's rapid progress on the novel was diverted by the appearance of yellow fever in New York City; his dear friend Elihu Hubbard Smith contracted the disease and died, and Brown may have had a mild case himself, from which he recovered after leaving the city environs for Perth Amboy, New Jersey (300), although it appears that his work on the novel, once it had been interrupted by the plague, was not resumed. Instead, he turned to other projects—the writing of *Ormond*, then the first part of *Arthur Mervyn*, and then *Edgar Huntly*, all of which he wrote between December 1798 and the middle of 1799. When Brown undertook the editorship of the *Monthly Magazine* in April 1799, he soon needed copy to fill its pages and presumably took the unfinished *Stephen Calvert* out of a drawer and began serializing it in June of that year. Arner's further inference, which seems quite plausible, is that by January 1800, he had exhausted what he had written of *Calvert* to date; hence, there were no installments of it in the February and March issues of the magazine, at which time "he pushed the work through to a rather hasty conclusion, completing the final three installments just shortly before their appearance in April, May, and June of 1800" (301). *Calvert* thus has a curious place in the narrative of Brown's brief and intense career of novel writing, both the second and the fifth of his novels, so to speak. As I will argue, these material circumstances of writing and publication—the interruption of the writing, the hiatuses in publication, and the truncated ending—have a number of profound implications for understanding the novel.

Brown left readers hanging, on the last page, with the protagonist, Stephen, about to meet his long-lost twin brother, Felix, who at that point was about to enter from the next room. A note appended to the final serial installment averred that "the reader's fancy has now a clue to all that has heretofore bewildered him, and will easily image to itself the consequences of such a meeting as is now about to take place." Stephen waits with "tremulous" frame and a "heart [that] throbbed as if [he] were on the eve of some fatal revolution" (SC 272) for his brother's entrance, and his own "suspenses" (272) at this moment cue and match those of the tremulous reader—particularly the reader of the original serialized version, who, as I will discuss, finds the materialized intervals and deferrals involved in this attenuated form of print publication resonating strangely with a tale that itself involves so many crucial delays, hesitations, interruptions, and postponements. But while Stephen's suspenses "were quickly at an end" (272), the reader's are left to throb, as it were, endlessly.

Although it has been customary to consider the unfinished state of *Calvert* as a mere accident of circumstances and as a formal defect of an abortive work, it is better to treat it as an incentive to critical speculation and to read it as a peculiar sort of literary experiment—perhaps not a fully intended effort in a genre we might call the *fragment*[4] but possibly a half-purposeful acknowledgment of the fundamental incompleteness of any work of literary art (which always needs to be "realized," as the theorists of *Rezeptionaesthetik* would say, in the reader's imagination).[5] *Calvert* would count, then, as a particularly blatant gesture toward the epistemological uncertainty and narrative inscrutability that Brown assiduously cultivated in many other ways virtually everywhere in his writing. This uncertainty or inscrutability is particularly tantalizing in *Calvert* because the tale involves dramatically explosive issues of race and sex that were among the most difficult for any writer to address in the period in which Brown wrote. He must have wondered how his bold approach to such dangerous topics—homosexual sodomy, the violent brutalization of children and women, the sexual exploitation of slaves, and weirdly concatenated erotic rivalries, to mention the most salient—would be received by readers, and he may finally have been unable, or unwilling, to follow out to their logical conclusions the daringly radical plot lines he had boldly set in motion.

If Brown had completed *Calvert* as he seems to have intended (as a five-part novel; more on this later), it would have been his longest fiction by a good measure. It would have been his most ambitious and adventurous, too. For a long time, *Calvert* has been consigned to the margins of Brown's corpus, but more recently, it has begun to be recognized for its (not fully realized) thematic and formal risks, and it counts as a key source for understanding both the history of early American sexuality and the history of slavery and race. It is the first American fiction to refer unmistakably to homosexual relations, when one of the main female characters, Clelia Neville, explains that her flight from Ireland to America was prompted by the unexpected discovery of her husband's unnameable "propensities," "pollutions" (SC 204), "depravity" (205), "abominable crimes" (206), "vices," and "enormities" (208), which her "own eyes were allowed to witness" (205) but which, in the classic phrase, "have not a name which [she] can utter" (204). The nature of these acts is unmistakably suggested by the fact that Clelia previously ascribed Belgrave's marital negligence and cruelty to "his attachment to some other woman," only belatedly coming to realize "that his associates were wholly of his own sex" (205). *Calvert* is also, arguably, the first American fiction to approach unflinchingly the matter of sexual violence in the context of institutionalized slavery: a character, Ambrose Calvert, who is depicted as a rampantly violent slave owner—as well as an abusively domineering husband and father—bequeaths his plantation and his human property to Stephen Calvert, whom he has never met but who is a distant relation; Stephen's extreme impressionability and established moral weakness look as if they will provide him with inadequate means to resist the temptations that his sudden and unaccustomed ownership of slaves will inevitably present to him.

We can't adequately measure the importance of *Memoirs of Stephen Calvert* unless we allow ourselves to ask where Brown was apt to have been going with themes and plots like these, which he set in motion but didn't follow to their likely ends. Much of the novel that we have, in its fragmentary form, is preparation. Stephen narrates from the seemingly recent past, retrospectively giving us the distant background for direly calamitous events that he ascribes to his own subsequent moral degeneration, but he never gets around to describing these events. The meaning of the novel in a sense depends exactly on what is absent: the outcomes of the plot lines that are initiated but not completed.

One of the few critics who has given *Calvert* extended attention, Norman S. Grabo, observed, "If he really intended to extend the story, [Brown] has planted a number of possibilities capable of interesting development," noting the "possibility of international intrigue," the opposition between Catholicism and Protestantism, two landed estates that remain to be settled (the slave plantation in America and Stephen's ancestral home in England), and the "real story of Clelia and Belgrave" (Grabo 148); in addition, "Felix's story has not yet been told," and the mystery of his supposed past relationship with Clelia remains to be clarified (148–149). What will happen to the erotic triangle formed by Stephen, Felix, and Clelia? And for that matter, what will happen to the erotic triangle formed by Stephen, his friend Sydney Carlton, and his cousin Louisa?

> [H]ow will Sydney emerge from his meddling orchestration of events and emotions? As Brown typically works, he could well emerge as the crucial figure of the book. Will Louisa and Clelia bring their contrasting characters and reputations into clearer adjustment? Will the new brother Felix prove to be Louisa's true soul mate?...No, I should say that though there are possibilities aplenty, they are merely hints for the kind of complications Brown could work out in four more volumes.   (149)

The "slave issue and miscegenation" have been prepared as conditions for further events, "to say nothing of Belgrave's alleged homosexual adventures" (149). In short, according to Grabo, "Brown has some shockingly good prospects before him" (149). More recently, Shapiro has speculated that Clelia might even have turned out to be a man (2004, 235). In what follows, I will offer some of my own speculations and link these to the material question of the text's serial publication, while suggesting, most generally, that Brown finally left these implications properly to the reader's imagination.

It is important, for several reasons, to take careful account of the novel's serial magazine publication. This was the only form in which *Calvert* was available to readers during its author's lifetime, and there is evidence that Brown took calculated artistic advantage of serial form. Because Brown inserted into the middle of its serial run (i.e., in March 1800) a strange contrived incident, in an interpolated "Note on Stephen Calvert"—featuring an engaged listener to Calvert's supposedly orally delivered tale who, frustrated by its interruption, writes to the magazine editor to protest its hiatus and to express his eagerness for its continuation—we know that fundamental questions of readerly reception were consciously present to Brown as he wrote this novel. This "Note" is itself a curious device, an artifact of *Calvert's* irregular "piece-meal" (SC 272) publication in the *Monthly Magazine, and American Review*, a short-lived journal Brown edited, between June 1799 and June 1800. The "Note" is a metafictional jeux d'esprit that purports to be from someone identified only by the initial "H.," who pretends that a friend recently introduced Stephen Calvert to him and claims that he had been listening raptly to Stephen tell his tale by "a winter-evening's fire," only to have Stephen abruptly rise, snatch his hat, and depart without explanation before finishing.[6] It becomes clear soon enough that this is a playful allegory of reading and a way of apologizing for a two-month suspension of the narrative's publication (no installment had appeared in February and only this "Note" in March). The presumably fictive letter from "H." is followed by a bracketed and italicized note from "E." (the editor, presumably): "[*The narrative of Calvert was interrupted for good reasons, with which, however, it would be absurd and impertinent to teaze the reader. The obstacles are now removed, and the tale will be resumed in the ensuing number, and punctually continued. E.*]" (MM, March 1800, 173). It is hard to avoid the suspicion that Brown is covering for a momentary lack of material (as Arner surmised) by taking the opportunity to play a game of narrative arousal and deferral. The fact that the ensuing April installment is exceptionally lengthy adds to the suspicion that Brown had been holding material back, staging the publication hiatus deliberately. It is difficult, as well, to avoid the suspicion that the idea of an abrupt cessation of the tale has here crossed Brown's mind.[7] Slyly, he keeps the reader waiting in suspense not only for the usual one month between installments but for an exacerbating three, this "teaze" directly following Clelia Neville's stunning announcement that she cannot marry Stephen because she is "*a wife already!*" (MM, January 1800, 30; italics in original).[8]

The entire narrative is framed (as other Brown novels were) as a direct written address from the writer, Stephen, to an unspecified "friend" (SC 71) who has demanded an explanation of Stephen's self-exile in the Michigan wilderness and for whom the written narrative evidently continues and supplements a prior oral transmission of Stephen's tale. Again, Brown is foregrounding temporal gaps, not only between the two tellings of the tale (first oral, then written) to this unnamed friend but also between the long-ago events related in the tale and the doubled narrative discourse itself. Other narrative contrivances contribute in additional ways to the sense that Brown is up to something unusually complicated and radical on the formal level. At the very end of *Calvert*'s last serial installment in the *Monthly Magazine* (June 1800), Brown appended this post-script, more or less speaking (once again) as author and editor at once:

> P. S. Calvert's story is a five-act drama. Here ends the *first* act; and this being in itself complete, the links connecting it with ensuing acts being only afterwards unfolded, it is thought best to stop the piece-meal publication of it here. The reader's fancy has now a clue to all that has heretofore bewildered him, and will easily image to itself the consequences of such a meeting as is now about to take place.   (272)

This peculiar and gnomic postscript itself encloses several mysteries. Since the "*first* act" has just ended on a note of high suspense—Stephen, to repeat, is about to meet his long-lost twin brother, Felix, who is poised to enter the scene from the next room—it seems perverse to claim, as the postscript does, that this is "in itself complete" or that we can "easily image" to ourselves the multiple "consequences" of such an improbable and potentially volatile meeting. The story up to this point is very distinctly *not* complete; in fact, it has been nearly all backstory and preparation for what are repeatedly called the dire "calamities" (71, 73, 145, 148) that are in store for Stephen and that will be the cause of the deep "guilt and remorse" (72) from which he presently suffers. And we can actually imagine all sorts of strange outcomes potentially proceeding from this momentous encounter. It would be fair to say that nearly all of this "first act" has consisted of elaborate foreshadowings of unspecified catastrophic events yet to come—none of which was ever to be "unfolded" to us except in our speculations, our "fancy," as Brown calls it.

Other mysteries abide here as well. Why assimilate this prose fiction to a "drama" of "five acts"?[9] Why indulge in a tautology about "links" being "only afterwards unfolded," when, by definition, literary narrative proceeds by way of connections that need both their before and after parts in order to make sense (the impossible alternative would be the case of "links" to what ensues being somehow already "unfolded" in what has gone before)?[10] And is Brown implying that the four following acts are already written (or at least mapped out in his mind) but that he is tired of "piece-meal" magazine serialization, with its own uncertainties? (In addition to stalling out in February 1800, publishing no installment of the novel that month or the next but, instead, the "Note on Stephen Calvert" in the March issue, there had earlier been the curious omnibus September–December issue of the magazine published at the end of the previous year, with its single installment of *Calvert*, effectively a prior four-month hiatus).[11] And does he mean to publish the remainder together, all at once, rather than dole it out irregularly over the course of many months, as the first "act" has been issued? Or is this all an authorial ruse?

It is difficult not to feel somewhat "teazed" or even misused by this postscript, since it really does nothing to clear up the reader's "bewilder[ment]" but only perversely amplifies it. That may be the point: it seems reasonably clear that questions of narrative connection and readerly comprehension are on Brown's mind, and this odd postscript (along with the interpolated March "Note on Stephen Calvert") serves to place them squarely on ours. That is to say, Brown here invites his readers to reflect on their own receptive situations, to begin to recognize and analyze the structure of literary engagement in the very moment(s) of their own most acute readerly frustration.

A reader who feels invited to let his or her "fancy" produce what was to follow might find that the extant plot of *Stephen Calvert* already contains a great deal of potentially controversial material, chiefly having to do with irregular sexual liaisons and ugly racial relations (and with volatile connections between the two), and it is conceivable that Brown, having started up so many scandalous plot lines, found himself unable to follow them out—whether because of taboos on explicit expression or because, as a still young novelist, he could neither handle the dire complications that had arisen nor manage the complex narrative scale he had projected. One thing is fairly certain, however, about what Brown had planned for the future development of the novel: the eponymous hero's virtuous cousin Louisa was going to die, and it was somehow going to be Stephen's fault. Stephen at one point in his writing of this memoir soliloquizes to Louisa, "I must forget that cruel fate that made me the engine to destroy thee," but he resolves in spite of this willful forgetting that he will nevertheless do "justice to thy memory" (193). There is a hint earlier on that Louisa might kill herself: she says that if Stephen goes to Europe, as he threatens to do, and loses his moral integrity, as she and Stephen's mother fear he would, "life would be insupportable" (169).[12] Perhaps there were going to be many causes of Stephen's deep and haunting "guilt and remorse" (72), but his moral responsibility for Louisa's ruin was surely meant to be one of them.

What was going to follow from the reunion of Stephen and his long-lost twin brother, Felix? On the one hand, Stephen has always longed for his brother and wondered about his twin's unknown fate. On the last page of the novel as we have it, he is shivering with excitement at the prospect of finally meeting Felix. On the other hand, it has been strongly implied that Felix in the past was on intimate terms with Clelia (which partly explains why she thinks Stephen has known her in the past and why she is perplexed by his presently seeming to pretend not to know her), and it is possible that the brothers would have become rivals for her affection. It is possible, too, that Brown was contemplating something less conventional than the Gothic rivalry of two men for possession of one woman, possible that he was imagining a threesome or some other even more unprescribed or inventive arrangement. (When Stephen has yearned painfully for years after his lost twin brother and yearned achingly in the present for Clelia, why should he not now love them as a pair?) The Gothic convention that Eve Kosofsky Sedgwick described and analyzed, in which the *homosocial* rivalry between two men shades imperceptibly into a *homoerotic* attraction for which the woman serves as a legitimating conduit, is vividly present in *Calvert* (certainly between Sydney and Stephen vis-à-vis Louisa, perhaps between Felix and Stephen with Clelia, and potentially between Belgrave and any of these others) but was not brought to explicit conclusion.[13] Homosocial/homosexual rivalry subsequently found more veiled expression in other Brown novels.[14] Here, Stephen has Sydney Carlton as a vexatious rival for Louisa's affection; his brother Felix as a potential rival for Clelia's; and, offstage, Clelia's allegedly sodomitical husband, Belgrave, as a vindictive rival, too, and one whose express homosexuality could potentially destroy the homosocial alibi for these male-male connections. If one merely does the math, the combinatorial possibilities for erotic trouble amid this tangle of affections and rivalries is boggling.

Europe is consistently presented in the tale as the locus of erotic mischief and sexual depravity. Early on, Stephen learns that he has a landed estate to be reclaimed in England, but his mother persuades him to stay in America and live a simple, virtuous life rather than run the risk of moral decay that is, to her mind, inevitably associated with Europe and with landed wealth. (He consents to stay at home but privately defers the claim on European land and title until after his mother's death.) Stephen frequently ponders the possibility of leaving romantic failure behind in America and taking the risk of going to Europe (and he does impetuously embark for Ireland at one point, only to have his ship founder and a rescue vessel take him back to Baltimore). If Brown had completed the novel, would Stephen eventually have fulfilled his purpose of going to Europe—perhaps in the company of his brother, Felix, who would have shared in his English inheritance and whom we have every reason to believe has had a different and more sophisticated life than Stephen, including an ostensible past affair with the married Clelia? And would Stephen, when abroad, have acquired or further exacerbated the "habits of corruption and idleness" (71) that he owns up to on the first page? Or would Belgrave have come to America in pursuit of Clelia and of the property she inherited from her aunt, which (along with her father's estate) legally belongs to him?

Clelia certainly fears that Belgrave's "vengeance" (226) will seek her out in one fashion or another. His angry plotting may even be the source of the rumors that have reached Philadelphia that Clelia is "sensual and fickle" (224), "an adultress, and a profligate," and a "hypocrite" (225), whose dire story of her husband's unnameable depravity was artfully contrived (Sydney believes) to distract suspicion from her own immorality. Louisa does extract from Stephen an admission that Clelia, even after belatedly telling him of her married condition, nevertheless not only continues to admit him to her house for private, unchaperoned late-night meetings (themselves, in Louisa's view, deeply improper) but has directly hinted to Stephen that her marital status need not be a bar to their sexual intimacy.

> Has she [Clelia] never wept at those ties [Louisa asks Stephen] which oblige her to treat you merely as a friend? Has she never painted the felicity attendant on indissoluble union with you, and maligned the power which forbids it?...At moments when your feelings are most active, does not a momentary doubt insinuate itself as to the validity of that bond which inthralls your Clelia to another?...Why, then, (do you not sometimes ask) should it hinder her from giving [you] the natural proofs of that attachment?...Have not such reveries as these sometimes, however rarely, fluctuated in your thoughts[?]...Have not soliloquies escaped you, at moments when memory was most full of the blandishments and graces of this friend, in which an hearer would distinguish such sounds as Unnatural restraints! Arbitrary institutions! Capricious scruples!   (219–220)

The perversity of this scene—virtuous Louisa inciting Stephen to entertain erotic fantasies of transgressive relations with Clelia and dwelling on this delicious fantasy herself as she stimulates his ready imagination—adds a pornographic thrill to the introduction of a set of intellectual and political questions about the "arbitrary" and "unnatural" moral codes that prescribe marital fidelity. This certainly sounds as though Brown was considering having Stephen become a freethinker about sex, perhaps intellectually persuaded as well as sensually suborned by a "faithless wanton" (218) into erotic antinomianism and practical libertinism (coached, so to speak, by the secretly and parasitically lascivious Louisa). Might this have turned out to be the "fatal revolution" (272) in his life, intimated on the novel's final page, producing what Stephen repeatedly refers to as his "depravity" (119, 143), his "versatile and sordid temper" (196), and leading to the "endless series of disasters and calamities" (176) that we have been led to expect but never get to see?

The novel as we have it contains repeated intimations of European revenge, sometimes even reaching across the ocean to America: Stephen's maternal grandfather "had been pursued by the vengeance of an hereditary enemy" and had died of wounds received (75); Stephen's father fled to Pennsylvania to protect himself and his family from "paternal vengeance" (83) and feared that "cruel and implacable" retribution might instead be wreaked upon his young son (i.e., Felix) who was left behind (91); Stephen's father's death by drowning in the Schuylkill River may be the result of "that vengeance that had been threatened" (94). Thus, when Clelia avers, "What expedient the malice of Belgrave may employ to hurt my reputation, or regain his power over my person, I know not" (211), readers might well expect the sodomite to show up in Philadelphia and bring corruption with him. That is, Stephen might have been ruined by going to Europe, or European degeneracy might have been imported to America—the groundwork for either one (or both) of these possibilities seems to have been carefully prepared in the fragmentary novel as we have it.

What was going to follow from Stephen's unexpected inheritance of a plantation and its slaves? We are told that Ambrose Calvert, the distant cousin who leaves his property to Stephen (having thrown his only daughter, Louisa, out of the house and disinherited her in contempt), is entirely decent in public but utterly depraved in private—a consummate moral hypocrite. Not only is he emotionally abusive to his wife and daughter, but his violence takes physical form as well; needless to say, his slaves are subject to even worse torments than his wife and child. Ambrose Calvert employs his eldest slave, Caesar, as overseer of the plantation in his absence but forbids Caesar to punish the other slaves physically; he reserves that activity for his own pleasure, of course, but he knows as well that "habits of command, and the influence of example, had a tendency to deprave" those who possessed such authority (107), and he needs to keep Caesar uncorrupted. While Ambrose has an "imperious temper" (107) to which his penchant for violence is attributed, we also see that his "tyrannical prerogatives" (107) as a slave owner have enabled that temper to grow toxic.

We readers know that Stephen, too, has a serious talent for hypocrisy and self-deception and is deeply susceptible to circumstantial influences. Will owning and commanding slaves corrupt him, despite his initial philanthropic resolution, upon inheriting them, that the "slaves would henceforth receive the treatment that was due to men, and their happiness be as sedulously promoted as it had been heretofore counteracted" (SC 106)? It is seldom noted that Stephen grew up with at least one slave in his mother's household, "an old negro, who was family property" (249), whose enslaved condition he does not protest; on the other hand, he does free one of the slaves who belonged to Calverton, a "female negro" (237), who then becomes a servant in Clelia's household.

In the *Monthly Magazine* during the run of *Calvert*, race and slavery received judicious discussion several times. Brown reprinted an essay, "Observations on the Conformation and Capacity of the Negroes," attributed to "Professor Blumenbach," that argued (among other things) that "the negroes, in their mental faculties, are not inferior to the rest of the human race" (MM, September–December 1799, 454).[15] An apparently original essay, "Thoughts on the Probable Termination of Negro Slavery in the United States of America," appeared in February 1800 and tried to imagine the historical "consequences" of racial difference and of the changing demographics of racial populations in the wake of the prohibition of slave importation (MM, February 1800, 81). Although this essay expresses the expectation that enlightened sentiment, voluntary manumission, and the anticipated higher birth rate among whites will eventually extinguish slavery, the author ("H.L.") concludes by shying away from "that terror which prevails among us respecting negro insurrections" and declines to "speculate upon the consequences which will follow from this slow, and gradual, but universal freedom of the blacks" (84). Brown as editor was certainly willing to entertain what, to some readers, must have seemed daring opinions concerning race and slavery. Having given slavery a critical role in the story of Stephen Calvert, what venturesome "consequences" might have ensued from it?

Slave owning apparently ruined Ambrose Calvert, who not only (it is strongly implied) fathered at least one slave child, Althea, but then beat and killed her as well (SC 104). Would Stephen, his "sexual impulses" (110) at a constant fever pitch and his amorous proposals refused by both Louisa and Clelia, have found himself unable to resist the sexual temptation that ownership of slaves presented? Characters in *Stephen Calvert* are often referred to as "slaves" of their passions and impulses or figured as "enslaved" by powerful circumstances (99, 108, 124, 138, 144, 164, 165). Did Brown perhaps have in mind, for the remainder of the novel, a complex and searching exploration of the psychic distortions and moral contaminations that the institution of slavery entailed upon its perpetuators? Was Stephen, who early in the tale is mistaken for a black man (a rumor goes around that the person who saved Clelia Neville from the fire that engulfed her house—Stephen, in fact—was recognized by an onlooker as a former slave [126]), going to follow Ambrose Calvert into the practice of miscegenation and the habit of sexually violent—even murderous—domination? At several points in the tale, he seems on the verge of forcing himself upon Louisa or Clelia in moments of angry arousal and abject humiliation (he would "exact" [135] obedience to his will or "extort" [150] Louisa's consent to marry him, he says, and he believes that by "assailing her constancy" in a moment of weakness, he could "triumph over her scruples" [170]; at another point, he threateningly declares to Clelia that he will "hearken not to scruples...I will argue or supplicate no more, for thou shalt be mine" [188]). Would he have followed in the footsteps of Louisa's unloving father, Ambrose, and become her second domineering abuser? Such an outcome seems distinctly probable, given the groundwork Brown has laid. Was this to be part of the chain of calamities that he tells us, in distant retrospect, were woefully to characterize his life? And were these depravities somehow going to involve the foreshadowed death of Louisa? Louisa is ready at one point to believe that Stephen might have coerced or raped Clelia: "She [Louisa] looked at me with eyes of terror and pity, and clasping her hands, 'Have you, indeed, betrayed her [Clelia]? Have you debased yourself? Have you acted vilely by a woman and a stranger?'" (194). Stephen denies having done so, but Louisa makes him repeat his denial, asking him again if he had "injured" Clelia, and his protestation that Clelia's "innocence" is intact and that she is as "pure" as before makes it clear that he understands the specificity and gravity of Louisa's suspicion (194). Would this have been Clelia's fate eventually, or was this debasement reserved in Brown's mind for Louisa herself, meant to be the precipitating cause of the self-destruction for which Stephen then felt unassuageable "guilt and remorse" (72)?

What was going to follow from the appearance in the tale (as part of Clelia Neville's backstory) of the nasty homosexual rake Belgrave, her abusive English husband? By most scholarly accounts, Belgrave is the first appearance in an American novel of a character with what could be called a durable homosexual orientation (although it is profoundly ahistorical even to put it in those terms). How does Brown phrase it? He leaves it to Clelia:

> Cohabiting with him, I became acquainted with transactions and scenes, which, at a distance, could not possibly have been suspected. Under a veil of darkness, propensities were indulged by my husband, that have not a name which I can utter. They cannot be thought of without horror. They cannot be related....For some enormities, which my subsequent experience brought within my observation, so far from knowing them by name, they had never occurred to me as possible. In brooding over my suspicions with respect to Belgrave, I fashioned, as I imagined, the most horrid images of voluptuousness and insensibility; but far different, far more flagrant was the guilt, far more savage the pollutions to which he was habituated....So open, so shameless was his conduct, that, at length, my own eyes were allowed to witness————. I cannot utter it—I was frozen with horror. I doubted whether hideous phantoms, produced by my own imagination, had not deceived me; till my memory, putting past incidents together, convinced me that they were real.   (203–205)[16]

Clelia has fled to America to escape her miserable marriage to this abominable man, but she seems to fear that Belgrave or perhaps an agent of his will in some fashion pursue her (and Stephen's own backstory contains intimations of angry nobles from the Old World finding their perceived enemies in America and exacting mortal revenge).[17] Might Brown have been pondering the prospect of bringing this European monster to Philadelphia?

There is a minor but important tradition in scholarship and criticism about Brown's work that assimilates his writing to a poststructuralist or deconstructionist model of meaning.[18] This present chapter might be thought to participate belatedly in this tradition, since it attempts to describe certain formal absences and textual traces in *Memoirs of Stephen Calvert* and claims that the signification of this fragment of a novel is generated as much by what is left out of it—the four unwritten "acts," the unrealized plot complications, the twin brother who is forever about to arrive but never shall do so—as by the text we do, in fact, possess. Brown invites such a reading by leaving the novel unfinished and by requiring readers at its provisional end to imagine what would have come after. The plot is characterized by a long series of deferrals and interruptions, postponements and delays, and by a narrative frame that loops back upon itself and highlights the promised but intermitted "endless series of disasters and calamities" (SC 176) alleged to have characterized Stephen's life. Those absent calamities—produced by Stephen's unspecified "depravity"—are, we might say, what the novel most insistently proffers to us, "teazes" us with. Are homosexual sodomy and violent racial domination the absent presences that define American experience but cannot be directly uttered in American literature? Just as the narrator, Stephen, has absented himself from the American "world" that he found too "abundant in temptation and calamity" (71) for him to preserve his integrity while stationed within it, so has the author of *Calvert* withdrawn himself from the scene of writing and left readers to puzzle out its traces unguided, challenging us to imagine what he has nevertheless told us cannot be imagined.

NOTES

1. SC 73. Page citations will default to the Kent State edition, although there will be occasion to cite from the original serialized *Monthly Magazine* publication as well. *Calvert* has not always been conveniently available in print. The only previous edition in the twentieth century was *Memoirs of Stephen Calvert*, Hans Borchers, ed., Vol. 2 in the Studien und Texte zur Amerikanistik series (Frankfurt am Main: Peter Lang, 1978).
2. The narrative specifies this as "a plan of insurrection in favor of Charles Stewart, which had long been meditated by the English catholics" (SC 79) and inspired by the "spirit of Charles the Ninth, and of Guy Faux" (80), which would seem to set the action sometime prior to 1660; in *Stephen Calvert*, the fictional restoration plot is foiled, however. A rough calculation of the three generations (from Stephen's grandfather's day to his own present youth) suggests that Stephen is living in the early to mid-eighteenth century.
3. Stephen's acknowledged bookishness—"my preceptors were books," he avers—and its apparent deleterious effects justify Sarah F. Wood's assimilation of *Calvert* to her model of "Quixotic fictions." "Stephen Calvert is the most self-consciously Quixotic of Brown's protagonists, beguiled by the books he reads into contracting unrealistic, romantic notions about the women he meets" (Wood 141).
4. Brown did, in fact, from around this time forward, publish fragmentary works that he labeled as such: "Death of Cicero, a Fragment" (1800), "The Household. A Fragment" (1800), "New Year's Day. A Fragment" (1804), "Somnambulism: A fragment" (1805), "Pressing. A fragment" (1806), "The Value of General Rules. A Fragment" (1806), and "Insanity. A Fragment" (1809). On the literary history and theory of the fragment, see Elias; Tronzo; Jung. See also and especially Matthew Pethers's acute essay on the early American novel, fragmented form, and serial fiction, which discusses *Calvert* in some detail. I am grateful to Pethers for sharing this essay with me before its publication.
5. See, for a classic statement, Iser, esp. 274 ff. Edward Cahill has ably explored the thematics and politics of imagination in *Calvert* (Cahill 2012, esp. 183–184, 195–196.
6. "Note on Stephen Calvert," MM 2.3 (March 1800): 172. The sympathetically aroused reader, avid for the story's continuation, is described here: "let us once have but fairly entered on the tale, and the inertest curiosity will not fail to exclaim at every interruption, 'what next?'" Although the tale did resume in April, it finally ended abruptly in June.
7. Questions of delay, deferral, procrastination, and anxious waiting abound in the action of the novel, and much turns on these repeated protractions. They cannot all be listed here, but two central examples—Stephen's delay in returning the inherited slave plantation, Calverton, to its rightful owner, Louisa; and Louisa's decision, instigated by Sydney Carlton, to defer her marriage to Stephen "for many years, perhaps forever" (SC 40), or until he gains moral maturity—may serve to call up the rest.
8. Unfortunately, the Kent State edition of *Stephen Calvert* renders this apparently intentional textual gap invisible, since it does not indicate where one serial installment ends and the next begins but runs the serial together. The Kent State edition also omits this "Note on Stephen Calvert" (which it calls "presumably fictional" [SC 357]), apparently judging it to be not a part of the text proper (the Borchers edition prints it as a sort of appendix, out of sequence [182–183]). I would contend that the "Note" ought to be included as an essential

component of the novel's experiment in manipulating narrative expectation and frustration and as a formal counterpart to the "P.S." that ends the novel (which the Kent State and Borchers editions both include, in its proper culminating position). Jared Gardner discusses this "Note" briefly; see Gardner, 771 n. 50. The breaks between serial installments, I would further claim, should not be presumed to be mere formal accidents, since Brown edited the magazine they appeared in and therefore had some control over the meting out of the story; on the contrary, and since they plainly operate strategically as part of Brown's metafictional performance, they should be assumed to be meaningful aspects of the novel's form.

9. A partial answer to this question would refer to the long prose fictions of "Mademoiselle Scuderi," one of which Stephen ostensibly finds Louisa reading in the garden at one point (SC 192). These vastly attenuated novels, such as *Clélie* (10 vols., 1654–1661; trans. John Davies and G. Havers as *Clelia, an Excellent New Romance the Whole Work in Five Parts*, 1678), were usually printed in five-volume English translations. As it happens, the names of characters visible on the page as Stephen peruses this book ("Statira, Lysimachus, Perdiccas" [192]) belong, in fact, not to a work of Madeleine de Scudéry but to her contemporary La Calprenède's *Cassandre* (5 vols., 1642–1650; trans. Charles Cotterell as *Cassandra the Fam'd Romance: The Whole Work, in Five Parts*, 1652). A trivial mistake on Brown's part, attributable to his haste in composition? A confusion due to his borrowing of Clelia Neville's name from Scudéry? Or a calculated feint of some kind, part of his metafictional game?

10. A curious detail: the typeface used for the magazine included several relatively unusual ligatures, one of them linking the lower-case characters *c* and *t* whenever they happened to appear together in that order; thus, in the passage under discussion here, the words "act" and "acts," as well as the word "connecting" (!), all feature these connected letters.

11. The dateline of the masthead for this omnibus issue of the magazine featured an asterisk after the "Sept. Oct. Nov. & Dec. 1799." The asterisk led to a footnote: "The unavoidable delay which has attended the publication of the last number, occasioned by the necessary removal of the Publishers from the city during the late epidemic, has induced them, to avoid *anachronisms*, and the *appearance* of successive delays, to conclude the present year with the publication of the first volume. The first number of the second volume will commence in January, 1800, and will be continued, it is hoped, without any interruption.— As there is, at present, nothing in the nature of the work that demands a strict observance of particular divisions of time, we trust our readers will approve of the form which the present number has assumed" (MM, September–December 1799, 401).

12. Clelia also intimates that she might be capable of suicide, that sorrow might drive her to commit "some fatal act of despair or resentment" (SC 206).

13. Sedgwick 1985; Sedgwick 1990.

14. Shapiro notes that in *Edgar Huntly*, which he calls *Calvert's* "intertext" (Shapiro 2004, 233) and which Brown wrote directly after *Calvert* and partially serialized in the same magazine, resorts to "circumlocution" (237) of various kinds to portray the same-sex eroticism that appeared to be heading for more direct depiction in *Calvert*. See also Shapiro 2007; Comment.

15. This is excerpted from Johann Friedrich Blumenbach. See discussions of this excerpt by Levine (30–31) and Shapiro (2008, 279–280).

16. Much of this language was omitted from the two nineteenth-century editions that included *Calvert*, those overseen by William Dunlap (Dunlap 1815) and Henry Colburn.

17. Stephen's proud and irascible Roman Catholic grandfather, Sir Stephen Porter, is thought perhaps to have caused the murder of his son Stephen (a convert to Protestantism who knew of his father's dangerous involvement in a plot to kill the king and reestablish Catholicism in England). Stephen Calvert, Sr., had fled to Philadelphia with his French Huguenot wife (whose surname he adopted) and one of their children, and in his new life in hiding in America, he ordinarily took precautions against expected paternal revenge; thus, his death in mysterious circumstances in the Schuylkill River, on a rare night when he suspended his usual caution and traveled abroad after dark, raises suspicions of murder, although in typical Brown fashion, it is also intimated that he may have either committed suicide or died merely by accident.

18. For example, Seltzer; Kreyling; Hesford.

WORKS CITED

Arner, Robert D. "Historical Essay." In Charles Brockden Brown, *Alcuin: A Dialogue and Memoirs of Stephen Calvert*, Sydney J. Krause, S. W. Reid, and Robert D. Arner, eds., 273–312. Kent, Ohio: Kent State University Press, 1987.

Bennett, Maurice J. "A Portrait of the Artist in Eighteenth-Century America: Charles Brockden Brown's *Memoirs of Stephen Calvert.*" *William and Mary Quarterly*, 3rd series, 39.3 (July 1982): 492–507.

Berthoff, W. B. "Adventures of the Young Man: An Approach to Charles Brockden Brown." *American Quarterly* 9.4 (Winter 1957): 421–434. Reprinted as "Adventures of the Young Man: Brockden Brown's *Arthur Mervyn.*" In Warner B. Berthoff, *American Trajectories: Authors and Readings 1790–1970*, 53–68. University Park: Pennsylvania State University Press, 1994.

Brown, Charles Brockden. *Memoirs of Stephen Calvert*. Hans Borchers, ed. Studien und Texte zue Amerikanistik, Vol. 2. Frankfurt am Main: Peter Lang, 1978.

Brown, Charles Brockden. *Memoirs of Stephen Calvert*. In *Carwin, the Biloquist, and Other American Tales and Pieces*, I: 157–256, II: 1–287, III: 1–82. London: Henry Colburn, 1822.

Brown, Charles Brockden. *Memoirs of Stephen Calvert*. In *MM* (June 1799): 71–112; (July 1799): 112–136; (August 1799): 136–151; (September–December 1799): 151–167; (January 1800): 167–188; (March 1800): 172–173; (April 1800): 188–237; (May 1800): 237–255; (June 1800): 255–272.

Cahill, Edward. *Liberty of the Imagination: Aesthetic Theory, Literary Form, and Politics in the Early United States*. Philadelphia: University of Pennsylvania Press, 2012.

Comment, Kristin M. "Charles Brockden Brown's *Ormond* and Lesbian Possibility in the Early Republic." *Early American Literature* 40.1 (2005): 57–78.

Elias, Camelia. *The Fragment: Towards a History and Poetics of a Performative Genre*. New York: Peter Lang, 2004.

Ferguson, Robert A. "Literature and Vocation in the Early Republic: The Example of Charles Brockden Brown." *Modern Philology* 78.2 (November 1980): 139–152. Reprinted as "The Case of Charles Brockden Brown." In Robert A. Ferguson, ed., *Law and Letters in American Culture*, 129–149. Cambridge, Mass.: Harvard University Press, 1984.

Gardner, Jared. "The Literary Museum and the Unsettling of the Early American Novel." *English Literary History* 67 (2000): 743–171.

Grabo, Norman S. *The Coincidental Art of Charles Brockden Brown*. Chapel Hill: University of North Carolina Press, 1981.

Hesford, Walter. "'Do You Know the Author?: The Question of Authorship in Wieland." *Early American Literature* 17.3 (1982–1983): 239–248.

Iser, Wolfgang. *The Implied Reader: Patterns of Communication in Prose Fiction from Bunyan to Beckett*. Baltimore and London: The Johns Hopkins University Press, 1974.

Jung, Sandro. *The Fragmentary Poetic: Eighteenth-Century Uses of an Experimental Mode*. Bethlehem, Pa.: Lehigh University Press, 2009.

Kreyling, Michael. "Construing Brown's *Wieland*: Ambiguity and Derridean 'Freeplay.'" *Studies in the Novel* 14.1 (1982): 43–54.

Levine, Robert S. *Dislocating Race and Nation: Episodes in Nineteenth-Century American Literary Nationalism*. Chapel Hill: University of North Carolina Press, 2008.

Neff, Brian C. "Frightening Masculinity: Gothic Affect and Antebellum Manhood." Ph.D. dissertation, Pennsylvania State University, 2010.

Pethers, Matthew. "The Early American Novel in Fragments: Writing and Reading Serial Fiction in the Post-Revolutionary United States." In Patrick Parrinder, Andrew Nash, and Nicola Wilson, eds., *New Directions in the History of the Novel*, 63–75. New York: Palgrave, 2014.

Sedgwick, Eve Kosofsky. *Between Men: English Literature and Male Homosocial Desire*. New York: Columbia University Press, 1985.

Sedgwick, Eve Kosofsky. *Epistemology of the Closet*. Berkeley: University of California Press, 1990.

Seltzer, Mark. "Saying Makes It So: Language and Event in Brown's *Wieland*." *Early American Literature* 13.1 (1978): 81–91.

Shapiro, Stephen. *The Culture and Commerce of the Early American Novel: Reading the Atlantic World-System*. University Park: Pennsylvania State University Press, 2008.

Shapiro, Stephen. "In a French Position: Radical Pornography and Homoerotic Society in Charles Brockden Brown's *Ormond or the Secret Witness*." In Thomas A. Foster, ed., *Long before Stonewall: Histories of Same-Sex Sexuality in Early America*, 357–383. New York: New York University Press, 2007.

Shapiro, Stephen. "'Man to Man I Needed Not to Dread His Encounter': *Edgar Huntly*'s End of Erotic Pessimism." In Philip Barnard, Mark L. Kamrath, and Stephen Shapiro, eds., *Revising Charles Brockden Brown: Culture, Politics and Sexuality in the Early Republic*, 216–251. Knoxville: University of Tennessee Press, 2004.

Slawinski, Scott. *Validating Bachelorhood: Audience, Patriarchy, and Charles Brockden Brown's Editorship of the* Monthly Magazine and American Review. New York and London: Routledge, 2005.

Tronzo, William, ed. *The Fragment: An Incomplete History*. Los Angeles: Getty Research Institute, 2009.

Wood, Sarah F. *Quixotic Fictions of the USA 1792–1815*. Oxford: Oxford University Press, 2005.

CHAPTER 8

....

CLARA HOWARD; IN A SERIES OF LETTERS

....

PHILIP BARNARD

> The irony of the novel is the self-correction of the world's fragility: inade-
> quate relations can transform themselves into a fanciful yet well-ordered
> round of misunderstandings and cross-purposes, within which everything
> is seen as many-sided, within which things appear as isolated and yet
> connected, as full of value and yet totally devoid of it, as abstract fragments
> and as concrete autonomous life, as flowering and as decaying, as the inflic-
> tion of suffering and as suffering itself.
>
> Georg Lukács, *The Theory of the Novel* (75)

IN its long-perceived status as the least interesting of Charles Brockden Brown's
published novels and as the least read of them in consequence, *Clara Howard* (June 1801)
offers a striking example of the way outdated assumptions can continue to shape ongoing
interpretations. Considered alone or, most often, together with *Jane Talbot* (December
1801)—the final published novel, which shares its epistolary format and vexed reception
history ("the consensus losers"; Krause 184)—*Clara Howard* received virtually no serious
attention in the nineteenth and the first half of the twentieth century, except insofar as
it was subordinated to the four best-known novels, thereby marking their priority,
and made to legitimate an enduring but misinformed narrative about Brown's corpus
and development. The two 1801 epistolary novels, in that account, marked a decline in
and/or emasculation of Brown's literary achievement and thereby signaled a calamitous
transition from Gothic Prometheanism to feminized sentimentality. Often the two titles
were also taken as signposts for a presumed turn from youthful radicalism toward
conservatism or a supposed abandonment of fiction tied to all these other factors. All
these assumptions are now exploded, to use a Brownian formula, but this reception
history's long shadow still minimizes attention to both novels.[1]

Although commentators as early as Lillie Deming Loshe in 1907, for example, could point out that *Clara Howard* deepens Brown's exploration of female subordination and presents more challenging complexities than early commonplaces allowed, fragmentary observations remained undeveloped (Loshe 45–49). Even with the 1986 Kent State scholarly edition and the closer scrutiny it began to occasion, later twentieth-century readings continued to construe the 1801 novels in terms of gendered stories of decline or defeat. For Leslie Fiedler in 1960, they mark "an effort at winning the great female audience; but more than that, they are further steps toward silence" (Fiedler 152). Norman Grabo in 1981 tried to alter chronology in order to speculate that they were written prior to the earlier novels, since "they are more easily comprehended as incomplete steps toward the realization of the major fictions than as later fallings off" (Grabo 142). Steven Watts's 1994 account articulates both the last gasp of the decline narrative and the transition beyond it. On the one hand, *Howard*'s "vapid prose and inane plot" make it "without doubt…the weakest of all Brown's novels" (Watts 134) and mark the author's supposed imaginative decline and turn toward conservatism (131–143). On the other hand, Watts finds that the 1801 novels engage critically with newly dominant post-Revolutionary liberalism: in both, "sentimental forms and language masked an important cultural realignment at the heart of the stories" (143), and *Howard*'s gloomy world of market pressures exposes "a fascinating configuration of gender and ideology" (136).

From the 1970s and '80s to the present, albeit in small numbers, scholarship has moved beyond the early reception tropes toward a wholesale revaluation of prior assumptions about *Clara Howard*. It is remarkable that all the latter-day discussions, that is, all chapter or article-length discussions of the 1801 narratives since Witherington in 1974, reject the decline narrative entirely and work toward new theses about *Howard* and its relationships to the other writings.[2] Indeed, it may be that in an era when aesthetic ideology has loosened its hold and scholars enjoy more powerful conceptual tools for exploring cultural history, *Howard* and *Talbot* are only now beginning to come into their own. Where earlier scholars referred to them primarily to underwrite a received narrative, latter-day readings parse their thematic and formal complexities and their curious (re)emphasis on conventions of sentimental fiction in two interrelated ways. On the one hand, in the widest sense, recent readings affirm that these novels develop prescient allegorical commentary on larger shifts in the world-system and its characteristic media or, in other words, that they problematize characteristic generic (epistolary, sentimental, and more widely novelistic) codes in ways that register transitions between old and new regimes after the Revolutionary era or between late-feudal-to-republican early modernity and the triumphant bourgeois liberalism of the new settlement. On the other hand, as concerns Brown in particular, these conclusions imply that the two 1801 novels stand as important elements in a coherent arc of production that extends from the author's earliest narrative experimentation around 1790 to the multigeneric writings of the 1802–1809 years.

Certainly, future discussions of *Clara Howard* can confidently jettison the assumptions that shaped early reception. Minus the "Gothic" furniture (and even that is not entirely absent), *Howard*'s epistolary format, its sentimental marriage-plot elements, and its relation to Brown's conception of romance as a form of conjectural history and an instrument of political education are all fundamentally congruent with the rest of the fictional output before 1801. Neither *Howard* nor *Talbot* marks an anomaly, departure, or interruption vis-à-vis the rest of the prior corpus in any of these senses, and earlier presumptions about their alleged aesthetic weakness, as recent readings demonstrate, are symptomatic of the critical paradigms that produced them.

Epistolary form is basic to virtually all of Brown's fiction. Indeed, the *only* major fiction that does not incorporate the letter form in some basic manner is the 1805–1806 *Historical Sketches*, written several years later. Thus, *Howard*, in 1801, in no way departs from a prior generic-formal dominant in Brown's corpus, whether understood as "Gothic," as first-person nonepistolary narrative, or the like. From the 1789–1793 "Rhapsodist" and "Henrietta Letters" (along with the narrative experimentation in the correspondence of these years) to the 1798 "Series of Original Letters," "Jessica and Sophia" (c. 1799–1800, posthumously published in Allen 108–169), and the 1801 novels, Brown employs the format consistently, and epistolary form is thus the rule and not the exception up to 1801. The so-called Gothic novels meld epistolary and memoiresque formats, never abandoning the basic potentials of the letter form and on the contrary emphasizing them: *Wieland*, *Ormond*, and *Edgar Huntly* are notably framed as voluminous single letters, written to a nameless relative of Clara Wieland, to I. E. Rosenberg, and to Mary Waldegrave. Brown's "devotion to the form is exceptional," as Elizabeth Hewitt notes in chapter 14 in this volume, and enacts his conviction, up to 1801, at least, that Samuel Richardson's and Jean-Jacques Rousseau's formal legacy is the most direct path to a fictional exploration of interrelated psychological and social concerns. Epistolary narrative, Brown writes in 1793, is the best format in which to explore "personal behaviours" in order to know "Life and Manners" (Letters 249). Via one aspect of epistolarity, Brown's fictional letters continually emphasize the letter writer's isolated point of view, the inherently limited and inadequate perspective of individualized subjects outside wider social exchange, the well-known blindness and precipitation of isolated and stressed Brownian protagonist-narrators. Via another, as the epoch's primary medium of interpersonal written communication, its basic form of social media, letters materialize fragile social connections and a potential for dialogue that provides testimony about surrounding damage. The contradictory potentials of sensibility, from solipsism to community, are dialectically implicit in epistolary form throughout Brown's fictions.

Likewise, troubling and inconclusive endings, which are never resolutions, involving courtship and marriage outcomes, the stuff of *Clara Howard*'s "sentimental" plot, always emphasizing female subordination and structured inequalities, are everywhere in Brown's other fictions. To cite the absolute minimum, only the best-known endings, recall Clara Wieland's depressing conclusive marriage to Pleyel; Constantia Dudley's reported self-defense in killing the possibly predatory suitor Ormond, which theoretically enables her somewhat disturbing arranged betrothal to the reactionary I. E. Rosenberg; or the possibly pregnant Mary Waldegrave's suspended engagement to Edgar Huntly, as the latter's betrothal to Clarice Wyatt is arranged by Edgar's wealthy Irish patron Sarsefield. The exception is possibly Arthur Mervyn's anticipated affectionate marriage to the wealthy Sephardic divorcée Achsa Fielding (yet her former husband haunts Arthur in a nightmare), which concludes *Mervyn, Second Part* in September–October 1800, only eight months before *Clara Howard* in June 1801. In this light, the similar but more sodden conclusion of *Howard*, as the heiress Clara finally consents to marriage with rural up-and-comer Edward Hartley (arranged by her father, the wealthy patron Mr. Howard), appears as a further turn on the conclusions of *Huntly* and *Mervyn* alike but, in any case, is firmly in line with the previous published romances.

Finally, as James Dillon noted in 1998 (252–254), *Clara Howard* provides a forceful example of the romance model of fiction writing that Brown articulated most famously in "Walstein's School of History" (September 1799) and "The Difference between History and Romance" (April 1800), the latter published fourteen months before *Howard*. In this model, fiction and history are two sides of a generic coin, and fiction is an instrument of political education as it provides a mode of conjectural history encouraging the reader to consider the pressures and causes, the larger social and economic forces and contexts, that shape actions. Howard resolutely dramatizes Walstein's observations about senti-mental genre conventions, that is, that "property" and "sex" are "the most extensive source of our relations" and that if the sentimental novels that explore their interrelation have "frequently excited contempt and ridicule," it is "not because these topics are intrin-sically worthless or vulgar, but because the historian was deficient in knowledge and skill" (Walstein 409). In contemporary parlance, the subject matter of sentimental novels allows the romancer to explore the political and cultural economies of sex-gender relations.

In short, it is more accurate to view the 1801 novels as a "culmination" and reflection on Brown's initial arc of narrative production than as any falling-off from its supposed heights (Witherington 274; Gardner 2000, 747). To understand what sort of transition *Howard* may mark and whether it is best understood as an "ending" or a "beginning" in possible periodizations of the corpus, we need to look elsewhere.

I. Paradox and Antinomy

As noted, latter-day readings of *Clara Howard* concur that the narrative's complex turns on epistolary and sentimental conventions, which we should also understand as variations on the "sex and property" problematics identified in Brown's model of romance writing as conjectural history, register the pressures and conditions of newly dominant liberalism. If *Talbot* is a "*Bildungsroman* of desperation" (Shapiro 127), recog-nizing that the progressive aspirations of the Woldwinite novelistic program have been foreclosed, then *Howard* stands as Brown's *Entzauberung* of the novel, that is, his obser-vation of an epochal "Disenchantment" with and in the novel form and the ascendant liberal order and diktat of market culture to which it is tied, since now, after the Revolutionary age, the novel concludes its "rise" and becomes the flagship of bourgeois literary history. Citing Moretti's condensation of Georg Lukács' thesis, in *The Theory of the Novel*, that the novel form first "diagnosed" a post-Revolutionary "disenchantment of the world" around 1800, we can suggest that *Clara Howard* reflects on a world, and on a generic form, "where the rules of bourgeois existence are both ineluctable and bankrupt" (Moretti 41).[3] Latter-day readings of *Howard* suggest this orientation via analyses of its conceptual and formal paradoxes, as well as reflections on the cultural-historical politics of its sentimental conventions.

As steps toward this larger historical perspective, Sydney Krause in 1984, Bruce Burgett in 2001, and Erica Burleigh in 2011 unpack the novel's conceptual antinomies or paradoxes and the ways they are structured into the triangular marriage-plot dilemma that drives the narrative. Clara Howard, an émigré "heiress" (CH 54), and Edward Hartley, a young Pennsylvanian rising from "peasant" (53) origins to urban respectability, are in love, and their marriage, a class misalliance, has been arranged by Clara's wealthy father. But Clara virtuously refuses to marry Hartley when she learns that he previously (and virtuously) committed himself, from benevolence more than love, to the recently impoverished and mysteriously disappeared Mary Wilmot. Clara commands Edward to find Mary and honor his commitment, and thus, the beleaguered young man lurches through a series of physically and emotionally damaging encounters that finally lead to Mary's virtuous refusal to marry Edward because she knows his true love is Clara and a miraculous deus ex machina (in this case, money ex machina) resolution in which Mary's wealth and class status are restored by a virtuous admirer and secret benefactor, the wealthy patron Sedley, allowing both virtuous couples to anticipate (but not actually achieve) betrothal as financial qua domestic felicity in gentry-class marriage. Clara and Mary turn out to be cousins, equally distinguished by aristocratic descent (and wealth), yet at the narrative's conclusion, Hartley nearly dies and struggles to recover from an emotional and physical breakdown brought on by his tribulations. Despite a veritable orgy of heteronormative virtue, love and money (sex and property) collide and coalesce, leaving the reader puzzled about the precise degree of irony involved in their unholy alliance. The novel performs a continual dance of separation that undermines the convention of a comic or resolving marriage, and Brown provides the skeleton of a sentimental novel but not its soul.

Concentrating on the central dilemma or paradox, it is apparent that the novel engenders an atmosphere of continual frustration, as Clara's virtuous principles contradict her affectionate desires and entail Hartley's frenzied and self-damaging attempts to fulfill them. Krause's initial perspective on this paradox was that if the characters "make a fetish of their altruism...to the point almost of perversity" (Krause 190), this is Brown concluding his novelistic phase by testing and correcting Godwinian principles. Burgett expands the same antinomies and the models of gendered subjectivity they register, tying them to contrasts between a Kantian "disembodying logic of republican self-abstraction" in Clara and a more "reactionary"-normative gendered embodiment of liberal citizenship in Hartley (Burgett 14). Thus, the novel marks a "contemporary ideological shift" linked locally to "the national understanding of the relation between gender and polity, sentiment and reason" and more widely to a world-systemic shift in regimes of gendered subjectivity that occurred "almost two centuries ago" (in 1801) (19). Burleigh glosses the paradoxes in terms of contrasting juridical models that Brown explores from the late-1780s legal cases recorded in Allen to *Alcuin* and the 1801 novels. *Howard*'s focus on marriage negotiations offers a "sophisticated" and gender-sensitive critique and contrast between "contractual" legal codes (and their abstract concept of equality) and "equity"-based codes, in a narrative that ultimately "question[s] the very premise of equality under the law" (Burleigh 750) in ascendant liberal jurisdiction.

These readings usefully locate cultural-historical referents for *Howard*'s antinomies. Keeping these logics in mind, other perspectives on the novel's structure allow for further unfolding of its enigmatic core of interrelated formal-thematic paradoxes. Jared Gardner in 2000 and Michelle Burnham in 2004 examine the novel's echt-Brownian narrative disjunctions and windings to produce insights into the novel's paradoxically "antinovelistic texture" and mode of "resistance to an emerging liberalism" (Burnham 263). Gardner draws a hopeful conclusion from what most recent readers regard as a downbeat tableau (Gardner 2000, 765). He proposes that letters and epistolary form provide a polyphonic counterpoint to individualized point of view in prior generic conventions and thereby point forward, both in Brown's own corpus and in the wider print culture, toward a new "editorial function" that bridges the divide between an outdated individualistic focus and a newer vision of community, allowing a greater degree of rational reflection. *Howard* "undermines the idea of a universal code of virtue" even as it "articulates the attendant risks of liberal relativism in Edward's descent into savagery" (his final emotional-physical breakdown) (762). Burnham focuses on the text's vertiginous temporalities and paradoxical narrative emptiness, generated by its nested and recursive narrative structures. In one sense, "nothing happens" in *Howard* (Loshe 48), and Burnham aptly describes the narrative as "one of frenetic inactivity, a series of impasses en route to no destination" (Burnham 271), arguing that "its epistolarity offers a politically charged representation of historical time" in which revolutionary potentials are foreclosed. The novel "resists not only liberal individualism but also the linearity and closure of both novelistic and nationalist narrative" (263).

In the temporal disjunctions and deferrals that Burnham first observed carefully, the reader reencounters familiar Brownian tropes concerning the limitations or blind spots of any individual's point of view and dense relational webs or backstories that reveal larger forces and networks of circumstance shaping surface action, here primarily involving aristocratic misalliances affecting inheritances and international mercantile networks generating them, including US intervention in the Mediterranean in defense of these networks.[4] Even as the basic dilemma is introduced in Letters 1–2 (as Edward embarks on his frustrating quest, after Clara and Mary both refuse marriage in deference to each other) and Edward departs from New York in March to search for Mary in Philadelphia, he visits his former rural home in Hatfield, Pennsylvania, and discovers misplaced letters from Mary written five months earlier, the previous November, from nearby Abingdon, which partly explain and partly obscure Mary's poverty and her mysterious disappearance (CH 9–17). Temporal discontinuities and overlapping letters, often introducing missing or deferred information (from both the characters' and readers' perspectives, each with different effects), immediately play a role in the narrative development and often trigger the three protagonists' perpetually hasty and ineffective decision-making. Virtually all of the narrative's key events have occurred before it begins, and all that remains is to dance forward toward an anticipated (but never achieved) resolution.

Most of novel's thirty-three letters are brief, but the primary backstories informing and explaining the action appear in two lengthy missives that constitute the text's informational core and provide interludes of nested subnarratives occupying more than one-third of the entire text. In Letter 13, by far the text's longest at more than thirty-nine pages in the Kent State edition (37–76), Edward spins out backstories explaining (1) his "peasant" origins and rise under the patronage of aristocratic British émigré Mr. Howard, Clara's father, including his tortured admission that he remains an abject "slave" of pre-Revolutionary class ideology (CH 53); (2) Mary's prior relations to the shadowy Sedley and his sister Mrs. Valentine; (3) Mary's self-enforced poverty after her wealthy father's and later her radical brother's deaths, when she refused to draw on $5,000 of uncertain and thus suspect origin, inexplicably held in the deceased brother's bank account; (4) the merchant Morton's revelation (which later proves misleading) concerning the mysterious fortune, which leaves Mary free to take possession of the $5,000; and (5) Clara's command to Edward that he search out Mary after she learns the information previously related. Thus, at the end of Letter 13, halfway through the narrative, the reader is brought back again to the temporal point of the narrative's beginning in March, now with the fuller contextual detail available from Edward's perspective at that time. In a *Tristram Shandy*-esque manner, minus the comedy, the narrative has gone halfway through before it can begin.

In Letters 27 and 28 (119–139), Mary emerges from hiding for the first time and addresses Clara by letter (but not Edward, who disappears in a hysterical breakdown near Philadelphia, succumbing to despair after the women's refusals to accept his proposals), since the two women were too embarrassed to speak when they actually encountered each other in New York by chance (CH 109). These two letters supply the remaining backstory necessary to the conclusion (all concerning events that occurred before the narrative ever began), explaining that the Virginia planter-class Sedley turns out to be a supremely disinterested benefactor and patron and thus a worthy marriage partner for Mary, freeing (gentry) Clara to accept (peasant) Edward after he recuperates from his virtue-induced and laudanum-fueled collapse.

"Moral causes and daily incidents" may have replaced the "prodigious and singular," as Brown famously wrote in a post-*Huntly* letter announcing his decision to change strategies in "Book-making" (Letters 463), but the world of *Clara Howard*, occupied with the coercive logic of sex and property, appears as grim, insecure, and alienating as that of the "Gothic" narratives. As Clara observes in her concluding letter to Edward, "This is a land of evils; the transitions of the seasons are quick, and into such extremes. How different from the pictures which our fancy drew in our native land!" (CH 146).

II. CRITICAL HISTORIES OF FORM

Clara Howard's staging of interrelated formal-thematic conundrums linked to rising liberalism becomes clearer when we consider the novel's intertexts or, put another way, when we consider ways in which it reflects critically on the progressive aspirations of late Enlightenment and Revolutionary era novel forms. Although his essay primarily addresses *Jane Talbot*, Shapiro offers the most extensive statement on the way the 1801 novels enact critiques of earlier Rousseauvian and Woldwinite modes of novel writing and their progressive aspirations, and in this respect, his argument provides an important gloss on *Howard* as well. Shapiro's reading outlines two stages or aspects of the formal-generic history in which the 1801 novels intervene.

First, in an argument that can be related to Burgett's reading of the novel's enactment of "male masochism," the sentimental novel and its gendered codes of sensibility mobilize a new model of "male feminization" (Shapiro 121) that is co-opted by emerging bourgeois liberalism. The man of feeling, here *Howard*'s Hartley, appropriates a certain cultural capital via sensibility but one that no longer offers a critical purchase on the new dominant: "The [generic] traffic in gender appropriation also clarifies why the senti-mental novel shifts from its earlier male-authored, female-protagonist novels to later male-authored, male-protagonist ones, and why the later novels will routinely introduce a woman's tale only in order to provide the narrative syntax for what will later become a man's" (123). Second, the Woldwinite novels of the 1790s, from Thomas Holcroft's *Anna St. Ives* to Brown's own prior work, are increasingly stymied by the "competing generic dictates of politics and literature" (116), that is, the way the psychologized and gendered predicates of sentimental form ultimately prove incompatible with the more abstract egalitarian and emancipatory ideals of the radical novelists. This impasse in the Woldwinite novel's development had already been observed by scholars such as Josie Dixon and Katherine Binhammer, but Shapiro's analysis summarizes the generic history of the problem and clarifies the seeming contradiction between sentimental convention (tending toward marital resolution) and *Howard*'s underlying drive to complicate, frustrate, and imply the futility of the generic formula (if we understand the goal to be a progressive or emancipatory novelistic practice). Indeed, if male protagonist Edward Hartley, in his rise toward urban respectability, is recently "emancipated from [his] servitude" as a watchmaker (CH 47, 40)—and likewise if a crucial plot turn in *Jane Talbot* occurs in the shop of a watchmaker—this image may offer a literalization of Brown's tinkering with the gears and springs of the novelistic apparatus ("My genius was always turned toward mechanics"; CH 40).

For Shapiro, then, the 1801 novels are the point at which the Woldwinite novel considers its own past activity (Shapiro 125), developing a critical perspective on its investment in generic codes that accompany the triumph of reaction. Moving well beyond Krause's initial notion that these novels simply "test" abstract Godwinite principles, this perspective shows Brown developing a far wider reflection on the cultural stakes of the (epistolary, sentimental, Woldwinite) novel at the moment of the phase shift between the Revolutionary era and the nineteenth-century bourgeois dominant. This helps us understand the novel's revision of sentimental and Woldwinite tropes, as well as what is often viewed as Brown's curious decision to reemphasize a classic epistolary format that, by 1801, was rapidly becoming residual. This line of reading was confirmed and underlined in a surprising way in 2007, when Leonard Tennenhouse pointed out that *Howard* develops a rather extensive reference to Henry Mackenzie's *The Man of Feeling*, a touchstone in the tradition of (male) sentiment and its generic forms. Tennenhouse observed that Brown's name "Edward Hartley" combines "Huntly" with Mackenzie's protagonist "Harley" and, echoing Burgett, Burleigh, and Shapiro, argues that the entire novel provides a critical gloss on Mackenzie and his tradition by inscribing "moral feeling and contractualism as two sides of the same coin of masculinity" (Tennenhouse 83).[5] Further (although not noted in Tennenhouse), we can observe that Mackenzie's character "Edward Sedley," the miraculously benevolent patron whose sudden appearance and generosity conclude the 1771 novel, reappears in the names of Brown's two prospective husbands, peasant Edward Hartley on the one hand and planter Sedley on the other, providing another major referent for the novel's ironic glosses on sentimental precedent.[6] In its reflection and critical variations on the sentimental tradition, *Howard* indeed seems to affirm that this genre's "vision of equality-based liberalism insufficiently thinks through the ramifications of social change, and that this incomplete critique unsettlingly reinscribes gender difference by reinforcing class ones" (Shapiro 117). Crudely put, *Howard* intimates that in the last analysis, it is property that determines sex and that its frantic performances of enlightened virtue and benevolence can do nothing to alter or ameliorate this law of social gravity.

III. *CLARA HOWARD* WITHIN BROWN'S CORPUS

In its insistent recycling of motifs and situations drawn from all of his previous novels and in its metafictional allusions to aspects of his own biographical situation in 1801, *Clara Howard* may be the most autobiographical of Brown's fictions. One question for future inquiry should be how this novel's complex autobiographical elements, both literary and personal, articulate with the larger questions it raises on all levels. This ensemble of questions, yet to be posed and answered in adequate detail, can be outlined in two large points that await greater development.

First, from the earliest reviews, critics have noted the way *Howard* recycles plot situations, motifs, names, and other features from Brown's earlier novels, especially *Edgar Huntly* (Ringe 440–441, 453). Space here does not allow a full review, but all of Brown's previous novels are referred to in this manner, and the list is sufficiently long and detailed that it raises the question of Brown's purpose in such extensive borrowing, recycling, repurposing, review, and allusion. From *Edgar Huntly*, echoed in "Edward Hartley," one notes the way the marriage dilemmas (one man, two women) and mysterious fortune left behind in the bank account of Mary Wilmot's deceased brother recast the situation of Huntly and Mary Waldegrave, as well as a host of topographical references, from the Powles Hook ferry on the Hudson to Hartley's native Hatfield and Mary Wilmot's Abingdon, Pennsylvania. Hatfield is in the Walking Purchase territory near Solebury, and Abingdon is where Edgar's fiancée, Mary Waldegrave, takes refuge in the prior novel.

Clara's and Mary's independence as troubled but strong-minded, sophisticated, gentry-class female protagonists echoes Brownian characters from Henrietta in 1793 to Clara Wieland, Constantia Dudley, Achsa Fielding, and so on. The vast wealth that enables the behind-the-scenes agency of Sedley and his sister, Mrs. Valentine, replays Ormond's practices as a "secret witness," and indeed, Sedley at the novel's end acts as "the secret advocate" (CH 143) whose machinations conclude but do not resolve the novel's windings. Hartley's aspirational path from rural "peasant" to urban professional, through a preliminary romance with one woman before a deferred union with a wealthy cosmopolitan, likewise reshapes that of *Arthur Mervyn*. Although early commenters were quick to chalk up this recycling to authorial laziness or hasty borrowings, that is, signs that Brown's "imagination" was flagging, in light of recent commentary, it makes more sense to ask how this insistent pattern of reference serves to double or reinforce the novel's critical review of the contradictions of earlier epistolary, sentimental, and Woldwinite novel forms with a glance back through Brown's own catalog. *Clara Howard* seems to self-consciously prompt the reader to refer back to the earlier output and ask what has changed.

Second, *Howard* presents a series of autobiographical motifs or echoes that tie the novel to Brown's situation in late 1800 to early 1801 in ways that have no parallel in the earlier or later fictions. This network of allusions links the novel to Brown's own courtship letters, written simultaneously with *Howard*, as well as to the interrupted timetable of *Jane Talbot*, begun and possibly completed before *Howard* but published only afterward, and the slightly earlier essay series "The Scribbler" (August 1800), which points forward to the conclusion of *Mervyn, Second Part* and both 1801 novels. Reading these texts in reference to one another generates a number of questions for future commentary. In August–September 1800, Brown traveled from New York to Philadelphia for what was intended as a visit but became a permanent return tied to his courtship of future spouse Elizabeth Linn and attendant pressures to establish a level of financial stability that was a sine qua non for the marriage. Despite his literary labors and some degree of cultural and social capital following the earlier writings, Brown's family had recently forced him to renounce a 1798–1799 courtship with Susan Potts because neither of them had income sufficient for marriage (Letters 452 n. 1, 915). In the courtship letters, he had to insist to Linn repeatedly that the relationship with Potts was over (Letters 478 n. 1, 481 n. 1, 486 n. 1). Thus, while commentators have always taken as gospel Paul Allen's assertion that *Howard*'s courtship triangle is based on a law-era incident involving Brown's friend John Davidson (Allen 44–48; Ringe 437–440), it appears as or more likely that this plot motif registers tensions Brown experienced during an ongoing transition between the courtships with Potts and Linn. The novel's anxious topography, leading from New York to Hartley's collapse in Philadelphia, revisits Brown's peregrinations of late 1800–1801.

Given the artificial, generically self-conscious tone of the courtship letters, in which Brown studiously performs the role of solicitous and self-disciplining beau, the question arises of whether *Howard* involves a critical reflection on or imaginative transformation of the ritualized emotional performance, heteronormative compliance, financial pressures, and fantasy structures involved in the author's own negotiations of the vicissitudes of sex and property (see Shapiro, as well as Hewitt's suggestive discussion of the courtship correspondence in this volume's chapter 14; Burnham likewise noted intertextuality with the courtship letters [267]). If this perspective seems unduly speculative, consider the overlapping timetables for the composition of both 1801 novels (outlined fully in Ringe 441–445) and their intersection with the courtship letters. The best evidence indicates that Brown commenced work on *Talbot* in late 1800 or very early 1801, immediately following the completion and publication of *Mervyn, Second Part* in late September or October 1800. Then he put it aside by March 10, writing to Linn, "I mean not to publish 'Jane Talbot.' My reasons for a change of plan, I will tell you, when I have your ear" (Letters 492). He turned instead to *Howard*, which then appeared in late June (*Howard*, like *Ormond*, was composed in four to eight weeks), followed by *Talbot*'s publication in December 1801. Thus, the dates of the courtship letters, written between late February and late April, overlap with those of *Howard*'s composition. In what senses the latter can be read as critical reflection on or some other transformation of the former emerges, therefore, as a necessary topic for analysis; at the very least, it indicates Brown's calculated distance on the stylistic features of both "series of letters," to cite *Howard*'s subtitle.

The final element in this ensemble of texts and allusions is the August 1800 essay series "The Scribbler."[7] That narrative series rescues its underfunded and anxiety-ridden writer-protagonist and his sister, Jane, from poverty with the miraculous appearance of a benevolent patron, in a turn that directly prefigures the money ex machina device of Sedley in *Howard* (or of Fielding in *Mervyn, Second Part*, whose conclusion was likewise written after "The Scribbler"). The novel's first paragraph, with Hartley's opening lament "Why do I write?" and melancholy longing after the disappearance of his interlocutor, Mary, who would previously "read, and ruminate on the scantiest and poorest scribble that dropped from my pen" (CH 5), refers back to the premise sketched out in "The Scribbler" and likewise suggests Brown's preoccupation with the problematic returns and potentials of novel writing (and heteronormative discipline) at this point in his development. Without minimizing "The Scribbler"'s continuity with the metafictional allegories of beleaguered writers in prior essay series "The Rhapsodist" (1789) and "The Man at Home" (1798), one can observe the topoi that link the narratives of this moment, as the "Scribbler" writes from New York and strolls *flâneur*-style on the same iconic Battery walk that reappears in Hartley's encounter with Morton, the source of *Howard*'s mysterious $5,000 (CH 66), and repeatedly in the courtship letters (Letters 519 n. 1).

IV. PROTO-MODERNISM

What, then, can we make of *Clara Howard*'s critical reflections on the novel form and that form's ideological implications at a crucial juncture in its history and in Brown's own development, both literary and biographical? *Howard* has always been perceived as difficult to parse—witness two hundred years of frustration with the challenges it presents—but perhaps its resistance to interpretation and willful opacity are an intentional literary effect. Perhaps this novel responds to different questions from the ones it has traditionally been made to answer.

The novel's paradoxical emptiness and air of futility or frustration have been noted repeatedly. We observed earlier that it was Loshe who first remarked, in a constructive sense, that "nothing happens" in *Howard* (Loshe 48). Burnham rightly emphasized this readerly estrangement effect, describing "the narrative's unusual quality of paralytic velocity" and "frenetic inactivity" (Burnham 267, 271), the "almost dizzying" reversals and deferrals that "(re)produce desire through delay" (266) as the text "retracts as quickly and as definitively as it promises satisfaction or resolution" (269), generally producing an "antinovelistic effect" (243). Burleigh likewise notes the narrative's curious manner of withdrawing the fundamental conventional promise of narrative pleasure, arguing that both 1801 novels are "largely uninterested in producing emotional responses in their readers" (Burleigh 752).

These observations open onto what we can call the proto-modernism or emergent modernism of *Clara Howard*. While latter-day readings have demonstrated that *Howard* articulates a critical perspective on new conditions of bourgeois liberalism in the post-Revolutionary era as it recognizes the limits of radical Enlightenment aspirations for the novel as an instrument of political education from Rousseau and Mackenzie to William Godwin and Brown's own prior production, a forward-oriented historical optics suggests that the novel also inaugurates new strategies in response to this transitional juncture. Although this aspect of Brown's writing is still frequently underestimated, we know that part of his literary achievement was the development of formal strategies that genuinely merit the adjective *radical* and whose full scope and complexity were not only prescient but well beyond the expectation horizon of his audiences. The narrative theatrics and deep irony effects that structure and undermine Sophia Courtland's first-person reportage in *Ormond* or the critical reflections on the cultural politics of historical romance and emergent neo-antiquarian nostalgia in the *Historical Sketches* are arguably the most radical formal gestures in American literary history before later nineteenth-century proto-modernists such as Herman Melville, Walt Whitman, or Emily Dickinson. Earlier than but somewhat analogously to other presciently modernist writers in the following generations, Brown was a gifted formal chameleon, who sharpened his skills by emulating and hybridizing generic models from Alexander Pope and Samuel Johnson to Rousseau or Godwin but who, in texts such as *Ormond*, *Howard*, and the *Historical Sketches*, pushes beyond received strategies to posit new and experimental ones.

The "antinovelistic" or proto-modernist effects in *Howard* entail at least four gestures that point forward toward generally accepted "modernist" and/or avant-garde practices. First, as the citations in the previous paragraph attest, and in keeping with its critical review of prior generic models, this novel tends away from representational conventions toward a dynamic of abstraction that registers new forms of alienation, most dramatically allegorized in the overdetermination of all possibilities by economic forces personified in Sedley and literalized in the suffering and final collapse of Hartley, a "slave" of class-based "self-contempt" to the last (CH 53).[8] Second, the narrative refuses the reader the aforementioned fundamental conventional promise of aesthetic pleasure; its plot is reader-unfriendly by design, analogous in this respect to countless later proto-modernist or avant-garde performances, from Melville's *The Confidence Man* to Jean-Paul Sartre's *Nausea* or William Faulkner's *As I Lay Dying*. Appearing only eleven years after Immanuel Kant's *Critique of Judgment* (1790) and eight years after Friedrich Schiller's (epistolary) *Letters on the Aesthetic Education of Man* (1793), the two inaugural monuments of bourgeois aesthetic ideology as the new romantico-modern dominant, this novel implies that future readers should take seriously Brown's implicit working through and rejection of aesthetic idealism in *Howard* and the very different *Historical Sketches*.

Third, as an extension and corollary of this abstraction and refusal, *Howard* presages the basic avant-garde presumption that valid art is anti-institutional art, implicitly negating, attacking, and abolishing the predicates of official or dominant forms. The narrative's critical perspective on prior novelistic conventions articulates this negation. Finally, *Howard* minimizes psychology effects in its protagonists, who seem reduced to action figures whose forward motion results from and likewise betrays their self-identified and self-defeating principles. While Brown encourages his readers to dis-identify with or take a critical distance on earlier protagonists and narrators such as Clara Wieland, Sophia Courtland, or Edgar Huntly by exposing their "unreliability," *Howard* seems to empty out its characters' interiority and discourage projective identification in a more extensive manner. This effect is registered in Gardner's observation that *Howard* is "organized without the totalizing narratives and central consciousness of the conventional novel" (Gardner 2000, 763).[9] As Shapiro and Kamrath note in this volume's chapters 12 and 13, on the 1803–1809 political pamphlets and 1807–1809 "Annals," and as we see in the 1805–1806 *Historical Sketches* as well, Brown's post-1801 narratives and fictions (with qualified exceptions in *Memoirs of Carwin*, "Somnambulism," "Insanity: A Fragment," etc.) tend to abandon individual subjects as characters and instead construct their dramatis personae out of larger historical units such as dynastic families, partisan factions, or the nation-state. From this perspective, the emptying out of subjectivity in *Howard* appears as Brown's first step toward this later narrative production, in which the "historical" slope of the romance-writing model replaces the "fictitious" one.

Although most treatments of the 1801 novels lump the two titles together and have difficulty drawing basic distinctions between them, a proto-modernist perspective on *Clara Howard* provides one starting point for understanding their differences. As noted earlier regarding the novel's composition timeline, *Howard* is actually the final novel undertaken in the course of the 1797–1801 sequence that begins with the now-lost *Sky-Walk*, since it was composed after *Talbot* was well under way and possibly completed. Its likely status as a concluding or retrospective gesture may have something to do with its curious length. While *Talbot* runs to around 83,400 words, in line with the other published novels, *Howard* comes to only about half that size, roughly 44,250 words. Whereas *Talbot* still offers hermeneutic footholds and thematic resting points, such as explicit ideological antagonists condemning Godwinism, theft, forgery, and other interest-generating narrative action, *Howard* directs attention away from this level of narrative convention and suggests another mode of ascent. Providing no antagonist to be expelled, no resolution to fulfill the romance's forward motion and culminate in readerly pleasure, and negating or minimizing other central aspects of conventional narrative mechanics, it stands as a key turning point in Brown's literary career.

Notes

1. In his "Historical Essay" for the 1986 Kent State edition, Donald Ringe reviews the reception history prior to the 1980s (452–459). It is no exaggeration to say that 170 years of reception history can be summarized in two formulations: for E. T. Channing in 1819, *Howard* and *Talbot* "are so very inferior to and unlike the others, that they require no particular notice"; and for Martin Vilas in 1904, *Howard* has lapsed into "sickly sentimentalism" (quoted in Ringe 456, 459).

2. Burnham surveys most of the key statements in this development, from Krause (1981) to Decker (1994), Burgett (1996), and Gardner (2000). Along with Shapiro (2001) and Burleigh (2011), these are the crucial readings.

3. "Disenchantment," Max Weber's *Entzauberung*, theorizes the progressive draining away of "magic" in the course of modernization-as-rationalization, the moment when "one can, in principle, master all things by calculation" (Weber, "Science as a Vocation"). Lukács adapts this concept in *Theory of the Novel* (1915) to chart the transformation that occurs after the Revolutionary era, as the novel concludes its "rise" and becomes as the central narrative form of the newly dominant liberal-capitalist stage of the world-system, reflecting its characteristic geoculture of ever intensified alienation. See Moretti.

4. Mary Wilmot's father, a "German" who anglicized his name from "Veelmetz" (CH 98) and made his fortune "in an English mercantile house," is originally from Altona, now part of present-day Hamburg and then a Jewish enclave and separate municipality with a concentration of cosmopolitan merchants, analogous to the Jewish enclave in the Comtat Venaissin (in Provence) that is referred to in the backstory of Achsa Fielding in *Mervyn, Second Part*. Thus, one minor implication is that Mary, like Clara Wieland's paternal grandmother, has Jewish parentage from the Hamburg community (see *Wieland*'s chap. 1). Similarly, the merchant Morton (*Howard*'s variant on the Weymouth merchant figure in *Huntly*) explains that he amassed a mercantile fortune "in Europe and the West Indies" before losing much of it to Barbary piracy, which he survived thanks to "agents of the United States, in consequence of a treaty being ratified between *us* and the government of Algiers" (CH 46), an allusion to William Bainbridge's ransom payments to the dey of Algiers in 1800. As with all of Brown's novels, the historical references and allusions embedded in *Howard*'s web of backstories frame and provide implicit commentary on the surface action and will repay detailed future examination.

5. The extraordinarily belated recognition of this reference stems partly from a long-standing confusion of names that originated early in the publication history. In *Howard*'s first English edition, Edward Hartley's name was changed to "Philip Stanley," and the novel was somewhat obtusely retitled *Philip Stanley; or, The Enthusiasm of Love* (London: Minerva, 1807). All subsequent US printings until the Kent State 1986 scholarly edition retained Brown's main title, *Clara Howard*, but adopted the British subtitle and non-Brownian name for the male protagonist, thereby effacing the allusion to *The Man of Feeling*. Even recent commentary occasionally takes the male protagonist as "Philip Stanley," perpetuating the misreading effect.

6. Brown reverses Mackenzie: whereas Mackenzie gives the protagonist a surname only (Harley) and the mysterious benefactor two (Edward Sedley), Brown inverts the same three names

to give the protagonist two (Edward Hartley) and the benefactor one (Sedley). Mackenzie's character name Sedley reappears in Brown's circle as John Elihu Hall's pseudonym for his 1804 contributions to the *Port Folio*. As a contributor to Brown's *Literary Magazine* in 1806–1807, Hall uses the pseudonym "Valverdi" (Letters 569 n. 1).

7. As of 2006, "The Scribbler" was known in two very different versions and three printings: an 1809 version, a distinct posthumous 1822 version, and a posthumous fragment in Dunlap 1815 that partly matches the 1822 text (Gardner 2006). The 1800 text (five installments in the *New York Commercial Advertiser*, August 12–16, 1800) is a fourth, newly recovered addition to the group and the original source for the 1815 and 1822 printings, which has come to light only after the 2006 discussion and in the course of ongoing work for Jared Gardner and Beth Hewitt, eds., *The American Register and Other Writings, 1807–1810*, forthcoming as Vol. 6 in the Bucknell *Collected Writings* edition.

8. Note that whereas the aristocratic-class and merchant-class inheritances behind the Howard-Wilmot (Veelmetz) fortunes are clearly presented in the novel's backstories, Sedley's sinister nature as a genteel personification of veiled, mobile, rapacious capital derived from Tidewater slavery remains implied and thus more subterranean in its ubiquitous corruption. For example: "Sedley's usual place of abode was his father's house in Virginia, but he chiefly passed his time in Philadelphia, where he resided with his sister [Mrs. Valentine], who was a lady of great merit, and left, by her husband's death, in opulent circumstances" (CH 61).

9. See also James Decker's conclusion that *Howard* is "uncannily 'modern'" (Decker 28) and Wil Verhoeven's affirmation (via Eagleton) that the 1801 novels are "dismantling the ideological self-identity of our routine social behaviour" (Verhoeven 164).

WORKS CITED

Binhammer, Katherine. "The Political Novel and the Seduction Plot: Thomas Holcroft's *Anna St. Ives*." *Eighteenth-Century Fiction* 11.2 (January 1999): 203–222.

Brown, Charles Brockden. "The Scribbler" (in 5 parts). *Commercial Advertiser* (New York) 3.887–891 (August 12–16, 1800), 2 (for each installment).

Burgett, Bruce. "Masochism and Male Sentimentalism: Charles Brockden Brown's *Clara Howard*." *Arizona Quarterly* 52.1 (Spring 1996): 1–25.

Burleigh, Erica. "Incommensurate Equivalences: Genre, Representation, and Equity in *Clara Howard* and *Jane Talbot*." *Early American Studies* 9.3 (Fall 2011): 748–780.

Burnham, Michelle. "Epistolarity, Anticipation, and Revolution in *Clara Howard*." In Philip Barnard, Mark L. Kamrath, and Stephen Shapiro, eds., *Revising Charles Brockden Brown: Culture, Politics, and Sexuality in the Early Republic*, 260–280. Knoxville: University of Tennessee Press, 2004.

Decker, James. "Reassessing Charles Brockden Brown's *Clara Howard*." *Publications of the Missouri Philological Association* 19 (1994): 28–36.

Dillon, James. "'The Highest Province of Benevolence': Charles Brockden Brown's Fictional Theory." *Studies in Eighteenth-Century Culture* 27 (1998): 237–258.

Dixon, Josie, "Revolutionary Ideals and Romantic Irony: The Godwinian Inheritance in Literature." In Keith Hanley and Raman Selden, eds., *Revolution and English Romanticism: Politics and Rhetoric*, 147–168. Hemel Hempstead, UK: Harvester Wheatsheaf, 1990.

Fiedler, Leslie. *Love and Death in the American Novel* (1960), rev. ed. New York: Stein and Day, 1966.

Gardner, Jared. "From the Periodical Archives: 'The Scribbler,' by Charles Brockden Brown." *American Periodicals* 16.2 (2006): 219–228.

Gardner, Jared. "The Literary Museum and the Unsettling of the American Novel." *English Literary History* 67.3 (Fall 2000): 743–771.

Grabo, Norman S. *The Coincidental Art of Charles Brockden Brown*. Chapel Hill: University of North Carolina Press, 1981.

Krause, Sydney J. "*Clara Howard* and *Jane Talbot*: Godwin on Trial." In Bernard Rosenthal, ed., *Critical Essays on Charles Brockden Brown*, 184–211. Boston: G. K. Hall, 1981.

Loshe, Lillie Deming. *The Early American Novel, 1789–1830* [1907]. New York: Frederick Ungar Publishing Co., 1958.

Lukàcs, Georg. *The Theory of the Novel: A Historical-Philosophical Essay on the Forms of Great Epic Literature* [1920]. Trans. Anna Bostock. Cambridge, Mass.: The MIT Press, 1971.

Mackenzie, Henry. *The Man of Feeling* (1771). Maureen Larkin, ed. Peterborough, Ont.: Broadview Editions, 2005.

Moretti, Franco. "Centenary Reflections." *New Left Review* 91 (January–February 2014): 39–42.

Ringe, Donald A. "Historical Essay." In Sydney J. Krause and S. W. Reid, eds., *Clara Howard; in a Series of Letters with Jane Talbot, a Novel*, Vol. 5 of *The Novels and Related Works of Charles Brockden Brown*, 433–474. Kent, Ohio: Kent State University Press, 1986.

Shapiro, Stephen. "'I Could Kiss Him One Minute and Kill Him the Next!': The Limits of Radical Male Friendship in Holcroft, C. B. Brown, and Wollstonecraft Shelley." In Walter Göbel, Saskia Schabio, and Martin Windisch, eds., *Engendering Images of Man in the Long Eighteenth Century*, 111–132. Trier: Wissenschaftlicher Verlag, 2001.

Tennenhouse, Leonard. *The Importance of Feeling English: American Literature and the British Diaspora, 1750–1850*. Princeton, N.J.: Princeton University Press, 2007.

Verhoeven, Wil. "'Persuasive Rhetorick': Representation and Resistance in Early American Epistolary Fiction." In A. Robert Lee and Wil Verhoeven, eds., *Making America, Making American Literature: Franklin to Cooper*, 123–164. Amsterdam: Rodopi, 1996.

Watts, Steven. *The Romance of Real Life: Charles Brockden Brown and the Origins of American Culture*. Baltimore: Johns Hopkins University Press, 1994.

Witherington, Paul. "Brockden Brown's Other Novels: *Clara Howard* and *Jane Talbot*." *Nineteenth-Century Fiction* 29.3 (December 1974): 257–272.

CHAPTER 9

....

JANE TALBOT, A NOVEL

....

STEPHEN SHAPIRO

NEITHER time nor the critics have been kind to *Jane Talbot*. While Charles Brockden Brown's last published fictions, *Clara Howard* and *Jane Talbot*, share many themes and motives with his so-called main, Gothic fictions, they have been frequently separated from his earlier romances by nearly every critic. These later epistolary novels' change in form and tone has made it easier for them to be marginalized, if not usually simply ignored, for reasons telegraphed by Brown himself. In an April 1800 letter to his brother James, Brown responded to his sibling's criticism of *Edgar Huntly*'s "gloominess and out-of-nature incidents" (Letters 462–464), admitting that even if the complaint was not justified, "most readers" would nonetheless agree with its negative judgment. Hence, to increase sales, there "is a sufficient reason for dropping the doleful tone and assuming a cheerful one, or, at least substituting moral causes and daily incidents in place of the prodigious or the singular." For most postwar critics drawn to Brown and appreciative of what is perceived as his fiction's greatest attraction, the prose of moody eccentricity, these lines have been taken as a sign of Brown's personal creative failure and loss of intellectual self-confidence. When read as a sign of artistic burnout, the last published novels are seen as Brown's capitulation to the dictates of a post-1800 literary marketplace that is taken to be simultaneously more feminized and more commercialized and as his retreat to the protective cover of a more conservative political vision.

Not until Witherington's 1974 essay was there any focused, let alone moderately favorable, discussion of *Jane Talbot*. Even after the renewed interest in and examination of Brown's corpus that began in the 1970s, *Jane Talbot* has had only a few dedicated considerations (Ringe; Krause; Shapiro; Brückner 2004; Brückner 2012; Burleigh). The paucity of discussion is regrettable, since Brown's last published fictions can be read as a critical and perceptive diagnosis of his own contemporary moment's cultural elements, rather than as a symptom of personal failure or pathetic fallacy telegraphing his early demise from tuberculosis. Instead of *Jane Talbot* (and *Clara Howard*) being "embarrassing concessions to convention and conservatism" (Krause 185) or capitulations to dominant mores and politics, these novels take these elements as their object of analysis. Coming at the end of the 1790s European revolutions and broad campaigns for republican governments and social relations, the subject of *Jane Talbot* and *Clara Howard* is the defeat of radical energies, their theme is the means by which an alliance of progressive sensibilities is disrupted, and their realization is that the new forces of control to be contested are now not those of regal authority or executive administration, as so many eighteenth-century writers proclaimed, but rather the nascent power of the nation-state grounded on free-market capitalism and ideologies of the liberal self that would be produced through disciplinary techniques of behavioral, emotional, and sexual normalization.

While the notion that Brown is the putative "father" of the American novel has long been discredited by the acknowledgment of many other, and many female, authors, there is nonetheless still a case to be made that with *Jane Talbot* and *Clara Howard*, Brown stands as one of the first creators of the *modern* American novel, if by that description we mean a novel treating the civil society of political and economic liberalism as it was coming into perceptible view and practice by the early 1800s. As a register of the onset of liberalism's domination and the damage caused by its cultural forms, especially that of bourgeois heteronormativity, *Jane Talbot* deserves be considered the start of a line that can be drawn through the later works of similar-minded authors such as Herman Melville and David Foster Wallace. Rather than revealing Brown's stymied failure of imagination, the 1801 novels operate as his investigation into an emerging form of social hegemony and mode of domination that has both replaced older ones while also grinding down the agents of progressive, alternative perspectives and psychologizing this potential of collective difference as individual dysfunction. Brown's insight is that the perceived antagonists that his slightly earlier romances array themselves against were not as powerful threats as imagined and that the strategy of opposition to them distracted progressives from perceiving the rise of a more powerful beast. Moreover, the replication of plot devices in these novels from Brown's prior works ought to be read less as a lack of continued innovation and more as a careful reexamination of the past's figures to assay their practicality within a changed time.

To explore this viewpoint, we might begin by asking two interlinked questions. First, why did Brown allow *Jane Talbot* to be called a "novel" on its published title page, rather than his previously preferred term "romance," which he considered the category defining his prior longer fictions? Second, amid the chorus of disapproval that greeted *Jane Talbot*, why did one of Brown's most engaged and sympathetic readers, Mary Wollstonecraft Shelley, daughter of William Godwin and Mary Wollstonecraft and wife of Percy Shelley, call *Jane Talbot* a "very stupid book," a stronger condemnation than her feeling that *Clara Howard* was merely "stupid" (Shelley 1987, 53)? What was Mary Shelley's particular aversion to this book by a writer she championed and arguably later drew on for inspiration and recital in her own novels from *Frankenstein* to *The Last Man*?

From the beginning of his 1797–1801 flurry of long fiction writing, and indeed from around 1793 on, Brown understood his narrative work as romances, a form he differentiated from novels not by differences in perceived aesthetic value, cultural status, or intellectual rigor but by their purpose. For Brown, a romance was a retrospective attempt to assay the causative formation of sociohistorical events and patterns. This speculative effort had formal implications for Brown as he fashioned a narrative style that often models forensic inquiry for his readers through his characters' frequent self-interruption of breathless events with wordy passages of balanced argument and counterargument. Additionally, the complexities of trying to discern causation in what may seem to be a forest of contingencies were enacted through a profusion of convoluted subplots that challenge the most skillful commentators seeking to convey even the most basic plot summary to their readers. If romance is speculative cultural history, the novel form, in Brown's hands, is used as a portrait of contemporary, or emerging, society, a project that necessitates different formal and narrative techniques.

Unlike Brown's romances, these novels have plots that *can* be easily described, not least as they involve generic scenes, such as the proposed midnight elopement plan, which his readers would easily recognize, having seen them in other tales many times before. The time setting of *Jane Talbot* (and *Clara Howard*, which can from here on be taken as inferentially linked to *Jane Talbot*) is notably different from that of Brown's other works. While *Wieland* is set in colonial days, *Edgar Huntly* in the 1780s, and *Ormond* and *Arthur Mervyn* in 1793, or roughly six years before the date of the novels' actual composition and publication, *Jane Talbot* and *Clara Howard* either are contemporaneous or seem to occur immediately prior to their publication. While Brown's previous tales are set in "other" cities or locales of extraordinary events, *Jane Talbot*'s Philadelphia and *Clara Howard*'s New York–Philadelphia trajectory are more familiar places of quotidian interaction. Brown's turn from the seeming fantastical and difficult to cognize to the familiar, from the romance to the novel, is not a symptom of Brown's "tiring invention" or "artistic cowardice" (Krause 185) but a formal change chosen as the most apt for a different project from that which motivated the previous romances.

It would be an error to see *Jane Talbot*'s epistolary composition as a capitulation to the perceived tastes of female readers, since the epistolary novel was already, by the start of the nineteenth century, a form becoming unfashionable, if not obsolete. Brown's decision to adopt an epistolary novel format for action set in the present was perhaps made less to satisfy contemporary readers' tastes than to indicate how the protagonists' chosen form of self-expression was itself already receding from view in a time increasingly organized by different social values.

The shift from romance to novel may also explain Mary Shelley's disapproval. In Brown's fiction, the conflict over space and geography involves questions about the collision of different visions of society. The challenge of producing a material location for the communication and enactment of progressive or bourgeois dissident cultural sensibilities runs throughout Brown's writing. Yet these alternative communicative nodes (forest enclosures, reading and writing rooms) are constantly under risk of forcible entry or surveillance by a voyeuristic figure whose intrusion brings the threat of a broader revelation or publicity that will further disempower these alternatives. This spatializing of struggle stages Brown's understanding of the hardships facing the expression of new group ideas and interaction within the undertow of the old regime. If the onset of nineteenth-century bourgeois hegemony, as a substantively different kind of power from what eighteenth-century writers had focused on, is the core concern of *Jane Talbot*, Brown's prospective insight about the incipient form of social dominance was precisely what Mary Shelley found so distasteful.

Throughout the mid- and late 1810s, Percy and Mary Shelley sought out and celebrated Brown's romances. Percy Shelley's six favorite literary works, according to Peacock, were Friedrich Schiller's *Robbers*, Johann Wolfgang von Goethe's *Faust*, and Brown's *Wieland*, *Edgar Huntly*, *Ormond*, and *Arthur Mervyn* (Peacock 35–36). Shelley wanted to build a summer house modeled after the one described in *Wieland*. *Ormond's* Constantia occupied "one of the highest places, if not the highest in [Percy's] idealities of female character" (Peacock 36). In 1818, adopting the pseudonym "Pleyel," the name of a character in *Wieland*, Shelley published a poem composed the year before, titled "To Constantia, Singing," which seems to be written as the imagined lyric to a song Constantia performs for Ormond (Bieri 47). Mary Shelley first heard *Edgar Huntly* as Percy read it to her in 1814, and she, in turn, read Brown's romances in succession during her own coming into authorship. It was likely the young couple who persuaded Godwin to read Brown at this time, a move that may have helped reactivate Godwin's interest in returning to produce fiction. When Godwin then published *Mandeville* (1817), Shelley thought it his best novel, perhaps because Godwin acknowledges in his preface that he was heavily influenced by *Wieland*, along with Joanna Baillie's *Montfort*. The impact of Brown's writing on Mary was such that after reading William Dunlap's biography, she wrote in 1826 that, while she disliked the United States, it had not been "barren of good... it produced one man whom I am sure I should have liked—the Author of Weland [sic]," "poor dear Brown—What a delightful person he seems to have been" (Shelley 1980, 402, 499).

If the Shelleys and Godwin were committed readers of Brown, then why did they complain about *Jane Talbot*? Krause argues that Brown here put "Godwin on trial" to test the philosopher's ideas in practice and then found them ineffective. Yet if this is so, then Brown's romances could also be similarly interrogative vis-à-vis Godwin. What differentiates *Jane Talbot* from the other work is that it does not simply explore Godwin's (and Wollstonecraft's) precepts but has a main character who openly identifies himself through Godwin's writing. For protagonist Henry Colden is described by Mrs. Fielder as someone who, having read Godwin's *Political Justice*, changed "in a moment, the whole course of his ideas" (JT 228) and turned into a proselytizer. Thus, more specifically, it is not ideas of Godwin in themselves that seem tested in the book but Godwinism as a cultural movement, a collectivity created by the shared reception of a set of ideas or critical perspectives. Yet in *Jane Talbot*, Brown found this culture unable to thrive, precisely at the moment when the Shelleys were attempting, on the other hand, to revivify the politics of Mary's parents and create a (Romantic) milieu partially grounded on these ideas. In this light, *Jane Talbot's* implicit doubt about the efficacy of the Shelleys' project may have been one that Mary was not willing to hear in the 1810s. She may, however, have better accommodated herself to it when reading Dunlap's biography of Brown in the 1820s, at a time when she herself had come to recognize the cultural power of the liberal nation-state.

Brown's perception of the transformation occurring in the post-1800 modern period opens *Jane Talbot*, as Jane records an instance of her abandonment of past beliefs and acceptance of a new political consciousness. Jane relates a pivotal moment from her childhood to Henry Colden. She describes seeing a group of strange men entering her mother's bedroom, to take her mother away, as Jane believes. Jane's father holds her back, despite her struggles and shrieks. Jane faints, awakens to discover that her mother has died and been buried, and then compulsively visits her mother's grave several times a day. She thus experiences the primal trauma of her mother's loss as caused by male violence and the heartless force of patriarchy. Growing up, Jane has a barely concealed dislike of her bullying brother and hapless father and happily moves in with an older woman, Mrs. Fielder, a former friend of her mother's and now a maternal surrogate. Yet after meeting Henry, Jane learns to differentiate between biological sex and its cultural codification in gender. Jane tells Henry that she used to think her difference from her brother Francis ("Frank") was "merely that of sex; that every boy was boisterous, ungrateful, imperious, and inhuman, as every girl was soft, plaint, affectionate. Time has cured me of that mistake, and so it has introduced me to men full of gentleness and sensibility" (JT 156).

Jane's newfound awareness that it is not biology but gender fashioning that matters, stands as her first utopian glimmer of a new world grounded on sentiment and sociability shared between women and men. Yet this opening for a new experience-system of feeling is then immediately opposed by Mrs. Fielder. When Mrs. Fielder sees Jane's "perverse spirit," her "sensibility," "inattention to anything but feeling," and "proneness to romantic friendship," she has Jane quickly married off to Talbot, a man twice her age, who was "addicted to industry," "regular and frugal in his manner and economy," and "satisfied with ignorance of theories" (JT 223). Against Jane's religiosity, Talbot "seldom went to Church" and, when there, "seldom spared a thought from his own temporal concerns" (223–224). Mrs. Fielder's orchestration of Jane's marriage to Talbot, a man lacking in intellectual or sensual excitement, was meant to limit Jane's energetic intellect and experimental idealism in favor of noncontemplative industry and a regulated personality. For Mrs. Fielder, Jane is a "zealot" whose mental ferment is infantilized as a narcissism that desires someone who would share her "sympathies," someone "who saw everything just as you saw it. Who could emulate your enthusiasm, and echo back every exclamation which chance should dictate to you" (223).

Mrs. Fielder's attempt to damp down Jane's emotional affect and extraworldly ideals results in a loveless (and childless) marriage in which Jane is meant to be Talbot's business helpmate, more than an object of desire. Indeed, Mrs. Fielder stands for the rise of a new sexless bourgeois propriety that disdains emotion of any kind. She seems to oppose not just Jane and Henry's but any kind of love match. Called Mrs. more as a status title than as evidence of former matrimony, she had even broken from Jane's mother when the latter married Jane's father. Mrs. Fielder's opposition to Jane's marriage with Henry, thus, is not simply her dislike of Henry's ideals but the threat that Jane's union with him could present companionate emotional support as an ideal that might, in turn, be emulated by others. While Jane is fervently religious and Henry a deist, Jane is attracted to him as a companion of similar feeling. He has a likewise "bookish," "visionary and romantic" nature, with allegiance to the power of ideas (225). Yet Jane seeks emotional currency and the affective flow of informality and intimacy more than ideas in themselves. She repeatedly chides Henry (Colden) for his "cold" communications and admits that she would have melted before Frank's demands had he spoken to her with fraternal sympathy.

Caught in an emotional tomb with Talbot, when Jane meets Henry, he reignites her earlier "notions of kindred among souls: of friendship, and harmony of feeling" (226). But after Mrs. Fielder is given an anonymous letter that seems to suggest Jane's sexual infidelity with Henry, she threatens to disinherit Jane and throw her into poverty if she marries him after Talbot has died. The bulk of the ensuing novel involves Henry and Jane's tumult and indecision over the degree to which they will, or even can, resist Mrs. Fielder's demand for conformity to her standard of behavior.

Brown thus apprehends the language of sentimental crisis but uses its syntax for a different purpose. The dominant tale of the sentimental narrative throughout the eighteenth century was a story about virtue in distress, the tale of a wayward youth's fatal fall, epitomized in the story of an aristocratic-like rake's seduction and abandonment of a young woman. The seductive attraction of new mores, represented by Henry, however, is very weak in *Jane Talbot*. The force bearing down on Jane instead is conveyed by a marriage to a dull man who clearly has little erotic interest in Jane or in anyone else, for that matter. Brown alters the generic elements of the eighteenth-century sentimental tale in this manner to suggest that the real forces to contend with are not the libidinally staged vestiges of gentry power but the onset of new agents dedicated to social conformity as an aid to nation-statist mercantile commerce and its liberal political economy.

Ostensibly a sentimental tale about a young couple's attempts to unite against their elders' disapproval and threats to their financial security, *Jane Talbot* articulates the psychological hardship of the cultural and political defeat, in the new century, of eighteenth-century progressive or utopian thought and politics. From the opening loss of Jane's mother onward, the novel depicts the challenges of internal exile, as the utopian adventure associated with the French Revolution and Woldwinite ideals is thoroughly overwhelmed and seems definitively consigned to the past. Left in its wake is an embittered exhaustion in which past ideals involving communitarian movements to reconstruct society are denied, former allegiances to these notions are experienced as criminal liability or psychological abnormality, and some former dreamers become actively hostile to their earlier visions of social alteration.

For instance, Jane's first effort to secure domestic equipoise occurs when she moves in with Mrs. Fielder in hopes of later marrying her father's adopted nephew. This plan is quickly destroyed by her brother, Francis, who is often called Frank by her, even though he stands for guile, not frankness. Frank's combination of financial speculation and the costs of keeping a mistress drives Jane's father into debt, but not before Frank has defrauded Jane of the small savings that were meant to be her financial endowment for the future. When Jane initially resists Frank's pleas for money, he cynically whistles Ça ira ("It Will Be Fine"), the popular tune associated with the French Revolution. Frank later escapes his debt by fleeing to France. Though he has no radical politics, he rises in the republic's army and becomes wealthy by expropriating the property of the émigré comte de Puységur (Antoine Hyacinthe de Chastenet, 1752–1809) and then legitimizing the larceny by marrying Puységur's sister.

Like Julien Sorel in Stendhal's *The Red and the Black* (1830), Frank stands as an example of the nascent arrival of self-interested charlatans eager to appropriate the language of republican ideals for selfish gains. It is not simply that Frank's name echoes both Benjamin Franklin and *Wieland*'s "Frank" Carwin to indicate the deployment of manipulative self-interest through dissimulating language. Frank's ventriloquism, as he whistles the French revolutionary tune, is a mundane version of Carwin's biloquism, but Brown has Jane's brother do so in a far less supernatural way than Carwin, to indicate how normal and commonplace such deceits have become in the emerging liberal order. The extraordinary plot devices that Brown used to convey his romantic explorations are no longer necessary, because the forces of social containment have become so prevalent as to become normative and hence able to be described in commonplace plots.

Although appearing as little more than a passing reference, Frank's acquisition of the historical figure Puységur's lands also conveys Brown's message about the collapse of eighteenth-century notions of progressive sentiment or sociability. As students of Franz Mesmer, the three Puységur brothers, and particularly Amand-Marie-Jacques de Chastenet, marquis de Puységur (1751–1825), are considered the figures who bring hypnosis into its modern form (Ellenberger 70–74; Regourd). While Mesmer portrayed animal magnetism as a social fluid that could be used to heal ailments, often through group use of the *baquet*, a water-filled vat with protruding iron bars that individuals held to the areas of their ailments while linking hands in a group chain, the marquis de Puységur helps shift hypnosis from its perceived status as a feature of vitalist animal magnetism to being understood as part of the machinery of the individual's mind, a move that helps lay the conceptual ground for the later notion of the unconscious. The marquis also used an elm tree for a form of hypnosis in which individuals confessed things that they would not have admitted otherwise. Because such an arboreal apparatus of public revelation of personal matters appears in the iconic elm tree that features in *Edgar Huntly* and reappears metamorphosed into an oak in the short tale "Somnambulism. A Fragment," Brown may have been using these tales to investigate psychological interiority in its early formulations. However, Frank's appropriation of Puységur's land represents the force of new money that is, in the novel's terms, literally stealing the philosophical territory of the Enlightenment era from underneath its feet. Whereas the eighteenth century's claim was that a rake could be reformed through sentiment's power of social reformation, by the new century that *Jane Talbot* describes, selfish Frank neither is punished nor suffers any trouble or challenge to the rewards he achieves through his deceptions (Shapiro).

Brown records this absence of a moral ending as evidence of his generation's overall increasing willingness, in the new century, to forgo their earlier vision of sociality in favor of naked self-interest. Jane's first fiancé, Risberg, for whom she sacrificed good relations with her family, likewise abandons her when he discovers her family's new poverty and then quickly marries a wealthy Englishwoman. Henry, Jane's romantic companion, experiences the betrayal of radical fraternity, as Mrs. Fielder's opposition to him is based on his early letters illustrating his attraction to deistic Godwinism, letters that were forwarded to her by an old friend of his. Henry and Jane usually find that even when they can reveal their betrayal by ostensible friends, it does nothing to change their current disempowerment, as speaking truth is now ineffectual.

Unlike Brown's other romances, which explore the potential for and breakthrough of other social visions but often stage their containment, *Jane Talbot* presents a grim world where the best that can be imagined is some form of exile, sanctuary, or relief from the forces grinding down alternatives. As readers, we discover Jane and Henry's romance only in the past tense. There is no description of the initial courtship, only retrospective attempts to justify it. The moment of electric reorganization is long over, its promise negated, and the task remaining is how to deal with its ruins at a time when reaction is enshrined.

In the world they now face, Jane and Henry's youthful enthusiasm is voided, leaving them with little spirit of radical dissent, and the couple is caught instead in an anomic lack of industry and malaise of "idling." Half bemoaning, half proclaiming his difficult integration into a rationalized society that is fitting itself for the pursuit of profit, Henry laments:

> I cannot labour for bread; I cannot work to live. In that respect I have no parallel. The world does not contain my likeness. My very nature unfits me for any profitable business. My dependence must ever be on others or on fortune....I am not indolent, but my activity is vague, profitless, capricious. No lucrative or noble purpose impels me.   (JT 267)

For a generation that has had its opportunities x-ed out by the containment of political and cultural radicalism, the sole remaining avenue of resistance appears to be the solitary rebellion of preferring not to do anything and slacking off. Placed within a society that has little use or tolerance for either their past ideals or present diffidence, Jane and Henry find themselves increasingly treated as psychological deviants. The damage in being labeled as misfits leads them to a desire for approval and acceptance, even if it means further abandoning the pursuit of their beliefs. Though she has repeated examples of the dangers of internalizing Frank's insults and snaps, for example, his imperious demand that the "oddity" (Jane) should *"be quiet!"* (167), Jane's deep longing for the certainties of acceptance within her family, situated as a microcosm of the society from which she feels expelled, usually leads her to accept submission, whether before Frank's bullying sarcasm or Fielder's dictates. Despite Henry's claims that Jane has "labored to bestow on me that inestimable gift Self confidence!" his persistent low self-esteem often divorces the couple from potential resources of resistance (310).

A core Woldwinite principle is that sociability and sentiment can exist without descending into vicious decadence because of the expression of the mind's rational control. The stoic regulation of the mind and body becomes the mechanism for enabling and then controlling embodied passions. Yet Jane and Henry's disempowerment and inability to deploy reason to overcome prejudice mean that they increasingly depend on the epistolary as an autoerotic replacement for interpersonal (and hence social) communication. When Jane psychosomatically feels a pain where the absent Henry once touched her, she places his letter to her breast. But it is her own touch that warms her, rather than Henry's, and the letter becomes like a mesmeric *baquet*, a device that is meant to allow a cure through self-suggestion but that also operates like an instrument of erotic fetishism. Left alone, Jane increasingly sexualizes writing, for example, when she comments, "My desk is, of late, always open: my papers spread: my pen moist" (203). Writing becomes a spastic, compulsive, and isolating activity that, as with contemporaneous scares over masturbation, is conceptualized as draining the body's vital activity. Jane and Henry increasingly describe their writing not as composing thoughts for rational communication but— recalling the August 1800 "Scribbler" series, which anticipates the 1801 novels in this respect—as "scribbling" in the sense of a body unleashed from self-control. Henry then says that his repeated act of writing to Jane for hours results in his fatigued body being left "listless and spiritless" (271). The spurting mind's spillage leaves the mental and physical constitution spent.

As their writing becomes divorced from reason, the two become bereft of their own identity. Thus, they increasingly experience themselves as inauthentic. This loss of self-possession appears in the ease in with their own handwriting becomes forged by others in ways that misrepresent them before the world. The novel's active mystery is Mrs. Fielder's receipt of a letter purportedly written by Jane, which implies her adultery with Henry while Talbot still lived. Jane, on reviewing the letter, is befuddled about the slippage between what is said in the body of her text and the document's signature as verificatory sign of her authentic self.

Jane cannot feel entirely surprised at how quickly identity can slip away, since she has herself "counterfeit[ed] in a strange hand" (221) an envelope to trick Mrs. Fielder into reading a letter that she said she would not otherwise have read. Henry similarly feels distanced from and unfairly conjoined to his past letters about deism. What finally cements Jane's refusal to participate in Frank's speculations is not the loss of the money she needs for basic survival but her discovery that a virtuous act is worthless in the traffic of the public market. Going to collect a watch at an artisan's shop, she overhears one speculator croaking that Frank has paid him off with Jane's check, and she is outraged "that my name should be prostituted by the foul mouths of such wretches" (195). Upset at the trading of her name by these men in the shop, she refuses Frank any more money, in the hope that the end of currency will stop the circulation of her personal name. As she is amazed that her attempt of social prophylaxis fails, she learns the impossibility of putting her name back within a closed network of unsullied meanings, outside the glare of publicity.

As Jane and Henry increasingly realize the inability of writing by itself to repair society, as well as the fragility of letter writing as a safe space, they begin to seek out different strategies. The first effort, by Jane, is to revise her earlier notion of female-female benevolence by expanding its realm to include members of other classes. When Jane seeks out a laboring-class family after the 1797 yellow fever plague, she discovers that the woman, Mrs. Henning, has become widowed and is in need of housing. After Jane arranges for

Mrs. Henning to rent an apartment, she imagines that she may escape Mrs. Fielder's control by becoming Mrs. Henning's lodger. Considering the possibility of abandoning her social status by entering within this lower-class lifeworld, she revises her earlier faith in female community by extending it across classes. The potential for this intramural class alliance among women, however, is quickly blocked by two instances of renewed male aggression.

First, her brother, Frank, unexpectedly comes back to return the $1,500 he had divested from Jane. Because Frank never offers himself as reformed in any way, his inexplicable appearance instantly makes the arrangement with Mrs. Henning unnecessary, so the character now vanishes from the reader's consideration of this alternative. Frank's sudden departure suggests that Brown wishes to register the strength of the undertow that will prevent anyone from leaving the shore of middle-class rule.

The magnetism of inclusion within middle-class privilege is such that even Henry ultimately seeks it out and overlooks another possible alternative community of writers. Henry discovers that the forged letter that has the effect of blocking the couple's relationship was written by Jane's friend, Miss Jessup. This friend belongs to the same generation as Henry and Jane and shares with them a tenuous financial existence and status as an outsider who is rarely taken seriously as a thinker. Henry discovers from a servant that Miss Jessup is a hyperactive writer like himself and Jane, someone who wrote "well: fast: neatly" and "would make a good clerk," and was "much addicted to the pen.... Was always scribbling. Was never by herself three minutes but the pen was taken up: would write on any pieces of paper that offered: was frequently rebuked by her mother for wasting so much time in this way" (336–337). Yet despite Miss Jessup's similarity to the couple and her addiction to writing as economically nonproductive labor, Henry mercilessly demonizes her. After discovering her forgery, he rushes to confront her, even though she is ill (fatally, as it turns out). When she greets him with a complaint about her social isolation, Henry, instead of taking the hint of possible reconciliation, accuses her so fiercely that it overwhelms her. Insisting that she write a confession that will exculpate Jane, he demands Miss Jessup's signature, despite her cries of weakness, and will even manhandle her body to do it. "All I want, said [Henry], are but a few words. You cannot be at a loss for these. I will hold: I will guide your hand: I will write what you dictate.... I did not stay for her consent, but seizing the pen, put down hastily these words" (352).

The encounter between Miss Jessup and Henry is the dynamic climax of the novel, since it marks what Henry will sacrifice in order to be embraced by acceptable society. Bullying a bedridden Miss Jessup and forcing his will on her body, Henry enacts a symbolic, Carwin-like, equivalent of sexual coercion. Yet by violating not her actual body but her literary-mediated one, the body that writing creates, Henry's violence goes beyond the corporeal to smash the vision of social betterment that the medium of writing was taken to represent. It is no surprise, then, that he miscalculates the value of the confession, which is easily discounted. For by forcing Miss Jessup's hand and showing brutal disrespect for community among writers, he destroys the sanctuary where a collective of youthful resistance could potentially be inscribed. Forcing Miss Jessup to write *against* her written self, Henry gives the literary over to Mrs. Fielder's social oversight and approval. After this meeting, the promise of the literary shrinks, as shown by the novel's decreasing frequency of letters, rapidity of response, and completeness of description.

The damage comes not only with Henry's resort to an aggressive masculinity but also with his hierarchical class prejudice. Just as Jane had experimented with cross-class alliance, so, too, has Miss Jessup. The latter's servant, Tom, is also "very fond of reading and writing" (337). But neither familiarity among writers, here between Tom and Miss Jessup, nor the creation of a literary world not defined by class relations can occur. Henry's bullying of Miss Jessup and his inability to imagine nonbourgeois culture follow a previous act in which he forced another woman to give up writing. When he visits the servant Mrs. Secker to extract a piece of Miss Jessup's handwriting that would confirm the forgery, his forcefulness overwhelms her: she "denied and confessed alternately that she had possessed some of Miss Jessup's writing: at length she began to weep very bitterly" (337). When Mrs. Secker complains of her treatment by Miss Jessup (an accusation that might also embed one against her other former employer, Henry, who had previously dismissed her for petty theft of a silk cravat and stockings, the vestimentary markers of his social rank), Henry opines, "It was always disagreeable to me to listen to the slanderous prate of servants: I am careful, whenever it intrudes itself, to discourage and rebuke it" But due to his resentment of Miss Jessup, he allows the maid "to run on in a tedious and minute detail of the capricious, peevish, and captious deportment of Miss Jessup" (333). However, Henry's brusque and moralized refusal to sympathize with Mrs. Secker (or Miss Jessup) destroys any potential alternative social links that Jane might have created. While the young women tentatively handle the fabric of cross-class connection, Henry increasingly insists on validating himself as a master in order to counter Mrs. Fielder on her terms.

Thus, if the weakened position of progressive ideals is *Jane Talbot's* theme, Brown's analysis is that bourgeois dissident ideals ultimately failed because their proponents were not willing to extend their critique of aristocratic-inflected gender relations into ones about emerging class differences. *Jane Talbot* ends in a generic comedy plot of matrimony, but its "happy end" occurs after Henry's eschatological transformation, in which he divests himself of any feature of challenge to authority that his marriage to Jane would previously have represented. As Henry transforms himself from being a weak marginal to a muscular success, *Jane Talbot* finally becomes his Bildungsroman insofar as he becomes a man of Christian-legitimized, nationalist capitalism.

Jane Talbot's conclusion chronologically spins out over the years, but in accordance with the shriveling of the literary, the delay is marked by only a handful of letters. Stymied by the failure of Miss Jessup's confession to effect change and restore his reputation, Henry joins his his brother-in-law's commercial expedition to China. In his absence, his sister, who has established contact with Jane, informs her that her brother-in-law, Montford, has returned with news that the ship's crew mutinied against him and Henry and that Henry abandoned ship on a desert isle. Four years later, he returns to America after having been rescued and taken to Tokyo. In what may be the first American literary description of pre-Perry Japan, Henry describes its inhabitants in savagelike terms that might have been otherwise applied to Native Americans (425–425). This turn indicates that the attitudes of domestic settler colonialism are being prepared for use and extension for early American imperialism.

Jane, too, in her own way, joins with an outlook of nationalism and imperialism. While Henry is away, she purchases "maps and charts and books of voyages" (412) to study. These "displays of Shoal, Sand-bank, and Water" stand as another eroticized outline of where Henry's body might be. Yet as her "freakish and perverse" fancy turns to a new "attachment to Geography" as a substitute for Henry's letters, which she can no longer receive, she begins to replace the "emotion and empathy" of informal interpersonal contact with the study of the sea links between nations (Brückner 2012, 192–193). By internalizing the coordinates of nineteenth-century nation-statism and imperial sea adventures, she intertwines her desire for Henry with the logbooks of the capitalist world-system.

Likewise, Henry finally leaves Japan when a Dutch East India trader takes him to Hamburg. In Germany, he accidentally meets Jane's new suitor, Cartwright, who, after discovering Henry's identity, dutifully gives up his claim on Jane. On learning of Jane's whereabouts, Henry heads home, but not before writing to his brother-in-law that he has been physically and psychologically changed. He claims that the hardships of the journey have made his body more muscular and allowed his mind to accept religion, "the living and delightful consciousness of every tie that can bind man to his divine parent and judge" (427). Declaiming his "past misconduct" and "depth of my former degeneracy" (428), Henry is scoured of his former deistic beliefs, which he now regards as a disability of effeminacy and degeneracy. The novel's final letter, from Jane to Henry, relates how Jane has been befriended by the Montfords, his sister and her husband, and mentions a deathbed confession by Miss Jessup to Mrs. Fielder about her fraud that, in turn, allows Mrs. Fielder's deathbed benediction of Henry and Jane's union and Jane's complete inheritance of Mrs. Fielder's fortune.

The conditions for this domestic conclusion and confirmation of bourgeois security rest on the pair's acceptance not simply of the form of increasingly dominant nationalist civil society but its content as well. Against Henry's early radicalism lie the older regulatory authorities of Mrs. Fielder and Talbot as an iron cage of mercantile industry and lack of intellectual enthusiasm. Unable to mount a challenge to this refrigeration of a radical politics and sentimental erotics, Henry believes he has two options of reaction: he can accentuate his marginality through awkwardness, triviality, isolation, and bodily self-destruction (as do so many of Brown's romance characters), or he can himself embrace the violent militancy of capitalist acquisition. He chooses the latter.

When the merchant ship mutinies, it illustrates Henry's increasing distance from community with the laboring or craft classes, and his travels through the East is his baptism into authority or regeneration through the work of mercantile accumulation. It is noteworthy that, on Henry's trip home, the midpoint of his return is not Jacobin Paris but the trading port of Hamburg. His youthful radicalism is replaced by the perceived maturity of normalcy, where literary energy laced with erotic desire is given over to unenthusiastic geniality, the personalized informality of those who feel they have nothing to contest. Mrs. Fielder can finally give her blessing to the couple's marriage, not only because the coupling of Jane and Henry no longer carries any threat of social turbulence but also because their early resistance actually better prepared them to adopt the nascent forms of nationalist capitalism that the prior generation of middle class, like Talbot or Mrs. Fielder, would still have found challenging.

Returning to Philadelphia, Henry settles among a young generation consisting of his brother-in-law Montford, Harriet (the sister of Henry's early friend, Thomson), and Jane's third suitor, Cartwright. This new community is superficially the ideal of shared sentiments that the novel strove for at its beginning, except that this new constituency has replaced the previous experimental intellectual and literary milieu with a contented reflection of normative society. The fractious young world that included the deist Thomson and the independent and amateur writer Miss Jessup has (literally) died and been replaced by the conservative harmony of the Montfords' world, where youth has been stripped of oppositional energy. The consolidation of this generation is actually tragic, because its fraternity does not mean anything other than smoothly fitting in with dominant social currents; its newness is bereft of any utopian transformation. Henry's previous dread about his authenticity is replaced by the bovine contentment of one who has the assurances of a predetermined curriculum vitae and the benefits awarded to one who never needs to disturb the shallows of his mental coast. The novel ends with Jane's apostasy against what she had earlier called "our hopes and opinions." Declaring that she can "write no more" (431), she now gives over feminine expression and self-ownership to Henry's patriarchal control. The plan of gender equality is erased in favor of more conventional social patterns.

Jane Talbot and *Clara Howard* end categorically with the realization that the philosophical projects of the radical Enlightenment and 1790s that challenged the eighteenth-century regime were not able to compete with free-market liberalism, disciplinary normalization, and nationalist imperialism. While Godwin, Wollstonecraft, and their associated writers could critique the old regime, they poorly perceived the onset of distinctively new forces that would become dominant. The ideals of the 1790s were thus better understood as a response to the past than as preparation for the future.

Consequently, readers have misunderstood *Jane Talbot*'s "badness." Brown's novels ultimately stand as both a record of the shifting composition of power within the early national period and a sign of the novel form's failure to withstand its own incorporation within nation-statist liberalism. If Brown seems to abandon the romance form with which he is still primarily identified (during the same years in which Godwin did as well), this retraction seems less a sign of any creative exhaustion than the reverse, an articulation of heightened awareness of the novel's vastly decreased efficacy to convey the recent past's ideals of social betterment within a society swiftly abandoning those ideals. Brown's renewed focus on journalism and interest in historico-geographical writing in particular stands as his search for a more effective form of creative politics in the new century. Since Brown did not live long enough to fully develop these modes of nonnovelistic literary communication, the full potential for these pathways remains open for consideration.

WORKS CITED

Bieri, James. *Percy Bysshe Shelley: A Biography, Exile of Unfulfilled Reknown, 1816–1822*. Newark: University of Delaware Press, 2005.

Brückner, Martin. *The Geographic Revolution in Early American: Maps, Literacy, and National Identity*. Chapel Hill: University of North Carolina Press, 2012.

Brückner, Martin. "Sense, Census, and the "Statistical View." In Philip Barnard, Mark L. Kamrath, and Stephen Shapiro, eds., *Revising Charles Brockden Brown: Culture, Politics and Sexuality in the Early Republic*, 289–309. Knoxville: University of Tennessee Press, 2004.

Burleigh, Erica. "Incommensurate Equivalences: Genre, Representation, and Equity in *Clara Howard* and *Jane Talbot*." *Early American Studies* 9.3 (Fall 2011): 748–780.

Ellenberger, Henri F. *The Discovery of the Unconscious: The History and Evolution of Dynamic Psychiatry*. London: Fontana, 1970.

Krause, Sydney J. "*Clara Howard* and *Jane Talbot*: Godwin on Trial." In Bernard Rosenthal, ed., *Critical Essays on Charles Brockden Brown*, 184–211. Boston: G. K. Hall, 1981.

Peacock, Thomas Love. *Peacock's Memoirs of Shelley with Shelley's Letters to Peacock*. H. F. B. Brett-Smith, ed. London: Henry Foude, 1909.

Regourd, François. "Mesmerism in Saint Domingue: Occult Knowledge and Vodou on the Eve of the Haitian Revolution." In James Delbourgo and Nicholas Dew, eds., *Science and Empire in the Atlantic World*, 311–322. London: Routledge, 2008.

Ringe, Donald A. "Historical Essay." In Charles Brockden Brown, *Clara Howard; in a Series of Letters with Jane Talbot, a Novel*, Sydney J. Krause and S. W. Reid, eds., 433–474. Kent, Ohio: Kent State University Press, 1986.

Shapiro, Stephen. " 'I Could Kiss Him One Minute and Kill Him the Next!': The Limits of Radical Male Friendship in Holcroft, C. B. Brown, and Wollstonecraft Shelley." In Walter Göbel, Saskia Schabio, and Martin Windisch, eds., *Engendering Images of Man in the Long Eighteenth Century*, 111–132. Trier: Wissenschaftlicher Verlag, 2001.

Shelley, Mary. *The Journals of Mary Shelley, 1814–1844*, Vol. 1. Paula R. Feldman and Diana Scott-Kilvert, eds. Oxford: Clarendon Press, 1987.

Shelley, Mary. *The Letters of Mary Wollstonecraft Shelley*, Vol. 1. Betty T. Bennett, ed. Baltimore: Johns Hopkins University Press, 1980.

Witherington, Paul. "Brockden Brown's Other Novels: *Clara Howard* and *Jane Talbot*." *Nineteenth-Century Fiction* 29.3 (December 1974): 257–272.

PART III

THE HISTORY-
FICTION NEXUS

CHAPTER 10

....

HISTORY, ROMANCE,
AND THE NOVEL

....

GRETCHEN J. WOERTENDYKE

"WHEN a writer calls his work a Romance," writes Nathaniel Hawthorne in his preface to *The House of the Seven Gables* (1851), "it need hardly be observed that he wishes to claim a certain latitude, both as to its fashion and material, which he would not have felt himself entitled to assume, had he professed to be writing a Novel." More than half a century after Charles Brockden Brown, Hawthorne's defense of romance against the novel, which he characterizes as like "sticking a pin through a butterfly," became a canonical theme for twentieth-century Americanist scholarship.[1] But Hawthorne's commitment to, and theory of, romance owes much to the influence of Brown's romances, his editorial writing, and his early essays on forms of history. Brown's fascination with romance cast the foundation for American Renaissance writers such as Hawthorne, Edgar Allan Poe, Washington Irving, and Herman Melville to build upon.[2] The mixture of historical self-consciousness, social critique, and philosophical depth that Brown assumes from Woldwinite writers such as William Godwin and Mary Wollstonecraft is what authors and critics came most to identify with the American genre.[3] Horace Walpole, working to define a "new species of romance"—as a blend of "the ancient and the modern"—early on established a language with which writers such as Brown could imagine a history without history and represent truth in fictional form (Walpole 7). So while Hawthorne defined romance against the novel, Brown used the category of history to chart the features and possibilities of romance.

This is in part because by the mid-nineteenth century, Hawthorne's romances were theorized and understood *as* forms of history, rather than as "marvelous stories" or Gothic tales, with their recognizable departure from reality. In the wake of the rise and proliferation of realistic prose fiction in the eighteenth century, the concept of the fictional existed as such for the first time.[4] The publication of Daniel Defoe's *Robinson Crusoe* (1719) helped to establish what Lennard Davis calls the "news/novels" matrix.[5] Once a distinction between the novel (fiction) and the news (fact) became a commonplace, fiction faced other sorts of obstacles in defining its moral, purpose, and audience. The conditions of possibility for romance emerged in this late-eighteenth-century context. In the early American and French revolutionary context, one in which suspicions over the immorality of the novel remained, authors such as Brown and Godwin adorned fiction with history first and foremost to authorize forms of fiction. Unlike the novel, which traveled the path forged by Defoe toward philosophical and representational mimesis, romance offered writers expansive imaginative license and provided the possibility for new theories of fiction and history. Modern romance arises out of ways of understanding and mediating history, the conjectural history of Scottish Enlightenment figures such as David Hume, Adam Ferguson, Dugald Stewart, and Adam Smith and the philosophical history of Godwin. After the rise of the novel and self-consciousness of the romance, the form became a Walpolean blend between Old and New World histories. Romance is for Brown the *only* genre of historical writing in which readers might make past peoples and events approximate their own contemporary moments and their own projection of a future existence.[6]

For Brown, fiction was singularly capable of interpreting the chaotic conditions of modern life while also creating a prehistory of the new nation. If historians were to describe verifiable events, limited by the discrete connection between time and place, then Brown's romancer relied on conjecture. "How wide, then," he writes, "if romance be the narrative of mere probabilities, is the empire of romance?" (Difference 253). Such expansiveness allowed Brown not only to explore eighteenth-century concerns about female education, immigration, slavery, revolution, and citizenship but also to create possible futures wherein varying outcomes, and their impacts, might be tested against the individual and the nation. Unlike Enlightenment historiography and, later, the realist novel, romance is utterly unmoored by verisimilitude, providing a space for experimentation and the opportunity to trace the paths of various hypotheses, back and forth in time.

This chapter looks at Brown's fictional-historical essays—from early works such as "The Rhapsodist" (1789) and "Walstein's School of History" (1799) to later statements on romance such as "The Difference between History and Romance" (1800), "Romances" (1805), and "Terrific Novels" (1805)—in order to explain how he draws on Enlightenment conjectural history and Godwinian philosophical history to develop a coherent and far-reaching theory of fiction. In Brown's system, temporal freedom allows the romancer a capacity to sympathize with the conditions of modernity, out of which every action must be weighed against its various possible outcomes. This spirit of invention situates Brown neatly within his late-Enlightenment context, as he adapts Scottish conjectural history to the different conditions of the United States and makes possible a New World romance. His remarkably contemporary theories remap early national prose across popular, historical, and philosophical registers; perhaps most especially, they reframe the way we understand American Renaissance writers such as James Fenimore Cooper, Irving, and Hawthorne.[7]

I. Everyday History

Brown's earliest published writings reveal a commitment to historical representation, inaugurating a lifelong attempt to determine the role of fiction in any portrayal of historical truth.[8] *The Columbian Magazine, or, Monthly Miscellany* published Brown's first essay, "The Rhapsodist," in four monthly instalments from August through November 1789. Brown, then eighteen years old and just beginning a career in law with Alexander Wilcocks, wrote in imitation of the popular essays found in *The Spectator*, under the fictional persona "the rhapsodist." What we might identify as the fictional-historical essay labors to account for the complex social, philosophical, and political problems of the early nineteenth century; it becomes the form of mediation he returns to throughout his career as a novelist, editor, essayist, and theorist. In this first essay, however, Brown only briefly sketches the larger concerns that come to dominate most of his writing and, instead, considers the life of an author. In "The Rhapsodist," Brown introduces a coy, unnamed narrator, staging strategies of concealment and disclosure around what it means to be an author and what responsibilities he should carry for readers. In it, too, are the outlines of concerns that appear in his later writing, including discernment, truth, prejudice, custom, and the importance of translating the most sophisticated tenets of Enlightenment thought into "the ease and convenience of organs of speech" (Rhapsodist 467).

Although Brown hides behind a fictional character, his narrator's central preoccupation is with being truthful, despite having readers who are "willing to be deceived" (465). The rhapsodist is concerned most with a work's "unity of design," which is only to be found through mimesis—"as they have really passed before the eyes of the describer"— in the "artless and unpremeditated language" of the author (467).[9] His focus here is on reason as a prerequisite of representing truth in its most authentic form, which in turn "confirm[s] the reasoning" (467). For Brown, an *idea* of truth governs the rhapsodist and is achieved by the poet or theologian who retreats into nature for solitary thought. The idea of excellence that Brown imagines is drawn from Cicero and becomes the inspiration for many of his characters, including Clara, Pleyel, and Theodore in his later *Wieland; or, The Transformation* (1798). These characters, like the rhapsodist, must have the inclination and capacity to strive toward an unattainable truth, even if what is produced is only a "mere exaggerated copy, taken injudiciously from some true original" (Rhapsodist 539).

But the rhapsodist's contemplations are inchoate, vacillating between a longing for freedom apart from the material conditions of a society that makes authorship impossible—"the melancholy fate of castle builders" (540)—and a theory of history and of storytelling that requires the writer to abstract himself from present conditions in order to fully comprehend the contemporary moment in a longue durée. Brown's emphasis on temporality becomes the foundation, and theory, of romance as the vehicle singularly capable of mediating, representing, and resolving the conditions of early national crises for American readers and writers. According to Brown:

> We are too much interested in the scene that passes before us to believe it unreal. The conclusion of every act, and the final catastrophe of the drama, affect much more nearly than the fading colours of a vision, and the unsubstantial images of sleep. But perhaps it is necessary to abstract our attention from surrounding objects, to transport ourselves some million of years forward from the present date of our existence, in order to form a rational conception of the present life, and of our own resemblance to the phantom of a dream.   (538)

Only through imagining a future are we able to comprehend, and make rational judgments about, contemporary existence. Brown yokes this possibility of understanding the present in its relation to the past and the future to his concern with the interiority of human experience as it negotiates "the final catastrophe of the drama" in the language of romance. Only through abstraction are we to recognize *ourselves* in the drama unfolding, and only through prolepsis are such abstractions made possible.

The resemblance between Brown's earliest attempts to describe the work of the romancer as both separate from and more sophisticated than that of the historian and Godwin's descriptions of the same is uncanny.[10] Godwin's fascination with the individual's motivations is one Brown shared and is most visible in his romances. Like Brown, Godwin believed romance was better suited to represent truth than the narratives produced by historians. The purpose of true history (romance), for Godwin, was to help individuals to make sense of "the machine of society" (Godwin 1988, 362). This required the study of minute features that make up common people's lives. By avoiding the historian's propensity for abstraction and grand narratives of state and nation, the romancer was free to uncover the authentic motivations of men and, thus, the mechanism whereby power was so meticulously preserved. Godwin writes: "Laying aside the generalities of historical abstraction, we must mark the operation of human passions; must observe the empire of motives whether groveling or elevated; and must note the influence that one human being exercises over another, and the ascendancy of the daring and the wise over the vulgar multitude." He concludes, "It is thus, and thus only, that we shall be enabled to add, to the knowledge of the past, a sagacity that can penetrate into the depths of futurity" (Godwin 1988, 363). Unlike Brown's call to "abstract our attention" in order to project ourselves into the imaginary future, Godwin's use of "abstraction" suggests linearity, objectivity, and facticity, an abstraction that fails to comprehend the messiness of human agency within networks of power.[11]

Godwin's belief in romance as authentic history, however, is undermined by his conviction that "to write a romance is a task too great for the powers of man," for "to tell precisely how such a person would act in a given situation, requires a sagacity scarcely less than divine" (Godwin 1988, 372). Brown avoids this retreat from romance, and Godwin's polarizing thought process, in two important ways: first, he turns away from the universalizing impulse of Godwin, whose faith in the "system of the universe" supersedes the local, or regional, laws that dictate Brown's theory; and second, rather than adopting the Enlightenment dialectics of Godwin's essay, Brown thematizes this tension between romance and history telling across the broad range of his writing. Brown's preface "To the Public" in *Edgar Huntly* (1799), for example, remains a feature of early American literary nationalism for critics. The preface states:

> America has opened new views to the naturalist and politician, but has seldome fur-
> nished themes to the moral painter. That new springs of action, and new motives to
> curiosity should operate; that the field of investigation, opened to us by our own
> country, should differ essentially from those which exist in Europe, may be readily
> conceived. The sources of amusement to the fancy and instruction to the heart, that
> are peculiar to ourselves, are equally numerous and inexhaustible. It is the purpose
> of this work to profit by some of these sources; to exhibit a series of adventures,
> growing out of the condition of our country, and connected with one of the most
> common and most wonderful diseases or affections of the human frame.   (EH 3)

The "moral painter" or romancer, Brown offers, has ample materials out of which to create his tale; moreover, such a tale must be drawn from the regional conditions of the writer, "incidents of Indian hostility" in *Edgar Huntly*. Faithful to those details "peculiar to ourselves" and therefore essentially distinctive from Europe, Brown's preface theorizes the fictional-historical romance as contingent upon the topography, and humanity, of a region just outside of Philadelphia. Recent critical assessments by Meredith McGill, Lloyd Pratt, and Trish Loughran insist that we attend to local economies, regional identities, and what Loughran calls "nation-fragments" over and beyond Benedict Anderson's monolithic nation-novel paradigm. "[I]t was not the connectedness of early American print cultures or the commonness of common texts that enabled U.S. founding," Loughran reminds us, "but instead the very localness of early print cultures that made founding possible in the first place" (Loughran 10–11). Rather than making him the father of the American novel, then, Brown's novelistic and essayistic fictions suggest a profound influence on the formation of the regional romance.

Perspectival uncertainty, the incapacity to represent truth, and a suspicion about language more generally become central themes around which most of the Brown archive coheres. Again, the example of *Edgar Huntly* is instructive. The tale opens, as does *Wieland*, with a narrator who complies with a request to tell a story; each relates horrific incidents that defy belief and thwart the teller's ability to make sense of, or write clearly about, the facts. *Edgar Huntly* echoes "The Rhapsodist" when the narrator explains, "Till now, to hold a steadfast pen was impossible; to disengage my senses from the scene that was passing or approaching; to forbear to grasp at futurity … could not be" (EH 5). As in the earlier essay, Brown suggests that distance, whether temporal, physical, or imaginative, is a necessary precursor to analytical thought and the kind of reasoning that allows for futurity.

The explicit concerns raised by Godwin in his theoretical essay characterize the actions, motivations, and descriptions narrated in Brown's romance. When, for instance, the narrator of *Edgar Huntly* suggests that "[i]n proportion as I gain power over words, shall I lose dominion over sentiments; in proportion as my tale is deliberate and slow, the incidents and motives which it is designed to exhibit will be imperfectly revived and obscurely pourtrayed" (EH 5–6), Brown highlights the delicate balance between knowing, feeling, and telling so foundational to his theory of romance and history. In *Edgar Huntly*, as in most of his writing, Brown both enacts and theorizes aesthetic experience at once, producing a form of cosmopolitanism previously unavailable to early American readers. Brown yokes eighteenth-century British Enlightenment theories of history, from Hume, Stewart, and Smith, to a form of regionalism wholly dependent on the topographical and sociopolitical locale of Brown's Philadelphia. By making geography generative, Brown offers what Ezra Tawil calls a "jagged American aesthetic," which, while related to Godwin's own developing sense of philosophical romance as bound up with an imaginary future and beyond conjectural histories of the present, cannot be entirely subsumed by either one (Tawil 120).

II. THE REGIONAL ROMANCE

By the time Brown published "Walstein's School of History," in *The Monthly Magazine, and American Review* (1799), his ideas about the form and purpose of romance acquired the narratological depth of his longer fiction, combined with the rhetorical power and clarity of his progressive philosophy. Published contemporaneously with the first part of *Arthur Mervyn; or, Memoirs of the Year 1793* (1799–1800), the essay is a multilayered fiction, which draws from Friedrich Schiller's moral and political philosophy, as well as German romanticism more generally. In it, Brown constructs the model intellectual environment, led by the fictional professor of history at Jena, Walstein (modeled on Schiller), whose two books, histories on the life of Cicero and the Marquis of Pombal, provide the basis for a select group of attentive students' tutorial. Through the voice of Walstein, Brown characterizes the historian's methodology as inventive when scant details are available in order to deepen the insights, issues, and progress of the story. The historian aims "[t]o illuminate the understanding…charm curiosity, and sway the passions" through his "copiously displayed and artfully linked" scenes (Walstein 337). To achieve this, the true historian must "assume the person of Cicero" in order to illustrate the kinds of connections between individual and society, out of which "truth flows" (337, 407). The somewhat paradoxical method requires the historian to act as if he *were* the subject (Cicero), so that "events" might be "artfully linked" and which, if done well, would produce a greater truth. This truth does not come from mimesis or transcription of dates and occurrences but, rather, through art, or the inventive agency of the writer.

Through the figure of Walstein, Brown articulates relations of parts to whole, meant to supplant the kinds of "abstract systems, and theoretical reasonings" to which a richly complex human history is frequently reduced. More important, for Brown, such abstractions flatten the experiences of the varied parts—those individuals in the larger society for whom representation is scarcely considered or provided. It is this aspect of Brown's Walstein essay, his sense of sociopolitical reform intertwined with his aesthetic theory, that educates his reader. "Walstein's School of History" illustrates a tension between the different parts (such as the nine students "more assiduous in their attention" to Walstein than the "negligent and heedless crowd" [335]) but simultaneously works to minimize sociopolitical hierarchies. More to the point, the historian must recognize distinctions without prejudice and without such distinctions dictating the subject or method of historiography. The historian, and thus, Walstein rejoins: "[T]hough few may be expected to be monarchs and ministers, every man occupies a station in society in which he is necessarily active to evil or to good" (408). Brown's attention to other stations highlights the degree to which the many parts are more influential than monarchs and ministers on the entire social fabric.

The implications of these passages for historical writing, and, by extension, for sociopolitical reform, are stark and put into relief many of the critical debates about Brown's political leanings, especially entrenched since Steven Watts's infamous segregation of the pre- and post-1800 publications.[12] Far less visible, however, are the implications for Brown's theory of romance. His return to romance here is subtle compared with other points in the essay, but nevertheless, it reinforces his idea that true histories are provincial, cleaving to the site of proximate influence and located in an identifiable region. In acknowledging that sites of power exert great influences over many, Brown writes: "It may seem best to purify the fountain, rather than filter the stream; but the latter is, to a certain degree, within our power, whereas, the former is impracticable" (Walstein 408). Real change cannot happen at the source but is possible at its outer reaches. Brown's mixed metaphor—the fountain and the stream—hints at Old World art forms in contrast to the natural world of the new republic; moreover, it underscores his belief that truth, reform, history, and romance need to be rooted in local geography, even written by local writers, and concerned with local readers.

Brown's "romantic" view of writing history depends on the local topography foremost because it comes to symbolize the heart of its people and the sympathies of the historian's readers. The sympathetic capacity of the historian generates an intimacy with the past, an intimacy that parallels the private histories within families and creates the conditions of possibility for engaging the common reader. This romantic sensibility makes the common reader, and the popular, a constitutive part of the romancer. The role Brown imagines for the literary overall is quite expansive and is utterly bound up with popular conceptions. Returning to "Walstein's School of History," "There are two ways in which genius and virtue may labour for the public good," Brown argues, "first by assailing popular errors and vices, argumentatively and through the medium of books; secondly, by employing legal or ministerial authority to this end" (338). Brown concludes by indicting Cicero and Pombal for their failure to recognize the essential power and reach of literature and for neglecting to speak to and about the broadest possible audience: "Their fate may evince the insufficiency of the instrument chosen by them, and teach us, that a change of national opinion is the necessary prerequisite of revolutions" (338). Attending to the stream rather than the fountain and marking public histories with the language of privacy, Brown illustrates the revolutionary potential of literature to alter the national sociopolitical landscape.

Brown's belief in the ideological function of literature situates him quite neatly within the contemporary debates over its role and power on both sides of the Atlantic in the late eighteenth century. In the wake of the French Terror of 1793, literature increasingly came to be considered a dangerous weapon if wielded by the wrong hands. The Alien and Sedition Acts of 1798 in the United States and the suspension of habeas corpus in England put writers and print under surveillance in ways that encouraged them to adopt literary strategies as alibis for sociopolitical beliefs. The rise and popularity of the Gothic romance in the 1790s might be understood as an outgrowth of social tensions and fear over the violence manifested by Jacobinism. As William Hazlitt hints, the "gothic vogue fed off the revolutionary anxieties of its readership" (cited in Miles 2002, 44).[13] In T. J. Mathias's deeply conservative and satirical poem *The Pursuits of Literature* (1798), for example, he lampoons Matthew Lewis's *The Monk: A Romance* (1796) as "a new species of legislative or state-patricide."[14] Mathias's remarkable conflation between literature and violence against the state is of a piece with widely read anti-Jacobin literature in the period, including Edmond Burke's *Letters on a Regicide Peace* (1795), the *Anti-Jacobin Review*, and the government-sponsored *British Critic*. In the United States, counterrevolutionary writers such as William Cobbett writing as Peter Porcupine adopted similar rhetorical strategies in order to encourage paranoia and fear over a host of radical possibilities.[15]

Mathias, like Cobbett, believed that literature had the power to create, shape, and ultimately destroy nations. In the third part of *The Pursuits of Literature*, he writes: "Wherever the freedom of the press exists, (and with us may that freedom be perpetual!) I must assert that Literature, well or ill conducted, is the great engine by which, I am fully persuaded, all civilized states must ultimately be supported or overthrown" (III: 1). The deluge of counterrevolutionary criticism coincided with the new, national sanctions to the same "free speech" Mathias claimed to support. In addition to the suspension of habeas corpus, the "great engine" of literature, which included Thomas Paine's much maligned *Rights of Man* (1791–1792), led to the treason trials of radical writers such as Paine and members of the London Corresponding Society, including its secretary, Thomas Hardy. Mathias, Cobbett, and Burke feared replication of 1793 and French revolutionary ideals on British and American soil. And, as Burke wrote during the nascent French Revolution in *Reflections on the Revolution in France* (1790), literary writers were in no small part responsible for the broad appeal of Jacobinism. These debates throughout British and American print culture in the 1790s existed in the "discursive shadow" of the Gothic, which made the genre's "terror" pregnant with radical and dangerous implications for the stability of the nation (Miles 2002, 46).

What becomes customary in literary and political discourse in the late eighteenth century, from both sides of the political divide, is the conviction that Gothic romance and Jacobinism were one and the same. This conflation is made possible because of a broad and acute fear of the relationship between the popular and large-scale violence against the nation-state. The French Revolution, as the most terrifying illustration of this link, functions as the engine out of which Gothic anxieties were produced and consumed by late-eighteenth-century writers, readers, and literary critics. Such convictions make Brown's appeal to the common reader seem radical, however, by framing romance as the ideal instantiation of history. In place of Jacobin excesses, Brown invites readers to reimagine revolution in its most "romantic" valences, as productive of the new nation, rife with democratic possibilities. To be sure, Brown's romances and later writing make visible the unpleasant possibilities as well, often staging national horrors as private histories, as in the case of the Wieland family. Nevertheless, in the internal dynamics of its plot and the fate of its characters, Brown's work imparts a sense of urgency about the common reader and his ability to adjudicate between imaginary and real worlds.

III. Description and Interpretation: The Science of Romance

In "The Difference between History and Romance," published in *The Monthly Magazine, and American Review* (2.4, April 1800), Brown takes up the assumptions about what distinguishes the two forms, namely "truth" and "fiction," in order to argue for the romancer as the superior observer, conjecturer, and overall scientist of human behavior. The essay argues that while such differences between history-as-truth and romance-as-fiction seem reasonable as theories, these suppositions fall apart when put into practice. This is the result of readers' natural tendency to conjecture, regardless of whether the narratives are "fictitious" or "true." Since true narratives often relate events and conditions fairly unknown, the reader becomes "prone to arrange them anew, and to deviate from present and sensible objects, into speculations on the past or future" (Difference 251). Put another way, true histories inevitably turn the common reader *into* a romancer. So while the historian "carefully watches, and faithfully enumerates the appearances which occur," the romancer, whether writer or reader, "adorns these appearances with cause and effect, and traces resemblances between the past, distant, and future, with the present" (251). He is a "dealer...in probabilities" rather than certainties.

Using the example of Mount Vesuvius's volcanic eruption, Brown claims for the historian only the "noises, the sights, and the smells" of the event; but the romancer's role is far more complicated and three-dimensional. Most fascinating is that the romancer is deemed the true scientist, the chronicler who describes, predicts, and stratifies enormously sophisticated events, such as a volcanic eruption, and their consequences for human existence across geographic and temporal regions. He describes, first, "the *contemporary* ebullitions and inflations, the combustion and decomposition that take place in the bowels of the earth," before exploring "the origin of things...the centrical, primary, and secondary orbs composing the universe, as masses thrown out of an immense volcano called *chaos*" (251–252; emphasis in original). In this way, historians "catalog" while romancers "arrange" and "dispose" ultimately to "inform you," the reader, about causes and effects. Brown's romancer par excellence is Sir Isaac Newton, and the essay is arguably Brown's least romantic and most dispassionately argued statement on the superiority of romance as narrative history. Nowhere is this more apparent than when Brown explains the mutually constitutive relations of actions and human motivations:

> The motive is the cause, and therefore the antecedent of the action; but the action is likewise the cause of subsequent actions. Two contemporary and (so to speak) adjacent actions may both be faithfully described, because both may be witnessed; but the connection between them, that quality which constitutes one the effect of the other, is mere matter of conjecture, and comes with the province, not of *history*, but *romance*.   (252–253; emphasis in original)

The romancer is singularly capable of blending these fundamental characteristics of historical method—description and interpretation—essential for linking each moment within the expansive arc of human existence. Only the romancer comprehends that "[t]he delineation of tendencies and motives implies a description of the action; but the action is describable without the accompaniment of tendencies and motives" (253). An important distinction between Brown's earlier essay "Walstein's School of History" and "The Difference between History and Romance" lies with his conception of the reader. In the former, the reader *is* a romancer; here, the reader justifies the romancer's methodology. In the absence of blending description and interpretation, the "mind of the reader" is vulnerable to misinterpretation, the narrative gap wherein historical and human error can thrive. "The writer," Brown concludes, "who does not blend the two characters, is essentially defective" (253).

Brown is responding to a tension between the "moral" and the "tendency" of writing, introduced by Godwin's "Of Choice in Reading," which appeared in *The Enquirer* in 1797. Godwin argues that we mistake literature's "moral" for its "tendency" to the detriment of writers but, more important, of readers: "the true moral and fair inference from a composition has often lain concealed for ages from its most diligent readers" (Godwin 1797, 135). While the moral is "that ethical stance . . . which the work may most aptly be applied," the tendency is "the actual effect it is calculated to produce upon the reader" and which the writer cannot completely predict or control. This lack of control over a work's tendency is the result of the unknowable "mind of the reader" (136). This is why, for Godwin, "the moral of a work is a point of very subordinate consideration, and that the only thing worthy of much attention is the tendency" (137). So while Brown and Godwin share a conviction about the principal importance of the reader, Brown aims to assert authorial agency in order to better manage the consequence and effect of a work on its reader. For Brown, the historian merely "supplying the builder with materials" leaves too much to chance; but the romancer "hews these stones into just proportions, and piles them up into convenience and magnificent fabrics" (Difference 253). He interprets and shapes the raw materials, presenting an ideal blend of action and motivation, and guides the reader toward the desired effect. Brown's "empire of romance" is "absolute and undivided over the motives and tendencies of human actions" and even has "very extensive" power over "actions themselves" (253).

More explicit than the nascent formulations in "The Rhapsodist" but gesturing toward "Walstein's School of History," Brown's letters to his friend Joseph Bringhurst, Jr. (1767–1834) illustrate how deeply and personally his faith in the fictional as the most apt vehicle for truth actually was. A fellow student of Robert Proud's Friends Latin School, Bringhurst engaged in a "poetical correspondence" with Brown and Elihu Hubbard Smith in *The Gazette of the United States* throughout 1791.[16] Writing under the pen name "Birtha," Bringhurst, who joined Brown as a member of the Society for the Advancement of Useful Knowledge, frequently expressed concern over education and literacy, partic- ularly over readers' capacity to discern value and truth. But Brown expanded on these general concerns provocatively in his letter to Bringhurst of December 21, 1792. In it, he compares the relative fictionality of Samuel Richardson's *The History of Sir Charles Grandison* (1753) and the Bible. He proposes, "If I ask what is the gospel history more than a Romance, will you not be startled?" Brown then justifies at some length why the question is, to some extent, irrelevant:

> But why should a question startle you which, however it be answered, is of no importance. As a lesson of instruction it is indifferent to me whether the Subject of this narrative be a real or fictitious being. This question would be indeed important, if it related to one who is supposed to have lived in my own time, and within the reach of my own immediate observation; because If it were true, I should then be a witness of those actions, and consequently, be more benefited by the example, but since this narrative is the only proof of his existence since he is seen and known by me only as he is represented here, the truth of the tale is in reality an objection to it, for this narrative is useful to me, only as it furnishes incitements to and sets before an object of imitation, were it a romance, the picture would probably have been more accurate and uniform, and this is it, that renders it less instructive to me, than the history of Grandison.   (Letters 207)

Imploring Bringhurst not to be offended by the parallel, Brown explains, "That one is truth and the other fiction is of no importance to one who considers both as moral lessons," concluding that Richardson's novel, "as a work of invention, [is] more accurate and uniform, and consequently more instructive," than ecclesiastical history. The 1792 letter resonates with Brown's later essay as well in its insistence that history, whether true or false, is always mediated regardless of the generic, rhetorical, or literary forms of mediation. According to Brown, we know Jesus through the Bible, and therefore the story is as much a romance as Richardson's novel. The letter illustrates the ways in which Brown's theories of fiction and history have profound philosophical, theological, and epistemological ramifications for the work of writing. But perhaps, as Brown suggests in a later letter to Bringhurst, on July 29, 1793, his preference for romance is best understood as his belief that true history becomes visible in the "habits, manners and opinions" of common existence:

> In the history of man there is this great and evident distinction. He is either a solitary, a domestic or a political being. It is domestic history that pleases me beyond all others. So far as the Characters of men are influenced by political events, political history is interesting, but . . . the personal character of individuals, their visages their dress, their accent their language their habits, manners and opinions; their personal behaviours I am desirous of Knowing. Life and Manners, I must repeat, is my favourite science. These are the materials of conversation.   (Letters 261)

In his letter of 1792 to Bringhurst, Brown describes Richardson's novel as romance, a generic slip that corresponds with critical conventions of the late eighteenth century that used the two terms interchangeably. But in the letter of 1793, he describes novelistic features as those that make up his "favourite science." His interests are "personal" and located in the "habits" of everyday existence. Brown's interest in the everydayness of the past reflects his engagement with Hume's *History of England* (1754), particularly. Both writers made the difficult narrative problem of historical distance a central preoccupation, one in which the minute details of life might make the past "temporarily present" for readers.[17] Such histories provide the materials out of which modern romance emerges, and romance is for Brown *the* genre of historical writing in which readers might make past peoples and events approximate their own contemporary moments and their own projection of a future existence.

IV. SYMPATHETIC READERS AND DISTANT GEOGRAPHIES

Brown embraces romance as the form of writing best able to represent a history that "connect[s] a by-gone time with the very Present that is flitting away from us," in the words of the later *House of the Seven Gables* preface. Hawthorne betrays an anxiety about connecting history for readers, in ways that would encourage sympathy for distant times and places. Such sympathy is needed, Hawthorne suggests, in order to develop individual, regional, and national self-consciousness about the present moment in time. Brown's writing betrays similar anxieties by making the reader the site of meaning around which all of his writing hinges. Often writing in epistolary form, Brown's fictional romances figure several readers at once, each adjudicating circumstances that "approach as nearly to the nature of miracles as can be done by that which is not truly miraculous" ("Advertisement" to *Wieland*, W 3). Whether featuring an unidentified correspondent, a primary character within the fictional world, or the reader of the text, Brown's romances deftly navigate between narrative seduction and disavowal. As Clara reassures her reader at the start of *Wieland*, "the tale that I am going to tell is not intended as a claim upon your sympathy" (W 5). It is this tension that seems to destabilize Brown's faith in romance and aligns his later writing with Godwin's suspicions. One might read the methodical attention to balancing description with interpretation in order to mitigate the vicissitudes of the reader's mind in "The Difference between History and Romance" as early evidence of Brown's wavering faith in readers as well.[18]

Brown's attention to history and geography is especially striking. In early writing, he understood regional space as a fixed variable, a "firm and immortal basis" against which the romancer contemplates history and the "traces [which] are for ever visible . . . its vestiges preserved entire to the remotest period of futurity" (Rhapsodist 538).[19] Brown's later essays, however, invert the relations between history and geography. In these essays, Brown fixes time in a particular moment in order to range beyond the borders of the nation. Many of his late writings feature discussions about international politics and geographic proximity but perhaps none more so than the 1803 pamphlet *An Address to the Government of the United States, on the Cession of Louisiana to the French, etc.* Here, the coordinates of geography and history are dynamic, as Brown negotiates the relationships between France, Saint-Domingue, and Louisiana. An "ordinary citizen" accidentally discovers a French plot to infiltrate and colonize Louisiana, a discovery made in a letter written to Napoleon, which is included in the pamphlet. Brown's pamphlet emphasizes the horrors of slavery and colonial mismanagement and offers a familiar urgent plea for readers to "awaken . . . from this fatal sleep" simultaneously (AG 32). While his fictional citizen underscores the danger of association with St. Domingo, by virtue of institutional slavery and French revolutionary doctrine, the consideration of four interrelated geographical regions suggests the way in which Brown becomes a distant reader. Distant reading, "where distance . . . *is a condition of knowledge*," offered Brown a means of mediating geography through the "devices, themes, tropes" of genre (Moretti 57).

Using the same strategies that helped him define romance as a literary genre distinctive from both conjectural and philosophical histories of the Scottish Enlightenment, Brown reconfigures scale on a geographic plane. That is, historical time and narrative temporality move into the background, which allows a space for the regional to come into the foreground. Brown's increasing attention to the nation's international relations, especially in the hemisphere, suggest that he may be the most cosmopolitan and versatile of romancers, capable of translating contemporary cultural geography into a long, and variegated, historical sweep.

In one final example of this turn to geography, Brown writes in "Annals of Europe and America," published in the *American Register* in 1808:

> Though it requires no extensive research to discover instances of selfish and iniqui-
> tous policy in the history of all nations, and especially in British history, mankind
> seldom extend their view beyond the present scene, and the recent usurpations of
> the French in the free cities and small states of Germany, in Switzerland, and Italy,
> excluded from the view of political observers the more ancient or distant examples
> of similar iniquities in the conduct of Great Britain. Even the recent conduct of that

power in Turkey was as egregious an instance of political injustice as the imagination can conceive; but it was transacted at a distance…and affected a race of men too much unlike ourselves to awaken our sympathy.   (Annals, II: 67).

Familiar tropes and anxieties are found throughout the passage: a concern with the reader's ability to see "beyond the present scene" (67); how the writer, who translates geographic relations, should negotiate distance; and if it is possible to "awaken [the] sympathy" of readers for people who remain "too much unlike ourselves" (67). Shifting the pastness of time into the background allows Brown to place the presentness of geography in into the foreground. For Brown, then, history is implicit in the shift to geography, just as nation supplants the category of history as such in Hawthorne's romances. Brown not only makes possible a form of fiction self-consciously historical in the eighteenth century but also introduces the grounds on which history becomes the latent content of romance in the nineteenth century.

Brown's capacity as a romancer to perform distant reading for those less able to bridge the gap between cultures, times, and regions seems a fitting conclusion to his long-standing intellectual commitment to parsing literature and history. Taken in full, Brown's writing highlights the degree to which we need to read him as not only the first romancer and literary critic in American letters but, more astonishingly, the nation's first cultural theorist. Understood this way, Brown prefigures far more than the Romantic writing of Irving, Hawthorne, and Poe; he prefigures the contemporary critical debates about temporality, nation, and scale that continue to shape the discipline and its return to his writing.

Notes

1. Richard Chase writes, "The fact is that the word 'romance' begins to take on its inevitable meaning, for the historically minded American reader, in the writing of Hawthorne. Ever since his use of the word to describe his own fiction, it has appropriately signified the peculiar narrow profundity and rich interplay of lights and darks which one associates with the best American writing" (Chase 20–21).
2. Both Poe and Irving were heavily influenced by the fiction and theories of Brown, though both, for the most part, avoided romance novels in favor of the romantic tale, romance Gothic tale, and other forms of writing.
3. The term is used in Barnard and Shapiro's notes in the Hackett editions of Brown's novels in order to distinguish between British radicals of the 1790s known more generally as Jacobins but also to highlight formal and generic influences that writers such as Godwin, Wollstonecraft, and Thomas Paine had on Brown's fiction, in tandem with the politics of writing, not apart from it. See Barnard and Shapiro xv.
4. See McKeon; Gallagher.
5. Davis identifies news/novels as a "discourse…characterized by a disinclination to distinguish between fact and fiction as a signifier of genre" (Davis 51).
6. Stewart coined the term "conjectural history" in his "Account of the Life and Writings of Adam Smith" (Stewart 293). See also Hume 1757; Ferguson. Hume 1754 is a philosophical history, not a conjectural history.

7. Mark Kamrath argues that Brown's theories of history and romance prefigure postmodern assumptions about historical truth marked by the "linguistic turn" in historiography, by charting his "changing rationalist and romantic conceptions of the past but also challeng[ing] historians and literary scholars alike to reconsider how inquiry into the 'art of the historian' in Brown's day informs and complicates issues of historical representation in our own" (Kamrath 233).

8. Samuel's Johnson's interest in everyday life is found across his writings, an especially clear example of which comes in a discussion between Johnson and William Robertson, a historian, on April 29, 1778. Johnson claims: "I wish much to have one branch well done, and that is the history of manners, of common life." Cited in Phillips (152).

9. Brown's "unity of design" prefigures Poe's description of literature that should produce a "unity of effect" in the reader; see Poe (163).

10. See Clemit; Godwin 1794. All available evidence points to the impossibility of Brown's having read Godwin's then-unpublished essay, which makes the similarity of the two remarkable. Godwin's "Of History and Romance" was written while *The Enquirer* was in press in 1797.

11. Brown's "theory of romance as socially engaged conjectural history...goes beyond Godwin and Wollstonecraft, however, by considering the nature and implications of fictional production more explicitly and in more nuanced ways than did the English writers" (Barnard, Kamrath, and Shapiro 19).

12. Watts writes, "On or about April 1800 Charles Brockden Brown changed" (131).

13. Robert Miles draws on William Hazlitt's *Lectures on the English Comic Writers*, published in 1907, wherein he locates the anxiety for Gothic romance in a more generalized anxiety produced by the transition between an old world and a new modern condition. Also see Miles 2008.

14. See McEvoy ix. See also Mathias.

15. Cobbett lived in Philadelphia from 1792 to 1802, during which time he published several inflammatory political pamphlets and edited the weekly *Peter Porcupine's Gazette*.

16. Bringhurst fled from Philadelphia to Delaware in 1793 during the yellow fever epidemic that Brown chronicles in *Arthur Mervyn* (1799–1800). See Bennett 279–280.

17. See Phillips 34.

18. See Brown's essays "Romances" and "Terrific Novels."

19. I discuss Brown's importance to American regional romance in Woertendyke 12–15.

Works Cited

Barnard, Philip, Mark L. Kamrath, and Stephen Shapiro. "Charles Brockden Brown and the Novel in the 1790s." In Theresa Gaul et al., eds., *Blackwell Companion to American Literature*, Vol. 1, *Beginnings to 1820*. Malden, Mass.: Blackwell Publishing, forthcoming.

Barnard, Philip, and Stephen Shapiro. "Introduction." In Charles Brockden Brown, *Ormond; or, The Secret Witness, with Related Texts*, ix–lii. Indianapolis: Hackett Publishing, 2009.

Bennett, Charles E. "A Poetical Correspondence among Elihu Hubbard Smith, Joseph Bringhurst Jr., and Charles Brockden Brown in 'The Gazette of the United States.'" *Early American Literature* 12.3 (Winter 1977): 279–280.

Brown, Charles Brockden. "Romances." LM 3.16 (January 1805): 6–7.

Brown, Charles Brockden. "Terrific Novels." LM 3.19 (April 1805): 288–289.

Chase, Richard. *The American Novel and Its Tradition*. New York: Gorian Press, 1978.

Clemit, Pamela. *The Godwinian Novel: The Rational Fictions of Godwin, Brockden Brown, Mary Shelley*. Oxford: Clarendon Press, 1993.

Davis, Lennard J. *Factual Fictions: The Origins of the English Novel*, 2nd ed. Philadelphia: University of Pennsylvania Press, 1996.

Gallagher, Catherine. "The Rise of Fictionality." In *The Novel*, Vol. 1, *History, Geography, and Culture*, Franco Moretti, ed., 336–363. Princeton, N.J.: Princeton University Press, 2006.

Godwin, William. *The Enquirer: Reflections on Education, Manners, and Literature, in A Series of Essays*. London: G. G. and J. Robinson, 1797.

Godwin, William. "Of History and Romance." In *Caleb Williams*. Maurice Hindle, ed., 359–374. New York: Penguin Classics, 1988.

Godwin, William. *Things as They Are; or, The Adventures of Caleb Williams*. London: B. Crosby, 1794.

Kamrath, Mark. "Charles Brockden Brown and the 'Art of the Historian': An Essay concerning (Post)Modern Historical Understanding." *Journal of the Early Republic* 21 (Summer 2001): 231–260.

Loughran, Trish. *The Republic in Print: Print Culture in the Age of U.S. Nation Building, 1770–1870*. New York: Columbia University Press, 2007.

Mathias, T. J. *The Pursuits of Literature*, 5th ed. London: T. Becket, 1798.

McEvoy, Emma. "Introduction." In Matthew Lewis, *The Monk: A Romance*, vii–xxx. New York: Oxford University Press, 1995.

McGill, Meredith. *American Literature and the Culture of Reprinting, 1834–1853*. Philadelphia: University of Pennsylvania Press, 2003.

McKeon, Michael. *The Secret History of Domesticity: Public, Private, and the Division of Knowledge*. Baltimore: Johns Hopkins University Press, 2005.

Miles, Robert. "1790s: The Effulgence of Gothic." In Jerrold E. Hogle, ed., *The Cambridge Companion to Gothic Fiction*, 41–62. Cambridge: Cambridge University Press, 2002.

Miles, Robert. "The Romantic-Era Novel." In Robert Miles, *Romantic Misfits*, 133–219. New York: Palgrave, 2008.

Moretti, Franco. "Conjectures on World Literature." *New Left Review* 1 (January–February 2000): 54–68.

Phillips, Mark Salber. *Society and Sentiment: Genres of Historical Writing in Britain, 1740–1820*. Princeton, N.J.: Princeton University Press, 2000.

Poe, Edgar Allan. "Philosophy of Composition." *Graham's Magazine* 28.4 (April 1846).

Pratt, Lloyd. *Archives of American Time: Literature and Modernity in the Nineteenth Century*. Philadelphia: University of Pennsylvania Press, 2010.

Radcliffe, Ann. "On the Supernatural in Poetry." *New Monthly Magazine* 16. 1 (1826): 145–152.

Tawil, Ezra. " 'New Forms of Sublimity': *Edgar Huntly* and the European Origins of American Exceptionalism." *Novel: A Forum on Fiction* 40.1/2 (Fall 2006), 104–124.

Walpole, Horace. "Preface to the Second Edition." In *The Castle of Otranto: A Gothic Story*, W. S. Lewis, ed., 7–12. Oxford: Oxford University Press, 1964.

Watts, Steven. *The Romance of Real Life: Charles Brockden Brown and the Origins of American Culture*. Baltimore: Johns Hopkins University Press, 1994.

Woertendyke, Gretchen J. *Hemispheric Regionalism: Romance and the Geography of Genre*. New York: Oxford University Press, 2016.

CHAPTER 11

....

HISTORICAL SKETCHES

....

PHILIP BARNARD

HISTORICAL *Sketches* is the name scholars have used since the 1950s to refer to a book-length ensemble of historical-fiction fragments that was composed certainly during the 1803–1807 years of Charles Brockden Brown's *Literary Magazine*, where several elements of the ensemble appeared in 1805, and likely during 1805–1806 alone. Although the greater part of the ensemble appeared posthumously in the Allen/Dunlap biographical miscellanies in a confused and poorly edited form, and its elements have never been published together, its overall conceptual and narrative coherence makes it clear that the *Sketches* constitute an unfinished work that stands as one of Brown's major and most ambitious fictions. In its scope and achievement, not to mention its volume—at about 114,500 words overall, the ensemble is considerably larger than any of the published romances—the narrative is an exceptional project in every sense and must be understood as a key work essential to any account of Brown's larger literary career.[1]

However, as a result of Brown's tangled reception history, the editorial disorganization of the fragments and their unavailability in any unified or widely available form, and the considerable intrinsic challenges of the narrative itself, it is still the case that the *Sketches* remain little known even to most scholarly readers producing research on Brown. This state of affairs should begin to change soon, as an edition of the *Sketches* is scheduled to appear by 2021 as Volume 5 of the ongoing Bucknell *Collected Writings* edition.[2] As of 2018, however, knowledge of and accumulated scholarship on this key work remain limited and primarily confined to description and initial efforts at interpretation. Future and more detailed explorations of the sprawling narrative will produce insights into Brown's engagement with changing literary-intellectual, sociocultural, and political-economic dynamics in the post-Revolutionary and rapidly liberalizing landscape of the 1800s and the Napoleonic era.

I. TEXT(S)

....

To clarify the textual state of the *Sketches* and the problems it creates even today, one can begin with a simple table of the fragments or segments that make up the ensemble as we know it at present, printed in the *Literary Magazine* and in the Allen and Dunlap (1815) biographies. Each source contains material not in the other two, although Allen and Dunlap overlap and use the same typesetting for almost half the text. The following list updates the Barnard account of 2004 (329 n. 3), with no assumptions regarding sequence or chronology, simply listing the fragments in the order in which they appear in their first printings.

Printed and overseen by Brown in 1805 (23,403 words total):

1. "A Specimen of Agricultural/Political Improvement"
   1a. LM 3.17 (February 1805): 86–93   4,311 words
   1b. LM 3.17 (February 1805): 120–128   5,142 words
2. "A Specimen of Political Improvement"
   2a. LM 3.18 (March 1805): 201–205   2,521 words
   2b. LM 3.18 (March 1805): 214–225   7,527 words
3. "The Romance of Real Life"
   LM 4.26 (November 1805): 392–396   2,263 words
4. "The Ivizan Cottager"
   LM 4.27 (December 1805): 428–431   1,639 words

Posthumously transcribed and printed in Allen/Dunlap, 1811–1815 (91,091 words total):

5. Allen/Dunlap (Vol. 1)
   5a. Allen/Dunlap 170–222   19,484 words
   5b. Dunlap 223–258   12,724 words
6. Allen 242–262   7,585 words
7. Allen/Dunlap 262–299   14,473 words
8. Allen/Dunlap 299–322   8,726 words
9. Allen/Dunlap 322–358   14,070 words
10. Dunlap 359–396   14,029 words

Total: 114,494 words for the ensemble

Fuller discussion of textual questions will await the scholarly edition, but a minimal understanding of their implications permits some idea of the problems that have confronted readers of the *Sketches* to the present. Until the mid- to late twentieth century, the ensemble's dating and indeed its full extent remained unclear. Working separately but arriving at similar conclusions regarding textual-archival issues, Kennedy and Berthoff (1945 and 1956) established that the *Literary Magazine* elements are part of the ensemble, minus the short "Ivizan Cottager" piece, identified in Barnard. The Allen version of the biography only became available in facsimile editions as of 1975. Kennedy, Berthoff, and subsequently Bennett were able to date the entire ensemble to the *Literary Magazine* years 1803–1807, noting that fictional events in the Allen/Dunlap segments occur as late as December 1804 (fragment 8, 322) and 1805 (fragment 5, 170, 184).

More recent information suggests a more specific dating of the *Sketches'* composition. As a result of work for the *Collected Writings* edition's Volume 3, *The Literary Magazine*, forthcoming in 2019, it has become evident that the number and quantity of Brown's original contributions to that magazine, relative to reprinted material not written by Brown, fell off significantly in 1806 and declined further in early 1807, when Brown began composing the voluminous "Annals" for the new *American Register*, the first volume of which was fully composed by July 1807 and surveys the same Napoleonic geoculture that the *Sketches* refer to in fictional form (AR 1: iv). Given that internal dates take the Allen/Dunlap fragments' narrative to 1805 and that several closely related historical-fiction pieces, with analogous narrative techniques and concerns, appeared in other 1805 issues of the *Literary Magazine*, overlapping with the *Sketches* and registering Brown's ongoing engagement with the project at that time, it is reasonable to suggest that the ensemble was composed primarily in 1805–1806, when no other large projects were under way: that is, after 1803–1804, when Brown composed and published two lengthy political pamphlets, as well as the 450-page Volney translation and annotation, and launched the *Literary Magazine* while writing a large proportion of its contents; and before 1807, when he began composing the book-length "Annals" and other materials for the *American Register*.[3]

Additionally, this dating of Brown's corpus of writings underscores the fact that the *Sketches* stand as the latest version of a career-long series of narrative plans, themselves related to Brown's evolving model of romance as conjectural history, elaborated from the 1789–1793 period of early experimentation onward. Attention to this sequence of plans incidentally accounts for much of the pre-1950s confusion regarding the *Sketches'* period of composition, as early commentators beginning with William Dunlap often conflate or confuse these early plans with the *Sketches*. Two Alloa fragments, for example, one from 1793 and the other around 1801, are all that remains of a prior pseudo-historical narrative project analogous to the *Sketches* in many respects. These brief fragments describe the invasion and administration of Japan by a Greek people called Alloans, who reform Shintoist religious institutions in order to secure their "dominion" (in the 1793 fragment) and conduct vast Asian wars against Mongol, Tartar, and Chinese antagonists, managing territories and populations calculated in the millions (in the c. 1801 fragment). Additionally, the 1793 fragment is chronologically and conceptually related to the architectural images, a set of thirty-eight drawings and plans in Brown's hand and from the same moment, that outline and compute architectural monuments and regulated built spaces (campuses, monasteries or abbeys, palaces, cathedrals, etc.), much like those described in the *Sketches* more than ten years later.[4] Whether these Alloa pieces are the same as or continuous with those noted in Elihu Hubbard Smith's diary in October and December 1796 and February 1797—when Smith hears Brown read from "notes toward his *great plan*, drawn from reading Coxe's 'Russian Discoveries'" (Smith 238, 256), or refers to projects featuring his "Aloas & Astoias, his Buttiscoes and Carlovingas" (272, 289)—remains uncertain. But the 1793–1796/97 and 1801 range of dates created by these references reminds us that the *Sketches* must be understood as the culmination of a career-long series of projects, conceived and elaborated before, possibly during, and after the better-known 1798–1801 phase of long romances.[5]

The posthumously printed fragments were poorly transcribed from Brown's manuscript. Neither Allen nor Dunlap seems to have read the texts carefully, and it is entirely possible, even likely, that more of the manuscript existed and was lost, since Dunlap describes passages included in his version of the biography as "a selection" (258). Evident typographical errors and misreadings pose manageable problems (scrambling some names and dates),[6] but, more important, the sequencing of the fragments remains problematic. Without developing examples, suffice it to say that the Allen/Dunlap elements are confused in this respect, if indeed Brown had established a final sequence, and may occasionally run together smaller segments better understood as distinct. Thus, Bennett (234–236), White, and Kamrath (121) all note that the elements, as printed and listed above, seem to require some degree of reordering. White, for example, in unpublished notes circulated in 2006, proposes a reorganization in four groups (using the fragment numbers above) as 1-4, 8-7, 9-10-6, 5.

Finally, in the absence of any authoritative or more appropriate title or name, *Historical Sketches*, applied to the entire ensemble, was introduced by Berthoff in 1956. His initial version was simply "Sketches," using quotation marks and no italics. After gaining currency since that time and evolving to the italicized form—which always carries a *soupçon* of surreality, oddly appropriate for this narrative full of invented texts, in that it refers to a book that, Borges-like, exists nowhere but in the commentary of its readers—this title has entered standard usage and will be employed for the forthcoming scholarly edition. Brown, of course, supplied titles for the *Literary Magazine* segments that apply to those texts in a subsectional manner, but the titles that appear with the disorganized Allen/Dunlap segments—"Sketches of Carsol" (Allen 170), "Sketches of a History of Carsol" (Dunlap 170), and "Sketches of the [or, alternately 'a'] History of the Carrils and Ormes" (Dunlap 258, 262)—were added by the compilers, the first without comment by Allen and the last two by Dunlap, who identifies them as his own invention (258).

II. Geography, Systems, Management, Power

On first encounter, the *Sketches* ensemble is bewildering and overwhelming in its enormous chronological scope, cast of characters, and multitude of interwoven episodes and concerns, all brought together into a series of variations on the grand question of representing historical transformation and change. While any first-time reader of Brown's fiction observes that Brownian narrative is complex and initially disorienting, the *Sketches* pose extreme challenges, both intrinsically and because of their fragmented state. Existing scholarship, for example, has not yet achieved the straightforward-sounding but elusive goal of describing the narrative fully and accurately, as this requires a cataloging of its episodes, subepisodes, and *fabula-syuzhet* structure—that is, a reconstruction of the narrative's implied fictional chronologies and geographies and of the way they are restructured in its narrative form—that has not been established.[7]

For purposes of basic description and provisional analysis here, however (updating my 2004 commentary to this end), one can describe the narrative in terms of three interrelated levels and emphases.

First, on an immediately narrative or plot level, the ensemble recounts the long history of an Anglo-European dynastic family named the Carrils and of their territories and doings across a complicated and world-systemic topography. The narrative's spatial dimension highlights the dynamics of center-periphery relations, uneven development, and their role in historical transformation, by emphasizing semiautonomous estates, "lordships," kingdoms, and other territories whose relative isolation sets the stage for and, geographically speaking, provides a precondition for its many systems of management, administration, and reform, which develop in tension with metropolitan forces represented by multiple centers of authority such as the Vatican or attested European monarchies that appear here in a counterfactual manner. Thus, the family's holdings are situated in mostly attested peripheral and insular administrative divisions or territories, such as the Isle of Athelney (Somerset), Beverley in the East Riding of Yorkshire (isolated by rivers on all sides), or Altamura (Apulia, southern Italy); semiautonomous "Palatine" counties or estates and divisions such as Rutland; and islands such as the Isle of Wight, Jersey, Guernsey, Alderney, Sark, Herm, Sardinia, Ibiza, Rhodes, and so on. The narrative's topography seems to begin with the British Isles, emphasizing their peripheral and isolated administrative regions such as Orme on the Welsh coast, Walney on the northwest coast in the Palatine county Lancashire, or Sir Arthur Carril's holdings on an unidentified peninsula in Scotland, but projects systemically to the Mediterranean, North America and, notably, to a distant non-European colony on the fictional island Serendib, which likely refers to Ceylon (White).

While the greater part of the narrative concentrates on the family's early-modern sixteenth-to-eighteenth-century history up to 1805, it ranges over eighteen centuries and flashes back to medieval and Renaissance episodes considered as parts of the family's genealogical narrative and claims to continuity, which appear as more or less naked fictions designed to reinforce present power. The episodes range from world-systemic, enormously consequential events, such as sectarian wars of religion, insurrections, or sociopolitical reforms and transformations that shape the fates of entire populations, to love affairs and other localized incidents that directly affect only smaller circles. It is the large-scale repercussions of the small-scale incidents that matter, however, for example, in the way Countess Pamphela Carril's amusing illicit affair with her lover and administrative puppet Alfonzo serves to consolidate her authority over the male political rivals and administrators around her (fragment 7, 278–283). In this respect, indeed, the narrative's vast scope and cast of characters are striking examples of the way Brown's post-1800 romances tend to intimate that the primary factors in historical change are not individuals but the wider actions, interests, and strategies of administrations and populations.

The narrative's proliferation of islands and isolated, insular domains or micro-territories and its fascination with large-scale, world-systemic transformation partly reflect the massive upheavals of the revolutionary and Napoleonic eras, when, for example, the "mediatization," secularization, and territorial redistribution of the Holy Roman Empire at the time of its dissolution in 1802–1803, just before the *Sketches'* composition, generated the largest territorial-administrative transformations in modern history in the Mediterranean and European regions that figure in Brown's narrative.[8] Since the narrative pastiches enlightened third-person historiography in the style of Hume, William Robertson, or Edward Gibbon and involves a disorienting host of characters, places, and incidents, all related within a web of nested backstories and subnarratives that combine fictitious with attested historical figures and events repurposed in this setting, much work will be necessary to adequately inventory its wide-ranging references and allusions, to ask what sorts of patterns they form, what intertexts they indicate, how they relate to the rest of Brown's corpus, and so on. At the same time, however, the text parodies early-Romantic antiquarian obsessiveness with encyclopedic detail and obscure reference, in a manner that functions as a sort of hermeneutic lure for readers who do not attend to its ironic dimensions and reflections on historical narrative and generic form.[9]

Second, against this stage setting or dramatic backdrop of dynastic history and world-systemic geography or topography, on a more mediated and conceptual level, the narrative describes governmental and disciplinary systems in which cultural practices function as social-ideological technologies. That is, it describes a range of organizational-administrative systems that reflect on modes of management, governmentality, and power. As noted, the text's emphasis on isolated or peripheral, primarily agrarian territoriality facilitates and amplifies these systems and their effects. The many examples have variously positive or negative, constructive or damaging outcomes and effects and lead the reader to consider the text's fascination with these systems and their dynamics in and of itself, beyond any single episode or example. In this respect, the *Sketches* prove ready-made for consideration via the Foucauldian analysis of liberalism and its relation to evolving system concepts of governmentality and biopower. In their larger implications, indeed, the *Sketches* register the emergence of a new liberal-capitalist dominant whose rationalizing and quantifying principles are supplanting prior mercantilist-absolutist systems at the time of the ensemble's composition. Read in this light, the ensemble's dramatization of the way its systems produce alternately (or simultaneously) "positive" and productive or "negative" and oppressive effects anticipates Foucault's 1979 argument that a basic paradox of market liberalism consists in the way its mythologized concept of freedom is anything but "natural" and must, in fact, be *produced* via evolving schemes of administration: liberalism's "improvements" and generation of ever greater economic productivity, what it mythologizes as "freedom," is only made possible through and as a function of administrative constructs, by ever more regulatory and disciplinary systems of governmentality (Foucault 2008, 51–73).

These systems have been the central focus of interpretative efforts thus far—albeit with differing assumptions and conclusions and not yet coordinated with Foucauldian models—primarily in Berthoff (1954 and 1956), Watts, Barnard, and Kamrath. The narrative's systems and forms of management or organization appear in an impressive array of variants—political, ecclesiastical, military, educational, agricultural, architectural and other art forms, and so on—but all enact the text's fundamental organizational drive and relate to the (re)production of power. Often, these systems' and structures' properties or effects are computed mathematically, producing the text's proliferating statistics, measurements, and continual gestures of quantification.

The *Sketches'* systems and forms of management appear in two groups we can describe roughly as governmental institutions and cultural-artistic practices. On the one hand, the ensemble surveys institutional systems that constitute, pace Louis Althusser, "Ideological State Apparatus" modes of interdependent state, church, juridical, etc., power via large-scale or system-wide administrative and managerial structures. On the other hand, it provides a complementary, quasi-Gramscian focus on the soft power of elite and popular cultural forms and practices as they serve to secure consent, cement ideological domination, or fuel antisystemic struggles. Monumental architecture, sculpture, elite and popular poetry, plebeian forms of print culture such as almanacs, and the writing of history itself are described at length, often in exhaustive detail. Dynastic or other territorial organizer-managers, such as the eighteenth-century Sir Arthur Carril, and likewise culture-organizing figures, such as his architect, Sarchi, design and oversee "structures" that intervene in changing social dynamics. The text's governmental-institutional systems and cultural-artistic technologies operate with relative autonomy yet mirror one another, with the soft power of the artistic-cultural practices acting as social technologies related to the hard power of the governmental systems of management.

To cite one of many examples that juxtapose these elements, consider the *Literary Magazine* fragments "A Specimen of Agricultural Improvement" and "A Specimen of Political Improvement." As the titles suggest (slipping from "Agricultural" to "Political" between two installments with no explanation, underlining the kinship and overlap of the texts' varied systems), the episode describes extensive managerial "improvements" that Sir Arthur C[arril] has made, during the narrative's eighteenth century, to lands in Scotland inherited by marriage, and the description is divided in a manner that reflects the larger narrative's dual emphases on institutional and cultural systems in relation to the reproduction of power, and on power's simultaneously liberating and oppressive effects. The segment's first half, the two March installments, provides copious statistics as it surveys the reforms through which Arthur increases his estate's agricultural-economic productivity. Its second half, the two April installments, provides equally copious measurements and computations as it describes the systemic features of the territory's architectural monuments, culminating in a baroque allegory concerning systemic order, disorder, and inevitable transformation in the water-channeling system of the "castle of C—" (fragment 2b).

The complexity of Arthur's managerial reforms or improvements (reorganizing the territory's overall political economy as concerns agriculture, religion, laws, education, prisons, urban planning, etc.) defies simple description, such that even the tireless narrator remarks: "To unfold minutely all the parts and branches of his system would demand a volume: I have found the greatest pleasure in studying this system, but cannot, at this time, pretend to give you more than a very loose and brief sketch" (127). As noted, the *Sketches'* systems produce alternately constructive or damaging outcomes. A few episodes define the extremes, describing primarily "utopic" (e.g., sixteenth-century Felix Carril's reforms in fragment 10) or "dystopic" (e.g., Michael Praya's Inquisition-like system in fragment 5a) processes, but most, like Arthur's systems in this episode, produce mixed effects. Thus, Arthur's reforms benefit the estate's population on the one hand, generating a higher standard of living by modernizing a prior, less rationalized regime. But on the other hand, they discipline the population in oppressive ways, as the reforms entail new, more rigorously policed systems of farming, land tenure, education, temperance, and so on. The reformer figures as a benevolent, paternalist landlord but likewise as a despot. Arthur's achievements exist in time, overturning a past dispensation and destined themselves to be overturned by future change: "Great as this revolution was, and long the period in which it was effected, sir A— had the happiness of seeing all his schemes accomplished…and might entertain a well founded hope of enjoying, for at least another thirty years, the contemplation of a structure which he had been the same number of years in building" (128).

The narrative's emphasis on systematicity and change and its examples of "structure" or "system" (these nouns appear repeatedly) are subsequently literalized and shifted to the cultural-artistic register in the two April installments, where the narrator describes lesser architectural monuments before devoting the final installment to a survey of the allegorical "castle of C—," whose two central towers housed both a prison and a "monastic, or collegiate…community" that fulfilled "clerical or studious functions" (223). In that structure, a vast, self-replicating system of channeling and intricate calculation, reminiscent of the surreal complexity of Giovanni Battista Piranesi's "invented" architectural fantasies (c. 1745–1750), controls and structures the flow of water, instrumentalizing its force for "improvements," but the marvelous structure is eventually brought to ruin as time and gravity overwhelm the carefully engineered system. Thus, the agricultural-political improvement segments illustrate the *Sketches'* concern with modernizing institutional and cultural system structures and their relations to the dynamics of historical change.

If the *Sketches* develop such system structures and play out their transformations by way of registering large-scale shifts in Brown's world-system, that is, the shock waves of geopolitical and geocultural change generated by revolutionary and Napoleonic upheavals, which mark the epochal transformation of early-modern absolutist and mercantilist regimes into the perpetually modernizing liberal capitalism of the romantico-modern nineteenth century, then future discussions should consider the text's relations to evolving contemporary system models of liberalizing social organization and management, from variants of mercantilism such as Colbertism or Cameralism in the Germanies to the physiocrats, Arthur Young's agrarian-improvement models, and so on. Arthur Carril's improvements in his isolated Scottish estate, for example, shift his lands' political economy to a more productive and hence profitable regime, but one that is more akin to the top-down models of cameralist theory than to the laissez-faire imaginary of Scottish-school "civil society."[10]

III. HISTORY AND ROMANCE

On their third, more abstract and formal level—following the plot-level spatio-temporal panorama of dynastic history and geography and the second-level survey of systems and forms of governmentality or organizational power—the *Sketches* proposes a metafictional and metageneric consideration of historical-fictional narrative and its social functions and implications in the post-Revolutionary, liberal ascendency. In the ironic perspective established by its narrative voice and the larger implications of its reflection on romance as a narrative genre, the ensemble offers a critical perspective on historical fiction's status and effects as institution and practice in the 1800s and on the logic and claims of historiography in its premodern, enlightened, and emerging early-Romantic liberal forms.

Even the briefest examination reveals that the narrative's many examples of history writing appear as frankly ideological-political tools, with no pretension to simple "truthfulness"; see, for example, the accounts of the propagandistic "Carsola Restaurata" composed by the minister Pareiro (fragment 5a, 184–187), Nicholas Kampsi's invented history (fragment 5a, 214–218), many episodes concerning hagiographic legends, or the farcical episode in which the ridiculous ballads of an itinerant tinker named Ralf are received as inspired songs of bardic tradition, translated into Latin, and elevated into canonical accounts of the life of a legendary Saint Ulpha, all as a means of consolidating the power of a later and similarly named Countess Ulpha (fragment 7, 293–296). That the ensemble produces a reflection on history-as-narrative was noted as early as Berthoff's 1954 dissertation—"The striking consequence is that History itself is the larger meaning of this 'history'" (290)—although Berthoff's more frequently cited 1956 article notably omits this question. However, this key dimension of the ensemble remains significantly underestimated and underappreciated in most commentary.

Along with Brown's evolving reception history, contrasting perspectives on the *Sketches'* generic logic and narrative voice constitute the major fault line in the scholarship to date. Berthoff and Watts follow dated reception tropes according to which Brown rejects Woldwinite critical perspectives after 1800 and, crucially, endorse a tradition of interpretative literalism dating back to Dunlap. That is, they do not factor in the text's narrative voice or take account of indirection, irony, and other rhetorical effects as significant devices framing its contents, implicitly arguing that Brown is identical with the text's narrator and thus endorses the systems or modes of management the narrative describes. The *Sketches* would thereby affirm an "antirevolutionary," Burkean-Eliotic vision of "cultural order" (Berthoff 1956, 154) or a backward-looking "nostalgia for certain organic, medieval social forms" (Watts 171).[11] My earlier commentary and that of Kamrath, by contrast, abandon the periodization of Brown's career around a supposed conservative turn and approach the text's generic structure and narrative voice as constructions themselves requiring analysis, reaching very different conclusions regarding the ensemble's wider implications. At least two key features of the *Sketches* are best considered on this formal-generic level of the narrative.

First, the ensemble's anonymous, third-person, omniscient narrative voice—presumably male, although unmarked as to gender and leaving grounds for uncertainty, given the narrative's typically Brownian turns on structured inequality and empowered female actors—plays a central role and can no more be conflated with Brown-the-author than effaced in construing the narrative's contents. All of Brown's narratives, from the early letters, periodical essays, and novels to the pamphlets and "Annals," as we know, manipulate narrative voice in sophisticated ways, and the *Sketches* are no exception. The *Sketches'* narrative pastiches historical style and modulates a dry and detached—alternately ironic, sardonic, sarcastic, humorous, and bemused—perspective that echoes Gibbon, for example, as it dismisses the superstition and priestcraft involved in deceptions concerning relics, hagiography, and various primarily Roman Catholic practices (Barnard 312, 317, 320–323). Unlike the earlier and better-known fictions, which employ epistolary-memoiresque formats to problematize first-person perspectives, the *Sketches*, in keeping with their composition during a period when Brown employs primarily distantiated, third-person editorial personas, problematize the dynamics and generic markers of conventionally historical narrative style.

Second, that irony, satire, and humor, albeit of a decidedly dry and deadpan variety, play a significant role here may seem surprising, as the complexities of Brownian style often lead readers to assume that these are generally absent. Nevertheless, in its variations on wry and distanced inflection, the *Sketches'* narrative voice produces a fundamentally critical perspective not just on this or that foible or eccentric episode of dynastic history but on the narrative's constant depiction of the ways in which history writing and art, and a host of related frauds, deceptions, and "soft" cultural practices, serve to legitimate, empower, mythologize, rationalize, and otherwise reinforce and glorify the claims of the Carrils and other figures of power. In a classic metafictional manner, the narrative voice interrogates its pseudo-historical evidentiary material and discourages interpretative deference before the power traditionally mediated in historical discourse, thereby encouraging readers to entertain a healthy skepticism regarding the limits of history understood conventionally, as an authoritative account of Ranke's proverbial *wie est eigentlich gewesen* or, to adapt the Woldwinite formula, "things as they were."

Primarily via these modulations of narrative voice, as they refer back to episodes of fictitious history writing, hagiography, and vernacular prose legends in invented versions of Bede and other Anglo-Latin and premodern histories, the *Sketches* remind the reader that history, especially in its pre-Enlightenment forms, acted primarily as an instrumental discourse legitimating and glorifying power. In this emphasis, Brown's experimental narrative anticipates Foucault's discussion of history-as-discourse's relation to evolving early-modern and liberal regimes of power and constructions of identity (Foucault 1997, 65–69). Space here does not allow fuller development of examples, but two areas of deflationary or demythologizing emphasis stand out.

First, in a narrative extensively concerned with ecclesiastical institutions, beliefs, traditions, legends, and practices, the narrative voice is relentlessly anticlerical and dismissive of theist illusions. Even as it acknowledges the church's efficacy as a means of social and ideological control, it categorically rejects belief as credulity and superstition. It is not unreasonable to suppose that this critical spotlight on priestcraft and mostly Christian religious delusion is one important reason the ensemble was never brought to press during Brown's lifetime, as it would have contradicted his carefully constructed nonpartisan position in the *Literary Magazine*. In this connection, it is notable that the antitheist emphasis is strategically absent only in the 1805 episodes that appeared publicly in that magazine.[12]

Second and likewise, despite earlier claims that the narrative affirms or enacts the emergent cultural nostalgia and reactionary medievalism of the Napoleonic-liberal phase, the ensemble is adamantly antimedievalist, so much so that, as a thought experiment, it can be read to great effect as a broad satire and inversion of Novalis's restorationist fantasy in *Christendom or Europe* (1799), one of the founding texts of romantico-modern literary reaction. The ensemble pastiches, satirizes, and dismisses the era's emerging "invented tradition" of Romantic neo-medievalism as national-racial essentialism and a new compass for identitarian reference after the traumas of the revolutionary age (cf. Foucault 1997, 115–138). The previously mentioned episode concerning the ridiculous bard Ralf, for example (fragment 7, 293–296), targets the contemporary neo-medievalist vogue for the Ossianic poems, and indeed, the central name "Carril" partly constitutes a broad reference to Ossianism, as Carril is the name of an important bard in James Macpherson's forgeries, which Brown dismissed in a series of (mostly republished) articles in 1805–1806 issues of the *Literary Magazine* (Barnard, 324–325, 330 n. 9–10), during the probable period of the ensemble's composition.[13]

The *Sketches'* anticlericalism and critical pastiche of neo-medievalism lead us to this third level's second key feature or dimension, which is the narrative's critique of emerging romantic historicism, a reflection on the cultural politics of genre that relates the ensemble to Brown's key theory of romance as conjectural history and to epochal developments in post-Revolutionary literary culture, as it transforms print culture from performances of rational debate in the public sphere (the late-Enlightenment "republic of letters") to privatized aesthetic experience in a liberal marketplace and emerging "cultural" sphere that binds subjects together with the newly invented traditions of nationalism(s). Here again, far from articulating a break with the earlier fictional or long-narrative production, *Sketches* further develops earlier concerns—recall the closely related projects undertaken from 1793 on—and, in this regard, can be understood as an extension or new stage of the critical reflections on generic form that figure centrally in the 1801 novels *Clara Howard* and *Jane Talbot*.

At this point in Brown's reception history, it is evident that his narratives, from the early fictional experiments to the 1805–1809 years of *Sketches* and "Annals," consistently develop a Woldwinite-related theory of romance as conjectural history and political education. Elaborated from 1792 to 1793 on (and thus coextensive with the ongoing projects for a *Sketches*-like pseudo-historical narrative) and most familiar from the "Walstein's School of History" and "Difference between History and Romance" essays (1798–1799), this model of historical fiction holds that fictional and historical narrative are socially engaged mediums or tools for considering historical dynamics and should be understood as two sides of a proverbial coin. The mixture of historical and conjectural elements in "fictional" (romance) and "historical" (romance) narratives leads their audiences to consider how forces and institutions shape behaviors and outcomes and likewise affirm that history entails interpretation and an inevitable degree of narrative conjecture or construction. On its face, this model attests that Brown never approached historical narrative naively, as a "transparent" medium, and viewed it consistently, via Woldwinite and other late-Enlightenment discussions, as a socially and ideologically fraught medium or technology. It also reminds us that Brown did not conceptualize or approach his narrative production in terms of a fiction/nonfiction distinction but rather in terms of the varying focus and utility of narrative forms as socially engaged instruments. In its fullest implications, the theory presents romance as a medium for contemplating the dynamics of historical change (Barnard, Kamrath, and Shapiro forthcoming).

Whereas the best-known romances, *Wieland*, *Ormond*, *Edgar Huntly*, and *Arthur Mervyn*, extrapolate the theory along the lines of the "Walstein" essay to develop enlightened fictions that, in principle, encourage readers to consider how social context shapes character and action in individuals, the lesser-known 1801 romances, *Clara Howard* and *Jane Talbot* inflect the model, focusing critically on the predicates of their generic forms, that is, the cultural-ideological implications of received late-Enlightenment generic formats, such as the sentimental or Gothic, which Brown combined to develop his style of narrative. As this volume's chapters on the 1801 novels argue, those narratives mark Brown's realization of the strategic limits of these earlier formats, from his engaged perspective, and produce a critique not of the principles informing the romance model but of the generic precedents previously employed and now perceived as no longer adequate, in the new liberal dispensation of the 1800s, for the goal of transmitting these principles in literary form. While the goal of producing "romance" narratives that provide exempla and encourage critical engagement with "things as they are" remains, the later writings, beginning with the 1801 titles, move forward from the earlier emphasis on understanding how context shapes individual actions and produce more insistent critical reflections on generic forms and their relations to larger structures of power. This is not merely a complex way of saying that Brown's narratives or romances scale up from dramatic-fictional forms centrally depicting individuals (Clara or Edgar) to political-historical forms (pamphlets, historical fictions, and "Annals") focusing on populations (seen in terms of partisan factions, dynasties, or nations) as dramatic actors but, rather, that, as Brown's career advances, the romance model produces increasingly sophisticated reflections on the dynamics of historical transformation and on generic forms understood as transistors of ideological transformation.

From this perspective, we can venture a concluding argument about how the ensemble's anticlericalism, antimedievalism, and demystification of naive "historicist" illusions relate to its systems of management-power and allegories of transformation, and how these features articulate together in an eccentric generic form that produces not a Gibbon-, Robertson-, or Hume-like tale of progressive demystification (an affirmation of stadial progress toward civil society absent in the *Sketches*) but a prescient registration and rejection of the large field of emerging Romantic cultural-historical and generic tropes that, after Katie Trumpener, one can refer to generally as "bardic nationalism." Considered as a gesture of metageneric innovation and experimentation, the ensemble can certainly be read via Trumpener's account of the way the Romantic novel form is centrally concerned with problems of culture and change, such that its "conceptual ambition and formal experimentation" generate new antiquarian-focused and historical-fiction forms that mediate the contradictions of the period's liberalizing world-system, both riven and related by center-periphery modulations and tensions: "the early national tale evokes an organic national society, its history rooted in place: the historical novel describes the way historical forces [from land improvements to colonial aggression] break into and break up this idyll" (Trumpener xii–xv). As Trumpener notes from her comparatist perspective, semiperipheral and peripheral writers in the Romantic period, writers like Brown, develop their own "strange cosmopolitanism" and responses to the emerging ideology of nationalism, in function of their location in the world-system and ideological relation to the period's newly dominant liberal-imperial imaginary (xiii, 67–127).

Gary Kelly's concept of an early-Romantic "quasi-novel" category that utilizes bold formal-generic experimentation to negotiate the period's phase shift in the social functions of print culture likewise provides useful angles from which to understand the *Sketches'* generic reflections (Kelly 167–171). Kelly's account situates the period's anti-quarian and neo-historicist generic experimentation as a feature of the contemporary world-system and a symptom of its shifts, allowing us to consider the *Sketches'* relations to formally analogous (while ideologically distinct) generic experiments from John Thelwall's *The Peripatetic* (1793) to Susanna Rowson's *Reuben and Rachel* (1798) and the 1802–1809 nostalgic annalism of Washington Irving as it leads to his generic break-through in *The Sketch-Book* (1819). Finally, Roland Barthes provides a useful formal model with his notion of the discursive *logothete*, the creator of obsessional, metage-neric, and formally overwhelming textual structures and systems such as those of Sade, Charles Fourier, Ignatius of Loyola, or Brown. Barthes's concept is useful here, as it defines three basic formal-organizational drives that operate dramatically throughout the *Sketches*: "self-isolation" (*s'isoler*), the enabling function of the ensemble's host of isolated territories; "articulation" (*articuler*), the combinatory function that constantly reshuffles narrative options on the thematic and metafictional levels, generating pro-liferating scenes or examples; and "ordering" (*ordonner*), the incessant production of taxonomies, categories, and measurements (Barthes 3–10).[14]

However we conceptualize the metageneric and formal experimentation that generates the *Sketches'* pastiche of emergent Romantic neo-medievalism and annalism (with its associated nostalgic cult of Catholicism, which seduces literary reactionaries from Novalis and the Schlegels to Henry Adams and T. S. Eliot) and continual staging of idyllic or darkly Gothic forces of historical transformation, it seems manifest that the ensemble anticipates and rejects Romantic nationalism and historicism, with their attendant ethnoracial and cultural-linguistic essentialism, in a manner that is characteristic of Brown's conception of romance. As Kamrath, Shapiro, and I have argued collaboratively elsewhere, one of the most prescient and notable features of the

Brownian version of romance, that is, one of the conceptual properties that separates Brown's approach to narrative most decisively from that of most of his contemporaries, is precisely the way it addresses the problem of considering or representing historical transformation. Brown develops the keyword *romance* in a manner that is distinct from the earlier, medieval, and early-modern sense of romance as tales of misalliance that allegorize the disintegration of feudalism and the advent of the modern state and mercantile capitalism (e.g., a noble lady and a subordinate male like the Countess Pamphela and Alonzo in fragment 7) and likewise distinct from the emerging liberal concept of (historical) romance as a cultural device that allows the reorganization of history from the perspective and with the norms of a triumphant industrial-capitalist bourgeoisie (e.g., as evoked in the fanciful present-day [1805] tale of Miss Tenbrook in fragment 3, titled by Brown "The Romance of Real Life").

As it extends and develops Brown's conception of romance during the later, more insistently "historical" phase of his literary career, the *Historical Sketches* ensemble brings the model forward from its late-Enlightenment conception into the geoculture of the liberalizing, early-Romantic nineteenth century. In this form, the romance model "no longer looks to fabulate or obscure the tensions within society as a distracting alibi for a declining order, as was true for early modern romance. Nor does it dissimulate the violence inherent in the establishment of a new (bourgeois) order, as was soon to be the case for the historical romance of the early nineteenth century. Instead, Brown's notion of romance situates the generic mode as an inquiry or speculative assay into the conditions through which historical transformation occurs. Thus, rather than the earlier or later versions of romance, which deploy mythological tales to direct attention *away* from large-scale social change, Brown's version of romance foregrounds the dynamics of change, or the project of encouraging awareness of those dynamics, as the very *purpose* of romance" (Barnard, Kamrath, and Shapiro, forthcoming).

NOTES

1. Compare *Edgar Huntly* (94,900 words), *Ormond* (94,620), *Jane Talbot* (83,415), *Wieland* (82,740), *Mervyn, Second Part* (77,480), *Mervyn, First Part* (71,910), and *Clara Howard* (42,250).

2. Provisionally titled *Historical Sketches and Fragments*, the scholarly edition will be edited by Philip Barnard, Yvette Piggush, and Ed White.

3. *The Literary Magazine and Other Writings, 1802–07*, edited by Robert Battistini, Michael Cody, and Karen Weyler, will appear in 2019 as Volume 3 of the *Collected Writings* edition. At least three directly *Sketches*-related fictional pieces appear in 1805: "Richard the Third and Perkin Warbeck" (LM 3.17 [February 1805]: 108–110, in the same issue as *Sketches* fragment 1); "Kotan Husbandry" (LM 3.19 [April 1805]: 303–307); and "Ciceronians" (LM 3.21 [June 1805]: 404–405). See the commentary in the forthcoming scholarly edition. Examination of the magazine's contents, both original and reprinted, during the period of the *Sketches*' composition, will reveal many connections between the fictional ensemble and the periodical texts.

4. Alloa is the name of a town in Scotland, continuing Brown's long practice of repurposing geographical place names. The early Alloa fragment, in the Ransom Center, University of Texas, is on the same paper (watermark "SL" for papermaker Samuel Levis) and in the same chirography as the 1793 Ellendale and Godolphin fragments, which provide the earliest formulation of the theory of romance as conjectural history (Letters 841), and the Ransom architectural drawings; this group can now be confidently dated to 1792–1793. The second fragment, at the Historical Society of Pennsylvania, is in a distinctly later hand, with the more refined and modernized chirography of the 1801 courtship letters. Both fragments will be included in the *Collected Writings* Volume 5, *Historical Sketches and Fragments*. Virtually the only previous commentary is Bennett, who remains uncertain about the fragments' dating (175–180), and Axelrod (98–102).

5. Likewise, as concerns compositional chronology and possible dating of the *Sketches* and its predecessors, Brown's autumn 1806 letter to Susan Linn echoes Smith's earlier mention of a "great plan" when he writes, "I have undertaken to compose a great book, and have limited myself in my engagements with a bookseller, to one year, within which to complete it" (Letters 652, 653 n. 6). While the book-length "Annals," the first volume of which was complete around six months later, by July 1807, is the likeliest reference, the nature of the "great book" remains unspecified, and thus there is a less probable but still plausible possibility that the passage refers to the *Sketches*.

6. For example, Kennedy pointed out early on (p. 1679) that the sentence in fragment 5, Allen/Dunlap 171, that adds up to the date 1810 ("These funds have been reduced to their present state, since 1725, that is, for 85 years") clearly involves an error in the same passage that brings the present date of that narrative to "1805."

7. Berthoff recognizes the necessity of such a reconstruction with a very rough attempt at periodizing the text into seven historical "ages" or "eras" (Berthoff 1954, 278–279).

8. *Mediatization* is a term historians use to describe the modernizing restructuration of the Germanies that occurred when the thousand-year-old Holy Roman Empire, a vast, multiethnic, multireligious patchwork of semiautonomous territories, was abolished and reorganized beginning in 1802–1803, that is, immediately before Brown undertook the *Sketches*. The *Sketches* seem to echo several administrative and geocultural aspects of this transition. Mediatization was a dual process of territorial reorganization and "secularization" in which vast ecclesiastical lands were transferred to nonchurch authorities and became the property of aristocratic families or newly organized civil administrations, in processes and struggles that figure in many of the *Sketches*' episodes. Likewise, the semiautonomous administrative status of "Palatine" territories such as the British one emphasized in fragments 6–7 and 9, was an important feature of the empire (although not limited to it) and is additionally linked to Brown's immediate context in that most eighteenth-century German immigrants to Pennsylvania were "Palatines" from the declining Rhineland territories of the empire. Finally, one can recall that the Holy Roman Empire originated with the ninth-to-tenth-century Carolingian dynasty that features prominently in the *Sketches*, and that the Northumbrian scholar Alcuin, referred to by Brown in his 1798 Wollstonecraftian dialogue, was an Anglo-Latin literary intellectual of this milieu, that is, a figure of the same type as Bede and others pastiched throughout the *Sketches*.

9. Pre-1950 readers, in an era still heavily invested in such Romantic antiquarianism, worry the text's encyclopedic references in a symptomatic manner: see, for example, Fricke in 1911 (53) and Kennedy's response to Fricke in the late 1920s (1690–1690a). Brown joked about such antiquarianism and its obsessive bibliomania in his November 21, 1806,

letter to fellow editor and contributor John Elihu Hall. From an etymological reflection on the word "Adversaria," the title of Hall's series in the *Literary Magazine*, Brown segues into a lighthearted review of seventeenth-century encyclopedic dictionaries dear to "Erudites" (which he consulted in the Logan Library) and notes that his only personal copy of such a compendium is the 1677 Thomas Holyoke folio-sized Latin dictionary and listing of "The Proper Names of Persons, Places, and other things necessary to the understanding of Historians and Poets." In this light, the *Sketches*' fictional Isle of Holioke (fragment 8, 300–312; fragment 9, 322, 342) likely involves a humorous derivation of Holyoke's name, itself involved in Latin joking and etymological punning in Brown's letter (Letters 655–660).

10. Cameralism was a body of administrative and economic theory and practice in German-speaking states from the seventeenth to the early nineteenth centuries. It provided a conceptual framework for governing absolutist states with a corporatist, top-down social and economic structure. Notably, it reflected the complexity of the political-territorial system of the Holy Roman Empire, whose reorganization as of 1802–1803, as noted earlier, seems to be referred to in the *Sketches*. See, for example, the discussions of cameralism in relation to the physiocrats and mercantilism, considered as inflections of emergent liberal models, in Foucault 2007, 15–27, 67–70; Foucault 2008, 51–73, 291–316.

11. Marchand anticipates (xliii–xliv, n. 124) and Martinez follows (184–206) this line of interpretation.

12. Kamrath contextualizes the ensemble's anticlerical emphasis in terms of contemporary struggles over church-state separation in the early republic (Kamrath 113–133); likewise, Barnard explains how some of the text's anticlerical episodes are likely directed at the clerical-reactionary partisanship of contemporary Federalists (Barnard 315–317). This line of argument connects the *Sketches* back to *Wieland*'s cautionary allegory of elite cultural-religious fanaticism.

13. See, for example, "On the Authenticity of Ossian's Poems" (LM 4.26 [November 1805]: 354–365), in the same issue as fragment 3, "The Romance of Real Life."

14. In this connection, recall Barthes' famous observation that a little formalism drove one away from history, but a lot drove one back to it.

WORKS CITED

Axelrod, Alan. *Charles Brockden Brown: An American Tale.* Austin: University of Texas Press, 1983.

Barnard, Philip. "Culture and Authority in the *Historical Sketches*." In Philip Barnard, Mark L. Kamrath, and Stephen Shapiro, eds., *Revising Charles Brockden Brown: Culture, Politics, and Sexuality in the Early Republic*, 310–331. Knoxville: University of Tennessee Press, 2004.

Barnard, Philip, Mark L. Kamrath, and Stephen Shapiro. "Charles Brockden Brown and the Novel in the 1790s." In Theresa Gaul et al., eds., *Blackwell Companion to American Literature*, Vol. 1, *Beginnings to 1820*. Malden, Mass.: Blackwell, forthcoming.

Barthes, Roland. *Sade, Fourier, Loyola* (1971). Richard Miller, trans. New York: Farrar, Straus and Giroux, 1976.

Bennett, Charles E. "The Charles Brockden Brown Canon." Ph.D. dissertation, University of North Carolina, Chapel Hill, 1974.

Berthoff, Warner B. "Charles Brockden Brown's Historical 'Sketches': A Consideration." *American Literature* 28.2 (May 1956): 147–154.

Berthoff, Warner B. "The Literary Career of Charles Brockden Brown." Ph.D. dissertation, Harvard University, 1954.

Foucault, Michel. *The Birth of Biopolitics: Lectures at the Collège de France, 1978–1979*. Michel Senellart, ed. Graham Burchell, trans. New York: Palgrave Macmillan, 2008.

Foucault, Michel. *Security, Territory, Population: Lectures at the Collège de France, 1977–78*. Michel Senellart, ed. Graham Burchell, trans. New York: Palgrave Macmillan, 2007.

Foucault, Michel. *Society Must Be Defended: Lectures at the Collège de France, 1975–76*. Mauro Bertani and Alessandro Fontana, eds. David Macey, trans. New York: Picador, 1997.

Fricke, Max. *Charles Brockden Brown's Leben und Werke*. Hamburg: Otto Meissner Verlag, 1911.

Kamrath, Mark L. *The Historicism of Charles Brockden Brown: Radical History and the Early Republic*. Kent, Ohio: Kent State University Press, 2010.

Kelly, Gary. "The Limits of Genre and the Institution of Literature: Romanticism between Fact and Fiction." In Kenneth R. Johnston, Gilbert Chaitin, Karen Hanson, and Herbert Marks, eds., *Romantic Revolutions: Criticism and Theory*, 158–175. Bloomington: University of Indiana Press, 1990.

Kennedy, Daniel Edwards. "Charles Brockden Brown: A Biography" (c. 1923–1945). Typescript with manuscript additions. Charles Brockden Brown Bicentennial Edition Records (bulk 1917–1995). Special Collections and Archives, Kent State University Libraries, Kent, Ohio.

Marchand, Ernest. "Introduction." In Charles Brockden Brown, *Ormond*, ix–xliv. New York: American Book Company, 1937.

Martinez, Inez. "Charles Brockden Brown: Fictitious Historian." Ph.D. dissertation, University of Wisconsin, 1979.

Trumpener, Katie. *Bardic Nationalism: The Romantic Novel and the British Empire*. Princeton, N.J.: Princeton University Press, 1997.

Watts, Steven. *The Romance of Real Life: Charles Brockden Brown and the Origins of American Culture*. Baltimore: Johns Hopkins University Press, 1994.

White, Ed. "Historical Sketches Order." Email message to Philip Barnard and Mark L. Kamrath, July 25, 2006.

CHAPTER 12

···

POLITICAL PAMPHLETS

···

STEPHEN SHAPIRO

THE cluster of longer writings discussed as the political pamphlets occupies an outsize place in considerations of Charles Brockden Brown's work.[1] The writings grouped in this category include *An Address to the Government of the United States, on the Cession of Louisiana to the French, etc.* (1803); *Monroe's Embassy, or, The Conduct of the Government, in Relation to Our Claims to the Navigation of the Missisippi* [sic], *etc.* (1803); *The British Treaty of Commerce and Navigation* (1806/1807?); and *An Address to the Congress of the United States, on the Utility and Justice of Restrictions upon Foreign Commerce, etc.* (1809). Although few nonspecialists encounter these pieces or are even aware of the historical controversies they address, the pamphlets have become a magical touchstone for negative summary evaluations of Brown, which often tendentially seek to separate the long romances of the 1790s (*Wieland, Edgar Huntly, Arthur Mervyn,* and *Ormond*) from the different forms of expression ("novels," journalism, geography, speculative fiction) that Brown later produced. Steven Watts's claim that "on or about April 1800 Brown changed" to become a "defender of bourgeois values" (Watts, 131–132) neatly captures the nineteenth- and twentieth-century received charge that Brown's last decade was spent advocating conservative or market-oriented positions. This spontaneous conversion theory, however, much like the Wieland father's spontaneous combustion, may prove less self-evident on further examination.

Before we examine each pamphlet more closely, five contexts or concerns should frame this discussion. The first raises the question of this group category's coherence and sequence. Should these writings be taken as unproblematically building on one another in a relatively smooth fashion? This chapter's claim is that the two 1803 works ought to be considered as fundamentally different from the 1809 *Address* and that the 1806/1807 *British Treaty* should not be attributed to Brown at all. As discussed here, there has been a variety of thoughtful discussion on attribution questions concerning the *British Treaty* and Brown's possible authorship. The current view, however, rejects attribution to Brown. If the *British Treaty* is removed from consideration, then what may have previously been seen as a consistent stream of interventions on governmental policy now looks like the output of two discrete moments, 1803 and 1809.

Furthermore, ought the 1803 works be treated similarly to the 1809 *Address*? The 1803 *Address* and *Monroe's Embassy* are substantively different from the 1809 *Address* in several basic ways. While both 1803 pamphlets were published anonymously and have a fictional narrator, the 1809 *Address* is not only printed under Brown's name but begins, somewhat unusually in Brown's corpus, by drawing the reader's attention to his prior writing and his Quaker background. In this light, the 1809 *Address* has an entirely different attitude to and threshold of unadorned facticity and authorial relation to the reader.

Additionally, as discussed below, the 1809 *Address* abjures the zesty complaints of the 1803 pamphlets and is more measured in tone and composition. While the earlier pamphlets are replete with literary devices, the 1809 text has few. Unlike the 1803 pamphlets, which seem to have been rapidly composed around themes on which and using modes in which Brown had never published before, the 1809 *Address* is the result of a longer period of reflection. Throughout the 1807–1809 years, Brown composed the book-length "Annals of Europe and America" for his *American Register* (see chapter 13 in this volume). In what were recognized as the most comprehensive accounts of contemporary European and American political events written to date in the United States, Brown was compelled to devote considerable time and effort to studying foreign events and materials in order to digest and comment on them for his readers. This lengthy, premeditated process led directly to the 1809 *Address*, specifically as parts of the 1808 "Annals" were reused, lightly edited, by Brown in the later *Address*. While Brown has often been criticized for writing and publishing in haste, his celerity in composition should not lead us to overlook the way in which, throughout his career, he seems to have thought about, taken notes on, and planned his approach to materials that occupied him for longer periods of time.

In this regard, the 1803 pamphlets do seem anomalous insofar as they were conceptualized and generated in a very short time. While the 1809 *Address* is the last long publication of Brown's known to us, it belongs within a web of materials on national political history that Brown was producing. These works include an 1804 translation and annotation of Comte de Volney's *A View of the Soil and Climate of the United States of America*; the *Historical Sketches*, a sprawling speculative history, composed likely in 1805–1806, which was not brought into final or complete form; and the two-volume *A System of General Geography*, a prospectus for which was publicly advertised and one volume of which was privately circulated, but which was lost after his death. Several of Brown's obituaries mention his fatally interrupted work in progress on this topic. Since "geography" as a category at that time intertwined lists of climate and topography with quasi-anthropological notions of collective mentality and temperament alongside matters of political economy, topics that would later be separated into the disciplines of geography, sociology, economics, and political science, this lost study would have possibly been Brown's conclusive statement on intellectual and social questions that he had been grappling with for at least a decade. The 1809 *Address*, then, can stand as an inferential avenue into what the *Geography* might have said, given its combined subjects. In this light, the 1809 *Address* has arguably more links and continuities with Brown's earlier writing, albeit in changed conditions and form of address. Just as Brown used his editorship in the 1800s to publish for the first time some of his writing from the 1790s, such as *Memoirs of Carwin the Biloquist*, the 1809 *Address* recuperates earlier themes and consideration about the social formation of history and culture. In this light, it is not insignificant that virtually all scholarly treatments of the political pamphlets make little or no mention of the 1809 *Address*, since doing so requires a greater grounding in Brown's other works than is necessary for the relatively discrete and disconnected 1803 pieces.

Third, Brown's work in the early years of the nineteenth century needs to be contextualized within the overall climate for anglophone progressives. The new century saw so great a concerted wave of repressive conservatism that practically no progressive writer active during the 1790s continued to confront reaction publicly. Nearly all fell into strategic silences, often based on the pressing need to ensure financial survival. Even the most otherwise dauntless figures, such as Thomas Paine, held back. The best comparative examples and models for Brown here, as always, remain William Godwin and Mary Wollstonecraft. After Wollstonecraft's death in 1797 and in the new political climate, Godwin voluntarily removed himself from public view. From 1805, he stopped writing novels and ran a children's bookshop under the name of his new wife (St. Clair, 279–298). He then proceeded to write books for children under various pseudonyms. The most frequently used was Edward Baldwin, a narrator who was described as a country gentleman. Baldwin's *Fables Ancient and Modern* was praised by the *Anti-Jacobin*, a journal nearly dedicated to harassing Godwin and his associates but one that was unaware of Baldwin's real identity. Among Godwin's other pseudonymous publications were histories of England (1805), Rome (1809), and Greece (1821). This phase of Godwin's reclusion and retreat to safe, uncontroversial topics is largely forgotten because in the mid- to late 1810s, he returned to publishing novels under his own name, after encouragement from his son-in-law Percy Shelley and daughter Mary (St. Clair).

This is to say that there are remarkable similarities between the shapes of Godwin's and Brown's careers and interests in historical writing. Yet while we understand Godwin's overall trajectory with little reference to a few years in the early nineteenth century, the same moment has been given a far more conclusive weight when considering Brown. Yet if Brown had not died in 1810, it is not impossible to imagine that he, like Godwin, would have actively returned to the forms and projects of the 1790s. The unfortunate contingency of Brown's fatal and unexpected illness, then, has perhaps unfairly conditioned the ways in which his achievement has been constructed.

Fourth, the period surrounding the 1803 pamphlets was also anomalous for Brown. After the 1798 yellow fever plague in New York City took the life of Elihu Hubbard Smith, Brown's housemate and one of his closest friends and supporters, his stays in New York became more frequently interrupted as he and his literary associates gradually scattered apart. A visit to Philadelphia in 1800, initially planned as temporary, resulted in a permanent return to that city. At that time, Brown seems finally to have given in to his family's concerns about financial stability, and he began working with his brothers' mercantile shipping and trading firm. While Brown's family had initially paid for his apprenticeship to one of Philadelphia's most established and prestigious lawyers, at a time before university law schools existed, Brown famously abandoned law in order to hazard a full-time literary career. Years of no formal employment, or even sporadic attempts at it, were probably underwritten by the largesse of his maternal grandmother, Elizabeth Lisle, a member of the Philadelphia Grandee Quaker elites and owner of large urban real estate holdings, and the relative indulgence often given to a family's younger children (Brown was the fourth of five brothers and six siblings overall). After the 1801 romances *Jane Talbot* and *Clara Howard*, which can both be read as Brown's critical investigation of and loss of faith in the novel's ability to house progressive ideals (see the chapters on them in this volume), Brown enters a phase where he has no ongoing or explicit literary or belletristic project. Possibly tasked with handling legal correspond-ence for his brothers' Atlantic shipping enterprises, Brown may have acquiesced to the absence of a literary life due to another reason, that is, family pressures blocking or delaying his eventual marriage to Elizabeth Linn on the basis of his need to secure proper financial stability. If both *Clara Howard* and *Jane Talbot* are obsessed with older family members' obstructive interference in the marriage plans of younger characters by leveraging concerns about money, these antimatrimonial plots may register Brown's own frustration at having to delay his marriage until late 1804 or, in other words, until after the relative success of the 1803 pamphlets may have persuaded their Philadelphia publishers, the Conrads, to back Brown's editorial project for a new journal, *The Literary Magazine, and American Register* (1803–1807).

Lastly, the environmental and familial context for the pamphlets points to a twofold problem in how scholars have or have not come to terms with the years after 1800. Because American politics have until recently been dominantly understood as a category defined, if not monopolized, by official political-party skirmishes over electoral victories, the history of the United States has been presented as best understood by using Thomas Jefferson's election in 1800 as a breaking point that closes off the period of the early American republic. On the other hand, Andrew Jackson's 1828 election is taken as the beginning of the antebellum period leading to the Civil War. Such frameworks make at least three fundamental moves, or mistakes, that structurally obscure the so-called early national period. First, they overprioritize political-party dynamics and thereby underestimate the central role of social and cultural transformations, forgetting that even the language of representative democracy implies the secondariness or belatedness of politics' "representation" of other social developments. Second, they overhomogenize political parties by focusing on the figure of the president, forgetting that all political parties are, in fact, coalitions and alliances in constant internal tension over policies and directions. This was never more so than with Jefferson's presidency, which cannot be used to simply identify positions as Democratic-Republican or Federalist. Audiences today are magnetized by theatrical representations of Alexander Hamilton and Aaron Burr, Jefferson's first vice president and assassin of Hamilton in 1804, partly because of the manifold and complex positions occurring in that period. As time goes on, and in a larger perspective, these complexities tend to become homogenized in ways few living at the time might have felt. All of Brown's pamphlets are clearly in opposition to Jefferson's foreign policy, but this opposition cannot automatically be taken as either an attack on the Democrat-Republicans or as an endorsement for the Federalists. In this respect, the conservative conversion thesis rests on too gross a view of the period.

Moreover, treatments of the United States cannot be understood coherently in isolation from global skirmishes. Throughout this period, nearly every feature of American society, including dress, clothing, and physical comportment, was shaped by the pulses of conflict between Britain and Napoleonic France (Shapiro). If we are to understand history by the rise and fall of men, then the career of Napoleon provides a more robust framework than the flash and disappearance of any single US president. North America, like Haiti, was caught in a changeable ecology contoured by Anglo-French (and likewise Spanish) tensions, and tactical positions in the New World often changed rapidly. The 1803 pamphlets are magnetized by fears of military conflict and possible invasion by France. By 1809, the enemy at hand, however, was the British, a country that during the War of 1812 actually did invade and burn down the White House. Static accounts of the Democratic-Republicans as pro-French and the Federalists as anti-French do not respond well to the period's dynamism.

In this light, an overall question emerges about how contemporary scholars understand the transitional outset of the nineteenth century and define what it means to be "conservative" in that period. Often, this is taken to mean a combination of demophobic politics with support for a free-market, free-trade ideology alongside exceptionalist ethnonationalism and heteronormative notions of gender relations. Today, from our present perspective, this cluster of outlooks, then categorized as liberalism (Wallerstein), appears as a force of reaction. Yet the early nineteenth century was in the process of transition and was rapidly reconfiguring a constellation of "long-eighteenth-century" concepts and ideals—involving bourgeois-dominated arguments in favor of communal sensibility (sentiment, sociability), doctrines of republicanism based on a selective excavation and interpretation of classical Greek and preimperial Rome, and principles of laissez-faire economics based on labor more than land—as part of a prolonged "revolutionary" effort to confront absolutist states grounded on monarchical sovereignty and/or aristocratic powers linked to Caribbean plantations.

The nineteenth century was the phase when the bourgeoisie became more confident in their ability to assume power, so that we see the transformation of long-held rhetorical positions, from socially oriented communitarianism to individualized competition, from international republican theory to nationalist imperialism, from laissez-faire dislike of internal governmental controls over the domestic market to claims for free trade directed against foreign governments' imposition of tariffs. Such reconfigurations involving multiple elements are never simple to orchestrate or uniformly synchronized in their transformation. Hence, if we now speak of a "long eighteenth century" and a "long nineteenth century," this suggests a period of overlap, including the initial decades of the 1800s, as a time of combined and uneven development. The period's development is uneven, on the one hand, because not all of these features become transformed synchronously in all regions of the world-system, and a plethora of variations emerge, including internally contradictory ones. It is combined, on the other hand, in the way Antonio Gramsci spoke of a "passive revolution" as a period when social groups that ought to be in conflict are actually coming together in a policy consensus, despite, or rather even because of, heated partisan conflicts (Gramsci 105–120).

In contrast to the politicians' sound and fury, this phase of the early national period is marked in reality by the ongoing formation of such a larger consensus. Much of the ire that Federalist politicians spurred was due, in large part, to the small set of New England factions that were coming to the inconvenient realization of their historic decline from their perceived authority and unquestioned regional privilege throughout the eighteenth century. A variety of factors converged to diminish New England's significance. Its agricultural backcountry became less productive due to the splintering of farms equally among male children, rather than inheritance primogeniture. The mercantile shipping trade began to fade as capital investment moved to new forms of industrialization or slightly southward with the rise of mid-Atlantic cities. Population growth in other regions left the New England states comparatively smaller. The popularity of rising denominations—Presbyterian, Baptist, and Methodist—undermined the religious authority of the region's Congregationalists. Yet despite their waning influence, the New Englanders are often granted outsize attention due to their cultural tendency toward heavy self-promotion (unlike other groups such as mid- and southern Atlantic Quakers) through the print public sphere and universities to which later scholars are often personally or professionally linked and on which their resources often depend.

An older political history of the period tacitly acknowledged the rising consensus by calling this phase the "Era of Good Feelings" due to the Democratic-Republicans' electoral dominance over a fading Federalist party, before it was in turn replaced by the Whigs. It is commonplace to assume that there were two competing visions for the future of the United States. In this narrative, Jefferson represented a nation based on farming for domestic consumption and Atlantic mercantile trade that would exchange these staples for ones that were not produced within a largely decentralized agrarian nation. On the other hand, the Federalists are seen as supporting a centralized nation promoting finance and manufacturing. This version of the era's political tensions, however, overlooks its more complex underlying concerns involving slavery, native territory, and the financial arrangements underpinning their relation to the world market. The transformation of Atlantic slavery to a more internally generated system involved shifting the locus of coerced labor from the production of sugar, and its links to alcohol production (rum), to cotton for textiles. The reorganization of the geography and density of slavery away from the coasts and inland to service a cotton trade revivified by new technologies, such as the cotton gin, vastly lowered production costs and created unexpected links between the South and the industrializing northern states and western European lands in ways different from and greater than the eighteenth-century colonies had experienced. Despite its self-assumed grandeur, the Virginia of George Washington and Jefferson was mirroring New England's shrinking economic significance. The states encompassing the new cotton fields, whose products were shipped via the Mississippi through New Orleans's port, however, were very differently linked to Atlantic commerce, especially as Britain was making its own transition toward industrial textile production. The importance of these new goods along with population pressures on the densely populated seaboard drove American immigration toward the frontiers.

These movements led inescapably to encounters and confrontations with Native American nations, and the resulting settler colonization led to repeated, if not routine, dispossession and genocide of indigenous peoples. Dunbar-Ortiz argues that frontier immigration by the so-called Scots-Irish, Scottish Protestants who populated Ulster Plantation, brought the patterns of anti-Catholic violence and land grabs to America, so that the violence of imperial British sectarianism became the template for later Anglo-Indian and US-Indian encounters. Underscoring both the economies of slavery and frontier expansionism were webs of credit and financial arrangement that grounded the attendant commodity chains linking the fluvial Mississippi with Atlantic and global oceanic trade. In many ways, then, the question that ought to guide our reading of the 1803 and 1809 pamphlets is not whether they are Federalist or Democrat-Republican in orientation but how they respond to the interconnected new trinity of slavery, native dispossession, and the new phase of the capitalist world-system, with its liberal ideologies of nationhood and individuality (Wallerstein).

The background to Brown's 1803 pamphlets looks to the changing landscape of America's empire beyond its eighteenth-century horizons. However, the larger irony is that Brown's initial 1803 *Address* would shortly be made irrelevant by events, thus limiting its actual effect. The context for the pamphlets began when Spain signed an ostensibly secret Third Treaty of San Ildefonso on October 1, 1800, to return Louisiana and New Orleans to France in exchange for Napoleon's support of Spanish rule in Tuscany. The name given to this transfer was *retrocession*, or *cession* for short, since New Orleans had originally belonged to France. News of the imperial trade spread quickly in the United States, causing fear, probably rightly, that Napoleon sought to recreate a French empire in North America. Although the transfer was scheduled for late 1803, the Spanish intendant or territorial governor unexpectedly closed the port to Americans, meaning that there was no place to store or distribute goods intended for the Caribbean and Atlantic trade. Americans could not say whether this closure was an individual act destined shortly to be overruled by Spanish authorities or an intentional provocation by the Spanish, effectively inviting the Americans to invade New Orleans, since Americans felt that Spain would rather have the United States control the region than the French but did not want to risk giving it to the Americans and thereby losing the opportunity to wrest European lands from the French.

The crisis, then, was twofold. First, it involved the entire status of the Mississippi as a crucial trading route for the emerging economy and potential barrier that needed overcoming in order for the nation to expand westward. That America ought to take possession of New Orleans was felt almost uniformly among political elites. Democratic-Republicans and Federalist politicians had few differences of opinion about the desirability of and need for acquiring control over New Orleans. The debate was about the *method* chosen. Should the United States attempt to negotiate with Napoleon through diplomatic channels or simply invade, leaning on a rising population of frontiersmen who were already armed, nearby, and belligerent? Second, since the United States did not have a standing army at that time, its military capability could not be assured against the experienced French forces. For the later War of 1812 would show that American militias were no match for a professionalized, regular army. Hence, while Jefferson did initiate plans for a military invasion, his first instinct was to attempt a diplomatic solution, even though few Americans had confidence in French trustworthiness. Whether Jefferson actually believed diplomacy would work or proposed diplomacy as a stalling tactic to win more time for assembling a military force is open for debate. In any case, that question did not have to be answered, since France unexpectedly offered to sell New Orleans and its associated territory to the United States in what is known today as the Louisiana Purchase.

Napoleon had two primary reasons for selling the land and abandoning French aspirations for a New World empire. First, a brief pause in the conflict between Britain and France, signed into effect by the 1802 Treaty of Amiens, broke down. With conflict resuming, Napoleon needed money for the next round of war, and one of the easier and more immediate ways to raise cash was to sell off property, in this case to Jefferson. Second, the sale of New Orleans was forced on Napoleon in many ways due to his failure to crush the Haitian Revolution. Napoleon dispatched an army to quell black liberation, but it was stymied by disease, and nearly a third of the French forces died from yellow fever. In need of money and unwilling to sacrifice troops who would be necessary for European campaigns, Napoleon abandoned Haiti and surprised American diplomats by making it clear that he would trade all of his American territorial claims beyond New Orleans for a good price.

The 1803 *Address* begins with a series of literary devices that immediately telegraph its status as a constructed text to its readers. The first is the device of its presentation by an anonymous "obscure citizen" not otherwise involved in political matters and measures (AG 3). The declaration is meant to appeal to the reader as a vox populi or common sense of the crowd. Yet because this rhetorical trick had become familiar throughout the eighteenth century, few readers took it at face value, and indeed, for most it served as indirect confirmation that they were getting information from a political insider. If the first element made the piece seem more authentic, the second undermines this appearance, as the narrator says that he has been given a document, purportedly an intercepted letter from a French counselor to Napoleon, by another American traveler in France.

While the framing device presents itself on the one hand as a direct channel to the heart of international affairs, it does so on the other hand through the Gothic tale's paraphernalia of intrigue, confidential disclosure, and revelations of corrupt designs beneath the surface. The seepage between facticity and fictional craft was perhaps very quickly perceived. Less than a month after the *Address*'s publication, the *Providence Phoenix* wrote, "The report goes that the celebrated pamphlet concerning Louisiana humerously [sic] attributed to a French Counselor of State, is the production of a *novel* writer of great celebrity in our capital cities; and this *brochure* was issued, not in a serious view but to try public taste in that *novel* walk of *Romance*." Using the keywords of romance—*novel, walk* (which seems to allude to *Edgar Huntly*'s Norwalk or Brown's lost novel *Sky-Walk*)—the *Phoenix* easily indicates Brown's authorship and suggests that the

Address should be read less for its political persuasion than as a calling card for literary fiction. Given that regional newspapers commonly republished news and information previously circulated in New York or Philadelphia newspapers, Brown's authorship of the pamphlet was likely known almost immediately in those two cities, and the report gives the strongest indication of how at least one group of contemporary readers contextualized the *Address*.

The literariness of the *Address* continues further, as the nature of its form will be familiar to those who know the style of Brown's other writing. The French counselor gives contradictory advice to Napoleon and presents arguments that are then followed by reverse claims. While the American narrator ends his address, after presenting the intercepted letters, by urging the US government to "STRIKE" and militarily occupy New Orleans (AG 56), the intervening complexity of the positions taken and then negatively evaluated can likewise have the effect of voiding the narrator's conclusion in advance. Because the American narrator simply ignores the counselor's list of factors that weaken and undermine the United States, his concluding call for invasion is left hanging as possible evidence of his own position's irrationality. Consequently, situated in the wake of Brown's romances, the 1803 *Address* might be taken as a case study of the mentality of those who advocate war. Everything depends on whether critics consider the narrator's explicit *thesis*, on the one hand, or Brown's *motivation* in presenting this expression for the reader's adjudication, on the other, as the argumentative and conceptual core of the piece. Or, alternatively, like Carwin, is the *Address* double-tongued and thus able to be read by both pro- and anti-invasion forces as confirming their positions?

Whatever one decides about Brown's intent, the lasting contribution of the *Address* is not its momentary politics but its articulation of a particularly modern and emergent view of political economy. The *Address* abandons long-standing considerations of international affairs based on legal right and the legitimacy of the state's actions, in favor of claims that nations pursue their own interests and merely deploy law to legitimize or sanitize these interests. As mentioned, this move marks the author's awareness but not necessarily endorsement of an emerging liberal political economy that is displacing the one girded by the continuing authority of a sovereign. The *Address* also indicates that the main force of historical change is not the actions of individuals considered in isolation, be they virtuous or vicious, corrupt or considerate, but a matter of the group action of a population. The shift from the molecular investigation of the individual (in this case, Jefferson) to the molar treatment of the mass belongs to what Michel Foucault calls biopower and biopolitics, as the large-scale momentum of population in the nineteenth century.

The French counselor argues that after the absolutist state and the tumult of the Revolutionary era, a new kind of power is emerging. Despite Napoleon's impressive victories on the battlefield, the counselor proposes that the power of the nineteenth century will be based not on "military exploits" but rather on the combination of four elements: population, the juridically backed bureaucratic state, the global market of international trade, and national identity. The French counselor proposes that these components, with an emphasis on population and profit seeking, are the factors on which governmental policy ought to be determined. In this amalgam of group interest with biopower, the counselor breaks away from eighteenth-century shibboleths to argue that policy should be shaped by a realistic consideration of force, rather than an effort to seek self-justifying precedent.

Thus, the arguments that increased population and ease of transportation and communication require expansion, and hence the invasion of Louisiana, bid farewell to Adam Smith's notion that trade is amicable and harmonizing. The counselor advocates a more modern-looking "free trade" perspective in that he views the globe as formed by a set of competitors. In this situation, each nation needs to consolidate its domestic harmony in order to best other nations in a competitive environment where the market produces inequality. Unlike Smith's laissez-faire economics, which sought to remove and neutralize the state, the French counselor perceives that in a post-Enlightenment-era, post-laissez-faire moment, the state needs to intervene, not to protect against commodity price increases but rather to create a market or, more precisely, to create the conditions under which a growing population will establish a market. The counselor thus perceives that markets are delimited or defined not by national limits but by those regions into which markets can expand. Anticipating the language and logistics of nineteenth-century imperialism, this restores the importance of territory but not within the older logic of feudalism. Instead, land is necessary as a staging ground for expanding the global marketplace.

Arguing from this viewpoint, the counselor has no place for concepts of exceptional national identity. The claims he makes are beyond morality, as he assumes that all nations act in a similar fashion. The classic claim of disinterested force, that is, the attempt to justify one nation's acts as better than the bad or unjust behavior of another's, appears mythological. In this sense, morality ought to have no place in considerations of state policy, since the interests that motivate any one nation are the same for the others. In this, the counselor generally refuses to assert any civilizational distinction between white Americans and Europeans and blacks in Haiti or elsewhere. The sole distinction the counselor recognizes in this regard is between American Indian (and other aboriginal peoples) and other groups. The exclusion of indigenous peoples has been the source of most recent critiques of the 1803 *Address* (Gardner; Doolen).

The counselor argues that France has lost Haiti not only as a result of the ravages of yellow fever but, more significantly, because of the black experience of liberation. Drawing attention to the transformation of the French peasantry into world-conquering soldiers in Napoleon's army through the transvaluation of revolution, the Haitian Revolution has transformed "a million helpless and timorous slaves" into "men, citizens, and soldiers" (AG 8). As Haiti is henceforth closed to the French, the counselor briefly considers Australia as a substitute, before arguing for a French recolonization of Louisiana. He reasons that the English are preoccupied with their other colonies in Ireland and India. The Americans are ill equipped to resist because of their self-weakening partisan disunity, self-complacent greed, and self-created internal threats of black slave rebellion and Native American resistance. The unnamed American narrator now interrupts the French counselor's letter to encourage an American invasion into a territory (and further into a continent) "which God and Nature have made ours" (52).

Shortly after the *Address, Monroe's Embassy* was published. This pamphlet is shorter and less rhetorically complicated than the 1803 *Address*. Furthermore, the tonal shifts and compositional style may possibly indicate that Brown was not the piece's sole author. The pamphlet's more heated nature is indicated by its signature, Poplicola. Using a Roman name, in this case that of a figure associated with opposition to the return to Roman monarchy, was a standard move for political polemics. The piece emphasizes familiar Brownian themes about the difficulty of ascertaining complex causal forces that shape historical events and consequentially cautions against the certainty of predictions. In this sense, *Monroe's Embassy* can be read as pushing many of the claims of the 1803 *Address* into the background. Instead, the piece is driven by a sense of urgency.

As Poplicola reveals himself to be a backcountry farmer, he argues that there is no time for diplomacy, since his perishable crops will rot, bankrupting himself and other farmers, as well as the merchants who need to trade these goods. Because of immediate time pressures, Poplicola urges invasion as the most expedient action to preserve the national economy. Matters of national honor or legal right are irrelevant in the face of business need. With its direct address and lack of encapsulated narratives, *Monroe's Embassy* is less literary and disencumbered of the counterconsiderations presented in the 1803 *Address*. The pamphlet's tense expression of need may be related to Brown's family's anxieties about the unsteady finances of its mercantile trade, which, judging by the lawsuits conducted by them, was deeply dependent on the smooth continuation of the New Orleans trade. Work on Brown's letters has led to the recovery of thirty-five lawsuits previously unknown to scholars, thirty of which were adjudicated in the New Orleans County and City courts in 1805–1807, revealing the Brown brothers' considerable interests in that port (Barnard, 522–523). At some point, these legal records will be made available via the Brown Electronic Archive project.

Unlike the 1803 *Address*, which was the only one of Brown's publications to go into a second edition in his lifetime, *Monroe's Embassy* did not garner much notice, as the success of the Louisiana Purchase put an end to invasion debates, and American politics moved on to other matters.

In late 1806 or 1807, *The British Treaty* was published in an initially anonymous form. The question of whether *The British Treaty* should be attributed to Brown has occasioned a small scholarly controversy. The pamphlet has a lively and rebarbative style, often including highly personalized and insulting attacks on James Madison and Jefferson, over their policy of expanding the territorial size of the United States. The strongest (and only) claim for Brown's authorship comes from William Dunlap, who had been a close companion of Brown's in the 1790s and New York period. Dunlap was in touch with Brown more sporadically during the 1801–1810 years following the author's return to Philadelphia, but in 1814, Brown's widow and executors called on Dunlap to complete a long-delayed posthumous biographical miscellany originally contracted with Paul Allen in 1811. Dunlap finished the project promptly and published the biography in 1815, mainly by padding Allen's text with previously unpublished material, and in the course of his commentary attributed *The British Treaty* to Brown without offering any commentary or rationale for his claim. Due to Dunlap's (relative) authority, based on access to Brown's surviving papers during his work on the biography, some later scholars accept his claim, partly because it chimed with the reception-history commonplace, itself related to struggles over the construction of his legacy, that Brown broke bad (conservative) in the new century.

Yet there have been strong arguments against this attribution. In 1952, David Lee Clark observes that the pamphlet's openly insulting ad hominem attacks are out of keeping with any of Brown's other writings and that its unnamed narrator claims to have known Madison as a youth, a chronology that would rule out Brown (Clark 260–261). Warner Berthoff concurred, noting additionally that the pamphlet is written in a style of "sustainedly easy vigor and polemical grace which Brown rarely, if ever could rise to" (Berthoff 405, 405 n. 1). Other questions remain. *The British Treaty* was published without any information regarding the printer-publisher. All of Brown's other pamphlets and post-1800 novels and magazines were consistently and openly printed by Philadelphians John Conrad (and brothers), H. Maxwell, or T. & G. Palmer. Additionally, *The British Treaty*'s second London edition (1808) lists Gouverneur Morris as the author. Since Brown was a prolific reader and editor of political matter published overseas in these years, the question arises of why he did not challenge that attribution if he was indeed this pamphlet's author. In his 2012 edition of writings by Morris, J. Jackson Barlow includes the pamphlet and provides several arguments for its attribution to Morris, while admitting that there can still be room for doubt and opening the door to the possibility that a third and still unknown writer, someone other than Morris (or Brown), may be the pamphlet's author.

On a preponderance of evidence, *The British Treaty* is not considered here to be Brown's. Dunlap may have initially attributed it to Brown for a range of reasons. After 1800, Dunlap was no longer in frequent contact with Brown, as they were no longer geographically proximate and had personal lives going in different directions, especially after Brown's marriage. Dunlap may have seen the pamphlet among Brown's papers when he was asked by the family to rescue the incomplete biography and, knowing of Brown's work on the 1803 and 1809 pamphlets, assumed that this publication was Brown's as well. On the other hand, by the 1810s, Dunlap was himself more consciously trying to downplay his own cultural politics of the 1790s. In a self-protective gesture, and possibly with the assumption that a similar move was necessary to establish Brown's reputation, Dunlap might have welcomed polemics against Jefferson, given that at this point, nearly all those within the American literary marketplace tended to align themselves with the Federalists.

The last pamphlet is Brown's 1809 *Address*, written under very different circumstances. At this point, Britain was America's main foreign antagonist, especially as it was threatening the highly profitable carrying trade between Caribbean goods and European markets and the sanctity of American vessels, as British forces boarded American ships to impress sailors. In response to these actions, and in what ranks as one of the most self-destructive economic policies in US history, Jefferson passed the Embargo Acts that after late 1807 made it illegal for American merchants to trade with either Britain or France, which had mutual blockades on each other. The effect of

Jefferson's policy was almost instantaneously to destroy US commerce and harbor employment. The consequences of this policy were so obvious that Jefferson was forced to lift the embargo fifteen months later. Hence, Brown's 1809 *Address*, suggestively conceived throughout 1808, was published just as its rebuttal of Jefferson's policy became pointless. As timing is all in political skirmishes, the *Address*'s effects were marginal.

The greater and enduring interest, then, of the 1809 *Address* lies in Brown's authorial self-positioning and how he argues in favor of lifting the embargo. For almost the first time in his writing, Brown writes *as himself* and abandons the techniques of quiet irony and duality of presented positions. Although the piece seeks to dismantle the logic behind Jefferson's foreign policy, the *Address* is equally, if not more, a condemnation of the Federalist style in confronting Jefferson. Brown reiterates his earlier claims but then abandons the manner used in the 1803 pamphlets. He rejects the claim that nations or individuals act rationally, since they operate to satisfy their own interests, rather than toward what may be actually fair and balanced. While this can be read as a dismissal of earlier Woldwinite arguments about striving for social betterment, it may more simply reflect a greater awareness of large-scale forces afoot. For if all social and international action is based on interest, then there is simply no point in pretending that one's own nation's acts are morally superior or legally justified. Nations act on "no principle but ambition and measured by no rule, but power" (AC vii). Instead, as he did earlier in *Monroe's Embassy*, Brown suggests that the best policy needs to be aware of the tempo of events and ready to act at the propitious moment. In this instance, however, Brown the narrator argues that waiting, rather than striking, is the best option. The *Address* begins by criticizing those who attack Jefferson by denouncing him as unpatriotic. Brown suggests that patriotism is not necessarily a positive value, resting as it does on chance in the accident of one's birth. He suggests that arguments should avoid combining strained efforts to "reason" through excessive citation of so-called facts, with intemperate accusations that the addressee is delusional. One either chooses the path of pacific, respectful dialogue or indulges in vicious polemics, but the two cannot be combined.

Discounting partisan style, Brown argues against the embargo on two broad lines. First, the embargo will not actually work, since neither Britain nor France will feel its effects; the pipeline of trade already afloat will continue, and such powerful nations have the ability to source goods elsewhere or do without. Second, as someone familiar with maritime commerce, Brown reminds the reader that innumerable strategies of illegal trafficking will subvert the embargo in real fact (indeed, the backstories of *Arthur Mervyn* emphasize a catalog of such strategies). Reiterating a point from *Monroe's Embassy*, Brown argues that the embargo's primary victims will be American farmers who have planted goods that cannot now find a market. If Jefferson idealized an agrarian republic, his foreign policy will damage this ideal more than Federalist plans for the nation. Brown ends the essay by arguing for a middle way that consists in building up the US domestic market so that it can decrease reliance on foreign trade. Overall, the *Address* seeks to separate party politics from the administration of state policy, implicitly suggesting that the emergent political-party system is not a good mechanism for the proper management of the nation.

Readings of the pamphlets have fallen into three patterns. The first presents the pamphlets as nonliterary oddities, a view often taken by the mid-twentieth-century biographical writers (Warfel; Clark, Axelrod, Ringe). This construction is likewise affirmed by those critics who endorse the general narrative of decline after the 1798–1800 phase of Brown's New York-based romance writing. Since Brown's noteworthiness was initially argued on the basis of those now canonical long fictions, and in a period when accurate attribution of periodical publications was even more difficult than it remains today, the *Bicentennial Edition* (Krause), for example, included only the long fictions and omitted the shorter stories, implicitly classifying everything else as a production of lesser significance. At present, the Charles Brockden Brown Electronic Archive and the ongoing Bucknell *Collected Writings* edition are establishing the importance of Brown's "other" fiction as a further exploration and extrapolation of Brown's 1790s ideas but in texts that respond to the alteration and evolution of cultural conditions that were created by emerging political and economic liberalism; nationalism and imperial expansion; confrontations between the two modes of capitalist regimes, one based on wage labor and the other on slavery; and the rise of bourgeois mores, including identities of heteronormative gender and sexuality. Brown's realization that many of the social analyses of the 1790s had imperfectly seen the onset of these features meant that he was in search of new forms of expression that could better convey and respond to the rising new social ecology.

Brown seems to have used his post-1800 long fictions (see the chapters in this volume on *Jane Talbot*, *Clara Howard*, and the *Historical Sketches*) to critique the efficacy of the novel as a form. The first decade of the nineteenth century can be read not as the absence or degradation of cultural forms but rather as an explosive growth of new, experimental ones. Few of these forms (journalistic excerpting, geography, speculative histories) garnered enough density to be recognized as a category. The "novel," on the other hand, by the late 1810s and '20s in Europe and by the 1840s in America, becomes intelligible not only as one form of creative culture but as the *dominant* literary form, and indeed to such a degree that it has been allowed to rewrite the period before its hegemony. Hence, well-known scholarly accounts imagine a linear, always upward *rise* of the novel and regard pre-1840s generic developments in often anachronistic ways.

A second pattern involves a split in the criticism regarding Brown's relationship to Americanness, a category initially considered as a positive and then more negatively since the 1970s. Scholars have recently condemned the pamphlets as evidence of Brown's (tacit) acceptance of imperialism, dispossession of Native Americans, and racial discrimination (Watts; Gardner; Doolen, Looby, Kafer, Hsu). Even more recently, a third mode has been to (begin to) consider the literariness of the pamphlets and to acknowledge that efforts to use political-party labels to assign blame (usually) do not capture the complexities of the period's spectrum of positions (Levine). Mark Kamrath has brought attention to the way that the 1803 *Address*'s rhetorical tactics bear resemblance to the long fiction of the 1790s and cautions against oversimplifying or assuming links between Brown's opinions and those of the French counselor. Despite its length, the 1809 *Address* has received practically no analysis, given the assumption that it merely reinscribes the perceived directions of the 1803 pamphlets, even while the basic change of concerns, from the French to the British in the years leading to the War of 1812, suggests the need for interpretative differentiation.

A challenge for considering the pamphlets is to see them as individual texts with their own particularities, even as they share continuities. From the perspective of Brown studies, the ultimate value of the pamphlets lies not in what gratifying or distressing perspective we find they convey but in the ways they encourage us to think about the early 1800s as a time that was cross-hatched with internal transformations and possibilities for cultural expression, not all of which survived in ways that are easily categorizable today.

NOTE

1. This discussion draws on my "Historical Essay" within the forthcoming Bucknell *Collected Writings* edition's Volume 4, *Political Pamphlets*, edited by Mark L. Kamrath, Stephen Shapiro, and Maureen Tuthill.

WORKS CITED

Axelrod, Alan. *Charles Brockden Brown, An American Tale.* Austin: University of Texas Press, 1983.

Barlow, J. Jackson. "The British Treaty (1807/08)." In J. Jackson Barlow, ed., *To Secure the Blessings of Liberty: Selected Writings of Gouverneur Morris*, 423–424. Indianapolis: Liberty Fund, 2012.

Barnard, Philip. "The Letters of Charles Brockden Brown." In Celeste-Marie Bernier, Judie Newman, and Matthew Pethers, eds., *The Edinburgh Companion to Nineteenth-Century American Letters and Letter-Writing*, 511–524. Edinburgh: Edinburgh University Press, 2016.

Berthoff, Warner B. "The Literary Career of Charles Brockden Brown." Ph.D. dissertation, Harvard University, 1954.

Clark, David Lee. *Charles Brockden Brown: Pioneer Voice of America.* Durham, N.C.: Duke University Press, 1952.

Doolen, Andy. *Fugitive Empire: Locating Early American Imperialism.* Minneapolis: University of Minnesota Press, 2005.

Dunbar-Ortiz, Roxanne. *An Indigenous Peoples' History of the United States.* Boston: Beacon, 2014.

Foucault, Michel. *History of Sexuality*, Vol. 1, *An Introduction* (1976). New York: Vintage, 1981.

Gardner, Jared. *Master Plots: Race and the Founding of an American Literature, 1787–1845.* Baltimore: Johns Hopkins University Press, 1998.

Grabo, Norman S. *The Coincidental Art of Charles Brockden Brown.* Chapel Hill: University of North Carolina Press, 1981.

Gramsci, Antonio. *Selections from the Prison Notebooks.* Quintin Hoare and Geoffrey Nowell Smith, eds. and trans. New York: International Publishers, 1971.

Hsu, Hsuan. *Geography and the Production of Space in Nineteenth-century American Literature.* Cambridge: Cambridge University Press, 2010.

Kafer, Peter. *Charles Brockden Brown's Revolution and the Birth of American Gothic*. Philadelphia: University of Pennsylvania Press, 2004.

Kamrath, Mark L. *The Historicism of Charles Brockden Brown: Radical History and the Early Republic*. Kent, Ohio: Kent State University Press, 2010.

Kamrath, Mark L., and Philip Barnard, eds. The Charles Brockden Brown Electronic Archive and Scholarly Edition. www.brockdenbrown.ucf.edu, December 30, 2011.

Krause, Sydney J., general ed. *The Novels and Related Works of Charles Brockden Brown: Bicentennial Edition*. Kent, Ohio: Kent State University Press, 1977–1987.

Levine, Robert S. *Dislocating Race & Nation: Episodes in Nineteenth-Century American Literary Nationalism*. Chapel Hill: University of North Carolina Press, 2008.

Looby, Christopher. *Voicing America: Language, Literary Form, and the Origins of the United States*. Chicago: University of Chicago Press, 1996.

Ringe, Donald A. *Charles Brockden Brown*. New York: Twayne, 1966.

Shapiro, Stephen. *The Culture and Commerce of the Early American Novel: Reading the Atlantic World-System*. University Park: Pennsylvania State University Press, 2008.

St. Clair, William. *The Godwins and the Shelleys: A Biography of a Family*. Baltimore: Johns Hopkins University Press, 1991.

Wallerstein, Immanuel. *The Modern World-System IV: Centrist Liberalism Triumphant, 1789–1914*. Berkeley: University of California Press, 2011.

Watts, Steven. *The Romance of Real Life: Charles Brockden Brown and the Origins of American Culture*. Baltimore: Johns Hopkins University Press, 1994.

CHAPTER 13

"ANNALS OF EUROPE AND AMERICA" AND BROWN'S CONTRIBUTION TO EARLY AMERICAN PERIODICALS

MARK L. KAMRATH

"Philadelphia, Mr. Charles B. Brown, editor of the American Register; as an annalist he acquired much reputation."

Obituary, *Boston Gazette*, March 5, 1810

THE study of American periodicals has a long history, beginning with Frank Luther Mott's *A History of American Magazines 1741–1850* (1930) and then being updated by works such as Michael T. Gilmore in *The Cambridge History of American Literature* (1994) and other studies. Gilmore remarks that while periodicals evolved out of newspapers on both sides of the Atlantic, American periodicals "accommodated the popular reading habits of the nascent liberal order and opened their pages to voices that disputed established hierarchies" (1: 558). Charles Brockden Brown's contributions to and editing of periodicals were closely connected with his understanding of the relationship between "history" and "romance" and his willingness to challenge the political status quo. This is particularly true, I want to suggest, in the last periodical he edited, the *American Register; or, General Repository of History, Politics, and Science*, which he published from 1807 through 1809 and which illustrates the arc of his democratic sensibilities but also the importance of more closely examining Brown's extensive periodical work both as an author and as an editor and his efforts to enlighten his readers.[1]

To begin, while Brown contributed to American periodicals as early as, possibly, 1788, it was his involvement with the New York Friendly Club that prompted him to seriously consider launching a monthly magazine.[2] In late December 1798, he wrote to his brother Armitt about his plan: "Eight of my friends here, men in the highest degree respectable for literature and influence, have urged me so vehemently to undertake the project of a magazine and promised their contributions and assistance to its success, that I have written and published proposals. Four hundred subscribers will repay the annual expense of sixteen hundred dollars" (Letters 449). Although it is difficult to fully identify his friends, we know that Elihu Hubbard Smith, a physician, and William Dunlap, a playwright, were among the closest and influenced his thinking on a range of topics. Nevertheless, it is in this context that Brown began his career as a magazine editor.[3]

The Monthly Magazine, and American Review, published between April 1799 and December 1800, sought initially, says David Lee Clark, to "exclude all political and controversial matter" and to focus primarily on "Original Communications, Selections, and Poetry" but over time did address the difficulties of (quoting Brown) being "entirely free from theological and political polemics" (131, 133, 151). Brown, to be sure, contributed essays and reviews to the magazine and, as Clark points out, was particularly focused on the question of American literature and authorship (137). He routinely defended American genius and literary production and featured material on American customs and manners, science and geography, and agriculture. Brown provided his readers with essays on such things as emigration, Philadelphia water works, the American language, the role of female politicians, intimacy between youths, and punishment, along with reviews of speeches and sermons. He also promoted historical writing in relation to specific colonies, the Revolution, and the overall progress of the country (Clark 149).

The period from 1803 to 1807 is when Brown edited and contributed to *The Literary Magazine, and American Register*. As Michael Cody points out, during this time, Brown published fifty-one monthly issues and used the magazine to "remain active in America's shifting ideological and cultural life" (9–10). "Like inn, tavern, coffeehouse, and street corner conversations," says Cody, "the magazine ranges through topics from politics and literature to yellow fever and dogs" (20). It discusses classical literature, female education, newspapers, and a host of other subjects, including marriage, revolution in Saint-Domingue, vaccination, the rise of religious sects, drunkenness, and death. In any given issue, readers would encounter essays on the lives of George Washington and Thomas Jefferson, along with titles such as "Why the Arts Are Discouraged in America," "Abolition of Slavery in New Jersey," "Death of Hamilton," "Remarks on Female Dress," "Terrific Novels," "Pestilence and Bad Government Compared," and "Literary Blunders." Unlike Joseph Dennie and others, argues Cody, Brown did not seek to establish any editorial authority or voice; instead, he sought to "moderate" reader conversations and "advance the interests of miscellaneous literature" (20–21).

Brown's last magazine, the *American Register*, was a semiannual work published from January 1807 through 1809 and focused heavily on foreign and domestic events as well as laws and public documents. Unlike his first attempt at editing, here Brown eventually embraced political matters. In his opening preface, for example, he remarked, "In properly distributing and proportioning the materials of a work of this nature, the compiler can only be guided by experience. And he must make several trials before his collections completely settle." Further, he hoped that his "Abstract of the Laws and Public Acts of the United States" would be of "some value to the lawyer and political enquirer" (Annals I: iii).

By the time he reached Volume 5 of "Annals of Europe and America, published in the *American Register*, he remarked in his preface that the magazine was "a work previously unattempted in America" and was "particularly designed to be a repository of American history and politics" (Annals V: iii). Most important, and drawing on his training as a lawyer, his experience as a novelist, and his abilities as an editor, Brown says of his editorial plan:

> The Register includes a comprehensive abstract of all the laws passed by the general government. This is not introduced for the benefit of the lawyer, to whom the originals only are of any service, but as the most important historical documents. The laws of the United States, from the nature of the government, relate almost wholly to the levying and collection of revenue; to the formation, distribution, and maintenance of a military force by land and by sea; to the modeling and government of frontier territories; to the public intercourse with the Indian tribes; and to modes of conduct with regard to foreign nations. Regulations on these points are closely connected with the current history of the nation and are absolutely necessary to be known by those who would be acquainted, not with municipal law but the political condition of their own country.   (Annals V, iii–iv)

Brown's editorial policy, in other words, changed as he moved from being a "compiler" of documents to a historian who was trying to focus the diverse interests of his readers on the current history and politics of the country. In an effort to educate a broad range of readers about recent events and their impact on a young democracy, he made careful use of public documents, historical narrative, and foreign news. In addition to his "Annals of Europe and America," he included historical sketches, chronicles, abstracts of laws and public acts, and obituaries. He also continued to provide sections entitled "Poetry" and "Review of Literature."[4]

Turning specifically to Brown's "Annals of Europe and America," for the better part of fifty years, since the 1960s, Brown's Gothic novels *Wieland* and *Edgar Huntly* have traditionally garnered the most reading and enthusiasm, both in scholarly circles and in the early American literature classroom. Since the publication of *Revising Charles Brockden Brown* in 2004, there has been more focus on Brown's other novels as well as his nonfiction, specifically his periodical writing, historical sketches, and political pamphlets. What has emerged since this time is a clearer picture not only of Brown's understanding of the relationship between "history" and "romance" but also of his capacity for historical analysis and writing contemporary history.

That is, if in the early 1800s, both sides of the Atlantic were in a state of cultural, economic, and political flux, and imperial ambitions, regardless of nationality, abounded, Brown's "Annals of Europe and America" represent an important moment in the history of early republican democracy and American historiography. Published in the *American Register* from 1807 through 1809, Brown's "Annals" provide a unique view of historical events in both Europe and America, his capacity as a novelist to write "history," and his status as an ironic historian.

Peter Novick writes, "Anyone interested in what professional historians are up to...might well begin by considering 'the objectivity question,'" arguing that a central question that has concerned historians from one age to the next has been the meaning and function of "objectivity" and bias in historical narrative (1). Contrary to consensus historiography, the late Enlightenment period, dating back to the writing of Pierre Bayle's *Historical and Critical Dictionary* (1696), articulates a consciousness of how difficult it is to write history with "perfect impartiality" (Bayle 109). Like Bayle and, later, William Godwin in "Of History and Romance" (1797), Brown inquired into the relationship between history and fiction in a historically self-conscious way.

To illustrate: the publication of "Walstein's School of History" and "The Difference between History and Romance," published in the *Monthly Magazine* in 1799 and 1800, respectively, offer Brown's earliest and clearest thoughts on historical writing and provide perspective on his later "Annals." In "Walstein," for example, Brown uses a fictional persona to explore models of "right conduct" and the limits of historical representation. In asserting that "Walstein was conscious of the uncertainty of history" and that one "can only make approaches to the truth," Brown's historical self-consciousness resonates with that of Godwin and others who understood the limitations of reason and language in representing the past (Walstein 336–337).

In "Difference," Brown specifically identifies how difficult it is to make distinctions between the writing of history and fiction. He writes that "History and romance are terms that have never been very clearly distinguished from each other" and that both the historian and the romancer attempt to represent the truth at some level. However, he also notes that the writer of history is a "dealer, not in certainties, but probabilities, and is therefore a romancer" (Difference 251). For Brown, in other words, the boundary between "history" and the "novel" was fluid, not hard and fast, and historical writing was an imaginative, subjective undertaking as much as it was a factual, objective one.

Brown's interest in the subject of history and the role of the imagination continued to evolve and manifested itself in his novels, later essays and reviews, and particularly his "Sketches of a History of Carsol" and "Sketches of a History of the Carrils and Ormes." His *Historical Sketches*, ten fragments tracing the imagined history of an English family from the Middle Ages to Brown's own time, serves as a workbench, from as early as 1803 to around 1806, where he examined the institutions and power structures of ecclesiastical and civil government. As in his novels, his historical sketches explore the histories of individuals and families; unlike them, however, they trace "domestic history" through successive generations. Further, just as Brown's Louisiana political pamphlets of 1803 contain political commentary and irony, so his historical fragments, as Philip Barnard has observed, interrogate the status quo and register cultural commentary about oppressive religious and political regimes (Barnard 318–319). In short, his imagined histories form a historiographical bridge between his novels and his "Annals of Europe and America," marking his readiness to historicize events in Europe alongside those in the United States.

I. "Annals of Europe"

Published in the first five volumes of the *American Register* and modeled in part after the British *Annual Register*,[5] Brown's "Annals of Europe and America" ran from 1807 until 1810, when Brown died, and Robert Walsh continued the remaining two volumes. In both cases, authorship of the "Annals" is complicated by the fact that Brown (and later Walsh) borrowed material from various sources, including Philadelphia newspapers, a common practice during the time. Despite this, Brown, like his contemporaries, also sought to be historically self-conscious and to avoid bias in his historical narrative. His appreciation of the imagination and its role in reconstructing is evident in his opening statement, where he writes:

> POLITICAL transactions are connected together in so long and various a chain, that a relater of contemporary events is frequently obliged to carry his narration somewhat backward, in order to make himself intelligible.... An active imagination is apt to carry us very far backward on these occasions; for, in truth, the chain of successive and dependent causes is endless; and he may be said to be imperfectly acquainted with the last link, who has not attentively scrutinized the very first in the series, however remote it may be.   (Annals I: iii)

Similar to his earlier questioning of the relationship between "history" and "romance," here Brown articulates a consciousness of the constructed aspects of historical writing—the role of the "imagination" in historicizing the past and understanding cause and effect, politically or otherwise. It is an understanding of history that would shape Brown's own historical writing as he sought in each volume to more effectively integrate historical sources into his historical narrative.

"Annals of Europe" itself appears in the first four volumes of the *American Register* and is dominated by analysis of Napoleon's rule in Europe, especially his march through the Mediterranean and eastern Europe, and the spread of British empire in India and South America. It is a narrative, in other words, that is attuned to the expansion of European nationalism, revolution, and war, along with the ways political and economic self-interest clashed with an emerging ethos and ideology of human rights in the early 1800s.

Of Napoleon, for instance, Stuart Woolf writes that despite his regime's restrictions on individuals, Napoleon's "administrative, fiscal, and juridical reforms" carried over in European states after his empire fell (243). In England, in fact, there was significant "sympathy" for Napoleon during his rule. In the United States, Napoleon's campaigns were covered in various newspapers, periodical publications, and occasional histories (Semmel 14). Tracts such as *Political & Theological Disquisitions on the Signs of the Times, Relative to the Present Conquests of France* (1807) and *Identity of Napoleon and Antichrist; Completely Demonstrated* (1807) highlighted interest in the convergence of biblical or millennial prophecy and current events. Local Philadelphia papers such as *Poulson's*

American Daily Advertiser and Duane's *Aurora General Advertiser* were among those printing news about Napoleon's success and defeats.

Brown's analysis of Napoleonic rule begins by conceding that in the years leading up to 1806, it was "well known" that France "defeated, repulsed, disarmed, or subdued" countries such as England, Spain, and Austria and that the English refusal to surrender Malta sparked war between the two countries and caused France to renew aggression against Austria (Annals I: 6). Turkey, Russia, and Prussia, he observes, were the only powers to stay out of war, at least initially. The French, Brown observes, "were not blind to the obvious policy of disuniting these allies, and that dexterity and artifice, in which the French excel all other nations were exerted for the purpose, but entirely without success" (Annals I: 15). Likewise, Brown says, France may be seen as conducting a policy of bribery in order to gain the "connivance and neutrality" of a particular country for its benefit (Annals I: 34). For example, the offering of Hanover to Prussia may be seen as a prime instance of Napoleon's use of territorial acquisitions to pacify a country while continuing to expand his empire. The French invasion of Poland and Napoleon's promise that he would make them "once more a nation," also is accounted for by Brown (Annals I: 58).

While the French defeat at Eylau in 1807 and the Treaty of Tilsit are covered by Brown, along with Napoleon's campaigns into Italy and Portugal, efforts to wait until events have unfolded before assigning cause and effect begin to emerge as a trademark of his historical writing. To be sure, Brown's historical narrative lapses into subjective, even ironic, commentary, as when he compares the egotism and "vanity" of Napoleon to the "imperial trappings and barbarous pomp of Charlemagne," depicts the ruler of Spain as a "prince verging upon idiocy and dotage, enslaved by the most ridiculous passions and devoted to the most childish pursuits," or comments on other types of "absurdity" (Annals I: 13, 17). But he attempts to demonstrate objectivity by stating his desire to delay analysis of a particular historical event.

Aside from critical representations of Napoleon and stereotypes about the French as masters of "subterfuge and sophistry," Brown's historical analysis also astutely remarks on how European countries typically relate to one another—a perception that would later inform his "Annals of America" (Annals I: 17). Early on, Brown comments on the absurdity of thinking that "gratitude or justice has any concern in the intercourse or compacts of nations"; the "selfish principle," he remarks, dictates that "deference and favour" toward another are greatest when something is to be gained (Annals I: 34). Of European nations' treatment of one another, Brown further remarks, "in seizing all within our reach, we act like the rest of the world, but in abstaining from the prey, when none can force us to abstain, we display an equity and moderation singular and meritorious" (Annals I: 45). In applying this principle to Napoleon, Brown suggests that he has shown restraint in regard to Austria, Tuscany, Rome, and the German princes and that Napoleon's efforts to require that Lutherans and Catholics be given the same religious and political rights qualify a view of him as absolute dictator. Brown's attempt, in other words, to objectively render historical analysis of Napoleonic rule also begins to engage the policies of empire building or territorial expansion of other countries, most notably the British Empire in India and South America.

As France pursued territorial expansion, England was extending its colonial reach on several fronts, one of which was South America and another India. In the "Annals of Europe," Brown is conscious of the relationship between race and gender in colonial constructions of the other and the ways, for instance, in which peoples inhabiting South America were generally thought by Europeans to be "discontented with their government, and ripe for any revolution; to be the prey of domestic faction; and disabled, by effeminacy, indolence, and a long inexperience of war, for any effectual resistance" (Annals I: 24). It is, however, on the topic of South America and the British withdrawal from Buenos Aires in 1807 that Brown tentatively associates American expressions of imperialism with English ones and also comments ironically on British colonialism.

Analyzing how Spanish colonial subjects view Spain and are mistakenly characterized as indolent, cowardly, or effeminate, Brown remarks that Americans imagine that all those colonized by Spain, like the former American subjects of Great Britain, desire separation from Spain in the Americas and that

> we have even harbored the gross delusion, that a wretched adventurer, at the head of two or three hundred men, picked up in our cities, could work a revolution in South America, and that the initial spark only was wanting to kindle a rebellion in Peru or Mexico. The grossness of these delusions is now made evident by the failure of so many formidable expeditions to La Plata.   (Annals I: 28–29)

Brown's assessment here of how military ambitions can co-opt political ones plays out more fully in his "Annals of America" when he examines the causes and effects of Francisco de Miranda's failed invasion of Venezuela. But even here, in his brief allusion to the "gross delusion" of adventurers like Miranda, he demonstrates his willingness to analyze the ideological mindset that prompts individuals in one country to determine that a revolution is needed in another. Brown's interest in the dynamics of political liberation and self-gain is a consistent theme in the "Annals."

Like Thomas Paine and William Duane, Brown examines British colonial rule in India. In Philadelphia, where Brown lived, the *Philadelphia Monthly Magazine* (1798), Duane's *Aurora General Advertiser* (1795–1812), and *Poulson's American Daily Advertiser* (1801–1839) all printed news about British military operations, mutinies in India, or native resisters such as Tipu Sultan. Just as Duane, in fact, wrote about "the injustice of the English government in India" and the "massacres of millions for commercial purposes in India, or Asia" (33) so Brown used his novel *Edgar Huntly* (1799) to interrogate a colonial ethos in India and the political status quo.[6]

It is in the "Annals," though, where Brown's Quaker beliefs about natural rights and the influence of Godwin's *Enquiry concerning Political Justice and Its Influence on Morals and Happiness* (1793) become apparent. Recalling Edmund Burke's December 1, 1783, "Speech on Mr. Fox's East India Bill" and his condemnation of "Indian suffering" (381) under East India Company practices, Brown probes how "the rights of men" were "cruelly violated" (Burke 386), stating:

Though it requires no extensive research to discover instances of selfish and iniquitous policy in the history of all nations, and especially in British history, mankind seldom extend their view beyond the present scene, and the recent usurpations of the French in the free cities and small states of Germany, in Switzerland, and Italy, excluded from the view of political observers the more ancient or distant examples of similar iniquities in the conduct of Great Britain. Even the recent conduct of that power in Turkey was as egregious an instance of political injustice as the imagination can conceive; but it was transacted at a distance, was aimed against infidels and the perpetual enemies of christian Europe, and was not crowned with success. The conduct, likewise, of the same government in India was a tissue of bare-faced usurpations on the rights of others, for which the usurper never deigned to allege any other motive than his own interest. But these were likewise afar off, and affected a race of men too much unlike ourselves to awaken our sympathy.   (Annals I: 67)

Brown's historical analysis here is highly insightful for his time, particularly in his observation that England, like France and like other countries in the past, has also pursued a "selfish and iniquitous policy" in regard to other continents and peoples. His reference to acts of British "political injustice" in Turkey not only recalls Godwin's critique of political institutions and the oppression of individuals but also targets injustices toward India. Saying that "the same government in India was a tissue of bare-faced usurpations on the rights of others," Brown fully interrogates the extent to which political self-interest motivates countries like England to ignore or condone atrocities abroad. He also identifies the racist dimensions of colonialism and why a lack of "sympathy" for others mutes any moral outcry concerning the oppression of other peoples.

Brown's "Annals of Europe" and analysis of European imperialism and colonialism conclude with the impact of Napoleonic aggression toward the Mediterranean and eastern Europe, particularly Turkey, Russia, Prussia, and Portugal, and with the effects of English military assaults on Denmark. He assesses not only the conduct of France and England but also the various alliances between them and other countries as each competed for geographical and military advantage. He details, for instance, Prussian territorial interests, Russian military maneuvers, and how the Russian forces retreated from the French to the Prussian town of Eylau in 1807. Likewise, Brown examines the Treaty of Tilsit (signed by France and Prussia in 1807), its political and economic repercussions, and remarks, self-reflexively, "It is not the historian's province to indulge in conjecture with regard to the future.... There is nothing, however, more certain than that the conduct of nations is regulated by their power" (Annals II: 59).

Nowhere, however, in the "Annals of Europe" is his historical self-consciousness more evident than when he reflects on the difficulties of determining the truth and the role of public or official documents in doing so. Such efforts distinguish Brown's historical narrative from others of his time. In his account of Napoleon's evacuation from Portugal in September 1808, for example, he consciously appends primary sources in an "Appendix" to his narrative titled "Official Papers Relative to the Evacuation of Portugal by the French Army," indicating his desire to have his historical narrative supplemented by primary documents such as "Report of the Court of

Enquiry, Appointed to Examine the Conduct of British Commanders in Portugal, and Proceedings Thereupon" (Annals IV: 31–39).

While other parts of his "Annals" would reflect increasing use of footnotes to record this type of commentary and how "no conscientious historian" should rely on "Private and anonymous information" (Annals IV: 23), Brown was clearly moving toward the belief that his own historical objectivity, and the historical understanding of his readers, might be best served by greater access to public, historical documents themselves—a belief that was to be forged further as he turned more fully in 1809 to writing his "Annals of America."

II. "ANNALS OF AMERICA"

In contrast to the "Annals of Europe," Brown's "Annals of America" register greater experimentation with regard to narrative form and a more ironic tone with regard to historical content. That is, as Brown became more attuned to European imperialism and colonialism and how "self-interest" motivated nation-states to act, he also became more conscious of how an imperial ethos impacted the course of recent events in America as it sought to expand its empire after 1800. Specifically, his coverage of the Aaron Burr conspiracy, the *Chesapeake* affair, Jefferson's embargo, and events associated with the Republican Caucus of 1808 illustrates his novel approach to "history"—his capacity for writing "dialogically" or in an ironic, politically conscious way.[7]

To begin, part of the backdrop for Brown's historical writing is a filiopietistic tradition of historical writing that assumed that providential design and national destiny in America were synonymous. This belief in American exceptionalism can be traced back to colonial historians such as William Bradford, Edward Johnson, Cotton Mather, and others in such works as *Wonder-Working Providence of Sions Saviour in New England* (1653) and can be found in contemporary histories such as Mercy Otis Warren's three-volume *History of the Rise, Progress, and Termination of the American Revolution Interspersed with Biographical, Political and Moral Reflections* (1805). As historian Michael Kraus observes of early explorers and historians, the "need to render unto God a statement of actions done in His name, and the desire to thank Him for beneficent guidance also found an outlet in our earliest historians" (22). George H. Callcott concurs, writing of nationalism after 1776 that "Americans never fully rejected their Puritan past, never fully embraced Enlightenment skepticism, never entirely broke the line between the Great Awakening that began in 1740 and the Great Revivals, which began in 1757" (16). Among the many historians, he asserts, who began their careers as clergymen and embraced the idea of a special destiny for America were Jedidiah Morse, Jeremy Belknap, Benjamin Trumbull, Jared Sparks, and George Bancroft.

Against this paradigm of US historiography, Brown's historical writing about American events aimed, like his writing about European events, to be impartial and objective; similarly to Washington Irving's *History of New York* (1809), it employed ironic commentary. Unlike Irving, though, Brown in "Annals of America" (begun two years prior to Irving's history) does more than mock New York's political elite or ridicule historical religious claims for displacing the American Indians and colonizing America. Amid the political turbulence of the 1790s and the Napoleonic Wars, Brown aimed to write a philosophically self-conscious and politically objective account of recent US history—and to avoid a teleological understanding of events, or a set of biases, in his search for historical truth.

To illustrate: Brown's *Address to the Government of the United States, on the Cession of Louisiana to the French, etc.*, published in January 1803, and *Monroe's Embassy, or, The Conduct of the Government, in Relation to Our Claims to the Navigation of the Missisippi* [sic], published in March 1803, both address the importance of Louisiana relative to French and American interests and argue for domestic security. Using a fictitious French counselor in the first pamphlet and the pseudonym "Poplicola" in the second, Brown's speakers, not Brown himself, articulate a nationalist stance. At the same time, his narrative can be ironic in that he is conscious of the prior "necessity of gin to disable, of fraud to betray" an "oppressed" race (AG 22), that is, Native Americans. In other words, Brown constructs narrative personas in these pamphlets whose perspectives both affirm and undercut common assumptions concerning, for example, national self-interest and the racialist and imperialist underpinnings of expansionism or Manifest Destiny.

In the "Annals" several years later, Brown echoes the position of Republican Samuel Harrison Smith, editor of the pro-Jefferson *National Intelligencer*, who favored the purchase of Louisiana from the French (as opposed to a Federalist position that favored the use of military troops). He remarks:

> Great therefore was the anxiety occasioned by this transfer, in all who reflected on the rapid progress of our population, and its speedy diffusion to the shores of the Pacific ocean, provided no untoward check or obstacle should rise up in its way.... The supposed value of this territory to France made it hopeless that any pecuniary price would be thought equivalent to it, and that she would give up so splendid an inheritance for a few million of dollars. Happily, however, the experiment was made, and she consented to sell us all her claims in North America, for a sum which it was easy and convenient for us to pay.   (Annals I: 70)

Brown expresses here sentiments that are clearly nationalist. However, he is also conscious of the "evils of internal dissension and rebellion," and the potential for French slavery and oppression in Santo Domingo to spark rebellion in a territory like Louisiana, when he observes that "instead of approaching nearer," these "evils" are "every day removed to a greater distance; the gulf which divides the master and the slave is becoming gradually narrower" (Annals I: 66).

Brown, like others, followed developments in the Spanish borderlands and Spanish America, especially as they concerned the actions and rhetoric of men such as Aaron Burr and Francisco de Miranda. He initiates his analysis of the Burr conspiracy to take over New Orleans or to inhabit Mexican territory by reflecting on his own position as an impartial historian. "In proportion," he writes, "as historical truth is connected with the reputation of living individuals ought an upright historian to scrutinize with accuracy, and decide with caution" (Annals II 84). Similar to his self-conscious posture in the *American Register* prefaces, and even his earlier periodical reviews and essays, Brown is careful in his assessment of the Burr conspiracy to take a balanced, unbiased approach. He notes, for example, that no "eminent person in the United States was so generally known to be actuated by ambition, by the appetite for power and office, and to have this passion less tempered and modified by the kindred lust of wealth," but he also observes that few can compare with Burr in "courage, activity, and enterprize." Burr, he continues, has "[g]reat talents," yet his lust for pleasure and the consequences of his duel with Alexander Hamilton prompted him to capitalize on the "favourite pursuit of men of enterprize in America"—the "purchase and settlement of new lands" (Annals II: 84, 86).

Brown's historical narrative interrogates the "adventurer" mentality prevalent at the time insofar as he assesses how war with Spain would impact men interested in territorial expansion west of the Mississippi River. "A war with Spain," he writes, "therefore, naturally fills the bold and adventurous mind with images of golden candlesticks and silver platters. Mexico is the native country of dollars, the treasures of which are only defended by unarmed monks or disaffected slaves" (Annals II: 87). Similar to his earlier use of irony in his political pamphlets, Brown's analysis addresses American ambitions of conquest that extend from Jefferson to common adventurers such as those who joined Burr on his clandestine trip down the Mississippi River. "The fate of Miranda," he continues in a footnote,

> who proceeded with great pomp to *revolutionize* South America, at the head of a fleet of three small vessels, and an army (including major-generals and admirals) of three hundred men, will also instruct us in the chimerical nature of such projects, and, at the same time, in the abundance of that spirit which leads some of us to embark in them. It should seem as if we thought the times of Cortez and Pizarro were returned, and as if forty soldiers on horseback, equipped in our manner, were still equal to the conquest of an empire in South America. Wilkinson, with ten thousand troops, would make as little impression on Mexico, as Miranda, with his three hundred, did on Terra Firma.   (Annals II: 87–88)

Both the failed English expeditions to La Plata in 1806 (and the invasion of Buenos Aires) and Miranda's failed invasion and liberation of Venezuela represent, for Brown, a rejection of the idea that a few good men or "adventurers" (Annals II: 88), armed with bullets and a desire for gold bullion, could reenact the kind of colonial ventures Hernán Cortés and Francisco Pizarro practiced—and that elements of the American Revolution could be exported by ambitious individuals.

While trying to withhold judgment about Burr until sufficient time had passed, Brown continues to remark on the difficulties of being objective and locating historical truth. Of events, legal depositions, and documents concerning Burr and New Orleans after he was captured and went to trial and the probability of finding out "the truth," Brown remarks: "Amidst this labyrinth, it is incumbent on a pen studious of impartiality to proceed with caution; but the due caution, on occasions like the present, leads to no certainty, and is obliged to content itself with leaving the reader to decide on his own conclusions of the credibility of witnesses, and the probability of events" (Annals II: 98). Brown's efforts at impartiality are accompanied by self-consciousness about the absence of certainty in historical inquiry and knowledge and likewise by his awareness that historical interpretation is ultimately a subjective and constructive activity for both the historian and the reader. That is, historical representation and truth are the result of multiple events, witnesses, and voices.

Brown's ironic assessment of American imperialism becomes most explicit in his response to commentary published in New Orleans defending General James Wilkinson and claiming the Burr "expedition" aimed to "raise the standard of natural rights, political liberty, and free trade" (Annals II: 103). Brown responds in a footnote comparing Burr to Miranda:

> This miserable cant must have been the favourite rhetoric of Miranda and Burr, and it is evident that such views must have been admirably calculated to give success to the intrigues of Burr at New Orleans. Burr's letter professes no intention of plundering banks and seizing ships, and his agents merely talk of the probable necessity of borrowing some specie and vessels. In another place he says, "the president's proclamation against Burr had reached New Orleans about the 6th of January, but produced no extraordinary sensation there. So far as Burr's designs were conceived against Mexico, *they excited no manner of uneasiness.* It indeed surprised the good people of Louisiana not a little to find the government so extremely solicitous about the territories of their neighbours, after having shown so much indifference as to the protection of their own." These passages, in a publication expressly designed to expose Wilkinson's conduct to contempt and abhorrence, on the principle that the danger from Burr was imaginary, are very extraordinary. This pamphlet, indeed, though written with opposite intentions, reflects strong probability on the opinion that Burr had formed the plan of a Mexican expedition at least, and that New Orleans supplied him with many partizans. Burr's designs might naturally enough, in this state of things, excite no uneasiness among the American settlers at New Orleans, but the guardians of the nation were bound to be very uneasy on this account, because the most flagrant mischiefs could not fail to follow a war entered into thus unjustly and wantonly with France and Spain. And for what end?[8] To gratify the lust of plunder and adventure, in a few unsettled individuals, who have the insolent folly of clothing their lawless views, under the stale, bald, flagitious pretences of giving liberty and independence to those whom they murder or despoil.
> (Annals II: 103–104)

Brown characterizes both men as "adventurers," as men motivated by personal interest or gain, not political altruism or the true desire to "raise the standard of natural rights, political liberty, and free trade." He challenges, in other words, the ideology of American exceptionalism insofar as he identifies the self-interest and "lust of plunder" of men like Burr as driving the expansion of American empire. As Brown continued to examine the Burr conspiracy and events like the *Chesapeake* affair and Jefferson's embargo, he increasingly understood, and distanced himself from, the emerging discourse of American destiny and providential favor.

For instance, with the June 22, 1807, incident of the *Chesapeake,* when the British *Leopard* opened fire on the US ship and killed three American sailors because of its refusal to turn over four "deserters," Brown analyzes the British habit of positioning squadrons and single frigates along the coast and mouths of rivers to "obstruct the commerce of the United States" (Annals III: 4). Acutely conscious of competing claims and the unreliability of sources, Brown writes, "As long as mankind are endowed with the same passions, there will never occur a quarrel between individuals or nations, in which either party is wholly blameless," and "to repeat anonymous tales, or record oral rumours, would be unworthy of historical veracity or dignity" (Annals III: 10–11). While his analysis insightfully accounts for how different elements of the American public reacted around the country and how the Federalist Party was "loudest and most vehement" in its call for retaliation, it also accounts for how the *Chesapeake*'s captain was investigated for supposedly failing to observe the *Leopard*'s hostile maneuvers and prepare for battle (Annals III: 20).

Moreover, Brown's history becomes critical of US political assumptions and foreign-policy practices when he poses questions about the principles that actuate political conduct, American or otherwise. In stating that no nation insists upon "a claim" because it is "just and equitable" but rather because "what is beneficial will always appear to be just," Brown asserts that the "impulse" driving American demands is "derived from the perception of national benefit alone" (Annals III: 48). Unlike earlier parts of the "Annals," where Brown is critical primarily of the motives and actions of other countries, here he is willing to question US claims against England and admit the "justice" of those claims to be "arrogant and useless" when measured against their intent. Both countries' appeal, asserts Brown provocatively, "to past times, to musty volumes, to diplomatic rolls, to definitions of national equality or political independence, is a futile and nugatory parade.... Usage and justice are in the mouths of both, but in the hearts of neither" (Annals III: 48).

Just as the *Chesapeake* affair enabled Brown to raise questions about US political motivation, self-interest, and "national benefit" (Annals III: 48), so Jefferson's controversial embargo policy in 1807 became a major subject of political disagreement. As scholars have observed, Jefferson's decision to stop exports to England because of neutrality violations ultimately strangled American productivity and, as constitutional historian Leonard Levy has argued, undermined protection against "self-incrimination," the "right to trial by jury," due process in regard to confiscating personal property, and "freedom from unreasonable searches and seizures" (Tucker and Hendrickson 204). Brown's historical analysis accurately records how "the wheels of foreign commerce" came to a grinding halt and weighs the arguments of its proponents and opponents (Annals III: 68). While relatively neutral for most of his analysis, Brown eventually remarks on the embargo's limited or neutral effects, saying that the "benefit" of one country is the "evil" of another (Annals III: 75) and that the US government was "obliged to pause in its hostile career," because as an "engine of public vengeance," the embargo had a negative impact, both economically and morally, on the American public (Annals V: 3–4).

To be sure, his political pamphlet *An Address to the Congress of the United States, on the Utility and Justice of Restrictions upon Foreign Commerce, etc.* (1809) comments more forcefully on the embargo, saying that the American "system of *political* justice is as narrow, selfish, depraved, unfeeling, as that of European states" (AC 37) and positions Brown in the dissenting tradition of Godwin, Paine, and Duane. It flatly challenges assumptions about American exceptionalism or uniqueness. Nevertheless, his "Annals of America" lay the groundwork for such ideas in a historically self-conscious and enlightened way.

With the absence of a "redeemer nation" rhetoric or a filiopietistic perspective in his "Annals" (Tuveson vii), Brown increasingly put distance between himself and a discourse of Manifest Destiny and institutional power, causing the editors of the *Boston Ordeal* on April 29, 1809, to remark, "though we recommend to our author not to show so evidently the democratic impulses of his feelings, in the historical narrative; yet we cannot but consider that his book may be rendered an important acquisition to the literature as well as politics of the country" (*Boston Ordeal* 257).[9]

Further, if Brown's prefaces to the *American Register* (1807–1809) chart a distinct evolution in his thinking about the importance of public documents as a basis for historical understanding, an evolution that would prompt him to conclude in his last volume that "Public documents are the only legitimate bases of history" (Annals V: iii), his "Annals" reflect that ethos—the idea that history is not a monological enterprise but, rather, the integration of multiple voices, perspectives, and details. Nowhere does Brown's assessment of the recent past become more provocative or novel than toward the end of his historical narrative, when he addresses congressional proposals to amend the Constitution, the debate over relocating the nation's capital to Philadelphia, and Stephen Bradley's controversial 1808 Republican Caucus memo.

For instance, by 1808, as Federalists such as Senator James Hillhouse sought to respond to Jefferson with amendments to the Constitution that included limitations on presidential terms and House and Senate confirmations of appointments made by the president, Brown began to include speeches from congressional debates in his "Annals" in lieu of his historical narrative. One instance of this is Brown's inclusion of Hillhouse's April 12, 1808, *Propositions for Amending the Constitution of the United States*, which addresses "schemes" to alter parts of the Constitution, the "scourge of party rage," and the potential for party interest, bias, and power to contaminate democratic processes and, ultimately, the integrity of the early republic (Annals V: 7, 11). Typical of this is Hillhouse's statement in the speech that "Ours is a *free representative republic*, deriving all power from the people, and when amended, as I propose for the purpose of checking *party spirit, executive influence*, and *favourtism*, will correctly express the *public opinion* and declare the *public will.*" (Hillhouse 22).

While Brown does not include Hillhouse's italics in his transcription of the speech, he nevertheless increasingly integrates public documents and language like this in his historical narrative as part of his effort to render an impartial historical account of a particular event. Further, in the larger context of his "Annals," Brown's integration of Hillhouse's voice with his own accords with his own growing concern about the integrity of democratic processes relative to election processes and amendments to the Constitution.

The 1808 Republican Caucus, in particular, brings Brown's historical consciousness and political consciousness into sharp relief, revealing his "democratic" leanings in political matters and his willingness to engage an alternative form of historical representation. In his last chapter of the "Annals," Brown inserts Senator Stephen Bradley's controversial memo requesting select congressmen to attend a Republican Caucus in order to nominate suitable candidates for president and vice president, namely, James Madison. Of the incident, John Quincy Adams wrote in his diary entry of January 23, 1808, that "there has been much question as to Mr. Bradley's authority to call this convention," especially since it "omitted" five members of the Senate and twenty-two of the House of Representatives (Adams I: 505–506). Of the memo itself, Brown remarks:

> One of the most singular transactions which happened during this session, was a formal and public convention of a certain party in the legislature, to influence the impending election of a president. The genius of the constitution displayed itself on this occasion in a remarkable manner. It afforded a curious example of the subtlety and power of party in moulding every thing to its own purpose and advantage.
>
> (Annals V: 80)

Brown's concern, like that of the Republicans who would protest the meeting, was that such practices could compromise the democratic process and thus the representative rights of the people. The summons, he remarks, "could not but disgust and anger who had not the same political views with the projectors of this meeting, and was certainly couched in a style too dictatorial and official" (Annals V: 80). In addition to Representative Edwin Gray's objection to the meeting, Brown prints in the "Annals" a protest drawn up by Gray, John Randolph, and seventeen members of Congress, a letter that was published on March 7, 1808, in Jefferson's *National Intelligencer*.

The letter protests the caucus on several grounds but primarily because Bradley's call for the meeting was "private," or behind closed doors, and therefore "without discussion or debate" of the whole body of Republican representatives (Annals V: 81). That is, according to Randolph and others, the secret meeting was not only "in direct hostility to the principles of the constitution" but also a "gross assumption of power not delegated by the people" and "an attempt to produce undue bias in the ensuing election of president and vice-president" (Annals V: 84). Similar to the ways in which James Cheetham, William Duane, John Binns, and other activist Republicans viewed caucuses as short-circuiting the nomination process, Brown understood the potential for caucus proceedings of this sort to undermine a republican form of government. By inserting such documents into his historical narrative, Brown sought not only to be impartial in his historical narrative and to let the facts speak for themselves but also to graft his reader-oriented, interrogative approach to novel writing into the "Annals." By substituting the discourse of public documents for his own, Brown illuminates historical moments such as the Republican Caucus of 1808 in democratic, critical way—a manner that runs counter to a romantic or idealized conception of the past and casts doubt on teleological certainty.

In closing, Brown's "Annals of Europe and America" comes to question the idea of US history as destined or exceptional. His self-conscious, dialogical method of historical writing and concern with the uncertainty of history become at once ironic and radical insofar as he sought to avoid party bias and to represent historical truth in imaginative yet provocative ways. Toward that end, he eschewed a providential rhetoric and sympathetically rendered oppressed others in India, commented ironically on the imperial dimensions of US exceptionalism in the American West, and interrogated political self-interest when it appeared in the Republican nomination process. He came to understand American self-interest, political power, and imperialism relative to that of Europe—and as threats to American democracy as he knew it.

Brown's instinctual resistance to individual and institutional oppression, like that of Paine and other Americans during the late Enlightenment period, is in line with what Robert Berkhofer calls a "postmodernist challenge to traditional history" or "a revision of the normal history paradigm" (3, 197). Unlike historians of his generation or even later, Brown understood the subjective nature of historical writing and sought to render historical truth without bias and with an awareness of its constructed and contingent nature. Further, just as Howard Zinn aimed to raise "the political consciousness of the readers of history" (Berkhofer 216), so Brown's history provocatively seeks to engage his readers, "the people," in the political present. As in his novels, he deconstructs historiographical conventions in an effort to promote critical thought and understanding.[10]

In the end, what this analysis amounts to is the need to further explore and understand Brown's vast body of periodical literature relative to the print culture of his era and even his other writings. As digital access to the Brown archive and the American Periodical Series makes clear, Brown's periodical contributions and his career as an editor of three magazines positioned him to be part of a transatlantic discourse about a range of topics concerning late-eighteenth- and early-nineteenth-century America. Such topics included not only global capitalism and expansion but also political, economic, social, religious, and racial issues, as well as the growth of various literary genres. This body of texts, when studied through the use of database search engines and poststructural and cultural theories, offers alternative ways of understanding the dynamic complexity of early republican literature, culture, and democracy—and Brown's efforts, philosophically, to educate and empower his readers.

NOTES

1. Parts of this chapter are from *The Historicism of Charles Brockden Brown: Radical History and the Early Republic*, published by the Kent State University Press, 2010. Used by permission of the publisher.

2. Brown may have contributed "Utrum horum Mavis, elige" to *The American Magazine, Containing a Miscellaneous Collection of Original and Other Valuable Essays in Prose and Verse, and Calculated Both for Instruction and Amusement* in May 1788. There is more certainty about authorship or attribution of his contributions to *The Columbian Magazine, or, Monthly Miscellany* in 1789. See "Primary Bibliography" in the Charles Brockden Brown Electronic Archive and Scholarly Edition.

3. For further information on the Friendly Club, authorship, literary networks, Brown's periodical publications, and early American print culture, see Waterman.

4. For readings of how the *American Register* continues to explore issues found in Brown's novels and even his method of writing, see Kamrath 2010 and Gardner.

5. Begun on April 24, 1758, when James and Robert Dodsley hired Edmund Burke to serve as editor, the British *Annual Register* was a yearly publication devoted to history, politics, and literature. Although it changed over time, it contained an essay about British and world historical events and a collection of state papers, or official letters, documents, speeches, and accounts. The historical part of the publication provided analysis, for example, of the Seven Years War (1756–1763) and its causes and effects. It attempted to be nonpartisan with its political content, and it reviewed significant books and featured essays, poetry, and writings of scientific interest.

6. For additional information on Brown's inquiry into British colonial rule in India and the East India Company, especially as represented in *Edgar Huntly*, see Kamrath 2004.

7. For an in-depth discussion of how Mikhail Bakhtin's *Dialogic Imagination* opens up ways of reading Brown's historical narrative, see "Empire and the 'Annals of Europe'" (chap. 5) and "American Exceptionalism and the 'Annals of Europe'" (chap. 6) in Kamrath 2010.

8. Jerome McGann has astutely pointed out the "interrogative" nature of Brown's novel writing, as in *Edgar Huntly*, which is also clearly present in his annals about Europe and America.

9. For contemporary views on Brown's political leanings, see Thomas Boylston Adams's letter to John Quincy Adams on November 30, 1802, where Brown is depicted as "a *small*, sly Deist, a disguised, but determined Jacobin, a sort of Sammy Harison [sic] Smith in 'shape and size the same'" (Adams 1). Also see Benjamin Pollard's review of Brown's *American Register* and "Annals" in the April 15, 22, and 29, 1809, issues of the *Boston Ordeal*. As Brown biographer Daniel Edwards Kennedy points out, the review comments on Brown's "lapses of correctness and deviations from authority" (Kennedy 1971–1972).

10. In our own modern era of social fracture, conspiracy thought, "fake news," and aggressive misrepresentation of facts and knowledge for political purposes, Brown's historical writing speaks to the importance in a democracy of philosophical inquiry and responding to the misleading rhetoric of demagogues.

Works Cited

Adams, John Quincy. *Memoirs of John Quincy Adams, Comprising Portions of His Diary from 1795 to 1848*, 12 vols., Charles Francis Adams, ed., 1: 505–507. Select Bibliographies Reprint Series. Freeport, N.Y.: Books for Library Press, 1969.

Barnard, Philip. "Culture and Authority in Brown's Historical Sketches." In Philip Barnard, Mark L. Kamrath, and Stephen Shapiro, eds., *Revising Charles Brockden Brown: Culture, Politics, and Sexuality in the Early Republic*, 310–331. Knoxville: University of Tennessee Press, 2004.

Bayle, Pierre. *A General Dictionary, Historical and Critical* [etc.] (1695 and 1697), 10 vols. London: Bettenham, 1734–1741.

Berkhofer, Robert F., Jr. *Beyond the Great Story: History as Text and Discourse*. Cambridge, Mass.: Harvard University Press, 1995.

Boston Ordeal. April 29, 1809, 257–262.

Burke, Edmund. "Speech on Mr. Fox's East India Bill," December 1, 1783. In *The Writings and Speeches of Edmund Burke*, Paul Langford, gen. ed., Vol. 5, P. J. Marshall and William B. Todd, eds., 378–451. Oxford: Clarendon Press, 1981.

Callcott, George H. *History in the United States 1800–1860: Its Practices and Purposes.* Baltimore: Johns Hopkins University Press, 1970.

Clark, David Lee. *Charles Brockden Brown: Pioneer Voice of America.* New York: AMS Press, 1966.

Cody, Michael. *Charles Brockden Brown and the Literary Magazine: Cultural Journalism in the Early American Republic.* Jefferson, N.C., and London: McFarland, 2004.

Duane, William. *Politics for American Farmers, Being a Series of Tracts Exhibiting the Blessings of Free Government... Compared with the Boasted Stupendous Fabric of British Monarchy.* Washington City, D.C.: R. C. Weightman, 1807.

Gardner, Jared. *The Rise and Fall of Early American Magazine Culture.* Urbana: University of Illinois Press, 2012.

Gilmore, Michael T. "The Literature of the Revolutionary and Early National Periods." In *The Cambridge History of American Literature*, General Editor, Sacvan Bercovitch and Cyrus R. K. Patell, Associate Editor, 539–693. Cambridge: Cambridge University Press, 1994.

Hillhouse, James. *Propositions for Amending the Constitution of the United States; Submitted by Mr. Hillhouse to the Senate on the Twelfth Day of April, 1808, with His Explanatory Remarks.* New Haven, Conn.: Oliver Steele, 1808.

Kamrath, Mark L. "American Exceptionalism and Radicalism in the 'Annals of Europe and America.'" In Philip Barnard, Mark L. Kamrath, and Stephen Shapiro, eds., *Revising Charles Brockden Brown: Culture, Politics, and Sexuality in the Early Republic*, 354–384. Knoxville: University of Tennessee Press, 2004.

Kamrath, Mark L. *The Historicism of Charles Brockden Brown: Radical History and the Early Republic.* Kent, Ohio: Kent State University Press, 2010.

Kennedy, Daniel Edwards. "Charles Brockden Brown: A Biography" (c. 1923–1945). Typescript with manuscript additions. Charles Brockden Brown Bicentennial Edition Records (bulk 1917–1995). Special Collections and Archives, Kent State University Libraries, Kent, Ohio.

Kraus, Michael. *The Writing of American History.* Norman: University of Oklahoma Press, 1953.

McGann, Jerome. "Re: Interrogatory Method of Brown's Novel Writing." Received by Mark Kamrath, 2014.

Novick, Peter. *That Noble Dream: The Objectivity Question and the American Historical Profession.* New York: Cambridge University Press, 1988.

Semmel, Stuart. *Napoleon and the British.* New Haven, Conn.: Yale University Press, 2004.

Tucker, Robert W., and David C. Hendrickson. *Empire of Liberty: The Statecraft of Thomas Jefferson.* New York: Oxford University Press, 1990.

Tuveson, Ernest Lee. *Redeemer Nation: The Idea of America's Millennial Role.* Chicago: University of Chicago Press, 1968.

Waterman, Bryan. *Republic of Intellect: The Friendly Club of New York City and the Making of American Literature.* Baltimore: Johns Hopkins University Press, 2007.

Woolf, Stuart. *Napoleon's Integration of Europe.* New York: Routledge, 1991.

PART IV

WRITINGS IN
OTHER GENRES

CHAPTER 14

....

LETTERS

....

ELIZABETH HEWITT

EPISTOLARY writing finds expression everywhere in Charles Brockden Brown's work. His earliest-known fictional work, the unpublished "Henrietta Letters," offers the beginnings of an epistolary novel. He first entered the world of print when he was only eighteen years old as "The Rhapsodist," a letter writer delivering his periodical essays to the *Columbia Magazine* (1789). Brown continued to write as an epistolary essayist throughout his life, finally publishing as "The Scribbler" in *The Port Folio* in 1809, just a year before his death. Perhaps more familiarly, his first published novel, *Wieland* (1798), takes a loose epistolary form insofar as it is structured around the conceit that its protagonist, Clara Wieland, writes the narrative as a letter. And Brown's final two published novels, *Clara Howard* and *Jane Talbot* (both published in 1801), are conventional epistolary novels, organized entirely around familiar correspondence. Brown's predilection for letters is not surprising, since for a young man who came of age at the end of the eighteenth century, his leisure life would have been surrounded by epistolary writing, taking the form of familiar correspondence, novels, and periodical essays. Moreover, for a young man whose parents intended him to practice law, his formal education, which began at the age of eleven, would have emphasized business correspondence as well as good handwriting. Alas, Brown's chirography was decidedly mediocre in his younger years, but his extant correspondence nevertheless reveals him to be a prolific letter writer, corresponding with family, friends, and business associates throughout his short life.

Brown's active engagement with eighteenth-century epistolary culture is entirely predictable, and yet in many ways, the intensity of his devotion to the form is exceptional. Writing in a period in which the popularity of both the epistolary novel and the periodical essay was waning, Brown remains steadfastly committed to both forms throughout his career. In what follows, I describe the particular ways in which his dedication to epistolary writing manifests itself throughout his life. This will let us discover the ways Brown's work was critically informed by his understanding of the particular affordances of the modern letter, which is to say the epistolary form as it existed in a world in which an increasing number of people had access to literacy, pens, paper, and the post office.

Within this landscape, the letter offered Brown a vehicle for two kinds of literary projects, one psychological and the other sociological. Following in the footsteps of Samuel Richardson, whom Brown describes as "the sublimest and most eloquent of Writers" (Letters 208) and Jean-Jacques Rousseau, whose epistolary writing Brown praises as possessing "transcendant excellence [and] a model of pathetic eloquence" (32), Brown understands the familiar letter as a repository for psychological interiority. He saw the letter as an ideal mechanism by which to deliver realistic novelistic characters. But epistolary writing was equally important to another project central to Brown's writing: detailed illustrations of the broader social geography in which his characters interact. Thus, even in his nonepistolary novels, such as *Edgar Huntly* or *Arthur Mervyn*, letters are fundamental to his storytelling, in that they can capture the intricacies of social interaction; letters link characters in a myriad of social and economic attachments across the globe.

Although he never left the eastern seaboard of the United States, Brown was likewise linked to many different communities through his own correspondence. Only a small fraction of the letters he wrote have survived, but the 179 extant letters nevertheless reveal Brown to use the form for heterogeneous social functions. In fact, although almost all the surviving correspondence is to family and friends, these letters reveal Brown to play a variety of social roles: passionate friend, dutiful brother, considerate reader, indefatigable author, virtuous suitor, sensible father, solicitous brother-in-law, to name a few.

We might consider, for example, the two largest clusters of letters within the corpus. The first includes forty-three letters written between 1792 and 1797 to Brown's friend Joseph Bringhurst, who, like him, was a Philadelphian Quaker.[1] Integral to this set are also the twelve surviving letters Brown wrote to their third friend, William Wood Wilkins. The second-largest group includes thirty-eight letters to his future wife, Elizabeth Linn, of which twenty-eight are the courtship letters Brown wrote within a three-month period in 1801 before their marriage. Both long epistolary sequences are similar in that they involve intimate expression to people who were emotionally important to Brown. And in both cases, Brown clearly conceives of letter writing as a critical component of the affectionate relationships he is establishing. In one of his early letters to Linn, for example, Brown "insist[s]" that she write back, saying that her letters will provide "the only proof admissible that you have not forgotten me" (474). But it is also the case that the "Charles Brockden Brown" who serves as author and protagonist in each sequence of letters is not the same. Indeed, he may not even retain any integrity within the confines of a single letter, as Brown himself suggests in a letter to Bringhurst, asking, "Would you imagine that all parts of the letter which lies before you, were the production of the same hand, or written within the same hour?" (35).

And so, if Brown is drawn to epistolary writing at least in part because he sees it as the vessel for self-expression, then his letters also reveal his understanding of identity as a product of managed and mutable performance. In his letters to Bringhurst and Wilkins, Brown performs the part of a volatile and mercurial young man, and he fashions his letters accordingly. He thus can ask his friends, "Is it not preposterous to be very anxious of propriety and *Method* in a familiar letter?" (16). Later he will apologize, "I am afraid I have, in this letter, miserably banged and buffeted propriety—of Style and Penmanship" (191). Largely modeling his persona from Johann Wolfgang von Goethe's *The Sorrows of Werther* and Rousseau's *Julie, or the New Heloise*, Brown establishes himself as a man so overcome by sentiment and passion as to have no command over his epistolary method. In one letter, he asserts, "I dare not send you the second letter. . . . It is full of the incoherences of moonstruck Fancy and ungoverened passion. It would appear too much like the ravings of a Lunatic" (46). Elsewhere, he announces that his "fertile pen" has filled the voluminous pages (and these letters are some of Brown's longest) with "the jarring dictates of excursive fancy, elevated reason or ungoverned passions" (39).

Brown also establishes himself as the clear protagonist of the correspondence, and his letters to Bringhurst and Wilkins consistently orient themselves around, as he puts it, "the study of myself" (27). Brown is quite aware of this rather exclusive focus on himself, and he routinely asks his correspondents if they grow weary the subject of "Self." He proposes to Wilkins, for example, "that if you do not like the subject on which I have hitherto so copiously written, I wish you would furnish me with a more instructive and delightful topic, and relieve me from the irksome necessity of talking of myself" (13). The egoism coupled with the tumultuous style of these letters easily lend themselves to interpretations that emphasize emotional disclosure. Yet it is also clear that this disclosure is a very studied affair: when Brown's friends respond in a panic to his letters that intimate his consideration of suicide (once again signaling the influence of Goethe's *Werther* to these early letters), Brown realizes that he has played his part too well.[2]

He performs a very different role in his letters to Elizabeth Linn, written a decade later, where Brown presents himself as a rational supplicant. "Tis true. Eliza is *preferred* by me," he announces sensibly before closing this letter with the restrained observation, "thou, only beloved friend, can tell me how wide the field that must be crossed before Eliza equally prefers C.B.B." (477). Noting that he is "oddly composed" (482), Brown works throughout these courtship letters to establish himself as possessing emotional equipoise. The letters to Linn also differ from his earlier ones in that instead of proposing epistolary writing as the means by which he can both study and disclose his innermost self, he declares letters to be a necessary but inadequate medium: "My inmost soul is not to be heard or seen. Into that you cannot enter. You must rely for your knowledge of my sentiments, on my words & looks. If *they* mislead you who but I am to be blamed: or rather to be pitied: for my happiness requires that you know me for what I am" (284).

We could attribute these substantial differences in self-presentation and epistolary style to age and maturity, given that almost a decade separates the man who wrote letters to his friends from the man who wrote letters to his fiancée. And certainly, this narrative of the volatile young romantic brought into submission by bourgeois domestication through marriage was one that dominated Brown scholarship for generations.

But this biographical reading of his correspondence is substantially undermined by something also common to both longer sequences, which is Brown's consistent manipulation of fiction and fact. Sometimes he tells stories about himself that we know to be untrue (that he is a young widower or that he spent his childhood in a prison), and sometimes he incorporates fictional scenarios into his letters. As the editors of *Letters and Epistolary Writings* explain, Brown uses his letters "as a sort of laboratory for the development...of ideas and techniques concerning fiction writing, presenting ideas for narratives, condensed versions of narratives, [and] fictional narrative sketches" (833). Fundamental to this literary experiment is Brown's tendency to obscure the difference between genuine familiar correspondence and fictionalized tale. Moreover, he does not provide his readers with any criteria by which they can discern fact from fiction, which has, as we will see, led to considerable difficulty in assessing the generic status of some manuscript texts in Brown's corpus. But we can make productive use of this difficulty by taking Brown's epistolary practices as a cautionary tale against reading letters as transparent expressions of self, since he clearly theorized all epistolary writing—whether autograph manuscripts to real people or printed epistolary fictions—as textual inventions of self and community. Philip Barnard proposes we read Brown as engaged in "epistolary performance[s]," in which the author variously "construct[s]" and "calculate[s]" identity and voice (Barnard 516).

This performance extends into the corpus of "real" letters, even those letters that would seem to require the transparent expression of authentic sentiment. Love letters, for example, exemplify an epistolary subgenre defined by emotional candor. But instead of only reading Brown's "real" letters to Linn as expression of his affection and love, we might see them as an experiment through which Brown interrogates the style and literary form of heterosexual romance. The very fact that these letters were retained, for example, gives us some indication of the generative role epistolary writing played in the social act of courtship; the letters were preserved and bound as a textual souvenir of a relationship that only later would become a marriage. Notably, however, Brown's sequence does not actually record a relationship, since none of Linn's letters were included in the bound set. This fact suggests that despite Brown's evident solicitousness toward his future bride's opinions, her writing was not considered crucial to the narrative he was constructing with these courtship letters.[3] The epistolary fiction scripted through these letters is not so much about two lovers as it is about one lover's apprehension of the other. Brown's epistolary fiction represents himself as a successful wooer. I call these letters a fiction, even though the participants were very much real people, because Brown himself frames them in these terms. The sequence notably begins with a letter to an unnamed correspondent, dated eight weeks earlier, in which Brown transcribes a dialogue *about* his future wife. Although the letter is anomalous in its addressee and its dating, we know that it was integral to the entire sequence, because the puncture holes in the manuscript's margins indicate that it was bound with the set. As such, we must read this first letter as a kind of framing device for the courtship letters to Linn that follow, effectively translating the whole into a kind of epistolary fiction. It seems likely that Brown borrows the framing device from Rousseau, who likewise offers a dialogue as a preface to his own famous epistolary fiction, *Julie*.[4]

Like Rousseau, Brown wishes to tell a story about writing's power to secure intimacy. Brown's dialogic letter thus begins with one individual asking, "Pray tell me what sort of woman is this, we are going to see" (*Letters* 468). His friend responds by asserting his own nescience: "You have made a strange request of me. What pretensions have *I* to a knowledge of her character? I am not her brother; her kinsman....I enjoy not the confidence of her intimates. I am not master of a single page of her past history. I have heard, neither the eulogies of friends, nor the aspersions of her enemies" (468–469). The letter continues in the same vein, offering us an animated conversation concerning their incomplete knowledge of Linn, who has given neither man "the key" by which they might "enter...her bosom" (470). Brown thus establishes the remaining letters as the record of the quest to gain access to the recesses of Linn's self. Indeed, the concluding sentence of the first letter states, "If you wish it, I will endeavor, by future attention to these particulars, to attone for past negligence" (471). By establishing this as the transition to the love letters that follow, we are required to read them as an "endeavor" to gain access to the bosom that Brown had earlier neglected. We might here be reminded of Carwin's desire in *Wieland* to gain the "key" to Clara's "inmost soul" by perusing her diary (W 205). Brown's investigatory project is, however, somewhat different from Carwin's in that he gains access to Linn not by reading her writing but by writing her as a character within his own courtship letters. In some ways, Linn engaged in a similar project after her husband's death, when she provided Brown's correspondence to his first biographers, Paul Allen and William Dunlap, who used it to produce their *Life of Charles Brockden Brown*. As was the case with numerous nineteenth-century projects that documented lives in letters, these early biographies of Brown presuppose that editors can arrange and organize epistolary writing so as to generate a person.

What makes Brown's investment in literary letters so compelling, I suggest, is that he so frequently calls attention to the mediated and performative quality of all epistolary writing. It is for this reason that readers are often unable to discern the difference between "real" and "fictional" letters. When, for example, the editors of the recently collected edition of Brown's letters constructed the census of his extant correspondence, one of the first conundrums was to determine the status of what had been designated a letter from Brown to his childhood friend John Davidson. It was addressed to a real person and signed "C.B.B.," and scholars had not surprisingly assumed the letter to be genuine and had classified it as such. Yet it became clear that it should not be read as a "real" letter to Davidson—or at least not only as such—but rather as the final letter in a longer exchange that scholars had designated as the "Henrietta Letters." At sixty-eight manuscript pages, this seventeen-letter sequence has presented a difficulty for critics ever since 1948, when David Lee Clark first published them, describing them as the remnants of a real correspondence between Brown and a unidentified woman named Henrietta (also called variously Harriot, Hariot, and Henriette), even as Clark also conceded that the text might constitute a "youthful attempt to write a novel in epistolary form" (Clark 55). Since Clark's publication, critics have been divided regarding their generic status, some insisting that it be read biographically while others determined it to be an example of Brown's earliest fiction writing.[5]

But as we have seen from the cases of his letters to Bringhurst, Wilkins, and Linn, this distinction between "real" and "fictional" is not one that entirely signifies for Brown. Brown, for example, mentions to Bringhurst that he is "devot[ing] almost all my leisure to the transcription" of the Henrietta letters, which would seem to imply their fictionality (Letters 52). Yet in the very next sentence, he asserts, "I think I have already assured you that those letters are genuine, and I suppose you easily perceive that one of the parties in this correspondence is myself," thereby cultivating the text as an authentic document (52). In another letter to Bringhurst, he recollects, "It was in the Summer of the Year 1788, during my Connection with the excellent and amiable Henrietta G—— that I first read the Eloisa of Rousseau" (89). Some literary historians have taken this sentence to corroborate that the relationship between Brown and Henrietta was real (and had occurred in 1788), but there are several reasons the sentence might instead imply the fictionality of the epistolary romance. First, the self-conscious reference to Rousseau's *Julie* signals that this is the generic mode in which the correspondence is written. Like Rousseau's wildly popular novel, Brown's "Henrietta Letters" scripts an exchange in which the primary topic is deferred erotic consummation. And so we might read Brown here as slyly metatextual, describing his own lover's perusal of a fiction that serves as the model for his own. Second, the representation of Henrietta that Brown offers in his letter to Bringhurst contradicts the portrait of Henrietta that is offered within the letters themselves. To Bringhurst, Brown announces that Henrietta owned a copy of *Julie* "in the original" and that she had read it before he did. In the "Henrietta Letters," however, she does not own the novel, nor does she know French; indeed, in one letter, Henrietta asks that C.B.B. teach her French so that she can read Rousseau, complaining, "You can at any time without my assistance be personally acquainted with the Authour of Eloisa and the social Compact" (690). This discrepancy would seem to suggest that Henrietta is a character of Brown's invention who can or cannot speak French, depending on the story into which she is being written.

In Brown's correspondence with Bringhurst, Henrietta needs to know French because her knowledge of "the Eloisa of Rousseau" is a crucial plot point in the tale he spins to his friend. Brown tells Bringhurst that Henrietta has judged *Julie* to be "the most seductive and pernicious book that she had ever read" (89). Henrietta's objections to the novel lead her to ask Brown to compose a "similar performance, in which different maxims should be incultivated, of which love and friendship in all their purity and sublimity should form the basis, and in which the triumph of virtue over the most lawless and impetuous passions, of duty over inclination, should be as vividly and forcibly described as I was able" (89–90). In making this directive, she gives him some artistic license: he can write in either epistolary or narrative form, and he can follow either a Richardsonian or Rousseauian style. Brown takes up her challenge, and "by writing almost incessantly from Sun rise to Midnight for thirty days," he is able to complete his "Romance, in the epistolary form and after the manner of Rousseau though somewhat more voluminous than 'Julie'" (90). Later in the letter, Brown goes further and insists that his novel is even "more voluminous than *Clarissa*." Given that *Julie* runs to about four hundred print pages and *Clarissa* is three times longer, this rate of composition necessarily strains credulity. Not only is it impossible that Brown could have written this "voluminous" romance in thirty days, but there is nothing in the historical record to indicate that he wrote it at all.[6]

Except, of course, Brown does write the romance insofar as he provides a lengthy summary of the imaginary novel in his letter to Bringhurst, thereby constructing a dizzyingly elaborate framed epistolary fiction, one that rivals contemporary experimental fiction in its inventiveness. Brown establishes himself as a character in a love story with a woman he designates as "Henrietta G," and this romance comes into being through a variety of epistolary texts. First, Brown writes and then transcribes a manuscript consisting of sixteen letters between "C.B.B." and "Henrietta." Second, he frames these sixteen letters with a missive to Davidson about their erotic correspondence. Third, he refers to the relationship in his correspondence with Bringhurst and Wilkins. Fourth, he uses one of these letters to describe Henrietta's challenge to write an epistolary novel, one that he will reproduce in abridged narrative form in the letter. And in this summary of his imaginary novel, Brown remarks on his deep identification with the protagonist, saying that "in every work of this kind, the character of the writer, such as it, really, is, or such as he imagines, or wishes it to be, may be found" (90).[7] As if to make explicit the depth of this identification, Brown calls his hero "Julius Brownlow," a name that obviously blurs the borders between real and fiction, in that "Julius" is a transparent reference to Rousseau's "Julie," and "Brownlow" is a variation of his own name. Brown had, in fact, signed himself in an earlier letter to Wilkins as "C.B. Brownlow Gentie" (23). And so Brown establishes himself not just as the protagonist of the "Henrietta Letters" but also as the protagonist of the imaginary epistolary novel he writes for the imaginary Henrietta.

Given this representational *mise en abyme*, it is no wonder that Brown's readers are so continually perplexed. Indeed, at the risk of exacerbating our interpretative vertigo, we might even understand the "Henrietta Letters" as Brown's first attempt to respond to the invented challenge to produce a more virtuous, dutiful, and lawful *Julie*. After all, the central topic that animates the entire exchange is the moral propriety of the correspondence, which is the selfsame animating concern of Rousseau's *Julie*. Unlike Richardson's *Clarissa* or Pierre Choderlos de Laclos's *Les liaisons dangereuses*, Rousseau's epistolary novel was not arranged as a seduction plot. Indeed, Rousseau boasted that the excellence of his *Julie* was located not in the romance or sexual scandal but in the plotlessness of its epistolary matrix, that a "chain of interest, which being concentrated among three people, is maintained for six volumes without episode, without romantic adventure, without wickedness of any sort" (Stewart xvii). Brown likewise constructs his epistolary fiction without plot or episode; the letters between Henrietta and C.B.B. are almost exclusively about the quality and purpose of their letters.

The sequence opens on an optimistic note, as Henrietta's first letter extols the reciprocal pleasures of letter writing: "I am never so happy as when employed in writing to my friend; and I am willing to perswade myself that he recieves no less pleasure from answring than I from the composition of my letters" (Letters 677). The exchange she describes, in which both participants in a binary correspondence take and give equal amounts of gratification, is the fantastical ideal of letter writing. Yet this perfect reciprocity is disrupted just as soon as C.B.B. responds, a rupture that his letter accentuates in the first two sentences of his reply: "What obligations do you continually heap upon me! How shall I discharge them?" (678). Already assuming the role of debtor, C.B.B. uses his own letter as the occasion to heap praises on his beloved. He further insists that any excellence to be found in his epistolary style is a consequence not of his "proficiency in the art of writing" but rather of his natural response in "contemplation of [her] charms" (679). He conceives of letter writing as the expression of "the Suggestions of [his] heart," in which there is nothing of "the dress of borrowed or artificial Sentiments" (679). These first two letters thus reveal a schism in their respective epistolary theories. For Henrietta, letters require managed and crafted writing to occasion another person's pleasure. For C.B.B., the letter's function is spontaneous and unstudied expression that casts a blind eye on the reader's response.

This disagreement, as it turns out, has already been a source of conflict between the two correspondents, as we discover when C.B.B. recollects an earlier letter he had written to Henrietta "for which you so often and severely chided me" (682). We are never privy to the text of this letter, but it remains a central topic of the epistolary sequence. When Henrietta replies, for example, she scolds him for mentioning it again:

> But the letter—Oh! My capricious and unaccountable friend! As thou valuest the continuance of my regard, let me not again be affronted at the mention of it. How would you be induced to write in that inexcusable licentious manner? I read it with indignation and regret, but let this be the last time, that you recall to my remembrance that epistle or the circumstances which produced it.   (682)

Her response to this letter would seem to disprove her own theory of reciprocal pleasures, since what was for C.B.B. the unrestrained articulation of his "native character" (679) is for Henrietta an "affront" and source of "indignation."

The censored letter also highlights what appears to be another central concern to Brown, which is the fundamental paradox of intimate correspondence. On one hand, the love letter is required to articulate passionate sentiment and offer itself as prophylactic for physical erotic contact. On the other hand, the linguistic representation of eros works too well and allows for an intimacy that exceeds physical presence, making the letter an almost hyperbolically sexualized object. And so, even as Brown seems to intend his "Henrietta Letters" as a romance in which, as his imaginary Henrietta requests, "love and friendship in all their purity and sublimity should form the basis" (689), their conversation relentlessly revolves around the possibility of "licentious" discourse. We might also note that the fact that the illicit letter is censored (we are not able to read it, and Henrietta insists that it not be a topic of conversation), even as there is a veritable "discursive explosion" about it, would seem to corroborate Michel Foucault's crucial thesis about sex and discourse (Foucault 7). Henrietta and C.B.B. talk about little else than that they should not talk about sex. Indeed, even when Henrietta tries to shift the genre of their exchange to a "literary correspondence," asking C.B.B. to write her the "more cool collected and dispassionate" letters of a "tutor" and not those of a "lover" (Letters 688), she also confesses that she prefers those parts of his letters that "are fraught with tender and pathetic sentiments" over those in which he "expatiates on cold and barren topics" (700). And for his part, C.B.B. declares Henrietta's epistolary skill—her "powers" at letter writing—to be solely responsible for unleashing his "lawless Imagination" (707).

His lawless imagination, however, never seems to transgress Henrietta's standards of propriety, since she also announces that she will "never part with these precious manuscripts," which will provide her with "exhaustless sccenes [sic] of entertainment" (734). And although she chastises him for the earlier letter, and although their correspondence centers around whether C.B.B. can contain his passion in prose, both lovers agree that his "purity and delicacy" are unimpeachable (715). And so, unlike the epistolary fictions of Richardson or Rousseau, in which the letters represent sexual actions that happen off the page, in Brown's letters, sexuality is only textual, and his fiction's only plot is the exchange of letters. Perhaps it is a consequence of this plotless quality that scholars have assumed the authenticity of the "Henrietta Letters." Why would anyone invent a fiction in which literally nothing happens?

Brown actually offers an aesthetic theory on behalf of this plotlessness within the "Henrietta Letters." His epistolary protagonist and alter ego articulates a literary "design" in which fiction should strive to "relat[e] every domestic incident, and account every dialogue, and describe[e] every scene that shall occur within a certain & assynable period with the most excessive and elaborate minuteness. Relations in which no circumstance, however frivolous and inconsiderable, should be omitted, and pictures in which should be comprised every appendage" (725). Brown describes here a hyperrealistic fiction dedicated to a scrupulous and exhaustive accounting of domestic intercourse. For such a literary project, plot would not involve the arrangement of selected incidents and actions but instead the patient transcription of such incidents and actions as they occur over a "certain & assynable period" of time. No wonder, then, that Brown is so drawn to the epistolary form, which is perfectly suited for the task of sketching the mundane details of quotidian life. Moreover, because the letter writer fashions his or her text as an act of communication, mimesis (what is told) becomes indistinguishable from diegesis (the act of telling). Epistolary fiction thus offers a structure by which Brown can bundle these communicative acts into a corpus whose integrity consists solely of texts devoted to the "most excessive and elaborate minute" representation of domestic life.

Because Brown has been canonized in American novelistic history for his use of extraordinary events (murder, seduction, plague), the literary theory he outlines in the "Henrietta Letters" might not seem to resonate with his work. And yet even in his most "Gothic" novels, there is a relentless emphasis on the transmission or relay of information from one person to another. Thus, even when his novels are not written in a conventional epistolary form, they stress letters as a primary medium through which social communication is forged, and the promise or impossibility of this communication often becomes a theme of equal importance to the sensational events that would seem to occupy the novel's plot. Clara Wieland tells the story of her brother's crime in a letter, but this story is frequently interrupted and challenged by other interlocutors. Edgar Huntly likewise is structured as a letter, and while this conceit largely disappears as the novel continues, correspondence remains critical, for example, in the question of whether

Edgar should burn his dead friend's letters. In *Arthur Mervyn*, the eponymous protagonist writes, reads, and delivers letters, and even more crucially, his credibility is tested by the letters that circulate throughout the fictional world. In *Ormond*, the antagonist, Thomas Craig, writes epistolary fictions that precipitate many events of the novel, including Stephen Dudley's financial ruin.[8] Brown was clearly drawn to epistolary writing since, more than any other fictional form, it draws attention to *telling*—to the sheer mechanics of establishing meaning between individuals.

Brown himself plainly expresses his preference for epistolary writing in a 1795 letter to Joseph Bringhurst. He writes, "The epistolary and narrative forms of Composition have each their respective advantages, but I have no doubt about the superiority of the former if it were well executed" (Letters 297). Brown's own practices give us a clear sense of why he conceives it as the superior form. Established in the eighteenth century as the paradigmatic form of self-disclosure, the letter can convey psychological interiority, but this same fact also leads Brown to consider the ways interiority, or identity, is also manufactured by epistolary performance. Moreover, as the crucial communicative technology of the eighteenth century, epistolary writing is particularly well suited to convey social and economic entanglement. Epistolary fiction may emphasize dyadic correspondence, but each correspondent is linked to numerous other nodes in a communication network, and so epistolary novels, as Jared Gardner explains, allow authors to "orchestrate a complex nexus of voices and sources" (Gardner 9).[9] This latter fact is perhaps one reason Brown confesses to Bringhurst that he finds the epistolary form the more difficult one in which to write. Indeed, Brown explains that because narrative fiction "is in itself, an easier task," he has decided to start with the narrative form (Letters 297). Five years and four novels later, Brown returns to the challenge of epistolary fiction with the publication of *Clara Howard* and *Jane Talbot*. Historically, these novels are the most overlooked; they are the only two that have not been reprinted in any affordable scholarly or classroom edition, for example.[10] Yet, as we can see from Brown's own meditations on epistolary writing, we should instead read them as the apotheosis of Brown's novelistic career.

Notes

1. Because Bringhurst retained his correspondence, which was ultimately donated to the Bowdoin College Library, this is the single largest repository of Brown letters.
2. For a longer discussion of these letters and the critical tendency to read them as autobiographical revelation, see Hewitt.
3. Each letter in the sequence contains two sets of holes, which were used to thread the entirety into a notebook. Sometime before the manuscript made its way to the Harry Ransom Center at the University of Texas libraries in the 1950s, the manuscripts had been unbound. It is conceivable, then, that Linn's texts had originally been incorporated into the larger set and were later destroyed, but there is also no evidence to suggest this. For more on the manuscripts, see Letters 471 n. 1, 831–832.
4. The first edition of the novel did not include the dialogue preface, but Brown would have been well aware of the preface to the second edition, since it was incorporated into all

subsequent editions that Brown would have read, including the English-language translation first published in 1769. The first American edition of the novel was published in 1796 as *Eloisa: or a Series of Original Letters, Collected and Published by J.J. Rousseau, Citizen of Geneva* (Philadelphia: Samuel Longscope, 1796) and took its text and title from the original English translation. All these English-language editions include Rousseau's dialogic preface at the beginning, calling it "A Dialogue between A Man of Letters, and M. J. J. Rousseau." Notably, one of the first topics raised in the dialogue involves the authenticity of the letters. The text's reader insists that his assessment depends on whether "It is a real, or fictitious correspondence" (xi).

5. The former position is argued by Eleanor Tilton (304–308) and the latter by Peter Kafer (51–56). The editors of *Letters and Early Epistolary Writings* judge the texts to be a fiction, observing that all evidence suggests Brown transcribed the 1792 manuscript from an earlier composition. The entire text is reprinted in *Letters and Early Epistolary Writings* (677–776), and an extensive discussion can also be found in the "Historical Essay" (Letters 838–842). For longer commentaries on the "Henrietta Letters" and their role in Brown's correspondence, also see Hewitt; Barnard.

6. The editors of *Letters and Early Epistolary Writings* note the "implausible rate of composition, even for a writer like Brown who often was able to write very rapidly," proposing that the claim should be "understood as part of the larger fiction concerning Henrietta" (100–101 n. 12). In his introduction to the contemporary English translation of Rousseau's novel, Philip Stewart comments on *Julie's* length, comparing it to *Clarissa* and declaring "length" to be "one of its characteristics" (Stewart xx).

7. It is entirely possible that this claim was also motivated by the widespread belief in the eighteenth century that Rousseau was himself the hero of his novel and that the eponymous heroine was actually the real Sophie d'Houdetot (Stewart xi).

8. Cynthia S. Jordan notes that "five of his six novels are written in an epistolary format," which signals that "the narrator's point of view should constitute a thematic concern" (80).

9. Gardner is here referring to Hannah Webster Foster's epistolary writing, but he also argues for the importance of Brown's late return to epistolary fiction in an extensive reading of *Clara Howard* (16–22).

10. Gardner offers a brief history of the critical rejection of *Clara Howard* and *Jane Talbot*. Michelle Burnham also records this critical history and makes an argument on behalf of the significance of the epistolary writing to Brown's career in her reading of *Clara Howard*. Burnham argues that Brown uses letters in *Clara Howard* to "trade," not in a "vertical epistolary effect," in which the emphasis is on "single individual subjectivities," but in a "horizontal one," which emphasizes "the intersubjective dependencies of selves represented through the exchange of letters over time" (264).

Works Cited

Barnard, Philip. "The Letters of Charles Brockden Brown." In Celeste-Marie Bernier, Judie Newman, and Matthew Pethers, eds., *The Edinburgh Companion to Nineteenth-Century American Letters and Letter-Writing*, 511–524. Edinburgh: Edinburgh University Press, 2016.

Burnham, Michelle. "Epistolarity, Anticipation, and Revolution in *Clara Howard*." In Philip Barnard, Mark L. Kamrath, and Stephen Shapiro, eds., *Revising Charles Brockden Brown: Culture, Politics, and Sexuality in the Early Republic*, 260–280. Knoxville: University of Tennessee Press, 2004.

Clark, David Lee. *Charles Brockden Brown: Pioneer Voice of America*. Durham, N.C.: Duke University Press, 1948.

Foucault, Michel. *The History of Sexuality*, Vol. 1, *An Introduction* (1976). Robert Hurley, trans. New York: Vintage Books, 1990.

Gardner, Jared. *The Rise and Fall of Early American Magazine Culture*. Urbana: University of Illinois Press, 2012.

Hewitt, Elizabeth. "The Authentic Fictional Letters of Charles Brockden Brown." In Theresa Gaul and Sharon Harris, eds., *Letters and Cultural Transformations in the United States, 1760–1860*, 79–98. Burlington, Vt.: Ashgate, 2009.

Jordan, Cynthia S. *Second Stories: The Politics of Language, Form, and Gender in Early American Fictions*. Durham: University of North Carolina Press, 1989.

Kafer, Peter. *Charles Brockden Brown's Revolution and the Birth of America Gothic*. Philadelphia: University of Pennsylvania Press, 2004.

Stewart, Philip. "Introduction." In *Julie, or the New Heloise: Letters of Two Lovers*, Philip Stewart and Jean Vaché, eds. and trans., *The Collected Writings of Rousseau*, Vol. 6, ix–xxvi. Hanover, N.H.: Dartmouth College Press, 1997.

Tilton, Eleanor. "The 'Sorrows' of Charles Brockden Brown." *Publications of the Modern Language Association* 69 (1954): 304–308.

CHAPTER 15

....

POETRY

....

MICHAEL C. COHEN

THE fact that Charles Brockden Brown wrote poetry may surprise early Americanists and even some Brown scholars. Yet poetry and poetics were important to Brown's formation as a writer, and he participated enthusiastically in the social and cultural practices that the writing and exchange of poems made available to people of his time. Brown's poems—approximately fifty texts attributed to him, as well as several others that are possibly his—stretch from his schooldays in the 1780s to the years just prior to his death in 1810, and they range from long neoclassical satires to epistolary squibs and epigrams, thus covering the entire span of his career and including most of the dominant genres of his era.[1]

About half of Brown's poems were published during his lifetime, appearing in newspapers, monthly magazines, or his novels, and all appeared anonymously or used pseudonyms. After Brown's death, William Dunlap included two unpublished poems in *The Life of Charles Brockden Brown* (1815). Brown's ten epistolary verses were included in the 2013 volume of Brown's letters, four poems come from Brown's novels *Wieland* and *Ormond*, and one is transcribed in Thomas Pim Cope's diary (1978). While many of the unpublished poems are found only in manuscript notebooks (they will be published, along with all of his extant verse, in *Collected Writings*, Vol. 7), Brown intended most for sociable purposes: he sent them in letters to friends, who on occasion recorded them in their journals and notebooks; he left them in places where he had traveled, such as "They Came at Noon" (1801), written on the wall of an inn near Albany (Cope 72–73); and in one instance, he inscribed a poem on the flyleaf of a companion's copy of Samuel Johnson's didactic novel *Rasselas*.

Brown published poems in the major periodicals of the day, including the *Gazette of the United States*, the *Weekly Magazine*, and the most prominent journal of belles-lettres, the *Port Folio*, and he published a smaller number of poems in journals he edited: "Monody on the Death of George Washington" and "A Negro's Lamentation" in the *Monthly Magazine*; "To Laura, Offended" and "To Clara" in the *Literary Magazine*; and "Devotion: An Epistle" (his longest poem) in the *American Register*. The latter two publications were based in Philadelphia, the cultural and political capital of the early national period, as well as the center of Brown's literary operations. A few were reprinted in New York City periodicals (Brown's home during the 1797–1800 novelistic years) and a few others in Boston papers. A very select number of the poems appeared in more far-flung locations such as in the *State Gazette of North-Carolina*, which published "An Inscription for General Washington's Tomb Stone" in 1789. Because controls over copyright were loose and practices of exchange and reprinting well established, Brown's works were likely reprinted in other cities and publications, and the readership of his poems may well have been broader than that of his novels. Thus, if Brown's poems no longer distinguish him as an early American author, they fully identify him with the literary climate in which he developed.

Brown grew up aspiring to be a poet. As he explained in a letter to Joseph Bringhurst, Jr., in 1792, while pondering his education as a younger man:

> I began to consider to what particular pursuit I was led by predominant propensity, and at *that time* concluded that grammar Rhetorick and poetry were the sciences to which I felt the strongest attachment, and of these therefore I thought it incumbent upon me to form some regular and Analytical System, which should furnish the materials of reflexion, and which should serve as my lode star my guiding luminary through the grammatical Rhetorical and Poetical library; by which I should be able to enroll in its proper class and assign its proper station to every new idea with which study or reflexion should furnish me.   (Letters 112–113)

Brown's system making was common to eighteenth-century pedagogy, and his forays into verse emerged out of an intensive education in the British poets of the seventeenth and eighteenth centuries. Brown's family was thoroughly poetic. His father, Elijah, kept more than a dozen notebooks and commonplace books in which he transcribed favorite poems culled from his reading in the thick stream of periodicals circulating through Philadelphia in the 1780s and 1790s. Held today at the Historical Society of Pennsylvania and written in a meticulously neat script adorned with typographical flourishes, these books cataloged a range of different poetries: extracts from long poems such as William Cowper's *The Task* or Mark Akenside's *Pleasures of the Imagination*; topical poems such as "The African," by William Lisle Bowles or "The Little Chimney Sweeper," copied "from one of the late London papers"; and verses on local events such as "To Doctor Moyes, on his Lectures Delivered in Philadelphia," which was taken from a 1785 issue of the *Pennsylvania Packet*.

Elijah Brown was a fan of the Della Cruscan poets, a coterie of authors including Robert Merry ("Della Crusca"), Hannah Cowley ("Anna Matilda"), and Mary Robinson ("Laura Maria"), whose emotive and sentimental poems, addressed to each other in an elaborate, Italianate style, enjoyed a wide vogue around the Atlantic in the 1780s. Elijah copied many of their *Poems on Various Subjects* (1787) into a notebook that also includes some of Brown's juvenile verse. The Della Cruscan influence would be important to Brown's development as a poet and a writer, particularly in the self-conscious use of literary personas addressing specific individuals through the periodical in a kind of literary game that invited readers to guess the identities of the participants. Like the Della

Cruscans, Brown's correspondents adopted monikers that held consistent over the years: "Birtha" (Bringhurst), "Ella" (Elihu Hubbard Smith), "Laura" (Deborah Ferris), "Stella" (Ruth Paxson), and "Clara" (Elizabeth Linn).

Elijah Brown bequeathed his appreciation for poetry to his children. In a letter from 1788, Charles reported receiving from his brother Armitt the gift of a volume of Alexander Pope, "which contains his satires and imitations of Horace," and it inspired him to emulate the most influential poet of the eighteenth century. As he explained:

> I strove to catch some of his spirit, and the success that attended my Endeavours has at the same time pleased me and discouraged me, the facility with which I wrote has revived the former good opinion I entertained of my own talents, but my ambition looks higher than the Musa Pedistris of such poetry—But when I reflect upon my haste in other Instances, and the several serious and pathetic strokes which I have indulged in this piece which I thought to render sacred to humour only, has encouraged me a little to think of something more elevated.   (Letters 3)

In thanks for this gift, Brown composed a neoclassical satire, "Epistle the First," though, in spite of the ambition described in the letter, he asked Armitt for a little fraternal leniency: "Wouldst thou my honor'd Brother & my friend / The joys of Poesy with Business blend, / Amuse thy leasure with my Idle lay / Nor judge too hardly what the muse shall say." This poem well expresses Brown's youthful poetic aims, to entertain his friends and to challenge the vices of his age.

> I leave the humbler Bards and wishing rise
> Higher than Pindar or the lofty Skies
> To stand the horror of an age of Night
> And shine as bright as Pope or e'en as bright
> As polish'd Flaccus who the times has sung
> And lash'd the vices that from greatness sprung.

Addressing satirists from Horace to Pope, whose epistles scanned "the manners of a vicious Age / With partial envy or satiric rage," Brown's poetry shoots for the highest ideals, the reform of culture and country. Elijah Brown inscribed this poem in one of his manuscript books, where he copied eight other works by his teenage son but also noted having omitted many other pieces. In 1788, Charles reported writing "at least one hundred lines a day," and this pitch of poetic activity continued into his twenties; in 1792, he confided to his friend William Wood Wilkins that "the poetical fervor is upon me," while he joked with Bringhurst about how "rapidly and inevitably I catch the poetical contageon, and slide into verse as an overloaded promontory sinks into the ocean" (Letters 4, 22, 15–16).

Most of this early verse emerged from Brown's years at the Friends Latin School, where he studied Greek, Latin, and some modern languages and where he developed early interests in history, belles-lettres, and philosophical speculation. While we lack details about the school's curriculum, composition and oratory were likely to have been included, as the poem "On Some of His School Fellows" bears the marks of a pedagogical exercise. Regardless, it is clear that poetry occupied a primary place in Brown's imagination during his adolescence and that he shared this interest with his closest schoolmates, including John Davidson, Bringhurst, and Wilkins. These early works were written for and about these friends, family, and the bustling literary and cultural world of Philadelphia in the 1780s. They vary in genre and style, from lengthy neoclassical satires such as "The Times" and "The Rising Glory of America" to several poems written to a romantic interest (perhaps to Dolley Payne, who later married James Madison) and more lighthearted fare such as the playful "For the Grocer's Window," composed for Brown's brothers James and Joseph to entice passers-by into their recently opened shop:

> The best of the kind,
> Put up to your mind,
> And here to be got very handy;
> Vinegar, and Rice,
> Melases, and Spice,
> Good spirits, and excellent brandy...
> American Beer
> Enquire for here
> For bottle, or Cask, as you love it,
> As good, I'll be bold,
> As ever was sold,
> To tell you a lie I'm above it.

Elijah Brown's note before "To Estrina," a break-up poem possibly written after Dolley Payne's 1790 marriage to attorney John Todd, claims that his son "requested me to transcribe it fair, before he gave it to the printer"; however, no early publication of this poem has been identified (it would appear in a Baltimore periodical in 1805, with the title "To Elvira"). There remains some uncertainty about Brown's first published poem. Daniel Edwards Kennedy identified the monitory "Utrum horum Mavis, elige," published in 1788 in Noah Webster's New York periodical the *American Magazine*, as Brown's first work in print. Although the content of "Utrum," a set of hortatory principles for young men, does resemble some portions of Brown's juvenile verse, there is no direct evidence linking it to Brown, who at the time had no New York connections that might have helped him place a poem in the foremost periodical of the day—and had he done so, it seems likely that Brown's father would have noted the fact (the editors of Webster's bibliography have attributed the poem to Webster). Moreover, a companion piece, "An Address to the Ladies," which Kennedy also assigned to Brown, is almost certainly not Brown's work, since it had appeared in Boston periodicals in 1781, when Brown was ten years old.

There is stronger evidence that Brown's first publication was "An Inscription for General Washington's Tomb Stone," which appeared in an unlikely location, the *State Gazette of North-Carolina*, in 1789:

The shade of great Newton shall mourn,
And yield him Philosophy's throne,
The palm from her brow shall be torn,
And given to Washington alone.
His brows ever shall be adorn'd
With laurels that never decay,
His laws, mighty nations unborn,
And ages remote shall obey.
Him liberty crowned with her wreath,
Philosophy shew'd him her plan;
Whilst the Muses inscrib'd underneath,
The hero, the sage, and the man.
Let candour then write on his tomb,
Here America's favourite lies;
Whose soul for the want of due room,
Has left us, to range in the skies.

Here too, however, questions remain. Paul Allen first attributed the poem to Brown in his unpublished *Life of Charles Brockden Brown*. According to Allen, Brown wrote the epitaph for Benjamin Franklin, not Washington, which makes sense—the poem's references to Newton, philosophy, and laurels refer much more clearly to Franklin rather than Washington—and readers can note how, in the fourth line, "Franklin" fits the poem's meter better than "Washington" (Allen 17). According to Brown family lore, recorded decades later, Franklin, who was still alive, contacted Brown prior to the poem's publication in a Philadelphia newspaper and asked him to demur, since Franklin desired, so the story went, to write his own epitaph (Bennett 1974; there is no contemporary evidence, such as letters between Franklin and the Brown family or notations in any relevant diaries, to support this story). The poem may have made its way to North Carolina via Brown's older brother Joseph, then living in Edenton, where the *State Gazette* was published. However the poem reached the paper, no one knows who switched its subject from Franklin to Washington, and since Washington had just become president, the revised poem might have been perceived as a political attack.

In the 1790s, Brown's poetic writings expanded beyond the more limited circulation of his early work. His extant letters from the period include five poems addressed to Bringhurst, and since much of the correspondence between the two has been lost, including all of Bringhurst's letters, this likely represents only a portion of the epistolary poems they exchanged. These poems are lighter in tone and topic than the school verse and reflect on a sociable world of conversation, reading, and debate that they also make manifest. "A Peter-Pindarical Performance" and "Introduction to a Heroi-Comic Poem on Loo," for example, allude to the games and pastimes Brown enjoyed with his friends, while adopting the satirical, mock-heroic language characteristic of favorite authors such as Pope.

Attend! Ye sisters of celestial birth!
Forsake your starry homes and post to earth
With laughter under each expanded Wing;

> Of harmony and wit untwine the string.
> Be near while I, than Hercules more strong,
> Unloose the fettered hands of drooping song;
> Retread the tract that Homer trod before
> And spread the muses praise from shore to shore.
> For, lo! the phrenzy of my soul constrains
> On Fancy's sparkling neck to throw the reins
> In numbers to imbalm a lofty theme
> And pour, of various verse, the copious stream,
> And (to cut short my tale) in Cantos two,
> To sound the triumphs of heroic LOO.

Loo was a popular card game, and Brown's poem depicts it as a mock epic à la Pope's use of ombre in *The Rape of the Lock* or Marco Girolamo Vida's comic descriptions of chess in *Scacchia Ludus*. Brown's rhetoric and imagery hyperbolically inflate the trivial subject matter:

> Behold, with joy depicted in my face
> Of trumps the royal pair, or knave or Ace;
> At Sight of trumpless hand, proclaim a truce
> Or scoul, with rolling eyes, on worthless *duce*
> At ace succeeding ace astonished gaze
> Or of collected spoils a trophy raise.
> Or see around, the mighty ruin strewed
> And, wait, in speechless terror to be *looed*.

But while Brown envisioned the possibility of this heroi-comic mock epic, he had no plans to finish it. It was, like a game of loo, merely for fun: "Tell me whether you approve it. I would delineate the whole plan of the poem had I formed it. I have opposite pursuits and inclinations, and must resign the task of celebrating this *delightful*!!! game to some time-provided inclination-aided bard" (Letters 50). Bringhurst's approval of the joke was what Brown desired most, and the pleasures of writing and reading the poem with his friends would complement the joy of playing cards.

These poems wear their learning lightly and show Brown constituting a sociable world at the same time as he was clarifying his ambitions as an author. David S. Shields has demonstrated that poetry was central to the refinement of polite men and women across eighteenth-century North America. As he and others have shown, poems offered an ideal basis for inculcating sociability; a poem's content could provide didactic advice on how to behave, but, more important, poems were believed to instill civility through their form (the ideal correspondences between sound and sense or genre and language) and the social forums to which they gave rise: card game, tea table, salon, and coterie. At bottom, didactic poems such as "Utrum horum Mavis, elige" seek to improve civility by teaching young people to match exterior polish with inner cultivation, in contrast to coquettes, fops, blades, and idlers:

> But he whose wisdom, such desires withstood,
> Unites his pleasure with his greatest good,
> Knows not misfortune tho' a fair one frown,
> His wealth escape him, and his friends disown;
> But, firm in what he *is*, in what he *may* be blest,
> Feels an unvaried sun-shine in his breast.

In bringing together "what he *is*" with "what he *may* be," such poetry seeks to reform the sensibilities of readers, making them more attuned to distinctions between outer display and inner worth (a process that will get several twists of the knife in Brown's later Gothic fictions).

Didactic address was only one method for reforming sensibility and refining sentiment; conversation was another, as was composing and circulating verse in manuscript. When Brown inscribed a poem in Deborah Ferris's copy of Johnson's *The History of Rasselas, Prince of Abyssinia* sometime after 1790, his intent was to help guide Ferris's reading:

> Accept my friend this guide to truth,
> Where Eloquence and wisdom joined
> Instruct the steps of headlong youth
> To keep the path by Heaven assigned
> Though clad in sad and sober guise
> He comes on rueful things intent
> Yet not unwelcome to the wise
> Whose steps in search of truth are bent.
> Yet not so much the gloomy sage
> My friend must heed nor long pursue
> His steps through this disastrous page
> Nor deam his ghastly painting true.

Johnson's reflections on the pursuit of happiness had made *Rasselas* the most popular novella of the later eighteenth century, but whatever wisdom the novel might have contained, Brown did not hold it to be self-evident. Though it identifies the novel as a "guide to truth," Brown's inscription also warns Ferris not to take the "gloomy sage" too seriously. She should read and reflect but not feel herself bound to accept Johnson's world view (as Brown put it elsewhere, "All human reason is no more than this, / To guide our footsteps in the realms of bliss"). The inscribed poem thus undercuts the authority of the text it prefaces, while also marking the book in which it is written as a testament to Brown's friendship with Ferris. This is a good example of the social values expressed when like-minded individuals circulated poems and books among themselves.

The sociability of this epistolary and manuscript verse also characterizes a number of poems in print now attributed to Brown. Most prominent among these are four poems composed for a poetic correspondence in the pages of the Philadelphia *Gazette of the United States*, the leading Federalist paper of the 1790s. The exchange began in February 1791, when a poem celebrating Washington appeared in the *Gazette*. Entitled "The Volunteer Laureat, An Ode," it was signed by "Ella," who sought rather directly to get other poets to write her back. She published several more poems in the *Gazette* over the next month, before "Birtha" wrote in with a sonnet "To Ella." Ella responded with an "Ode to Birtha," and several weeks later, "Henry" chimed in with a poem mentioning Ella (his poem was first printed in the Philadelphia *General Advertiser* and then reprinted in the *Gazette* two days later). Ella's "Ode to Henry," published in the *Gazette* the following week, encouraged further entries from Henry, who willingly obliged. By that August, the three authors had produced thirty-five poems, making their correspondence the longest and largest in American literary history (and since several other poets published poems to Henry in Philadelphia newspapers during the run, the correspondence may be even larger if we look beyond the *Gazette*).

The authors never identified themselves, though Ella's identity was an open secret among the literati: she was Elihu Hubbard Smith. Smith had been experimenting with sonnets in his letters and journals and tried privately to recruit people to join his poetic correspondence in the *Gazette*. His friends began calling him Ella, and Brown referred to him that way in a 1793 letter to Bringhurst—whom Dunlap identified as "Birtha" in his copy of Smith's 1793 anthology *American Poems* (the first American poetry anthology), which included five of Birtha's contributions to the *Gazette* (Bailey). The identity of "Henry" remained unknown until the 1970s, however, when Bennett made the case that Henry was Brown (Bennett 1974 and 1977). Henry's first contribution to the series was a sonnet possibly addressed to the sisters "Payne," the subjects of some of Brown's other early verses, and "Henry" would go on to be one of his favorite fictional names. When Brown visited Smith in Connecticut two years later, he reported with pleased surprise to Bringhurst that the two of them were popular among Smith's friends, including several of the Hartford Wits, the leading poets of the day (Letters 229–232). As with Brown's epistolary poems of these years, his Henry poems wear lightly the literary sophistication that underwrote them. Most of the *Gazette* poems were Petrarchan sonnets, a form whose popularity had been revived by the Della Cruscans and Charlotte Smith. The addresses between Ella, Birtha, and Henry thus depended on a deep awareness of current literary trends; clearly, these authors knew what was popular in Europe, and they were eager to bring fashionable poetic forms to American contexts and readerships.

The Della Cruscan style used "the medium of a DAILY PRINT" to transmit "poetical Sympathy" between persons (allegedly) "unacquainted with each other, and reciprocally unknown" in an ostentatiously sentimental manner (*British Album*, "Preface"). Though this stylistic practice can fairly categorize many of the Ella-Birtha-Henry poems, only about half of these poems refer explicitly to their participation in a correspondence. The rest seem related to the sequence only by virtue of the author's pseudonym, and even the poems dedicated by one author to another seem otherwise abstracted from the publication setting. The most interesting poems are those that adapt the features of coterie circulation to riff on the context of newspaper verse, such as Ella's "Sonnet II. Sent to Mrs. ——, with a Song" (published March 19, 1791):

> Blest is the *Poet* if his songs can raise
> Some kindred genius that will catch the fire,
> With answering notes awake the trembling lyre,
> And give to far posterity his praise.
> Yet double pleasure fills his aged days,
> If chance, responsive to his fond desire,
> While from the lips of youth the notes aspire,
> In the warm breast the flame of virtue blaze.
> And still a greater pleasure, should he spy
> That while from Virtue's breast the music flows,
> Caught by the song, the voice, the speaking eye,
> In every heart the illustrious purpose glows.
> Even he, the Poet, nobler worth should warm
> By virtue, greatly rous'd, in —'s form.

Ella's sonnet explains that the poet earns posterity not only through the vehicle of the poem but also through the "kindred genius" awakened in those who hear it, "caught by the song, the voice, the speaking eye"—in other words, through poetry's milieu, which should be personal and interactive, whether mediated by music, voice, or writing. This imagined setting works in tension with the sonnet's place in the newspaper; since the poem does not literally come with a song (as it might if presented in a salon), the title plays up the fictiveness of its context. The sonnet thus pretends an intimacy its setting resists but also augments; written for a blank, the poem might address anyone. At the same time, those familiar with Ella might read themselves as the addressees, thereby heightening their sense of bonding amid the vaster anonymity of the newspaper's audience. And the encoded title alerts even uninformed readers to the possibility of an addressee they may or may not be able to identify.

Henry's first entry into this correspondence, a "Sonnet, Written after hearing a SONG sung by several SISTERS," is therefore typical:

> Hark!—hear'st thou not the sweetly swelling strain
> Of warbled music float along the air?
> Soft are the sounds,—the sister band how fair!
> How high flies rapture when it springs from *P*yn**.
> So round the Lyre the heavenly Muses stand,
> And charm the changing soul with varied joy;
> So Ella's lays the feeling heart command,
> And faintly hide Apollo in the boy.
> Hail charming group! for you shall Fancy rise,
> To you young Love his earliest homage pay;
> And while our souls his softened slavr'y stray,

> Your *Minds* preserve the conquest of your *Eyes*;
> Till ripe you fall, as Heaven and Fame approve,
> From Beauty's branch, into the lap of Love.

The opening question can only be rhetorical in the *Gazette*; no reader actually hears a song as he or she scans the poem's lines. But the unanswerable question makes for a neat springboard into the comparisons of the second quatrain, as the unheard song becomes a vehicle first to consider the power of the "Heavenly Muses" (poetry as an abstraction) and then to refer back to the *Gazette*'s verse, specifically "Ella's lays," which had been appearing there for two months when this sonnet was published. Yet when the sestet returns to a vision of the (non)singing sisters P*yn*, the poem doubles down on its initial description of an imagined occasion: we are back in a parlor, perhaps falling in love with these young women and their beauty, voices, and intellect. The sonnet's address is extratextual: as a poem first appearing in the *General Advertiser*, it refers to poetry in the *Gazette*, thus invoking Philadelphia's newspaper culture; then, as a poem addressed to "three sisters," their name only barely concealed, the poem seems to target its referents so precisely as to exclude its actual audience, the *Advertiser*'s readers. But even this apparently specific address is upended, since by the time the poem was published, Dolley Payne had been Dolley Todd for more than a year, so the supposedly real addressees no longer existed in the terms by which the sonnet addressed them.

The result is a metareflexive portrayal of newspaper poetry's pragmatics, the ways in which the publication context in the Federalist period contributes to the poem's meaning. Brown's sonnet compels readers to imagine a situation that structurally excludes them but then turns this exclusion into a metaphor for poetry: by imagining a song we cannot hear, we are able to feel (if not hear) the power of that unheard abstraction, poetry. While not all of the Ella-Birtha-Henry poems are like this, the sequence as a whole turns the newspaper from a publication format into a vehicle to reflect on the socially oriented practices readers use when they read poems.

In Brown's biography, the 1790s tend to be known as a period when he abandoned a legal career to pursue writing and literature. He spent time in New York with Smith, Dunlap, and other ambitious young writers, and his letters to Bringhurst offer early experiments in extended narrative fiction. He also began working with some of the newly prestigious magazines of the day. Jared Gardner, Michael Cody, and others have documented the meteoric rise of the magazine as the premier vehicle for literary culture in the Federalist United States. Bennett (1974) has made the case that Brown's work with magazines began with the *Columbian Magazine* in 1789 and that he was involved in the publication of the Philadelphia-based *Lady's Magazine* in 1792. Bennett attributed to Brown four poems that appeared in the *Lady's Magazine* that year: "Sonnet to Flora," "Constancy. Addressed to Miss P——s," "Verses—on Miss S——n," and "An Elegy Addressed to Miss P——'s." Like the Henry poems, the latter three of these verses seemed to address a coterie readership through print; based on occluded in-text references, Bennett surmised that "Constancy" and "An Elegy" were directed once again at Dolley Payne.

However, Brown wrote none of these poems, which all appeared during the 1780s in a London periodical also known as the *Lady's Magazine*. Although each was marked as "Original" to the Philadelphia *Lady's Magazine*, there seems to have been a pattern in the practice of reprinting materials from the London journal and modifying them for a Philadelphia readership, since each poem received a new title in Philadelphia that apparently addressed someone specific. While there is no evidence that Brown selected or adapted these poems, Bennett makes a strong argument that the Society for the Advancement of Useful Knowledge, to which Brown belonged, edited the magazine (just as the Tuesday Club had melded with the *Port Folio*), so Brown may have played a role in publishing these poems even though he did not write them. On the other hand, because it was standard periodical practice in the 1790s not to name authors, it is entirely possible, if not likely, that he published other poems that remain unidentified.

Brown's scribal practices continued through the mid-1790s in tandem with his forays into periodical publication and editorial work, and as with his earlier poems, these writings developed out of social relationships while simultaneously mediating and extending them. This was particularly true for Brown's relationships with women. Brown's interests in coterie exchange and circulation and his engagements with women writers in the 1790s may be linked to his readings of Mary Wollstonecraft, whose arguments about female education and reading are echoed in the "Henrietta Letters" of 1792, elaborated in several poems of the period, and developed further in courtship letters written between 1794 and 1804. David Lee Clark, Eleanor Tilton, Kennedy, and Bennett have noted Brown's poetic exchanges with a series of women, including Dolley Payne, Deborah Ferris ("Laura"), Ruth Paxson ("Stella"), Susan Potts ("Clara"), and Elizabeth Linn ("Clara"). During the 1790s, Brown composed many poems in the contexts of these relationships; Bennett speculates that most of the poems Brown published after 1801 were, in fact, written earlier, though there is no manuscript evidence to support this argument. The poems Brown wrote with Paxson were published in the *Weekly Magazine* as an exchange between Henry and Stella several years after the relationship had cooled (for a detailed reconstruction of this kerfuffle, see Letters 297–317). In the first poem, Henry sets the scene of composition for Stella:

> As lonely o'er my little fire,
> I sit and muse, and dream of fame,
> My hopes on Fancy's wing aspire
> To wealth, and rank, and sounding name.
> But ah! the little traitor Love
> Unbidden mingles in the theme;
> The fixed resolve dares disapprove,
> And stile the vision but a dream.
> "Ambition hence!" the urchin cries,
> "Thy solitary reign resign;
> Henry thy fate's in Clara's eyes;
> Thou'rt happy if the maid be thine.
> "And what avails the laurell'd brow,

> Or loud applause, or splendid store;
> Clara can happiness bestow,
> And canst thou Henry wish for more!"

The scene is almost purely conventional. The pastoral pseudonym Stella had a long history in coterie verse, dating back at least to Philip Sidney's *Astrophil and Stella*, and in the 1790s, many Stellas were writing or receiving poems in New York and Philadelphia magazines. Henry and Stella's poems maintain the Della Cruscanism of the earlier correspondence with Ella and Birtha, in that the pseudonymous address accomplishes much of the work. The subject of Henry's verse is not Stella but Clara (tentatively identified by scholars as Susan Potts), thus dislocating the poem further from its imagined conversational setting and rendering as topic the fictionality of the poems' themes and language. Stella renders this explicit in her response to Henry:

> Ingenuous Henry! may thy song,
> When pour'd on Clara's list'ning ear,
> In softest accents from thy tongue
> The most persuasive influence bear . . .
> May sacred friendship, serious power!
> Exulting, bless the youthful choice;
> With liberal hand each passing hour
> Improve, and crown your virtuous joys.

Though Henry has addressed Stella rather than Clara, Stella imagines the song poured into Clara's "list'ning ear," figuring the imaginative labor that readers of their exchange would undertake when eavesdropping (as it were) on them. The goal is "persuasive influence" on the virtues of "sacred friendship." Henry replies to this invocation two weeks later by also emphasizing the powers of personalized verse:

> Though long, my lyre, unstrung,
> Idle, neglected, thou hast hung,
> Thy notes in deep oblivion drown'd;
> Again, with trembling hand,
> At Stella's sweet command
> I wake thy slumbering wires and pour thy music round. . . .
> I lean o'er Friendship's hallowed shrine,
> And see her vestal flame serenely shine,
> As to the "serious power" in reverence I bend.

The Stella poems rely even more heavily on the mediating force of the periodical to secure their fiction of address. While the two quote each other's work, there is little pretense of privacy or personal connection between them: Henry addresses his lyre rather than his friend, while the object of his love is not Stella but Clara. The sequence is about prompting Henry to sing again, but while Henry's poems presumably evince ongoing literary production, the final song to Stella expresses his retirement: "In vain, with ardent eye and daring hand, / I touch again the soft responsive wires; / No melting music flows at my command, / Nor Muse the meditated strain inspires." What is more, this last poem ends with an editorial footnote that explains that it was "written under the pressure of an illness which, four weeks afterwards, terminated in death," and for this reason Paxson's niece later attributed the poems to Brown's friend Wilkins, who had died in 1795. The truth-telling voice of editorial authority in the press serves up a fiction in order to close out the sequence, while the public forum of the magazine lets the poet withdraw from public correspondence by way of a poem.

Cody has shown that America's periodical culture was much on the minds of Brown and his friends during this time. In 1797, Smith impressed on Joseph Dennie the idea that a magazine could be the ideal repository for "all the best smaller poems in our language"; if Dennie published correct versions of important authors from "Thos. Warton to Milton, & of Gilbert Wakefield to Pope...It would supersede the necessity of a large library of poetry; it would induce many to read what otherwise they might never think of; & could not fail of making some favorable impression on the minds & manners of the people at large" (Smith 327). He thought similarly about sonnets ("Sonnets are short; if well written, & on profitable subjects, they may do good"); in an era of business (and busy-ness), periodicals could best promote the civilizing features of verse, supplementing (if not replacing) polite institutions like the coterie or the salon (189). Brown had a saltier view:

> Even bad verses are pleasing to the readers of bad taste, and though good verses, are as rare in newspapers, as swallows in winter, yet they sometimes are met with, and delight us in proportion to their rarity. Bad verses are not disreputable to a newspaper, no more than bad English to a foreigner, because they are naturally expected; but poetry, very middling in a collection of elegant extracts, is super-excellent here, and surprises us, like just expression from a chimney sweeper
>
> (Letters 570–571).

This alignment of taste and value projects a hierarchy of forms that diminishes the newspaper in relation to more polite and elegant forms of communication. While the last clause may indicate that Brown lumped all poetry together as "middling" compared to other kinds of "elegant extracts," several later poems show him still valuing the social functions of verse. In "Alliteration" (1802), Brown defends these values by comically exposing some of the dangers to poetry presented by periodical publication. "Such are the charms in poetry we find, / To soothe the sorrows of the wounded mind," he begins, elaborating poetry's affective virtues:

> Yet, whilst we own the power of verse divine,
> And for the Poet's brow the wreath entwine,
> We see with sorrow half her empire lost,
> Her ends perverted and her meaning crost
> By bold intruders, who in every age,
> Assume her mark and venture on the stage;

> Then false conceits their glittering tinsel shew,
> And ranting rage contends with weeping woe.
> Alliteration proudly rears her head,
> And o'er the labored page her art is spread;
> R's P's and Q's in every corner rise
> And strike with ravishment our gazing eyes,
> Yet, whilst we praise a science so profound,
> We grieve that sense is sacrific'd to sound.

Notably, Brown compares poetasters with bad actors, "bold intruders . . . on the stage," who take over the poet's corner (the space in a newspaper reserved for poems) and "strike with ravishment our gazing eyes" with their "R's P's and Q's," much like a ranting actor might din in the ears of an overwhelmed audience. Ironically, Thomas Cooper's December 1799 performance, on the stage of Dunlap's New-York Theatre, of Brown's best-known poem, "Monody on the Death of George Washington," had been a disaster in just this mode. That poem begins as follows:

> No mimic accents now shall touch your ears,
> And now no fabled woe demand your tears;
> No Hero of a visionary age,
> No child of poet's phrenzy walks the stage;
> 'Tis no phantastic fate of Queens or Kings,
> That bids your sympathy unlock its springs;
> This woe is yours, it falls on every head;
> This woe is yours, for WASHINGTON IS DEAD!

While decrying "mimic accents" and "fabled woe," Cooper is reported to have spoken "in the very tones of Mrs. Melmoth, artificial and declamatory, ending his lines with a full cadence of voice, exactly in the manner of that actress when she repeats her Blackbird Elegy," before forgetting the remaining lines (Crito). Perhaps in response to Cooper's poor performance, Brown emphasizes in "Alliteration" how the versifier's "ranting rage" and "weeping woe" act like "glittering tinsel" that usurps the profound science of versification. His twist on Pope's famous dictum from *Essay on Criticism*—"'Tis not enough no Harshness gives offense, / The Sound must seem an Eccho to the Sense"—reaffirms his own career-long commitment to the formal values of poetry, especially its capacity to instill harmony through harmonious language.

Similarly, Brown's critique of alliteration as the confusion of cause and effect reiterates a point made in many of his essays from this time. Alliteration can be useful when it harmonizes sound and sense, but too many poets love alliteration's mere materiality.

> Thus sings Alliteration—and her theme
> To some, the height of poetry may seem;
> Yet may we hope this taste at length will fail,
> And common sense take up the pleasing tale;
> Then shall Alliteration have less power,

> Yet not be banish'd quite the muse's bower,
> Since still her art may have the power to please,
> If well employ'd, and introduc'd with ease.

Returning alliteration to its place as one rhetorical device among others would also mark the return of taste and common sense to poetry, which remains for Brown a profound science. In fact, in "The Poet's Prayer" (published in Dennie's *Port Folio* in 1801), the poet admits to have "oftener than discretion bade…rais'd / A secret invocation to the Muse," giving the lie, perhaps, to the now-dated notion that Brown had abandoned literary ambitions in his last decade. Brown's poet hopes that "worlds of intellect shall ope / Their gates to me, which ne'er the poet's knock / Obeyed, and throw wide their resplendent valves." The pursuit of knowledge rather than fame ("The phantom glory, the ignoble child / Of selfishness abhorred") drives Brown's verse to the end, as do the ideals of sociable understanding.

Because the story of Brown's career has almost always been organized around his long narrative fictions, it has been typical to claim that his major period of productivity occurred between 1798 and 1801 and that his literary writing tapered off thereafter, as he shifted into magazine editing and sought other paying work to support his young family. In a less novel-oriented account, however, it becomes possible to see that the reading, writing, and exchange of poetry remained important to Brown through the end of his life. Smith's diaries record dozens of instances between 1795 and 1798 in which he, Brown, Dunlap, William Johnson, Richard Alsop, and others would gather to read and discuss poetry, sometimes their own compositions or more often those printed in the latest issue of a periodical. For example, in December 1796, Smith noted, "I found Ch. B. Brown here, when I returned. A long & disputatious argument, 'On the difference between poetry & prose'—or rather on 'the wherein are poetry & prose distinct'; which ended, as such discussions usually do, without the conviction of either party; & with no clearer ideas on the subject, than before" (Smith 273).

This is not to say that scholars have been wrong to celebrate the importance of Brown's experiments in narrative fiction; it is instead to argue that there are valid reasons to read those fictions in the context of his experiments in other genres. Smith noted one afternoon how "Charles has been all day, writing verses. He read them to us—after a sad manner, this evening. He also read what he has composed of his novel" (290); later that year, Smith offered his commentary on Brown's dialogue *Alcuin* while simultaneously composing a series of sonnets for his friends, despite the fact that Brown had apparently come to "despise" sonnets (417). As a professional man of letters, Brown worked across many registers. In "A Negro's Lamentation, Written at Charleston," for example, Brown produced an early instance of a type of antislavery poem, the "lament" written in the voice of an enslaved person, that would become a prominent vehicle of abolitionist rhetoric in subsequent decades.

> What though I come from Afric's burning coast,
> And here, a captive, groan beneath the yoke;
> Yet, like great *Buckra*, I can have my toast,

> And like him, too, the gentle Muse invoke.
> Soft are the accents when, with soothing tone,
> My Angel cries her sweet-potatoe-pone;
> Which oft I've eat beneath the ev'ning sky,
> "And drunk delicious poison from her eye;"
> While her soft bosom, rising to the sight,
> With envy fill'd the black'ning clouds of night.
> Oft have I view'd her, at the close of day,
> *Jump* to the fiddle, lightsome on the Bay;
> Or heard her sing responsive on the lyre,
> While my heart beat with hope and fond desire.
> But bliss is fled! *Buckra*, for want of gold,
> The lovely nymph inflexibly has sold
> To some rich planter, man of high renown,
> *Who haunts vendues to knock poor Negroes down!*

While there is not enough evidence to conclusively identify Brown as the author of this poem, there are a number of intriguing connections to *Arthur Mervyn, Second Part*, likewise published in the fall of 1800 (Barnard and Shapiro). If this work is Brown's, it reveals him to have been expanding his poetic repertoire and also indicates hitherto underrecognized connections between his poetry writing, his novels, and his ventures in other literary and cultural fields.

During his last decade, Brown published several other experiments in different verse genres, including the anacreontic, a song on the pleasures of drinking ("The Water Drinker," actually an anti-anacreontic song) and the ranz-des-vaches, a Swiss herdsmen's song that had become enormously popular during the Napoleonic Wars ("A Rans de Vache of Tuscany"). His poem "To Laura, on her Attachment to Homer's Iliad," which appeared in the *Port Folio* in 1801, displays some of Brown's sharpest reflections on the literary and moral virtues of poetics. This later work reflects the confidence of a cosmopolitan belletrist offering his judgments on current tastes, proper reading, and good literary style. Meanwhile, the elaborate literary hoaxes of "A Rans de Vache of Tuscany" and "Solitary Worship," which both purport to be translations of early-modern European works but which are almost certainly Brown's own original compositions, show that he maintained a playful sense of the periodical's capacities for both deception and education.

In one of Smith's final diary entries, he records copying down a long poem by Samuel Taylor Coleridge to send to Alsop, before meeting Brown at dinner. Smith's voracious reading habits and his intense desire to stay apprised of literary developments from abroad clearly carried over to his close friend after Smith's untimely death in 1798. As Brown's many reviews attest, he remained current with the latest literary developments coming from England and Europe. He reviewed early US editions of Robert Southey's *Joan of Arc* and *Poems* for the *Monthly Magazine* in 1799; his review of the former included a lengthy disquisition on the development of epic poetry and its relation to the "progress of society" (226). For the *Literary Magazine*, he reviewed Peter Bayley's *Poems* in 1804, damning the work with faint praise but also jibing William Wordsworth and

Coleridge's *Lyrical Ballads* in the process (Bayley had dedicated his burlesque "The Fisherman's Wife" to "all admirers of the familiar style of writing, so popular in 1800," and Brown smirkingly noted that "if viewed in a serious light, it is vastly superior to 'The Thorn' or 'Idiot Boy' of Wordsworth" [19]). On the other hand, Brown extravagantly praised Walter Scott's 1805 *The Lay of the Last Minstrel* in the *Literary Magazine*, calling it "a very beautiful and entertaining poem, in a style which may be justly deemed original, and which affords evidence of the genius of the author" (99). He also commented on the controversy surrounding the legitimacy of the Ossian poems, which had been rekindled by the publication in 1805 of James Macpherson's spurious manuscripts. In a long essay on "The Latest Evidence Concerning the Authenticity of Ossian's Poems," published in the *Literary Magazine* that year, Brown staked a middle position (which, incidentally, many later scholars have endorsed), arguing against the existence of any authentic manuscript but supporting the idea of long-standing Gaelic oral traditions. "No well-informed person now pretends that Ossian is a historical authority, or that a collection of Gaelic poems any where exists, of which Macpherson's version is a faithful, or even a loose translation," Brown argued. "But there no doubt existed, before the times of Macpherson, a sort of general basis of tradition, on which the poems, whether collected or composed by himself, appear to have been founded" (354).

All told, Brown was probably among the most well-read students of poetry in the United States by the time of his death in 1810. Cope described Brown living in "fields of literary clover.... [his] friends are all learned Doctors. All intimately acquainted with the whole anatomy of language. They have probed to the bottom of its most latent principles, dissected every letter of the alphabet & can tell, to a little, the number & species of every particle of which each is composed. Chas. is equal to any of them. He has analyzed elements of thought. He has explored the innermost recesses of all articulate sounds. He can split the nerves of an idea & lay bare the sinews, bones & essential spirits of a conjecture" (Cope 79). Or, as Henry tells Stella, his earthly muse, in the final lines of "The Poet's Prayer":

> Thy friendly ear the tedious strain, though wound
> Through many a page, beyond the customed march
> Of poets, shall in vain strive to fatigue,
> Thou still shalt listen, still shall bend to hear
> His accents, harsh to others, sweet to thee,
> The accents of a friend are always sweet.

Even when the song is tedious, the accents of a friend are sweet.

NOTE

1. This discussion draws on work for *Poems*, Vol. 7 of the Bucknell *Collected Writings of Charles Brockden Brown*, edited by Michael C. Cohen and Alexandra Socarides, forthcoming 2019.

WORKS CITED

Bailey, Marcia Edgerton. *A Lesser Hartford Wit, Dr. Elihu Hubbard Smith, 1771–1798*. Orono: University of Maine Press, 1928.

Barnard, Philip, and Stephen Shapiro, eds. *Charles Brockden Brown's Wieland, Ormond, Arthur Mervyn, and Edgar Huntly, with Related Texts*. Indianapolis: Hackett, 2009.

Bennett, Charles E. "The Charles Brockden Brown Canon." Ph.D. dissertation, University of North Carolina, Chapel Hill, 1974.

Bennett, Charles E. "A Poetical Correspondence among Elihu Hubbard Smith, Joseph Bringhurst, Jr., and Charles Brockden Brown in *The Gazette of the United States*." *Early American Literature* 12.3 (Winter 1977): 277–285.

The British Album: Containing the Poems of Della Crusca, Anna Matilda, &c., 2 vols. London: John Bell, 1790.

Brown, Charles Brockden. "The Latest Evidence concerning the Authority of Ossian's Poems." *LM* 4.26 (November 1805): 354–365.

Brown, Charles Brockden. Review of *Joan of Arc: An Epic Poem*, by Robert Southey. *MM* 1.3 (June 1799): 225–229.

Brown, Charles Brockden. Review of *The Lay of the Last Minstrel*, by Walter Scott. *LM* 4.23 (August 1805): 99–102.

Brown, Charles Brockden. Review of *Poems* by Peter Bayley. *LM* 2.7 (April 1804): 17–19.

Brown, Charles Brockden. Review of *Poems* by Robert Southey. *MM* 1.2 (May 1799): 135–137.

Clark, David Lee. *Charles Brockden Brown: Pioneer Voice of America*. Durham, N.C.: Duke University Press, 1952.

Cody, Michael. *Charles Brockden Brown and the* Literary Magazine: *Cultural Journalism in the Early American Republic*. Jefferson, N.C.: McFarland, 2004.

Cope, Thomas Pym. *Philadelphia Merchant: The Diary of Thomas P. Cope, 1800–1851*. Eliza Cope Harrison, ed. South Bend, Ind.: Gateway Editions, 1978.

Crito. "Theatrical Communication" [review of Thomas Cooper]. *Commercial Advertiser* 1 (January 1800): 2.

Gardner, Jared. *The Rise and Fall of Early American Magazine Culture*. Urbana: University of Illinois Press, 2012.

Kennedy, Daniel Edwards. "Charles Brockden Brown: A Biography" (c. 1923–1945). Typescript with manuscript additions. Charles Brockden Brown Bicentennial Edition Records (bulk 1917–1995). Department of Special Collections and Archives, Kent State Libraries, Kent, Ohio.

Shields, David S. *Civil Tongues and Polite Letters in British America*. Chapel Hill: University of North Carolina Press, 1997.

Smith, Elihu Hubbard, ed. *American Poems* (1793). William Bottorff, ed. Gainesville, Fla.: Scholars' Facsimiles and Reprints, 1966.

Smith, Elihu Hubbard. *The Diary of Elihu Hubbard Smith (1771–1798)*. James E. Cronin, ed. Philadelphia: American Philosophical Society, 1973.

Tilton, Eleanor M. "'The Sorrows' of Charles Brockden Brown." *Publications of the Modern Language Association* 69.5 (1954): 1304–1308.

Warfel, Harry. "Charles Brockden Brown's First Published Poem." *American Notes and Queries* 1 (1941): 19–20.

Warfel, Harry. *Charles Brockden Brown, American Gothic Novelist*. Gainesville: University of Florida Press, 1949.

CHAPTER 16

....

SHORT FICTION

....

SCOTT SLAWINSKI

THOUGH still primarily known as a novelist, Charles Brockden Brown also wrote short prose pieces, including serial essays such as "The Rhapsodist" (1789), "The Man at Home" (1798), and "The Scribbler" (1800/1809); social-observation pieces such as "Portrait of an Emigrant. Extracted from a Letter" (1799); and anecdotes and short historical or anthropological works such as "Richard the Third and Perkin Warbeck" (1805) and "Kotan Husbandry" (1805). All contain elements of fiction and can be considered as part of a larger ensemble of Brownian short fiction, especially since the "short story" was not a fully formed genre at the turn of the nineteenth century. In addition to these pieces, however, Brown published eight tales that provide fertile ground for exploring the transition from early-modern short fiction formats to the Romantic and modernist "short story." These tales are of particular interest for the light they shed on Brown's own fictional method and for the ways they look forward to later practitioners of the short-story form such as Edgar Allan Poe and Nathaniel Hawthorne. Brown's reinterpretations of contemporary source material and revisions and reworkings of his own fictions cemented his foundational place in American literary culture not as an early harbinger of a more completely aesthetically realized form or as a literary founding father, but as one who saw writing as an endless series of opportunities for experimentation, the better to engage the diverse literary and cultural currents flowing throughout the Atlantic world at the turn of the nineteenth century.[1]

Reasons for the obscurity of Brown's short fiction are complex, ranging from limited availability prior to the digital age to scholarly focus on his Gothic novels to the general dominance of the novel as a fictional form. Nevertheless, although generally ignored in book-length studies of Brown, the short fiction is a crucial part of his oeuvre.[2] His tales develop the same themes and employ the same techniques as his novels, but they demonstrate Brown's artistry while working on a limited canvas. Gothic elements loom large, as do explorations of sensibility, gender roles, chance, and the mysteries of the mind. Frame stories, unreliable narrators, and conjectural reworkings of historical and contemporary events appear in the tales just as they do in the novels. Neatly packed into the compact space of short fiction, Brown's manipulations of these elements can often be more readily explored in the stories than in the novels.

I. "A LESSON ON SENSIBILITY" (1798) AND "INSANITY: A FRAGMENT" (1809)

Many of Brown's favorite plot devices appear in his first published short story, "A Lesson on Sensibility" (1798),[3] which relates the history of Archibald, a young man who falls in love frequently but superficially because his "sensibility had become diseased by an assiduous study of those Romancers and Poets, who make love the basis of their fictions" ("Sensibility" 71). As a merchant in Ireland, Archibald becomes romantically attached to a young woman of superior social status. Her family attempts to break off the match, forbidding her to see him. He travels to the Caribbean, where he forms a new love interest; meanwhile, his Irish lover remains true to him in his absence until her family deceives her into believing Archibald is false. Set to marry someone else, on her wedding day, she is found dead in her chamber, her death judged a probable suicide. When Archibald hears that his faithlessness caused her death, he immediately credits the tale, because he has been faithless. He returns to Ireland, where he asks to enter the tomb to view the body, but when the vault is opened, her corpse is found "not decently reposing in her coffin, and shrouded with a snow-white mantle, but,—naked, ghastly, stretched on the floor at the foot of the stair-case, with indubitable tokens of having died, a second time, a victim to terror and famine" (76). Archibald is led away from the scene "in a frenzy the most outrageous" (76).

Basic elements of Brown's Gothic novels are present in this brief tale: mental instability, deception, madness, horrible death.[4] The story also provides a lesson, however ambiguous, on sensibility. Most fundamentally, sensibility is a susceptibility to emotion, particularly to strong feelings regarding others. The eighteenth-century literary shift toward sensibility often produced sentimental fiction and poetry, which plied the reader for emotional reactions to its content. In Brown's story, to whose sensibility does the title refer? We are told that love is Archibald's "element" and that he "could not exist without it" (72); his head has been turned by books on the subject. Each time he meets a new potential love interest, he exhibits a superficial excitement which quickly passes despite his protestations to the contrary. When he courts the Butlers' daughter, love is his "ruling passion" (73). At the end of the tale, he has lost his mental balance entirely at the sight of the dead woman. Clearly, susceptibility to emotions takes a heavy toll on him. As for the Butlers' daughter, her fidelity to Archibald in the face of parental opposition may seem to indicate steadfast resolve. But stubborn resistance to the wisdom and authority of her elders goes against filial duty, and her utter rejection of logical argument underscores her unreasonable attitude. Her unshakeable loyalty to Archibald can thus be viewed as a type of sensibility. Does she attempt suicide, the ultimate tragic consequence of sensibility? Or, driven beyond her emotional limits by the purported faithlessness of her lover and the pressure to marry another, does she fall into some sort of catatonic trance that simulates death? If so, then her sensibility is the cause of her premature entombment and horrific death. Lastly, there are the Butlers themselves. In their "alarm" and "finding arguments ineffective" (73), they take extreme measures to break an attachment they deem "an evil of such magnitude" (73). Their revulsion against Archibald and their love for (or perhaps their desire to exert control over) their daughter—their feelings, in other words—drive them to use forced confinement and falsehoods against their own progeny. This is an extreme emotional response of another sort. If sensibility characterizes all the major players in this text, then from whom are readers to learn the lesson? Not to be, like Archibald, overly influenced by books and driven to a frenzy by a horrific sight? Not to be intractably dedicated to a particular emotion, like the daughter? Not to be so rigid in one's pursuit of goals to the detriment of oneself and those nearby, like the Butlers? Typically, Brown leaves this ambiguous.

Brown recycled this story a decade later but with significant alterations. In refurbishing the piece for Joseph Dennie's *Port Folio*, he added a frame story that entirely refocuses the tale from a lesson about sensibility to a commentary on madness, a change emphasized by his new title, "Insanity: A Fragment" (1809). This second version is condensed considerably, with many ruminations about emotion and motivations omitted; indeed, Brown seems to wink toward his original story when his narrator notes that he is conveying the "substance" ("Insanity" 165) of the tale but that it was initially told to him "with much greater minuteness" (167). Selective editing on the narrator's part removes much of the ambiguity of the original. In "Sensibility," the extent of Miss Butler's artifice when acquiescing to her family's matrimonial wishes is ambiguous, but in "Insanity," the narrator clarifies that it is all artifice; similarly, in the original, her suicide is given as a probability, whereas in "Insanity," it is stated with certainty. In "Sensibility," sentimental literature seems to be one root of Archibald's instability, whereas in "Insanity," Mr. Ellen denies that reading led to his kinsman's mental breakdown. The 1809 frame story allows for the key alteration, however, giving another turn of the screw, as Mrs. Ellen reveals that the entire episode "existed only in his own [Archibald's] mind" and that "the whole is a dream, regarded by him indeed as unquestionable reality" (168). The turn toward insanity in the second version modifies the focus from excessive emotionalism to psychological instability. As a result, a shift in genre also occurs: "Sensibility" foregrounds an eighteenth-century story of sensibility and sentiment, while "Insanity" foregrounds the Gothic horror tale, thereby foreshadowing the later work of Poe.

II. "THESSALONICA: A ROMAN STORY" (1799) AND "DEATH OF CICERO, A FRAGMENT" (1800)

While "Sensibility" and "Insanity" employ the conventions of sensibility and the Gothic, respectively, Brown develops his model of conjectural historical fiction in two other tales. Drawing on attested historical events as source material, "Thessalonica: A Roman Story" (1799)[5] recounts the story of a notorious massacre that took place in Thessalonica in 390 CE, when thousands of the city's inhabitants were murdered in retaliation for the death of the Roman general Botheric. The catalyst for the massacre was a riot that occurred when Botheric commanded the arrest of a favored charioteer for immoral behavior (Edward Gibbon claims the charioteer sexually desired Botheric's handsome slave boy). The city had been simmering with resentment for some time over the housing of Roman soldiers, especially those culled from the Germanic tribes of northern Europe. When Botheric rejected demands for the charioteer's release, Thessalonians attacked the garrison headquarters, killed Botheric and a number of other soldiers, and dragged the commander's body through the streets. Apprised of the incident, Emperor Theodosius I flew into a rage and ordered a retaliatory strike against the city, possibly at the instigation of his ruthless advisor Rufinus and despite a request for leniency from Ambrose, bishop of Milan. The troops treated the populace as enemies rather than Roman citizens in revolt. They gathered the Thessalonians into the hippodrome under the pretense of an exhibition, and an unbridled and indiscriminate massacre followed. Theodosius recalled his order, but by then, his troops had already butchered seven thousand Thessalonians (Gibbon notes that some sources put the number as high as fifteen thousand). The blame for the massacre fell on the emperor, and Ambrose chastised him to repent his sin.

In Brown's hands, this source material is transformed into a commentary about irrational behavior, the psychology of occupation and mob violence, effective governance, and the utility of standing armies. Brown retains a few historical facts: there was a riot in Thessalonica in 390 that killed Botheric and instigated the massacre. Gone is the charge of sexual immorality and the charioteer's arrest as the fuse that ignites the popular revolt, and Botheric is slain not at his headquarters but at the hippodrome just before the games begin. No mention is made of the people's resentment regarding the billeting of troops or of Ambrose and his efforts to calm Theodosius, and in place of the seven thousand slain, Brown hints at a toll closer to thirty thousand or more. Brown embellishes the tale with additional characters and other inventions and in so doing refocuses the story away from the slaughter—though he does not shrink from indulging his Gothic impulses for blood and horror—and onto the psychology of mob violence. He chooses as his narrator Julius Malchus, Thessalonica's prefect and chief magistrate, a person who is in a position to collect all the facts of the case and "deliver to you, and to posterity, a faithful narrative" ("Thessalonica" 117). The story makes clear the need for such a narrative. The tale that reaches Theodosius I, though "minute," presents an "exaggerated and fallacious picture of the tumult" (112). Malchus's narrative reshapes received history by exposing the motivations of the mob, the soldiers stationed in the garrison, and Theodosius's conniving advisor Rufinus.[6]

In "Thessalonica," Macro, a townsman, becomes the catalyst for the violence, and his crime is not sexual immorality but simple intoxication. Two guards injure him when he drunkenly attempts to enter the games through a reserved entrance, and though some witnesses attempt to bring the soldiers to their commanding officer for judgment, others are incensed and retaliate, dismembering one guard while forcing the other to flee. During the melee, "the weaker were overpowered, and scores were trodden to death or suffocated" (101). At this precarious moment, Botheric arrives with a twenty-man retinue. In Brown's version, Botheric is neither a northern barbarian nor an unsympathetic character. He recognizes the situation's volatility and seeks to calm the crowd. Random chance (rather than the crowd's thirst for blood) escalates the violence when Eustace, a soldier recently flogged and discharged by Botheric, wounds the general with a rock. Outraged by the assault and encircled by the Thessalonians, the soldiers "determined to open a way by killing all that opposed them" (103). Bloodshed begets bloodshed, and the soldiers are "mangled by numberless wounds, or trampled into pieces," and after their deaths, the "assassins contended for the possession of the dismembered bodies, and threw the limbs, yet palpitating, into the air, which was filled with shouts and imprecations" (103). Brown's alterations are significant. By changing the riot's catalyst, he shifts its cause away from the Thessalonians' desire for bread and circuses (i.e., their favorite charioteer) and onto mob psychology. He also complicates the origins of mob violence by creating a balance between those citizens who try to quell the potential for a riot and those who demand vengeance, and he places the blame for the situation on the army far more than on the crowd. The irrational behavior of Macro and Eustace contributes elementally to the ensuing slaughter, but the army's actions catalyze the anarchy that follows. As a result, the mob's actions become sympathetic, because the Thessalonians have witnessed both undue force exerted against Macro and the slaughter of their neighbors and kinsmen as the soldiers rip their way through the crowd.

Thessalonica is victimized again when the army's report reaches Theodosius. Walimer, Botheric's successor, confidently expects the emperor to order the army to carry out some form of retribution; he desires not justice but the "advantage of proceeding in the business of revenge with the sanction or connivance of the government" (106). This is key, because while Walimer is plotting the army's revenge, the civil government is investigating the riot, uncovering its causes, and executing justice. Officials discover Macro's drunkenness and order his ignominious execution. More important, Eustace's key role in the violence is uncovered and his attempted flight frustrated. These events position the army as the center of trouble and the Thessalonians as victims. Brown is by no means sanctioning mob violence, but he is making the crowd's actions comprehensible and showing how violence can rise incrementally and almost imperceptibly in a crisis.

Brown also uses the massacre to illustrate the dangers of a strong military and a weak government. On numerous occasions, Brown's narrator mentions the threats the soldiers pose. In the original altercation, the citizens' consensus is that the soldiers were "first assailants" (115), and the army's willingness to use violence as its tool of choice lends credence to the rumor that "the soldiers had received orders to massacre the people" and that "Botheric had directed a general massacre" (103). Malchus regularly recurs to the fear of the soldiers once "freed from the restraints of discipline" (104), to a "dread of the vengeance" (105) the army would inflict, to the "cruelty" of the soldiers should Botheric's funeral "exasperate" their grief, and to the expectation of "indiscriminate massacre and havoc." Even some senators regard them with suspicion and "at the approach of night, secretly withdrew from the city" (110).

The general weakness of the civil government compounds the problem of reining in the military. While Malchus does purpose justice for Botheric and the other men, Macro's conviction and Eustace's release to Walimer do nothing to avert the massacre. Moreover, the city relies on the military to maintain order rather than its own ability to restrain lawlessness. When informed of Macro's death at the hands of the mob, the magistrates can do nothing but hope that "the popular indignation would be appeased by this victim," because on previous occasions, they had employed the military "to vindicate their authority by the aid of the soldiers," a course the crisis has rendered "now impracticable or hazardous" (108). Only with the utmost difficulty has Malchus repeatedly quieted the crowd and encouraged it to disperse, efforts whose effectiveness prove transitory.

The imperial government, dominated by the emperor and his associates, is no more effective. Absolute monarchy reigns in the person of Theodosius, who is subject to extremes of temperament, and the story exposes the danger of power residing in one individual. On another level, however, "Thessalonica" exposes the threats to any government when its support structure is corrupt. In Brown's version of events, Theodosius's temperament is manipulated to serve Rufinus's ambitions and desires. His adviser abuses the trust Theodosius places in him by previously forming a secret political alliance with Botheric to accumulate power: Rufinus would control the civil government while Botheric controlled the military, a plan scuttled by Botheric's death. Rufinus instead uses the crisis to enhance his position and attempts to recover some of the ground he lost through Botheric's demise. Lastly, the story exposes the imperial government's inability to control the military. Although Walimer does receive the orders he desires from the emperor, he is also fully ready to resort to extralegal means to exact revenge for Botheric's death. Directly after his expressed desire for the imperial government's imprimatur for his actions comes his stated belief that "If the Emperor should refuse justice, it would then be time enough to extort it" (106). He clearly believes that the military is in a position to gain its point despite the emperor's power. The entire incident at Thessalonica serves to expose the dangers of weak government.

Finally, Brown cannot help but be Brown in composing "Thessalonica." The volume of bloodshed in the story underscores his Gothic impulses: Botheric and his company as well as Macro are dismembered, and thousands perish bloodily by the sword in this historical representation, far more than in the historical tragedy itself. Beyond the bloodshed, though, Brown at the close of the tale inserts the psychological element so prevalent in his most famous works. Rather than ending with the slaughter, as Gibbon does, Brown allows his narrator to expatiate on the survivors' mental and emotional states. Those who escaped are "in the fruition of melancholy and despair" (117). Memories of the carnage "pursue them to their retreats, and deny them a momentary respite." The narrator continues:

> Some have lost their terror only by the extinction of their reason; and the phantoms of the past have disappeared in the confusion of insanity. Others, whose heroic or fortunate efforts, set them beyond the reach of the soldiers, were no

sooner at liberty to review the past, and contemplate their condition, than they inflicted on themselves that death which had been, with so much difficulty avoided, when menaced by others. Their misery was too abrupt, and too enormous, to be forgotten or endured.   (117)

The survivors appear less well off than the victims. In addition, in these final paragraphs, Brown brings his own narrator's reliability into question. Malchus explains that he is one of the survivors who suffers from "the full fruition of melancholy or despair." He further claims that the "period of forgetfulness, or of tranquil existence in another scene, is hastening to console me" (117). What does he mean by this? Is he dying and expecting a better existence hereafter? Is he contemplating suicide but must first finish his narrative? Or is he slipping into the insanity to which others have succumbed, and is that the "tranquil existence" he mentions? Unsurprisingly, Brown leaves his narrator's state ambiguous and his future murky. Clearly, though, Brown's interests in "Thessalonica" remain fixed in psychology even as he engages in political commentary.

Around the time he was writing "Thessalonica," Brown also published "Death of Cicero, A Fragment" (1800). Originally appended to *Edgar Huntly*, this "fragment" is an imagined letter from Cicero's slave Tiro to the orator's friend Atticus; it describes Cicero's final days after being sentenced to death. Tiro takes up the tale after Cicero has parted company with his equally doomed brother, narrating the statesman's attempted escape to the East. Taking refuge in a hut when unfavorable sea winds delay his flight, the orator begins to lose heart, telling Tiro, "Let their executioners come; I am willing to die" ("Death" 12). Later, when Cicero stops at his villa at Formia, a disgruntled slave informs the searchers of his master's whereabouts. Alerted to the approaching threat, Cicero flees, but on the way, his entourage encounters the searchers, led by Laenas, who allegedly, by some questionable accounts, was once defended by the orator in court. Confronted with his fate, Cicero halts his servants' defense of him, stands before Laenas, and offers his head. Cicero's executioners leave with the severed head, and the "fragment" closes with Tiro's reflections on Cicero and the events of his final days.

Generally, the retelling of Cicero's final moments is accurate in its essentials, demonstrating that Brown had carefully studied Appian and Plutarch, among others. Brown departs, however, in some interesting ways. Most prominently, as Oliver Scheiding notes, Tiro, Brown's alleged eyewitness to the statesman's final moments, actually was not with Cicero during his flight. Additionally, while Cicero did go ashore, according to Plutarch, he began walking back to Rome rather than bedding down in a hut, and although several accounts make mention of informants betraying the orator, Brown invents the disgruntled slave. Also of interest is the absence of the centurion Herennius, who is the statesman's executioner, not Laenas, and many accounts claim that Marc Antony wanted not just the statesman's head but his hands, too, because they wrote the philippics against him. Clearly, Brown does not pay strict attention to the historical facts as they were known to him.

Scheiding represents "Death of Cicero" as counterbalancing the idea of history as exemplary (articulated in "Walstein's School of History"). Accordingly, Tiro's attempt to render a faithful narrative of Cicero's final moments is undercut by interpretative gestures that expose the subjective nature of historical accounts. Tiro holds a "limited understanding of the events and the internal causes which finally 'led' to Cicero's death" (Scheiding 1998, 45), and thus, unreliability characterizes his "eyewitness account" (45). Moreover, he is not present for every event and relies on the accounts of others to fill in the narrative. Tiro, then, is a typical Brownian narrator in his unreliability, but there is another dimension to his unreliability as well. He often replaces his own observations and beliefs with those of others around him, particularly Cicero's. A prominent example appears once he has failed to persuade Cicero to remain aboard ship for the night. Faced with his master's determination, Tiro "endeavoured to find reasons for approving" of the plan to land ("Death" 9). Later, though well aware that visiting any of Cicero's villas invites danger, Tiro "now reflected that Formia being situated within a mile of the sea, might be the best asylum to which he [Cicero] could betake himself" (21). This rationalizing brings Tiro's judgment into question and appears even at the final moment of crisis. He asks himself, "Should I stand a powerless spectator of the deed? Might I not save myself at least the ignominy and horror of witnessing the fall of my master, by attacking his assassins or falling on my own sword?" (41). He defers acting, however, when "the remembrance of duties, which his death would leave to be performed by me and of the promises by which I was bound" (41). This is curious behavior for one who only a few paragraphs earlier determined to defend Cicero at the cost of spilled blood. Of course, Brown was bound by the historical record, which suggests Tiro played a leading role in collecting the orator's writings for posterity, but by writing Tiro's internal dialogue, Brown not only explores the cause and effect of Cicero's actions, in keeping with his own meditations in "The Difference between History and Romance," but also casts doubt on Tiro's own motivations. Was it the impulse to service or to self-preservation that motivated Tiro to acquiesce when facing Cicero's imminent murder? Is the fictional Tiro's claim to a dedicated and vigorous defense of Cicero's life a way of vindicating his own inaction to posterity? This, too, suggests the subjective nature of historical narrative.

Brown's interest in Cicero, in this tale as well as in *Wieland* and other texts, has often been read as a political commentary about the early republic. "Death of Cicero" also deals with another of Brown's favorite themes, however: the role of chance and coincidence in people's lives. While Tiro attempts to explain Cicero's end through human action and inaction, at least two key causes of the failure of Cicero's flight can be attributed to Dame Fortuna. First, the refugees "had scarcely got on board...and made our bargain with the master when the wind, which had lately been propitious, changed to the southeast, and with this wind, the master declared it impossible to move from our present station" (5). Just as it appears that Cicero's escape will succeed, a sudden change in the weather derails his intentions, perhaps also adding to his sense of fatality. Cicero's choice of refuge is equally important. Tiro explains that the villa to which Cicero retires had already been searched and found vacant, making the assassins' return unlikely, but in this villa resides the slave, "whose temper was remarkably perverse and malignant" (28). Though advised to sell this slave of "turbulent and worthless character" (28), the orator forgets to do so. While this could be chastising Cicero for busying himself so much with Roman affairs that he neglects his own, it equally suggests chance's role in human fate. Should Cicero be faulted for putting the state before the management of his own villa? Cicero's dedication to service ironically undoes him and, combined with the ill wind that halts his flight, suggests the inevitability of events, something Cicero considers as his willingness to flee wanes.

III. Seduction Plots and Violence against Women in "The Trials of Arden" (1800), "A Lesson on Concealment" (1800), "The Romance of Real Life" (1805), and "Somnambulism" (1805)

While he drew on classical history to compose his Roman stories—albeit in a way that "adorn[ed] these appearances with cause and effect, and trace[d] resemblances between the past, distant, and future, with the present" (Difference 251)—Brown also culled his own era for source material. In "The Trials of Arden" (1800) Brown revised the events surrounding a sensational New York City murder trial to tell the tale of Arden, wrongly charged with murdering his patron's daughter and a victim of mob violence.[7] Arden's situation resembles the case of Levi Weeks, who was accused of murdering Gulielma Sands, whom some believed to be his fiancée. Allegedly, Weeks had carried her off to be married but instead cast her down a well to be rid of her. The case thrilled and horrified New Yorkers, and the succeeding trial involved several notable public figures, including the defendant's "dream team"—former Treasury Secretary Alexander Hamilton, future Vice President Aaron Burr, and future Supreme Court Justice Brockholst Livingston. Outside the courthouse, handbills vilified Weeks, and enraged spectators called for his crucifixion. Tremendous drama ensued during the three-day trial, and at the end, the jury retired for a mere five minutes before returning a verdict of not guilty. New York City residents largely rejected the jury's verdict, casting insults and threats at Weeks when they spotted him in the street. His northern life unbearable, he eventually found peace and prosperity in Natchez, Mississippi. Much of this material Brown shaped into "The Trials of Arden."

While the source material is important, it is also worth examining Brown's piece as fiction. Arden's trials begin when he abruptly resigns his position as tutor in the Finch family shortly before the corpse of Harriet Finch is found in a nearby grotto. Arden is charged with her murder because he is seen entering the grotto around the time of her disappearance; circumstantial evidence strongly tells against him, but the jury acquits Arden, and popular outrage forces him to flee the city until the truth surrounding

Harriet's death comes to light. With all of Harriet's property willed to him, Arden thrives until his untimely death during the American Revolution.

Obviously, "Trials of Arden" employs many typical Brownian devices for fiction, from Harriet's Gothic murder to Arden's suspicious behavior and questionable trustworthiness to the use of the frame story. At the center of this tale is another ubiquitous target of Brownian analysis: the shaping or warping influence of social norms, especially those derived from prescribed gender roles and marital choices. Most of the characters wish to marry, and this desire drives the story's action. Wingate is betrothed to Harriet, but she prefers Arden. Harriet's actual murderer, Mayo, years before aspired to her hand. Anne Brudenel loves Arden, but he cannot marry her until he can support her. Harriet's desire to marry Arden catalyzes all subsequent actions. That she chooses him and is the one who lures him into a web from which he almost does not escape is key. In essence, she plays the rake, he the victim of seduction. Realizing that he is charmed by Harriet and that she loves him, he intends to withdraw from the Finch household rather than create domestic conflicts. It is Harriet who, petitioned by her father and Wingate, seeks a "private marriage" ("Arden" 31) to be publicized later. She advocates presenting a false acquiescence to Wingate's desire to marry her to maintain peace in the household, intending to reveal all at the last moment. Arden protests, but she is "unconvinced by his arguments" (31) and proceeds to sweep away all his objections to her plan of secretly marrying. Like a seducer, Harriet causes Arden to doubt his own judgment: He "fluctuated, wavered, in one mood he promised compliance with Harriet's wishes, and afterwards, when solitude and deliberation had time to sway him, he retracted those promises. He was unhappy, undetermined, and changeful" (32). Even after he resolves to resist her, he changes his mind, worrying she might attempt suicide. A victim of her charms, he is wooed by Harriet but wary of the consequences of her proposals. In "Trials of Arden," Brown turns the ultrapopular seduction story[8] of the vulnerable virgin in the hands of the manipulative rake upside down, demonstrating the fluidity of stereotyped gender roles and sexuality.

"A Lesson on Concealment; or, Memoirs of Mary Selwyn" (1800)[9] provides another example of how Brown reworks the sentimental seduction plot. This story is arguably Brown's most complex piece of short fiction, employing all the typical elements of a Brown tale. It opens with a letter from the bereaved Molesworth to Henry Kirvan that inquires about the circumstances surrounding the death of Mrs. Molesworth. A party to her secret, Henry's response explains how she had come to believe her past was catching up with her. Flashing back to his own history, Henry relates his employment under Haywood, during which he witnesses the unusual meeting of his employer and a stranger, their departure together, and Haywood's flight. Henry learns that the stranger was one Selwyn, whose married sister Haywood had seduced, leading ultimately to the husband's suicide, and that Haywood had just murdered the brother in a duel. The sister, Mary Selwyn Colmer, had fled her domestic establishment and was presumed dead. After Haywood's flight, Henry gains employment with Molesworth, a physician, and, falling ill, is nursed by Mrs. Molesworth. Her strong resemblance to her brother Selwyn causes Henry to identify her, after which she unfolds her tale of coerced marriage, seduction, flight into rural anonymity, and second marriage to Molesworth. Unfortunately, Henry's recognition of her increases her anxiety that her past will be revealed, which causes a fatal decline in her health. Though he promised to keep her secret, Henry divulges it in an attempt to alleviate the emotional distress of the bereaved husband.

Like "Trials of Arden," this lengthy story reworks the seduction tale, first through the use of a Richardsonian epistolary correspondence and second through plot devices such as the illicit sexual encounter and the sentimental distresses of the heroine and those around her. Although he draws on these conventions, Brown is not interested in retelling a multitold tale, and thus he departs from the genre in significant ways. Notably, Brown's victim is a married woman rather than a naive maiden, and the moment of seduction is left almost untold, condensed into a mere paragraph. More significantly, as Fritz Fleischman observes, it is her obedience to the wishes of others (namely, the men in her life) that brings on the tragedy rather than her disobedience and concealment (Fleischmann 331). Most important, rather than suffering an imminent death during childbirth as punishment for her sexual sin, Brown's heroine survives her encounter with her seducer. Although initially in an emotional turmoil that leads to two suicide attempts, Mary eventually settles in rural Connecticut, where she meets and marries Molesworth. Though anxious about moving to Philadelphia, where visiting New Englanders might recognize her, she ultimately, albeit briefly, achieves happiness with her new husband. Hers is a history of sin, repentance, and redemption, with her death resulting from misplaced obedience and secrecy rather than illicit sexual conduct. Her brief success story anticipates, to a limited degree, those of the heroines of the mid-nineteenth-century sentimental novel.

Even as it restyles the seduction plot, "Concealment" remains quintessential Brown and contains his favorite conventions. Secrecy drives the plot. Both Mary and Haywood hide their tryst, and Henry conceals Mary's identity until her death. Moreover, it is Mary's disguised identity that arouses curiosity in Henry, who, having "rashly plunged into the stream too far to recover my footing" ("Concealment" 185), flails about in an investigation that ends in destruction. Coincidence also plays a central role. Henry just happens to be taken in by the man whose wife had been the lover of his former employer. Tragedy usually characterizes Brown's denouements, and in "Concealment," Molesworth's domestic establishment has fallen to ruin, but preceding Mary to the grave are her brother, husband, and stillborn child. Molesworth meanwhile must deal with the revelations of Mary's past. Further, Henry's willingness to mask Mary's past and then, against her expressed wishes, to yield it to the one person she did not wish would know it places him in a suspicious light. His own moral failings in this matter and his changeable willingness to keep her secret open him up to questions of reliability. After all, Molesworth (and readers) have only his perception of the story's events by which to judge. Finally, there is the issue of the story's "Lesson." Though Brown claimed on at least two occasions a desire to lay moral imperatives before the reader, the lesson of his tale remains debatable, seemingly both for and against the use of secrecy.

Published five years later, "The Romance of Real Life" (1805) demonstrates Brown's continued interest in social position, marriage, and the lives of women. This brief tale, presented as a self-sufficient short narrative in Brown's *Literary Magazine* but also as one element of the much larger and mostly unpublished *Historical Sketches* (1805–1806), provides the backstory for the marriage of Mary Tenbrook to the grandson of the Earl of W—.[10] Aiming to concentrate the family wealth, the earl intends to wed his young grandson to a wealthy cousin. While in Italy, however, the grandson meets Mary, the daughter of a rich German banker settled in London who intends to divide his fortune among virtuous Mary's four profligate brothers while leaving her only a small inheritance. Her refusal of a prearranged marriage and her youngest brother's insinuations that she is the consequence of his mother's infidelity further alienate Mary from her father. The earl's grandson falls in love with Mary and secretly weds her; shortly thereafter, the earl recalls his grandson so that the arranged marriage to his cousin can take place. Rather than confront his grandfather with his marriage and conversion from Catholicism to Protestantism, the grandson conceals himself for two years, until, weary of his life, he sets out to face his grandfather, only to learn of the man's death and his inheritance of the family fortune. He publicly weds Mary, and her rise in social position reconciles her with her father. The youngest son asks Mary's forgiveness just before his death, and her other three brothers drown while crossing the Thames to visit their father, leaving Mary with the banker's entire fortune.

Brown is clearly reworking material from "Lesson on Concealment" here but allowing for a different outcome. Instead of acquiescing to the arranged marriages, both Mary and the earl's grandson resist this fate by marrying each other. Whereas nearly all of Mary Selwyn's troubles stem from her willingness to marry against her inclinations, these characters ultimately prosper through their resistance.[11] Brown also reverses the consequences of concealment, since the grandson's silence regarding his marriage and whereabouts lead not to his destruction but to his prosperity. While Brown appears to turn the lesson of "Lesson on Concealment" on its head, it is the grandson's decision to confront his wealthy relative that leads to his inheritance, and it is his public acknowledgment of Mary that results in her reconciliation with her own family, circumstances that mitigate the seriousness of the secrecy. Mary, in fact, declares her resolution of never "acknowledging or receiving him as her husband, till he chose to act with candour and uprightness" ("Romance" 395). While the narrative might begin with the grandson, it is Mary who ultimately dominates this story with her strength of character. Even though by 1804 Brown was supposedly a settled, married ex-novelist who disavowed his fictional writings, "Romance" shows his continued interest in many of the themes that drive his fiction, and for once he allows his characters a happy ending.

In 1805, Brown published "Somnambulism: A Fragment"[12] in his *Literary Magazine*, a tale he might have written during an earlier period when he featured sleepwalking in the now-lost *Sky-Walk; or, The Man Unknown to Himself* (1798) and in *Edgar Huntly* (1799). No doubt, Brown gained some insight into somnambulism through his close friend Dr. Elihu Hubbard Smith, and numerous pieces had been written on the subject by the time Brown came to produce his own story. The most prominent of Brown's sources was Erasmus Darwin's *Zoonomia* (1794), but he might also have read about sleepwalking in various encyclopedia articles, Benjamin Rush's work, or Benjamin Gooch's piece about a sleepless man from Madrid. According to Sydney J. Krause, "somnambulism was universally considered a sign of infirmity, a disease centered in the nonvolitional (we would say autonomic) system, which, since it took possession of a person, mind and body, belonged in the twilight realm of dementia" (Krause 336). Darwin phrased it more bluntly when he claimed that no perfectly sane person sleepwalks. The tale's epigraph reinforces this medical backdrop by offering the reader a purportedly factual account extracted from the *Vienna Gazette* of June 14, 1784, which provides additional testimony to the possibility of murder-while-sleepwalking.[13]

The tale opens during a visit to the narrator's family by the Davises, father and daughter. Quite taken with the daughter, the narrator, Althorpe, suffers intense disappointment when the Davises are suddenly called away and undertake a night journey. Althorpe, who hopes to win daughter Constantia's affections away from her betrothed, tries to persuade them to wait until morning; he also offers to escort them, tendering vague notions of danger as his reasons. The father refuses his offer, partly because he suspects it stems from an attachment to Constantia, and, although he considers following them secretly, Althorpe ultimately falls asleep, dreaming that he did escort them and killed a potential assassin. Meanwhile, the Davises spot a figure in the road during their journey. To Mr. Davis, the person appears to be Althorpe, but they also know that a local idiot named Nick Handyside sometimes escapes his family home, roams the countryside, and howls occasionally. One of these noises causes the horse to bolt, smashing the carriage against a tree. Mr. Davis initially follows the driver in pursuit of the horse but then turns back to stay with his daughter; still at a distance, he hears a gunshot and returns to find his daughter with a fatal head wound. Awakening in the morning, Althorpe learns of the incident, and, piecing together their journey, he discovers that an unidentified individual had paralleled their course.

The headnote to the tale tells a similar story, leading readers to believe that Althorpe follows the Davises in his sleep and shoots Constantia rather than see her wedded to another. This correspondence brings the narrator's stability, and thus his reliability, into question. Scholars have also rightly noted that the families of Althorpe and Constantia appear to differ in social station, making any union between them a transgression of class boundaries. What has gone unnoticed, however, is Althorpe's young age as an impediment to any attachment to Constantia. He is variously called "young man" ("Somnambulism" 335, 338, 341), "young friend" (338, 342), "young Althorpe" (341, 342), and "young rogue" (341). Moreover, Constantia describes him as "Ardent and rash," possessing "all the fiery qualities of youth, unchastised by experience, untamed by adversity," and "capable no doubt of extravagant adventures" (341). Mr. Davis notes how youths of his age act gallantly toward women (338). Althorpe, too, admits as much when he debates whether he has failed to profit from experience with "similar follies" (339) such as needlessly following the Davises on their journey. He displays his emotional inexperience by fancying himself in love with Constantia after only a few days' acquaintance and reveals how his "emotions arose to terror" at the thought of the potential risks of a night journey and how his "passions . . . were incontroullable" when he allowed them free rein (337). He recognizes that his age and place in the family should have made "silence and submission" his "peculiar province" (337). Even the introductory note serves to emphasize Althorpe's immaturity by describing the murderer as either a "young man" or a "youth."

By way of contrast, while the *Vienna Gazette* calls the victim a "young lady," Brown painstakingly emphasizes Constantia's maturity. She is called youthful only three times, and two of those involve her keener eyesight when compared with her father's; the third instance occurs when Mr. Davis proposes that they walk a short distance on their journey, and calling her "young lady" could easily emphasize her vitality and strength rather than her age. When she is not referred to by name, Constantia is most often simply "the lady." She herself remarks on her maturity when she claims she is "not so much a girl as to be scared merely because it is dark" (338). Later, her sophistication appears in her analysis of Althorpe: "He is rash and inconsiderate. That is the utmost amount of his guilt. A short absence will show him the true state of his feelings. It was unavoidable, in one of his character, to fall in love with the first woman whose appearance was in any degree specious. But attachments like these will be extinguished as easily as they are formed" (342). She further comments that the "period of youth will soon pass away" (342) but predicts Althorpe will not learn from his experiences. That she recognizes all this in Althorpe strongly implies that she has already passed through the stage he currently occupies. She demonstrates mature wisdom and insight in these passages, all of which distance her own state of development from Althorpe's. Social position does play a role in "Somnambulism," for it appears that Mr. Davis is a merchant while Althorpe's uncle is a farmer, and, as Michael Cody observes, Althorpe represents the conflict between eighteenth-century rationalism and nineteenth-century romanticism, but the difference in the age and level of maturity in the young people is also a significant parallel issue (Cody 2002).

Just as he did in his novels, Brown absorbed the intellectual and historical currents of his era and translated them into his short fiction. He is, indeed, one of the most historically grounded authors in the American literary tradition. As his stories demonstrate, his interests ranged widely, from law to sciences, psychology to sociology, history to the macabre. While his novels have received overwhelming attention, his short stories remain relatively unknown and unanthologized, yet they are as compelling as his novelistic efforts and, when closely analyzed, provide as rich a field for understanding Brown's interests, artistry, and culture.

NOTES

1. Duncan Faherty and Sian Silyn Roberts also make this point elsewhere in the volume.
2. The only modern collection of the short fiction is *Somnambulism and Other Stories*, edited by Alfred Weber (1987). All of the short fiction will be included in forthcoming volumes of the Bucknell University Press *Collected Writings of Charles Brockden Brown*.
3. No detailed analysis of this story has appeared.
4. The story also lends itself as possible source material for Poe's Madeline Usher in the "indubitable tokens...on her snow-white mantle" (75) of the young woman's attempts to claw her way out of her grave.

5. Oliver Scheiding (1997) uses this story to explore Brown's understanding of fiction and history, while I have studied its presentation of masculinity.

6. Brown outlines his interest in events and motivations in "The Difference between History and Romance" (1800).

7. See Slawinski 2009 for a full exposition of the case as Brown's source material and Slawinski 2002 for the story's depiction of masculinity. These are the only two extended discussions of "Arden." Later significant mobilizations of "true crime" narratives for fictional ends include, of course, Poe's "The Mystery of Marie Roget" (1842) and Theodore Dreiser's *An American Tragedy* (1925).

8. Beginning in the 1740s with Samuel Richardson's *Pamela* (1740) and *Clarissa* (1748) and lasting into the nineteenth century, the story of the threatened virgin and the immoral rake proved quite marketable, and even Sukey Vickery's *Emily Hamilton* (1803), which rejects seduction as a central plot device, includes one successful seduction offstage. Moreover, the seduction story's familiarity allowed Hawthorne to dispense with its retelling in *The Scarlet Letter* (1850), focusing instead on the psychological consequences of seduction.

9. Besides my own work, Warner Berthoff has used "Lesson on Concealment" to describe Brown's "method in fiction," while Fritz Fleischmann has discussed it and Hannah Webster Foster's *The Coquette*.

10. The *Historical Sketches* are a sprawling, novel-length ensemble of fragments, most of which appeared posthumously in Dunlap's biographical miscellany (1815). Recounting the eighteenth-century history of the fictitious Carrill and Orme families and the lands they rule, they culminate in the contemporary world that is the setting of "The Romance of Real Life." Critically neglected, "Romance" was reprinted in the *Cincinnati Literary Gazette* on September 18, 1824, under the heading "Moral Tales."

11. Brown also resisted a prearranged marriage, and family disagreement surrounded his union with a non-Quaker.

12. Michael Cody sees "Somnambulism" as exploring the tension between neoclassical and Romantic ideals, William J. Scheick understands it as exposing the instability of design, and Stephen Shapiro reads it as related to homoerotic desire.

13. It is also possible that Brown fabricated this epigraph.

Works Cited

Berthoff, Warner. "'A Lesson on Concealment': Charles Brockden Brown's Method in Fiction." *Philological Quarterly* 37 (1958): 45–57.

Brown, Charles Brockden. "Death of Cicero, A Fragment." In Charles Brockden Brown, *Edgar Huntly; or, Memoirs of a Sleep-Walker*, III: 3–48. Philadelphia: H. Maxwell, 1800.

Brown, Charles Brockden. "Insanity: A Fragment." PF 1.2 (February 1809): 165–168.

Brown, Charles Brockden. "A Lesson on Concealment; or, Memoirs of Mary Selwyn." MM 2.3 (March 1800): 174–207.

Brown, Charles Brockden. "A Lesson on Sensibility." WM 2.16 (May 1798): 71–76.

Brown, Charles Brockden. "The Romance of Real Life." LM 4.26 (November 1805) 392–396.

Brown, Charles Brockden. "Somnambulism: A Fragment." LM 3.20 (May 1805): 335–347.

Brown, Charles Brockden. *Somnambulism and other Stories*. Alfred Weber, ed. Frankfurt am Main: Peter Lang Verlag, 1987.

Brown, Charles Brockden. "Thessalonica: A Roman Story." MM 1.2 (May 1799): 99–117.

Brown, Charles Brockden. "The Trials of Arden." MM 3.1 (July 1800): 19–36.

Cody, Michael. *Charles Brockden Brown and the* Literary Magazine: *Cultural Journalism in the Early American Republic.* Jefferson, N.C.: McFarland, 2004.

Cody, Michael. "Sleepwalking into the Nineteenth Century: Charles Brockden Brown's 'Somnambulism.'" *Journal of the Short Story in English* 39 (Autumn 2002): 41–55.

Fleischmann, Fritz. "Concealed Lessons: Foster's *Coquette* and Brockden Brown's 'Lesson on Concealment.'" In Klaus Schmidt and Fritz Fleischmann, eds., *Early America Re-Explored: New Readings in Colonial, Early National, and Antebellum Culture,* 309–348. New York: Peter Lang, 2000.

Gibbon, Edward. *The Decline and Fall of the Roman Empire,* Vol. 2. New York: Modern Library, 1932.

Krause, Sydney J. "Historical Essay." In Charles Brockden Brown, *Edgar Huntly; or, Memoirs of a Sleep-Walker,* Vol. 4 of *The Novels and Related Works of Charles Brockden Brown,* Sydney J. Krause and S. W. Reid, eds., 295–400. Kent, Ohio: Kent State University Press, 1984.

Scheick, William J. "Assassin in Artful Disguise: The De-Signed Designs of Charles Brockden Brown's 'Somnambulism.'" *Profils Américains* 11 (1999): 27–45.

Scheiding, Oliver. "'Nothing but a Disjointed and Mutilated Tale': Zur narrativen Strategie der Doppelperspektive in Charles Brockden Browns historischer Erzählung 'Thessalonica: A Roman Story' (1799)." *Literaturwissenschaftliches Jahrbuch im Auftrage der Görres-Gesellschaft* 38 (1997): 93–110.

Scheiding, Oliver. "'Plena Exemplorum est Historia': Rewriting Exemplary History in Charles Brockden Brown's 'Death of Cicero.'" In Bernard Englier and Oliver Scheiding, eds., *Re-Visioning the Past: Historical Self-Reflexivity in American Short Fiction,* 39–50. Trier: Wissenschaftlicher Verlag Trier, 1998.

Shapiro, Stephen. "'Man to Man I Needed Not to Dread His Encounter': *Edgar Huntly*'s End of Erotic Pessimism." In Philip Barnard, Mark L. Kamrath, and Stephen Shapiro, eds., *Revising Charles Brockden Brown: Culture, Politics, and Sexuality in the Early Republic,* 216–251. Knoxville: University of Tennessee Press, 2004.

Slawinski, Scott. "A Tale of Two Murders: The Manhattan Well Case as Source Material for Charles Brockden Brown's 'Trials of Arden.'" *Early American Literature* 44.2 (2009): 365–398.

Slawinski, Scott. *Validating Bachelorhood: Audience, Patriarchy, and Charles Brockden Brown's Editorship of the* Monthly Magazine and American Review. New York: Routledge, 2002.

PART V

POLITICS
AND THE
WORLD-SYSTEM

CHAPTER 17

BROWN AND THE WOLDWINITES

ABIGAIL SMITH STOCKER

In the early twenty-first century, literary study no longer approaches print cultures as autonomous formations within nation-states. Rather, it understands all literatures, whether British and American, circum-Atlantic, or global, as being in conversation with one another. No early American fiction writer demonstrates the need for postnational perspectives more than Charles Brockden Brown. In addition to other radical Enlightenment sources such as the Encyclopédistes, he gravitated especially toward the philosophy and fiction of the circle of British radicals around William Godwin and Mary Wollstonecraft, and they, in turn, eventually acknowledged and echoed the work of the American writer. By the late 1790s, along with his associates in the Friendly Club of New York City and others, Brown adapted and expanded both the arguments and the literary strategies of the Godwin-Wollstonecraft group, and his circle collectively participated in a correspondence with them.[1]

I. BROWN'S NEW YORK CIRCLE AND THE WOLDWINITES

Brown and fellow Friendly Club members, especially his closest New York associates, Elihu Hubbard Smith and William Dunlap, read widely, often categorizing authors according to their philosophical and moral agendas. In this context, Godwin's *Enquiry Concerning Political Justice* resonated so loudly with the member's collective sentiments that it became a touchstone by which they measured other philosophical works (Waterman 95). As early as 1795, Brown referred to *Political Justice* as a book to which "I appeal, as to an Oracle" (Letters 302). Club members sympathized with Godwin's questioning of established authority and institutional religion and agreed that social ills could be addressed through sincere social inquiry, patient moral reform, and universal education.

From that point on, as the group read, they began to classify works from similarly minded authors as Godwinian. These included poets Robert Southey and Samuel Taylor Coleridge; scientists Erasmus Darwin, Thomas Beddoes, and Joseph Priestley; and the core British radicals of the late eighteenth century: Tom Paine, Thomas Holcroft, Robert Bage, Mary Hays, Helen Maria Williams, Elizabeth Inchbald, and, most important, Mary Wollstonecraft (Waterman 97). Reflecting the critiques of female subordination in the Godwin-Wollstonecraft circle, the New York group likewise welcomed the participation of women in their philosophical discussions, without, for all that, making them actual members of the Friendly Club (133–134).[2]

Together they engaged in contemporary debates over women's rights and treated their female interlocutors according to their commonly held belief that women possessed an intellectual capacity equal to that of men. On all these grounds, Philip Barnard and Stephen Shapiro have proposed the term *Woldwinites* as a general identifier, merging the two writers' names and acknowledging the equal importance of Wollstonecraft and other women writers in the radical movement (Barnard and Shapiro 2008, xv n. 11). While Brown and his closest associates were engaged with the work of the entire circle of British writers, this keyword likewise refers to Brown's particular focus on Wollstonecraft and Godwin as the central figures in the London group. The conservative press had framed the couple as de facto leaders of the radicals after Godwin's *Memoirs of the Author of A Vindication of the Rights of Woman* shocked the reading public following Wollstonecraft's death in September 1797. In what was then an extremely unconventional biography, the bereaved husband described an intelligent and long-suffering woman but also revealed frankly that she had conceived two children out of wedlock, pursued an affair with the married painter Henry Fuseli, and twice attempted suicide. Readers of the *Memoirs*, especially the counterrevolutionary press, took the biography as evidence that Wollstonecraft's philosophical writings were essentially linked to an unchecked sensibility and a dissolute personal life.

Wollstonecraft's landmark protofeminist treatise, *A Vindication of the Rights of Woman*, was presented by conservatives as a manual for deviant female behavior. The main arguments of the *Vindication*, including its affirmation of women's equality in the political and social spheres, its critique of the role of education in female subordination, and its rational model for social transformation, were influential after the book's appearance in 1792. The influence of the book and its author alike, however, were drowned out by the atmosphere of scandal that followed the publication of Godwin's biography in January 1798. The perception that Wollstonecraft's public writings were informed by her private excesses allowed critics to dismiss the work of all Woldwinites as texts that not only sought philosophical reform but also aimed to upset every aspect of life, from the home to the pulpit to the state house. Next to Wollstonecraft, Godwin was deemed the worst of the radicals for his part in her second extramarital conception and his reckless retelling of her indiscretions. His *Political Justice* was revisited for controversial material, and his comments in the first edition about reforming the current institution of marriage were exposed to public ridicule and misinterpretation.

In this context of heated press attacks and widespread demonization, Brown continued to affirm the two writers and arguably worked to redeem their most salvageable beliefs while at the same time addressing the shortcomings and limitations of their ideas and the enlightened behavioral models they had come to represent. Brown engages with Wollstonecraft and Godwin in both his essays and his fiction, developing his theory of romance writing from Woldwinite precedents and enacting it by placing his fictional characters in moral dilemmas of domestic and public life in order to encourage readers to weigh the consequences of social and economic inequalities on all levels. In this manner, Brown adapted and extended the British writers' theories and fictional models, effectively situating himself as a second-wave American Woldwinite.

Brown planned and wrote his best-known novels and key theoretical texts during the 1795–1799 period, when the New York Friendly Club flourished. Smith and Dunlap wrote extensively in their diaries from this period, detailing the group's activities: books they read together, discussions they had, literary and theatrical projects on which they worked, and the correspondence they kept. Among the first books the Friendly Club read were those written by Godwin and Wollstonecraft. At some point between spring 1793 and fall 1795, the Friendly Club read Godwin's *Political Justice* and *Caleb Williams* and Wollstonecraft's *Rights of Woman* (Waterman 97). At this early stage, long before the couple's romantic relationship, like many other contemporary readers, the club members understood that the two writers were closely related in an intellectual and ideological sense. In a letter from November 1795, Smith details a discussion he had with Susan Tracy and a Mr. Lewis in which these three works were considered together. Smith's diary also displays a letter that Tracy had written on the *Vindication* and remarked that he found much sense in it. This diary entry shows that the Friendly Club believed it was impossible to achieve the social reform outlined in *Political Justice* without treating women as intellectual equals and expanding their rights.

Not a month before, in October 1795, had Dunlap attempted a correspondence with Godwin and Holcroft, in which he complimented Holcroft on his treatment of the independence of women in *Anna St. Ives*. Dunlap flattered both of his correspondents, for he was interested in creating a dialogue with them about philosophical issues. In offering Godwin criticism on a point of Roman history in *Political Justice*, Dunlap seemed to be attempting to make it clear that he and his New York associates were serious intellectuals. He described his own literary coterie and asked about Godwin's association with Holcroft.

Both men responded politely to Dunlap, encouraging his work and offering their assistance, while reminding him that they were very busy. Their responses read as polite brush-offs rather than real commitments to involve themselves with a stranger in New York. Godwin's diary reveals that he did not consider the Friendly Club members among his extensive acquaintance. Godwin's silence regarding Dunlap's correspondence in the diary, in which he diligently chronicled the letters he received and wrote on a daily basis, shows how little he thought of the exchange. Although Godwin did not mention Dunlap's letters, he was curious about the American and read his republican play, *The Archers; or, Mountaineers of Switzerland*, in June 1796.

Dunlap had sent Holcroft several of his plays, including *The Archers*, and Holcroft's response arrived in the winter of 1796. He criticized Dunlap's play as "common" and said it needed much improvement (Dunlap 1833, 1: 310). This slight from a revered author had to hurt Dunlap, and in his next letter to Holcroft, in July 1797, he tried to save face by claiming that since writing the play, he had experienced a moral enlightenment based on inquiry and justice.[3] His reference to the philosophy of Godwin is unmistakable and leads us to consider what took place for Dunlap intellectually between writing the two letters.

This was an active time for the New York circle. Brown stayed with Dunlap at his Perth Amboy, New Jersey, residence from fall 1796 to spring 1797, and Smith was a frequent visitor. After reading Wollstonecraft's *Letters Written during a Short Residence in Sweden, Norway, and Denmark* (1796), the group discovered Bage's novel *Hermsprong; or, Man as He Is Not* (1796), which reminded them of Godwin's *Caleb Williams* (1794). In November 1796, Smith and Brown discussed converting *Hermsprong* into a dramatic comedy. The project never materialized, although in January 1797, Dunlap did stage a play titled *Tell Truth and Shame the Devil*, in which he mentions Godwin. During this period, while Brown stayed at Dunlap's home, he began writing his dialogue on women's rights, *Alcuin*, which he published in the Philadelphia *Weekly Magazine* as *The Rights of Women*. This echo of Wollstonecraft's treatise reflected the mood in the house. In spring 1797, the Friendly Club read Hays's *Emma Courtney* (1796), sympathizing with her critique of women's education, and in July, Dunlap noted in his diary that he was reading the *Vindication* for the second time.[4] By August, one month before Wollstonecraft's death, Brown was circulating a copy of *Alcuin's* parts I and II to the entire group.

It is likely that the Friendly Club group and their female friends returned to the *Vindication* in June 1797, when news of Godwin and Wollstonecraft's marriage reached New York. This remarkable attention to the news of these two writers' lives suggests that the New York group desired to have a greater intimacy with their British contemporaries. Indeed, it was after reading the *Vindication* at the end of July that Dunlap finally decided to respond to Holcroft and tell him about his Godwinian enlightenment.

The Godwin-Wollstonecraft marriage was not confirmed until October and was followed only three weeks later by news of Wollstonecraft's death. If the former was exciting, the latter was devastating, and Brown's New York circle, men and women alike, were likely deeply affected by her passing. There was, however, to be some consolation, for the group would soon have a closer relationship with the Woldwinites. In January 1798, Thomas Cooper, the twenty-year-old ward and pupil of Godwin, moved to the United States to jumpstart his acting career. The Friendly Club immediately sought his acquaintance and barraged him with questions about the London literary circle. Dunlap was most interested in Cooper's recollection of the affecting scene at Wollstonecraft's deathbed. After satisfying their curiosity, Cooper maintained a working relationship with the Friendly Club, and in December 1799, he performed the monody that Brown composed for George Washington's death (Allen 367).

Perhaps the Friendly Club's friendship with his ward was enough to convince Godwin of the worth of his American counterparts. In July 1798, just six months after Cooper's arrival in America, Godwin read the first two parts of Brown's *Alcuin* (Godwin *Diary*,

July 19, 1798). His interest in Brown's work was rekindled in June 1812, when he read *Arthur Mervyn*, and later in May and June 1816, when he read *Wieland, Edgar Huntly, Ormond, Clara Howard,* and *Jane Talbot* (June 21, 1812; May 22, June 4, June 13, June 23, June 28, 1816). There is good reason to believe that it was his daughter and son-in-law who recommended these books to him. His daughter, Mary Wollstonecraft Shelley, had read them in 1814 and 1815; her husband, Percy Bysshe Shelley, demonstrated a thorough knowledge of Brown's novels as early as 1813 (Williams 56; Sickels 1116). According to one critic, Brown's influence can be seen in Percy Shelley's novels and some of his poems; there are motifs from *Edgar Huntly* in *Zastrozzi,* from *Wieland* in *St. Irvyne* and *Rosalind and Helen,* and from *Arthur Mervyn's* scenes of pestilence in *Laon and Cythna* (Sickels 1117–1126). Mary Shelley acknowledged her use of yellow fever scenes from *Arthur Mervyn* in her 1826 novel, *The Last Man.* Moreover, many critics have studied the similarities between *Wieland* and *Frankenstein,* which Mary Shelley began writing in the summer of 1816, just one year after reading *Wieland.* Pamela Clemit views *Wieland* as a pivotal milestone in the development of philosophical fiction and marks its place on that continuum from Godwin's novels to Mary Shelley's (Clemit 105–138).

Godwin himself eventually acknowledged the reciprocal influence of Brown in the preface of his 1817 novel, *Mandeville,* when he cited *Wieland* as a source and called Brown a "person of distinguished genius" (Allen 368). In the same year, Godwin formed a lasting relationship with two former associates of Brown: John Howard Payne, an actor, and James Ogilvie, an essayist, lecturer, and emissary for Godwin in America. Godwin frequently dined and attended the theater with the two men separately. During this period, Brown's novels were read and admired by other British Romantics surrounding the Godwin and Shelley circle, including William Hazlitt, Thomas Love Peacock, and John Keats, who noted that Brown's books were not only "powerful" but actually exceeded those of Godwin in "plot and incident" (quoted in Clemit 107).

Throughout the Romantic era, writers in the United States, Great Britain, and Europe consistently understood Brown in conjunction with Godwin. In 1803, the German translation of Brown's *Ormond; or, The Secret Witness* was attributed to the British philosopher (Barnard and Shapiro 2009, viii). In 1824 the long-running *Blackwoods Magazine* in Edinburgh began referring to Brown as the "Godwin of America" (Waterman 99). And in 1846, Margaret Fuller, the American women's rights advocate, recognized the similarity between the two writers and the possibility of a reciprocal influence.

II. "MORAL INDEPENDENCE" IN THE WOLDWINITES AND IN BROWN

Long before the Friendly Club, Brown read Wollstonecraft and Godwin in his father's library. Brown concerned himself with these writers more than any other British radical, and they are the two he addresses most directly in his writings. While there is a great deal of crossover in the writings of the Godwin-Wollstonecraft circle, two crucial points set the couple apart. One is the issue of marriage. As a result of the scandals surrounding *Memoirs*, their critics found them complicit in the same moral crime against traditional domestic unions. Brown's treatment of marriage reflects this. He provides a long discussion of marriage reform in *Alcuin* and echoes Wollstonecraft's most famous work in the title of the magazine version. In *Jane Talbot* (1801), he mentions Godwin by name and features a young couple who is kept from marrying because the groom once held Godwinian principles. The eponymous heroine must overcome her impetuous nature through patient self-control and the help of the strict government provided by her guardian. This may refer to Wollstonecraft, who was hampered by her excessive sensibility and favored spirited action to effect change in desperate situations. This is in contrast with the sober rationality of Godwin, who taught the benefits of patient inquiry and gradual reform.

For Brown, it may be Wollstonecraft's lifestyle that poses the most difficulty. In political terms, Wollstonecraft's impetuosity translated into a reasoned apology for the carnage that followed the French Revolution. Most Woldwinites, like Godwin, rejected the idea of revolution as a punctual and violent eruption—associated with the beheadings of Louis XVI and Marie Antoinette and Maximilien Robespierre's Reign of Terror—and instead affirmed a model of gradual social change. Wollstonecraft did not. Although she had come to appreciate the value of calm and measured social change, which in Godwin's eyes was the only kind of reform that could endure, she argued it was necessary to spur that change with a decisive event. She believed that the revolution of the mind that had taken place in France required a new government to support it and that all peaceful solutions to gaining this end had been exhausted. But Wollstonecraft was not a Robespierre-style revolutionary. Once events had been set in motion, she felt it was important to form the new constitution through a democratic process adhering to historic precedents.

Wollstonecraft was a mass of contradictions. She praised collective action in theory. In practice, she often (rashly) defied social constraints on women on her own, thereby endangering the social movements she supported in principle. When an anonymous contributor to Brown's *Monthly Magazine*, calling himself "L.M.," eulogized Wollstonecraft in August 1799 in "Reflections on the Character of Mary Wollstonecraft Godwin," he dubbed her unconventional actions "schemes of independence" (Anonymous 330). L.M., possibly a member of the Friendly Club, complained that Wollstonecraft forced premature change by refusing to regulate her passions for the common good, thereby ignoring Godwin's argument that rational sentiment, a social practice of sincerity and truth, would eventually lead toward progress. In *Political Justice* (book 8, chapter6), Godwin argued that individualized "moral independence" is immoral in that it jeopardizes the well-being of the community and threatens to thwart potential social progress already under way. Godwin argues that absolute independence is impossible, since no action can be performed in a vacuum, without beneficiaries or victims. Nonetheless, he maintains that an effort should be made to end social injustice and, for this reason, recommends a "natural independence" that requires individuals to adhere to reason and be mindful of working within and around social customs already in place.

Brown's narratives feature themes similar to Godwin's dichotomy of moral and natural independence. He places characters in situations where they must devise ways of confronting the defective social institutions and long-held prejudices that exert damaging pressures on their lives. They must endure inconvenient and oppressive restrictions as they painstakingly seek a mode of independence that results in the most good. The struggle takes place at a personal level, and with this microcosmic view, Brown reminds his readers that a revolution of the mind must occur before a larger political change can take place.

Before the published novels, Brown formulated these ideas in the fictional *Alcuin; A Dialogue* (1798). A strong-willed woman, Mrs. Carter, debates with the schoolmaster Alcuin, named after an eighth-century Carolingian rhetorician and scholastic. As part of their wider discussion of women's rights, Mrs. Carter and Alcuin dwell at length on the topic of marriage. Echoing Wollstonecraft's *Vindication*, Mrs. Carter complains that the existing institution of marriage subjugates women and that marital bonds are formed without the parties' mutual respect. Just as she is on the brink of winning the verbal contest, however, Alcuin trumps her grievances with a practical consideration. He asks her how an individual might act to bring about the changes she suggests. She is either unwilling or unable to prescribe a mode for putting her theories into practice, so Alcuin follows up by cautioning Mrs. Carter that marriage is a custom of long standing and that to alter it is presumptuous (AL 66–67).

Even in the imagined utopia that Alcuin envisages in the dialogue's part III, Brown does not presume to alter the institution of marriage. When Alcuin describes the egalitarian society in the paradise of women, Brown interrupts the tale just before he can explain the utopian solution to marriage. Marriage becomes the theme for the remaining discussion (54–67), making it the most important consideration on the question of women's rights in the entire work. The most controversial reform that Brown recommends is divorce when marriage is not based on friendship. He is not willing to provide a revolutionary path by which women can form a moral independence from established social institutions. Change, apparently, must be gradual or not at all.

Wollstonecraft and Godwin agreed that marriage should be based on friendship. They rejected arranged marriage for property and political advantage, believing that marriage should be affectionate and based on a union of mutual respect and shared responsibilities. At the same time, Wollstonecraft argued that children had a duty to accept a spouse selected by kind and generous parents, even if they did not agree with their parents' choice. It was not rational, in her view, for a child to oppose the will of a kind parent, who not only had the best interest of the child at heart but also had the wisdom of experience.

It is not difficult to point out many examples of damaging arranged marriages or misalliances in Brown's fiction. In *Wieland*, all of the family's problems begin with the hasty rejection of an arranged marriage. The grandfather of Clara and Theodore marries a woman from a merchant family against the wishes of his aristocratic parents, who then disinherit him. He and his wife soon die, orphaning their son. Their son becomes a religious zealot to escape an abusive apprenticeship. His religious devotion eventually leads to his mysterious death in a flash of light at his self-made temple and the untimely grief-driven death of his own wife. Once again, the consequence is that Clara and Theodore become orphans. Left without parents or schooling, they devise an uncommon family community, one susceptible to delusion and destruction. When Theodore murders his wife and children, the reader may reason that an earlier precipitate act of independence from parental design bears such force that the cumulative effect after three generations is mass murder.

In *Memoirs of Stephen Calvert*, the paternal line is similarly corrupted by a clandestine marriage. Stephen Calvert, Sr., marries a peasant girl in secret without the knowledge of his aristocratic father. Unhappy with the marriage and believing that Stephen has exposed his role in the Jacobin uprising, his father tries to kill him. Stephen's suffering is compounded by the fact that the woman his father had chosen for him was actually his childhood sweetheart; if he had been patient and not married the peasant girl, he could have had it all, an affectionate marriage as well as his patrimony. Instead, Stephen's indiscretion causes a lifetime of fear in which he must move to America to protect his growing family. Eventually, he drowns mysteriously, possibly because his father's men caught up with him. Brown leaves this question open, though, suggesting that Stephen may have committed suicide to escape regret and guilt over his untimely marriage.

To demonstrate the value of patience, Brown also shows that the lessons learned by the mistakes of ancestors can improve circumstances for their progeny. With each generation, it becomes a little easier to work around parental authority and established marriage traditions. Ultimately, the couples at the center of the action in *Wieland* and *Memoirs of Stephen Calvert* are able to marry for love but not until they experience trials in the process of partner selection. Clara Wieland must allow for the passage of time to clear her name and restore her honor before she can marry Henry Pleyel. Stephen Calvert, Jr., must realize that marrying for money is not a pure motive before he can be with Clelia Neville.

It is in *Jane Talbot* (1801) that Brown provides his most complete novelistic treatment of marriage reform in reference to Woldwinite discussions. He attempts to reconcile the traditional and radical positions through the deliberations and arguments of rational and sympathetic characters and the concerted opposition of their guardians. The eponymous heroine and her suitor, Henry Colden, do not have to endure a litany of family tragedies or confront tyrannical parents. Because their parents are kind, however, it is reasonable that the young people should have their approval before they can wed. To this end, the couple must suffer, reform, or outlive many obstacles, not least those posed by their penchant for new philosophies and radical behavior. Henry is distracted by Godwinianism, and Jane is ruled by Wollstonecraftian impetuosity. Before they can marry, they must prove to their guardians that they have digested these philosophies properly, taking from them only the most salubrious and rational ideas.

Over the course of the novel, Henry disavows his prior, youthful Godwinian tenets. Whereas he once agreed with the first edition of *Political Justice* that the emotional need for marriage was cowardly, he now checks Jane's affections for him when they do more harm than good. This position is still Godwinian, but it refers to the more inclusive second edition of *Political Justice* and the idea of benevolent justice. Jane adopts this theory as a way of mediating between her passions and calm reason. She declares that love does not have to be cold to be rational; instead, she claims, just love is dependent on such vigor in its practice and "confers bliss not only on ourselves but on another" (JT 151). This kind of love enacts justice in the equal portion of ecstatic happiness that it provides to both parties. Although Jane argues for the benefits of passion, she acknowledges that the greater good may require these passions to have boundaries.

It is Henry's Godwinian inquiry that allows Jane to reform her impetuous character. Jane finds that she must draw on her own religious beliefs to counteract the errors in Henry's first-edition principles, which included atheism. Thus, she not only makes Henry truly pious but also fortifies her own convictions. The strengthening of her faith shows the reader that this sort of rational reflection, which is promoted in the second edition of *Political Justice*, is compatible with religion and right action.

Thus, the novel's characters experience an emotional growth that would have been thwarted by a premature sexual union if it were not for the efforts of Jane's guardian, Mrs. Fielder. Her part in the couple's happiness arguably suggests that Brown believed that (reasonable) parental approval was crucial to the formation of a healthy marriage. The couple should be dutiful to their parents and heed the lessons of precedent and tradition. Mrs. Fielder's benevolent authority deserves obedience and respect. Since she cares for Jane, she seeks to guide her toward decisions that will preserve her happiness. This warrants her involvement in Jane's procurement of a proper partner. Brown emphasizes that Jane's deference to her guardian does not prevent her from practicing her own beliefs; it merely guides her in the development of her beliefs so that they steer her in the course of right action. She welcomes the counsel of Mrs. Fielder even when it is to the detriment of her relationship with Henry, yet she also reminds Mrs. Fielder that the onus is on her to prove that her advice should be heeded.

Jane's caveat tentatively echoes Wollstonecraft's argument in the *Vindication* that there is a duty to parents but also a duty *on* parents. Children should be dutiful, but parents forfeit that duty if they are tyrannical toward their children. Brown allows for the airing of this opinion, yet it is not until Mrs. Fielder is on her deathbed that she finally gives her consent for Jane and Henry to marry. Only then, with the passing of the former generation, is it acceptable for them to do so.

In *Jane Talbot*, on this reading, Brown came closest in his fictions to providing a solution to philosophical reform of old institutions. Mrs. Fielder's last-minute approval implicitly provides hope that institutions are malleable and open to reason. They are restrictive but may serve positive purposes when they preserve social virtues and benefits using the knowledge that was available when they came into being. Since they are animated by good intentions, they require only that individuals work patiently within their boundaries, enacting gradual change and minimizing disruption. In this way, Jane and Henry create a natural independence from the unjust restrictions of an aging institution while maintaining its sanctity and improving it.

This optimism may have been a mere flash in the pan, however, in the evolution of Brown's thought. Although he continued to believe that natural independence was possible as an effective means of producing social reform, he also criticized the damaging effects of established institutions that are not as rational and kind. *Ormond* and *Edgar Huntly*, for example, show how this intransigence harms individuals, and especially women, who fall outside the mold. In these narratives, victimization causes uncontrolled reactions to perceived injuries and suggests that it is extremely difficult for individuals to act rationally if they have been mistreated. In other words, the subjects of inequality and subordination are impelled to act morally independent by abusers who have corrupted them and pushed them beyond the limits of patience and tolerance.

In *Ormond*, Brown presents one of his most progressive female characters, Martinette de Beauvais. As a refugee from Robespierre's Reign of Terror, a veteran of the American Revolution, and a gender-bending single woman, she is arguably the most revolutionary character, male or female, in the Brown canon. Yet, according to Martinette, her unconventional life was a product of forces beyond her control. At two points in her education, she is forced to study traditionally masculine subjects by members of the same patriarchal institutions that would condemn her for such knowledge. The first time this happens, she applies herself to masculine subjects to avoid the lecherous advances of her ecclesiastical tutor, who, as a debauched priest, represents the corrupted institution of religion. Later, she inadvertently learns about politics when her guardian, who is married to a government official, carries her off to another country to prevent her from seeing her suitor. This second time, she is driven so far in her studies by the stress of separation from her lover that once she is reunited with him, she sees no alternative but to follow him into battle in the American Revolution.

This marks the beginning of Martinette's moral independence. To become a soldier, she assumes male dress, wields swords, and partakes in rigorous exercise. Soon she remarks that her soul has become "a stranger to the sexual distinction" (O 202). In her unsexing, she embodies widespread fears concerning Wollstonecraft's radicalism and the French Revolution. While Brown refers positively to Martinette's residual feminine attributes of dignity and grace, he also implies that she lacks the conventional manners that invite normal social interaction. Her tendency to speak freely, defying social decorum and custom, are hasty movements toward familiarity that are not matched in her unfeeling character. Although she is worldly and energetic, her conversation and deportment are guarded and lacking in sympathy. Her masculine attainments have had an adverse effect, causing her reason to eclipse her femininity and rendering her incapable of friendship and love. After her lover's death, Martinette appears friendless and isolated, with no living relatives except for a guardian she cannot tolerate. After his death, she apparently decides to move back to France. On this reading, Martinette's uncertain situation illustrates the destructive effects of morally independent behavior and the corrupt institutions that forced it upon her.

With the voice of Ormond, who may be Martinette's lost brother, Brown alludes to the fallacy that motivates those who exercise moral independence.[5] Ormond comments on the difficulty of applying abstract principles to actual practice. In his theoretical convictions, he epitomizes Godwinian thinking, promoting patience instead of revolutionary action. In the extended summary of Ormond's principles in the novel's chapter 12, it is the duty of the philosopher to inquire into the nature of a just society. It is impossible, however, for one person to ensure the happiness of mankind on his own, and thus, the philosopher, like Martinette and everyone else, is corrupted by his social environment. In consequence, society must experience fundamental change from within before reformers can expect to create beneficial change from without, and one must be satisfied with acting for oneself as opposed to by oneself and contrary to the common interest. It is only with benevolent motives toward others and deference to the common good that one may hope to improve one's condition in society (O 112–118).

Yet despite his rational and benevolent philosophy, Ormond is himself corrupted by the society in which he lives and thus acts selfishly against custom. He abuses his socially granted power as a male and persuades his lover, Helena, to reject propriety and join him in a marriageless sexual partnership. This scheme ruins her and renders both of them miserable, leading to Helena's suicide. This turn echoes Wollstonecraft's suicide attempts and seems to dramatize the worst of what can happen when followers of her philosophy act independently of social norms. For Helena and Martinette, the system has failed to change in time to save them from their fates. Society mistreats them, corrupts them, and expels them. They drift into a limbo for those who are damaged by intransigent institutions and await the salvation of adequate reform.

Brown continued to study the moral independence of women in inhospitable societies in the 1805–1806 *Historical Sketches*. Numerous illustrations of female subordination appear in the novel-length *Sketches*, embedded within the larger narrative concerning the patriarchal dynasties of the ancient Carrill and Orme families. Lady Jane Carril and Countess Pamphela, two of the narrative's matriarchs, both suffer as a result of their arranged marriages formed to secure dynasties and political allegiances. Wollstonecraft argued that women who were subject to such marriages paid with their happiness for the political ambitions of men. Potentially, their families could improve their social standing but only at the cost of marriages without love and affection. Godwin argued that such marriages embodied social corruption on every level and mirrored the politics of despotism. The experiences of Lady Jane Carrill and Countess Pamphela in the *Sketches* suggest that these arranged marriages ultimately prove destructive to dynastic ambitions by corrupting future generations through the process of victimization.[6]

In the first example, the Carrils arrange Lady Jane's marriage to the unfaithful and abusive Count of Florac. In fear for her safety, she flees with her son and daughter to England, but the damage caused by Florac's brutality is complete; she is never equal to the emotional task of being a mother. Lady Jane practices a laissez-faire attitude toward parenting, sending the daughter to be brought up by an aunt and dealing laxly with the son because of her obsessive ideas about securing his fortune. The rigid system by which her marriage is arranged instills in her a fixation on wealth without guiding her in the exercise of her judgment for the interest of her children. Lady Jane's misguided parenting leads her son into a life of depravity, drunkenness, and promiscuity. He dies young, becoming what Brown calls a "martyr of maternal folly" (Dunlap 1815, I: 316). The narrator echoes Wollstonecraft's *Vindication* when he or she suggests that "the greater number of women's follies proceed...from the tyranny of man" (*Vindication* 265). Lady Jane learns nothing but depraved notions under the harsh tutelage of a power-hungry patriarchy.

In a second example drawn from the *Historical Sketches*, Countess Pamphela exhibits a more natural independence in that her actions do not harm anyone and her change in circumstance is not willful. However, the speed of her emancipation and her subsequent immoderate behavior seem to confirm that her independence remains a moral one. Pamphela's father forces her to marry against her will to satisfy his political ambitions, but he and her new husband both soon die, leaving her in control of her own affairs. She never remarries, choosing instead to remain single for the rest of her life. This abrupt transition from subjection to autonomy, minus patient deliberation and rational inquiry, spoils Pamphela's temper. As a result, she has an exaggerated perception of her own abilities. She is impossibly prudent, dexterous, studious, and pious and becomes deluded about her powers as the community matriarch. Although the narrator treats the episode ironically, possibly suggesting that Pamphela is manipulating her audience to serve her interests, on a literal reading, she comes to believe that her body is the second incarnation of an earlier Saint Pamphela and invincible to disease and death until the time of her choosing. With no female peers to serve as a guide to her governance, her sense of her own singularity and importance is distorted (Dunlap 1815, I: 277–283).

It is significant that in all of her unusual accomplishments, Pamphela also promotes the equality of the sexes, exhibits masculine ambition, and has a passion for politics. These all reflect a Wollstonecraft-like character, but the narrative emphasizes that, unlike Wollstonecraft, Pamphela never reduces her opinions to practice. However eccentric, she never engages in immoral acts like those chronicled in Godwin's *Memoirs*. Her passive role in the change of her condition appears significant; it makes her morally superior to those, like Wollstonecraft, who would force the alteration of institutions and endanger social stability.

A final example of Brown's many reworkings of dilemmas that refer to the concept of moral independence is his final short tale, "Insanity: A Fragment" (February 1809). This narrative is a retelling of Brown's published short story "A Lesson on Sensibility," from May 1798. The two narratives may serve as bookends to his career and a final return to the Woldwinite theories that Brown had approached enthusiastically in the 1790s. The later, 1809 version of the story seems to test natural independence as a means of reform for a dishonest and unjust system.

In both versions of the narrative, two impassioned lovers dutifully follow the dictates of patience but meet with a terrible fate. In this tragic outcome, the tale suggests that Godwin's notion that institutional change could be wrought at a personal level with due diligence was a chimera if that institution was unwilling to change its moral outlook. It is one thing if a moral outlook is benevolent and sincere, but if an institution uses dishonest means to preserve its traditions, then it is impermeable to reason and reformation.

The problem with Wollstonecraftian independent action, however, is that it is rooted in sensibility and thus prone to excess. In the 1798 "Lesson on Sensibility," Miss Butler is overcome by her passions in spite of herself. Her irreproachable sincerity and keen sensitivity aid her in forming intimate relationships; however, her extreme sensibility prevents her from deliberating on the sincerity of others. As a result, she succumbs to the flattery of the hot-blooded Archibald. When her parents take action to separate the two lovers,

Archibald is incensed while Miss Butler remains calm. She reasons that a patient attitude and a strong will may eventually enable her to marry the man she desires, so she submits and follows her parents' rules. By being master of herself in this instance, she feels that she is exerting her independence, and according to Godwin, this would be the way to proceed: by natural means, without any rash action.

Her parents have no intention of playing fair, and they resort to force to keep the lovers apart by telling Miss Butler that Archibald has been unfaithful to her. This dishonesty proves to be the fatal blow to her patience and reason, and she eventually takes her own life. Ironically, the parents' falsehood turns out to have some truth in it. Although they have, in fact, unearthed Archibald's true infidelity, their interference is catastrophic, as the guilt Archibald feels over his former lover's death causes him to lose his sanity.

"A Lesson on Sensibility" ends here, but the 1809 "Insanity" modifies the tale with the conclusion of a new framing narrative. In it, the veracity of Archibald's narrative is under dispute; his relatives argue over whether he is already insane and has made up the entire story. Both the 1798 and 1809 versions play upon the moral dilemma of patience and reason in the face of adversity, but the fact that Brown questions the reliability of the main narrative in "Insanity" may suggest that by the end of his career, the author has grown frustrated with this theory. The later version of the narrative does not imply that Miss Butler's patient trust will change the minds of her parents. Her plight is doomed from start to finish simply because she is at the mercy of a corrupt authority that cannot be trusted to act justly and honestly.

Whereas Brown's novels arguably provided positive moral exempla—if you follow these rules of action, you will be rewarded—there is no such promise here. The lovers in these two tales abide by the will of their parents to avoid a clandestine marriage, but still they suffer. With a reading of the narrative as an enactment of dilemmas related to the notion of moral independence, Archibald's madness is a consequence of social evils that can only be alleviated through the enlightenment of that society (Weber 16). In this, his final story, Brown suggests that until that time when society shall adhere to a sense of sincerity and justice, the feasibility of steady reform shall remain the chimerical creation of idealists.

Notes

1. Much of this chapter originates in a chapter from my doctoral thesis for the University of Aberdeen, supervised by Janet Todd, to whom I am greatly indebted. I would also like to thank Michael Plaxton at the University of Saskatchewan College of Law for his readings of early drafts.
2. See also Teute, 149–181.
3. I track the source of this enlightenment in my doctoral thesis, Smith 245–258.
4. On Dunlap's reading *Rights of Woman* for what would be the second time, see Smith, 256.
5. The "factual" nature of all narrated claims about Martinette and Ormond, for example, their kinship, remain uncertain because the novel's narrator, Sophia Courtland, is an intemperate, counterrevolutionary partisan whose unreliability is emphasized in numerous ways throughout the narrative.
6. Clemit calls this corrupt breeding of victims "inherited conditioning" (130).

WORKS CITED

Allen, B. Sprague. "William Godwin and the Stage." *Publications of the Modern Language Association* 35.3 (1920): 358–374.

Anonymous ("L.M."). "Reflections on the Character of Mary Wollstonecraft." MM 1.5 (August 1799): 330–335.

Bage, Robert. *Hermsprong; or, Man as He Is Not*, 3 vols. London: Minerva Press, 1796.

Barnard, Philip, and Stephen Shapiro. "Frontispiece." In Charles Brockden Brown, *Ormond; or, The Secret Witness, with Related Texts*, viii. Indianapolis: Hackett, 2009.

Barnard, Philip, and Stephen Shapiro. "Introduction." In Charles Brockden Brown, *Arthur Mervyn; or, Memoirs of the Year 1793 with Related Texts*, ix–xliv. Indianapolis: Hackett, 2008.

Brown, Charles Brockden. *Historical Sketches*. In Dunlap 1815, I: 170–396.

Brown, Charles Brockden. "Insanity: A Fragment." PF (February 1809): 165–168.

Brown, Charles Brockden. "A Lesson on Sensibility." WM (May 19, 1798): 71–76.

Clemit, Pamela. *The Godwinian Novel: The Rational Fictions of Godwin, Brockden Brown, and Mary Shelley*. Oxford: Clarendon Press, 1993.

Darwin, Erasmus. *Zoonomia; or, The Laws of Organic Life*. London: J. Johnson, 1796.

Dunlap, William. *History of the American Theatre*, 2 vols. London: R. Bentley, 1833.

Dunlap, William. *Tell Truth and Shame the Devil, a Comedy in Two Acts. As Performed by the Old American Company, New-York, January 1797*. New York: T. & J. Swords, 1797.

Godwin, William. *The Diary of William Godwin*. Victoria Myers, David O'Shaughnessy, and Mark Philp, eds. Oxford: Oxford Digital Library, 2010. http://godwindiary.bodleian.ox.ac.uk.

Godwin, William. *Enquiry concerning Political Justice. The Political and Philosophical Writings of William Godwin*, Vol. 3. Mark Philp and Martin Fitzpatrick, eds. London: Pickering, 1999.

Godwin, William. *Memoirs of the Author of A Vindication of the Rights of Woman*. Pamela Clemit and Gina Luria Walker, eds. Peterborough, Ont.: Broadview, 2001.

Hays, Mary. *Memoirs of Emma Courtney*, 2 vols. London: Robinson, 1796.

Holcroft, Thomas. *Anna St. Ives*. Peter Faulkner, ed. London: Oxford University Press, 1970.

Shelley, Mary Wollstonecraft. *Frankenstein; or, The Modern Prometheus*. London: Lackington et al., 1818.

Shelley, Mary Wollstonecraft. *The Last Man*. London: Henry Colburn, 1826.

Shelley, Percy Bysshe. *Laon and Cythna*. London: Sherwood et al., 1818.

Shelley, Percy Bysshe. *Rosalind and Helen, a Modern Eclogue*. London: C. and J. Ollier, 1819.

Shelley, Percy Bysshe. *St. Irvyne; or, The Rosicrucian*. London: J. J. Stockdale, 1811.

Shelley, Percy Bysshe. *Zastrozzi, a Romance*. London: G. Wilkie and J. Robinson, 1810.

Sickels, Eleanor. "Shelley and Charles Brockden Brown," *Publications of the Modern Language Association* 45.4 (December 1930): 1116–1128.

Smith, Abigail M. *The Reception of the Life and Work of Mary Wollstonecraft in the Early American Republic*. Ph.D. dissertation, University of Aberdeen, 2009.

Teute, Frederika J. "A 'Republic of Intellect': Conversation and Criticism among the Sexes in 1790s New York." In Philip Barnard, Mark L. Kamrath, and Stephen Shapiro, eds., *Revising Charles Brockden Brown: Culture, Politics and Sexuality in the Early Republic*, 149–181. Knoxville: University of Tennessee Press, 2004.

Waterman, Bryan. *Republic of Intellect: The Friendly Club of New York City and the Making of American Literature*. Baltimore: Johns Hopkins University Press, 2007.

Weber, Alfred. "Introduction." In Charles Brockden Brown, *Somnambulism and Other Stories*, ix–xxiii. Frankfurt am Main: Peter Lang, 1987.

Williams, John. *Mary Shelley: Literary Lives.* New York: St. Martin's Press, 2000.

Wollstonecraft, Mary. *Letters Written during a Short Residence in Sweden, Norway, and Denmark* [London: J. Johnson, 1796]. In Janet Todd and Marilyn Butler, eds., *The Works of Mary Wollstonecraft*, 6: 237–348. New York: New York University Press, 1989.

Wollstonecraft, Mary. *A Vindication of the Rights of Woman: With Strictures on Political and Moral Subjects* [London: J. Johnson, 1792]. In Janet Todd and Marilyn Butler, eds., *The Works of Mary Wollstonecraft*, 5: 79–266. New York: New York University Press, 1989.

CHAPTER 18

BROWN AND WOMEN'S RIGHTS

FRITZ FLEISCHMANN

THE question of women's rights and roles in the family and the commonwealth engaged Charles Brockden Brown's interest throughout his career. From the early "Henrietta Letters" to the fictional empires of his last decade, Brown identified gender and sexuality, and the definitions of masculinity and femininity, as constitutive elements of public and private life. Influenced by the ideas of Jean-Jacques Rousseau and then of Mary Wollstonecraft, William Godwin, and their circle, energized by discussions in the Friendly Club, Brown posed these questions directly in his fictional dialogue *Alcuin* and in the characters and plots of some of his fictions published between 1798 and 1801. In Brown's fictional world of failed parents, tyrannical brothers, business chicanery, and shifting social hierarchies, of uncertain masculinities and conflicted civic life, women appear as victims and survivors, foils and collaborators, interrogators and counter-models, whose memorable humanity and strength of mind beg the question of their equality with men.[1]

I

If government emanates from the people, who "the people" are becomes the subject of political theory.[2] "Are not women born as free as men?" John Otis had asked in *The Rights of British Colonies Asserted and Proved* (1764), and the American Revolution had "initiated a wide-spread, ongoing debate over the meaning of women's rights" (Zagarri 2). In 1776, New Jersey began allowing women to vote in federal and state elections (a right revoked in 1807); after 1792, Wollstonecraft's *A Vindication of the Rights of Woman* had popularized the term *women's rights*; in 1798, Judith Sargent Murray's *The Gleaner* congratulated her "fair country-women" on "the happy revolution which the few past years has made in their favor" (Zagarri 1–4). In Essay 88 of *The Gleaner*, Murray's Constantia places her hope in the new republic: "Yes, in this younger world, 'the Rights of Women' begin to be understood; we seem, at length, determined to do justice to THE SEX; and improving on the ideas of a Wollstonecraft, we are ready to contend for the *quantity*, as well as *quality* of mind." She appeals explicitly to her enlightened readers: "*The idea of the incapability* of women, is…in this *enlightened age*, totally *inadmissible*"; the author proposes to "establish the female right to that *equality with their brethren, which…is assigned them in the Order of Nature*" (Murray 703, 705, 709).

In his *Retrospect of the 18th Century* (1803), Brown's friend Samuel Miller noted "the change of opinion gradually introduced into society, respecting the importance, capacity, and dignity of the *Female Sex*" (quoted in Zagarri 19). However, not only was this "change of opinion" mainly limited to notions about women's capacity for education, but it would take decades for such ideas to move beyond what historian Lucia McMahon has called "mere equality" and to allow women to aspire to public roles (McMahon x). As for political rights, the longing for stability and order among the new nation's leaders was stronger than their willingness to consider the extension of rights to new categories of persons.[3] Still, "for a few brief decades, a comprehensive transformation in women's rights, roles, and responsibilities seemed not only possible but perhaps inevitable" (Zagarri 8).

Even while progressive voices were calling for such a transformation, however, public sentiment was beginning to turn against them. Wollstonecraft's *Vindication* had been widely read and discussed,[4] but the publication of Godwin's *Memoirs of the Author of A Vindication of the Rights of Woman* in 1798 was seized upon by the swelling anti-Jacobin furor to associate Wollstonecraft and women's rights with sexual libertinism, sympathies for the increasingly mistrusted French, and a general subversion of social hierarchies, religion, and political stability. In the United States as well as Britain, Wollstonecraft's "piety and moral stringency…were ignored in favor of a caricature of godless female lubricity" (Taylor 246).[5] For an author like Brown, in search of a public and a living, to write about such a charged topic as women's rights, closely associated with Wollstonecraft, necessitated a strategy that allowed a full exploration of the issues but also a modicum of ambiguity—or deniability. This strategy[6] or method is what caused some of Brown's initial readers in the world of the Friendly Club,[7] as well as modern critics, to wonder what he really meant to say. Thus, Cathy N. Davidson claimed that *Alcuin* "was surely one of the former works that [Brown]…disavowed" in his 1803 "Editor's Address" (Davidson 72), whereas Sydney J. Krause, reading Brown "in context with the women's issues that were debated in his [own time]," concluded, "No writer in Brown's time—and for a considerable time thereafter—would make a more positive statement about the essential capabilities of women, more than validating their entitlement to fully equal rights with men" (Krause 2000, 350, 375). Brown's most thorough and direct examination of this question is staged in *Alcuin; A Dialogue* (1798).

II

A possibly unfinished[8] piece of fiction framed by a first-person narrator, *Alcuin* is full of ironic wit and choreographs a dizzying dance through a maze of arguments. Brown published a version of Parts I and II in the Philadelphia *Weekly Magazine*, entitled "Rights of Women," before the book publication overseen by Elihu Hubbard Smith in New York, titled *Alcuin; A Dialogue*. Today, most critics refer to the work as a dialogue; Fredrika Teute calls it a novel. Reader response may be affected by whether one reads it as a book or as a magazine serial.[9]

The text as we know it today begins with a male and ends with a female speaker. "I called last evening on Mrs. Carter,"[10] Alcuin[11] begins. He has been invited by the widowed Mrs. Carter's brother, a physician, whose household, "the favourite resort of the liberal and ingenious" (AL 3), she supervises. Alcuin looks for conversation that "blends...utility and pleasure" (5), an environment modeled on the Friendly Club, among whose circle the dialogue was first read. Before he gets to Mrs. Carter's salon, the narrator spools off pages of autobiographical reflection. He is both poor and proud, shy and self-confident, lonely yet hesitant to venture into society. Toiling amid urban noise as an underpaid schoolmaster, he still extols his own condition: although deprived of health, peace, money, and leisure, he is "the happiest of mortals" (6), an ironic allusion to his creator Brown, who had experienced the life of a Philadelphia schoolmaster in 1793–1794 (Kafer 74–76) and was, like Alcuin, a "[dealer] in fiction" who feared that his "stock" of experience was all too "slender" (6).

Listening to the political conversation in the room, Alcuin approaches his hostess with this question: "Pray, Madam, are you a federalist?" (7). Her response is incredulous. She has often been asked to listen but never for her opinion; "the women's province" excludes politics, whereas men "consider themselves in an element congenial to their sex and station" (7). Jumping to defend the status quo, Alcuin must defend women as they are, ascribing their intellectual deficits to the "limited sphere" in which they properly belong (9). By contrast, his hostess is critical of women and therefore of the circumstances that shape them, echoing the *Vindication*. Such parallels abound; just as Wollstonecraft had asked for equal treatment of women by the French revolutionaries, Mrs. Carter derives her demands for women's political rights from the American Revolution.

Arguments about rights typically arise where rights are denied or contested. For women's rights, the argument for restriction historically is about difference and its varieties (physiology, intellect, etc.), typically connected to a larger order (such as God or nature), or about long-standing, naturalized traditions. Inequality may also be justified where hierarchies of power are seen as guarantors of social order. In the case of *Alcuin*, the dialogue's opening exchange establishes that Mrs. Carter is a political creature, a person who has thought about the polis and formed an opinion. Thus, the premise of intellectual (or other) difference that underlies her disenfranchisement is already called into question, her right to reason established. Alcuin, a John Adams of gender politics, faces an uphill struggle against the first of Brown's strong women characters.[12]

Alcuin will admit "that the sexes are essentially equal" (10); that humans are shaped by their environment—compared with which "[t]he differences that flow from the sexual distinction are as nothing in the balance" (10); that gender is a social construct. But he denies specific injustices against women: "The evil lies in so much of human capacity being thus fettered and perverted" (11). He does not dispute Mrs. Carter's claim that "the same principles of truth and equity must be applicable to both" men and women (19), but he claims that the gendered division of labor tends to favor women, who end up with the more pleasant tasks and have more leisure (19–21), a claim rejected by Mrs. Carter for leaving out the majority of women. Alcuin's strategy here and else-where is to downplay what he considers the minor question in favor of the major one: "Human beings, it is to be hoped, are destined to a better condition on this stage, or some other, than is now allotted them" (21). This strategy—expanding the question only to defer it—inevitably shores up the status quo.

We see this again in Part II, after Mrs. Carter criticizes the new Constitution for denying equal rights to women. Alcuin defends this restriction, as the Constitution also restricts the political rights of minors, slaves, recent immigrants, and the poor. Is Mrs. Carter pleading for all disenfranchised categories? No: "I plead only for my own sex" (28). Although this is a tactical move to counter Alcuin's, Mrs. Carter here reflects the contemporary discourse on women's education that made "gender the only relevant category" while downplaying differences of race and class (Kelley 6). Mere physical difference, the reason for women's exclusion, should not disqualify anyone from voting or holding office. The dialogue, pointed and often funny, ranges over a vast ground, including married women's property rights, women's education, and forms of government. Alcuin's method is sophistic, that of Mrs. Carter Socratic. She gets him so tangled up in his own contradictions that at the end of Part II, we see him in total defeat. He admits women's intellectual equality, garnishes this admission with the sentimental claim for women's higher nature, resorts to flirting with his hostess, and ends up spouting pure Wollstonecraft: men's assumption of superiority "is a branch of that prejudice which has so long darkened the world, and taught men that nobles and kings were creatures of an order superior to themselves" (33).

When Alcuin returns to the salon a week later, he claims to have been transported by his "good genius" (35) to an island "paradise of women," a socialist utopia where labor and leisure are shared equally by all and where there is no difference between the pursuits of men and women or in the way they dress and behave; all are guided by the principle of functional utility. Alcuin reports on his conversation with a kind inhabitant. This guide interprets Alcuin's questions about *gender* as questions about *sex*, that is, anatomical differences, and refuses to give him "a physiological dissertation" (43). Asked about the "moral or political maxims" derived from sexual differences, the guide insists that all humans are rational and must be treated the same. When Alcuin inquires about the institution of marriage, the guide's answer is short: "I do not understand the term" (49), and upon further inquiry, the guide once again thinks Alcuin is asking about sex: "You cannot at this age be a stranger to the origin of human existence" (49).

With this topic, the report from the "paradise of women" is brought to a halt. Alcuin wonders about the propriety of discussing sex with his hostess—who promptly reprimands him for "sophistry," to which "the proper antidote is argument" (52). She launches into a long discourse on the evils of marriage, criticizing the submission expected of married women, the loss of their property and lack of control over their children, even going so far as to say (with Godwin) that a common dwelling is not an essential ingredient of the married state and arguing for "an unlimited power of divorces" (58). But she rejects insinuations that she is an opponent of the institution of marriage per se; she merely wants to reform it to remove its present injustices. Alcuin is skeptical: "A general corruption of manners" would result from widespread divorce, "till the whole nation were sunk into a state of the lowest degeneracy" (65). Mrs. Carter's response is cutting: "Pray thee . . . leave this topic of declamation to the school boys" (65). If "anger in her own cause" is the emotion "most frequently denied" to an educated woman of Brown's time (Ferguson 179), Mrs. Carter's outbursts of open anger legitimate that emotion and emphasize the singularity of Brown's text. Provocatively, Alcuin proposes "to adventure a few steps further." If "marriage has no other criterion than custom," are there any universal principles that define it? If not, what should one do if the marriage customs of one's country do "not conform" to one's "notions of duty" (66)?

This sort of antinomian radicalism is a dangerous teaser.[13] If "marriage" is merely conventional, why can't anything be called marriage? If it's not perfect anywhere, why can't individuals question it according to their "notions of duty"? Mrs. Carter rejects Alcuin's "perversion of language" (67) and answers his question with a forthright definition: "Marriage is an union founded on free and mutual consent. It cannot exist without friendship. It cannot exist without personal fidelity. As soon as the union ceases to be spontaneous it ceases to be just. This is the sum. If I were to talk for months, I could add nothing to the completeness of this definition" (67).

Alcuin presents many familiar Woldwinite ideas.[14] Parts I and II draw heavily on Wollstonecraft's critique of women's condition within a larger democratic argument. In Parts III and IV, Brown turns to Godwin: "Alcuin's Utopia is Godwin's" (Borghi 19), and *Political Justice* informs Mrs. Carter's critique of marriage (Krause 1982, 422). However, Godwin also becomes Mrs. Carter's target when she distances herself from "that detestable philosophy which scoffs at the matrimonial institution" (70). Like Wollstonecraft, she wants to reform marriage, not abolish it.

Brown's familiarity with the writings of Wollstonecraft and Godwin is well documented; he was also familiar with the feminist writings of their associate Mary Hays and other members of their circle.[15] His friend Ruth Paxson, under the pseudonym "Constance," published the "Wollstonecraftian Sketch 'A Contrast'" in the *Weekly Magazine* around the same time in 1798 as Brown's "Rights of Women" appeared there (Letters 305 n. 1). And as editor of the *Monthly Magazine*, Brown published "Reflections on the Character of MARY WOLLSTONECRAFT GODWIN" in August 1799, a thoughtful defense of Wollstonecraft that makes her sound just like Mrs. Carter: affirming marriage as an institution but finding its current laws and customs "particularly for women unjust, tyrannical, and oppressive" (333). The author hopes that "the efforts which have been made, will not be lost, but that their influence may tend to equalize the condition and privileges of the sexes, without entrenching upon the necessary guard of civil institutions, or confounding their salutary regulations with the exercise of despotic tyranny" (334).

Of course, identifying the provenance of *Alcuin*'s ideas does not necessarily identify Brown's own views.[16] To hear his voice in *Alcuin*, one must read it not as apprentice work but as a significant creation. Doing so, Peter Kafer finds intentionality. After defining the American republican system, *Alcuin* reviews its internal contradictions; then "the text vaults...into a Quakerly-Godwinian vision of a more rational, egalitarian, just society. And *then* Brown finishes by setting up the basis for a critique of *that* visionary system" (Kafer 96), ending "in an imaginative realm that will be the frame of Brown's novels: the realm of *what if*" (99–100).

In addition to the political arguments, the male-female dialogue has its own dynamic. Both debaters are abstractions as well as mimetic characters, but while Alcuin's positioning commits him to nothing, Mrs. Carter realizes that arguments have consequences— different ones for a woman from those for a man. As always, Brown counts on the reader's intelligence:[17] "When you read, your books ought to be considered as a text to which your imagination must furnish supplement and commentary" (Letters 695).

Readers have often found it difficult to avoid taking the character Alcuin's views as Brown's. But most of the irony in the dialogue is at Alcuin's expense; he is an unworldly naïf, skewered by a sophisticated woman. That Brown considers him a fool is evident not only from the zigzag of Alcuin's arguing but also from at least one of his positions on which we do have Brown's opinion. When Alcuin pays flirtatious compliments to Mrs. Carter toward the end of Part II, he grounds his claim that women are "on the whole, the superior" sex on the feelings inspired "by the mere graces of their exterior, even when the magic of their voice sleeps, and the eloquence of the eyes is mute" (33). Arner (280) rightly recognizes this view of women's sexual superiority as that of John Gregory, whose *Father's Legacy to His Daughters* had been harshly criticized by Wollstonecraft. What Brown thought of Gregory is clear from his March 30, 1801, letter to his future wife, Elizabeth Linn: "Dr. Gregory was an egregious fool, Eliza. Never consign thy conversation & behaviours to his government. If I remember rightly, his errors are properly exposed, in the 'Rights of woman'" (Letters 512).

If Brown's own self-image, as outlined in the fictional letter to Susan Godolphin in 1793, was that of "a utopian reformer" (Watts 68), by the time of *Alcuin*, Arner's view that Brown is skeptical of utopian panaceas would be supported by Mrs. Carter's insistence that specific rights and concrete reforms are more important than theoretical claims and visionary solutions. That Brown may not have advocated a total revolution in gender roles is suggested by Smith's letter to his sister (quoted in Teute 165): rather than "mingling in the active occupations of politics & war," Smith writes, Brown thinks that women should "cultivate science in retirement, correct opinion by their writings, & improve men by their example."

To the enlightened reader, in any event, *Alcuin* is not a Rorschach inkblot but an intellectual fencing match with a score. By the end, Mrs. Carter has simply landed most of the hits; the case she makes for women's rights "is that compelling, that simple"

(Krause 1982, 426). By contrast, Alcuin's defensive retreats and turns to generic radicalism provide no remedy for specific injustices, such as the captivity of women in marriage and their civil disenfranchisement. His last recourse is to an imagined "paradise" where everything has been resolved; not only has gender as a social relation disappeared, but so has social injustice in general. It is important that Alcuin comes back from his "voyage" still defending the social world in which he finds himself; the radical visionary is a reactionary sophist. Mrs. Carter's performance, however, is a ringing affirmation of women's right and ability to reason, an affirmation of the progressive ends as well as the pragmatic means of reform, with sober sensitivity to what ideas might have a chance in the new American republic.

III

In Alcuin's world of male politicians, women are not expected to have a voice; Mrs. Carter rejects utopian visions and gives voice to women's concerns in the here and now. In *Wieland*, a woman's self-critically rational voice tells a tale of a fragile paradise lost through male madness and eccentricity, cracked open by its own tensions and the intrusion of the outside world. In *Ormond*, paternal failure starts a young woman's initiation into a world of men where women are objects, where utopian conspiracies are concocted by murderous misogynists, and where the only happiness comes from the company of other women. The strength of the novel's heroine, Constantia Dudley, is tested not only by the economic catastrophe that befalls her family but also by the civic catastrophe of Philadelphia's 1793 yellow fever epidemic, all set in the political hothouse of the American 1790s.[18]

Stephen Dudley, an artist and intellectual living a life of aristocratic ease in New York, has raised his daughter like a rational being, instructing her in all the arts and sciences at his command. This education prepares her for dealing with her father's bankruptcy and decline, followed by her mother's death; when we meet her, she is managing the family's much-reduced affairs in Philadelphia. By the time Constantia meets Ormond, she has already dealt with pestilence and poverty, been rescued from a rape attempt, and, against her father's wishes, rejected a marriage offer that would have restored their prosperity. In a novel about sexual politics, her reasons for this rejection are stated explicitly and at length.

Spurred by Balfour's marriage proposal, Constantia reflects about "the genuine principles" of marriage:

> Now she was at least mistress of the product of her own labor. Her tasks were toilsome, but the profits, though slender, were sure, and she administered her little property in what manner she pleased. Marriage would annihilate this power. Henceforth she would be bereft even of personal freedom. So far from possessing property, she herself would become the property of another.   (O 84)

She will not manipulate a man by the "hateful arts of the sycophant" which Rousseau had recommended and Wollstonecraft had criticized, and, contra Godwin, she is "too wise to place an unbounded reliance on the influence of truth" (84). Her conclusion that "[h]omely liberty was better than splendid servitude" (85) frames her personal decision in terms of the American Revolution.

Ormond's views on marriage are part of a political philosophy "intimately identified with the Godwinian model" (Krause 1982, 420). His "discourse" is quite different from his "actions" (O 114–115), however, which are driven by his desire for personal power (116). Convinced "that the intellectual constitution of females was essentially defective" (117–118), he regards his lover Helena "merely as an object charming to the senses" (120). Since she has not been taught to reason, Helena's artistic talents do not enable her to face poverty (again, the result of paternal failure) with rational composure as Constantia has, dooming her to a life of dependence as Ormond's kept mistress.

Ormond is a case study in the double standard that Wollstonecraft had so bitterly attacked. Despite his belief in women's intellectual inferiority and the glaring power he wields over Helena, Ormond claims that theirs is a voluntary union and that Helena only needs "to reason justly" (123) to deal with the social ostracism attendant on her status. No wonder that his "maxims were confuted in the present case" (126). Ormond is attracted to Constantia precisely because of her intellectual capacities. But his need for "absolute power over the conduct of others" (177) turns his courtship of Constantia into a power struggle. When persuasion fails, he threatens rape, a sort of violence he has practiced since his youth (263–264). As he prepares to violate Constantia, alive or dead, he tells her (as he had told Helena) to reason her way to consent: submitting to rape is "an illustrious opportunity to signalize your wisdom and your fortitude" (282). What she withholds is "in [his] power to extort" (283). This is about power, not sex; if Ormond's rage is fired by Constantia's refusal of consent, threatening to violate her corpse is an argumentative ploy to compel consent rather than an expression of intent.

Ormond's demise at the point of a penknife (a writer's tool, a tool of reason) wielded by a woman leaves no doubt about Brown's sexual politics. Not a rake but an enlightened reasoner, at least in his own mind, Ormond instrumentalizes reason to justify his own ends. Seduction relies on power; violence postures as passion; consent means constraint. Ormond lives out a fantasy of omnipotence that suspends the volition of all others. So completely rational does his hubris seem to Ormond that he reacts to the puncturing penknife with "a look of terrible upbraiding" but no resistance; he falls "as if struck by lightning" (291).

In the novel's world of failed fathers, fraudulent business partners, and manipulative reformers, communities of women appear to offer the only safe retreat; "female homo-sociality" becomes "a respite from the structures of patriarchy" (Stern 187). Constantia develops a great fondness for the aptly named Martinette, growing "daily more enamored" of her (189), although taken aback by her friend's sanguinary exploits (she is, or may be, Ormond's sister). Martinette is a truly liberated woman dedicated to a radical search for freedom, a woman "with a soul that was a stranger to the sexual distinction" (202). Despite her hesitations, Constantia continues to be fascinated by Martinette, as she is by

Ormond, attracted by their unconventionality and self-assurance. By her own report, though, Sophia is the great object of Constantia's love, and their reunion throws them into a three-day "state of dizziness and intoxication":

> The ordinary functions of nature were disturbed. The appetite for sleep and for food were confounded and lost, amidst the impetuosities of a master-passion. To look and to talk to each other, afforded enchanting occupation for every moment. I would not part from her side, but eat and slept, walked and mused and read, with my arm locked in her's, and with her breath fanning my cheek.   (250)

Ormond mocks their "romantic passion for each other" (256), but Sophia describes it as a great celebration: "O! precious inebriation of the heart! O! pre-eminent love! what pleasure of reason or of sense, can stand in competition with those, attendant upon thee?...surely thy sanction is divine: thy boon is happiness!" (250).

The critical discussion of how to sort the different models of womanhood in *Ormond*—the beautiful but dependent Helena, the rational and resourceful Constantia, the exotic Martinette, proponent of revolutionary violence, and the sentimentally savvy Sophia, the narrator—also circles around the question of Brown's gender politics—and of his politics in general.[19] Brown, ever attentive to names, may have named Constantia after Murray's character or after his friend Ruth Paxson, who published as "Constance," but Constantia may simply be an allegory for constancy, just as "Clara" Wieland retains the clearest mind amid her muddled clan. The conservative Sophia is a worldly-wise businesswoman, and Martinette's name may allude to Jean Martinet, French drillmaster under Louis XIV, or to Marie Antoinette (Comment 68); it is also reminiscent of Mars, the god of war. Martinette is warlike, an enthusiast of war, like her brother; the difference between Martinette and Ormond is that she kills for a cause, whereas he kills for self-gratification. Where Constantia remains "constant" to her ideals under pressure, Martinette may represent the violence of the French Revolution. Although constancy is a conservative principle, it does not preclude change; in such a reading, Constantia could be seen as Girondin, Martinette as Jacobin.

At the very least, it can be said that Brown is clear on a woman's right to self-determination, even if he leaves much to the reader to figure out. And obviously, men are gendered, too. What positive models of masculinity does *Ormond* have to offer? If the title character "exposes the narcissism that underpins patriarchy" (Lewis 48), such exposure extends to most of the male characters in the novel. Ormond's narcissism is manifested in his need to control[20] (the "secret witness" of the subtitle is a secret manipulator), but the childlike selfishness of Constantia's father is only a different version of patriarchal entitlement.[21] Constantia's becoming the quasi-parent of the one and the killer of the other puts an end to both. In the end, another patriarchal custom also appears to yield before the power of female networks: Sophia's telling Constantia's story to the mythical I. E. Rosenberg makes her a kind of marriage broker, ending the patriarchal exchange of women between men,[22] preparing the possible spouse to appreciate the kind of woman Constantia has become—and is yet to become.

IV

....

When Margaret Fuller (1810–1850), the greatest feminist thinker of her age, reviewed a reprint of *Ormond* and *Wieland* in 1846, she greeted Brown as a kindred spirit: "it increases our own interest in Brown that, a prophet in this respect of a better era, he has usually placed his thinking royal mind in the body of a woman...a conclusive proof that the term *feminine* is not a synonym for *weak*" (Fuller 63). If Fuller had known *Alcuin*, she might also have recognized in Mrs. Carter's constitutional critique and realistic assessment of women's roles the ideas of her friend Neal, himself an avid reader of Brown's novels and an unbending advocate of women's rights in his own time. Brown anticipated Fuller by almost half a century in insisting that the constraints that contemporary gender roles imposed on women were neither divinely ordained nor naturally given but were only the result of habit and tradition and therefore changeable. Seeing these constraints held up against the idea of a rational, self-governing republic, Brown's readers could judge for themselves why and how they would need to be changed.

NOTES

1. This chapter includes language from Fleischmann 1983 and 2000.
2. For an overview, see Ferguson 80–123; quotation from Otis on 96.
3. Paradigmatic for this position is the reasoning John Adams gave against extending political rights to new categories of persons. In his response on April 14, 1776, to his wife Abigail's famous request to "remember the ladies" in the new nation's laws, John Adams grants that his "masculine systems" are the product of convention and nothing else but still defends social hierarchy as a guarantor of peace and order. This is one of the arguments raised in *Alcuin* to justify voting restrictions. See Ferguson 150–191 for an illuminating overview of the parallels between the (lack of) rights of Indians, slaves, and women.
4. Susan Branson found that while most American magazines of the 1780s and '90s favored the status quo for women, new ideas were in circulation: "Accepted or not, Wollstonecraft's ideas reached a broad audience" (Branson 50).
5. On Wollstonecraft's reception in the United States during the 1790s, see Janes; Thiébaux; C. M. Brown; Branson. For fuller discussions of women's rights in the early republic, see Branson; Botting; Ferguson; McMahon; Zagarri.
6. According to Philip Barnard and Stephen Shapiro, Brown was a lifelong progressive who dealt with the conservative reaction strategically by making his fictions deliberately readable in opposite ways. "Fictions are...narrative experiments" for Brown, "a form of conjectural or counterfactual history" (Barnard and Shapiro xxvii). This reading develops a line of Brown scholarship that goes back at least to Warner Berthoff, who had described for Brown a "method in fiction": the use of narrative as "an instrument for *discovering* ideas, for exploring and testing them out" (Berthoff 46). Although, for a writer, the membrane between "method" and "strategy" is thin, Brown's lifelong commitment "to the postulates of the Enlightenment" (Harry Levin, quoted in Verhoeven 10) is beyond doubt.
7. Elihu Hubbard Smith reports some early reader responses to Parts I and II of *Alcuin* in his August 25, 1798, letter to Brown: "Some difference of opinion exists, as to the merits of the

respecting arguments; some doubt the soundness of your conclusions" (Letters 386). On August 29, he reports that "Mrs. S. Johnson" (wife of his friend Seth Johnson) "is anxious to know how all this is to end. She ... thinks there is much truth delivered on either side of the debate: but is at a loss to know what is the writer's ultimate design. From what she has seen, she infers his object to be to render women satisfied with their present civil condition. I cannot pretend to enlighten her" (Letters 393).

8. Part III and possibly Part IV were not published until five years after Brown's death, when a long section III was included in the Allen/Dunlap biography. Whether there was yet another part of *Alcuin* that Dunlap chose not to publish in 1815 "remains an open question" (Letters 405 n. 3). For the full publication history, see the Kent State edition's "Textual Essay" by S. W. Reid and "Historical Essay" by Robert D. Arner.

9. "Reading *Alcuin* in book form," Catherine O'Donnell Kaplan writes, "one cannot but expect resolution." Since Brown himself authorized the *Weekly Magazine* publication and since he may have intended to sell it as a serial to Joseph Dennie's *Farmer's Weekly Museum* (Dunlap 1930, 133), Kaplan thinks that with intended serial publication, Brown may have been writing "for a genre that demanded ever more writing, not climax and conclusion" (Kaplan 82).

   For the changes Brown made for the *Weekly Magazine*, see Arner 290–298. Arner sees these alterations driven by "the wish to remove from 'The Rights of Women' any references that could in any way be construed as espousing radical republican views, particularly those that might be seen to tie the dialogue to American supporters of the French Revolution" (294).

10. This character is named after a contemporary of Brown's, the poet, translator, and bluestocking Elizabeth Carter (1717–1806). In "Henrietta Letter" VII, Brown calls her "[t]he deepest of female Scholars" yet "still a woman" with "all the delicacies of her sex" (Letters 687).

11. The name refers to the Carolingian scholar Alcuin (c. 735–804), a native of Northumbria, later abbot of St. Martin at Tours, whose works include educational treatises in dialogue form. In the *Weekly Magazine* version, the name is changed to Edwin.

12. In the "Henrietta Letters," probably composed and revised between 1788 and 1792, the character "C.B.B." writes that he "never conceived that the minds of women were naturally inferior to those of Men" (Letters 720). Henrietta is thus an early instance of Brown's fictional women who can hold their own in a debate.

13. Dangerous not only because it suggests an intellectual position that Mrs. Carter is not ready to embrace but also because Alcuin has been flirting with her, in which situation this line of suggestion may develop "into a genuine if temporary threat to her chastity" (Arner 285). For more on the perceived dangers of mixed-sex friendship, see Waterman.

14. Of course, these are not the only ones, as Borghi and others have shown, nor is there complete agreement on the weight they carry. Teute, for example, argues that *Alcuin* should be read not so much in the context of Wollstonecraft and Godwin but against Erasmus Darwin's notion that all natural organization arises from sex and that affection pervades the universe.

15. E. H. Smith refers to Hays in two letters to Brown (Letters 387, 393).

16. In his "Historical Essay," Arner reviews *Alcuin* scholarship through 1982. Substantial discussions since then include Fleischmann 1983; Vickers; Amfreville; Kierner; Schloss; Teute; Edwards; Kafer; Kaplan; Botting; Waterman.

17. For an extended discussion, see Fleischmann 2000.

18. See Barnard and Shapiro for an overview of the novel's themes, issues, and contexts.

19. Readings of Martinette, in particular, diverge widely. Kristin Comment sees her as "a figure of sexual excess" held up as a warning (Comment 65). Paul Lewis, by contrast, thinks that Martinette, "for all her deviation from gender norms, serves neither as monster nor villain but as role model" (Lewis 40). Hana Layson thinks that "Brown's meditation of sexual injury becomes sharply critical of republican masculinity and rationality and of Wollstonecraft for so eagerly embracing them" (Layson 163). For the most consistently progressive reading, see Barnard and Shapiro xxvii–xxxi.

20. Abandoning Helena for Constantia, a woman who is his mental equal, does not mean that Ormond abandons his wish to control. As a case study of patriarchal narcissism, *Ormond* anticipates (and perhaps helped to inspire) the tales of Brown's admirer John Neal (1793–1876), who developed the problem of the male would-be feminist in such tales as "Idiosyncrasies" and "Ruth Elder." See Fleischmann 2012.

21. Dudley's narcissism seems mitigated by the fact that he has given his daughter an enlightened education not usually available to women. But the point is that even enlightened men cannot shed the sense of entitlement that is part of their gendering. Versions of such entitlement from the same period of Brown's writing can also be found among the men in "A Lesson on Concealment; or, Memoirs of Mary Selwyn," published in the March 1800 number of Brown's *Monthly Magazine*. Other examples are Jane's weak father and rakish brother in *Jane Talbot* (1801), counterpointed by the male feminist Colden.

22. On this theme in *Wieland* and *Carwin*, see Van Leeuwen 10. For Ludloe as double-tongued reformer in *Carwin*, see Edwards 290 ff.; Tupan 45–46.

WORKS CITED

Amfreville, Marc. "Un obscure dialogue au siècle des Lumières: *Alcuin; or, The Rights of Women* de Charles Brockden Brown." *Revue française d'études américaines* 92 (2002): 86–97.

Arner, Robert D. "Historical Essay." In Charles Brockden Brown, *Alcuin; A Dialogue with Memoirs of Stephen Calvert*, Vol. 6 of *The Novels and Related Works of Charles Brockden Brown*, Sydney J. Krause and S. W. Reid, eds., 273–312. Kent, Ohio: Kent State University Press, 1987.

Barnard, Philip, and Stephen Shapiro. "Introduction." In Charles Brockden Brown, *Ormond; or, The Secret Witness, with Related Texts*, ix–lii. Indianapolis: Hackett, 2009.

Bayless, Martha. "Alcuin's *Disputatio Pippini* and the Early Medieval Riddle Tradition." In Guy Halsall, ed., *Humor, History and Politics in Late Antiquity and the Early Middle Ages*, 157–179. Cambridge: Cambridge University Press, 2002.

Berthoff, Warner. "'A Lesson on Concealment': Brockden Brown's Method in Fiction." *Philological Quarterly* 37 (1957): 45–57.

Borghi, Liana. *Dialogue in Utopia: Manners, Purpose and Structure in Three Feminist Works of the 1790s*. Pisa: ETS, 1984.

Botting, Eileen Hunt. "Protofeminist Responses to the Federalist-Antifederalist Debate." In Ian Shapiro, ed., *The Federalist Papers*, 533–558. New Haven, Conn.: Yale University Press, 2009.

Branson, Susan. *These Fiery Frenchified Dames: Women and Political Culture in Early National Philadelphia*. Philadelphia: University of Pennsylvania Press, 2001.

Brown, Chandos Michael. "Mary Wollstonecraft, or, the Female Illuminati: The Case against Women and 'Modern Philosophy' in the Early Republic." *Journal of the Early Republic* 15 (Fall 1995): 389–424.

Brown, Charles Brockden. "The Editors' Address to the Public." LM 1.1 (October 1803): 3–6.

Brown, Charles Brockden. "A Lesson on Concealment; or, Memoirs of Mary Selwyn." MM 2.3 (March 1800): 174–207.

Comment, Kristin M. "Charles Brockden Brown's *Ormond* and Lesbian Possibility in the Early Republic." *Early American Literature* 40.1 (2005): 57–78.

Davidson, Cathy N. "The Matter and Manner of Charles Brockden Brown's *Alcuin*." In Bernard Rosenthal, ed., *Critical Essays on Charles Brockden Brown*, 71–86. Boston: G. K. Hall, 1981.

Edwards, Justin D. "Engendering a New Republic: Charles Brockden Brown's *Alcuin, Carwin* and the Legal Fictions of Gender." *Nordic Journal of English Studies* 2.2 (2003): 279–301.

Ferguson, Robert A. *The American Enlightenment, 1750–1820.* Cambridge, Mass.: Harvard University Press, 1994.

Fleischmann, Fritz. "Concealed Lessons: Foster's *Coquette* and Brockden Brown's 'Lesson on Concealment'." In Klaus H. Schmidt and Fritz Fleischmann, eds., *Early America Re-Explored: New Readings in Colonial, Early National, and Antebellum Culture*, 309–348. New York: Peter Lang, 2000.

Fleischmann, Fritz. "'A Right Manly Man' in 1843: John Neal on Women's Rights, Masculinity, and the Problem of Male Feminism." In Edward Watts and David Carlson, eds., *John Neal and Nineteenth-Century American Literature and Culture*, 247–270. Lewisburg, Pa.: Bucknell University Press, 2012.

Fleischmann, Fritz. *A Right View of the Subject: Feminism in the Works of Charles Brockden Brown and John Neal.* Erlanger Studien 47. Erlangen: Palm & Enke, 1983.

Fuller, Margaret. Review of *Wieland* and *Ormond*, both reprinted in New York by W. Taylor, 1846. *New-York Daily Tribune* (July 21, 1846): 1; reprinted, *New-York Weekly Tribune* (July 25, 1846): 1. In "American Literature," *Papers on Literature and Art* (1846), 2: 146–150. Reprinted in Bernard Rosenthal, ed., *Critical Essays on Charles Brockden Brown*, 62–64. Boston: G. K. Hall, 1981.

Janes, Regina M. "On the Reception of Mary Wollstonecraft's *A Vindication of the Rights of Woman*." *Journal of the History of Ideas* 39 (1978): 293–302.

Kafer, Peter. *Charles Brockden Brown's Revolution and the Birth of American Gothic.* Philadelphia: University of Pennsylvania Press, 2004.

Kaplan, Catherine O'Donnell. *Men of Letters in the Early Republic: Cultivating Forums of Citizenship.* Chapel Hill: University of North Carolina Press, 2008.

Kelley, Mary. "'Vindicating the Equality of Female Intellect': Women and Authority in the Early Republic." *Prospects* 17 (October 1992): 1–27.

Kierner, Cynthia A. "Introduction." In Charles Brockden Brown, *Alcuin; A Dialogue*, Cynthia A. Kierner, ed., 3–40. Lanham, Md.: Rowman and Littlefield, 1995.

Krause, Sydney J. "Brockden Brown's Feminism in Fact and Fiction." In Klaus H. Schmidt and Fritz Fleischmann, eds., *Early America Re-Explored: New Readings in Colonial, Early National, and Antebellum Culture*, 349–384. New York: Peter Lang, 2000.

Krause, Sydney J. "Historical Notes." In Charles Brockden Brown, *Ormond; or, The Secret Witness*, Vol. 2 of Sydney J. Krause and S. W. Reid, eds., *The Novels and Related Works of Charles Brockden Brown*, 389–478. Kent, Ohio: Kent State University Press, 1982.

Layson, Hana. "Rape and Revolution: Feminism, Antijacobinism, and the Politics of Injured Innocence in Brockden Brown's *Ormond*." *Early American Studies* 2.1 (Spring 2004): 160–191.

Lewis, Paul. "Charles Brockden Brown and the Gendered Canon of Early American Fiction." *Early American Literature* 31 (1996): 167–188.

[M., L.]. "Reflections on the Character of MARY WOLLSTONECRAFT GODWIN." MM 1.5 (August 1799): 330–335.

McMahon, Lucia. *Mere Equals: The Paradox of Educated Women in the Early American Republic*. Ithaca, N.Y.: Cornell University Press, 2012.

Murray, Judith Sargent. *The Gleaner*. Introductory essay by Nina Baym. Schenectady, N.Y.: Union College Press, 1992.

Schloss, Dietmar. "Intellectuals and Women: Social Rivalry in Charles Brockden Brown's *Alcuin*." In Udo J. Hebel, ed., *The Construction and Contestation of American Cultures and Identities in the Early National Period*, 355–369. Heidelberg: Winter, 1999.

Stern, Julia. "The State of 'Women' in *Ormond*; or, Patricide in the New Nation." In Philip Barnard, Mark L. Kamrath, and Stephen Shapiro, eds., *Revising Charles Brockden Brown: Culture, Politics, and Sexuality in the Early Republic*, 182–215. Knoxville: University of Tennessee Press, 2004.

Taylor, Barbara. *Mary Wollstonecraft and the Feminist Imagination*. Cambridge: Cambridge University Press, 2003.

Teute, Fredrika J. "A 'Republic of Intellect': Conversation and Criticism among the Sexes in 1790s New York." In Philip Barnard, Mark L. Kamrath, and Stephen Shapiro, eds., *Revising Charles Brockden Brown: Culture, Politics, and Sexuality in the Early Republic*, 149–181. Knoxville: University of Tennessee Press, 2004.

Thièbaux, Marcelle. "Mary Wollstonecraft in Federalist America 1791–1802." In Donald H. Reiman et al., eds., *The Evidence of the Imagination: Studies of Interaction between Life and Art in English Romantic Literature*, 195–245. New York: New York University Press, 1978.

Tupan, Maria-Ana. *Genre and Postmodernism*. Bucharest: Editura Universității din București, 2008.

Van Leeuwen, Evert Jan. "'Though Hermes Never Taught Thee': The Anti-Patriarchal Tendency of Charles Brockden Brown's Mercurial Outcast Carwin, the Biloquist." *European Journal of American Studies* 1 (2010): 2–15.

Verhoeven, W. M. "'This Blissful Period of Intellectual Liberty': Transatlantic Radicalism and Enlightened Conservatism in Brown's Early Writings." In Philip Barnard, Mark L. Kamrath, and Stephen Shapiro, eds., *Revising Charles Brockden Brown: Culture, Politics, and Sexuality in the Early Republic*, 7–40. Knoxville: University of Tennessee Press, 2004.

Vickers, Anita M. "'Pray, Madam, Are You a Federalist?' Women's Rights and the Republican Utopia of *Alcuin*." *American Studies* 39.3 (Fall 1998): 89–104.

Waterman, Bryan. "'The Sexual Difference': Gender, Politeness, and Conversation in Late-Eighteenth-Century New York City and in Charles Brockden Brown's *Alcuin* (1798)." In Marguérite Corporaal and Evert Jan van Leeuwen, eds., *Literary Utopias of Cultural Communities, 1790–1910*, 23–46. Amsterdam: Rodopi, 2010.

Watts, Steven. *The Romance of Real Life: Charles Brockden Brown and the Origins of American Culture*. Baltimore: Johns Hopkins University Press, 1994.

Zagarri, Rosemarie. *Revolutionary Backlash: Women and Politics in the Early American Republic*. Philadelphia: University of Pennsylvania Press, 2007.

CHAPTER 19

SLAVERY, ABOLITION, AND AFRICAN AMERICANS IN BROWN

LEONARD VON MORZÉ

I. QUAKERISM AND ABOLITION

THANKS to Peter Kafer's 2004 study, the embeddedness of Charles Brockden Brown's fiction in the history of Pennsylvania Quakerism now seems clearer than ever. For Brown, one of the more complex legacies of Quaker history was the role that Africans played in it. While Quakers were the most reliably abolitionist among the major Christian denominations of the eighteenth century, their century-long preeminence in Atlantic commerce also included some involvement in the slave trade. In addition to high-stakes investments in West Indian commerce, the Brown family had some history of managing slave plantations. Brown's ancestor and namesake Charles Brockden (1683–1769) established a small plantation near Williamstown, New Jersey, east of the Delaware River, and owned at least one slave who was later manumitted by the Moravians (Clement 185–188). While the Philadelphia Quaker Meeting, the denomination's most important organizational entity, voted to bar slave owners from its ranks in 1774, Brown's eldest brother, Joseph, acquired many slaves by way of marriage in 1794. Charles expressed some unease on hearing the news; the event may have inspired an episode in the *Memoirs of Stephen Calvert*.[1] The questions raised by this family history haunted Brown's fiction, a key instance of his fascination with patriarchal legacies, surprise obligations, and the fate of laborers.

By the time of Brown's youth, the Quakers were fairly united in their abolitionist commitments, but they were no longer in a political position to implement reforms in a newly democratized Pennsylvania state legislature. Thus, a 1780 Pennsylvania law providing for the gradual abolition of slavery (the first in the new nation) reflected Quaker weakness rather than strength, insofar as it did less than later ordinances in other

Northern states to ensure the manumission of slaves (Nash 62–63). Pacifism was one main pillar of belief on which Quaker abolitionists took their stand; they recognized that the enslavement of Africans instigated internecine conflicts among African nations.[2] Quakers thought of slaves as morally damaged by their bondage, and they committed themselves to remedying the perceived ignorance of the newly free. A "paternalistic attitude" that Gary Nash calls uniquely Quaker often met with resistance from African Americans, who could not be blamed for finding themselves more at home with the message of personal deliverance to be found among Methodists and Baptists. It is perhaps unsurprising, then, that Quakers counted relatively few African Americans among their ranks (Nash 89–90).

Many of the young men in Brown's circle found themselves similarly resisting religious paternalism. Though not himself a Quaker, Brown's friend and mentor Elihu Hubbard Smith, for example, privately noted his dismay at a traveling party of British Quaker women who approached him "for an opportunity of addressing some advice to the *Blacks*"; he reported that the resulting discourse, delivered to one thousand African American listeners, contained "some appropriate advice" but also "ravings of the most absurd mysticism in terms full of metaphor; & in tones, hardly intelligible" (Smith, 130). In such cases, African American resistance to theological paternalism helped young white intellectuals to gain their own critical distance from church authorities. Smith was convinced of abolitionists' responsibility to create conditions in which African Americans could become, as he explained in print, their own "instructors in learning, and inculcators of morality" (Smith 1798, 28).

For all of Brown's critical distance from the paternalism of Quaker leadership, his fiction also demonstrates an awareness of Quakers' extraordinary commitment to the education of African Americans. Brown attended the Friends Latin School on Fourth and Chestnut at a time when the aging Anthony Benezet was still teaching just a couple of blocks away at the African School House in Willing's Alley. Quaker abolitionist Benezet (1713–1784) taught at both schools and is the most likely model for the mission of Edgar Huntly's dear friend Waldegrave, whose "religious duty compelled him to seek his livelihood by teaching a school of blacks" (EH 143). Despite continual struggles with money, the institution attracted visits from a wide range of Enlightenment observers, such as Benjamin Franklin and Brissot de Warville, who were interested in this demonstration of Africans' capacity for reason (Hornick 417).

The social issues affecting Philadelphia's black community were, then, not limited to slavery. Though, of course, slavery imperiled even free blacks, the institution was in rapid decline in the city by 1800, thanks to the Gradual Abolition Act passed twenty years earlier. The Free African Society, an influential group of the black elite formed in 1787, noted with alarm the growing antiblack sentiment among whites, especially among recent immigrants who competed with blacks for jobs. Though the most frightening manifestations of this trend appeared in the decades following Brown's death, some of the signs were already visible, particularly in executive and legislative attempts to limit black mobility to and around the state. Other states made less progress; in a footnote to his *Discourse*, Smith lamented in 1798 that the New York Senate had recently rejected an emancipation bill, the final version of which would not be passed for almost twenty more years.

II. Abolition in Brown's Circle

Brown never became a member of one of the era's many abolition societies. However, many of his closest associates from the 1780s on were engaged in various abolitionist projects, in which they attempted to enlist Brown.[3] The diaries of Elihu Hubbard Smith (which ends with Smith's death in 1798), Thomas Pim Cope (which begins in 1800), and William Dunlap (which extends throughout Brown's adult life) are particularly rich guides to abolitionist engagements in Brown's circle. In the 1790s, several of Brown's friends, including his eventual roommates Smith and William Johnson, were elected officers of the Manumission Society of New York, which published abolitionist addresses and maintained a school for the children of slaves. Society member Dunlap stayed with Brown in 1797 when he visited a gathering of abolition societies in Philadelphia. Abolitionism was the single most important political project linking these men across the lines of religion, party, and city of origin that otherwise separated them.

The major achievement of the Manumission Society of New York was its arrangement of education for freed blacks, but historians have cast some doubt on the coherence of its remaining activities. Far more lax than the Quaker Meeting, the Manumission Society condoned slaveholding among its members, a measure it deemed necessary for the formation of a large association in New York, which had, in the 1790s, more slaves than any other US city besides Charleston. More worrisome than the implicit acceptance of hypocrisy was the Manumission Society's arguable contribution to a political discourse for which Northern slavery could be seen as acceptable and humane precisely insofar as it exposed the brutality of its Southern counterpart (White 81–88).

Under such conditions, Brown's nonmembership in the Manumission Society might be read as a principled stance; the organization's contribution to establishing a regional distinction between North and South, in particular, is undermined in Brown's novel *Stephen Calvert*. In his home town of Philadelphia, Brown would have found an environment in which covert abolitionist practice supplemented the antislavery public sphere. Quaker tailor Isaac Hopper was the city's key player in the Underground Railroad which conducted slaves to the North; it has been suggested that the mysterious hiding place described at the end of the First Part of *Arthur Mervyn* represents a way-station on Hopper's railroad.[4] In the city's public life, the Pennsylvania Society for Promoting the Abolition of Slavery (or PAS, revived in 1784) could be seen as significantly more advanced in its moral integrity (few members owned slaves) than its New York counterpart.[5] As secretary of PAS, Walter Franklin, Brown's former classmate at the Friends Latin School and a member of its debating society, assisted in bringing numerous lawsuits to Pennsylvania's highest courts on behalf of slaves who sought emancipation. Beginning in 1794, Franklin argued a case against the constitutionality of slavery itself in *Flora v. Graisberry*, which took eight years before the High Court of Errors and Appeals finally rejected his arguments in 1802 (Letters 99 n. 4, 236 n. 8).

PAS efforts did not end after this setback. The journal of Thomas Pim Cope, whom Brown called his "best friend" on his deathbed (Cope 249), is a particularly sensitive record of the multifarious strategies of a leading PAS member, abounding as it does with responses to news reports of slave insurrections, firsthand observations of gratuitous cruelty against slaves, and notes on PAS organizational activities. A passionate abolitionist convinced of his friend's genius, Cope recorded in 1803 that he had made Brown "the offer of writing the History of Slavery" and that Brown had accepted. To his chagrin, however, Cope repeatedly noted that Brown made "small progress" on the volume (139, 182). Cope attributed Brown's breaking of "his plighted word" not to his friend's wavering on the importance of abolition but to his Godwinian freethinking which allowed him to dishonor promises and to prefer the world of the imagination to the responsibilities of "common life" (192, 174). From Cope's perspective, Brown's inability to complete the projected "History of Slavery" reflected his lamentable addiction to imaginative writing. Yet Brown's novels, as we will see, engage thoughtfully with the abolitionist movement; *Calvert* would be particularly valuable to the abolitionist movement as a critique of Northern complacency.

III. Redrawing the Lines: *Memoirs of Stephen Calvert*

Published in eight installments of the *Monthly Magazine* in 1799–1800, *Memoirs of Stephen Calvert* is Brown's fullest fictive representation of slavery. The story resists easy summary. Separated early in life from his identical twin brother, Felix, Stephen is renamed Felix in his brother's honor (to avoid confusion, however, I will continue to refer to the narrator-protagonist as Stephen). Stephen's renaming represents the family's attempt to recover a lost felicity in Pennsylvania, to which they relocate in an effort to escape a tangled family history. Stephen and Felix have had to be separated because classic battle lines within European society—Catholic versus Protestant, French versus English—have divided their family. This family history inverts traditional cultural alignments so thoroughly as to confound even Brown's most careful readers.[6] The first Calvert in America is one Gaspard Calvert, a French Huguenot who flees persecution around 1705 and founds Calverton in Pennsylvania, a slave plantation whose location will turn out to be crucial to the narrative. The Protestant Gaspard Calvert's act of settlement inverts the seventeenth-century story of the foundation of Maryland by the historical Calverts, English Catholics. Closer to the present is the secret marriage of the narrator's father, a Catholic Englishman named Stephen Porter, to a Protestant Frenchwoman, probably in the 1740s, inverting the familiar cultural narrative of Frenchwomen seducing Englishmen toward Catholicism. The narrator's grandfather, meanwhile, is a tyrannical Gothic figure who is about to complete a Jacobite terrorist plot to restore the Catholic pretender Charles Stuart to the British throne and to avenge Catholics' stolen birthrights.[7]

The narrator's father seeks to establish his family's freedom from its entanglement in European history by resettling near Philadelphia. Soon after their emigration, however, he dies mysteriously, a presumptive victim of his own father's vengeance. This event is followed in the narrative by another example of "paternal tyranny" (SC 100) that is equally disturbing, the abuse one Ambrose Calvert visits on his daughters. A distant relative of Stephen, Ambrose has taken over Calverton from his father-in-law, Gaspard. Ambrose's management of his slaves is a reign of terror whose victims include his own children. Utterly dissipated, Ambrose exults in inflicting physical tortures on slaves with his own hands. Brown reinforces that familiar inversion by which the slave owner becomes "the slave of ferocious and immitigable passions" until he dies, it seems, from sheer exhaustion (SC 98). Though Brown did not have to read Thomas Jefferson's *Notes on the State of Virginia* (1785) to develop the image, Ambrose's abuse recalls Jefferson's famous observation that "the whole commerce between master and slave is a perpetual exercise of the most boisterous passions" (Jefferson 236). Stephen's obvious compassion for the sufferings of Ambrose's white daughter Louisa at the hands of her father recalls Jefferson's exclusive concern about the damage to the character of the slave owner's children. Jefferson fails to mention that those children typically included slaves, and Brown goes beyond Jefferson in exposing Ambrose's sexual domination over his slaves. Althea, playmate and later maid to Louisa, has a complexion that betrays Ambrose's paternity. In a critical scene, Ambrose inflicts injuries on Althea that prove fatal while his acknowledged daughter Louisa looks on in horror (SC 102).

What does Ambrose's story have to do with the European backstory of political intrigue? The latter has introduced a set of historical realignments that Brown's plantation Gothic now extends to the division between North and South. Robert D. Arner observes that the family backstory reveals the extent to which an American ideology of innocence depends on its negative relation to European history. Stephen the narrator is guilty of "sentimental pastoralism" insofar as he symbolizes an America in flight from what Stephen himself calls "paternal vengeance" (SC 83).[8] Though Arner does not mention the subplot involving the slave plantation, this episode in the novel further undermines American pastoralism, remapping the history-versus-innocence opposition in relation to North and South. Brown indicates the cartographic location of Ambrose Calvert's plantation with care, suggesting that it straddles a key boundary line in early America. Early in the novel, the reader learns that Calverton is "on the bank of Delaware, just below its conflux with Schuylkill" (76).

The site's location in a Philadelphia suburb defamiliarizes readers' conception of the boundaries of the South, as established by the well-known separation of Maryland from Pennsylvania through the greatest of American boundary lines, the Mason-Dixon survey of 1763–1767, which had been prompted by a long dispute between the Calvert and Penn families. If Mason-Dixon was not yet shorthand for the North-South divide in Brown's day, it is nonetheless significant that the time of the narrative can be (very roughly) dated to the period of the line's survey, suggesting that *Calvert* undertakes a ghostly retracing of its cartographic coordinates, much as Edgar does in sleepwalking across the lines of the Walking Purchase in *Edgar Huntly*. Just as that earlier survey had done, Mason and Dixon had left their mark on Brown's family history. Brown's father, Elijah, had been raised in Nottingham, Pennsylvania, a village southwest of Philadelphia, which was divided by the surveyors into two separate towns in Maryland and Pennsylvania.[9]

The Mason-Dixon Line assumed a new importance in Brown's adulthood. After Pennsylvania began to abolish slavery, the boundary separating Pennsylvania and Maryland would mark the line between slavery and freedom. The cultural difference between North and South was, however, was not so clear in Brown's mind. While the name Calvert was closely linked to the fortunes of Maryland, Brown makes a point of locating Calverton on the Northern side of the line. Ambrose the Pennsylvanian is nonetheless represented as a "Southern"–style slave owner in the cultural codes of early America. Thus, Brown probes the purpose of representations of the difference between Northern and Southern slavery, as they were being formulated by his friends in the New York Manumission Society or by writers such as J. Hector St. John de Crèvecoeur, author of *Letters from an American Farmer* (1782). Crèvecoeur's Farmer James is a model yeoman who is nonetheless an owner of slaves, making his representation of the horrors of Southern slavery appear to validate an opposition between a Southern violent slavery and a gentler Northern version. As though in response to such a self-serving region-alism, Brown represents a Pennsylvania farmer in Ambrose who would fit well in Crèvecoeur's nightmarish Charleston. The inversion of historical boundary lines within the Calvert family tree upsets, then, the comforting notion of the *containability* of slavery—the hope that it might be kept within the boundaries of the South, just as a strong sense of regional identity was developing in early American culture.

These boundaries are not clarified by Stephen Calvert's accession to Calverton. Coming on the heels of his father's mysterious death, Stephen's inheritance owes symbolically to the murderous action of his tyrannical grandfather. Inheriting fifteen slaves, Stephen appears prepared to turn the plantation to "far better uses" than the previous owner (106).[10] Stephen wishes to marry Ambrose's disinherited daughter Louisa in order to transfer the property. His recognition that his proposal is morally suspect, insofar as it would allow him to maintain his control of Calverton, comes to him only after meeting Louisa and finding her ugly (114). Even his moral scruples, then, seem designed to facilitate the pursuit of deeper unexamined desires, while the ethical project of restitution leaves unperformed the higher duty of manumission. Just as Stephen is about to propose half-heartedly to Louisa, Stephen is saved by the apparent epistemological clarity afforded by his rescue of the lovely Clelia Neville from a house fire on High Street in Philadelphia. The consequent publication of a news story about this act of heroism leads to an extended passage of African American dialect, rare in Brown. The event gets into the newspapers because one of Stephen's slaves, Cuff, relates to a companion the conversation he had with another slave while they watched Stephen's heroic act. This relation is, in turn, over-heard by a newspaper editor:

"Ou' pop a man! uppa de latha like a rat. Ob bobs! what de debble! 'Prime,' says I, 'is'n da massa Cavut? No! ees! ees! it ee massa Cavut. What de debble if ee see me? teh Ceesa gim me floggin! Way! scampa! scud!'

" 'No, no,' says Prime: 'top; he be kill. Run uppa de latha. Massa Cavut sure enough.'

"So I top. Ebba body olla, Downa, downa! Massa Cavut no ere em: run uppa lika querril up oaka tree. No debble runna like im. In ee pop. No liffa de winda, but in ee pop, trough glass and all. Quash! ebba body olla. Prime olla. Me olla mo dan ebba body—'O massa Cavut! massa Cavut!'—Massa Cavut era no body bum me. So ou' pop massa wid 'oman in 'is 'and. Down de latha ee runna, mo fass dan ebba—'oman in 'is 'and 'till. Den I runna too; fear ee see me: teh Ceesa gim me floggin."

"Pray," said the apprentice, "who are you talking of, Blackee? the man who got the girl out of the window t'other night, at the fire? Do you know who he was?"
"Be sure I do. He my massa: ung massa Cavut. He be lif oba Kukill. I be lif wid im. He be come estaday oba de watta."

"Massa Cavut" was translated by a market-man, who lived near Chester, into Mr. Felix Calvert: and this intelligence being transferred to the printer, it found its way, by his contrivance, to the public.   (128)

For Stephen, the episode humorously confirms that a true account of an event sometimes does emerge, despite multiple narrators and the many false versions that also circulate. Yet Stephen also fails to examine the parts of the discourse that do not relate to his heroism. The newspaper apprentice, for example, interprets "de watta" not as the Schuylkill but as the Atlantic, resulting in the printed misinformation that the heroic savior of Clelia is "lately from Europe" (127), an important clue that his twin brother is already in town. The black dialect also indicates the speakers' precarious social position. Cuff's first thought is that he will be seen by Stephen and whipped by Caesar, Calverton's overseer, to whom Stephen has delegated the punishments once executed by Ambrose. Little wonder that Prime's shocking attempt to reassure Cuff consists of asserting the likelihood of Stephen's death. Cuff's discourse undermines Stephen's claim that he has put the institution of slavery on a new, humane basis. Despite Stephen's promise that upon his inheriting them, "the slaves will henceforth receive the treatment that was due to men" (106), Cuff anticipates a whipping, a fear likely to be realized now that the story has been transmitted to Stephen. For readers attentive to the tale's geography, the episode also provides concrete evidence of the plantation's location in the heart of Pennsylvania Quaker country. If Calvert had to cross "oba de...Kukill" (that is, the Schuylkill River), to arrive on High Street in Philadelphia, then the plantation must be to the southwest; if it were in New Jersey, Cuff would have instead have spoken of the Delaware River. The role of a market man familiar with the name of Felix Calvert further specifies Chester, Pennsylvania, as Calverton's probable location.

Cuff's expression of fear challenges the self-satisfaction of the Northern plantation owner who has his slaves whipped just outside the City of Brotherly Love. That Stephen has inherited, rather than purchased, his slaves simply makes his relationship to slavery one of psychological disavowal rather than rationalized exploitation, which is consistent with the theme of the evil twin. Stephen never completes his project of returning Calverton to Louisa and reveals little subsequent interest in his plantation. As Stephen weighs his options near the end of the narrative, his treatment of Calverton is a study in geographical containment. He sees that his three residences in the Delaware Valley correspond to three possibilities of *Bildung*: he could remain a "juvenile" in his mother's home in New Jersey, he could become a citizen in Philadelphia, or he could embrace the role of a "proprietor of spacious fields, and the master of a numerous household at Calverton" (248). None of these destinies appears, in the end, desirable, including the patriarchal form of slave owning. Just a few pages later, Stephen will flee to Europe; and though he quickly returns to America, his mysterious eventual relocation to the wilderness of Michigan (unexplained in the incomplete narrative we have), where all the fruits of his farm are "the product of my own labour" (71), suggests that he has sought to escape the corruptive influence of slavery.

The geographical confusion implied by the location of the Pennsylvania plantation continues to affect Stephen during his errant courtship of Clelia Neville. He describes his inability to win her as a confusion of the cardinal directions: "The wisest and soberest of human beings is, in some respects, a madman; that is, he acts against his better reason, and his feet stand still, or go south, when every motive is busy in impelling him north" (179–180). If his courtship cannot avoid going south, it is because the slave plantation whose stewardship he seems to have forgotten is not geographically containable; the elements of what may be called a plantation Gothic are culturally marked as Southern but actually stem from a site on the Northern side of the Mason-Dixon Line. So disoriented is Stephen that he is characterized as a "slave" four times in the context of romantic courtship and the questions of property that marriage entails; he seems to move in all directions at once, subject to the changing winds of his passions (108, 124, 138, 144). While it is, of course, preposterous and offensive for a slave owner to identify himself with the condition of being chattel, Stephen functions as a psychological prop for others, a replacement for the missing Felix, or the lost happiness, of his parents and of Clelia herself, who carries a portrait of the original Felix in her bosom. Perhaps, as one rumor suggested, Clelia's rescuer is, in some sense, an emancipated slave, another of Stephen's doubles (126). The representation of black and white characters as doubles is developed in the two novels to which we now turn.

IV. *ARTHUR MERVYN* AND *ORMOND*

As novels that may be called realist, both *Arthur Mervyn* and *Ormond* feature narrators and characters who visually scrutinize the world; likewise, both works situate their action in three specific historical contexts relevant to this chapter: Atlantic slavery, the Haitian Revolution, and the 1793 yellow fever epidemic. While these contexts went unnoted by academics working on Brown until a brief 1970 article by Charles Bennett that was the first to discuss Brown's racial politics, they now inform much of the interpretative work on these two novels.

The financial intrigue at the heart of *Arthur Mervyn* can now be recognized as a consequence of the exploitation of Atlantic slave labor, the transformation of human beings into capital. Caribbean slave labor provides the characters with their sources of capital and figures in the novel's central image of "horrible corruption" (AM 252). Wrapped in rolls of lead around the rotting corpse of Amos Watson are bills of exchange worth ten thousand pounds sterling from the sale of a Jamaica plantation. Thomas Welbeck has killed Watson and left him beneath the house like an African encased in a slave ship, enacting symbolic vengeance for the Middle Passage (Shapiro 285). The sale of another slave plantation, this one in Guadeloupe, is the source of the capital Vincentio Lodi has stashed in the leaves of a book. Lodi's father had been killed by a slave to whom he promised freedom but whom he later betrayed. Thus, the novel condenses the history of white flight from the Caribbean, as Europeans sought to take profits from the immensely wealthy colonies, selling to ever more adventurous risk-takers willing to hazard retribution at the hands of their slaves. The feverish acceleration of capital flows that resulted from the Haitian Revolution explains much of the novel's interest in the historically novel spectacle of what Arthur calls "floating or transferable wealth" (AM 56). The twin histories of Haiti and the plague are also economically evoked by the name of Dr. Stevens (the original narrator of the tale and Arthur's auditor), referring to Edward Stevens, a doctor-turned-ambassador from the West Indies who prescribed gentler alternatives to Benjamin Rush's doses of mercury and was perhaps the most radically pro-Toussaint of all the American representatives to Haiti (Zuckerman 189–90).

As the most successful slave insurrection in history, the Haitian Revolution functions as another context for *Mervyn*. Political autonomy, which the island's French planters had sought as an end in itself, was for the successful black rebels only a means to secure the complete abolition of slavery. The priority of social transformation meant that the revolution followed the French example rather than the American Revolution. The message that US slaves might not wait for abolitionists to make social change also could hardly be missed. Brown's Philadelphia became the home of many émigrés from the French colony. White planters arrived in large numbers, as did their slaves. Monetary aid flowed from white Philadelphians to the French planters, while their slaves (who actively contested their legal status as chattel, usually becoming servants or free laborers) won little sympathy, even from the city's black community. Shocking the city's residents, Frenchmen openly flaunted their sexual dalliances with "kept" women of color (Branson and Patrick 196–197). Such relationships exposed the monetary basis of relationships between the sexes, demonstrated one possibility of racial coexistence, and challenged the Manichaean dichotomy of black or white, introducing a culture for which subtle distinctions of parentage and skin color assumed enormous importance.

The racial politics of both Haiti and the United States figured in discussions of the causes and the course of the yellow fever epidemic. Some contemporaries believed that the disease arrived on the same vessels that brought French émigrés to the city from Haiti.

Race also figured in the retrospective debate over the contribution of African American workers during the 1793 outbreak of the disease. Encouraging African Americans to demonstrate their gratitude for the steps the state had taken to abolish slavery, prominent doctor Rush enlisted a large number of black volunteers to serve as nurses and doctors, such as the former slave Dr. James Derham. The Free African Society, founded as a mutual aid society for African Americans to help one another, stepped in to assist whites. Observing the resistance to the disease of some of the volunteers (who had likely developed immunity after contracting and surviving the disease in the Caribbean), Rush had surmised that blacks were constitutionally immune to yellow fever, an incorrect conclusion that contributed to more than three hundred fatalities (Powell 254). Despite having fled the city himself, Mathew Carey, the early republic's most successful publisher, printed an account of the outbreak in November 1793 that accused the black workers of profiteering. Two of Philadelphia's most important civic and religious leaders, Absalom Jones and Richard Allen, offered a mildly worded but decisive response, a rejoinder that Carey acknowledged and excerpted. In their response to Carey, Jones and Allen noted that two-thirds of the volunteers serving the sick were persons of color, cited many examples of white profiteering, and described the many casualties the community had suffered in spite of assurances of immunity to the disease.

In representing scenes from the epidemic, Brown generally validates Jones and Allen's contention that blacks had performed selfless service during the 1793 outbreak, with only a few exceptions. Brown leaves no doubt about their other key claim that some whites "acted in a manner that would make humanity shudder" (Jones and Allen 19). Nonetheless, servants are rarely full-fledged characters in Brown, and black servants and slaves are no exception to that pattern. Perfidious whites such as the younger Thetford, who sends a servant girl and a protégé (Wallace) to their graves (though Wallace survives it), suffer vengeance at the hands of black characters, as Thetford's faithful servant is replaced by "a black woman" (AM 160) who, despite the bidding of the generous man Medlicote, refuses to do her duty. The good Medlicote is served, in turn, by "a faithful black, who makes my bed, prepares my coffee, and bakes my loaf" (161). When Brown moves beyond servants and nurses, he offers passing glimpses of a collective identity of free black laborers. He pays special attention to the black cartmen who walked through Philadelphia, carrying the dead, transporting the sick, and sustaining what remained of the city's commerce. Perhaps Brown made them central to his portrait of Philadelphia because he would not have seen them during his time in New York, where African Americans were completely barred from this often well-paying profession; in Philadelphia, by contrast, carting provided one of the few routes to respectability for the black working class (Nash 150). In Chapter V of *Ormond*, the reader becomes acquainted with one black carter who is Constantia's "humble friend" (O 54). Earlier in this chapter, Constantia's white friend Mary Whiston has died from fever after being abandoned by her brother. In a novel full of predatory, faithless males, the carter listens to her tale "with respect" (53) and generously takes away the body of her friend at a time when corpses were thought to be potent carriers of disease. Representing a larger collective of free black labor, the carter offers the reader a glimpse of a social class on the move.

As the spectacle of the carter would suggest, Brown is fascinated by acts of looking, whether studied observation or furtive glances. Brown's analytical prose often takes in subject as well as object, viewer as well as spectacle, producing a realist mode engaged in bilateral experiments with racial character (Otter 58–69). Two scenes of looking have become key loci for interpretations of race in *Arthur Mervyn*. In the first such scene, in the First Part, Chapter 16, Arthur is on his way back to the Thetford residence in an attempt to rescue Wallace. But instead of Wallace, Arthur discovers two men whose characters look transparent rather than ambiguous. They are so starkly opposed that there can be no mistaking them: on the one hand, a supremely unselfish Italian noble-man, so beautiful that Arthur immediately hails him as "one in whose place I would willingly have died"; on the other hand, a perfidious, thieving servant, "a scar upon his cheek, a tawny skin, a form grotesquely misproportioned" (AM 147–148). One man is entirely selfless and dutiful, the other self-interested and faithless. Yet the two merge when Arthur "turns with the swiftness of lightning" toward the "tawny" man in the mir-ror, in the belief that "the dying man had started from his bed and was approaching me" (148). Black and white mirror each other, as though to suggest that Arthur's capacity for elevation as a poor white depends on his difference from those with dark skin.[11] The racially ambiguous term *tawny* is typical of Brown's representational mode. Skin and face often become the object of classificatory activities, particularly with regard to race. Yet phenotype and physiognomy never merely objectify or caricature the racial "other." When John Neal implausibly claimed that Washington Irving's portrait in "Adventures of a Black Fisherman" of "the round black head of Sam" ("his white eyes strained half out of their orbits; his white teeth chattering, and his whole visage shining with cold perspiration") was plagiarized from Brown's description of Carwin's face in *Wieland*, he succeeded in proving only how far removed Brown's representation of the body is from Irving's thoroughly racist caricature of terrified "Mud Sam."[12] For all his protagonists' search for racial difference, they are at least equally interested in racial resemblance. Having seen a "tawny" man in the mirror, Arthur will go on to marry a woman who is "tawney as a Moor," the foreigner Achsa Fielding (AM 432).

In the second scene of looking, in the Second Part, Chapter 17, Arthur sits on a stage-coach "in company with a sallow Frenchman from Saint Domingo, his fiddle-case, an ape, and two female blacks" (370). As they travel together, Arthur attempts "to discern the differences and samenesses" between "the features, proportions, looks, and gestures of the monkey, the Congolese, and the Creole-Gaul" (370). The unlikely presence of the monkey invites us to read the scene as a parody of the taxonomic activity of Enlightenment science. Yet the presence of a similar scene of looking in *Ormond* sug-gests that Brown's abiding interest in the act of visual discrimination was not simply parodic. Brown describes Constantia Dudley's practice of physiognomic reading, the tracing of character from facial features, in almost the same terms as Arthur's. Constantia had often met with faces that "conveyed at a single glance, what could not be imparted by volumes" (O 77), but Martinette de Beauvais's face seems to thwart her attempt at decoding. Representing the heterogeneity of Constantia's thoughts as she looks at her new acquaintance, Brown suggests that her mind becomes as confused as Martinette's features.[13] Fittingly, the reader learns that as Constantia examines the stranger, she is looking into the mirror without knowing it, for the two women deeply resemble each other.

Constantia is both alienated and attracted by Martinette's face (and race). The possibility of Martinette's mixed-race ancestry may be the source of this interpretative complexity: "The shade was remarkably deep; but a deeper still was required to become incompatible with beauty" (O 77). Having passed through the colony of Saint-Domingue, the dark-skinned Martinette in *Ormond* recounts a relationship with a French empire builder, mirroring the explicitly kept status of Helena Cleves, another character with a Gallic name (though, at the same time, *no one* keeps Martinette). The scene may reflect an encounter with a West Indian racial epistemology. The presence of Saint-Dominguans in Philadelphia challenged the Manichaean dichotomy of black or white, introducing an elaborate caste system of shades and hues. More important for US observers, perhaps, the refugees suggested possibilities for racial coexistence of which the republic had not yet dreamed.

V. Brown's Late Pamphlets

Early interpretations of Brown's major pamphlets in light of the abolitionist content in his *Literary Magazine, and American Register* (1803–1807) must now be somewhat qualified, given that electronic searches now allow us to identify many essays once confidently ascribed to Brown as reprints from London periodicals.[14] Yet Brown does not express fixed positions so much as inhabit different personas, blurring the lines between author and editor. If, as periodical editor, Brown sometimes left the articles' authorship ambiguous, as many other contemporary editors did, Brown the pamphleteer posed as an editor and translator of another's voice. In *Address to the Government of the United States, on the Cession of Louisiana to the French, etc.* (1803), Brown posed as "an obscure citizen" who has intercepted and dutifully translated the writings of a French adviser to Napoleon (AG 1).

Analysis of the racial politics of the *Address* should proceed from the interpretative consensus that the work expresses a "pragmatist" expression of "realpolitik" (Verhoeven 181; Levine 349). Notions of providence or national exceptionalism do not figure in the work, but neither does a humanitarian or rights-based discourse; slavery is presented here simply as an existential threat to the security and future development of the nation. The pamphlet's extraordinarily damning picture of American race relations shatters the myth of the nation's exemption from the revolutionary struggles of the rest of the globe. A comparison of the former French colonial slave regime with the United States must lead the observer to conclude that "the same intestine plague exists [in the latter] in a degree equally formidable," an indictment onto which he then piles a 124-word sentence enumerating slaves' many just causes for vengeance (AG 72). At the same time, however, the *Address* is not strictly pragmatic insofar as it sometimes appears to endorse features of what might be called a racial fantasy. By attributing the exclusive motive force for slave insurrections to French influence, the pamphlet is able to call for a strike against French incursions without demanding an end to American slavery.

The pamphlet's structure leaves open the question of how its views relate to those of the author, Brown. After a brief introduction by the "editor," the pamphlet's principal narrator, a French counselor to Napoleon, emerges. Both denouncing the servility of the former slaves and begrudgingly acknowledging their victory in Haiti, the counselor offers a kinetic account of how peoples are *made* over a static view of race. The counselor says that "the revolution has...on both sides of the ocean...changed an half a million of helpless and timorous slaves, the mere tools of the farmer and the artizan, the sordid cattle of the field, into men, and citizens, and soldiers" (10). The French and Haitian revolutions are treated as two parts of a single process, but the number cited here ("half a million") refers definitively to the slave population of Haiti.[15] While deferring to Napoleon's apparent conviction that climate was responsible for the French loss of Saint-Domingue, the counselor nonetheless rebukes those who would underestimate the Haitian revolutionaries, dismissing as absurd the prejudice that the spirit of revolution could not animate an African slave just as fully as a European artisan. From one angle, then, the Haitian Revolution can appear to be a model of collective action, the completion of a social revolution still lacking in the United States.[16]

Nonetheless, the French counselor's account remains a racial fantasy for one important reason: the *direction* of historical process lies entirely in the hands of a white patriarch, Napoleon, whose ideological seed can "propagate a new race of intellectual beings" (27), "race" being understood here as a colonial population whose shared conditions of settlement produce a common culture (additionally, it should be noted that Brown deleted this long section in a revised edition of the pamphlet). Napoleon is the first conductor of this mobile population; American slaves (who constitute a fifth of this supposedly "free" nation) are puppets who can be raised to rebel "at any moment" Napoleon desires (73). That Brown wishes not to attribute this implausible view to the counselor but to hint that American readers might also accept it is suggested by the lament for George Washington, who, had he remained both "founder" and "supreme magistrate" (61) of the nation, would have never allowed the national collective will to wither as it has, and by the concluding admonition to Congress to make the nation one, to "command us to rise as one man, and strike!" (92) Indeed, the pamphlet's narrator appears here to endorse a larger national myth of race that is simultaneously abolitionist and racist, insofar as slaves (and American Indians, not discussed in this chapter) are puppets incited by an alien sovereign. In *Monroe's Embassy, or, The Conduct of the Government, in Relation to Our Claims to the Navigation of the Missisippi* [sic], etc. another pamphlet of the same year, Brown's narrator repeats the attribution of the imminent "insurrection of our slaves" to French influence (ME 54).

While for us the evils of slavery need no demonstration, in Brown's era, the kind of argument used to make the case mattered a great deal. The state of emergency described in the *Address* might, in the absence of a call for the immediate abolition of slavery, have lent support to schemes of colonization (that is, plans for the removal of African Americans to Sierra Leone or elsewhere). Yet Brown, as editor of the *Literary Magazine*, was simultaneously reprinting texts critical of claims for the colonization projects being drawn up by America and British policymakers.[17] These reports would have lent support to Philadelphia's African Americans as they were rebuffing, nearly unanimously, the advances of those who invited them to emigrate from the United States. Brown's *Address* cannot, then, be taken as a brief for colonization but must be read as an exposé of the irresolvable political problem that slavery posed for the new republic.

NOTES

1. Brown to older brother James Brown, April 19, 1795 (Letters 291, 292 n. 4). The plantation was located near Edenton, North Carolina, a place later made famous by Harriet Jacobs.
2. Anthony Benezet makes this argument throughout his antislavery writings, and eighteenth-century visionary John Churchman, brother-in-law to Brown's grandfather William, had made the connection explicit in his *Account*, a text well known to Brown (Kafer 184).
3. I rely heavily here on the contextual materials gathered in Barnard and Shapiro 2008, 400–409.
4. Barnard and Shapiro 2008, xli–xliv.
5. Though they do not discuss Walter Franklin, an introductory account of the PAS is Nash and Soderlund 99–136.
6. Norman Grabo, for example, inadvertently normalizes the story in the course of his inaccurate summary; for example, the narrator's father is represented as an Englishman who defies his "anti-Catholic [actually anti-Protestant]" father when he "secretly marries a Catholic [actually Protestant] girl" from France (Grabo 144).
7. In a slightly later text, Volney (as translated by Brown) would, curiously, associate Federalists with political slavery, as they affirmed the necessity for a monarchical "power raised upon a politico-religious foundation, like that claimed by the Stuarts of England," as against the Republicans, who argue that "absolute power is the primary source of national vice and misery" and that it "manifestly tends to produce, diffuse, and perpetuate these errors and these passions, both in the master and the slave" (xii–xiii).
8. Arner in SC 309.
9. On Elijah Brown's Nottingham upbringing, see Kafer 18–26. On the division of the Nottingham lots between the Penns and the Calverts, see Ecenbarger 130.
10. Compare Mervyn's account of his relation to the property later revealed to be Welbeck's (AM 47).
11. For discussions of this important scene, see, for example, Christophersen 105–106; Smith-Rosenberg 250–256; Doolen 82–91; Goudie 187–189.
12. Neal 426; see Axelrod xvi.
13. See Barnard and Shapiro 2009, xxxiv–xxxix, 59 n. 3, n.4.
14. One such contextualization is Levine.
15. The president of the Colonial Assembly of Saint-Domingue said, notoriously, "We have not brought half a million slaves from the coasts of Africa to make them into French citizens" (quoted in James 122).
16. See Drexler. For the view that Brown defines American nationality against the alien, see Gardner 56.
17. E.g., the anonymous "Account of the Sierra Leone Colony" and "Account of the British African Colony at Bulam."

WORKS CITED

Anonymous. "Account of the British African Colony at Bulam." LM 6.35 (1806): 108–114.

Anonymous. "Account of the Sierra Leone Colony." LM 2.13 (1804): 538–541.

Arner, Robert D. "Historical Essay." In SC 273–312.

Axelrod, Alan. *Charles Brockden Brown: An American Tale*. Austin: University of Texas Press, 1983.

Barnard, Philip, and Stephen Shapiro. "Introduction," "Notes," and "Related Texts." In Charles Brockden Brown, *Arthur Mervyn; or, Memoirs of the Year 1793, with Related Texts*, ix–xliv, passim, 365–426. Indianapolis: Hackett, 2008.

Barnard, Philip, and Stephen Shapiro. "Introduction" and "Notes." In Charles Brockden Brown, *Ormond; or, The Secret Witness, with Related Texts*, ix–lii and passim. Indianapolis: Hackett, 2009.

Bennett, Charles E. "Charles Brockden Brown's 'Portrait of an Immigrant.'" *College Language Association Journal* 14 (September 1970): 87–90.

Branson, Susan, and Leslie Patrick. "Étrangers dans un Pays Étrange: Saint-Dominguan Refugees of Color in Philadelphia." In David Geggus, ed., *The Impact of the Haitian Revolution in the Atlantic World*, 193–208. Columbia: University of South Carolina Press, 2001.

Carey, Mathew. *A Short Account of the Malignant Fever*, 1st ed. Philadelphia: Carey, 1793.

Christophersen, Bill. *The Apparition in the Glass: Charles Brockden Brown's American Gothic*. Athens: University of Georgia Press, 1993.

Churchman, John. *An Account of the Gospel Labours, and Christian Experiences of a Faithful Minister of Christ*. Philadelphia: Crukshank, 1779.

Clement, John. "Charles Brockden." *Pennsylvania Magazine of History and Biography* 12.2 (1888): 185–193.

Cope, Thomas Pim. *Philadelphia Merchant: The Diary of Thomas P. Cope, 1800–1851*. Eliza Cope Harrison, ed. South Bend, Ind.: Gateway, 1978.

Crèvecoeur, J. Hector St. John de. *Letters from an American Farmer*. London: Thomas Davies, 1782.

Doolen, Andy. *Fugitive Empire: Locating Early American Imperialism*. Minneapolis: University of Minnesota Press, 2005.

Drexler, Michael. "Brigands and Nuns: The Vernacular Sociology of Collectivity after the Haitian Revolution." In Malini Johar Schueller and Edward Watts, eds., *Messy Beginnings: Postcoloniality and Early American Studies*, 175–199. New Brunswick, N.J.: Rutgers University Press, 2003.

Ecenbarger, Bill. *Walkin' the Line: A Journey from Past to Present along the Mason-Dixon*. New York: M. Evans, 2000.

Gardner, Jared. *Master Plots: Race and the Making of American Literature, 1787–1845*. Baltimore: Johns Hopkins University Press, 2000.

Goudie, Sean X. *Creole America: The West Indies and the Formation of Literature and Culture in the New Republic*. Philadelphia: University of Pennsylvania Press, 2006.

Grabo, Norman S. *The Coincidental Art of Charles Brockden Brown*. Chapel Hill: University of North Carolina Press, 1981.

Hornick, Nancy Slocum. "Anthony Benezet and the Africans' School: Toward a Theory of Full Equality." *Pennsylvania Magazine of History and Biography* 99.4 (October 1975): 399–421.

James, C. L. R. *The Black Jacobins* (1938). New York: Vintage, 1989.

Jefferson, Thomas. *Notes on the State of Virginia*, 2nd ed. Philadelphia: Mathew Carey, 1794.

Jones, Absalom, and Richard Allen. *A Narrative of the Proceedings of the Black People.* Philadelphia: Woodward, 1794.

Kafer, Peter. *Charles Brockden Brown's Revolution and the Birth of American Gothic.* Philadelphia: University of Pennsylvania Press, 2004.

Levine, Robert S. "Race and Nation in Brown's Louisiana Writings of 1803." In Philip Barnard, Mark L. Kamrath, and Stephen Shapiro, eds., *Revising Charles Brockden Brown: Culture, Politics, and Sexuality in the Early Republic,* 332–353. Knoxville: University of Tennessee Press, 2004.

Nash, Gary. *Forging Freedom: The Formation of Philadelphia's Black Community, 1720–1840.* Cambridge, Mass.: Harvard University Press, 1988.

Nash, Gary, and Jean Soderlund. *Freedom by Degrees: Emancipation in Pennsylvania and Its Aftermath.* New York: Oxford University Press, 1991.

Neal, John. "American Writers, No. II." *Blackwood's Magazine* 16.93 (October 1824): 415–428.

Otter, Samuel. *Philadelphia Stories: America's Literature of Race and Freedom.* New York: Oxford University Press, 2010.

Powell, J. H. *Bring Out Your Dead: The Great Plague of Yellow Fever in Philadelphia in 1793.* Philadelphia: University of Pennsylvania Press, 1949.

Shapiro, Stephen. *The Culture and Commerce of the Early American Novel: Reading the Atlantic World-System.* University Park: Pennsylvania State University Press, 2008.

Smith, Elihu Hubbard. *A Discourse, Delivered April 11, 1798: At the Request of and before the New-York Society for Promoting the Manumission of Slaves, and Protecting Such of Them as Have Been or May Be Liberated.* New York: T. & J. Swords, 1798.

Smith-Rosenberg, Carroll. "Black Gothic: The Shadowy Origins of the American Bourgeoisie." In Robert Blair St. George, ed., *Possible Pasts: Becoming Colonial in Early America,* 243–269. Ithaca, N.Y.: Cornell University Press, 2000.

Verhoeven, Wil. "Beyond the American Empire: Charles Brockden Brown and the Making of a New Global Economic Order." In Kevin Hutchings and Julia M. Wright, eds., *Transatlantic Literary Exchanges, 1790–1870: Gender, Race, and Nation,* 169–188. Burlington, Vt.: Ashgate, 2011.

Volney, C. F. *A View of the Soil and Climate of the United States of America.* Charles Brockden Brown, trans. Philadelphia: Conrad, 1804.

White, Shane. *Somewhat More Independent: The End of Slavery in New York City, 1770–1810.* Athens: University of Georgia Press, 2004.

Zuckerman, Michael. "The Power of Blackness." In Michael Zuckerman, *Almost Chosen People: Oblique Biographies in the American Grain,* 175–218. Berkeley: University of California Press, 1993.

CHAPTER 20

....

BROWN'S PHILADELPHIA
QUAKER MILIEU

....

ROBERT BATTISTINI

To inhabit the Quaker experience of eighteenth-century America is to enter a historiographical maze and to warp sanctified images of Revolutionary America as a contest between oppressed Patriots and cruel imperialists. Quakers understood political identity differently from most colonists, and their principles fit nowhere on the tidy binary demanded of the revolutionaries. They were widely misunderstood and distrusted. While the first half of the century was a period of great Quaker success and influence, the Revolution culminated a process of persecution, contraction, and diminution that began at mid-century. By 1800, Philadelphia was no longer a "Quaker city."

These changes ultimately decreased the diversity of Quaker opinion and practice, but Quaker experience was not homogeneous even during the lifetime of Charles Brockden Brown. Though Brown lived his life in two urban centers, his family had roots in the rural, Quaker enclave of Nottingham, fifty-five miles southwest of Philadelphia in Chester County. For Philadelphia, the pious Quaker countryside was present as denominational legend, family history, and an ongoing site of personal, social, and economic exchange. Even within the city, considerable variation existed in wealth and status.

One outlier was the family of Elijah Brown, a middling merchant censured by the Quaker Monthly Meeting. Even within Brown's family, not every child experienced the same Quaker context: the first three sons had conventional Quaker educations and became merchants, while the fourth, Charles, was educated with the children of Quaker grandees at the Friends Latin School and apprenticed for six years at the law office of Alexander Wilcocks, a member of the city's Anglican elite. This individual's Quaker milieu was no simple composite of Pennsylvania Quaker experience.

This chapter will briefly consider Quakerism in early Pennsylvania and Brown family history, before turning to the representation of Quakers in Brown's writings.[1] Earlier biographers often asserted direct links between "the liberal thinking of the Friends" and what Harry Warfel terms the "radical social philosophizing" of the mature Brown (Warfel 7, 27). But while Brown's work discovers myriad influences and his upbringing was undoubtedly a powerful one of them, the Quaker element is impossible to isolate from, for instance, his later Woldwinite reading and the Friendly Club.[2] Further, eighteenth-century Quakers were not "liberal" in the contemporary sense of the term, and the lessons of Brown's particular Quaker experiences likely complicated conventional Quaker principles. Rather than a predictable influence or set of conditions, Quakerism for Brown was a "special historical *context*" (Kafer 34).

I. EARLY QUAKERISM

Quakerism is often associated with progressive social politics and a distinctive, though still unambiguously Christian, theology.[3] Properly known as the Religious Society of Friends, the movement "flowered out of Puritan soil," developing "a distinctive emphasis within the Puritan tradition, and in a real sense the fulfillment of it" (Tolles 1960, 10–11). Quakers share with Calvinists a sense that "religion must be integrated with life on the natural plane," with no "cleavage between the spheres of divine and natural law" (Tolles 1963, 9–10). However, they differ from Calvinists in holding that God makes new revelations to individuals through "inward objective manifestations in the heart," or "the Inner Light" (Frost 22). Instead of elaborate biblical exegesis, Quakers cultivate this spiritual presence available to every person. Likewise, in their universalism or egalitarian concept of salvation, Quakers differ sharply from Calvinists. Rather than limiting redemption to an "elect," salvation is available to all. Not surprisingly, Quakers rejected what they saw as the "capricious" Calvinist notion of predestination (Frost 13) and spent little time in eschatological speculation; their concern was with a deity present before them. The Quaker Christ was made incarnate with every "hungred" given "meat," every "stranger" taken in, every naked body clothed, and every prisoner they "came unto" (Matthew 25: 35–36).

The Quaker relationship to secular government occasioned much persecution. Eighteenth-century Quakers advocated active obedience to government, which was instituted by God. If they disagreed with state policies, they bore witness by passive disobedience; however, Quakers "eschewed subversive plotting or cooperation with any activities intended to bring about the downfall of any regime" (Mekeel 2). Even so, Quaker allegiance was to a universal realm of religious practice, and thus they would not swear allegiance to a political state. Quaker pacifism follows logically from this position: no political state or earthly institution justifies killing or dying. Founder George Fox wrote, "Dwelling in the light...takes away the occasion of wars, and gathers our hearts together to God, and unto one another, and brings to the beginning, before wars were" (quoted in Tolles 1960, 9). Thus, Friends refused to bear arms and resisted "all violent methods of social control and social change."[4]

Two further aspects of Quaker practice are relevant to a discussion of Brown. One is the Quaker view of so-called pagans such as the Native Americans: if inner light is sufficient for salvation, does redemption require specific knowledge of Christian doctrine? William Penn asks this in *The Christian Quaker* (1674), eventually arguing a position that George Keith called "plain deism appearing with open face" (Frost 17). But by even posing the question, Penn created a precedent for affirming the idea of universal access to salvation, regardless of skin color or doctrinal expression.

Second, Quaker meetings enacted egalitarianism. Eschewing paid clergy and "liturgical decorum," allowing any member to speak, and encouraging women's participation, meetings enacted "populist religious theater." James Emmett Ryan invokes Milan Kundera's description of novels as "a fascinating imaginative realm where no one owns the truth and everyone has the right to be understood" to describe seventeenth-century meetings as "a potentially anarchic scene characterized by an unbounded narrative fraught with theological polyphony and gender trouble" (Ryan 11–12). Perhaps such meetings played some part in the complexity and ambiguity of Brown's fiction.

Historically, Quakers emerged from the radicalism of Commonwealth England as one of the "independent" churches persecuted by both Anglicans and Presbyterians: Diggers, Muggletonians, Fifth Monarchists, Ranters, and Quakers. Only the Quakers thrived past the Restoration (Frost 11). They were able to "suck in all the remnants of previous radical protest" (Sykes 139) and became unpopular with all manner of authority, for their mission had profound economic and political consequences:

> They were decrying the abuses of the law and the church, the iniquities attending on rich and poor, the inadequacies of the government.... Friends... in that uncertain epoch, were a powerful bogey to the new Puritan Establishment, to its uneasy hypocritical conscience.   (Sykes 139, 141)

Early Quakers disrupted Anglican and Presbyterian services, inviting persecution and martyrdom. Instead of the millennium, what followed was the Restoration of 1660, which proved to be no improvement (Taylor 265). Friends were "the most suspect" of Puritan Dissenters: "at least until 1672, to be a Quaker in England was to be the figure of an outlaw" (Sykes 145).

Without a 1667 aristocratic convert, William Penn, Quaker history would have been very different. Though most Friends were of middling economic status at best, Penn was wealthy gentry who found a powerful ally in the Roman Catholic duke of York (the future James II). To satisfy a debt to Penn's father, in 1681, Charles II granted Penn forty-five thousand square miles west of the Delaware (Penn had already been an investor in present-day southern New Jersey), and in 1682, the duke of York added the Swedish-Finnish-Dutch settlements to the south, present-day Delaware (Nash 7–10). In 1682, during "the fastest and most efficient colonization in the seventeenth-century English empire," twenty-three ships brought two thousand well-supplied colonists, and one year later, twenty ships brought two thousand more. By 1686, Pennsylvania counted more than eight thousand colonists. Besides Quakers, the colony welcomed non-Quakers and non-Britons; Penn promised equal rights and religious freedom to all. English, Irish, and Welsh Quakers immigrated, along with Anglicans, German Pietists (especially Anabaptists), and Dutch Calvinists (Taylor 266–267).

II. PHILADELPHIA FRIENDS, 1682–1800

Though Thomas Paine's first "American Crisis" is known for its "times that try men's souls," the longest "Crisis" essay is the third, published April 17, 1777:

> The common phrase with these people is, *"Our principles are peace."* To which may be replied, and your practices are the reverse; for never did the conduct of men oppose their own doctrine more notoriously than the present race of the Quakers...like antiquated virgins, they see not the havoc deformity has made upon them, but pleasantly mistaking wrinkles for dimples, conceive themselves yet lovely and wonder at the stupid world for not admiring them.   (138)[5]

Revolutionary Philadelphia provided a willing audience for Paine's anti-Quaker rage. The eighteenth-century history of these New World pacifists, in spite of some Friends' best efforts, was drenched in blood and opprobrium and characterized by decline and contraction.[6] In the words of Jack Marietta, they went from a "Church" to a sect (xii) but nonetheless refashioned themselves into a potent, if numerically minor, force in the United States.

The resentment of 1777 had its roots in Pennsylvania's good fortune during the first century of colonization. Its soil was excellent and its growing season ideal for exportable grains. The Delaware and Susquehanna Rivers provided easy transport for agriculture, and the climate was a temperate medium between New England's bitter winters and the Chesapeake's malarial heat. Pennsylvania benefited from its historical belatedness (prior colonies' mistakes became lessons), and from the start, Penn cultivated good relations with the Delaware (Lenni Lenape) Indians. He honored his treaties and "paid higher and fairer prices than his predecessors in other colonies." Peace was secured (for the first generation), and the devastation of a Metacom's War was avoided (Taylor 267–268). The colony prospered, and Quakers became a powerful commercial and land-owning community; they controlled the legislature and often counted among the wealthiest merchants in Philadelphia.

After 1750, Quakers themselves became sharply critical of this political and economic success; in this period, in Richard Bauman's words,

> It is evident that the character of Quaker involvement in the political community of Pennsylvania was not without a considerable element of compromise, expediency, assertiveness, contentiousness, and general reliance upon the human agency, which ran directly counter to the Quaker prescription of meek and selfless submission to the agency and protection of the Almighty.   (Bauman 217)

No act of "expediency" was more momentous than the 1737 "Walking Treaty," which defrauded the Delaware Indians of 1.2 million acres north of Tohickon Creek, thirty-five miles north of Philadelphia. An original 1686 treaty stated that the purchase was of land that could be walked at a reasonable pace, with breaks, in a day and a half. But James Logan, Quaker chief justice of Pennsylvania, acting on behalf of Penn's sons Thomas and John, cleared a path and hired three running "walkers" who covered sixty-four miles. To make matters worse, Logan negotiated with the Delaware's enemies, the Iroquois, to remove them from their land (Kafer 173–174).

The Walking Treaty came to symbolize the rapacity of Philadelphia elites, Quakers in particular. Brown famously set *Edgar Huntly* in the stolen territory, and the treaty is identified as a cause of later frontier violence in Matthew Smith and James Gibson's *Declaration and Remonstrance*. But in establishing the Quaker milieu of a late-eighteenth-century writer like Brown, we might ask how far responsibility and guilt transfer. Were all Pennsylvania Quakers of 1737 implicated? Logan was allied with the Proprietary Party, in opposition to the Quaker Party of the Assembly. He eventually opposed Quaker pacifism and, in acting for Penn's sons, placed himself in opposition to most of the community. Logan's actions may exemplify a strain of elite Quaker avarice in 1737, but the group's culture shifted dramatically throughout the century. Mid-century Quakers themselves publicized the injustice of the treaty. Israel Pemberton and his Friendly Association for Regaining and Preserving Peace with the Indians by Pacific Measures "shrilly averred that the Delawares had been defrauded in the Walking Purchase" (Marietta 188). As a result, Pemberton and other Quakers would soon earn the antipathy of Scots-Irish settlers. But for Friends of Brown's generation, the Walking Purchase was not a secret to repress or sublimate; it was a well-known incident that illustrated the consequences of greed. It probably spoke more to the legitimacy of Native American grievance than continuing Quaker responsibility.

By mid-century, these resentments became violent. In 1754, western Pennsylvania became a North American front in the global Seven Years War. After the defeat of British General Edward Braddock's army in July 1755, Native American allies of the French attacked German colonists at Tulpehocken and Moravians at Gnadenhutten. Throughout autumn and winter, "Indians continued to strike when they pleased," causing the Pennsylvania frontier to collapse as settlers fled eastward to Shippensburg, Carlisle, York, and Reading. Eventually, even Philadelphia was "almost crazy" with anxiety (Marietta 151). The Assembly was pressured to act, and, against the wishes of the Quaker elite, war on the Delaware was declared in April 1756. This was a terrific disruption to Quakers' sense of justice: "Friendship with the Delaware Indians had mythic importance to the pious Friends of the mid-eighteenth century" (Marietta 156–157). For Quakers, the Scots-Irish were intruders in the original relationship between Quakers and the Delaware; they believed the Delaware to be capable of deep understanding and a fine sense of justice, in contrast to the alleged barbaric ignorance of the Scots-Irish. Under these circumstances, Quakers were at odds with the Assembly. Six Quakers resigned in June 1756, and those who remained were disowned. In one stroke, Quakers relinquished their formal political prominence in Pennsylvania; they would never regain it.

The broader war raged until 1763. No longer in government, "how would Friends now fulfill the solemn, benevolent promises made in fabled meetings under an elm on the shores of the Delaware?" (Marietta 187). Even if first-generation elite Quakers had, metaphorically speaking, made timber for frontier forts out of that elm, mid-century Quakers appear to have been motivated by real concern for their traditional allies. However, for frontier settlers caught in the conflict, Quaker sympathy for the Delaware was proof of Quaker complicity in the attacks.

Britain began to win the war in 1759 at Quebec, but this did not stop a coordinated series of Native American attacks on British settlements in 1763. As had happened eight years earlier, panic spread through the frontier. But this time, the frontier people organized. On December 14, 1763, more than fifty men, mostly Scots-Irish from Lancaster County calling themselves the Paxton Boys, attacked a Conestoga Indian settlement, slaughtering six. Fourteen family members absent during the attack were moved to Lancaster City for safety, but the Paxton Boys pursued them and murdered all fourteen. Rumors spread that the next provocation would be a march on Philadelphia. In February 1764, the Paxton Boys terrorized Philadelphians (inspiring some young Quakers to take up arms) and marched as far as Germantown, where Benjamin Franklin, Joseph Galloway, and other city leaders persuaded them to return home (Bauman 109–110).

The aftermath of the uprising was to "remind Friends that they were an increasingly outnumbered and powerless minority in Pennsylvania" (Marietta 202). Not only had Quakers lost power and suffered economic reversals, but now they were despised by an increasing majority of Pennsylvanians. Their pacifism and sympathy for the Delaware were seen as invitations to violence and bloodshed that were visited almost entirely on the Scots-Irish, a less educated, poorer, and more recently arrived group.

The 1760s were dark times for Pennsylvania Friends, but the worst was yet to come. Quakers were mostly, albeit quietly, against the Revolution. Economic interests, ties between British and North American Quakers, and pacifism led Friends on both sides of the Atlantic to oppose the war (Mekeel 113). Their refusal to fight and abstention from partisan oaths incurred the wrath of the Revolutionary leaders, none Quakers: "Increased suspicions as to their true intents...caused the patriots to consider them Tories" (Mekeel 129–130). These suspicions flared into hysteria with a fabricated document, "an account of the position and forces of the American army...sent from the spuriously designated Quaker Yearly Meeting at Spanktown" (Mekeel 178). The Continental Congress recommended action, and in September 1777, seventeen Quakers, mostly leading figures, were arrested and exiled in Virginia. Brown's father was among them. The exiles, minus two who died, returned the following April, and harassment continued into the 1780s: "In addition to social obloquy, imprisonment, and personal abuse, there were heavy material losses" (Mekeel 201).

From the time of Brown's father's birth in 1740 to Charles's teenage years, Pennsylvania Quakers suffered enormous losses of political power, social prestige, and economic stature. They went from undisputed masters of the realm to a persecuted minority. But not all Quakers were disappointed by these changes, for there had always been undercurrents of resistance to the early-eighteenth-century community's worldly success: "The Revolution...disappointed none of the reformers. It was as much a disaster as anything they had predicted" (Marietta 251). Liberated from the compromises intrinsic to governance, post-Revolutionary Quakers increasingly withdrew from secular society.

Disownments increased during and immediately after the war; those who remained were particularly devout and committed. Both Richard Bauman and Jack Marietta read this withdrawal as a necessary precondition for the progressive social-reform work that Quakers soon undertook on behalf of women, Native Americans, African Americans, and prisoners (Bauman 228; Marietta 97–128).

Thus, Pennsylvania Quakerism was transforming dramatically during Brown's early adulthood. Surely, there was some influence on his own commitments, but Brown himself warns against equating Quaker practice with Woldwinite radicalism. In the 1805 *Literary Magazine*, reprinting a 1794 London *Monthly Review* piece on the "Origin of Quakerism," Brown concedes, "It is very remarkable, indeed, that in the internal order of this society [Quakers], in its legislative and judicial system, we see the most extravagant political reveries of Godwin and his followers realized." Even so, he asserts that Quaker systems and the "speculative politicians of the present age…build upon a very different foundation; and not only different, but irreconcileable: but while inferences are the same, the diversity of premises is overlooked or disregarded" (Brown 1805, 20).

Marietta makes a similar point: the eighteenth-century Quakers were not liberals. These Quakers, "in fact, showed no significant desire to free men and women of restrictions upon their behavior and character in the expectation that enlightenment, progress, and felicity would result" (Marietta 82–83). Though they may offer contemporary progressives much to celebrate, as devout Christians, they differed in significant ways from the radical Enlightenment that shaped Brown: they believed in a personal God who privately communicated with individuals, advocated obedience (though not deference) to earthly government, and avoided the kinds of encompassing critique of temporal systems that structured the Woldwinite agenda.

In sum, the history of eighteenth-century Pennsylvania Quakers was one of contradiction and violence. We can imagine four interpenetrating layers of Quaker history by the time Brown was a child. Friends appeared as persecuted religious rebels; a successful commercial minority presiding over a thriving colony; a politically powerful urban elite blamed for frontier violence; and, by 1777, religious eccentrics again alienated (at times through violence) from the dominant culture around them. They were persecuted persecutors, pacifists blamed for violence in their attempt not to be violent. Perhaps this paradoxical duality demonstrates Joanna Brooks's contention that imperialism and Quakers were incompatible (Brooks 46); for the Quakers, this incompatibility was a wrenching moment of cognitive dissonance. Why did they generate such hatred? The Quakers' response was to imagine that they ultimately were responsible for their contemporaries' opprobrium and that they had agency, even amid the complexities of the eighteenth-century world. Brown's major intellectual break with the Quakers was partly on this point of agency and control. His novels present characters enmeshed in complexities beyond their comprehension. Brown replaces the spiritual commitment of the Quakers with a profound grasp of systems—political, economic, social, and cultural— in both visible and subterranean realms, of which people are, at best, partially aware and by which they are shaped and limited.

III. The Brown Family

Brown interacted with Philadelphia's Quaker elite through family connections and his education at the Friends' Latin School, but his father, Elijah, was atypical.[7] The Browns arrived in America in 1677, before Penn's charter. They helped establish Nottingham in 1702 and, by the time Elijah was born in 1740, achieved some prominence there. Yet by 1757, Elijah turned to commercial opportunities in Philadelphia. The father's career was initially promising, especially after a favorable marriage to Mary Armitt in 1761. But then came "the disruptions of imperial politics, of local Philadelphia politics, and of the Revolution itself" (Kafer 30). By 1768, Elijah was in debt, formally censured, and provisionally disowned by the Philadelphia Monthly Meeting; he would never formally rejoin. Through Mary's relative Richard Waln, Elijah was able to recuperate some of his losses in 1770, but throughout his life, he worked at the margins of Philadelphia's commercial society. Ironically, his arrest and exile in 1777–1778 may have been his finest moment; he and the other sixteen became Quaker celebrities.[8] But by 1784, Elijah was again in debt, possibly experiencing debtor's prison (Kafer 43).

Elijah and Mary's children, then, grew up simultaneously within and alienated from the mainstream Quaker community. It is perhaps telling that Brown and all of his brothers were disowned for marrying non-Quakers.[9] Brown married Elizabeth Linn, daughter of a Presbyterian minister, in November 1804 and was disowned shortly thereafter. He probably came closest to a conventional Quaker experience in the five years he spent at the Latin School, where he received the best education available to a Philadelphia Quaker, since Friends did not ordinarily attend universities (Frost 108, 136).

IV. Brown on Quakers

Brown was a prolific writer in many genres, yet his published work suggests, at most, a modest investment in Quaker history and identity.[10] After a brief consideration of *Arthur Mervyn, Wieland,* and Brown's occasional periodical reflections on Quakers, I will conclude with a discussion of *Edgar Huntly.*

Arthur Mervyn is respectful, possibly ironic or wistful, in its consideration of rural Quakers. Arthur is not a Friend but, like Brown's father, Elijah, a young man leaving Chester County for Philadelphia. In the novel's First Part, as he resolves to escape the fever "at the first farm-house" (AM 122), Arthur encounters the Quaker Hadwins. He praises the farmer for blending "the simplicity of the husbandman and the devotion of the Quaker" with "humanity and intelligence" (123). He is charmed by the Hadwin daughters, who, though strangers to "elaborate education," possess curiosity and discernment. Arthur fancies the younger daughter Eliza, but he is not a Friend, and Hadwin is a "conscientious member." Hence, he will neither "feign conversion" nor "introduce discord and sorrow into this family" by a conquest of "Eliza's errors" (124–125). When Arthur revisits Philadelphia and Hadwin dies before his return, Eliza is willing to marry, but Arthur undergoes a "revolution of mind" and determines "to suppress that tenderness" he had felt, causing the girl to "burst into tears" (293–294). Eventually, Arthur marries a cosmopolitan Sephardic Jew, Achsa Fielding.

Arthur's choice of an urban sophisticate over the "guileless simplicity" of the Quaker farm girl may be an autobiographical flourish. Metonymically, Eliza is the best version of Nottingham; she proves her independent mettle by burning her father's will and embarks on a path of self-improvement under Arthur's guidance. Still, Arthur insists on "activity and change" and an "apprenticeship to fortitude and wisdom," which he assumes he could never find with a Quaker ingénue, even if she joins him in Philadelphia. Regardless of the autobiographical resonance, the narrative apparently favors the transatlantic exchange of revolutionary ideas in 1793 over rural Quaker roots, even when they appear in the form of "the sweetest voice, the most speaking features, the most delicate symetry" (293, 298).

Wieland (1798) explores religious devotion, and the Wielands may be read to echo aspects of Quaker thought and experience. The elder Wieland could allude to the Quaker ministers that Elijah Brown left behind in Nottingham; the internal combustion suffered by Wieland, Sr., may well be an irreverent literalization of the "inner light"; and Theodore's murderous "thirst for the knowledge of [God's] will" (W 165) may even satirize Quakers such as John Woolman who claimed direct instruction from God. Kafer reads the novel as an evocation of "the Brown-Churchman saga writ large, tracing it back to its seventeenth-century European mystical wellsprings" (Kafer 183).

Brown, though, does not invite such parallels. No characters are Quakers, and the Wielands' detailed spiritual inspirations are continental: Camisards, Moravians, and "calvinistic inspiration" (W 24). The elder Wieland's insistence that worship be "silent" and "performed alone" (11) is contrary to the social focus of the "Society of Friends." Theodore withdraws into a "thrilling melancholy" (23) in which he discovers God's will in the "bounty" of no "less sacrifice" than the murder of his family; this obviously differs from a Quaker focus on earnest amelioration of the world at hand. As is clear in *Edgar Huntly*, Brown could be critical of particular Quakers, but nowhere in his writings does he characterize Quaker practice as obsessive or violent. Rather, in his fictions, he presents mental imbalance—manifest in combustion, somnambulism, and murderous "mania"—as a reflection of dysfunction and injustice in wider realms.[11] Insofar as religious practice in *Wieland* is spiritual at the expense of the temporal, it is difficult to connect to the Quakers of Brown's work, who exhibit none of the Wielands' metaphysical fixations.

Beyond the novels, Brown occasionally discusses Quakers, especially in his final years. Typically, he informs and corrects. In addition to Brown's earlier-discussed comments in "Origin of Quakerism," another example is his commentary on Comte de Volney's footnote explaining Quakers in *A View of the Soil and Climate of the United States*. Volney is complimentary, averring (in Brown's translation) that, "impartially considered," Quakers are in their "theoretical and practical morality, more favourable than any other to the happiness of mankind." Volney's only reservation is their alleged antipathy to the physical sciences: "How can the truly devout condemn as profane the study of the works of God?" Brown's refutation is unambiguous: Quakers "deem the human character truly adorned and ennobled by skill in natural philosophy and history, and the sciences properly so called." In particular, Quakers "pay due respect to the physical and mathematical sciences," as well as admitting "the study of ancient and modern languages and literature into their schools." Only pursuits "chiefly or solely conducive to the amusement of the senses" are prohibited (Volney 358).

Brown's "Quakerism, A Dialogue" is another didactic moment. The Quaker speaker objects to exaggerated literary portraits, insisting that Friends are "neither better nor worse than other societies" and that, given the lack of Quaker writers, "in no play or novel that I have read, was the quaker ever justly conceived or faithfully portrayed." She explains that non-Quakers create Quaker characters who speak with "intolerable affectation," with "thou and thee...the formal style of *hath* and *doth*; and *loveth* and *lovedest*." Real Quakers, though, use only the "single *thee*." After explaining Quaker honorifics and calendar names, she provides a translation for her interlocutor: "Gentlemen and Ladies, will you favour me with your company on Tuesday evening, and you, Mr. Blank, may I see you in June?" becomes "Will you give me your company, *friends*, on *third-day* evening, and thee, friend Blank, shall I see thee in the sixth month?" After these trivialities, Brown's character concludes by distinguishing Quakerism from other religions:

> It is intended to supply a rule of universal action, and to supersede all other law and government. A community entirely of *friends* would need no other laws and institutions than the society has at present.   (Brown 1804, 250)

In only one published piece does Brown speak directly to his experience of growing up Quaker. Appearing in 1809, less than a year before his death, the political pamphlet *An Address to the Congress of the United States* begins with a personal "Advertisement," in which Brown predicts that the *Address* will be "condemned and disclaimed by all" and that he will be disregarded either for ignorance of maritime law or for being a "visionary...[with] my pacific doctrine, my system of rational forbearance and forgiveness carried to a pitch of Quaker extravagance." To this noble charge, Brown demurs:

> The truth is, I am no better than an outcast of that unwarlike sect, but cannot rid myself of reverence for most of its practical and political maxims. I feel a strong inclination to admit to an equality of rights and merits, men of all nations and religions; to pass the same sentence on the same conduct, even though the men who practice it bear, at one time, the name of French, at another of English, and at another of American: Sometimes that of federalists, and sometimes that of republicans.   (AC vi)

In this moment, at least, Brown admits both affection for and influence by progressive Quaker commitments to equality and justice. While "no better than an outcast," he suggests that he takes no pleasure—finds no subversive glee—in his disownment from the Society of Friends.[12]

Another piece from 1809 demonstrates the sort of disinterested judgment that Brown attributes to Quakers. In his "Sketch of the Life of General Horatio Gates," Brown reviews the persecution of Quakers during the Revolutionary War. Their being "favourably disposed" to Great Britain was a "practical consequence of their conscientious aversion to war." Because of the assumption of their "treason and rebellion," "it is needless to say" whether or not Quakers sided with Britain "independent of religious motives." Even so, Quaker sufferings "constitute no particular stigma against the American revolution," for "jealousy, intolerance, and oppression, belong of necessity to all revolutions" (Brown 1809, 484). In this valedictory assessment, Brown attributes the violence that touched him personally, as a child, to the pressures of historical transformation, rather than the Scots-Irish who were personally and corporately responsible for Quaker oppression. In this, the "Sketch" is a useful intertext for *Edgar Huntly*.

V. Reading *Edgar Huntly*

In February 1764, Philadelphians were terrified by the Paxton Boys' march toward their home. Though the march stopped at Germantown, Ed White reads this not as "an anticlimactic failure" but as an effective way of making the message of the earlier massacre clear: "they marched to affirm, defiantly, *past* actions" (White 114). The march continued by other means. On the presses of Philadelphia, a pamphlet war was begun by Matthew Smith and James Gibson's *A Declaration and Remonstrance of the Distressed and Bleeding Frontier Inhabitants of the Province of Pennsylvania*. Smith and Gibson defend the massacre of Native Americans with chilling logic that blames Philadelphia elites—Quakers in particular—for creating the need for such violence. They, the Scots-Irish, are still reasonable people—"extremity alone compels this"—and the "Indians" could hardly be expected not to indulge in "Insolence and Villainy":

> When it is considered...that ONAS [William Penn] had cheated them out of a great deal of Land, or had not given near sufficient price for what he had bought. And that the Traders ought also to be scourged; for that they defrauded the *Indians* by selling Goods to them at too dear a Rate...

Ultimately, their grievance is with the "Villany, Infatuation and Influence of a certain Faction," one with "the political Reigns [sic] in their Hand" that chooses to "tamely tyrannize over the other good Subjects of the Province!" (Smith and Gibson 89).

Some sixty-three publications were written in response, most famously Franklin's *Narrative of the Late Massacres*.[13] Franklin was not a Friend but a close ally at this point, voting in the Pennsylvania Assembly with the Quakers and taking over their positions after the 1756 resignation of six Quaker Assembly members (Tolles 1963, 248). The *Narrative* is an anomaly in Franklin's oeuvre. Instead of his customary logic leavened with wit, here Franklin writes with Gothic excess:

> You have imbrued your Hands in innocent Blood; how will you make them clean?—The dying Shrieks and Groans of the Murdered, will often sound in your Ears: Their Spectres will sometimes attend you, and affright even your innocent Children!... *Talking in your Sleep shall betray you, in the Delirium of Fever you yourselves shall make your own Wickedness known.* (Franklin 556 emphasis added)

If justice is not done—"the Wicked punished and the Innocent protected"—Pennsylvania can expect "no Blessing from Heaven," and with no security, the state can expect "Anarchy and Confusion" and "Violence...[will] dispose of every Thing" (557). *Narrative* suggests the power of Smith and Gibson's *Declaration*. If they are right, then Quakers are responsible for the cycle of violence, harming both the Scots-Irish and their traditional allies the Delaware. This is a devastating charge.

Edgar Huntly can be read as a belated response to Smith and Gibson. Rather than a pamphlet, Brown's work is an imaginative treatment, a novel with his only Quaker protagonist. Like Franklin, Brown imagines a sleep-induced "delirium" as a manifestation of such atrocities. However, Brown's unsound sleeper is a Quaker. Why write a novel in which a Quaker sleepwalks into the very territory stolen in 1737, encounters and murders Delaware warriors, and investigates an Irishman for murder?

This question has attracted scholarly attention. For Brooks, *Edgar Huntly* is the "apotheosis of the Quaker-Irish captivity narrative" (Brooks 42). After the Smith and Gibson *Declaration*, Quakers used "the 'savage' Scots-Irish to disavow their own implication in the anti-Indian violence at the Pennsylvania frontier" (38). They produced "Quaker-Irish captivity narratives" in which Quakers are captive to Scots-Irish rather than Native Americans, thereby redefining themselves as "conscientious people captive to their situation and to their proximity to the unmanageable violence of frontier Scots-Irish settler" (42). On Brooks's reading, *Edgar Huntly* "employs the Irish as a proxy for Indians and as the personification of historical responsibility," and the Irishman Clithero's death "liberates Huntly from captivity to broader questions of guilt and innocence" (43, 44). Brooks predicates her reading on the "essential contradiction between the 'Quaker peace testimony and British colonialism'" (46). Such a contradiction certainly exists, but this claim may distract from an understanding of Quaker history and culture. The Quakers were more committed to Native American harmony and peace than any other colonizing group in North America. Indeed, as discussed earlier, they suffered for their support of the Lenni Lenape. The fraudulent land deals were not made by a vote among Quakers, and Quakers groups decried the criminality of the Walking Purchase.

Another interpretation reads *Edgar Huntly*'s violence as exploration of the Scots-Irish treatment of Quakers. Kafer explains that Philadelphia Quakers associated barbarity with the Scots-Irish, not Native Americans. Brown, especially, would have remembered "two [Scots-Irish] 'savages' named James Loughead and James Kerr [who] had come to the Brown-Armitt residence…and arrested his father" (Kafer 182). On this reading, when Edgar imagines that his uncle and sisters have been killed by the Delaware and marvels, "I doubted whether I had not witnessed and shared this catastrophe" (EH 186), Brown is reimagining the 'catastrophe' of September 5, 1777.

Within Brown's Quaker milieu, however, neither reading may be persuasive. Whatever transgressions historical Quakers perpetrated, they were nothing like Edgar's orgy of violence. Edgar the character is a poor metonym for Pennsylvania Quaker experience. Friends typically celebrated the culture and restraint of the Delaware, and thus, the Edgar who slaughters panthers and warriors has not "turned Indian." But Edgar may well register the experience of the group of Pennsylvanians who could easily identify with the following:

> My father's house was placed on the verge of this solitude. Eight of these assassins assailed it in the dead of night. My parents and an infant child were murdered in their beds; the house was pillaged, and then burnt to the ground.   (EH 173)

This is the aggrieved voice of the *Distressed and Bleeding Frontier Inhabitants*; from this perspective, Edgar imaginatively inhabits the Scots-Irish experience. *Edgar Huntly* can thus be read as a meditation on how and why violence like Edgar's—or the Paxton Boys'—can occur. It may attempt to understand a Scots-Irish perspective that *did* feel the brunt of Native American attacks. In Brown's era, few Pennsylvania Quakers were vulnerable to the violence Edgar depicts. But the novel's Quaker Solebury still hosts an anomalous Delaware female elder, Deb, who refuses removal and uses Norwalk as a portal to the violence of the western frontier ("this rude surface was sometimes traversed by the Redmen, and they made, by means of it, frequent and destructive inroads into the heart of the English settlements" [172]). Through careful manipulation of this setting, Brown enables coastal readers to glimpse the terror of frontier life.

The question involves both the interpretation of this novel and our perspective on Brown's Quaker background. With its Quaker protagonist and representation of a primal scene of imperial and settler-colonial fraud, *Edgar Huntly* invites both biographical interpretations like Kafer's and readings like Brooks's that survey the historical sweep of Quaker-Indian relations ("The Irish Edny, like the Indian, is the carrier of the past, the symbol of guilt, and the scapegoat" [Brooks 44]). But we underestimate the novel's complexity by insisting on either extreme. Brown's novel poses its questions in a manner that transcends both perspectives: *Edgar Huntly* imagines a Pennsylvania Quaker imagining cultural others from whom he is deeply alienated––Irish immigrants, the Delaware, Scots-Irish settlers—and considers local conflicts against the backdrop of the wider Atlantic and imperial world that shapes them.

What, then, do Quakers mean for novelist Brown? *Edgar Huntly*, at least, does not situate Quakerism primarily as a religious or personal matter. Rather, Pennsylvania Quakers appear as one of many nodes in a complex geopolitical network. Edgar never leaves his rural setting, but the narrative situates his experiences within a global struggle between Great Britain and France, linking North America, Great Britain,

Europe, and South Asia. On this representation, imperialism damages the Lenape, the Irish, and settler-Pennsylvanians alike.[14]

The novel frustrates the reader's desire to take sides in its conflicts. It rejects the mythic notion of Lenape-Quaker amity embodied in the recurrent Elm; its action begins with the murder of a Quaker (Waldegrave) by a Lenape warrior seeking "vengeance" (EH 281) for "a long course of injuries and encroachments" that had "lately exasperated the Indian tribes" (173).[15] Deb, the Lenape matriarch who orchestrated the recent attacks, is proudly defiant: she "readily confessed and gloried in the mischief she had done" and "accounted for it by enumerating the injuries which she had received from her neighbors" (280). Given the history of colonial encroachment—the "progress of population" by which return to their ancestral home involves "multiplied perils" (172–173)—the reader is not likely to regard the Quakers as innocent victims. But even if Deb's pluck is appealing, the novel presents the Delaware men as little more than (mostly inept) killing machines. As mentioned, the narrative encourages the reader to empathize with the plight of the frontier Scots-Irish. Even so, the main Irish characters are not backcountry settlers: Lorimer, Sarsefield, and Clithero are not Presbyterian Scots-Irish immigrants and are difficult to assimilate to Smith and Gibson's people. The closest Brown's reader comes to actual frontier people are the drunken Selby, his abused wife, and the traumatized captive rescued by Edgar. Even as the narrative suggests sympathy for their situation, it does not depict the Scots-Irish with complexity.

Rather than encourage partisanship, *Edgar Huntly* depicts the broader system within which these parties struggle. After murdering a fifth Lenape, Edgar reflects on the way war engenders savagery:

> Such are the deeds which perverse nature compels thousands of rational beings to perform and to witness! Such is the spectacle, endlessly prolonged and diversified, which is exhibited in every field of battle; of which, habit and example, the temptations of gain, and the illusions of honour, will make us, not reluctant or indifferent, but zealous and delighted actors and beholders!   (202)

Indeed, Brown insists the violent disruption brought about by colonial aggression renders social or religious identities—even pious assertions of nonviolence—irrelevant. Echoing Smith and Gibson's *Declaration*, Brown demonstrates that before a panther— or when peering into a cave with five armed aggressors holding a captive—everyone becomes Edgar with a tomahawk.

The novel emphasizes the unpredictability, even futility, of individual action: "How little cognizance have men over the actions and motives of each other? How total is our blindness with regard to our own performances!" (278). Readers are thus likely to sympathize with many of Brown's characters; given his problematization of agency, blame is difficult to assign. But virtue is equally scarce, and Brown takes pains to show the inability of individual principle to effect real change, particularly the Quaker commitment to pacifism. Edgar is shocked by the violence of which he is capable: "I had imbibed from the unparalleled events which had lately happened a spirit vengeful, unrelenting, and ferocious" (192). He mocks his own rage for vengeance; he fails to "discover the romantic and criminal temerity of my project, the folly of revenge, and the duty of preserving my life" (187) and continues his slaughter, soon murdering four more Lenape. Thus, the Quaker fares no better, and perhaps no worse, than others in the novel.[16]

In *Edgar Huntly*, then, the Quakers are one more identity group. Brown invites qualified sympathy for one Friend confronting his inner savagery, but insofar as Quakers indulge Edgar's casual dismissal of Scots-Irish on the frontier as persons with "the intellectual mediocrity of clowns" (226), or insofar as their far-flung merchant networks contribute to the immiseration of locals like Weymouth (a native of Solebury, thus presumably Quaker himself), they may well be complicit in Edgar's lapse into violence. As Brown's only sustained portrait of a Quaker character, *Edgar Huntly* suggests that while the mature writer retained an acute sense of Quaker history and practice, he denied Quakers any unique status or virtue.

NOTES

1. For earlier treatments of Brown and Quakerism, see Hintz; Moses.
2. See Waterman for a critique of Quaker-centric readings. For the Woldwinite context, see Barnard and Shapiro 2006, xv.
3. See Tolles 1960 and 1963 for background and early history and Sykes for the Commonwealth context of early Quakerism. Frost explores Quaker theology, and Trueblood is useful on the "inner light" and universalism. Nash and Taylor provide accounts of the first two decades of Pennsylvania settlement and important contextual information.
4. Friends likewise emphasized "plain language" and the egalitarian *thee* and *thou* instead of *you*, which connoted social superiority. They rejected deferential titles (*mister* or *sir*) and bowing or uncovering their heads, as markers of unequal status (Tolles 1963, 8).
5. Hintz discusses Paine, the son of a Quaker, but remains unaware of the third "American Crisis" essay (Hintz 17–27).
6. Bauman, Mekeel, and Marietta are the best sources on the transformation of American Quakers in the eighteenth century.
7. Kafer provides the most extensive biographical information and family context.
8. See Kafer 36–37; while the others were arrested for their prominence or political activity, Elijah's arrest was essentially a police action, after he sold flour on the open market in violation of a wartime law.
9. Watts writes that the Brown clan "did not exactly fit the standard Quaker mold…[they] might be described as 'Quaker modernists'" (27–28).
10. *Wieland, Ormond, Clara Howard, Jane Talbot,* and the *Historical Sketches* make no direct mention of Quakers, and *Stephen Calvert* includes only a minor character who helps persuade Stephen's father to emigrate.
11. See Barnard and Shapiro 2009 for Brown's medical-physiological understanding of mental illness (derived from Erasmus Darwin) and Godwinian vision of human behavior reflecting broader social concerns.
12. In the 1805 *Literary Magazine*, Brown prints William Austin's favorable depiction of Quakers in *Letters from London, Written during the Years 1802 & 1803*, with an introductory compliment: "The following portrait of quakers is entitled to no small praise" (105).

13. See White on the Paxton Boys uprising.

14. For the global context, see Kamrath; Hinds; Barnard and Shapiro 2006.

15. See Krause for discussion of the elm tree, which alludes to a well-known "Treaty Elm" in Philadelphia that was held to mark the spot where, according to legend, Penn made a pact of eternal amity with the Delaware.

16. As Brown wrote in "Quakerism, A Dialogue," Quakers are "neither better nor worse than other societies" (Brown 1804, 248).

WORKS CITED

Barnard, Philip, and Stephen Shapiro. "Introduction." In Charles Brockden Brown, *Edgar Huntly; or, Memoirs of a Sleep-Walker, with Related Texts*, ix–xlii. Indianapolis: Hackett, 2006.

Barnard, Philip, and Stephen Shapiro. "Introduction." In Charles Brockden Brown, *Wieland; or, the Transformation, with Related Texts*, ix–xlvi. Indianapolis: Hackett, 2009.

Bauman, Richard. *For the Reputation of Truth: Politics, Religion, and Conflict among the Pennsylvania Quakers, 1750–1800*. Baltimore: Johns Hopkins University Press, 1971.

Brooks, Joanna. "Held Captive by the Irish: Quaker Captivity Narratives in Frontier Pennsylvania." *New Hibernia Review* 8.3 (2004): 31–46.

Brown, Charles Brockden. "Origin of Quakerism." LM 3.18 (March 1805): 194–195.

Brown, Charles Brockden. "Quakerism, A Dialogue." LM 1.4 (January 1804): 248–250.

Brown, Charles Brockden. "Sketch of the Life of General Horatio Gates." PF 2.6 (December 1809): 481–484.

Franklin, Benjamin. *A Narrative of the Late Massacres, in Lancaster County, of a Number of Indians, Friends of This Province, by Persons Unknown, with Some Observations on the Same*. Philadelphia: Anthony Armbruster, 1764.

Frost, J. William. *The Quaker Family in Colonial America: A Portrait of the Society of Friends*. New York: St. Martin's Press, 1973.

Hinds, Janie. "Deb's Dogs: Animals, Indians, and Postcolonial Desire in Charles Brockden Brown's *Edgar Huntly*." *Early American Literature* 39.2 (2004): 323–354.

Hintz, Howard William. *The Quaker Influence in American Literature*. New York: Fleming H. Revell, 1940.

Kafer, Peter. *Charles Brocken Brown's Revolution and the Birth of American Gothic*. Philadelphia: University of Pennsylvania Press, 2004.

Kamrath, Mark. "American Exceptionalism and Radicalism in 'Annals of Europe and America.'" In Philip Barnard, Mark L. Kamrath, and Stephen Shapiro, eds., *Revising Charles Brockden Brown: Culture, Politics, and Sexuality in the Early Republic*, 354–384. Knoxville: University of Tennessee Press, 2004.

Krause, Sydney J. "Penn's Elm and *Edgar Huntly*: Dark 'Instruction to the Heart.'" *American Literature* 66.3 (1994): 463–484.

Kundera, Milan. *The Art of the Novel*. Linda Asher, trans. New York: Harper & Row, 1988.

Marietta, Jack D. *The Reformation of American Quakerism, 1748–1783*. Philadelphia: University of Pennsylvania Press, 1984.

Mekeel, Arthur J. *The Relation of the Quakers to the American Revolution*. Washington, D.C.: University Press of America, 1979.

Moses, Richard. "The Quakerism of Charles Brockden Brown." *Quaker History* 75.1 (1986): 12–25.

Nash, Gary B. *Quakers and Politics: Pennsylvania, 1681–1726*, new ed. Boston: Northeastern University Press, 1993.

Paine, Thomas. "The American Crisis III" (1777). In Eric Foner, ed., *Thomas Paine: Collected Writings*, 116–146. New York: Library of America, 1995.

Ryan, James Emmett. *Imaginary Friends: Representing Quakers in American Culture, 1650–1950*. Madison: University of Wisconsin Press, 2009.

Smith, Matthew and James Gibson. *A Declaration and Remonstrance of the Distressed and Bleeding Frontier Inhabitants of the Province of Pennsylvania*. Philadelphia: W. Bradford, 1764.

Sykes, John. *The Quakers: A New Look at Their Place in Society*. Philadelphia: J. B. Lippincott, 1959.

Taylor, Alan. *American Colonies*. New York: Viking Press, 2001.

Tolles, Frederick. *Meeting House and Counting House: The Quaker Merchants of Colonial Philadelphia, 1682–1783*. New York: W. W. Norton, 1963.

Tolles, Frederick. *Quakers and the Atlantic Culture*. New York: Macmillan, 1960.

Trueblood, D. Elton. *The People Called Quakers*. New York: Harper & Row, 1966.

Volney, Constantin François. *A View of the Soil and Climate of the United States of America*. Charles Brockden Brown, trans. Philadelphia: J. Conrad, 1804.

Warfel, Harry. *Charles Brockden Brown: American Gothic Novelist*. Gainesville: University of Florida Press, 1949.

Waterman, Bryan. "Review Essay: Charles Brockden Brown, Revised and Expanded." *Early American Literature* 40.1 (2005): 173–191.

Watts, Steven. *The Romance of Real Life: Charles Brockden Brown and the Origins of American Culture*. Baltimore: Johns Hopkins University Press, 1994.

White, Ed. *The Backcountry and the City: Colonization and Conflict in Early America*. Minneapolis: University of Minnesota Press, 2006.

CHAPTER 21

BROWN, THE
ILLUMINATI, AND
THE PUBLIC SPHERE

ANTHONY GALLUZZO

IN an 1805 essay on the origins of Freemasonry, published in his Philadelphia *Literary Magazine*, Charles Brockden Brown evokes the Illuminati conspiracy scare that gripped the United States in the late 1790s, only to dismiss the entire phenomenon: "the charge of infidel and revolutionary principles, brought by Barruel and Robison, against the lodges of freemasonry, are now generally exploded" (Brown 1805, 335). The key texts of the conspiracy panic, Abbé Barruel's *Memoirs Illustrating the History of Jacobinism* (1797) and John Robison's *Proofs of a Conspiracy against all the Religions and Governments of Europe* (1797) ascribe the French Revolution and the radical convulsions that subsequently shook the Atlantic world to the machinations of the Bavarian Illuminati, a secret society dedicated to recognizably Enlightenment principles, whose members' attempts to infiltrate the government of Bavaria's Catholic and absolutist prince-elector led to the order's suppression in 1784. This small-scale and abortive conspiracy, rooted in the backward social conditions and stillborn intellectual life of eighteenth-century Bavaria, nonetheless came to occupy a central position in what we would now recognize as conspiracy theory writ large, more accurately described as conspiracy metaphysics.[1]

As distinct from the conspiracy thinking that characterized certain strands of eighteenth-century civic-republican discourse, this mythology purports to account for historically novel political and social transformations, such as the French Revolution, by recourse to the deliberate machinations of Masonic secret societies. Following Edmund Burke, Barruel and Robison discerned in the imagined activities of these secret societies—which they and their followers conflated with the protosecular *saloniste* and coffee-house culture of eighteenth-century *philosophes*, *Aufklären*, and projectors—a diabolically methodical plot against government, church, and the patriarchal family.

These texts, both published in 1797 in Great Britain and the United States, represent one important component in the counterrevolutionary offensive waged against "Jacobinism" throughout the Atlantic world during the later 1790s. William Pitt, his anglophile Federalist sympathizers in the United States, and their anti-Jacobin proxies in the popular press used this catch-all term of ideological opprobrium to discredit republican movements across the Atlantic world, whether they were in fact Jacobin revolutionaries or merely moderate reformers. The two authors read the French Revolution as simply one phase in a vast plan to overturn all "government" and "religion," orchestrated by a secret society that includes the actual Illuminati, a short-lived Freemason-like organization active in Bavaria from 1776 to the early 1780s, before it was suppressed by the German state's hereditary elector.

These conspiracy narratives mirror, in a scapegoating and schematic fashion, the stated goals of late-eighteenth-century radicals such as William Godwin, who, in his 1793 *Enquiry Concerning Political Justice*, offered a vision of "anarchy" or political simplicity, according to which the progress of truth secured through open and transparent debate, or the public use of human reason, would ultimately lead to the dissolution of church and state—two congealed forms of error—and toward human perfectibility itself. While the US iteration of the Illuminati scare, promulgated by an orthodox Federalist-aligned clergy, was refracted through the prism of the Calvinist jeremiad, it was also shaped by the long-term trajectory of a transatlantic democratic movement and public, galvanized by the French Revolution, and variously described as Jacobin, radical republican, and Painite. It was against this cosmopolitan threat that the forces of reaction fashioned a self-consciously conservative and nationalist movement that partly cannibalized the methods of their radical opponents and progenitors. In other words, the new defenders of the older order implicitly recognized that things had changed; restoration would increasingly require popular consent, and nowhere more so than in the formally republican United States.

I. The Illuminati Scare and the Transatlantic Counterrevolutionary Offensive of 1798

Historian Seth Cotlar identifies 1798 as the year of a Federalist counteroffensive aimed at Painite or radical democratic republicans throughout the United States. This was no easy task in a republican polity many of whose citizens identified with the French Revolution and saw in it a continuation of historical processes inaugurated by the American War of Independence, according to which the entire world would be reorganized along republican lines. The itinerant Thomas Paine, whose political theories informed so much of radical Atlantic Anglophone political culture in the later eighteenth century, functioned as a living emblem of this movement as he moved from the revolutionary United States to his native Great Britain and finally revolutionary France. Indeed, in the eyes of Federalist (and British) elites, this cosmopolitan ideal was not the only or even the most threatening aspect of the radical democratic movement of the 1790s. The spread of the relatively democratic and socially inclusive model of politics and public sphere promulgated by printer-publishers such as Benjamin Franklin Bache, Thomas Greenleaf, and their readers represented a clear threat to the reactionary ideal of a deferential and hierarchical republican order.

As Cotlar notes, "the belief that Painite ideas were so self-evidently true that mere dissemination would automatically generate mass political conversion and commitment was perhaps the greatest democratic conceit of the age" (Cotlar 35). In other words, such popular movements—often described, after E. P. Thompson's *The Making of the English Working Class*, as a nascent working class or at least an oppositional counterpublic— correspond closely to the ideal type of the "liberal bourgeois" public sphere notably formulated by Jürgen Habermas as a civil-society sphere of debate and discussion in which conventional distinctions of rank were ostensibly suspended on the assumption of a shared rationality, despite the persistence of very real exclusions based on race, gender, rank, and status.

This democratic public sphere was cosmopolitan in scope and aspiration. For example, the London Corresponding Society advocated for basic electoral reforms, such as the expansion of the franchise, which their US counterparts in the democratic-republican societies took for granted in a formally republican polity they wanted to democratize in a more substantive fashion. Both movements nonetheless shared ideas and personnel, as with the exodus of Anglo-Irish radicals who fled to the United States in the wake of Pitt's Two Acts, and a broad commitment to radical republicanism, manifested in their plebeian and middling memberships. The already existing democratic-republican societies, galvanized by the French Revolution, absorbed many of the new radical exiles. Although this movement was later partly incorporated within the Jeffersonian Democratic-Republican Party, it should not be identified with it, especially during this early period, when the marriage of immigrant and native-born Jacobins often produced a radicalism different from what was taken as the outer limit of centrist dissent.

This largely white, predominantly male movement pushed the logic of universal emancipation to its theoretical limit in this era, countering the various exclusion clauses that defined Anglo-American liberalism with a vision of universal rights and the political economy required in order to realize this goal. Mary Wollstonecraft's *A Vindication of the Rights of Woman* (1792) uses a republican logic, predicated on the equal rational capacities of both men and women, to argue for the rights of women to participate as active citizens in a hypothetical republican polity. Connecticut-born Abraham Bishop (1763–1844), who would later counter Illuminati panic narratives with his own republican theory of aristocratic conspiracy, offers an instructive example. Bishop's "The Rights of Black Men" (1791) proclaims the centrality of racial equality to any consistent application of Paine's program and celebrates the Haitian Revolution in the wake of the initial Saint-Domingue uprising.

In his *The Key of Libberty* (1978), Massachusetts's William Manning (1747–1814) followed Paine's arguments in *Agrarian Justice* and *The Rights of Man*, Part 2, calling for public banks and infrastructure projects, agrarian land reform, progressive taxation, and the end of inheritance. These principles opposed Alexander Hamilton's economic policies, but Manning understood them as preconditions for effective equality and the exercise of natural rights, the "rights of man." Building on Jean-Jacques Rousseau and a radical reading of John Locke, for whom the earth was held in common in the state of nature and labor alone confers right, this model assumes that existing accumulations of property are arrangements that can be altered through processes of political adjudication.

"Active" citizenship, as Cotlar notes, encompasses a model of collective political agency outside the circumscribed realm of electoral politics in the early United States. In its more bourgeois form, printers and their "reader-politicians" wrote, published, republished, and debated the various political issues of the day, such as the course of the continental revolution, Pitt's repressive measures, or Hamilton's excise taxes, exerting pressure on the state by way of concerted action, such as petition. This transatlantic democratic-republican movement's plebeian membership, however, continued to draw on traditions of crowd action related to traditional ideals of the moral economy. The so-called Whiskey Rebellion, inflated by Hamilton into a domestic insurrection that required a strong response on the part of a federal militia, may be understood in this manner.

The natural rights framework, at this stage and in this milieu, was inseparable from the collective exercise of self-government outside the state, elected or not. Natural rights necessarily entailed political rights, and it was only with the Federalist counteroffensive of the later 1790s that a passive conception of civil rights—in which racial, gender, and property relations were redefined as immutable social structures, outside the realm of political adjudication—was cemented. Likewise, with this transformation, "politics" for those outside an elite that was admittedly in a state of transition came to be identified with voting rights (for white male property owners). The Federalist reactionaries could not denounce these principles in the same manner as their British counterparts without undermining the republican principles that provided legitimation for the new US state or revealing the aristocratic exclusion clauses built into the foundational myths of public sphere and republican citizenship alike.

In this situation, the Illuminati conspiracy romances of publicists such as Robison and Barruel provided one solution to the dilemma insofar as these narratives recast popular uprisings as aristocratic plots in a novelistic mold. This manufactured panic was not enough to save the Federalist Party, whose leaders embraced a hierarchical and authoritarian social and political order, exemplified by the 1798 Alien and Sedition Acts, and proved untenable in a formally republican polity that was already moving, at the end of the eighteenth century, toward liberal capitalist social relations.

According to the standard accounts, the Federalist-era Illuminati scare begins with arch-Federalist minister Jedediah Morse's March 23, 1798, Fast Day Sermon, which he repeated and refined in the pulpit and the press during the months that followed. Morse elaborated on President John Adams's inflammatory representation of the United States as "at present placed in a hazardous and afflictive position" (quoted in Stauffer 229). Adams most directly refers to the US position vis-à-vis revolutionary France and its antagonist Great Britain, especially in the wake of the XYZ affair and the undeclared naval quasi-war, under the pro-British Federalist administration of Adams, between the ostensibly neutral American republic and the French.

The novel character of this crisis for Federalists such as Adams or Tory ministers under Pitt was related to the universalist claims of the French revolutionaries, which commanded significant support among anglophone populations, including colonized Ireland, where the United Irishmen led an abortive revolution in 1798 while waiting for French assistance that never materialized (see Bric). Rather than a conflict between sovereign powers, understood according to the model of national sovereignty established after Westphalia in 1648, the crisis of the 1790s consisted in an expanding democratic threat to this sovereign, and largely absolutist, order. Ironically, it was Great Britain's liberal constitutional monarchy that led the charge in defense of the old regime.

The US Federalist leadership found itself in an even more peculiar position, since the American revolutionary break with Britain was seen among French revolutionaries and a significant portion of the American population as the inauguration of a cosmopolitan, radical-democratic transformation of all political orders and social arrangements. In the US context, the French Revolution spurred many Americans, and Democratic-Republican societies and radical emigrés sought to help complete an unfinished revolution. It was against this unprecedented threat of social transformation that representatives of a status quo under threat first saw themselves as self-consciously conservative in a distinctively modern, specifically counterrevolutionary sense. Burke and his circum-Atlantic epigones understood that the old order was irrevocably changed by the so-called democratic revolutions of the late eighteenth century and the concurrent emergence of a new collective subject in those popular classes whose democratic aspirations needed taming, even as their formal consent was increasingly required to do just that.

The ideological architects of counterrevolution thus sought to reconfigure "the old" in order to "make privilege popular, to transform a tottering old regime into a dynamic, ideologically coherent movement of the masses" (Robin 43). In this manner, counterrevolutionary ideologists ranging from Burke to Robison and Timothy Dwight exploited the tension between the new, ostensibly bourgeois-liberal ideals of a sincere, transparent publicity and the secrecy of the Masonic lodges in which these norms were first promulgated, away from the censorious eyes of the absolutist state.

For the conspiracy romancers, the Illuminatist cabal cloaked a base will-to-power in ethico-philosophical garb, even as they pursued a diabolically principled plan to exterminate all religion and government. Robison promiscuously mixes his conspirators' motivations, to inconsistent but ideologically revealing effect:

> The more closely we examine the principles and practice of the Illuminati, the more clearly do we perceive [that their] first and immediate aim is to get possession of riches, power, and influence, without industry: and, to accomplish this, they want to abolish Christianity; and the dissolute manners and universal profligacy will procure them the adherence of all the wicked, and enable them to overturn all the civil governments of Europe; after which they will think of farther conquests, and extend their operations to the other quarters of the globe, or, till they have reduced mankind to the state of one indistinguishable chaotic mass.
>
> (Robison 209–210)

Adam Weishaupt's naive Rousseauvian belief in the restoration of a virtuous human community to a benevolent state of nature is transformed by Robison into its Hobbesian negative image, as the Illuminati seek to establish a war of all against all. Why anarchy and the triumph of "profligacy" are better suited for world conquest than the instrumental use of religious belief to secure the obedience of the multitude, in keeping with the ethos of Thomas Hobbes and a certain strand of absolutist raison d'état, is a question neither posed nor answered by Robison.

In fact, both the desire for "riches, power, and influence, without industry" (209) and the world conquest that supposedly drove the Illuminati better describe the Anglo-European ruling classes during the first age of empire, with the notable difference that these goals were masked by, if not accomplished through, a missionary Christian rhetoric. The overlap between an American militant Protestantism and Robison's own claims clearly impressed the Federalist clergy, who used pulpit and press to promote the Illuminati narrative from 1798 through 1799, nor were these elective affinities lost on either the moderate or radical republican opposition.

Writing in Massachusetts, Morse begins his sermon with a typically anti-Jacobin tirade against the French threat, to which he also ascribes the Democratic-Republican opposition to the Adams administrations, other insurrections such as the Whiskey Rebellion, and, most important, "the astonishing increase of irreligion." Morse introduces Robison's work to his American audience and ultimately draws a line from the Illuminati plot to "abolish Christianity, and overthrow all civil government" to the continual "declaiming against the Clergy, and endeavoring by all means" to "asperse their characters and to bring them and their profession into disrepute" (quoted in Stauffer 232).

Morse proclaims the presence of Illuminati agents in the United States, identified with the new "Jacobin Clubs" or the Democratic-Republican associations that constituted one important pole of opposition to the Federalist administrations of George Washington and Adams. According to Morse, French foreign minister Edmond Charles Gênet frequented these clubs, despite their preceding the overzealous French minister's ill-fated mission by several years. Morse further equates the Jacobins with the United Irishmen and finally the Illuminati, who were, we are to believe, behind the French Revolution and the democratic opposition to the Federalist administration alike. "Illuminate" Morse, as the republican opposition later dubbed him, adduced as evidence for these grand conspiratorial claims the existence of the Wisdom Masonic Lodge in Portsmouth, Virginia. This offshoot of the French Grand Orient Lodge had a largely French émigré membership. Although the membership of the Wisdom Lodge did not exceed one hundred people, consisting largely of French royalist exiles from Saint-Domingue in the wake of the Haitian Revolution, Morse linked this lodge to several other extant Masonic organizations, claiming that they "combined and organized (with other foreigners and some disaffected Americans)" and were "regularly instructed and directed by their masters in France" in order to revolutionize "this country" (quoted in Stauffer 299).

Morse offers a prime example of the American countersubversive discourse that would inform so much American nationalism in the nineteenth century and beyond. Writing in the context of the partisan extremism of the 1790s, Morse's efforts to attach

"American Jacobinism," a catch-all term for a vibrant radical democratic movement that encompassed native-born and émigré radicals, to conspiratorial foreign subversion establish a pattern that long outlived the conflicts of the moment. Although the Illuminati scare, coinciding with the Federalist 1798 Alien and Sedition laws that effectively criminalized dissent in the new republic, was one important factor in Thomas Jefferson's electoral victory of 1800, the victorious Democratic-Republican Party itself employed a more moderate conspiratorial anti-Jacobin rhetoric in order to marginalize the more radical elements of its electoral coalition.

While Morse introduced Robison's conspiracy metaphysics to an American audience, it was Yale president and Congregationalist "Pope" Timothy Dwight who elevated the Illuminati conspiracy to an "eschatology" (Lienesch 152). Dwight's 1799 Fourth of July sermon, *The Duty of Americans*, seamlessly blends anti-intellectualism, partisan scapegoating, and Calvinist end-times theology, providing one seminal rhetorical template for American nationalism and its corollary paranoid style. Dwight found in the conspiracy metaphysics of Robison and Barruel a perfect complement to his own campaign against the enlightenment infidelity of Voltaire, the Encyclopédists, and their Anglo-American devotés, to whom he ascribes "a systematical design to destroy Christianity, and to introduce in its stead a general diffusion of irreligion and atheism" (Dwight, 10–15).[2]

Rather than following fellow anglophones Robison and Morse, Dwight is ironically closer to the French Jesuit émigré Barruel, whose three-volume *Memoirs of Jacobinism* reduced the entire Enlightenment to an elaborate conspiracy. The publication of Barruel's work in the United States did not generate the same kind of response that greeted Robison's text, despite the hopes of Morse and others. Even while the Federalist campaign successfully fanned anti-Jacobin and French sentiment during 1798–1799, the Illuminati scare, understood in narrow terms, was eventually undone insofar as Morse insisted on the factual accuracy of Robison's claims. Yet while the empirical claims were proven false and the Federalists defeated, the narrative template persisted.

II. Brown's Treatment of the Illuminati Fantasy in *Memoirs of Carwin* and *Ormond*

Godwin and, to an even greater extent, Brown understood and indeed embraced the significance of ideological fictions in determining the shape of the new public sphere. Rather than simply equating "romance" with the philosophes' priestcraft and rejecting it altogether in favor of a reductively empirical conception of truth, Brown and Godwin alike insisted that an alternative model of fiction was central to any progressive political project. Brown outlines a radical model of romance in the key 1799 essays "Walstein's School of History" and "The Difference between History and Romance"; these texts can be read alongside his critical reflections on secret societies and anti-Jacobin conspiracy theories, all of which Brown understood as another, dangerous mode of fictionalizing to be countered through critically self-reflexive imaginative interventions, which presumably include Brown's own novels.

As we shall see, Brown ironically appropriates certain aspects of 1790s conspiracy discourse, as exemplified by the work of Robison, in the form of would-be fictional villains such as the titular character of *Ormond* (1799) and Ludloe in *Memoirs of Carwin* (1803–1805). These figures belong to Illuminati-like secret societies, while their aims reveal a closer kinship with the old regime the Illuminatists wanted to undo, at least according to the febrile imaginings of Jedidiah Morse and Dwight. Yet it is in these imaginings that we find the rudiments of a nationalist, and emphatically anticosmopolitan, ideology to come, vividly dramatized in Dwight's vision of virtuous Americans and their women reduced to "the dragoons of Marat and concubines of Voltaire" (Dwight 21).

The *Memoirs of Carwin the Biloquist* is significant in this regard. Although Brown's unfinished 1803–1805 prequel to *Wieland* (1798) was intended to clarify the eponymous character's enigmatic origins, this fictionalized autobiographical fragment only further obscures this figure, who is alternately depicted as hero and villain, libertine and victim. Rather than offering clarification, the narrative complicates the dialectical quality neatly captured in Clara Wieland's representation of Carwin as a "double-tongued deceiver," a characterization prompted by Carwin's "biloquial" vocation. In appropriating the voices of others—many of whom are in fact socially, sexually, and racially "other"—Carwin surpasses any mere ventriloquist, even as he employs these stolen idioms for his own ends.

This quality is exemplified throughout the *Memoirs*, which often confront the reader with figures who combine antithetical social and political categories. Carwin himself is simultaneously self-serving and perversely principled. In this way, he resembles his Janus-faced mentor, Ludloe (aptly named after the seventeenth-century commonwealth regicide), a seeming exponent of Godwinian utopianism who is also an oppressive opportunist.

Yet Ludloe has revealed himself as the leader of an Illuminati-like global secret society and threatened Carwin with sudden death if he should reveal the group's existence; we know from *Wieland*, the complete novel for which the *Memoirs* function as a kind of prequel, that Carwin ultimately flees Ludloe and his organization. Brown's juxtaposition of an Illuminati trope, straight out of Robison and Barruel, with Ludloe's Godwinian rhetoric has led many critics to read *Memoirs* as a counterrevolutionary Bildungsroman, in keeping with the conspiracy tracts that Brown certainly appropriates for his own purposes, despite his explicit rejection of anti-Jacobin conspiracy metaphysics and the politics that underwrite them.

Yet Brown reveals Ludloe's mystical theatrics, which at least initially conjure Weishaupt by way of Robison for the reader, as more ideological mystification in the vein of Pitt or Adams. Rather than offering a Godwinian or radical identification, Ludloe more closely resembles those ruling classes who simultaneously trivialized and demonized the popular transatlantic insurgencies that shook the transatlantic world during the 1790s, by reducing them to the machinations of artful schemers like those of the courts of the old regime. In an ironic reversal characteristic of Brown's novelistic method as outlined in

"The Difference between History and Romance," Brown dramatizes the extent to which it was the Federalist elites propagating myths of a cabal disingenuously using a democratic rhetoric in order to gain or hold power who most closely resemble cabals disingenuously using democratic rhetoric to gain or hold power. Brown pushes this mode of ironic conspiracy romance to its limit in *Ormond*.

Written in November–December 1798, *Ormond; or, The Secret Witness* was published in January 1799, at the height of the Illuminati scare in the United States. Described by two recent critics as "the most self-consciously radical fiction written in the United States before *Moby-Dick*" (Barnard and Shapiro ix), *Ormond* is a peculiar Bildungsroman that follows the fortunes of Constantia Dudley, an arguably protofeminist heroine, "conducted" by her eccentric father "to the school of Newton and Hartley" or educated in the rational fashion recommended by Wollstonecraft in her *Vindication*, a text much admired by Brown (O 33). The narrative begins with a swindle, as Constantia's father falls prey to the machinations of Thomas Craig, a confidence man who insinuates himself into the family business, initially posing as an English striver willing to work as an apprentice in the Dudleys' New York merchant house. A master of deceit and forgery in a novel that thematizes the centrality of imposture in both the early republic and the wider transatlantic world during the age of revolution, Craig ultimately embezzles everything from the Dudleys, forcing them into penury and out of New York.

The remainder of the novel takes place in Philadelphia, where the impoverished Dudleys face a series of tragic difficulties, including the death of Constantia's unnamed mother and the loss of her father's eyesight; these melodramatic woes preface the novel's extended account of the 1793 yellow fever epidemic, which Brown knew from personal experience. The narrative uses the epidemic as a vehicle to explore, in brutal detail, inequalities and discrepancies between rich and poor, black and white, native-born and immigrant, and men and women as they all labor under the emerging market order of the formally egalitarian United States. The epidemic also functions as an ambiguous emblem for the revolutionary and counterrevolutionary upsurge that gripped the Atlantic world during the 1790s, including the radical (and reactionary) diaspora communities that remade Philadelphia, as noted earlier. Constantia, in seeking to support her blind father and avoid eviction, accordingly encounters various transatlantic radical immigrants. More than any of the other novels Brown wrote in the later 1790s, *Ormond* offers its readers vivid depictions of the radical and reactionary émigrés and exiles who settled in the northeastern United States and reshaped its politics—most dramatically in the character Martinette de Beauvais, the cross-dressing radical veteran of the American and French revolutions—in addition to the largely royalist French planter diaspora that fled Saint-Domingue in the course of the Haitian Revolution.

Upon reencountering Constantia and her demands for financial relief in Philadelphia, the swindler Craig turns to Ormond, a business associate of an unspecified sort. After learning of Craig's schemes and the Dudleys' plight, it is Ormond who restores Constantia and her father to their former station in life, although in secret, as is his wont and perhaps in keeping with the novel's subtitle.

Using disguise (for example, as a black chimney sweep), Ormond spies on the Dudleys and delivers a letter with money to Constantia from an unnamed benefactor proclaiming his intention to make good on Craig's debt to the elder Dudley. Ormond also apparently discovers his attraction to Constantia during this voyeuristic scene of "secret witnessing," despite holding a belief, at this point, that she had an illicit affair with Craig, due to the latter's exculpatory falsehoods. The scene telescopes the novel's dizzying array of motifs and concerns, coming as it does in Chapter 14, after the Dudleys' precipitous descent into poverty, all due to the artful impostures of a con man. Aside from demonstrating the extent to which class position in the new republic is a precarious matter of life and death, the account of the plague that immediately precedes Ormond's first appearance notably includes various accounts of Philadelphia's free black community, relegated to collecting the diseased bodies of fever victims due to a mistaken belief that Africans were immune to the disease.

While Ormond's class transvestism and blackface performance can be linked to other versions of theatrical imposture in the novel, his capacity for "grotesque metamorphosis" and easy ability to move "from the highest to the lowest rank in society" (O 134) and back again—unlike the various plebeian and free-black figures who populate the first part of the novel—mark him as a representative of the ruling class in a distinctive way. While Ormond's disdain for conventional mores, including sexual morality, suggests the aristocratic libertine, the constant metamorphoses and international character of Ormond's powers and ambitions point to an emergent capitalist-class power. Finally, the combination of aristocratic and capitalist elements also suggests the Federalist project, with its mixture of aristocratic and liberal-capitalist elements.

Ormond appears a villain as he goes on to abandon his mistress, Helena Cleves, who kills herself as a result, in pursuit of Constantia, apparently entranced by her rational self-possession, which forces him to reconsider his low opinion of women. Yet upon Constantia's rejection and the prospect of her removal to Europe, Ormond kills her father, in addition to Craig, whom he at least initially frames, before attempting to rape and murder Constantia and threatening to violate her body after death. Yet Ormond's theatrical villainy and "remarkable facility in imitating the voice and gestures of others" (115) have led some readers to see in this character another, older version of Carwin the biloquist. Even more significant for our purposes, Ormond's "political projects," conducted in secret and described by the narrator as "likely to possess an extensive influence on the future condition of this western world" (111–112), have been taken to exemplify a conservative turn in Brown and to constitute his own fictionalized reiteration of the countersubversive Illuminati conspiracy romance.

Robert S. Levine and an earlier generation of Americanist critics contend that "like the conspirators of Barruel, Robison, and the Congregationalists, Ormond and his associates are Enlightenment rationalists who seek to impose their moral and political views on peoples throughout the world. Evincing no respect for national boundaries and identities, they are international utopianists who want to bring the many into unity through 'the subversion of all that has hitherto been conceived fundamental and, in the constitution of man and government'" (Levine 45). Levine identifies an "alarmist vision of American vulnerability" here, which he links to the Federalist-Congregationalist promulgation of Illuminati conspiracy theories, and argues that this vision "dominates the novel" (47). To his credit, Levine also identifies an enlightenment counternarrative—one much more in line with Brown's stated sympathies—that functions as a counterpoint to the reactionary melodrama of conspiracy romance.

Rather than two competing narratives, identified as "enlightenment" and "reaction," with an emphasis on the latter, as Levine argues, Brown's novel is an ironic conspiracy romance, as we learn in Chapter 23, when the narrator reveals herself as Sophia Westwyn (Courtland), "a friend of Constance and writer of this narrative," and develops claims to being "merely instrumental to the purpose" God "wills" (O 224). In the same way that both the radical Enlightenment and the French Revolution—"infidel philosophy" and "Jacobinical sedition" in the countersubversive lexicon—are Illuminati instruments employed by a diabolical cabal to destroy government, religion, the patriarchal family, and property, according Robison and Barruel, the narrator Sophia is merely serving God's ends. The predestinarian theology here is the Congregationalist sort espoused by the Federalist clergy behind the Illuminati scare in the United States, as Brown's readers would recognize, and, as such, at a far remove from the protosecular freethinking espoused by Constantia, of which Sophia later disapproves, even attributing her friend's penchant for Ormond to the absence of religion. For Brown, who favored the atheistic *Political Justice* over Christian holy writings in letters to his pious Quaker friend Joseph Bringhurst, Jr. (Letters 297–313), this opening identification is the first of several cues to the reader that our narrator—an orthodox anti-Jacobin in the mold of Dwight—is not a reliable one. As Brown implies here and elsewhere in the novel, the template for the Illuminati conspiracy romance is theological, hence its appeal to the New England Federalist establishment, a point that, as we have seen, Bishop developed at length in his own "Rights of Black Men," which proposes that it is the New England clerical elite that most closely resembles the fictionalized Illuminati cabal.

In this vein, narrator Sophia observes that the "difference between Europe and America, lay chiefly in this; that in the former, all things tended to extremes, whereas in the latter, all things tended to the same level. Genius and virtue, and happiness, on these shores, were distinguished by a sort of mediocrity. Conditions were less unequal, and men were strangers to the heights of enjoyment and the depths of misery, to which the inhabitants of Europe are accustomed" (O 236). As one critic underlines in regard to these observations, "Sophia here echoes an argument proposed by right wingers up to the present who maintain that the American Revolution was concerned with individual liberty and mercantile prosperity (in a 'classless' society), whereas the French Revolution focused on collective equality and undesirable or 'extreme' transformations. In this manner the pronouncement seems to use a patriotic sounding affirmation to articulate a deeper commitment to conservative principles" (Barnard and Shapiro 182 n. 4). Sophia's account of a "less extreme" and "less unequal" United States is doubly absurd in light of what is ostensibly her own narrative account of the Dudleys up to this point, including their dramatic fall into poverty and the brutally stratified vision of class and race relations in Philadelphia that occupies the first part of the novel. Indeed, it is precisely those extremes that Ormond, as rendered by Sophia, traversed through his blackface and class transvestite impostures. Here again, Brown signals his own distance from the narrator as he alerts his reader to her agenda in crafting a hyperbolic Illuminati romance after Robison and Barruel.

Keeping Sophia's ideological investments in mind, we should attend to the initial outline of Ormond's political philosophy, which she offers the reader following her allusions to his ominous "political projects" (O 111). She asserts, for example, that Ormond "distinguished between men in the abstract and men as they are" (112), offering phrasing that explicitly recalls Godwin's *Caleb Williams, or Things as They Are*, the 1794 novel that fictionalized the radical political principles outlined in his 1793 *Enquiry*. Sophia ventriloquizes Ormond, telling the reader that in his eyes, "the former [men in the abstract] were beings impelled, by the breath of accident, in a right or wrong road, but whatever direction they should receive, it was the property of their nature to persist in it." Godwin, like other radical Enlightenment intellectuals, rejected models of human nature that emphasized its innate character—indebted as they were to theological ideas of "original sin"—and emphasized the role of environmental factors such as social class. Understanding these conditions was the necessary prerequisite to altering them; yet for Ormond, no "single being could rectify the error. It was the business of the wise man to form a just estimate of things, but not to attempt, by so chimerical an enterprize as that of promoting the happiness of mankind" (112). While Ormond echoes the radical emphasis on the deterministic character of social forces and the necessity of addressing the structures that constrain and misshape individuals—proclaiming that the "principles of the social machine must be rectified, before men can be beneficially active" (112)—like Ludloe, he employs these principles in order to rationalize inaction and the pursuit of "nothing but his own good."

The hyperbolic discrepancies between Ormond's principles and the behavior they authorize link Sophia to Robison and Barruel's version of the Illuminati, whose radical projects mask diabolically selfish aims. Yet in emphasizing the extent to which Ormond—or Sophia—distorts and betrays these principles, Brown alerts his readers to these narrators' own agendas. So our narrator once again evokes the Godwin—one metonymic figure for transatlantic radicalism in general—who famously insisted on total sincerity no matter the circumstance, when she writes of Ormond that complete "sincerity" or candor was his "chief boast," a candor that is "disgusting to weak minds," since "he regarded not the happiness of others" (114). Sophia initially depicts Ormond's sincerity as a license for cruelty—one potential consequence of total truthfulness no matter the consequence—before revealing that Ormond is a master of disguise and imposture. Why? Because "the treachery of mankind compelled him to resort to it" (115)? This cynical accommodation to things as they are is the antithesis of Godwin's perfectionist moral philosophy, as even a casual reader of the anarchist philosopher would have recognized at the time.

We subsequently learn that Ormond considers women to be inferior beings, because they are fundamentally irrational. Ormond abandons his mistress, Helena Cleves, who commits suicide as a result, upon meeting Constantia, who represents a living refutation of these sexist notions. But these beliefs are again more consonant with the views of Dwight and those reactionary defenders of the old order who saw in Godwin, founding feminist Wollstonecraft, and the transatlantic radical movement a threat to patriarchal authority, which they rendered in the sexualized terms of seduction or an "Illuminati concubinage" that more closely resembled the condition of women under the old order, as noted earlier. In each of these cases, rather than arguments for a radical reconstitution of social relations, the positions that Sophia attributes to Ormond are peculiar apologias for the status quo, while his nearly superhuman powers of disguise and impersonation remain in keeping with the logic of duplicity that we find in all of the novel's characters, whether "good" or "bad," from Thomas Craig to Martinette and the Dudleys, who assume the name Ackworth upon relocating to Philadelphia. Sophia herself is more of a duplicitous secret witness than the titular Ormond, considering her unreliable and voyeuristic narrative, ostensibly assembled from Constantia's firsthand accounts and additional sources that Sophia keeps secret (3, 111–112).

Sophia's vision of Ormond as a diabolical Illuminatus can thus be seen as a red herring, a reassuring fiction, or both, for our decidedly unreliable narrator, especially when considered in relation to the brutal market society that Brown depicts throughout the novel, a social order that mandates duplicity and imposture as basic means of survival. Ormond, in fact, exemplifies the system of private-property relations, safeguarded by the Federalist constitution, that Sophia otherwise upholds as the key to the prosperous "mediocrity" that distinguishes the United States from Europe, even as she, or the countersubversive mindset she represents, is uncomfortable with the social pathologies that come with those relations. In this manner, Sophia resembles Dwight himself, who, in the words of critic Chandos Michael Brown, "did not have the critical distance to recognize in the spectre of the Illuminati conspiracy the displacement of an equally anonymous and implacable marketplace, or that capitalism more surely than Jacobinism would transform the seemingly permanent institutions of home, family, community; he feared social change in its most elemental form. The Illuminati, the Jacobins, Godwin and Wollstonecraft all joined in the grim liturgy of a black mass celebrating anarchy, divorce, suicide, and abortion, a devilish inversion of all that was right and good in the world" (C. M. Brown 403).

As we can see, Brown repeatedly highlights the discrepancies between his narrator and conspiracy romancer manqué Sophia's ideologically loaded intentions—to contain the chaotic and subversive social currents of the French-revolutionary-era Atlantic world within the Manichaean lines of counterrevolutionary conspiracy romance—and their effects on the attentive reader. This ironic method and style—which belies the explicit narrative voice of Sophia that so many commentators take as normative—is arguably its own form of imposture, employed by Brown the novelist for radical ends, in a way analogous to his most radical character Martinette's revolutionary drag. In the wake of the counterrevolutionary offensive of 1798 and the often explicitly reactionary nationalisms that followed the implosion of the French revolutionary upheaval, Brown's ironic and coded romance represents one possibility for writing self-consciously radical fiction in revanchist times, a kind of code for speaking in a time of reaction. And it is among those able to read or receive the code—a hermetic counterpublic—that radical hope resides, waiting for another opportune moment to resurface. Brown's radical fictions in this way entail an ideal readership that ironically resembles the Illuminati of conspiratorial dreams and nightmares.

Notes

1. A substantial scholarly literature explores this episode and the subsequent history of US conspiracy fantasies and countersubversive panics. Hofstadter, Wood, and Rogin provide foundational accounts, and the questions they raise are further developed in White, Waterman, Tanner, and Robin, among others.

2. Note that Dwight had not read Robison at this stage, drawing instead on Morse's summary and a positive review in a British monthly magazine. His perspective, even prior to the Illuminati controversy, nonetheless overlaps with Barruel and the line of argument pursued by many conservative Catholic, usually Jesuit, opponents of the Illuminati and the Aufklärung; namely, that the broadly critical rationalism we usually associate with the Enlightenment should be understood as a literal conspiracy against all sanctified authority. Reinhart Koselleck revives this theory in a philosophically sophisticated form for the twentieth century. Interestingly, for Dwight and his counterrevolutionary fellow travelers, the traditional protestant opposition to the Catholic Church as Antichrist—which still certainly characterized German polemics against Illuminism, through the 1780s—is seemingly irrelevant, as Protestants and Catholics make common cause against the "infidel" threat. Here is a salient example of a recognizably conservative ideology that, rather than simply restoring a status quo ante (in this case, before the Revolution or the perceived threat of secular enlightenment, when confessional differences were worth martyrdom and murder), reconfigures itself in the face of an epochal change. See Robin.

Works Cited

Barnard, Philip, and Stephen Shapiro. "Introduction" and "Notes." In Charles Brockden Brown, Ormond; or, The Secret Witness, with Related Texts, ix–lii, passim. Indianapolis: Hackett, 2009.

Barruel, Abbé [Augustine]. Memoirs Illustrating the History of Jacobinism. A Translation from the French of the Abbe Barruel, 4 vols. Hartford: Hudson & Goodwin for Cornelius Davis, 1799.

Bishop, Abraham. "The Rights of Black Men." In Tim Matthewson, "Abraham Bishop, 'The Rights of Black Men,' and the American Reaction to the Haitian Revolution." Journal of Negro History 67.2 (Summer 1982): 148–154. [Originally published in Argus (Boston), November 22, November 25, December 2, 1791.]

Bric, Maurice. "Ireland, Irishmen, and the Broadening of the Late-Eighteenth-Century Philadelphia Polity." Ph.D. dissertation, Johns Hopkins University, 1990.

Brown, Charles Brockden. "Origin of Free-Masonry." LM 4.26 (November 1805): 335.

Brown, Chandos Michael. "Mary Wollstonecraft, or, the Female Illuminati: The Campaign against Women and 'Modern Philosophy.'" Journal of the Early Republic 15.3 (Autumn 1995): 403.

Burke, Edmund. Reflections on the Revolution in France and on the Proceedings in Certain Societies in London Relative to That Event. Conor Cruise O' Brian, ed. London: Penguin Books, 2004.

Butler, Marilyn, ed. *Burke, Paine, Godwin, and the Revolution Controversy Revolution.* Cambridge: Cambridge University Press, 1984.

Clemit, Pamela. *The Godwinian Novel.* Oxford: Clarendon Press, 1993.

Cotlar, Seth. *Tom Paine's America: The Rise and Fall of Transatlantic Radicalism in the Early Republic.* Charlottesville: University of Virginia Press, 2011.

Durey, Michael. *Transatlantic Radicals and the Early American Republic.* Lawrence: University Press of Kansas, 1997.

Dwight, Timothy. *The Duty of Americans, at the Present Crisis, Illustrated in a Discourse, Preached on the 4th of July, 1798.* New Haven, Conn.: Thomas and Samuel Green, 1798.

Elkins, Stanley, and Eric McKitrick. *The Age of Federalism: The Early American Republic, 1788–1800.* Oxford: Oxford University Press, 1993.

Godwin, William. *Caleb Williams.* Maurice Hindle, ed. Middlesex, UK: Penguin Books, 1988.

Godwin, William. *Enquiry Concerning Political Justice* (1793). Isaac Kramnick, ed. Middlesex, UK: Penguin Books, 1976.

Goodwin, Albert. *The Friends of Liberty.* London: Hutchison, 1979.

Habermas, Jürgen. *The Structural Transformation of the Public Sphere.* Thomas Burger, trans., with Frederick Lawrence. Cambridge, Mass.: MIT Press, 1991 and 1998.

Hofstadter, Richard. *The Paranoid Style in American Politics and Other Essays.* New York: Alfred A. Knopf, 1965.

Klancher, John. "Godwin and the Republican Romance: Genre, Politics, and Contingency in Cultural History." *Modern Language Quarterly* 56.2 (1995): 145–165.

Koselleck, Reinhart. *Critique and Crisis: Enlightenment and the Pathogenesis of Modern Society.* Cambridge, Mass.: MIT Press, 1988.

Leask, Nigel. "Irish Republicans and Gothic Eleutherarchs: Pacific Utopias in the Writings of Theobald Wolfe Tone and Charles Brockden Brown." *Huntington Library Quarterly: British Radical Culture of the 1790s* 63.3 (2002): 91–111.

Levine, Robert S. *Conspiracy and Romance: Studies in Brockden Brown, Cooper, Hawthorne, and Melville.* Cambridge: Cambridge University Press, 1989.

Lienesch, Michael. "The Illusion of the Illuminati: The Counterconspiratorial Origins of Post-Revolutionary Conservatism." In Wil Verhoeven, ed., *Revolutionary Histories: Transatlantic Cultural Nationalism: 1775–1815,* 152–165. New York: Palgrave, 2002.

Manning, William. *The Key of Libberty, Shewing the Causes Why a Free Government Has Always Failed, and a Remidy against It; Written in the Year 1798, by William Manning with Notes and a Foreword by Samuel Eliot Morison.* Billerica, Mass.: Manning Association, 1922.

Robin, Corey. *The Reactionary Mind: From Edmund Burke to Sarah Palin.* Oxford and New York: Oxford University Press, 2011.

Robison, John. *Proofs of a Conspiracy against all the Religions and Governments of Europe, Carried on in the Secret Meetings of Free Masons, Illuminati, and Reading Societies. Collected from Good Authorities, by John Robison, A.M.* London: T. Cadell and W. Davies, Strand; Edinburgh: W. Creech, 1798.

Rogin, Michael. *Ronald Reagan, the Movie; and Other Episodes in Political Demonology.* Berkeley: University of California Press, 1987.

Smith, Morton James. *Freedom's Fetters: The Alien and Sedition Laws and American Civil Liberties.* Ithaca, N.Y.: Cornell University Press, 1956.

Smyth, Jim. *The Men of No Property: Irish Radicals and Popular Politics in the Late Eighteenth Century* New York: St. Martin's Press, 1992.

Stauffer, Vernon. *New England and the Bavarian Illuminati*. New York: Columbia University Press, 1918.

Tanner, Jakob. "The Conspiracy of the Invisible Hand: Anonymous Market Mechanisms and Dark Powers." *New German Critique* 103 (Winter 2008): 51–64.

Thompson, E. P. *The Making of the English Working Class*. New York: Vintage Books, 1966.

Twomey, Richard. *Jacobins and Jeffersonians: Anglo-American Radicalism in the United States 1790–1820*. John Murrin, ed. New York: Garland, 1989.

Waterman, Bryan. "The Bavarian Illuminati, the Early American Novel, and Histories of the Public Sphere." *William and Mary Quarterly* 62.1 (2005): 9–30.

White, Ed. "The Value of Conspiracy Theory." *American Literary History* 14.1 (2002): 1–31.

Wilson, David A. *United Irishmen, United States: Immigrant Radicals in the Early Republic*. Ithaca, N.Y.: Cornell University Press, 1998.

Wood, Gordon. "Conspiracy and the Paranoid Style: Causality and Deceit in the Eighteenth Century." *William and Mary Quarterly* 39.3 (1982): 402–441.

CHAPTER 22

···

BROWN, EMPIRE, AND COLONIALISM

···

ANDY DOOLEN

THE early American novel used to be widely regarded as didactic, foolishly sentimental, and overloaded with hackneyed plot contrivances. It was judged to be a poor imitation of English and European literary models. After an early phase of reception in which Charles Brockden Brown and other novelists were generally viewed as minor antecedents to the nineteenth-century flowering of US literary and print cultures, commentators such as Leslie Fiedler and Richard Slotkin shifted the prevailing consensus. They reconstructed the psychological, historical, and social complexity of his novels, and they identified Brown's many important contributions to literary nationalism and cultural independence.

The frontier was integral to Brown's critical revival. Fiedler and Slotkin moved far beyond the facile cliché that representing the western landscape and its indigenous inhabitants was something of a literary achievement for an early American author. Their compelling studies presented Brown as a pivotal figure in transforming the western landscape into a psychological and literary tableau of nation formation. In the classic *Love and Death in the American Novel* (1960), Fiedler countered the formalist summation that Alexander Cowie had offered nine years earlier in *The Rise of the American Novel*. Fiedler praised Brown for being an instrumental player, right alongside luminaries such as Theodore Jefferson, in the "psychic revolution" for cultural and national independence (Fiedler 32). Brown's reputation, at that time, for being an inferior novelist did not faze Fiedler, who explained that the intensity and disorder of Brown's novels resulted from the author's inspired attempts to invent a distinctive Gothic tradition for the new nation. More than any of his peers, Brown wrote with the acute understanding of how the settler nation's insatiable desire for territory was corrupting the republican experiment. The United States could not distance itself from the dark history of European colonialism in North America.

Brown's *Edgar Huntly; or, Memoirs of a Sleep-Walker* has been the central piece in the revisionist project initiated by Fiedler and Slotkin. The eponymous hero's trek into the

Pennsylvania wilderness—the symbolic equivalent of a national psyche scarred by violent struggles for supremacy—mirrors an ambiguous and fraught process of introspection and self-discovery. Tracking the fugitive Clithero into the Pennsylvania backcountry, Edgar Huntly wanders ever deeper into his unconscious, inevitably confronting the haunting childhood memory of his parents murdered by American Indians. Edgar is entrapped in this nightmare world, soon discovering his primitive side and becoming an Indian killer, subsequently leaving a trail of bodies behind him as he fights his way back to the safe precincts of white civilization. The realism of the frontier dissolves in the imagination of the Gothic novelist. His "sensibility and dreamlike style" converted the actual frontier into a grotesque and fanciful space, Fiedler writes, "bearing a fitful, largely accidental resemblance to the facts of history or geography" (Fiedler 154–155). In the criticism of Fiedler and Slotkin, the physical landscape in *Edgar Huntly* is projected through the distorted vision of dreamers and sleepwalkers, which causes the frontier to shimmer like a dreamscape and to lose its resemblance to historical reality. Likewise, the indigenous antagonists are not historical subjects. Brown's novel renders them into symbolic vehicles for exploring the savagery lurking inside Edgar himself.

The historical frontier vanished within this psychological paradigm and thus, along with it, the gritty geographical memory necessary for understanding colonialism and empire. Nevertheless, Fiedler and Slotkin guided scholars through the intricate wilderness settings in Brown's novels. In the ensuing decades, scholars trained in New Historicist and American studies approaches connected the symbolic frontier to actual histories of conquest and exploitation in North America. For these scholars, the true meaning of Edgar's errand into the wilderness was located outside the psychological dreamscape and within a series of social, political, and historical settings. From this perspective, Edgar constitutes a politically inflected national allegory: the nightmare that Edgar cannot outrun is the dark shadow of colonialism hanging over the new nation. His mission carries him inexorably back to the terror and genocide that gave birth to the putatively enlightened republic, an unsettling paradox of the North American experience that many scholars now believe inspired the distinctiveness of Brown's national voice.

The concept of the national allegory was essential to reviving Brown's legacy. However, this concept also obscured Brown's most revelatory insights for a simple reason: until relatively recently, the structures of colonialism and empire were excluded from prevailing historical accounts of nation formation. These structures were judged to be antithetical to the republican political system—a belief, summed up in any US history textbook, that chattel slavery or Indian dispossession or territorial expansion *contradicted* the nation's revolutionary laws and principles. Yet Brown's writings persistently deny the existence of a clear temporal boundary between British colony and American republic. In this version of literary nationalism, colonialism—a system of territorial acquisition, capitalist exploitation, and the domination of non-whites—was part and parcel of the Bildungsroman of a rising republic with imperial designs in North America. The remainder of this chapter examines this development in Brown's fiction and nonfiction writings.

I. The Novels

This brief sketch has emphasized Brown's career as a novelist because his extraordinary novels have been largely responsible for improving his status in American literary history. The pace of the recovery effort gathered momentum during the early 1980s, largely spurred by Kent State University Press, which released *Arthur Mervyn, Clara Howard, Edgar Huntly, Ormond, Jane Talbot, Wieland, Alcuin, Memoirs of Carwin,* and *Stephen Calvert.* Except for the philosophical dialogue *Alcuin,* all of these works are novels. The larger American literary canon was being revised at the same time, and Brown's critical fortunes have risen alongside fresh and capacious interpretations of the early American novel. As scholars developed more complex understandings of the ways American authors adapted sentimental, Gothic, picaresque, and historical forms to the early national experience, Brown's novels became known for their unique fusion of literary vision and sociopolitical critique. The stylistic and structural oddities that disappointed formalist scholars are now widely appreciated as Brown's seizure of the post-Revolutionary zeitgeist.

Edgar Huntly; or, Memoirs of a Sleep-Walker has guided this chapter thus far, in part because of its significance within the more historical, even postcolonial, critical models that continue to drive the recovery effort. Published in 1799, the novel follows Edgar Huntly in his quest to solve the murder of his friend Waldegrave. Edgar hides near the elm tree where the crime occurred, until one evening, he spots a mysterious character digging at the base of the tree, who turns out to be the immigrant Irish servant Clithero Edny. Edgar eventually tracks the Irishman to his home and questions him about the murder. Telling Edgar that he is a sleepwalker, Clithero rejects the insinuation that his nocturnal ramblings prove that he must know something about Waldegrave's murder at the elm tree; however, a guilt-ridden Clithero confesses, in a lengthy story about his life in Ireland, that he fled to North America after murdering, in self-defense, the crazed brother of his patroness Mrs. Lorimer. After winning Edgar's sympathy and support, Clithero inexplicably disappears, and Edgar pursues him into the Pennsylvania backcountry. In a surprising twist, we learn that Edgar, too, is a somnambulist. His serpentine journey through woods and caverns becomes increasingly sensational and disorienting. After awaking in the darkness of a cavern, unaware of how he came to be there, Edgar decides the time has come to return to civilization. The return journey is perilous: he encounters hostile Indians, butchering one of them with a hatchet; kills a panther; and escapes a mob of white settlers, who mistake him for an Indian and try to shoot him. Finally reaching the safety of Solesbury, Edgar discovers his old teacher Sarsefield newly married to Mrs. Lorimer, Clithero's former patroness, who disabuses Edgar of the notion that Clithero was innocent. In fact, he is a deranged killer, who shows his true colors in the final pages, when he commits suicide after his failed attempt to assassinate Mrs. Lorimer. Indeed, nothing is at it seems in *Edgar Huntly.*

Such bewilderment was a defining trait of Brown's literary nationalism. In her foundational analysis of the novel, Carroll Smith-Rosenberg argued that this narrative of confused identities articulated the double-consciousness of the post-Revolutionary generation. They "quite self-consciously fused two subject positions: the victorious postcolonial and the colonizer, heir to Britain's imperial venture in North America. Facing east, Euro-Americans positioned themselves as Sons of Liberty; facing west, they were the progenitors of a vast new empire" (Smith-Rosenberg 495). In other words, the post-Revolutionary generation recognized that it inhabited a settler nation and would not easily discard or forget the experiences, structures, and lessons of colonialism. Similarly, in their seminal work of postcolonial criticism, *The Empire Writes Back*, Bill Ashcroft, Gareth Griffiths, and Helen Tiffin revisit Fiedler's insight that Brown transformed English and European literary styles and forms into literary expressions of national independence. As they argue, Brown's project rehearsed the central conflict in settler literature between "the backward-looking impotence of exile and the forward-looking impetus to indigeneity" (135–136). In this light, Brown's novels did not so much inform the creation of an emerging national consciousness as they exemplified the challenges faced by postcolonial intellectuals in developing a distinctive national literature, which ably reconciled past and present, dependence and independence, colony and nation.

Edgar Huntly attempts to reconcile the colonial history of land theft in Pennsylvania with the guiding principles of republican society. The novel's most meaningful site is the "Treaty Elm," the legendary site of William Penn's supposed 1682 pact of friendship with the Lenni Lenape. The fictional descendants of the Lenni Lenape return in Brown's novel to attack the settlers who had dispossessed their ancestors. The Elm is a melancholy monument to the Quaker founder's desire for peace and friendship, which the subsequent history of frontier violence and land grabs had destroyed. The Elm evokes the notorious Walking Purchase Treaty of 1737, when Theodore Penn, son of the founder, swindled the Lenni Lenape by hiring trained runners to demarcate the purchase boundaries, which robbed them of their homelands and fueled a vicious cycle of frontier violence between incoming settlers and the Lenni Lenape.

In his influential analysis of the novel, Sydney Krause argues that the Elm conveys Brown's vision of generational decline. Edgar's inability to comprehend what is happening around him—his "blunted awareness being typical of the settlers' know-nothing response to the burden of history"—is evocative of the settler's obtuseness about the suffering of the Lenni Lenape (Krause 472). Brown's history of frontier violence established a color-blind pattern of generational decline, which afflicted whites and American Indians alike. The killing is the fault of "the dishonor of the sons," who failed to live up to the original pact of peace and friendship signed under the Elm. *Edgar Huntly* is best understood as being a "gloomy but enlightening gloss on determining events in the American experience" (479). For Krause, the novel's vision is primarily retrospective.

Contemporary scholars have positioned *Edgar Huntly* more immediately in the context of the 1790s. Brown's depictions of American Indians or Irishmen certainly evoke the colonial past, but they also refer to pressing contemporaneous issues. For instance, Jared Gardner traces the interrelationships between *Edgar Huntly* and the Alien and Sedition Acts. Fully grasping the ambivalence and confusion inherent in Brown's settler novel, Gardner argues that the portrayal of the Indian in *Edgar Huntly* embodies a host of "savage" threats against the new nation—most troubling of all, the threat of the alien (Gardner 53). The pairing of Edgar and Clithero, as doubles saturated with psychological and political significance, is telling because it literalizes their differences. The pairing establishes a fundamental association between Irishman and Indian: "Edgar claims his ownership of the forest, and the rights, skills, and qualities of the Indian, not by becoming an Indian, but by killing Indians; and it is the alien—who does himself fatally become the Indian—who allows Edgar to achieve this. Aliens become Indians; Americans become Indian killers" (75).

Brown's novel adapts the logic of the Alien and Sedition Acts. By putting his zealous protagonist on the trail of the dangerous Irishman and then having Edgar eliminate American Indians in the backcountry, Brown delves into the violent, racialized process of identity formation in the settler nation. The construction and the elimination of the foreigner, as Gardner notes, "is the precondition of national identity; without the alien, there is no American" (56). Brown's novel confronts a dilemma common to any settler nation: how to build a unique and common national identity in the aftermath of colonialism? Brown articulates an equivalence of the threat of the foreigner (Irish) with that of race (American Indian), which advances this nation-building project. The result is not merely the existential or ritualistic cleansing suggested by the mytho-psychological models of Fiedler and Slotkin. The Anglo-American protagonist, who resembles both Irish and American Indian, must expel these foreigners from the homeland by lethal force, if necessary. By the conclusion, Edgar has barely survived a brutal rite of passage, but he has succeeded in gaining the sort of self-awareness that makes him the ideal republican citizen.

Gardner's brilliant reading of *Edgar Huntly* proved to be the catalyst for some innovative reexaminations of Brown's literary nationalism. John Carlos Rowe identified the way Brown's novels "draw much of their interest and power from their settings in the unstable political landscapes of eighteenth-century Europe and North America," which made him wonder how readers "for so long have ignored or accepted as mere Gothic mechanics the colonial disturbances and anxieties so fundamental to his narratives" (Rowe 25–26). Brown's fictional worlds represented a microcosm of a settler ideology that expressly denied its complicity with the structures of British colonialism and imperialism. Brown's status as a national author makes him a fitting starting point for Rowe's study: by demarcating racial, ethnic, and political antagonists, Brown's "Gothic technology" was constitutive of US imperial power. Yet Rowe believes that this way of reading—of being attuned to the political function of the symbolic Indian—remains a partial measure. Critics should follow through by restoring to Brown's fictional Indians the "historical integrity" of their languages, beliefs, and traditions. Such an approach can expose the "secret complicity" that masked the connection between Brown's Gothic wilderness and the genocidal laws, treaties, and policies first adopted by European empires, then inherited, imitated, and adapted by an expansionist United States (39). For Rowe, it was not simply that Brown's novels "offer subtle endorsements of the imperial policies of the young republic as it expanded westward" but that the novels "*accompanied and complemented such imperialist practices*" (50).

In a similar vein, Brown's *Wieland; or, The Transformation* articulates the inability of the United States to transcend its histories of colonialism and empire. The novel recounts the story of two orphans, Theodore Wieland and his sister, Clara, who inherit a large family estate outside colonial Philadelphia. The siblings transform the neoclassical temple built by their zealous Protestant father into a pastoral cathedral for celebrating their Enlightenment ideals. However, they begin to hear mysterious voices, predicting a coming disaster for the family, and the creeping sense of doom gradually destroys their New World harmony. One evening, the voice of God whispers to Theodore, or so he believes, ordering him to kill his family. So he takes up an ax and butchers his wife, their four children, and a servant girl. Theodore also intends to murder his sister, but an enigmatic laborer named Carwin utters a startling confession that stops the carnage: he is a ventriloquist and the source of the strange voices. Stunned by the deception, which inspired his killing spree, Theodore commits suicide.

Brown's tale of violence in the Pennsylvania backcountry provided an alternative view of the American Revolution. As Ed White cogently argues, Brown resists "the nascent triumphalist historiography of the Revolution," which emphasized the actions of metropolitan elites within fixed chronological boundaries (1776–1787). He incorporates into *Wieland* a transhistorical undercurrent of subaltern resistance—connecting the colonial era (the Paxton Riots of 1763–1764 and the Carolina Regulations) to the war years (Shays Rebellion) to the present day (the Whiskey Rebellion and Fries Rebellion). This history of resistance defines the true scope and meaning of the American Revolution (White 42, 44). White traces the decisive influence of Robert Proud, Brown's former teacher. Proud had published his two-volume *History of Pennsylvania* in 1798 and 1799, and its account of backcountry violence, often perpetrated under the cover of religious enthusiasm, echoes throughout *Wieland* (White 43). Carwin embodies the struggle for power occurring in the Pennsylvania backcountry. Drawing on Gayatri Spivak's theory of the subaltern, White claims that Carwin's "biloquism"—Brown's neologism for ventriloquism—not only resists understanding and representation but also exerts inexplicable power over and torments the Wielands (52). In the end, Brown does not intend for the rural subaltern to refer to a specific subject or group but rather to a "materialized, subjunctive relation" of the United States during the 1790s, a "site of perennial disruptions" that erase any temporal or spatial boundaries between colony and nation (56).

Brown continued his study of the rural subaltern in *Memoirs of Carwin the Biloquist*. Begun during *Wieland*'s composition and completed when the text was serialized between 1803 and 1805 in Brown's *Literary Magazine*, *Memoirs of Carwin* relates the early misadventures of the backwoods trickster in the years before he enters the world of *Wieland*. David Kazanjian traces Carwin's biloquism back to the fleeting image, in the opening pages, of a "Mohock savage"; his piercing, reverberating scream teaches Carwin about his own latent verbal powers.

Placing the serial novel precisely at the turn-of-the-century intersection of US colonialism and aesthetics, Kazanjian claims that Carwin's allegorical, hybrid speech "render[s] a racial nation not so much by ritually excluding nonnatives as by ritually assimilating Indians into a white nativism" (Kazanjian 144). *Memoirs of Carwin* can be read as a national allegory, although not the monologic type generally associated with US literary nationalism. The Mohawk warrior's terrifying cry marks the ambivalence, the "tenuousness of an American literary aesthetic" (140). Brown attempts to produce the modern figure of a double-voiced US citizen, but his novel cannot silence the histories of dispossession and genocide. That this national project ultimately fails—both historically and aesthetically—should not diminish Brown's efforts to understand the "assimilative drive" and the "unfinished business" of white settler colonialism in the early United States (144).

Duncan Faherty excavates what he calls the "biloquial architectural landscape" in Brown's narratives. It is a decidedly settler-national landscape, where original structures (and articulations) coexist with their copies (and echoes). This doubling not only produces confusion and violence but also speaks to the fundamental ambivalence of early national history. For instance, Theodore and Clara believe that they have converted their father's temple into a space with a new meaning for a new generation; however, their Enlightenment cathedral turns out to be a palimpsest that cannot fully cover up their father's history of religious enthusiasm and missionary conquest. In Faherty's compelling reading, the idealistic Wieland siblings reflect the aspirations of an independent nation to break free of the past but be unable to avoid building atop the architectural ruins of colonialism (Faherty 54). In this light, Carwin's invasion of the Wielands' domestic space depends on the "myopic refusal" of Theodore and Clara to recognize that "no space can be safely occupied without addressing its history" (56). By refusing to see their inheritance in the larger context of colonialism and territorial expansion, they also fail to understand the stranger Carwin, who inexplicably torments them and devastates their utopian community.

These new approaches have improved our understanding of the interrelationships between *Edgar Huntly*, *Wieland*, and *Memoirs of Carwin* and the histories of settler colonialism and empire. Collectively, these approaches challenge conventional wisdom about the discontinuity between colony and nation. In a similar vein, Brown's *Arthur Mervyn; or, Memoirs of the Year 1793* reverses the gaze away from the western frontier and toward the Atlantic corridor connecting Philadelphia and the West Indies. Expelled from the family farm, Arthur wanders into Philadelphia at the height of the deadly yellow fever epidemic of 1793 and catches the disease. The heroic Dr. Stevens finds him in the street, nurses the youth back to health, and hears Arthur's amazing life story. While initially thinking Arthur an upstanding young man, Dr. Stevens soon learns that the dazzling opportunities of big-city life have led him astray. He experiences many hardships in Philadelphia, including being conned out of his clothes and money; dejected and penniless, he is about to return to the country when he meets the seemingly wealthy Welbeck, who turns out to be a criminal. He schools his rustic charge in getting ahead in the city, ultimately leading Arthur down the path of ruin. One fateful day, Arthur witnesses Welbeck murder a man and foolishly assists his mentor in burying the body in the basement. When Welbeck disappears, Arthur realizes the truth about his devious mentor. After an interlude in the countryside, Arthur risks his life by returning to the plague-ridden city to clear his name. By the end of *Arthur Mervyn*, Welbeck is dying in debtor's prison, and Arthur is poised to fulfill his plans to study medicine under Dr. Stevens. He decides to begin a new life, perhaps in Europe, after marrying a wealthy Jewish heiress. Is Arthur an honorable character faithful to the new nation's civic virtues? If we follow those readings that argue that Arthur may be a deceptive and self-interested narrator, it is impossible to say what drives him.

Brown's realistic account of the 1793 yellow fever used to be the novel's only selling point, which thankfully is no longer the case. Now viewed as much more than a relatively decent imitation of Daniel Defoe's *A Journal of the Plague Year*, *Arthur Mervyn* is prized by critics for its examination of the geopolitical ramifications of the yellow fever epidemic, which eighteenth-century observers speculated originated in the West Indies. The disease exposed the popular fear that commercial expansion into a contaminated Caribbean threatened the health and security of the United States. Increased contact with the West Indies might infect the nation with racial and political disorder. In two influential studies, Philip Gould and Teresa Goddu revised the conventional geographical boundaries of American literary history by positioning Brown's novel within the global slave economy. Goddu observes that the "specter of slavery lurks in every economic transaction. Money from slave societies ubiquitously circulates to America, revealing America's international and domestic economies' dependence on slavery" (Goddu 37).

Exploring this space in *Fugitive Empire*, I trace the novel's unease over infected money back to the thriving and unstable commercial traffic between the United States and the West Indies. A key plot twist in *Arthur Mervyn* involves a money belt, containing the liquidated assets of a West Indian plantation and buried in the basement with the murdered courier. After realizing his oversight and digging up the small fortune, Welbeck lands in prison and bequeaths the "lost treasure" to Arthur, who ventures into the South with the diseased money so that he can clear his name. Like the Fugitive Slave Law, however, Arthur's mission cannot contain the spread of the disease. By restoring the property to the Maurice family in Baltimore, he hopes to create a virtuous republican capital detached from the risks of the global slave economy and positively unlike a Southern economy based in racial exploitation and terror. Yet this image of the South as quarantine for runaway capital, I argue, merely reinforces a persistent problem: the spread of "clean" and "dirty" money could not be disentangled in a slaveholding republic (Doolen). The global slave economy, as the economic engine of the nascent US empire, made even the most virtuous citizens complicit with its corruptions.

Likewise, Sean Goudie claims that *Arthur Mervyn* registers Brown's ambivalence about US involvement in the global slave trade, specifically the "nation's diseased paracolonial commerce" with the West Indies. Whereas other scholars have observed how Brown's depiction of the yellow fever articulates popular fears of racial and political violence in the West Indies spreading to the United States, Goudie argues that Arthur's traumatic encounter with a West Indian "servant" during the epidemic foreshadows a "far more subtle, insidious *evolution*"; Arthur's interest in taxonomy shifts toward the classification of peoples in the United States (Goudie 179). His transformation ultimately reflects the convergence of racial science and public policy in the United States at a precarious moment. Disorder in the French and British West Indies had exacerbated race, ethnic, and class divisions in the United States, weakened the abolitionist movement, and fostered support for plans that would protect the slaveholding nation by removing free blacks from it.

Brown's awareness of the hazards of expanding commerce into this turbulent geography directly keyed the structure and thematics of *Arthur Mervyn*. The novel "exposes in unflattering ways the classificatory mechanisms used by the budding empire to constitute national character, to establish the boundaries between acceptable and unacceptable terms of identity for the nation and national citizen, and to devise frameworks for belonging and removal" (Goudie 182). Arthur's traumatic experience during the yellow fever epidemic reflects a growing awareness that the United States did not possess the power to control the dangerous sociopolitical cross-currents flowing throughout the US–West Indies corridor. In fact, as Goudie concludes, "[w]ithin and without the borders of Brown's text, West Indian and Anglo-American cultures and commodities clash and cohere in ways that resist hegemonic attempts to domesticate West Indian figures within their discursive constructions of a resolutely *white* empire" (198).

In sum, the ambivalences, ambiguities, and elusiveness of Brown's novels have encouraged critical speculation about the many interconnections between Brown, his writings, and the forces of colonialism and empire. One important result of these studies has been to cast doubt on what was once assumed to be the turning point in Brown's career. Whereas many earlier, pre-1980s commentators assumed that Brown turned toward conservatism in his later years, after his well-documented engagement with Godwinian ideas and other strains of radical thought in the 1790s, more recent scholarship tends to challenge this view. Over the last three decades, the reevaluation of Brown's novels, letters, and other writings has transformed his position in American literary history. Brown's biography and reception history now read like one of his widely admired, contradictory, and unpredictable novels.

II. Nonfiction Writings

Until recently, Brown's nonfiction writings attracted little critical attention relative to the novels. Their existence seemed to prove the assumption that a disillusioned Brown had abandoned the novel for the sharper partisan blade of journalism and pamphleteering after 1800. In addition to the essays published in his *American Register, or General Repository of History, Politics, and Science*, Brown wrote three popular pamphlets: *An Address to the Government of the United States on the Cession of Louisiana to the French, etc.* (1803); *Monroe's Embassy, or, The Conduct of the Government, in Relation to Our Claims to the Navigation of the Missippi* [sic], *etc.* (1803); and a strident attack on Jeffersonian trade policies entitled *An Address to the Congress of the United States, on the Utility and Justice of Restrictions upon Foreign Commerce, etc.* (1809). Moreover, his writing on science and geography seemed to confirm his post-1800 utilitarian trajectory.

He translated Comte Volney's *A View of the Soil and Climate of the United States of America* (1804) and was working on an extensive geographical study of the earth in the years before he died.

Steven Watts offers a partial explanation for why the "fledgling political writer" supposedly gave up on his literary career, joined his brothers in a business partnership, and promptly began beating the drum for commercial and territorial expansion. Watts argues that Brown matured quickly into "an ardent expansionist" whose "advocacy of American commercial activity and geographical growth was striking" (Watts177). In many of his writings, Brown articulates the merchant's conviction that the expansion of the United States would spread the benefits of republican civilization and protect the nation against the scourge of factionalism and sectional conflict. He supported the principle of free trade, defended US claims on the contested Louisiana Purchase, and condemned the Jefferson administration for an ill-conceived embargo and other restrictive trade policies (176). However, Brown believed that greed, factionalism, and sectional jealousies were undermining the civilizing mission of republican society. Commercial and territorial expansion might instigate a war, but military conflict could cure the republic and restore its original strength and virtue. When other scholars researched Brown's nonfiction writings during the 1990s, these writings seemed to corroborate the old theory that Brown, after 1800, had shifted his allegiance to the conservative Federalist politics of the commercial class to which he now belonged.[1]

As more and more scholars made the leap from Brown's novels to his nonfiction writings, it became increasingly difficult to describe these texts as purely political propaganda or utilitarian studies bereft of intellectual vigor and aesthetic experimentation. Brown continued to grow as a writer. "[I]t may be more accurate to say," as the editors of *Revising Charles Brockden Brown* write, "that Brown extends the epistemological, sociopolitical, and interpretive concerns of the novels into non-novelistic genres, producing historiography, journalism, statistical commentary, annotated translations, and political pamphlets that are closely related to and often bear clear rhetorical resemblance to the more familiar terrain of the novels" (Barnard, Kamrath, and Shapiro 255). This emphasis on Brown's nonnovelistic writings has greatly improved our understanding and appreciation of Brown's post-1800 fictional works, such as *Clara Howard* (1801), *Jane Talbot* (1801), *Memoirs of Carwin the Biloquist* (1803–1805), and the *Historical Sketches* (1803–1807). These later titles prove that Brown continued to experiment and mature as a wordsmith after 1800. His artistic powers never dissipated.

As a result, neglected texts such as the *Historical Sketches* have emerged in recent years to broaden our understanding of Brown's exploration of colonialism and empire.[2] Published in fragments in Brown's *The Literary Magazine, and American Register* and in the posthumous Dunlap 1815 biography, the *Historical Sketches* relates the fictional history of the powerful Carril family, spanning eighteen centuries, from their scandalous beginnings in the Roman era to their prominence in seventeenth- and eighteenth-century Europe. Brown traces the history of the Carril family back to an illicit relationship between authoritarian power and cultural capital. Philip Barnard rightly praises the

Historical Sketches as a literary achievement. An inventive mix of history and fiction, *Sketches* is continuous with the themes, styles, and preoccupations of Brown's most celebrated novels (Barnard 311–312).[3] Barnard rejects the prevailing thesis that the text is a product of Brown's post-1800 political conservatism. Quite the opposite, Brown is actually protesting against the "extremism of contemporary Federalists"; this is evident in his depictions of anti-Jewish violence, which evoke the "Federalists' use of ideological demonization and scapegoating to promote political repression" (Barnard 316). Aesthetic production was crucial to Federalist authority. Drawing on Hannah Arendt's insight that state institutional power is based in these creative acts of "constantly transforming reality into fiction," Barnard argues persuasively that *Historical Sketches* inevitably reveals Brown's main objective: to expose how the interrelationship of "aesthetic" and "political" representation facilitates the state's inexorable drift toward control and domination. Brown's *Historical Sketches*, which Barnard describes as "one of the earliest fully developed dramatizations of modern totalitarianism," ought to be central to any study of early US imperialism (316).

The "Annals of Europe and America," a narrative series published in the *American Register*, also demonstrates the complex interplay of history, fiction, and political commentary in Brown's later work. Mark Kamrath contends that "Annals of Europe and America" is a "dissident" "narrative" that takes aim at the European and US practices of colonialism and empire (Kamrath 362). Adopting a global perspective, and inspired by the writings of William Godwin and Thomas Paine, Brown condemns the British exploitation of India, Ireland, Egypt, and Denmark, and he wonders about the widespread usurpation of the "rights of others." Kamrath shows how Brown's critique of British colonialism "eventually lent itself to a stinging indictment of imperialist attitudes associated with American Exceptionalism—a reevaluation of America's prophetic promise" (375). Brown's ambivalence about an expansionist United States defines the "Annals of Europe and America." If the nation hoped to realize its destiny, then the moral imperatives of republican principles must guide their commercial policies (356). Profit must not be the primary objective in a republican society that believed the expansion of its commerce could free the world from tyranny.

I wish to conclude this chapter by discussing two 1803 political pamphlets about a smoldering crisis in Louisiana. The pamphlets are Brown's most controversial examinations of colonialism and empire. In 1802, Spain closed the port of New Orleans to upriver commercial traffic, infuriating the public and instigating calls for military action to restore US rights on the Mississippi River, even if such action required seizing New Orleans. The crisis worsened after news leaked of a secret Spanish-French treaty that transferred Louisiana territory to France, persuading Brown to take up his pen and compose the anonymous *Address to the Government*. The pamphlet masquerades as nonfiction, but Brown employs a literary device: a fictional letter written by a French foreign counselor to Napoleon. The counselor advises Napoleon that he should abandon plans to invade Haiti and concentrate instead on conquering Louisiana. Brown's pamphlet repeated the Federalist censure of the Jeffersonian party as hapless Francophiles unable to defend US interests against foreign aggression.[4]

The fictitious French counselor believes that France can defeat the United States by inciting a mass insurrection among disaffected slaves and American Indians. The fact that Brown seems to call for war by exploiting the nation's racial anxieties used to trouble critics, but the pamphlet no longer appears like malicious and one-dimensional propaganda. Attuned to Brown's experimental artistic tendencies, scholars have uncovered a more ambiguous and elusive text. Rather than proving that Brown had abandoned his youthful idealism and literary instincts, the pamphlet revealed the essential characteristics of the Gothic novelist. Robert Levine aptly labels Brown the "pamphleteer-fictionist" during this period when he supposedly had turned away from the Gothic themes of *Edgar Huntly* and *Wieland*; Brown evidently still enjoyed being the subversive artist and shocking his audience with terrifying conspiracies and "masterminding villains" (Levine 1989, 57).

Gardner's groundbreaking work on Brown's pamphlets collapsed the divide between the two halves of Brown's career. Gardner shows how the pursuit of the alien—and his inevitable removal—fuses together *Edgar Huntly* and *An Address to the Government*. By conflating the Irish alien and the indigenous outsider, Brown's novel offered an ideological framework for tracing a similar nation-building dynamic in the pamphlet, which conflated the French with American Indian and African American antagonists. These companion texts, in Gardner's ingenious reading, identify how racial difference, "conceived as the most perilous threat to American identity, thus becomes at the same time a cornerstone in the myth of nation-building" (Gardner 56). Far from being devoid of aesthetic complexity, the pamphlet had "learned the lessons of *Edgar Huntly*'s engagement with the logic of the Alien and Sedition Acts: constructing and exorcising the alien is the precondition of a national identity; without the alien, there is no American" (56).

In the years since Fiedler and Slotkin opened up fresh approaches to Brown's writings, scholars have moved beyond nation-centered frameworks and have developed alternative temporal and spatial frameworks for reading Brown's fiction and nonfiction writings. Scholars are now attuned to the significance of transnational histories; global commerce; revolutions and political violence in France, Haiti, and the United States; ideologies of racial difference; and territorial expansion. Their work has effectively reorganized the chronology of Brown studies. The once-sturdy boundary between Brown's liberal and conservative years and his fiction and nonfiction writings has become permeable.

As a result, scholars continue to broaden our understanding of Brown's nonnovelistic writings. For instance, in his contribution to *Revising Charles Brockden Brown*, Levine returns to the subject of aesthetic complexity in Brown's "biloquial" pamphlets. Scholars misread a pamphlet such as *An Address to the Government* because they mistakenly conflate Brown the author and the fictitious French counselor. By overlooking the ironic distance between the two, scholars cannot accurately decipher the pamphlet's racial politics. The French counselor certainly exploits fears of a slave rebellion, but Levine argues that the counselor was not Brown's mouthpiece. Brown hopes that his readers, if they adopt his narrator's skeptical stance, will reject the counselor's racist views and face up to the hazards of maintaining the institutions of slavery. As Levine concludes, Brown's racial rhetoric aimed to alert US citizens, particularly in the South, to a growing national crisis. Slavery was deepening party and sectional rivalries and undermining the harmony and the security of an expanding United States.

Levine shows how a transnational context of revolutionary struggle can alter our view of Brown's stance on the vital issues of race and nationhood, arguing that Brown's Louisiana writings do not share Jefferson's "fear and loathing of blacks" or his anxiety about a coming race war in the United States. In fact, Brown presented an expansionist agenda that both encouraged people to respect the rights of the slave rebels of Saint-Domingue and to question the assumptions of American exceptionalism. Brown adopts a "Federalist-nationalist postrevolutionary perspective," an intentionally awkward label that supports Levine's main point that the conventional national framework has prevented critics from understanding Brown's *spatial* dynamics (1989, 335). Brown simply looks different within this broader geographical framework. He was not unlike other Northeasterners, predominantly merchants and Federalist politicians, whose unstable mixture of self-interest and political idealism motivated their objections to Jefferson's restrictive trade policies and their support for a free Haiti.

Brown's body of work challenges contemporary readers to revise their assumptions about the putative contradiction between republic and empire. Like many of his contemporaries, regardless of their political affiliation, Brown developed a vision that reflected a consensus that territorial expansion and conquest would strengthen the American republic by solving the potentially catastrophic problems of racial conflict. His writings support the theory that the geographical diffusion of slavery through an expanding nation-state might eventually abolish the wicked institution. Rather than fearing the blowback from the extraordinary revolution occurring in Saint-Domingue, as Jefferson did, Brown supported the antislavery cause and affirmed the principle of black humanity. In many ways, Brown was in tune with the extraordinary promise of the Louisiana Purchase. It doubled the physical size of the country and inspired Federalists and republicans to dream of an "empire of liberty" that would only enhance the anti-imperial legacy of 1776.

The ameliorating effects of expansion not only promised to gradually abolish slavery and eliminate the threat of a large-scale insurrection but also to terminate frontier violence between land-hungry settlers and American Indians. As the republican system spread across the continent, American Indians inevitably would exchange their lands for new homes farther west. They would embrace the promises of annuities, farming implements, and, one day, assimilation into a republican society that had tutored them in the arts of civilization. In his analysis of Brown's writings about race between 1799 and 1805, Levine cautions against viewing Brown as a "multiculturalist before his time." Yet Levine rightly contends that Brown had adopted a "capacious vision of human possibility" that scholars are just beginning to investigate (Levine 2008, 343).

NOTES

1. On the interplay between Brown's commercial and intellectual impulses, see Gilmore.
2. Warner Berthoff's 1956 article on the *Sketches* made this recovery possible.

3. Barnard describes the textual problems involved in reading and examining this unfinished, fragmentary work, which runs upward of 260 pages and one hundred thousand words. These writings have yet to be published in a single volume, and it has only been since the mid-1970s that scholars have had access to a relatively fuller version of the text.

4. Shortly after the first 1803 pamphlet captivated a national audience, Brown published *Monroe's Embassy*, which specifically criticized the Jefferson administration for failing to assert US dominion over the Mississippi River and the largely uncharted Louisiana territory.

WORKS CITED

Ashcroft, Bill, Gareth Griffiths, and Helen Tiffin. *The Empire Writes Back: Theory and Practice in Post-Colonial Literatures*. London: Routledge, 1989.

Barnard, Philip. "Culture and Authority in Brown's *Historical Sketches*." In Philip Barnard, Mark Kamrath, and Stephen Shapiro, eds., *Revising Charles Brockden Brown: Culture, Politics, and Sexuality in the Early Republic*, 310–331. Knoxville: University of Tennessee Press, 2004.

Barnard, Philip, Mark Kamrath, and Stephen Shapiro, eds. *Revising Charles Brockden Brown: Culture, Politics, and Sexuality in the Early Republic*. Knoxville: University of Tennessee Press, 2004.

Berthoff, Warner B. "Charles Brockden Brown's Historical 'Sketches': A Consideration." *American Literature* 28.2 (1956): 147–154.

Cowie, Alexander. *The Rise of the American Novel*. New York: American Book, 1951.

Doolen, Andy. *Fugitive Empire: Locating Early American Imperialism*. Minneapolis: University of Minnesota Press, 2005.

Faherty, Duncan. *Remodeling the Nation: The Architecture of American Identity, 1776–1858*. Hanover, N.H.: University Press of New England, 2007.

Fiedler, Leslie A. *Love and Death in the American Novel*. New York: Criterion Books, 1960.

Gardner, Jared. *Master Plots: Race and the Founding of an American Literature, 1787–1845*. Baltimore: Johns Hopkins University Press, 1998.

Gilmore, Michael T. "Charles Brockden Brown." In Sacvan Bercovitch, ed., *The Cambridge History of American Literature: 1590–1820*. Cambridge: Cambridge University Press, 1994.

Goddu, Teresa A. *Gothic America: Narrative, History, and Nation*. New York: Columbia University Press, 1997.

Goudie, Sean X. *Creole America: The West Indies and the Formation of Literature and Culture in the New Republic*. Philadelphia: University of Pennsylvania Press, 2006.

Gould, Philip. "Race, Commerce, and the Literature of Yellow Fever in Early National Philadelphia." *Early American Literature* 35.2 (2000): 157–186.

Kamrath, Mark. "American Exceptionalism and Radicalism in the 'Annals of Europe and America.'" In Philip Barnard, Mark Kamrath, and Stephen Shapiro, eds., *Revising Charles Brockden Brown: Culture, Politics, and Sexuality in the Early Republic*, 354–384. Knoxville: University of Tennessee Press, 2004.

Kazanjian, David. *The Colonizing Trick: National Culture and Imperial Citizenship in Early America*. Minneapolis: University of Minnesota Press, 2003.

Krause, Sydney J. "Penn's Elm and *Edgar Huntly*: Dark 'Instruction to the Heart'." *American Literature* 66.3 (1994): 463–484.

Levine, Robert S. *Conspiracy and Romance: Studies in Brockden Brown, Cooper, Hawthorne, and Melville*. Cambridge: Cambridge University Press, 1989.

Levine, Robert S. *Dislocating Race and Nation: Episodes in Nineteenth-Century American Literary Nationalism*. Chapel Hill: University of North Carolina Press, 2008.

Rowe, John Carlos. *Literary Culture and U.S. Imperialism from the Revolution to World War II*. Oxford: Oxford University Press, 2000.

Slotkin, Richard. *Regeneration through Violence: The Mythology of the American Frontier, 1600–1860*. Middletown, Conn.: Wesleyan University Press, 1973.

Smith-Rosenberg, Carroll. "Subject Female: Authorizing American Identity." *American Literary History* 5.3 (January 1993): 481–511.

Watts, Steven. *The Romance of Real Life: Charles Brockden Brown and the Origins of American Culture*. Baltimore: Johns Hopkins University Press, 1994.

White, Ed. "Carwin the Peasant Rebel." In Philip Barnard, Mark L. Kamrath, and Stephen Shapiro, eds., *Revising Charles Brockden Brown: Culture, Politics, and Sexuality in the Early Republic*, 41–59. Knoxville: University of Tennessee Press, 2004.

PART VI

THE BODY
AND MEDICAL
KNOWLEDGE

CHAPTER 23

....

BROWN AND
PHYSIOLOGY

....

STEPHEN RACHMAN

Somnambulism, spontaneous combustion, ventriloqual psychosis, and yellow fever—these are the signature pathological and quasi-pathological conditions that mark the para-physiological terrain of Charles Brockden Brown's fiction. Situated as cultural pathologies and quasi-clinical conditions, they function as triggers for his plots and as engines of sociocultural critique, activating the questions of literary power that animate his fiction. In terms of forging American Gothic aesthetics, if Brown saw his own literary operations as an innovation in that European narrative tradition by dispensing with "[p]uerile superstitions and exploded manners; Gothic castles and chimeras" (EH 3), then he accomplished this by domesticating and rationalizing these European devices with American settings and a series of fascinating yet, at the time, vaguely understood physiological phenomena which he conceived of as both mysteries of the human organism and cultural pathologies.

This shift constituted a central element in Brown's thematic Americanization of the Gothic novel, politicizing it, transferring the balance away from patently superstitious sources of irrational terror toward ones if not exactly more rational, then rooted in fears based on mysterious phenomena found in contemporaneous discourses of nature and reason. An article on "Terrific Novels" that Brown edited in 1805 elaborated on this distinction. Gothic terror in its debased form attempted to "keep the reader in a constant state of tumult and horror by the powerful engines of trap-doors, back stairs, black robes, and pale faces: but the solution of the enigma is ever too near at hand, to permit the indulgence of supernatural appearances" (Brown 288). Brown's objection was not to terror per se but that the terrifying devices of standard Gothic fiction, even as it had developed in its relatively brief history to 1800, amounted to little more than jumpiness induced by scary atmospherics and costumery, the idiom of which did not rise (in his estimation) to a sufficient level of legitimate intrigue, falling into absurd patterns of panic, fear, concealment, and revelation. For Brown, Gothic anxiety's proper métier was not the trapdoor-riddled monk's castle or the black robe but the mental conditions aroused by fears of madness, disease, bankruptcy, politics, the ordinary violence of human passion, and, on the American frontiers, Native American treachery and captivity. The difficulties involved in Brown's shifting of Gothic stimulus away from the vocabulary of conventional fear toward more legitimate sources of anxiety are immediately present to any reader of his fiction. Haunted houses and hooded figures are immediately recognizable; physiological obscurities, histories of settler-native dealings, and financial woes are not. When one begins to travel beyond fear in Brown's Gothic, one encounters science and, more often then not, medical science. Thus, Brown's novels are freighted (in both positive and negative senses) with complex backstories and explanatory passages that invest the most fantastic and phantasmagorical aspects of his work with an imaginative intensity that maintains a realistic density; the patho-psychophysiological is a key category in this respect.

Brown's biography gives ample evidence of his interest in medicine and disease. William Dunlap describes him as having a delicate constitution, prone to illness that "incapacitated him from athletic exercise" (Dunlap 1815, I: 20) and led to a lifelong preoccupation with his own fragile health and an investigation into the mechanisms of health and disease. In a pre-Temperance era of grog shops and daily drams, he seems to have abstained from distilled alcohol and maintained a vegetarian diet. His galvanic friendship with Dr. Elihu Hubbard Smith and connections with other members of the New York Friendly Club, especially Drs. Edward Miller and S. L. Mitchill, were forged in large part through a shared enthusiasm for medicine, nature, politics, and literature and an educational vision that could synthesize and integrate these branches of knowledge. Brown's experiences with yellow fever epidemics, including the well-known episodes of 1793 and 1798 (Smith died during the 1798 epidemic, and Brown may have suffered a mild case in either of these years), were signal events in his life and, as Dunlap and all subsequent biographers have claimed, fundamental to his fictional productions.

All of these factors undoubtedly shaped the angle of Brown's literary vision toward the physiological; but this terrain was equally part and parcel of a widespread Enlightenment taxonomical project establishing rational catalogs of the natural world and human societies. One text he would make ample use of, for example, in his accounts of somnambulism in *Edgar Huntly* and of "mania mutabilis" in *Wieland*, was Erasmus Darwin's *Zoonomia*, which advanced a taxonomical schematic of human disease that purported to be more than heuristic but grounded in nature and physiology. Using the nervous system as a template, Darwin organized diseases as "disorders of irritability, sensation, volition, and association, according to the tier in the psychophysiological hierarchy they affected" (Porter 60). While precious little medical consensus coalesced around these disease taxonomies, they marked one of the signal ambitions of the era to systematize the problem of disease along natural lines, a problem that Brown eagerly took up and made a central feature of his literary projects.

In journals from the late 1780s or early 1790s, written during his participation in the Belles Lettres Society, a group he founded along with other former classmates from the Friends Latin School, Brown offered his own taxonomy of knowledge situating the concept of the human in conjunction with the natural. "The general and I believe the true division of science," he begins, "is into moral and physical. The object of moral science is the mind, the object of physical, matter: this is sufficiently plain" (Dunlap 1815, I: 18). Equating mind with spirit, Brown concluded that the mind (considered in the abstract) belongs properly to the philosophical area of metaphysics, but the study of the mind (in its interaction with the world) belongs properly to natural and social history. "Is there not a difference between the consideration of the mind in its essence or being," Brown rhetorically posed the question, "and the consideration of the mind, as it acts with relation to something else, just as we consider man in the several lights of a rational creature, and as a member of society?" (I: 18). Brown's budding interest in the mind under the pressure of social stimuli and the domain of knowledge under which such considerations fell was coupled with an interest in medicine and pathology. "Man as an animal," he reasoned, "is the subject of the science of medicine, which is nothing more than the art of curing diseases incident to the human body. But there are diseases incident to the mind also; is the cure of these the province of the physician, when the mind is affected by the disorders of the animal system, or when its diseases may be cured, by the application of external remedies? It is thus the province of the physician" (I: 19). In this early lucubration, Brown staked out the territory of the para-physiological, or the shared border between the mental/moral and the bodily/natural. Brown would come to situate his fiction in the interstices between the social, medical, and mental and the categories of knowledge that regulate understanding of these domains.

I. Combustion and Embodiment: *Wieland*

Whether interpreted as part of the tradition of the Richardsonian sentimental novel that exposes the fatuousness of sentimentalism (Ziff), an exploration of the tension between religious enthusiasm and Enlightenment rationalism in the new republic (Gilmore, Samuels; Tompkins), an inquiry into the unstable relationship between legal language and truth (Korobkin), a Gothic commentary on the friability of Enlightenment thought in the age of revolution (Fliegelman; Looby), a discourse on the dilemmas of authorship at the outset of the nation's literary existence (Christophersen; Ruttenburg), or even an oblique commentary on anti-onanism tracts (Temple), virtually all readings of *Wieland* hinge on an analysis of Brown's use of the interloper Carwin's ventriloquism, or "biloquism" as the text at times refers to it, and its relationship to the central characters of the novel. The religiously enthusiastic, voice-hearing murderer Theodore Wieland, his sister the would-be sentimental heroine Clara, and her conventional suitor Pleyel all face the challenge of Carwin's vocal illusions. Through the vehicle of ventriloquism and the crimes that may or may not have followed from it, Brown invites the reader to contemplate what might be termed the "natural" Gothic element within American existence. Looking in horror upon the body-strewn crime scene, Clara reflects: "I was not qualified, by education and experience, to encounter perils like these" (W 150). Clara cannot fully come to terms with either Carwin's ventriloqual mendacity or her brother's homicidal actions, because she is thrust into a world of "epistemological terror and moral confusion" for which no educational regime or experience can quite prepare her (Fliegelman 239–240). Much of the powerful social critique that *Wieland* has generated in the last few decades of scholarship flows from an analysis of the ways in which Brown's American Gothic explores these educational, epistemological, and experiential limitations and, in some sense, offers itself as the educational experience that Clara confesses to be lacking.

And yet, while the novel may call into question the certainties of reason and faith, Brown achieves this by occupying the para-physiological terrain of medical inquiry, as indicated in his prefatory "Advertisement" to *Wieland*:

> Some readers may think the conduct of the younger Wieland impossible. In support of its possibility the Writer must appeal to Physicians and to men conversant with the latent springs and occasional perversions of the human mind. It will not be objected that the instances of similar delusion are rare, because it is the business of moral painters to exhibit their subject in its most instructive and memorable forms. If history furnishes one parallel fact, it is a sufficient vindication of the Writer; but most readers will probably recollect an authentic case, remarkably similar to that of Wieland. (W 3)

For all the uncertainty that critics have made of *Wieland*, Brown offered psychopathology as an explanatory ground of the novel, in at least a preliminary way, as a medical-scientific discourse that provides at least some purchase on the mental latencies and "perversions" it delineates. The medical perspective that Brown urged his readers to consult may not provide full explanation for the behaviors and phenomena to be found in *Wieland* per se, but, unlike for Clara, it prepared the reader to accept the horrors of human behavior as extreme but plausible, alluding to an actual case of religiously induced familicide. Brown confers upon the physiological equal authority with the authorial (note that "Physicians" and "the Writer" are singled out in the "Advertisement" for capitalization).

Brown's concern with the verifiability of his most improbable Gothic effects manifests itself in a number of key moments in *Wieland*. The diagnosis of Theodore's condition is delivered through Clara's uncle Thomas Cambridge, whose military medical practice had exposed him to a broad spectrum of mental disorders, including cases of mania. "Unquestionably the illusions were maniacal," he assures Clara, "though the vulgar thought otherwise. They are all reducible to one class, and not more difficult of explication and cure than most affections of our frame" (179). Brown reinforces the doctor's opinion with a citation from *Zoonomia* on "mania mutabilis" (mutable madness), which describes a range of ideational and sensory (including auditory) hallucinations.

Of course, Carwin's mischievous ventriloquism creates a condition not found precisely in Darwin's *Zoonomia*, a collective hallucination in which Clara and Pleyel share to some extent in Wieland's hearing voices. In *Wieland*, it is not so much a question of either ventriloquism or psychosis but *both*: psychosis under the additional pressure of ventriloquism. The voice is both a disembodied phenomenon that can come from within or outside the body and a disembodied phenomenon that emerges with great precision from the forces of embodiment, either the manipulation of the uvula (ventriloquism) or mental irritation (mutable madness).

In a similar vein, while many careful readings of *Wieland* (e.g., Fliegelman) have interpreted Brown's cautious rendering of the elder Wieland's death by what appears to be spontaneous combustion as a calling into question of both religious and medical authority (the elder Wieland is extremely devout), the scene is carefully presented with a forensic air, from the ruling out of lightning strike as a cause, through a technical description of a "prelusive gleam" (19), to the fatal spark and explosion and its sequelae: fever, gangrenous putrescence, delirium, and death. This parallels the gesture toward medical corroboration of the opening preface. Just as the "Advertisement" alluded to an actual case of paternal familicide that might have been familiar to contemporary readers,[1] Brown similarly appended a footnote to the mysterious death of the elder Wieland, referring the reader to a Florentine medical journal and the French medical reports of Merille and Muraire for confirmation of the reality of such occurrences and to the research of Maffei and Fontana for further forensic speculation regarding the physiological basis for such a violent and bizarre physical phenomenon (19).

Brown's likely source for these details, a 1790 article in the London-based *Literary Magazine and British Review* reprinted in 1792 in the Philadelphia-based periodical *The American Museum* (Anonymous), does not call into question the reality of spontaneous combustion but rather speculates that "another principle" might be at work in causing the incineration of an "animal body" (Letters 148). Scholars have noted that Brown is an outlier in his (or his narrator Clara's) discussion of the elder Wieland's combustion, in that he does not connect it to alcoholism as a precondition, while virtually every other reported clinical case does (see, for example, *Wieland* 18 n. 12). He also parts company with the many fictional presentations of spontaneous human combustion (e.g., Herman Melville's *Redburn* with its burning corpse of a drunken sailor or Krook's combustion in Charles Dickens's *Bleak House*) that emphasize the connection with alcohol. Brown's omission may have more to do with his interest in contemporary debates about the internal cause of combustion than with a desire to instill in the reader skepticism of the paranormal. Brown's account of the death of the elder Wieland distinctly parallels the source article, which describes the death of an alcoholic Italian priest named Bertholi. However, the source article proposes that rather than "spontaneous burning"— via an ignition of internal vapors—its cause is an "electric commotion," which in conjunction with the victim's bodily chemistry, ignited the "phlogiston," a theoretical substance, now rejected, that was supposed to be the principle source of metabolic heat (Letters 147).

Brown takes care to inform the reader that Clara's source about her father's death (she was six at the time) was the skeptical uncle Cambridge who serves as a conduit of medical information and is wholly averse to supernatural explanation. Clara's meditation, however, cannot help but reframe her father's death by combustion in a way that pits the divine against the natural:

> Was this the penalty of disobedience? this the stroke of a vindictive and invisible hand? Is it a fresh proof that the Divine Ruler interferes in human affairs, mediates an end, selects, and commissions his agents, and enforces by unequivocal sanctions, submission to his will? Or, was it merely the irregular expansion of fluid that imparts warmth to our heart and our blood, caused by the fatigue of the preceding day, or flowing, by established laws, from the condition of his thoughts?   (W 19)

In this passage, the rationale for the removal of the alcoholic element of the spontaneous combustion narrative becomes clearer in two senses. First, the element of an obvious vice such as alcohol abuse would make visible precisely what Brown's discourse seeks to obscure—it would be a legible sign of sinfulness. Second, the removal of the alcoholic element reinforces the plausibility of the phlogiston hypothesis, which Clara describes as "the irregular expansion of fluid that imparts warmth to our heart and our blood." Through the elision of alcohol as a contributing factor—and alcohol-related volatile vapors as an explosive force—Brown can point directly to either physical laws or para-physiological forces brought to bear by "the condition" of the elder Wieland's "thoughts." Essentially, Brown offers what would have been the most current physiological theory of bodily combustion, not to call it into question as medical authority per se but to elucidate the Gothic mystery as a choice between religious teleology and the para-physiological, between disembodied forces of judgment and equally mysterious forces of embodiment.

This perspective permeates *Wieland* thematically and, at times, on the level of the sentence. Fred Lewis Pattee objected to Brown's style as being "grotesque with circumlocutions" (Pattee xli), exemplified in such sentences as: "He [Pleyel] was connected with this place by many social ties. While there he had not escaped the amorous contagion" (W 39). However roundabout this may appear as a description of someone having been in love, Brown's phraseology, rather than being arbitrarily circumlocutory, points directly toward a socio-physiological vision at the heart of his Gothic sensibility. In *Wieland,* love is a social contagion, a catching disease, simultaneously embodied and disembodied, disruptive of both the individual's physical health and the social equilibrium.

The larger theme of Carwin's ventriloquism reproduces these concerns using a similar set of literary tactics. When the secret of Carwin's vocal tricks are revealed, they appear, like the example of spontaneous combustion, as an obscure but documented phenomenon, requiring annotation, grounded by Brown in a physiological discourse. In an extended footnote, Brown refers to Jean-Baptiste de La Chapelle's 1772 study *Ventriloque ou l'engastrimythe* (*Ventriloquism, or the Engastrimyth*), a generally debunking account that, as Steven Connor has observed, brought skepticism to supernatural explanations of the phenomenon and "a sober and systematic investigation of the facts and the evidence afforded by the senses," yet it also conveyed an exaggerated "will-to-illusion" that grossly overstated the power and danger of ventriloquism (Connor 213–216). To a certain extent, even the most influential social critiques to which Brown's treatment of ventriloquism have been put, such as Fliegelman's theorization of voice and democracy in the early republic ("[it] seem[s] with a sardonic literalness to call into question all possible faith in the republican formula vox populi, vox Dei" [291]),[2] share La Chapelle's overstatement of ventriloqual power and a tendency to exaggerate Brown's investment in the spectral threat of ventriloquism as it shifts from sensory illusion to cultural deception. Carwin is presented not so much as a cultural mastermind as a prurient meddler or interloper (see Christophersen; Grabo). His ventriloquism, for all its disembodiment, takes on dangerous power not in and of itself as a form of deception but in its interaction with religious obsession/psychosis (Theodore) and ignorance of nature/physiology (Clara). In *Wieland*, the danger of ventriloquism "does not come from its actual power of deluding the senses," as Connor summarizes it, "but from its power of awakening uncontrollable fantasies of such power" (Connor 234).

The role of the physiological in Brown thus provides a relatively stable base of knowledge from which one might delineate these Gothic fantasies of power. This allows him to bound the Gothic impulses in a strategy of containment, keeping his own novelistic discourse from being construed or subsumed under yet another fantasy, or his authorship from becoming yet another form of ventriloquism, rendering Brown another version of Carwin. According to Connor, La Chapelle was the first to distinguish systematically between two kinds of ventriloquism: (1) engastromyth, or belly-talking, via an "inner voice" that seems to inhabit the body; and (2) throwing the voice, or the power to make a voice appear as if it were coming from far off (Connor 214). These two forms of ventriloquism become crucial to *Wieland*'s theme, in that the first form expresses the embodied voice and the second form expresses one that is disembodied. It is as if Brown has distributed these two forms of illusion to different characters. Theodore's mutable madness manifests itself primarily as an internal voice, and Clara experiences the illusions of Carwin as a voice coming from "far off." Furthermore, such oscillation between forms of embodiment and disembodiment around ventriloquism echoes the play between material and immaterial in Clara's weighing of the potential causes of her father's death—chemical imbalance or divine retribution? The relatively discrete but mysterious physiology of ventriloquism and the relatively discrete but perhaps even more mysterious physiology of spontaneous human combustion have parallel consequences. They intersect and are rhymes of each other in Brown's work. These two arcane para-physiological mechanisms point in the same direction: two forms of illusion that lead to greater social deception. *Wieland*, through its footnotes, its backstories, and obscure medical research, tries in the end to expose the threshold of natural knowledge around these mysterious topics in order to educate the reader to recognize precisely the place where such deceptions could take on explosive social force.[3]

II. Sleep Disorder
Clinic: *Edgar Huntly*

Like Washington Irving, James Fenimore Cooper, Lydia Maria Child, Catharine Maria Sedgwick, and many others who would follow, Brown used American settings and Native Americans to give his fictions a distinction from European models. What he said of *Edgar Huntly* remains generally true of all his novels: "It is the purpose of this work...to exhibit a series of adventures, growing out of the condition of our country" (EH 3). As Richard Slotkin observed, the Native American themes of *Edgar Huntly* (which Slotkin describes as a "gothic captivity narrative") "have a special significance for Americans and embody an essential and characteristic quality of the national experience." What is less remarked upon, however, with respect to the genre's Americanization is this other pathological component, the connecting of the conditions of the country to "one of the most common and most wonderful diseases or affections of the human frame" (Slotkin 375–376). For Slotkin, the disease component amounts to a device that serves to reveal national "psychology," and while that is certainly one of Brown's general objectives, Slotkin seems to construe Brown's use of "wonderful" to mean "fantastic," rather than the more accurate sense, "mysterious." In other words, Brown is not merely touting the exceptionalist wonders of the American wilds by coupling them with a commensurately wondrous mental typology. Rather, he is coupling that exceptionalist narrative with a furtive, strange psychology that is more than a psychology, in the sense that it is a disease, an affection, and a psychosomatic condition, in accordance with eighteenth-century mental and physiological concepts of both body and mind.

Of course, this is not to say that Brown's thematic usage of disease has not been discussed—quite the contrary—but rather that (1) while all substantive discussions of, for example, *Edgar Huntly* or *Arthur Mervyn* treat sleepwalking, they generally do so in order to point to symbolic or political social constructs and discourses which are allegorized with little attention to their medical-historical parameters, and (2) these analyses tend to neglect the ways in which Brown saw the introduction of the pathological as part and parcel of American Gothic discourse.

A fairly typical example of this mode of criticism can be seen in Paul Downes's perceptive 1996 essay on sleepwalking in *Edgar Huntly*:

> Sleep-walking is thus symptomatic for Brown's characters, but it is also the novel's way of theorizing the subjectivity of the postrevolutionary, post-Enlightenment citizen of democracy. Indeed, Edgar Huntly's study of just decision making in the new Republic anticipates more recent accounts of the place of contingency and undecidability in political intervention, even as its extraordinary figurations expose the novel to the persistent possibility of being read as the gothic registration of fantastic anxieties. Brown's sleep-walkers share a discursive space with postrevolutionary visions of the political representative as a "puppet" of the people (an image popular with Federalist polemicists) or as "monstrously" independent of his constituents'

intentions (a radically populist cry). But while these steadfastly dichotomized political perspectives reveal a shared investment in the self-present integrity of the subject of Enlightenment, Edgar Huntly finds the subject of democracy where the citizen repeatedly misplaces himself.   (Downes 417)

Downes reads *Edgar Huntly*'s use of the sleepwalking motif as a symptom of anxiety over the will of the post-Revolutionary democratic citizen, and he recognizes the Gothic anxiety that marks it, while paying scant attention to the medical theories regulating the metaphoric symptomatic it describes. Even as it explores the metaphoric possibilities of the trope of sleepwalking, this kind of approach thus elides, perhaps with some interpretative cost, Brown's theory of sleepwalking and its derivation from extant medical literature and Darwin's *Zoonomia*.

Considering Brown's engagement with the political ramifications of somnambulism, Justine S. Murison suggests that the "scholarly quandary" of *Edgar Huntly* lies in "whether Brown's twinned themes of psychology and politics can be extricated from one another" (Murison 265). We might modify this formulation further: the para-physiological cannot be separated from the political. If we consider the Gothic transference that Brown effects by Americanizing the genre, we see that rather than placing the violent, murderous impulses in supernatural sources, Brown locates them in the "most common wonderful of diseases or affections" (EH 3). This gives a good indication of what always interests Brown about pathology. The phenomena he dramatizes are common enough to be applicable to a wide array of social conditions. They are wonderful in the sense that their essential nature remains so fundamentally mysterious as to inspire wonderment. They are diseases or affections, that is, entities that impact upon the body (disease) or the mind (affection). It is this last connection, which has arguably been underdeveloped in the critical literature on Brown, that suggests that pathological conditions are simultaneously bodily and psychological and thus that American Gothic anxiety takes on a bodily dimension wherein the body is Gothicized. It becomes the object of Gothic horror.

In today's popular imaginary, somnambulism occupies a space between Lady Macbeth and modern newspaper accounts of the use and abuse of Ambien. In the Shakespearean version (which aligns in some ways most closely with Brown's moral etiology), murderous guilt troubles the sleeper, leading to unwitting perambulatory confession. In the Ambien version, a drug-induced reverie leads to violence on planes, unwitting indulgence in snack foods, and risky narcoleptic shopping trips. In the older version, the disease has a moral agency, while in the contemporary one, it seems to be about catatonic consumption or irritability. The contemporary version seems to have bodily, rather than moral, causes. In Brown's *Edgar Huntly*, we enter not only a world of Clithero and Edgar, sleepwalking doubles of each other, but one in which all characters are judged in minute detail based on the qualities of their sleep, its relative lightness or depth, its trouble or quietude. For example, here is Clithero describing his obsession with Clarice:

My thoughts could not long continue in this state. They gradually became more ardent and museful. The image of Clarice occurred with unseasonable frequency. Its charms were enhanced by some nameless and indefinable additions. When it met me in the way I was irresistibly disposed to stop and survey it with particular attention. The pathetic cast of her features, the deep glow of her cheek, and some catch of melting music she had lately breathed, stole incessantly upon my fancy. On recovering from my thoughtful moods, I sometimes found my cheeks wet with tears that had fallen unperceived, and my bosom heaved with involuntary sighs.

These images did not content themselves with invading my wakeful hours, but, likewise, encroached upon my sleep. I could no longer resign myself to slumber with the same ease as before. When I slept, my visions were of the same impassioned tenor.   (51)

This and other representations (sleep is described seventy-six times in *Edgar Huntly*) accord with close precision to descriptions of the disease found in Darwin's *Zoonomia*. Darwin viewed somnambulism as a form of reverie, which he defined as a disease of volition stemming from "violent voluntary exertions of ideas to relieve pain, with all the trains or tribes connected with them by sensations or associations." Sleepwalking, it followed, was "a part of reverie, the latter consisting in the exertions of the locomotive muscles, and the former of the exertions of the organs of sense; both which are mixed, or alternate with each other, for the purpose of relieving pain." Similarly, Brown's account of Clithero carefully charts the progression of his sexualized fantasies of Clarice from the conscious act of musing toward the increasingly involuntary. First, he can neither control the frequency with which mental pictures of the object of his obsession recur nor prevent the "sweetening" or intensification (the mental cheesecloth and sentimental soundtrack) that his "fancy" seems to supply to these images. Second, he cannot foreclose the lingering attention he bestows upon the details of these mental pictures, becoming the helpless voyeur of his own imagination. Third, he cannot control the physiological symptoms attendant on his mental arousal (involuntary sighing and crying), symptoms suggestive of a nocturnal ejaculation. Fourth and finally, he cannot control the hypnogogia of his reveries and prevent them from taking over his sleep. Brown describes Clithero's somnambulism in much the same terms, as an extension of the involuntary, unconscious symptoms of reverie:

> I started from my attitude. I was scarcely conscious of any transition. The interval was fraught with stupor, and amazement. It seemed as if my senses had been hushed in sleep, while the powers of locomotion were unconsciously exerted to bear me to my chamber. By whatever means the change was effected, there I was.   (77)

Brown furthermore insists on linking these conditions to pulse, which comes in for as much monitoring as do habits of somnolence. The linkage is made clear in passages such as one where Clithero asks, "Who knows not the cogency of faith? That the pulses of life are at the command of the will? The bearer of these tidings will be the messenger of death. A fatal sympathy will seize her. She will shrink, and swoon, and perish at the news!" (77).

In a second example, we see the sleep monitoring that preoccupies Brown:

> To sleep, while these images were haunting me, was impossible. I passed the night in continual motion. I strode, without ceasing, across the floor of my apartment. My mind was wrought to a higher pitch than I had ever before experienced. The occasion, accurately considered, was far from justifying the ominous inquietudes which I then felt. How, then, should I account for them?
>
> Sarsefield probably enjoyed his usual slumber. His repose might not be perfectly serene, but when he ruminated on impending or possible calamities his tongue did not cleave to his mouth, his throat was not parched with unquenchable thirst, he was not incessantly stimulated to employ his superfluous fertility of thought in motion.   (68)

Edgar Huntly thus exhibits an insistent watchfulness of others as they sleep that is at once clinical and sexual, and Brown's Gothic awareness of the body at rest curiously harks forward to the age of Ambien and a world of perpetual bodily anxiety. We may be reluctant to characterize this as an American or modern trait per se, but certainly Brown marked it out for scrutiny. His novels seem to suggest that the US postcolonial subject is hyper-vigilant about mental and physical contamination or, more allegorically (given the iconic Elm in *Edgar Huntly*) about dangers arising like a nightmare on Elm Street.

III. Yellow Fever and the Physiology of Fear: *Arthur Mervyn*

"Often have I wished," Brown writes in a confessional mode in his 1804 epistolary novel *Jane Talbot*, "to slide obscurely and quietly into the grave; but this wish, while it saddened my bosom, never raised my hand against my life. It made me willingly expose my safety to the blasts of pestilence; it made me court disease; but it never set my imagination in search after more certain and speedy means" (JT 383).

The "blasts of pestilence" that threaten Brown and his fictional surrogates Henry Colden, Arthur Mervyn, and Constantia Dudley come in the form of yellow fever epidemics. Brown's fictions reveal a good deal about his para-physiological vision with respect to yellow fever. His relation to this disease was more personal than his relation to the other medical phenomena that populate his novels. His descriptions of yellow fever are richer, more intimate, and, while coordinated with contemporary medical debates, also corroborated by direct experience. Brown may have contracted the fever in the outbreak of 1793 or that of 1798, to both of which he was exposed, despite his frail constitution and the urgings of his family to retreat to safer areas, and his proximity to multiple outbreaks may account for the suggestion that Henry Colden's exposure was motivated by a death wish. That Brown used the biblically-inflected Johnsonian phrase "blasts of pestilence" is indicative of his general physiological perspective. Yellow fever was a pestilence, a plague; its epidemic qualities were theoretically derived from miasmatic or ambient atmospheric disturbances. In this, he did not deviate from the thinking of his physician friend, Elihu Hubbard Smith, or Smith's teacher, Philadelphia physician and founding father, Benjamin Rush.

Despite Brown's extensive writings about yellow fever, his positions regarding the nature of the disease can only be inferred from general remarks in his fiction. The absence of a definite position may have to do with the fact that Brown saw himself as a literary authority and not a medical one, and he was careful to delimit his authority, especially given that his first audience for his literary productions included medical professionals in the Friendly Club circle. Smith, one of Brown's closest associates during this period, wrote extensively about yellow fever and was likely the greatest influence on Brown's understanding of the disease. As an anticontagionist, Smith did not hold that the disease could be communicated from person to person. Adherents of noncontagiousness believed that an epidemic such as yellow fever was better explained by Thomas Sydenham's theory of "epidemic constitution," in which general atmospheric changes occasioned by seasonal fluctuations produced diseases in susceptible persons. This theory was an eighteenth-century revival and extension of Hippocratic humoral thought (Durey 105–106). Rush modeled his hypothesis about yellow fever after Sydenham and, indeed, was sometimes styled the "American Sydenham". Smith followed his mentor Rush in this respect, and his journals conjecture on ways of testing Sydenham's various disease hypotheses (Smith 192; on Rush, see Powell xxi, 126, 164).[4] Smith suspected that yellow fever probably originated locally in decomposing organic matter that created miasma and, under the proper conditions (derived from Sydenham's theory of epidemic constitution), took on malignant or epidemic properties due to local atmospheric conditions and hygienic or dietary deficiencies or mental disturbances in the population. This miasmic corruption might enter a susceptible body, creating conditions of humoral imbalance and thereby a diseased state. Absent the later discovery that mosquitoes are the actual vector of the disease (though Smith does make observations about flies, mosquitoes, and standing pools of water), the anticontagionist perspective seemed to account for a mysterious affliction that struck great numbers of victims at once, broke out spontaneously at seemingly determinate intervals in locations without obvious contact between sick individuals, did not seem traceable to human contact, and tended to spare medical attendants (though Smith succumbed to it, many doctors and nurses did not).

In *Arthur Mervyn*, while Brown never offers a comprehensive theory of yellow fever transmission, he certainly uses anticontagionist terminology to characterize the diagnosis, and this perspective seems to have activated his para-physiological vision: "My new sensations conjured up the hope that my indisposition might prove a temporary evil. Instead of pestilential or malignant fever, it might be a harmless intermittent. Time would ascertain its true nature" (AM 182).

The classification of fevers into intermittent or pestilential/malignant was typical of anticontagionist perspectives, emphasizing the atmospheric, constitutional, and mental conditions that might render a fever harmless or life-threatening. At another moment, Arthur reflects with growing para-physiological consciousness that "this disease assailed men with different degrees of malignity. In its worst form perhaps it was incurable; but, in some of its modes, it was doubtless conquerable by the skill of physicians and the fidelity of nurses. In its least formidable symptoms, negligence and solitude would render it fatal" (133). The negligence he has in mind is fundamentally social: "Hunger and negligence had exasperated the malignity and facilitated the progress of the pestilence" (180). Because of the anticontagionist perspective, Brown's novel (Waterman 2005, 241), like Smith's investigation, provides a running commentary on stench and fetid areas, poor ventilation, and noxious unhygienic spaces.

Not surprisingly, given Smith's anticontagionism, he also concurred with Rush regarding treatment, generally bleeding and purging his patients. As scholars have pointed out (Hedges 310 n. 32), Brown makes no mention of bleeding patients, nor does he engage in the vigorous polemics surrounding bloodletting, He does, however, indicate the use of purgatives. In describing the Bush Hill emergency hospital's deplorable conditions, Arthur notes that "no suitable receptacle was provided for the evacuations produced by medicine or disease" (AM 173). Rather than engage in questions surrounding the therapeutics of bloodletting, Brown engages blood's relation to yellow fever through the para-physiological, specifically in terms of the impact of the mind on the body. At one point, after accidentally bloodying his own nose, Arthur contemplates why the bleeding suddenly stopped. "The blood," we are informed, "by some inexplicable process of nature, perhaps by the counteracting influence of fear, had quickly ceased to flow" (113). The impact of fear on blood flow was just such a nexus.

Brown's concern for Arthur turns on his mastery of fear and a general sense in which the panic that yellow fever engendered in the populace was a contributing factor to the disease's malignancy, not just on a social level but also on a physiological one. "Hitherto distress had been contemplated at a distance," Mervyn explains. "...Now the calamity had entered my own doors, imaginary evils were supplanted by real, and my heart was the seat of commiseration and horror" (134). Smith expressed a similar concern in his diary: "This whole City, is in a violent state of alarm, on account of the Fever"; it produced a terror in the populace that acquires "redoubled horror," "a malady of the mind a thousand times more dreadful & pernicious than all corporeal evils" (Smith 55, 62). In a sense, Brown returned to yellow fever again and again in his fiction because it concretely exemplified, as no other mass social experience in his life, the para-physiological relations at the heart of his Gothic vision. If he sought to provide a more plausible basis for Gothic fear in a local habitation, he did so by dramatizing a disease whose incidence of mass panic seemed to coincide with its malignancy. "We fear it," Brown wrote of yellow fever in 1796, "as we are terrified by dark" (Letters 371).

NOTES

1. An 1801 review of *Wieland* refers to the lurid James Yates family murders that occurred in upstate New York in 1781, to which Brown almost certainly alluded. An article about these crimes appeared in 1796 in a New York magazine and was soon reprinted in the *Philadelphia Minerva*. See Axelrod 53–63; Williams 643–645.

2. For similar approaches, see Looby; Judson; Wolfe.

3. This position aligns with Bryan Waterman's argument about Brown's literary practice participating in "the early Republic's culture of information, broadly conceived" (Waterman 2003, 215), in which medical knowledge serves as key branch of public information and necessary natural history.

4. For example, Smith records the following: "May have the way for discovering whether there is, as Sydenham conjectured, a regular succession of general diseases & a return of them, after determinate intervals" (192).

WORKS CITED

Anonymous. "Letter respecting an Italian Priest, Killed by a Electric Commotion, the Cause of Which Resided in His Own Body." *The American Museum, or, Universal Magazine, Containing, Essays on Agriculture—Commerce—Manufacture* 11 (April 1792): 146–149.

Axelrod, Alan. *Charles Brockden Brown: An American Tale.* Austin: University of Texas Press, 1983.

Brown, Charles Brockden. "Terrific Novels." LM 3.19 (April 1805): 288–289.

Christophersen, Bill. *The Apparition in the Glass: Charles Brockden Brown's American Gothic.* Athens: University of Georgia Press, 1993.

Connor, Steven. *Dumbstruck: A Cultural History of Ventriloquism.* Oxford: Oxford University Press, 2000.

Darwin, Erasmus. *Zoonomia or, the Laws of Organic Life in Three Parts... Complete in Two Volumes.* D. Carlisle, for Thomas and Andrews, 1803.

Downes, Paul. "Sleepwalking out of the Revolution: Brown's *Edgar Huntly.*" *Eighteenth-Century Studies* 29 (1996): 413–431.

Durey, Michael. *The Return of the Plague: British Society and the Cholera 1831–2.* Dublin: Gill and Macmillan, 1979.

Fliegelman, Jay. *Prodigals and Pilgrims: The American Revolution against Patriarchal Authority, 1750–1800.* New York: Cambridge University Press, 1984.

Gilmore, Michael. "Calvinism and Gothicism: The Example of Brown's *Wieland.*" *Studies in the Novel* 9 (1977): 107–118.

Grabo, Norman S. *The Coincidental Art of Charles Brockden Brown.* Chapel Hill: University of North Carolina Press, 1981.

Hedges, William L. "Benjamin Rush, Charles Brockden Brown, and the American Plague Year" *Early American Literature* 7.3 (1973): 295–311.

Judson, Barbara. "A Sound of Voices: The Ventriloquial Uncanny in *Wieland* and *Prometheus Unbound.*" *Eighteenth-Century Studies* 44.1 (2010): 21–37.

Korobkin, Laura. "Murder by Madman: Criminal Responsibility, Law, and Judgment in *Wieland.*" *American Literature* 74 (2000): 721–750.

Looby, Christopher. *Voicing America: Language, Literary Form, and the Origins of the United States.* Chicago: University of Chicago Press, 1996.

Murison, Justine S. "The Tyranny of Sleep: Somnambulism, Moral Citizenship, and Charles Brockden Brown's *Edgar Huntly.*" *Early American Literature* 44.2 (2009): 243–270.

Patee, Fred Lewis, "Introduction" to Charles Brockden Brown, *Wieland; or the Transformation and Memoirs of Carwin the Biloquist.* New York: Harcourt Brace Jovanovich, 1926, ix–xlvi.

Porter, Roy. "Medical Science and Human Science in the Enlightenment." In Christopher Fox, Roy Porter, and Robert Wokler, eds., *Inventing Human Science: Eighteenth Century Domains,* 58–71. Berkeley: University of California Press, 1995.

Powell, J. H. *Bring Out Your Dead: The Great Plague of Yellow Fever in Philadelphia in 1793*. Philadelphia: University of Pennsylvania Press, 1949.

Ruttenburg, Nancy. *Democratic Personality: Popular Voice and the Trial of American Authorship*. Stanford: Stanford University Press, 1998.

Samuels, Shirley. "*Wieland*: Alien and Infidel." *Early American Literature* 25 (1990): 45–66.

Slotkin, Richard. *Regeneration through Violence: The Mythology of the American Frontier 1600–1860*. Norman: University of Oklahoma Press, 1973.

Gale Temple. "Carwin the Onanist?" *Arizona Quarterly: A Journal of American Literature, Culture, and Theory* 65.1 (2009): 1–32.

Tompkins, Jane. *Sensational Designs: The Cultural Work of American Fiction 1790–1860*. Oxford: Oxford University Press, 1985.

Waterman, Bryan. "The Bavarian Illuminati, the Early American Novel, and Histories of the Public Sphere." *William and Mary Quarterly* 71 (2005): 9–30.

Waterman, Bryan. "*Arthur Mervyn*'s Medical Repository and the Early Republic's Knowledge Industries." *American Literary History* 15.2 (Summer 2003): 213–247.

Williams, Daniel E. "Writing under the Influence: An Examination of *Wieland*'s 'Well Authenticated Facts' and the Depiction of Murderous Fathers in Post- Revolutionary Print Culture." *Eighteenth-Century Fiction* 15.3–4 (2003): 643–668.

Wolfe, Eric A. "Ventriloquizing Nation: Voice, Identity, and Radical Democracy in Charles Brockden Brown's *Wieland*." *American Literature: A Journal of Literary History, Criticism, and Bibliography* 78.3 (2006): 431–457.

Ziff, Larzer. "A Reading of *Wieland*." *Publications of the Modern Language Association* 77.1 (March 1962): 51–57.

CHAPTER 24

BROWN AND THE YELLOW FEVER

SCOTT ELLIS

IN the middle of September 1795, Elihu Hubbard Smith wrote in his diary from New York City, "This whole City, is in a violent state of alarm, on account of the Fever. It is the subject of every conversation, at every hour, & in every company; & each circumstance of terror acquires redoubled horror, from every new relation" (Smith 57). Smith—a writer, editor, and intellectual and Charles Brockden Brown's close associate in New York—was also a physician, and his observation reflects his own experience treating victims of the yellow fever. The spread of this virus in New York City, two years following the devastating epidemic in Philadelphia, dominates Smith's medical attention and insights about its effect on the urban population. Smith's valiant efforts to assist victims of the fever presage the work of a few of Brown's future fictional characters, but they also showcase the personal and devastating effects of the epidemic. Three years later, Smith contracted the disease, and despite his best efforts helping others survive, he succumbed to it.

The yellow fever looms large in the life and work of Brown. The death of his close friend Smith and the widespread social upheaval associated with the fever's nearly annual recurrence shaped his world view and ultimately his fiction. While national and global events such as the French and Haitian revolutions, the Alien and Sedition Acts, and the Bavarian Illuminati panic all inform Browne's writing, it was the yellow fever epidemics, and his proximity to them, that figure most prominently in many of his novels and tales. While giving him a convenient if devastating metaphor for other types of contagion, the fever also affected him literally and created a social crisis through which he mapped his fictional and moral ideas. The yellow fever shaped Brown as a writer and thinker, and in turn, he worked to shape the fever into something manageable and understandable for himself and his readers.

I. OUTBREAKS, REACTION, AND SOCIAL EFFECTS OF YELLOW FEVER OUTBREAKS

The yellow fever is a virus normally found in Africa and South America, but trade and transportation brought it and its carriers to New York, Philadelphia, Boston, New Haven, Baltimore, and other urban commercial centers during the late eighteenth and early nineteenth centuries. During the late summer and early fall, particularly during the 1790s, residents of these cities witnessed a spread of yellow fever, whose victims suffered from severe pain of the head, back, and limbs; discolored eyes and skin; a high fever; nausea; and its telltale emission, black vomit. The largest outbreak struck Philadelphia in 1793, when nearly five thousand of the city's citizens succumbed (Horrocks and Van Horne vii). Although understood today, the yellow fever remained an enigma for Brown and his contemporaries. Chronicled by some of the most noteworthy of Philadelphia's residents, including physician Benjamin Rush and printer and publisher Mathew Carey, the epidemic of 1793 brought the city to a devastating halt, as city leaders and common citizens alike tried to comprehend the destruction and act appropriately. While many religious leaders interpreted the epidemic as the wrath of God, physicians such as Rush relied on their medical research to identify the cause of its transmission and tried to offer ways to stave off the disease.[1]

Medical concerns about the fever, however, were often overshadowed by political, racial, and economic interests. Indeed, the fever became a nexus for differing political parties and ideological factions to debate a host of social concerns. One of the central public debates involved racial identity, as the African American community came under the spotlight for its actions during the epidemics. Rumors circulated that African Americans were immune to the fever, and African American men were therefore pressed into service to help carry the dying to clinics and hospitals and the dead to their graves. This rumor, popularized by Rush, led to subsequent concerns about African Americans' conduct during period. In Philadelphia, accusations and rebuttals about theft and other inappropriate activities emerged in published accounts of the fever. Carey's account accusing African American nurses of theft and extortion was countered by Absalom Jones and Richard Allen, African American ministers who denied such accusations and articulated the risk and bravery of those who assisted the city with the dying and the dead (see Gould; Otter).

These racial debates coincided with political debates, which revealed broader partisan issues beyond the fever. Central to this political antagonism were the theories about the origin of the fever. Generally, Republican physicians, most notably Rush, argued that the fever was local, as squalor, poor sanitation, and the local climate fostered the epidemic. On the other hand, Federalist and nonpartisan physicians, including Edward Stevens and William Currie, generally subscribed to the importation theory, which argued that refugees (especially those from Haiti), cargo, and the ships used to bring them to port also brought along the fever (see Pernick). Such rhetorical arguments—in which economic practices were perceived as both causes and victims of the fever—pointed to a widespread belief that commerce and trade, both foreign and domestic, fostered the infectious epidemic, a symbolic link whereby transmission of goods parallels transmission of disease. These debates about the origin of the fever in turn led to radically different proposals for halting the fever. While one group argued for better sanitation, the other pushed for tighter controls on commerce, including a push for outright quarantine and cessation of trade with certain areas such as the West Indies. The 1798 *Letter from the Secretary of the Commonwealth of Pennsylvania*, for example, suggests that the state may cease trade in future summer months with both the Mediterranean and the West Indies and states that did not enforce quarantine laws ("Pennsylvania"). To hedge their bets, several states, including Pennsylvania, agreed to do both.

Regardless of the policies enacted, the fever had a profound effect on those citizens involved in commercial industries. Throughout its duration, the yellow fever epidemic severely damaged businesses and trade in both New York and Philadelphia. Carey, for example, explains that during the 1793 epidemic, the Board of Physicians in New York City threatened to publish the names of anyone secretly attempting to sell merchandise brought from Philadelphia. They considered such people to be "enemies to the welfare of the city" and urged residents to avoid the temptation of such profit (Carey et al. 43). Losing customers to disease and temporary emigration, merchants and commercial entrepreneurs sustained significant and consistent financial losses, which spread to artisans and laborers of all stripes. As businesses closed, craftsmen ceased their work, shipyards halted their traffic, and many middle- and upper-class residents fled to healthier environs, leaving the poor in their wake. Condie, Folwell, and Rittenhouse estimated that in Philadelphia during the beginning of August 1798, around forty thousand people—or approximately 75 percent of the city's population—fled the city, leaving the poorer citizens behind (Condie, Folwell, and Rittenhouse 55). Financially unable to leave their homes, impoverished citizens, the vast majority of the plague's victims (B. Smith 150), were left behind to languish in fear in the infected areas or followed others in the abbreviated migration to internment camps outside the fever-filled pockets of the city. Carey even notes that while some Philadelphia landlords agreed to withhold rent collection during the epidemics, others did not, placing an additional burden on those who could least afford it, an issue that Brown describes in his novel *Ormond*.

These published debates and pronouncements about the fever masked the fact that the print industry, the essential medium for communicating such opinions, was itself significantly affected by the epidemic, as some of the most prominent printers in New York and Philadelphia—Benjamin Franklin Bache, owner of the staunch republican *Aurora*, along with James Watters and (possibly)[2] Thomas Greenleaf—succumbed to the fever. Printing establishments whose owners and employees survived the fever suffered as well. In a compilation of reports and notices of the recent epidemic, Currie notes on September 5 that three Philadelphia printing presses had already ceased their operations and most printers had fled the city (Currie 59). Although necessary to both cities—especially when transmitting information about the fever—printing and distributing newspapers, magazines, pamphlets, and books proved to be a risky business, as the threat of contracting the disease challenged even the most ardent devotees of the profession.

One notable exception to this urban crisis in the book trade was the business of Hocquet Caritat, Brown's publisher in New York. According to George Raddin, the owners of two of the city's circulating libraries—Aarondt Van Hook and Gardiner Baker—died during the outbreak in 1798, leaving Caritat with the only significant New York establishment (Raddin, *New York of Hocquet Caritat*, 19). Having recently moved his library and bookstore from the unhealthy Pearl Street to the more fashionable[3] (and salubrious) Broadway, a location relatively free from the epidemic and frequented by both those who stayed in the city and those who fled to the countryside, Caritat enjoyed the unfortunate fruits the fever brought to him (Raddin, *Early New York Literary Scene*, 26–27). Caritat's location within the city allowed him to maintain his business despite the general decline in economic activity around New York.

II. THE YELLOW FEVER IN BROWN'S NOVELS

> Constantia had now leisure to ruminate upon her own condition. Every day added to the devastation and confusion of the city. The most populous streets were deserted and silent. The greater number of inhabitants had fled, and those who remained were occupied with no cares but those which related to their own safety. The labours of the artizan and the speculations of the merchant were suspended. All shops, but those of the apothecaries were shut. No carriage but the herse was seen, and this was employed, night and day, in the removal of the dead. The customary sources of subsistence were cut off. Those, whose fortunes enabled them to leave the city, but who had deferred till now their retreat, were denied an asylum by the terror which pervaded the adjacent country, and by the cruel prohibitions which the neighbouring towns and cities thought it necessary to adopt. Those who lived by the fruits of their daily labour were subjected, in this total inactivity, to the alternative of starving, or of subsisting upon public charity.   (O 55)

Thus begins the fifth chapter of *Ormond; or, The Secret Witness*, Brown's novel published in January 1799 by Caritat, only months after the epidemic in which Smith had perished. In Brown's novels *Ormond* and *Arthur Mervyn; or, Memoirs of the Year 1793*, along with the periodical series "The Man at Home," Brown positions yellow fever as a resonant symbol that affects nearly every facet of his characters' and readers' lives. Through this leitmotif, Brown speaks to the issues of race, commerce, class, and gender as they intersect with a subject that most of Brown's readers knew far too well.

Ormond recounts the travails of Stephen Dudley, a former apothecary, and his daughter Constantia, who are trapped in Philadelphia during the fever epidemic. Constantia, her father, and their friend and servant Lucy find themselves impoverished and isolated in the midst of Philadelphia's plague, a precipitous descent from their middle-class lives back in New York. In the novel, the yellow fever that engulfs the city's residents not only underscores the Dudleys' fall but simultaneously points to the inherent vulnerability of the market economy. By providing him with an unfortunately topical symbol with which his readers could identify, Brown used the epidemic to illustrate how the very economic structure that has alienated Stephen and his family coincides with the corresponding illness—both biological and metaphorical—latent within the urban centers of the United States.

The Dudleys' situation reflects that of many urban citizens whose lives were disrupted and often displaced during the epidemics. The mercantile stasis that accompanied even the suggestion of the yellow fever contrasted with the dynamic flood of wealthier city residents to areas safely outside the plague's grasp. As Constantia rightly observes, "To fly from the danger was impossible. How should accommodation at a distance, be procured? The means of subsistence were indissolubly connected with her present residence, but the progress of this disease would cut off these means, and leave her to be beset not only with pestilence but famine. What provision could she make against an evil like this?" (37). Work, the means through which she should be able to escape from her situation, is cut off from her. She loses her employment because of the epidemic (40) and therefore loses her ability to escape from their situation. Yellow fever has essentially foreclosed the possibility of the Dudleys' economic relief and has all but ensured their death. When Constantia relates that of the three hundred inhabitants of her neighborhood, two hundred die and only eight or ten escape with their health intact (58), we realize the dangerous depths to which the Dudleys have fallen. Beginning as an artist free from financial worries and traveling through Europe, Stephen now finds himself beset by unending anxiety and mired within the poorest, most unhealthy part of Philadelphia.[4]

In *Ormond*, the yellow fever resonates with real and symbolic illness; it signals a disruption of everyday urban life and points to the limitation of the occupational standard against which Stephen is judged, a limitation depicted through the failure of the apothecary to remedy the city's ills. In the quotation that begins this section, Constantia notes the evacuation of all businesses save one: "The labours of the artizan and the speculations of the merchant were suspended. All shops, but those of the apothecaries were shut" (55). Constantia's observation reinforces the earlier demise of her father, who, had he not squandered his own inherited shop in New York City, could still be in business in either city. Yet Stephen's failure is tempered by the inability of the city's apothecaries to curb the progress of the disease, a systemic (rather than personal) failure depicted by Brown soon after Whiston, the Dudleys' meddlesome neighbor, enters their apartment exhibiting symptoms of the fever. A journeyman cooper who has lost his job because of the epidemic, Whiston had planned to flee to the countryside and escape the fever, but his procrastination has led him to contract the disease. Observing these symptoms, Stephen understands the inexorable progress of Whiston's illness but recounts his previous training with medication and exhorts Whiston to "go home, and to take some hot and wholesome draught, in consequence of which, he might rise tomorrow with his usual health" (44). Despite Stephen's training and prescription, Whiston soon dies, a victim of the incurable fever. Whiston's death, regardless of Stephen's best efforts, underscores the inability of anyone, apothecaries included, to eradicate the epidemic and demonstrates that the illness affecting the city lies beyond the control of any profession.

Whereas the yellow fever serves a minor, if crucial, part in *Ormond*, it figures much more prominently in the first part of *Arthur Mervyn*, a two-part novel (or two novels spliced together) depicting the travails of its titular character through Philadelphia and beyond. The first part of the novel was published in the spring of 1799, mere months after the publication of *Ormond*, and situates the tale amid the most devastating yellow fever outbreak during the era, as its subtitle, *Memoirs of the Year 1793*, indicates. Mervyn, a naive youth who ventures forth to earn a living in the city, finds himself embroiled in fraud and deception, social and economic conditions embodied by the spreading virus.

The first part of *Arthur Mervyn* begins with a Dr. Stevens[5] finding a sickly young man, Arthur, leaning against the wall near his home. Recognizing symptoms of yellow fever, Dr. Stevens nonetheless decides to help the young man, nurses him back to health, and eventually persuades him to tell his story, which takes up most of the first part of the novel. As in *Ormond*, the first part of *Arthur Mervyn* is filled with accounts of deception, destruction, and struggle, but what distinguishes it from Brown's other works is the centrality of the fever. Even when he returns to the country after his initial foray to Philadelphia, the fever invades the narrative and draws Arthur back to the city. Indeed, the yellow fever is a central character in the novel, a character that affects others' behavior, destroys families and lives, and, one could argue, creates conditions for benevolence.

As we learn from Arthur about the events leading to his discovery by Dr. Stevens, we see how Brown uses the "innocent young man from the country who moves to the city" plot device as a lead-in to the much more complicated scenario with the fever. His association with the fraudulent Welbeck, his initial flight from the city to the country in search of honest work, and his relationship with the Hadwin family are all placed in greater relief upon the outbreak of yellow fever in Philadelphia. Despite the growing epidemic, Arthur decides to return to the city to find both Clemenza Lodi, whose money and manuscript he now has in his possession, and Wallace, the fiancé of Susan Hadwin, who has traveled to Philadelphia. Arthur's decision to return to the infected city despite the threat to his own health reveals the strength of his moral convictions, but it also redirects the narrative to explore a city under siege from the epidemic.

As Arthur travels against the tide of Philadelphia residents escaping the city, Brown begins to present horrifying details about the fever and its aftermath. For many readers, his descriptions of the fever show him at the height of his talent. The nearly empty marketplace now revealed "not more than a dozen figures; and these were ghost-like, wrapt in cloaks, from behind which they cast upon me glances of wonder and suspicion; and, as I approached, changed their course, to avoid touching me. Their clothes were sprinkled with vinegar; and their nostrils defended from contagion by some powerful perfume" (AM 139). Mervyn's quest for Wallace leads him to encounter not only those seeking to avoid infection but also those caught by the fever, the hospitals to which they are brought, and the people who traverse the city in order to pick up the dead. After nearly being buried alive, Arthur finds himself in a hospital, lying "upon a mattress, whose condition proved that an half-decayed corpse had recently been dragged from it.... You will scarcely believe that, in this scene of horrors, the sound of laughter should be overheard. While the upper rooms of this building, are filled with the sick and dying, the lower apartments are the scenes of carrousals and mirth. The wretches who are hired, at enormous wages, to tend the sick and convey away the dead, neglected their duty and consume the cordials, which are provided for the patients, in debauchery and riot" (173).

Brown presents his purpose for using the fever prominently in his Preface, in which he writes, "The influences of hope and fear, the trials of fortitude and constancy, which took place in the city, in the autumn of 1793, have, perhaps, never been exceeded in any age. It is but just to snatch some of these from oblivion, and to deliver to posterity a brief but faithful sketch of the condition of this metropolis during that calamitous period" (3). To this "moral observer," the epidemic "furnished new displays of the influence of human passions and motives" and therefore serves as a poignant if unfortunate canvas on which to portray a narrative about human corruption and benevolence.

III. Scholarly Approaches to the Yellow Fever in Brown's Work

To attend to the yellow fever in Brown's writings is to attend simultaneously to an unfortunate epidemic and an overdetermined metaphor, with scholars primarily focusing on the latter. For their part, scholars have read the fever as a mediating symbol reflecting a wide variety of late-eighteenth-century issues. Shirley Samuels connects the yellow fever to the French Revolution and other concerns about disorder to highlight how the family and the novel serve to counteract these dilemmas and enact order, whereas Julia Stern views the fever as commentary about rampant individualism and market capitalism. William Hedges compares and contrasts the conscientious responses to the fever by Rush and Arthur, suggesting that Arthur's reactions highlight the complex nature of moral action. Drawing on the means by which "romance" writers responded to conspiracy, Robert Levine argues that the fever symbolically addressed a fear of another alien import, the Illuminati. More recently, Siân Silyn Roberts suggests that the fever functions metaphorically by illustrating alternative patterns of community in which feelings can be transmitted without normal inhibition from one person to another. Louis Kirk McAuley takes a different approach and reads the fever as a metaphor for the impact of the dangers of print on society by contextualizing it with biased news and Thomas Jefferson's presidential campaign.

Most of the scholarship about Brown's use of the yellow fever epidemic examines it as a metaphorical device pertaining to other "contagions" facing the young republic.

However, other scholars examine the fever not metaphorically but literally as an object and origin of events that shape Brown's career and writing. Robert Ferguson, for instance, argues that the epidemic benefited Brown by disrupting normal social operations and allowing him to justify his writing as a chronicle of the fever. Taking this attention to authorship even further, Bryan Waterman suggests that we explore Brown's writing according to the "information revolution" of the late eighteenth century and examine how his work circulates with the increasing professionalization of medical discourse. Philip Gould and Samuel Otter situate Brown's use of the fever as it participates in the debates about contagion and race in the writings of Carey, Rush, Jones, and Allen. Shifting their attention to local debates about the fever to global commerce, Philip Barnard and Stephen Shapiro position Brown's use of the fever within the Caribbean slave revolt, the slave trade, and the rise of commerce. Their analysis reveals how the fever and local debates about it reflected and refracted Atlantic concerns about the French and Haitian revolutions and the increase of transnational trade. As these approaches suggest, the fever looms large for Brown not only as a metaphor but as a medical, social, and biological fact that resonated personally for many of Brown's readers. Through their examination of the fever as both metaphor and fact, though, scholars over the past four decades have enriched our understanding of the various functions of the fever in Brown's fiction.

These approaches to Brown's use of the fever usually explore its depiction in his novels, but as we move into further studies of the fever, we can perhaps get a better sense of its effect on his work by examining his early serialized narrative, "The Man at Home." This loosely connected cluster of thirteen installments, published in the *Weekly Magazine* from February to April 1798, consists of the ruminations of Bedloe, a debtor on the run from the law who has secluded himself in the tiny house of his washerwoman, Kate. As I will discuss, the yellow fever figures prominently in Bedloe's vignettes, but the disease and its social aftermath speak more generally to one of Brown's fictional principles: placing characters in troubling circumstances to test their response.[6] Indeed, I suggest that we examine the fever in the broader context of unusual but true events and phenomena (political revolutions, biloquism, somnambulism, etc.) that disrupt characters' lives and communities, forcing characters to forge new identities and challenge their moral principles.

Brown articulates this theory in his nonfiction essays "Walstein's School of History" (1799) and "The Difference between History and Romance" (1800). As he explains in the former, the social function of fiction (or "romance") is to articulate proper models of behavior by placing characters in situations of distress to facilitate their moral growth. Furthermore, by positioning these characters in decidedly social settings—he explains the importance of interpersonal interactions in everyday occurrences such as the marketplace or relationships—the writer can model responses for the reader: "The perfection of our character is evinced by the transient or slight influence which privations and evils have upon our happiness, on the skillfulness of those exertions which we make to avoid or repair disasters, on the diligence and success with which we improve those instruments of pleasure to ourselves and to others which fortune has left in our possession"

(Walstein 410). For Brown, the writer has a duty to place characters in conditions of stress and show how these situations affect the characters and those around them. In "The Man at Home," parts of which he later included in his novels, these "privations and evils" often include the fever, but to understand the fever's effect as it relates to Brown's ideas about fiction, we might do well to explore first an analogous subject that was well known and had a broad social impact. For many US citizens at the end of the eighteenth century, the problem of debt was real and devastating, disrupting lives and the burgeoning marketplace. This form of devastation, one that gave Brown a ready-made historical fact with which to examine motives and personal reactions, affected Brown's own father and, more well known to Brown's readers, a prominent Philadelphia resident.

IV. Social Disruptions in "The Man at Home"

"I know not whether my pen will afford me any amusement in my present condition," Brown's anonymous narrator begins the first installment. "I am without books, and am not permitted to leave my chamber." Explaining that he has cosigned a loan for a friend who cannot pay the debt, the sixty-year-old narrator, who is now hiding from his creditors, comments, "I am very well known in this city, and since I am desirous of making my fellow citizens believe that I have gone into the country, it is necessary to make myself a rigid recluse" (1–3). While such a claim may remain general enough for us, readers in Brown's Philadelphia would have immediately recognized his subject as Robert Morris, the great financier of the American Revolution.

During the war, Morris was instrumental in securing funds for the patriot cause, managing war accounts and providing General George Washington with hard currency to pay his troops (Sumner 1892, 18). A decade after the Treaty of Paris, however, this financial mastermind was headed toward personal bankruptcy. Morris had greatly overextended his wealth, creating land companies to buy millions of acres from New York to Georgia, which he hoped to resell at a large profit. To pay for his land speculation, Morris used much of his own fortune but borrowed thousands more, often using his good name as credit. When public rumors began to circulate in 1796 and 1797 that Morris could not pay his debts, his creditors wasted no time in recalling them. Since most of Morris's wealth now lay in land, and since the tense financial situation in the new republic during these two years forced citizens to hoard currency, he was unable to sell his lands and repay his debts. Unfortunately for many citizens in Philadelphia and beyond, Morris's financial failure affected them much more directly. As they began to grasp as much land as possible, Morris and his partner John Nicholson, at one time comptroller general of Pennsylvania, routinely endorsed each other's notes (Greenleaf, who was later imprisoned for debt, was also involved). For example, Morris would borrow money to purchase land, and Nicholson, using his status, would "back" the debt, called adding a "surety," by signing his name. In turn, Morris would likewise back Nicholson's debts. As Bruce Mann notes, this practice of "securing" one's debts was routine and assured the creditor that if the original debtor faulted on the payment, the backer would then be forced to pay (Mann 14–15). The problem with this practice is obvious, at least in the way Morris and Nicholson went about it. If Morris was backing Nicholson's debts and if Nicholson was backing Morris's debts, what would happen if both of them went bankrupt, as happened in this case?

Far from a problem limited to the debtors and creditors, though, this practice soon begins to affect the public at large when the Morris-Nicholson notes began to circulate, viruslike, as general currency. In other words, since bills obligatory and promissory notes were "assignable," meaning creditors could use them to pay their own debts, these cross-endorsed bills began to circulate widely through the region for debts large and small. People who had no direct connection with either Morris or Nicholson soon found these notes in their hand, and when the rumors of their financial troubles began to spread, those who possessed these bills sought to demand payment for their full value. Since the two could not immediately pay—their wealth was mainly vested in their land purchases—their notes lost value. The situation became so dire that people began to sell the bills at ten cents on the dollar in 1796 and three cents on the dollar a year later (Sumner 1891, 282). Morris and Nicholson went so far as to print proposals in Philadelphia newspapers in April 1797 admitting the deflation and offering to buy back their notes at twenty-five cents on the dollar (Sumner 1891, 284), and throughout that spring, notices appeared continuously in several papers about the limited worth of the Nicholson-Morris cross-endorsed and widely circulated notes.

The creditors' demands became so continual that in the fall of 1797, Morris was forced to retreat from Philadelphia to his country estate on the Schuylkill. Nicholson was in the Washington area at the time and knew he could not return to Philadelphia, either. Although Morris's retreat was initially a secret—rumors suggested that his absence from the public eye was part of his plan to flee to Washington—creditors quickly found Morris at his estate, which he called "Castle Defiance." According to law at the time, debtors could remain in their own homes without fear of arrest, but if they left their homes, they could immediately be detained and be forced to pay their creditors or sent to jail. As Brown's debtor-narrator remarks, "This chamber is my prison. I must confine myself to it, on penalty, if I leave it, of changing it for a prison indeed" (installment 1). In hindsight, Morris's self-confinement becomes almost comical: creditors disguising themselves hoping Morris would let them into the house so they might grab him; Morris sending out his gardener to detect spies; creditors starting "watch-fires" on his property; Morris, growing increasingly and justifiably paranoid, peering through his shutters at the creditors hiding behind trees (Young 230); and Morris only accepting written communication when placed in a bucket lowered from a second-floor window (Rappleye 506). "Have patience," he remembers shouting from his window to clustered creditors below, "and I will pay thee all" (Sumner 1891, 287). Such was the case for the great "Financier of the American Revolution," forcing Morris, like Brown's narrator, to become a man at home.

Given the simultaneity of Morris's collapse and the publication of "The Man at Home"—the first installment of the series was published on February 3, 1798, less than two weeks before Morris surrendered to the sheriff—readers of the *Weekly Magazine* would have undoubtedly understood the implicit connection between Brown's narrator and Morris. Debt has rendered the once prominent citizen an outcast, as his public status and identity, previously defined by complex and diffuse social and economic interactions, are simultaneously undermined. Reenacting such a situation throughout "The Man at Home," though, Brown presents us not with public accounts, which circulated widely in newspapers, but with the private thoughts and actions of the debtor. Readers were therefore granted imaginative access to the mind of this prominent citizen, who is forced by his devastating and very public economic collapse to redefine himself. At the center of an event whose effects rippled throughout his interconnected society of friends and strangers alike, Bedloe, the legal fugitive trapped by this situation, is paradoxically empowered to think and act in new ways.

Bedloe's accounts demonstrate that the isolation caused by this upheaval allows the reflective person to engage with whatever topics come to mind, thereby allowing him to use his own thoughts as the only guideline in his composition. In a moment of hyperbolic wit, he begins the sixth installment by explaining how he has written a poem of several pages, inspired merely by a broomstick. "The writer," he claims, "follows the train of ideas suggested by the sight of this useful instrument and is led by it on many an instructive and amusing ramble. His speculations, indeed, are bound together by no other affinity than this" (167). Invoking examples from *Paradise Lost* and William Cowper's *The Task*, and following Jonathan Swift, he proclaims that a simple object such as a broomstick may inspire schools, sects, and "sublime theories" that would spread throughout "the enlightened part of mankind," just as the fall of a leaf inspired investigation into the motion of the planets (168). His writings, in other words, possess value, regardless of the apparent insignificance of the topic. The narrator finally realizes that his self-confinement ironically allows him to think about the world anew. Not only does he reflect on unexpected kindness from people like Kate (whom he had likewise helped years before), but he also takes this time in isolation to examine linguistic differences of class, to encourage Miss De Moivre to write her own story, and to debate the justice of sending debtors to jail. In other words, the external narrative framework of the series—a fugitive debtor on the run from a social contagion of his own making—presents the narrator with a unique situation in which he can better understand himself and the world around him.

Given the broad social impact of debt and its effect on a broad spectrum of people, not just prominent citizens such as Morris/Bedloe,[7] it is no accident that the recurring theme in Bedloe's ruminations is a dramatic situation with similar social effects: the yellow fever epidemic. Like debt, the fever spreads quickly, disrupts lives, damages economic and emotional relationships, and often leads to isolation. For nearly all the people Bedloe writes about, the yellow fever has altered their lives and forced them—or those around them—to make crucial decisions and/or confront new relationships: Kate is left alone because her employers (the M'Farlanes) die from the fever, leading to

Bedloe's assistance (installment 2); Miss De Moivre buries her father, who succumbs to the fever (installment5); Baxter, who secretly watches this private burial, subsequently contracts the disease and recovers through the help of his wife (installment5); the veteran of the Revolutionary War who pens his tale (which was hidden in a trunk in Bedloe's room) dies from the fever after refusing aid (Installment 8); and Bedloe's unnamed friend benevolently stays in Philadelphia during the epidemic, observes Miss De Moivre, and helps her find assistance from Miss D____ (installment 10).

In each case, the fever is not merely the subject of the narrative but the catalyst for thought and action following the disruption of quotidian social relationships. In other words, the epidemic, like Bedloe's debt, places Brown's characters in situations in which they must make a critical decision, wrestle with an idea, or reach a conclusion. Such a use of the fever is made most explicit in installment 11, in which Bedloe's friends Harrington and Wallace debate the effects of the murderous actions taken centuries before by a secret tribunal in a Greek colony in southern Italy. This tribunal sought to eradicate dissenters, and for four months, it dispatched groups nightly to murder members of the opposition, who were always unaware of their impending plight. After discussing such "intestine commotions," they ultimately compare them to the effects of the recent yellow fever epidemic (320). Harrington draws an exact parallel between the two and argues that, like the brutal and mysterious acts of the tribunal, the fever killed indiscriminately and without warning, ultimately causing more hardship than the physical assaults by the tribunal. Wallace, on the other hand, sees little comparison and claims that "the Yellow Fever was, to me, the most fortunate event that could have happened" (322). When the plague spread through Philadelphia, Wallace was forced to abandon his store and leave for the countryside, where he regained his health and met and married a young woman with a good dowry.

The differences in these interpretations of the fever underscore Bedloe's point at the beginning of the installment, when he argues that calamities can ultimately be beneficial. While some people are driven to suicide by the thought of others' suffering, such behavior is anomalous, because, he argues, "[w]e are generally prone, when objects chance to present to us their gloomy side, to chance their position, till we hit upon the brightest of its aspects" (320). In other words, calamities such as isolation from debt or the fever force us to reflect or act on our situation, and such instances can define who we are and what we should become.

I suggest that the recurrence of the fever as a motif throughout the "Man at Home" series and in his novels is more than Brown's use of an easily recognizable event from which to develop a narrative. Instead, the cumulative effect of the fever on a variety of characters speaks to the redefinition of oneself during such a calamity. Disease is not merely a physiological fact but also a test of the mind. Like the effect of debt on Bedloe, the fever is a condition that mandates new thought and action following the destruction of normative social relationships, and, though devastating, it can lead to progress. As a "moral painter" (see "To the Public" in *Edgar Huntly*), Brown seeks local situations that will bring his characters to a moment of decision, and what better catalyst for such a moment than recent outbreaks of the devastating epidemic? The yellow fever affects and reflects many subjects—commerce, slavery, revolution, politics, and so on—but in Brown's writing, it figures first and foremost as an unfortunate yet identifiable social event that creates a situation in which reading, thinking, and action must take place without the usual social guideposts. For his characters, the yellow fever is a test, and, through his writing, Brown asks his readers to decide whether they pass or fail.

NOTES

1. See Rush 1794 and 1799 For an examination of Rush's opinions and the Philadelphia yellow fever epidemic of 1793, see Powell.
2. Frank Luther Mott suggests that Greenleaf may have died from tuberculosis rather than the yellow fever. See Mott, 134 n.
3. Monaghan and Lowenthal note that at the beginning of the 1790s, "[f]ashionable families were abandoning Queen (now Pearl) Street for Wall and Broadway" (103).
4. Condie, Folwell, and Rittenhouse argue that this lack of trade and business activity in general affected lower- and middle-class citizens significantly, since they could not work or obtain money to survive (62). For a cogent summation of the yellow fever and its symbolic relationship to economic instability, see Gould.
5. Shapiro suggests that the character of Stevens was probably based on Dr. Edward Stevens, a physician who came to Philadelphia and consulted with Rush about possible treatment (297).
6. For a recent articulation of this theory of Brown's designs in his fiction, see Barnard and Shapiro, xvii–xviii.
7. For a cogent explanation of the contemporary laws for debtors and the effect of debt on society at large, see Mease, especially 186–191.

WORKS CITED

Barnard, Philip, and Stephen Shapiro. "Introduction." In Charles Brockden Brown, *Arthur Mervyn; or, Memoirs of the Year 1793, with Related Texts*, ix–xliv. Indianapolis: Hackett, 2008.

Brown, Charles Brockden. "The Man at Home." WM I.1–13 (successive issues February 3– April 28, 1798): 1–4, 33–37, 65–67, 99–103, 133–136, 167–170, 193–195, 225–226, 257–261, 289–291, 320–323, 352–355, 383–386.

Carey, Mathew, David Rittenhouse, and American Philosophical Society. *A Short Account of the Malignant Fever, Lately Prevalent in Philadelphia*. Philadelphia: Mathew Carey, 1793.

Condie, Thomas, Richard Folwell, and David Rittenhouse. *History of the Pestilence, Commonly Called Yellow Fever, Which Almost Desolated Philadelphia, in the Months of August, September & October, 1798*. Philadelphia: R. Folwell, 1799.

Currie, William. *Memoirs of the Yellow Fever, Which Prevailed in Philadelphia, and Other Parts of the United States of America, in the Summer and Autumn of the Present Year, 1798*. Philadelphia: John Bioren for Thomas Dobson, 1798.

Estes, J. Worth, and Billy G. Smith. *A Melancholy Scene of Devastation: The Public Response to the 1793 Philadelphia Yellow Fever Epidemic*. Canton, Mass.: Science History Publications, 1997.

Ferguson, Robert. "Yellow Fever and Charles Brockden Brown: Context of the Emerging Novelist." *Early American Literature* 14 (1979): 293–305.

Gould, Philip. "Race, Commerce, and the Literature of Yellow Fever in Early National Philadelphia." *Early American Literature* 35 (2000): 157–186.

Hedges, William L. "Benjamin Rush, Charles Brockden Brown, and the American Plague Year." *Early American Literature* 7 (1973): 295–311.

Horrocks, Thomas A., and John C. Van Horne. "Foreword." In J. Worth Estes and Billy G. Smith, eds., *A Melancholy Scene of Devastation: The Public Response to the 1793 Philadelphia Yellow Fever Epidemic*, vii–xii. Canton, Mass.: Science History Publications, 1997.

Letter from the Secretary of the Commonwealth of Pennsylvania, by Direction of the Governor, Relative to the Late Malignant Fever; and Report of the Board of Managers, of the Marine and City Hospitals, in Reply. Philadelphia: Thomas and Samuel F. Bradford, 1798.

Levine, Robert S. *Conspiracy and Romance: Studies in Brockden Brown, Cooper, Hawthorne, and Melville*. Cambridge: Cambridge University Press, 1989.

Mann, Bruce H. *Republic of Debtors: Bankruptcy in the Age of American Independence*. Cambridge, Mass.: Harvard University Press, 2002.

McAuley, Louis Kirk. "Periodical Visitations": Yellow Fever as Yellow Journalism in Charles Brockden Brown's *Arthur Mervyn*." *Eighteenth Century Fiction* 19 (Spring 2007): 307–340.

Mease, James. *The Picture of Philadelphia*. Philadelphia: B. & T. Kite, 1811.

Monaghan, Frank, and Marvin Lowenthal. *This Was New York, the Nation's Capital in 1789*. Garden City, N.Y.: Doubleday Doran, 1943.

Mott, Frank Luther. *American Journalism; A History, 1690–1960*, 3rd ed. New York: Macmillan, 1962.

Otter, Samuel. *Philadelphia Stories: America's Literature of Race and Freedom*. New York: Oxford University Press, 2010.

Pernick, Martin S. "Politics, Parties, and Pestilence: Epidemic Yellow Fever in Philadelphia and the Rise of the First Party System." *William and Mary Quarterly* 29.4 (1972): 559–586.

Powell, J. H. *Bring Out Your Dead: The Great Plague of Yellow Fever in Philadelphia in 1793*. Philadelphia: University of Pennsylvania Press, 1949.

Raddin, George Gates. *Hocquet Caritat and the Early New York Literary Scene*. Dover, N.J.: Dover Advance Press, 1953.

Raddin, George Gates. *The New York of Hocquet Caritat and His Associates, 1797–1817*. Dover, N.J.: Dover Advance Press, 1953.

Rappleye, Charles. *Robert Morris: Financier of the American Revolution*. New York: Simon & Schuster, 2010.

Roberts, Siân Silyn. "Gothic Enlightenment: Contagion and Community in Charles Brockden Brown's *Arthur Mervyn*." *Early American Literature* 44 (2009): 307–332.

Rush, Benjamin. *An Account of the Bilious Remitting Yellow Fever, as It Appeared in the City of Philadelphia, in the Year 1793*. Philadelphia: Thomas Dobson, 1794.

Rush, Benjamin. *Observations upon the Origin of the Malignant Bilious, or Yellow Fever in Philadelphia, and upon the Means of Preventing It: Addressed to the Citizens of Philadelphia*. Philadelphia: Budd and Bartram, 1799.

Samuels, Shirley. "Plague and Politics in 1793: *Arthur Mervyn*." *Criticism—A Quarterly for Literature & the Arts* 27 (1985): 225–246.

Shapiro, Stephen. *The Culture and Commerce of the Early American Novel: Reading the Atlantic World System*. University Park, Pa.: Pennsylvania State University Press, 2008.

Smith, Billy G. "Comment: Disease and Community." In J. Worth Estes and Billy G. Smith, eds., *A Melancholy Scene of Devastation: The Public Response to the 1793 Philadelphia Yellow Fever Epidemic*, 147–162. Canton, Mass.: Science History Publications, 1997.

Stern, Julia A. *The Plight of Feeling: Sympathy and Dissent in the Early American Novel*. Chicago: University of Chicago Press, 1997.

Sumner, William Graham. *The Financier and Finances of the American Revolution*, 2 vols. (1891). New York: Augustus M. Kelly, 1968.

Sumner, William Graham. *Robert Morris*. New York: Dodd, Mead, 1892.

Waterman, Bryan. "*Arthur Mervyn*'s Medical Repository and the Early Republic's Knowledge Industries." *American Literary History* 15 (Summer 2003): 213–247.

Young, Eleanor. *Forgotten Patriot: Robert Morris*. New York: Macmillan, 1950.

CHAPTER 25

···

BROWN AND SEX

···

JORDAN ALEXANDER STEIN

I

···

FEW early American novels are sexier than Charles Brockden Brown's, and this fact stems very much from their author's design. Brown was fascinated by sex in the sense of both what is now usually called gender (the secondary sex characteristics that differentiate people in social environments) and in the sense of sexual activity (intercourse but also correlated circumstances such as marriage, reproduction, and inheritance). As Brown himself wrote in the second part of his essay "Walstein's School of History" (1799):

> Next to property, the most extensive source of our relations is sex. On the circumstances which produce, and the principles which regulate the union between the sexes, happiness greatly depends. The conduct to be pursued by a virtuous man in those situations which arise from sex, it was thought useful to display.
>
> Fictitious history has, hitherto, chiefly related to the topics of love and marriage. A monotony and sentimental softness have hence arisen that have frequently excited contempt and ridicule. The ridicule, in general, is merited; not because these topics are intrinsically worthless or vulgar, but because the historian was deficient in knowledge and skill.
>
> Marriage is incident to all; its influence on our happiness and dignity, is more entire and lasting than any other incident can possess. None, therefore, is more entitled to discussion. To enable men to evade the evils and secure the benefits of this state, is to consult, in an eminent degree, their happiness.
>
> A man, whose activity is neither aided by political authority nor by the *press*, may yet exercise considerable influence on the condition of his neighbours, by the exercise of intellectual powers. His courage may be useful to the timid or the feeble, and his knowledge to the ignorant, as well as his property to those who want. His benevolence and justice may not only protect his kindred and his wife, but rescue the victims of prejudice and passion from the yoke of those domestic tyrants, and shield the powerless from the oppression of power, the poor from the injustice of the rich, and the simple from the stratagems of cunning. (409–410)

The first three paragraphs neatly outline their author's sense of the ways both gender and marriage become bases for history and fiction, but the final one makes a further claim. Here Brown is interested not only in the social aspects of sex but also in the ways they relate to individual character, knowledge, motive, and action.

Sex, in this third sense, in relation to individual character, is usually called sexuality. Following the terms established by Michel Foucault's influential *History* (1976), sexuality is an epistemology, a way of knowing something. More specifically, Foucault understands sexuality as a type of knowledge distinguished by its ability to make totalizing claims about persons. If, for example, a woman has sex (or wants to have sex) with another woman, the epistemology of sexuality abstracts this inclination into a durable preference. A woman who has sex with another woman is *the kind of person* who does such things and may be recognized and identified as such by herself and others. Sexuality thereby offers a kind of knowledge that, in Foucault's well-known phrase, can be taken for the truth of the self.

This chapter considers the various things that sex does and can mean in Brown's corpus, with particular attention to his novels. Following on Brown's discussion in "Walstein's School of History," the chapter takes for granted that sex doesn't mean just one thing, but indeed has at least three different meanings: sex as gender, sex as marriage, and sex as sexuality. In this definitional multiplicity, Brown is not alone. It is common for sex to mean more than one thing. Indeed, many scholars influenced by Foucault have elaborated his critique by enumerating the many things, besides an inborn and essential truth of the self, that sexuality might help us to know. From their vantage, sex is plural; its meanings are almost always simultaneously social and individual, bodily and symbolic.

Brown's commitment, in his novels and elsewhere, to drawing together gender, marriage, and sexuality offers a nuanced sense of sex's plural meanings; however, that commitment provides more in the way of artistry that it does in analytical clarity. Though Brown's works depict sex in plural ways, the works are not consistent in their representations of the relationship *among* these plural aspects of sex or in their emphases on which aspects matter most. Sex accordingly has become an interpretative problem for readers of Brown's novels: what meaning or meanings for sex are being represented, and to what end? This chapter surveys scholarly attempts to make sense of Brown's engagements with sex in its multiple forms, in an effort to identify which meanings for sex might best serve readers of Brown's novels.

II

There are reasons scholars don't agree on what sex means. Indeed, the interpretative challenges around sex in Brown's novels are arguably intertwined with methodological developments in American literary studies as a whole. Americanist literary scholarship during the middle of the twentieth century gave Brown's novels far less attention than it gave to those of more securely "American" authors such as James Fenimore Cooper or

Nathaniel Hawthorne. These latter authors appeared more American, by virtue of the ease with which critics could interpret their novels according to an exceptionalist hermeneutic, one that emphasized the American landscape, Calvinist or New England national origins, the romance tradition, and an implicitly masculine individualism (Foerster). Brown's novels, by contrast, were far less explicit in their engagement with American national identity or with Calvinism, and several are set in urban rather than rural environs. Yet if Brown's novels felt to this generation of critics less representatively American than the novels of Cooper or Hawthorne, it is nevertheless the case that those who did pay attention to Brown's novels found them generally complicit with other exceptionalist themes. Larzer Ziff's influential 1962 essay defending Brown's literary merits argues that "for a half-century before the great literary movement in New England he [Brown] had perceived the theme and the manner of the American novel, which is to say that like all great literary artists he knew his culture better than it knew itself" (Ziff 57). Ziff's essay is representative of what can broadly be called a culturalist reading of Brown's novels, one that earns the novels their status as American by emphasizing the historical and social circumstances of Brown's composition. The culturalist interpretation of Brown thus reads his novels more in terms of concrete historical referents and less in terms of broad thematics.

Culturalist interpretations began to dominate Americanist literary scholarship in the 1980s and after, and it was perhaps not coincidental that critical interest in Brown's novels expanded in this same period. In a major historicist reconsideration of the aesthetic merits of antebellum novels, Jane Tompkins famously argued in 1985 that "nothing happens" in Brown's *Wieland* because the text is not interested in depicting human agency. Instead, it is a novel full of "casualties of history viewed from the perspective of men who had watched in fear the bloodbath that followed the French Revolution" (Tompkins 60). Where Tompkins uses the historical circumstances of the text's production to interpret its plot, Shirley Samuels, in an important 1990 essay, uses the same method to interpret its form: "the representative family-as-nation that was portrayed in numerous political pamphlets of the Revolutionary War found a fictional form in novels of the early Republic" (Samuels 51). Such readings of plot and form ultimately swelled critics' abilities to make explicit the kind of American themes in Brown's novels that had eluded an earlier generation of critics. Thus, Jay Fliegelman's introduction to a widely adopted 1991 classroom edition of *Wieland* emphasized the ties between the novel's theme and setting, on the one hand, and its depiction of social issues surrounding the American Revolution on the other. In the thirty years between Ziff's essay and Fliegelman's edition, *Wieland* had become, unquestionably and obviously, an early American novel (Stein).

The vicissitudes of *Wieland*'s critical fortunes are worth rehearsing here for the ways in which they bear on scholarly assessments of sex in Brown's novels more generally. Overwhelmingly, critics interested in sex in Brown's novels during the past four decades have pursued a culturalist approach. With some consistency, these critics (as I will elaborate) interpret sex in Brown's novels in relation to the social and historical circumstances surrounding Brown's life and writings. This is not to say that no interpretations concerned with sex in Brown's novels existed before 1980. Indeed, many critics of Ziff's generation read Brown's novels as Bildungsromans, and thus, themes of property inheritance and transfer, marriage, and knowledge acquisition were expounded as stories of masculine sexual development, however implicitly. Be that as it may, the culturalist approach of the past four decades has enabled many more explicit interpretations of sex in Brown's novels. Yet in the absence of a single agreed-upon meaning for sex, culturalist interpretations exhibit three tendencies.

The first group could be called *gender criticism*, and its primary focus is on the difference (or the lack of difference) between men and women. Brown's feminism and its consequences for his novels is of particular interest to this strain of criticism. Such criticism includes Fritz Fleischmann's account of the sexual politics of Brown's novels and, in particular, his very early identification of the influence of Mary Wollstonecraft's *A Vindication of the Rights of Woman* on Brown's depiction of women characters. Focusing on *Ormond*, Fleischmann notes the agon staged in the characters of Helena and Ormond, the former embodying all that Wollstonecraft despised about the education of women and the latter the "violations of human dignity" that come about through the abuse of patriarchal power (Fleischmann 57). Other critics see Brown less as intervening in the debates about feminism in the period than simply engaging them—and so the politics of Brown's novels remain hard to pin down. For example, Elizabeth Jane Wall Hinds argues that Brown's novels trouble the period's shifting ideals of republican virtue by exploring the ways the economic conditions of the early republic (including questions about the transfer of property) affect men and women unevenly. But she arrives at this conclusion about the thematic concerns of Brown's novels without making any definitive interpretation of Brown's own political concerns. Other critics, such as Sydney J. Krause, have lauded the emphasis Brown's novels place on resilient female characters, arguing that "[n]o writer in Brown's time—and for a considerable time after—would make a more positive statement about the essential capabilities of women, more than validating their entitlement to fully equal rights with men" (Krause 375). Similarly, Paul Lewis has argued that "*Ormond* pushed beyond familiar questions about woman's place to boldly feminist positions" (Lewis 38), yet what counts as feminism in Lewis's essay is the depiction of physical valor. While this definition is defensible, such unambiguous accounts of Brown's feminism tend to focus on his depictions of strong female characters rather than on the intellectual circumstances under which he labored to create them.

Ambiguity about Brown's feminism grows when gender criticism homes in not only on Brown's novels but also on his life. Focusing more on the intellectual origins for Brown's interests, many critics have noted the popularity of Wollstonecraft's writings within Brown's milieu, especially during his association with the Friendly Club in New York. Fredrika J. Teute and Bryan Waterman, for example, have offered detailed accounts of the ways in which *Alcuin* and *Ormond* register the intellectual debates within the Friendly Club about Wollstonecraftian feminism, in contrast with the "perhaps unconscious homosocial constitution" of the club (Waterman 98). Philip Barnard and Stephen Shapiro, in their critical introductions to editions of *Wieland* (2009) and *Arthur Meryn* (2008), have likewise connected Brown's depictions of female heroes with his reading and interpretation of the Anglo-Jacobin or Woldwinite feminism of the 1790s. Furthermore, the homosocial dimension of Brown's social life receives excellent elaboration in Catherine O'Donnell Kaplan's study of masculine self-fashioning the early republic through artistic and cultural pursuits. Kaplan demonstrates that horizontal (rather than hierarchical) social arrangements were part of the intellectual milieu of the Friendly Club and that they are not exclusively, or even primarily, of interest to Friendly Club members in cross-gender contexts. As these examples suggest, when critics look at Brown's life as a context for his views on gender, they are less likely to make unambiguous claims about his feminism. Instead, what becomes clear are some of the complex tensions between what Brown's novels represent and the conditions under which they were written.

A second group in the scholarship focusing on Brown and sexuality could be called *marriage criticism*, as it emphasizes social aspects of sex. While gender criticism focuses on the relations between men and women, gathering complexity by alternating in its attention between art and life, marriage criticism instead focuses on the relations between men and women in a domain that explicitly overlaps social and sexual interactions. In a very few cases, this strain of scholarship pursues a biographical line. Caleb Crain, for example, details the sympathetic relations that Brown rehearsed in his epistolary correspondence with male friends and extrapolates from these erotically charged exchanges larger themes in Brown's novels. Moving also from the life to the work, Steven Watts has argued that Brown's interest in sex and gender relations stems from his youthful flirtations with Deborah Ferris and Susan Potts, two young women not of the Quaker faith and therefore unacceptable to Brown's parents (Watts 58). The problem with this biographical line, however, is that it feels speculative and, indeed, in the case of Watts's interpretation, proves to be factually dubious (Letters 297–317, 910, 915). The scant documentation concerning Brown's sexual relationships, as well as the lateness of his marriage (in 1804, six years before his death and after the completion of all his novels), makes it difficult to substantiate any biographical ties to his fictional writings. Even Leslie Fiedler, whose influential *Love and Death in the American Novel* discussed Brown's marriage plots as imitations of Samuel Richardson's seduction novels, despaired of biographical interpretations, lamenting about how "confused do sentimental life and sentimental literature become" (Fiedler 73).

As an alternative, much of what I'm calling marriage criticism has pursued a more formalist approach to Brown's novels. In a pioneering contribution to this line of thinking, Cathy N. Davidson's 1981 reading of *Alcuin* focuses on the dialogic structure of that text's debate about marriage, concluding that "Brown employed the dialog form to explore ideas, not to advance or to substantiate them" (Davidson 82). Despite this open-ended interpretation of Brown's politics, Davidson succeeds in nailing down Brown's (and *Alcuin's*) themes: "discussion leads to questions of sexuality" (81). For Davidson, sexuality here means marriage and sexual activity—and for reasons I have already suggested, this definition is far from inevitable. Nonetheless, her point is not only to establish the thematic importance of sexuality but also to insist that the dialogical structure of *Alcuin* is what leads readers there. Rather than assume a biographical interpretation, then, critics interested in marriage have tended to ask about the ways a text's themes work with (and, in a few cases, against) a text's form. Marriage criticism has, in other words, emphasized the fictionality of Brown's novels. Though marriage criticism, to be sure, sees continuities between Brown and his time and place, it also pays thoughtful attention to the ways Brown's novels may be exploring fantasies or alternatives to the time and place of their composition.

Perhaps a clearer way of making the point would be to say that marriage criticism is interested to observe what (sex as) marriage does and does not make possible in the social world of the early republic. Generally speaking, however, the accounts are optimistic. Stephen Shapiro, for example, reads the end of *Arthur Mervyn*, where the eponymous hero marries a rich and exotic woman, as proposing "egalitarian miscegenation" (Shapiro 2008, 265) that works to overcome racism in a postslavery society. On this view, Brown's novel expresses a kind of erotic optimism that makes libertine behavior a playful means of securing a bourgeois order. Such locating of interracial possibility in marriage advances the idea that sexual activity is tied to social and cultural work. Yet where Shapiro sees that Brown's novels use marriage to broker social possibility regarding race, others have seen that marriage brokers social possibility for other kinds of identities. Kristen M. Comment, for example, has read the homoerotic dynamic between Constantia Dudley and Sophia Courtland in *Ormond* as an explicitly lesbian representation, which "reflects both the cultural fascination with lesbian possibility and patriarchal efforts to contain it" (Comment 59). At the same time, Comment's reading of *Ormond*'s plot leads to the conclusion that "the novel's ambivalent treatment of female independence leaves that containment tenuous at best and ultimately affirms the power of female homoerotic bonding it seeks to limit" (59). In this account, Brown's form exceeds his politics, and *Ormond*'s greatest success is its failure of authorial control. A different sense of optimism about narrative collapse comes through in Elizabeth Maddock Dillon's brilliant reading of *Edgar Huntly*, in which the eponymous hero's inability to maintain property is linked to his inability to follow the heterosexual narrative path (the "heteropathic narrative") of masculine desire for virtuous women (Dillon 161). Focusing on the formal absence of a marriage plot in *Edgar Huntly*, Dillon details the ways in which the novel's other aspirations (for property transfer and sympathetic exchange) are disenabled when a marriage plot fails to materialize. Complementing the kind of reading done by Davidson a quarter century before, Dillon's account of sex-as-marriage shows that gender and relations of sexual difference require a complex coordination, such that sex means lining up gender with heterosocial relations, with property, with social possibility, according to what anthropologist Gayle Rubin, in another context, has called a "sex/gender system."

A third grouping of scholarship on Brown and sexuality could be called *queer criticism*, and its emphasis steers toward neither gender nor marriage as such but rather to the social and sexual possibilities that emerge when those relationships break down. The primary effort of this strain of criticism is not to put Brown's novels into historical context so much as it is to see how the novels exceed or challenge what otherwise would seem to have been possible in the time of their initial publication. Suspicious of any possible determinism that resides in historicist readings of Brown, queer criticism of his novels is generally unconcerned with authorial intentions. Instead, queer criticism of Brown's novels is keyed to historical ironies, whereby the effects of texts or representations are open-ended and unpredictable.

Moreover, the version of sexuality that queer criticism tends to value most in Brown's novels is a plastic one, or what Thomas A. Foster, in another context, has called "an inconsistent and shifting mixture of acts *and* identities" (Foster xii). Thus, where a scholar like Comment might speak about "the cultural fascination with lesbian possibility" (Comment 59) in the early republic, what I'm calling queer criticism seeks instead to work outside any confidently emergent account of such social categories, in favor of what Bruce Burgett has called "queer history of sexuality" (Burgett, 122). In Burgett's usage, *queer* stands in tension with *history*, insofar as the latter term implies a normatively paced, progressive ordering of time. By contrast, a queer history of sexuality narrates social and erotic experiences that may have been present historically without ever having earned the dignity of a socially recognized category, as, for example, gay and lesbian identities have done. In a succinct distillation of these critical moves, Stephen Shapiro has argued that *Ormond* "differs from the period's emerging descriptions of same-sex sexuality as it conceptualizes homoeroticism more in terms of its group politics, rather than those of aberrant biological sex and its codification in gender roles" (Shapiro 2007, 357). By this account, the value of *Ormond* is in the way it can be read against not only emergent sexual norms in the early republic but also dominant sexual norms in our own period. While such work is by no means anti-historicist, its mode of historicism is insistently nonteleological.

As a strategy for working outside of such a teleological move toward contemporary sexual identities, many queer critical essays on Brown comply, implicitly or explicitly, with Eve Kosofsky Sedgwick's assessment of the Gothic more generally, that "even motifs that might ex post facto look like homosexual thematics (the Unspeakable, the anal), even when presented in a context of intensities between men, nevertheless have as their first referent the psychology and sociology of prohibition and control" (Sedgwick 116). That is to say, queer criticism engages sexuality in a way that is broadly social and yet not reducible to sex, gender, desire, bodies, or many of the other things that would seem most obviously to index it (as was more the case with marriage criticism).

Thus, some of the most exemplary queer critical essays on Brown's novels have tended to focus on the ways erotic experience can be understood as a relay between one body and something outside that body—such as a book. Reading, indeed, emerges as a central concern in much queer criticism on Brown's novels. Dana Luciano, for example, has argued that *Edgar Huntly* is a kind of metafiction, depicting "[a]ttachments to pleasure for its own sake," "pleasure not tied in to an instrumentalist teleology" that might otherwise be "dismissed as archaic, barbaric, infantile, pathological, or queer" (Luciano 3). In her interpretation, *Edgar Huntly* simultaneously endorses and undermines this latter judgment. Along the way, the novel shows how reading is a dangerously embodied activity (evocative of nonrational corporeal sensations) and shows this, moreover, in an evocative story that, by virtue of its medium, requires reading. To choose another example, Christopher Looby's searching analysis of *Memoirs of Stephen Calvert* has argued that Stephen's own reading of Mademoiselle de Scudéry's romances provokes him to understand that sexuality—"an imaginary composite of many different experiences, identifications, and performances (bodily sensations, gender determinations, forms of sexual conduct, erotic scripts, and so on)"—is an attribute of his person (Looby 843). Stephen's experience of reading becomes central to his sense of himself, but, Looby argues, it also becomes a focal point for his own readers, who are encountering Stephen as a character in a novel. That is, like Luciano's interpretation of reading in *Edgar Huntly*, Looby's interpretation of reading in *Stephen Calvert* operates on more than one level simultaneously. According to these queer critical accounts, Brown's novels evoke sexuality at the levels of both content and form and, indeed, insist that doing so is a fundamental project of these novels, which pursue the question of whether sexuality is, in Looby's phrase, "essentially a literary phenomenon" (Looby 841). Greta LaFleur has taken this point further, locating the cross-dressing plot of *Ormond* not in a woman's relationship to another woman but in the novel's relationship to the "wealth of American fiction published during the last decade of the eighteenth century [that] features female characters who disguise themselves or even live as men" (LaFleur 97). For queer criticism, contact between a body and a book counts as sexuality as much as if not more than contact between two bodies.

III

There is no single consensus on what sex means in the criticism of Brown's novels. We have seen, for example, that one strain of the queer criticism of Brown's novels tends toward analyses of the metafictional consequences of reading and that these analyses feel quite far, in scope and tone, from the confident estimations of Brown's politics that we saw among the gender criticism of these same novels. Critics who imagine that sex means marriage have had little reason to pay attention to scenes of reading in Brown's novels, just as a critics who imagine that sex evokes a queer cluster of desires and actions have not necessarily had much to say about Brown's feminism.

The fact that Brown's novels can sustain these multiple readings speaks to their artistic complexity, but the fact that none of the scholarship on Brown and sex recognizes a critical disagreement is worrisome. Working toward some consensus is necessary for scholarship to advance, and given the number of pages written on Brown and sex, the conversation should arguably be advanced much further than it is.

At the same time, acknowledging the lack of critical agreement about Brown and sex may itself be the way forward. At the least, critical *mésalliances* may be worth thinking through, as they point to things that we, as critics of Brown's work, may not yet understand—for example, why his feminism does not seem very queer or how his formal interests do and do not comply with particular political questions. In other words, for critics to maintain a plural account of sex in Brown's novels may be entirely productive, provided that one is prepared to acknowledge the incoherence within the critical conversation. This acknowledgment of the multiple and competing senses of sex in the criticism on Brown is crucial, I think, because it is impossible at present to predict which one sense (if any) will in the future yield the clearest and most productive analyses. We have yet to determine what sex means in Brown's novels.

Works Cited

Barnard, Philip, and Stephen Shapiro. "Introduction." In Charles Brockden Brown, *Arthur Mervyn; or, Memoirs of the Year 1793, with Related Texts*, xi–xliv. Indianapolis: Hackett, 2008.

Barnard, Philip, and Stephen Shapiro. "Introduction." In Charles Brockden Brown, *Wieland; or, the Transformation, an American Tale, with Related Texts*, ix–xlvi. Indianapolis: Hackett, 2009.

Burgett, Bruce. "Between Speculation and Population: The Problem of 'Sex' in Our Long Eighteenth Century." *Early American Literature* 37.1 (2002): 119–153.

Comment, Kristin M. "Charles Brockden Brown's *Ormond* and Lesbian Possibility in the Early Republic." *Early American Literature* 40.1 (2005): 57–78.

Crain, Caleb. *American Sympathy: Men, Friendship, and Literature in the New Nation*. New Haven, Conn.: Yale University Press, 2001.

Davidson, Cathy N. "The Matter and Manner of Charles Brockden Brown's *Alcuin*." In Bernard Rosenthal, ed., *Critical Essays on Charles Brockden Brown*, 71–86. Boston: G. K. Hall, 1981.

Dillon, Elizabeth Maddock. *The Gender of Freedom: Fictions of Liberalism and the Literary Public Sphere*. Stanford, Calif.: Stanford University Press, 2004.

Fleischmann, Fritz. *A Right View of the Subject: Feminism in the Works of Charles Brockden Brown and John Neal*. Erlangen: Palm und Enke, 1983.

Fliegelman, Jay. "Introduction." In Charles Brockden Brown, *Wieland and Memoirs of Carwin the Biloquist*. New York: Penguin, 1991.

Fiedler, Leslie A. *Love and Death in the American Novel*. New York: Criterion, 1960.

Foerster, Norman. "Factors in American Literary History." In Norman Foerster, ed., *The Reinterpretation of American Literature: Some Contributions toward the Understanding of Its Historical Development*, 23–39. New York: Harcourt, Brace, 1928.

Foster, Thomas A. *Sex and the Eighteenth-Century Man: Massachusetts and the History of Sexuality in America*. Boston: Beacon, 2006.

Foucault, Michel. *The History of Sexuality*, Vol. 1, *An Introduction* (1976). Robert Hurley, trans. New York: Vintage, 1990.

Hinds, Elizabeth Jane Wall. *Private Property: Charles Brockden Brown's Gendered Economics of Virtue*. Newark: University of Delaware Press, 1997.

Kaplan, Catherine O'Donnell. *Men of Letters in the Early Republic: Cultivating Forms of Citizenship*. Chapel Hill: University of North Carolina Press, 2008.

Krause, Sydney J. "Brockden Brown's Feminism in Fact and Fiction." In Fritz Fleischmann and Klaus H. Schmidt, eds., *Early America Re-Explored: New Readings in Colonial, Early National, and Antebellum Culture*, 349–384. New York: Peter Lang, 2000.

LaFleur, Greta L. "Precipitous Sensations: Herman Mann's *The Female Review* (1797), Botanical Sexuality, and the Challenge of Queer Historiography." *Early American Literature* 48.1 (2013): 93–123.

Lewis, Paul. "Attaining Masculinity: Charles Brockden Brown and Women Warriors of the 1790s." *Early American Literature* 40.1 (2005): 37–55.

Looby, Christopher. "The Literariness of Sexuality: Or, How to Do the (Literary) History of (American) Sexuality." *American Literary History* 25.4 (Winter 2013): 841–854.

Luciano, Dana. "'Perverse Nature': *Edgar Huntly* and the Novel's Reproductive Disorders." *American Literature* 70.1 (1998): 1–27.

Rubin, Gayle. "The Traffic in Women: Notes on the 'Political Economy' of Sex." In Rayna Reiter, ed., *Toward an Anthropology of Women*, 157–210. New York: Monthly Review, 1975.

Samuels, Shirley. "*Wieland*: Alien and Infidel." *Early American Literature* 25.1 (1990): 46–66.

Sedgwick, Eve Kosofsky. *Between Men: English Literature and Male Homosocial Desire*. New York: Columbia University Press, 1985.

Shapiro, Stephen. *The Culture and Commerce of the Early American Novel: Reading the Atlantic World-System*. University Park: Pennsylvania State University Press, 2008.

Shapiro, Stephen. "In a French Position: Radical Pornography and Homoerotic Society in Charles Brockden Brown's *Ormond or the Secret Witness*." In Thomas A. Foster, ed., *Long before Stonewall: Histories of Same-Sex Sexuality in Early America*, 357–383. New York: New York University Press, 2007.

Stein, Jordan Alexander. "Are 'American Novels' Novels? *Mardi* and the Problem of Boring Books." In Russ Castronovo, ed., *The Oxford Handbook of Nineteenth-Century American Literature*, 42–58. New York: Oxford University Press, 2011.

Teute, Fredrika J. "A 'Republic of Intellect': Conversation and Criticism among the Sexes in 1790s New York." In Philip Barnard, Mark L. Kamrath, and Stephen Shapiro, eds., *Revising Charles Brockden Brown: Culture, Politics, and Sexuality in the Early Republic*, 149–181. Knoxville: University of Tennessee Press, 2004.

Tompkins, Jane. *Sensational Designs: The Cultural Work of American Fiction 1790–1860*. New York: Oxford University Press, 1985.

Waterman, Bryan. *Republic of Intellect: The Friendly Club of New York City and the Making of American Literature*. Baltimore: Johns Hopkins University Press, 2007.

Watts, Steven. *The Romance of Real Life: Charles Brockden Brown and the Origins of American Culture*. Baltimore: Johns Hopkins University Press, 1994.

Ziff, Larzer. "A Reading of *Wieland*." *Publications of the Modern Language Association* 77.1 (March 1962): 51–57.

PART VII

LITERARY FORMS, AESTHETICS, AND CULTURE

CHAPTER 26

···

BROWN'S AMERICAN
GOTHIC

···

ROBERT MILES

IT is a remarkable coincidence of literary history that Charles Brockden Brown and Francisco Goya should in the very same year produce exactly the same trope for post-Enlightenment dystopia. In his 1799 collection of sketches, *Los caprichos*, or caprices, Goya includes the image that is possibly, apart from Henry Fuseli's *The Nightmare*, the single most iconic representation of the Gothic: *El sueño de la razon produce monstruos*, or, as it is usually translated, *The Sleep of Reason Produces Monsters*.[1] It shows the artist slumped over his desk, in sleep or reverie (the Spanish *sueño* means both) while about him flutter the totemic creatures of dark superstition (bats) but also wisdom (owls). In the very same year, Brown published his self-conscious experiment in American Gothic, *Edgar Huntly; or, Memoirs of a Sleep-Walker*. At a key moment in his story, Edgar tells us:

> Possibly, the period will arrive when I shall look back without agony on the perils I have undergone. That period is still distant. Solitude and sleep are now no more than the signals to summon up a tribe of ugly phantoms. Famine, and blindness, and death, and savage enemies, never fail to be conjured up by the silence and darkness of the night. I cannot dissipate them by any efforts of reason. My cowardice requires the perpetual consolation of light. My heart droops when I mark the decline of the sun, and I never sleep but with a candle burning at my pillow. If, by any chance, I should awake and find myself immersed in darkness, I know not what act of desperation I might be suddenly impelled to commit.   (EH 158)

It is typical of Brown's dense, abstract, cerebral style of fiction that this passage should contain a great deal for the reader to puzzle over, not least of which is the answer to the question here posed by Edgar: What desperate act? Doubling, of course, is a principle source of Gothic horror. Is Edgar the double of Clithero, a sleepwalker who appears to be, for much of the tale, a homicidal lunatic? As the story progresses, Edgar seems to mimic—indeed, seems to be catching—Clithero's propensity to sleepwalk, so much so that by the end of the novel, the reader is left wondering whose sleepwalking memoirs these are, Clithero's or Edgar's. Does the sleep of reason open up the possibility of homicidal madness of the kind that seems to afflict Clithero, whose secret grief turns on his interrupted attempt to knife his adopted mother, Mrs. Lorimer, for the best of reasons? Huntly also doubles Clithero in his propensity to justify his actions on the basis of benevolent intentions that almost always miscarry, including the benevolent action of pursuing Clithero in order to sound the mystery of his suffering, after observing Clithero, in the dead of night, digging a hole under the elm tree where Edgar's friend Waldegrave had recently been murdered. Brown's version of the sleep of reason thus contains an ambiguity: Do the "tribe of ugly phantoms" (158) that assail Edgar occur when reason sleeps? Or when reason daydreams?

Goya intends the same ambiguity. The obvious post-Freudian sense of Goya's image is that when we sleep, so does reason; as the ego nods, the id awakens. But Goya also means something else: he represents himself, possibly, as lost in reverie, not sleep; he indulges in dreams of reason, fantasies of utopias, successful revolutionary actions where evil is extirpated and the good inherit the earth as superstition is banished and reason reigns in peace. Goya's subscription to the image suggests as much: "The Author Dreaming. His only intention is to banish harmful superstition and to perpetuate with this work of fancy the solid testimony of Truth" (quoted in Nehamas 37). But as Goya's critics note, the image is subtly ironized. The "sleeper" is a melancholic, disappointed by the failures of the Enlightenment (Lázaro-Reboll); he is aligned with Don Quixote's hopeless forays in idealism, not "truth" (Ciofalo); and while the owls ought to signify Minerva, the goddess of wisdom, the name of the particular kind of owl depicted is, in Spanish, a byword for a prostitute (Ciofalo 433). For Goya, the promise of Enlightenment has fizzled out. The dark forces of the feudal past—the Catholic Church but especially the Inquisition—arise, like so many bats, in reaction, while the enlightened ones embark on hopeless schemes of improvement that miscarry or sink into libertinism. Once one is clued in to Goya's irony, a second way of interpreting the image emerges, one that prompts the question "do monsters appear when rationality nods, or are they Reason's hideous brood?" (Porter 236).

Goya's image is thus rife with dark antinomies: neither Enlightenment nor its Counter; neither superstition nor fantasies of reason; neither the old order nor the new. These same dark antinomies structure Brown's fictional world. In a classic study of the American Enlightenment, Robert A. Ferguson explains why this might be so. Ferguson contrasts an American sense of Enlightenment with a European one. In the American sense, Enlightenment is the natural Whiggish progress towards liberty, where feudalism is thrown out, the rights of man universally established, and representative government enshrined. Everywhere superstition and darkness surrender to reason and light. In the European sense, Enlightenment is just one more trick of an age-old pattern of power and repression. "Since the Revolution claims government by consent of the governed as the irreducible source of its achievement, self-determination becomes the sign and symptom of the Enlightenment at work in each succeeding generation" (Ferguson 22). This American sense runs into a countervailing European one: "For the European scholar, even self-determination can appear to be a social control as much as it is a political right, a methodology that has structured individuals into isolated monads and objects of manipulation" (23). The ever-renewing American drama of self-emancipation conflicts with the European sense of the hopelessness of doing so, of the inescapability of ideology, which, like a camera obscura, transforms schemes of idealism into something like their opposite. As in Brown's *Wieland*, dreams of an ideal new community based on the public goods of reason and fraternity disintegrate into private nightmares.

Ferguson's key point is that these caricatures together map out the extremes of a dialectical process that holds true on both sides of the Atlantic. Together they just tell us what the process of Enlightenment, of modernity, is like. Immanuel Kant's definition of Enlightenment—the struggle to know, to free ourselves from the immaturity of prejudice and superstition—is a continuing project, with defeat always an immanent possibility, then as now. Like Goya's "dream" of reason, both bats and owls are in play. But there is, of course, a difference in perspective.

> In Europe the Enlightenment must overcome the wreckage of human history, or, as Jefferson tells Priestley, "the times of Vandalism, when ignorance put everything into the hands of power and priestcraft." Not so, in America. Freed from the tyranny of the past, ideas, even the same ideas, flourish in a different way "under the protection of those laws which were made for the wise and the good." (Ferguson 34)

But what of the people who entertain these ideas? What of their virtue? Education? Sincerity? What if the revolution outruns the capacity of the people to keep up with the responsibilities that come with self-determination? What if rebellion lacks grace? These questions haunted post-Revolutionary America. As Ferguson puts it, the early years of the republic were born in rupture and nurtured in anxiety (25). "The American literature of the period thrives in the resonant space between the hope of blessing and the fear of curse. It defines itself in that crisis; this is where it holds its audiences. In so doing, early republican writings depend heavily on the process of the Enlightenment" (41).

Brown's American Gothic breathes within the claustrophobic space between the hope of blessing and the fear of curse. Live burial is the master trope of the Gothic. In Brown, the trope is inflected with the uncertain struggle of Enlightenment itself. This is evident is several ways, of which the most noticeable is the pathology of Brown's narrators. His novels typically embed narratives within narratives. In *Edgar Huntly*, Clithero's story is nestled within Edgar's, whose narrative is in turn addressed to his fiancée Mary, the sister of Waldegrave, the investigation of whose death initially prompts Edgar's interest in Clithero. The story of Sarsefield, the eventual husband of Mrs. Lorimer, Clithero's benefactress, is partly narrated by Clithero and partly by Sarsefield himself, in a letter near the end of the novel. None of the narratives is above suspicion; most are sunk in contradiction and constantly hint at their unreliability. Subjectivity appears to be a prison-house from which few escape into objective commentary and its enlightened spaces. As Edgar himself exclaims, "How little cognizance have men over the actions and motives of each other! How total is our blindness with regard to our own performances!"

(EH 278). The reader does well to take Edgar's advice and to doubt the reliability of his story, built as it is on his "blindness" to his "own performance." And yet, if we doubt Edgar's sincerity, we must also question these moments of seeming honesty and transparency. His candor may simply be another ruse. In order to get himself off one hook, he throws himself onto another. His opinions are thus rarely what they seem, being held for reasons that are not always disclosed, even to himself.

With their tenuous hold on self-knowledge, it is hardly surprising that the deeply held convictions of Brown's characters turn out to have shallow roots. Thus, we hear of how Waldegrave had changed, in a blink, from a progressive to a reactionary, from one holding the materialist shibboleths of the radical Enlightenment to a staunch defender of "Counter-Enlightenment" values.

> Waldegrave, like other men early devoted to meditation and books, had adopted, at different periods, different systems of opinion on topics connected with religion and morals. His earliest creeds tended to efface the impressions of his education; to deify necessity and universalize matter; to destroy the popular distinctions between soul and body, and to dissolve the supposed connection between the moral condition of man anterior and subsequent to death. (131–32)

The contemporary reader would know that it was William Godwin who deified necessity and Baruch Spinoza who universalized matter. Waldegrave holds the opinions associated with Thomas Jefferson's party in particular and Jacobins in general (Stewart). As Jonathan Israel has shown, these opinions were the common intellectual stock-in-trade of progressive thought in the eighteenth century, a strain Israel dubs "radical" because it was aggressively materialist in its outlook (Israel 8–17). Like all good participants in the republic of letters, Waldegrave promulgated his views through correspondence with Edgar:

> The intercourse now ceased to be by letter, and the subtle and laborious argumentations which he had formerly produced against religion, and which were contained in a permanent form, were combated in transient conversation. He was not only eager to subvert those opinions which he had contributed to instil into me, but was anxious that the letters and manuscripts which had been employed in their support should be destroyed. (EH 132)

There is no explanation for the switch. Whereas Waldegrave had formerly been a committed Jacobin, he was now, it seems, staunchly in the Federalist and Congregational camps. In terms of Ferguson's dialectic of the Enlightenment, Waldegrave does not move on to a synthesis but swings erratically between the opposite poles of aggressive emancipation from the superstitions of the past and their warm embrace. He shapeshifts from owl to bat. In the one mood, he looks forward hopefully to the blessings of the American Enlightenment; in the other, he clings to inherited authority, as if to ward off the curse that will descend for having embarked on the impious plan of revolution and earthly paradise. Meanwhile, Edgar seems utterly unconcerned by his friend's wild intellectual gyration, other than expressing the wish to keep the letters confidential, as Waldegrave had asked, in order not to embarrass his sister with the freethinking Edgar apparently still holds.

Brown's narrators are, so to speak, buried alive in discourse. Philosophical language does not take them nearer the light or even, for that matter, self-knowledge. Brown's characters never seem to understand what it is that motivates them. Without self-knowledge, sincerity is not a reliable indication of either character or motive. Clithero's confession has all the marks of being sincere, so much so that Edgar is won over, from his initial conviction that Clithero must be the murderer of Waldegrave to a belief in him as a noble-souled victim of circumstance who suffers principally from an excess of benevolence and tact. Clithero's plan of mercy killing "was the necessary result of a series of ideas mutually linked and connected. His conduct was dictated by a motive allied to virtue. It was the fruit of an ardent and grateful spirit" (91). Edgar's trust is, of course, immediately betrayed by Clithero, who, given the opportunity, recurs to his monomaniacal plan of assassinating Mrs. Lorimer. It is not just Clithero's language that appears to be so much disingenuous wind; it is Edgar's as well, as his lengthy analysis of Clithero is revealed as a tissue of self-deceptions.

The reader's growing sense of claustrophobia is intensified by the application of Brown's unstated principle that all discourse is suspect; we sense that we are surrounded by a medium that precludes a more distant, and holistic, viewpoint. In Brown, we are presented with many analytical trees but few woods. We are given warning of this at the start: "In proportion as I gain power over words, shall I lose dominion over sentiments. In proportion as my tale is deliberate and slow, the incidents and motives which it is designed to exhibit will be imperfectly revived and obscurely portrayed" (5–6). On the one hand, Brown is drawing a contrast, through Edgar, between speech and writing, one immediate, direct, and unambiguous, the other mediated, indirect, and shadowy (Gilmore 38). But on the other hand, he sketches a process similar to the one Sigmund Freud called secondary revision, where the more one translates psychic material into words, the farther one gets from its motive sources and meaning, and the more obscure it becomes. In *Edgar Huntly*, in particular, we never know whether the speaker wakes or dreams. Is the narrative we read simply the record of Edgar's "sleep" of reason when he is assailed by "a tribe of ugly phantoms"? His story is certainly fantastic.

It may even be a dream. One moment, Edgar repairs to bed, and the next moment, he awakens somewhere else, apparently buried alive, having become a full-blown sleepwalker. Did he catch the condition, absorbing Clithero's narrative owing to a surfeit of revolutionary sympathy? (Barnes). Or does it begin because Clithero's story triggers Edgar's own, deeply repressed, guilt? For much of the novel, the unexplained mystery is, if Clithero did not kill Waldegrave, who did? At the end, Edgar reports that a defiant Queen Mab exults in informing her captors that one of her countrymen, impatient for the uprising to begin, embarked on a quest for solo vengeance, which he wreaked upon the first European he chanced upon, and that, unfortunately, was Waldegrave. This confession is reported to Edgar, who in turn informs Mary. In other words, there is no corroboration for Edgar's account of Waldegrave's death in a narrative by a sleepwalker whose mind is, by his own admission, "fettered" (EH 164). He has the motive, as we learn that Waldegrave's death has left his sister a wealthy woman, on the strength of which she and Edgar plan to marry:

> This obstacle was unexpectedly removed by the death of your brother. However justly to be deplored was this catastrophe, yet like every other event, some of its consequences were good. By giving you possession of the means of independence and leisure, by enabling us to complete a contract which poverty alone had thus long delayed, this event has been, at the same time, the most disastrous and propitious which could have happened.   (156)

When the merchant Weymouth turns up, we discover that Waldegrave's inexplicable windfall was the result of a favor he had performed for Weymouth, who has returned to claim it. It seems Waldegrave had been keeping the money safe for Weymouth while the latter was away in Europe. A series of disasters had detained the merchant; the capital he had left with Waldegrave was now all that remained of his fortune. Without the money, Edgar and his fiancée cannot marry. Edgar writes Waldegrave's sister to say that, of course, they must return the six thousand dollars to Weymouth, a sizable sum. When Edgar speaks of his fiancée's misery, he refers to his own:

> I know the bitterness of this sacrifice. I know the impatience with which your poverty has formerly been borne; how much your early education is at war with that degradation and obscurity to which your youth has been condemned; how earnestly your wishes panted after a state which might exempt you from dependence upon daily labour and on the caprices of others, and might secure to you leisure to cultivate and indulge your love of knowledge and your social and beneficent affections.   (155)

Edgar's psychological disturbance and sleepwalking coincide with the destruction of his hopes of marital bliss but also of his dream of cultivating knowledge, thus "banishing harmful superstitions and perpetuating the solid testimony of truth." While Edgar addresses Waldegrave's sister, he might as well be talking about himself. He hints as much with his repeated "I know," suggesting knowledge that is, indeed, firsthand—in which case, what follows is Edgar speaking of himself in the third person, a practice in keeping with the weirdly dissociated subjectivity of many of Brown's other characters.

While there is no evidence, beyond the merely circumstantial, to implicate Edgar in his friend's death, it is an important principle of Brown's fiction that the reader should contemplate the idea that behind our plans for social and beneficent actions lie unfathomable motives. It is as true of Edgar as it of Wieland, Carwin, or Ormond. Something hidden from Edgar has apparently triggered his sleep of reason, which begins from the moment he awakens in Norwalk's Gothic crypt. From here on, Edgar's narration becomes more surreal but also, apparently, allegorical, as we question whether he sleeps or wakes. As Edgar himself puts it, he finds himself in "a species of delirium," or "wakeful dream." In another uncanny echo of Goya, Edgar terms his own *caprichos* "capricious combinations" (161). Particularly telling, however, is the way Brown casts Edgar's experience of live burial:

> My excruciating sensations for a time occupied my attention. These, in combination with other causes, gradually produced a species of delirium. I existed, as it were, in a wakeful dream. With nothing to correct my erroneous perceptions, the images of the past occurred in capricious combinations and vivid hues. Methought I was the victim of some tyrant who had thrust me into a dungeon of his fortress, and left me no power to determine whether he intended I should perish with famine, or linger out a long life in hopeless imprisonment. Whether the day was shut out by insuperable walls, or the darkness that surrounded me was owing to the night and to the smallness of those crannies through which daylight was to be admitted, I conjectured in vain.   (161–162)

There are several layers to this extraordinary example of Brown's American Gothic. As Eve Kosovsky Sedgwick long ago pointed out, live burial extends to language itself. As a Gothic trope, live burial figures as a differential boundary or perverse door. When we want out, the door keeps us in; when we want it to prevent ingress, it opens. The same is true for language itself. When in "Dejection: An Ode," Samuel Taylor Coleridge despairs of his ability to give voice to his grief, so that he is left in despairing isolation, it is as much a form of live burial as when, in Edgar Allan Poe's "The Cask of Amontillado," Fortunato's cries not to be entombed fall on the narrator's deaf ears. In both cases, language fails in bridging the gap between self and other. Brown's version of linguistic live burial occurs when often hyperrational narrators lose themselves in a reality others come to see as psychotic. Theodore Wieland's religious mania would be an overt example, his sister Clara's a more covert one. In this respect, Clara is closer to Arthur Mervyn, who, the more he reveals, the less he explains. The principle extends to characters whose voices, and rationalizations, come to us in some filtered version, such as Ludloe and Ormond, both self-indicting freethinkers. Ormond provides an especially striking example of perverted rationalism, such as his insistence on revenging himself for Constantia's refusal to fall in with his plans for freethinking concubinage, through rape, not for reasons of desire but as a form of rational amour propre that takes on the force, for Ormond, of a categorical imperative. Arguably, though, the classic instance of the Gothic principle in Brown's work, is Edgar Huntly's narrative. From this moment forward, when he awakens in his cave to begin a series of unlikely adventures armed with his trusty tomahawk—killing and eating a panther before vanquishing a quartet of fearsome Indian warriors while rescuing their young female captive—nothing is reliable. Does he sleep or wake? Is this a reliable narrative of sober facts and sound reasoning or a bizarre fantasy of heroic do-gooding? Brown leaves the question open.

If it is a fantasy, it is cleverly structured. As Huntly regains consciousness in his crypt, Brown reveals the way Edgar's imagination is divided between what we can call the American and European Gothics. His first thought is that he is a character from the European Gothic imagination, where live burial means the dread *lettre de cachet*, where innocent men are consigned to oblivion in the Bastille or some other stony medieval space, without due process. His second thought is that he has been "buried alive" (162) or entombed. These possibilities are rejected as he grows accustomed to his environment; he realizes, in time, that he is, in fact, in Norwalk, a labyrinthine, atavistic intrusion of the wild west into an area that is perhaps fifty miles northeast of Philadelphia but also fifty miles closer to New York. In his prefatory address to the novel, Brown advises his readers that he will find his sources for fear and horror not in the "puerile superstition and exploded manners; Gothic castles and chimeras" of the European Gothic but in American scenes of "Indian hostility, and the perils of the western wilderness" (3). Brown is not rejecting the European Gothic; rather, he is telling us that he wants to find the American equivalent in "sources of amusement to the fancy and instruction" that are "peculiar to ourselves" (3). While he wants to focus on a "series of adventures, growing out of the condition of our country," he does so by connecting them to "one of the most common and most wonderful diseases or affections of the human frame," that is, somnambulism or sleepwalking (3).

But the meaning of the American difference is only observable when placed next to its European foil, which is why Edgar's sleep of reason starts with the master trope of the European Gothic, live burial, but immediately segues into the clichés of Western horror: the wilderness as a labyrinth infested with predatory animals and vengeful, scalp-taking warriors. Ruminating on the meaning of Clithero's strange tale, Edgar gives away more than he intends. Its meaning lay outside the experiences related by the "romancers and historians" with whom he had communed. As a result, his "judgment was, for a time, sunk into imbecility and confusion." Edgar tells us that his "mind was full of the images unavoidably suggested by this tale, but they existed in a kind of chaos, and not otherwise than gradually was I able to reduce them to distinct particulars, and subject them to a deliberate and methodical inspection" (91). As he begins to give shape to the shapeless, the contours of his reading reassert themselves. American Gothic is dependent on the European, just as the American experience of the Enlightenment is inflected by the European, and vice versa.

Thus, when Edgar comes to tell Clithero's bizarre story, it falls into the classic pattern of European Gothic. Mrs. Lorimer's and Sarsefield's misfortunes begin with a prohibition against marrying for any other reason than dynastic alliance. Their misfortune is intensified by the machinations of the diabolical Wiatte, Mrs. Lorimer's twin brother, so that, together, brother and sister seem to embody the principle of the divided self, one as angelic as the other is evil. Clithero even speculates that they are telepathically connected (78). Wiatte's motiveless malignancy may be attributed, in Godwinian fashion, to the collective poison permeating a system based on tyranny and inequality, which pools where it may. In another Godwinian echo, Clithero himself is a Caleb Williams figure, a lower-caste lad of parts adopted by an upper-class patron. These Godwinian echoes intensify later in the novel, when Edgar himself plays Caleb to Clithero's Falkland, when he seeks to sound Clithero's psychic mystery by breaking into his cleverly contrived "chest." The point of these intertextual references is to make it clear that Brown's sleep of reason follows contours laid out for him by his reading, by the "romancers and historians" who condition his imagination.

Riddled with class-consciousness, Clithero cannot emancipate himself from his mind-forged manacles. He cannot believe that he should be permitted to express his love for Clarice, owing to their difference in rank. And when he realizes he can, owing to the freethinking precepts of his benefactress, Mrs. Lorimer, who encourages his court-ship of Clarice, a self-destructive, paranoid impulse drags him back down. Thus, in the crucial part of his narrative, Clithero refers to machinations, which entrap him, hinting at the existence of a deep-laid plot. Wiatte returns, it seems, from the dead. "The existence of Wiatte was the canker that had blasted the felicity of my patroness" (68). Now that Wiatte had returned, there was "something portentous" in his presence:

> If I trembled for the safety of her whom I loved, and whose safety was endangered by being the daughter of this miscreant, had [Sarsefield] not equal reason to fear for her whom he also loved, and who, as the sister of this ruffian, was encompassed by the most alarming perils? Yet he probably was calm while I was harassed by anxieties.
>
> Alas! The difference was easily explained. Such was the beginning of a series ordained to hurry me to swift destruction.   (68–69)

The dark hints do not cohere. Clithero suggests that Sarsefield is the puppetmaster. If so, it is hard to see how, given that the crisis was brought about through Clithero's own incautious detour through the "dark, crooked, and narrow lane" (71), where Wiatte was waiting for him. It may be that Wiatte knew that Clithero would take this detour as he returned from visiting Mrs. Lorimer's banker, but by the same token, Clithero might have guessed that this would be a place Wiatte might attack. How could Sarsefield have arranged for Wiatte to wait in ambush for Clithero in a lane that Clithero takes on impulse? More revealing, perhaps, is Clithero's account of his thought processes:

> In the course of my meditations, the idea of the death of this man had occurred, and it bore the appearance of a desirable event. Yet it was little qualified to tranquilise my fears. In the long catalogue of contingencies, this, indeed, was to be found; but it was as little likely to happen as any other. It could not happen without a series of anterior events paving the way for it. If his death came from us, it must be the theme of design. It must spring from laborious circumvention and deep laid stratagems.   (74)

In the moment of Wiatte's attack—first a pistol shot that grazes Clithero's forehead, followed by an attempted knifing—Clithero was "impelled by an unconscious necessity" (74). He represents himself as a mere automaton, just as, later, Edgar will so describe himself in his moments of life-and-death derring-do. But the suggestion arises that it was Clithero who was engaged in "laborious circumvention and deep-laid strategems" that permit him to realize his secret desire of dispatching Wiatte, the only obstacle to his dreams of domestic felicity. "[M]y sense was no sooner struck by the reflection from the blade, than my hand, as if by spontaneous energy, was thrust into my pocket. I drew forth a pistol" (71). Clithero does not describe the act of shooting Wiatte. It merely happens, without Clithero's active will. "He lifted up his weapon to strike, but it dropped from his powerless fingers. He fell..." (71). Not only is the act of shooting

Wiatte conveniently omitted from his narrative, but so is any explanation of why he was armed and ready.

Brown uses an interesting expression for Clithero's somnambulism, which overtakes him the moment after killing Wiatte. Previously, he was capable of regarding the world objectively. "Now my liberty, in this respect, was at an end. I was *fettered*, confounded, smitten with excess of thought, and laid prostrate with wonder! I no longer attended to my steps" (74; emphasis added). Unconsciously, he wanders back to the bankers' residence in his first act of sleepwalking. Elsewhere, Clithero speaks of being "fettered by reverie" (86). Waking in the pit, Edgar uses the same expression: "Surely my senses were fettered or depraved by some spell" (164).

In the sleep of reason, reason itself is fettered, much like language in Gothic moments of "live burial." In his *Enquiry Concerning Political Justice*, Godwin infamously argued that the assassin was no more to blame than the knife he wielded: both lay at the end of a long chain of cause and effect (chapter IV). Brown purposely cites this when he has Edgar defend Clithero's attempted stabbing. In the moment, Clithero is fettered by reverie; he acts spontaneously, in accordance with his conditioning, with (in Edgar's eyes) Clithero being no more guilty than the knife he wields. His actions are governed by what Hawthorne will call (modifying Godwin) a "dark necessity." But Brown's hints reveal that the decisive actions of his protagonists are shadowed by a compromising desire. Clithero wishes for Wiatte's death, because Wiatte is an impediment to his marriage to Clarice. Once we begin to realize that Edgar's story doubles Clithero's, we begin to regard in a darker light the obvious motive Edgar has for murdering Waldegrave, in order to marry his sister, inheriting her fortune. Edgar's exculpating, Godwinian rhetoric, deployed, ostensibly, to bring intellectual succor to Clithero, by the same token now appears as Edgar's self-exculpating gloss. Edgar presents himself in an American key. "The magic of sympathy, the perseverance of benevolence, though silent, might work a gradual and secret revolution, and better thoughts might insensibly displace those desperate suggestions which now governed him" (EH 111). This is the language of the American Enlightenment, or revolutionary sympathy. Optimistically, Edgar believes sensibility may cure Clithero's ills. But what we come to understand is that Edgar's version of Enlightenment is shadowed by the inescapability of the past. Brown's version of American Gothic emerges in those moments when the reader encounters, not uniquely American sources of horror, but European Gothic in America. To put it another way, *Edgar Huntly*'s American Gothic lies not in the Western content (Native Americans, panthers, wilderness) but in the doubling between Clithero and Edgar, Europe and America.

This aspect of American Gothic is well understood and has been much commented on (see Crow; Goddu; Martin and Savoy; Monnet; Ringe). As Charles Crow notes, the truth the American Gothic reveals is not the complaint of Hawthorne and Henry James that their America suffered from too little history but that it suffered from too much of the wrong, sanguinary kind, especially relating to the erasure of Native Americans and Africans from the nation's standard history (Crow 1–2). If Gothic horror relies on the return of the repressed, the repressed that returns in the American tradition is the stain of slavery and genocide (for instance, see Martin and Savoy, 129–130).

Brown's Norwalk is an early exemplar of this tradition. Norwalk is not just a literal instance of the wild west; it is also a symbolic representation of what will later be conventionally referred to as the "unconscious." With its ravines, circular paths, caverns, and promontories, it is a neatly circumscribed labyrinth, seemingly immense once one is lost inside it, but it is otherwise a discrete intrusion into the everyday normality of a modern, pastoral America. Nearly everything that happens there possesses a hallucinatory quality. While Brown is careful to cite an actual place, Solebury, in *Edgar Huntly*, it is less a verifiable piece of geography in the state of Pennsylvania than a state of mind, being, in its circular convolutions, and involutions, brainlike in its curiously bounded topography. It operates in the novel in an extremely complex way. Thus, Edgar, staggering out of its vicinity to the margins, where normality reigns, appears as a specter:

> This dwelling was far different from that I had lately left. It was as small and as low, but its walls consisted of boards. A window of four panes admitted the light, and a chimney of brick, well burnt and neatly arranged, peeped over the roof. As I approached, I heard the voice of children and the hum of a spinning-wheel....A good woman, busy at her wheel, with two children playing on the ground before her, were the objects that now presented themselves. The uncouthness of my garb, my wild and weather-worn appearance, my fusil and tom-hawk, could not but startle them. The woman stopt her wheel, and gazed as if a spectre had started into view.
>
> (EH 159–160)

In the conventional terms of American Gothic, Edgar is an instance of the return of the repressed, an overdetermined token of the violence on which the nation was founded, an abject embodiment of both the people the nation had to rid itself of, in order to become a nation, and the violence used to subdue them. Accordingly, Edgar takes on the guise of the specter at the feast, an unwelcome and gruesome reminder of a past that can only exist in the glorified form of Edgar's sleep of reason, where the savages he vanquishes are inhumane slaughterers of families and abductors of young girls, not Good Samaritans bringing gifts from the forests for which one might give thanks.

The complexity arises from the deeply intertextual nature of Norwalk as a representation of the American political unconscious. Brown cites the ideal of the new Adam, the American farmer, the nuclear family based on the biblical, "patriarchal" model that was so core to the Revolutionary self-understanding:

> There was nothing in the first view of his character calculated to engender suspicion. The neighbourhood was populous. But as I conned over the catalogue, I perceived that the only foreigner among us was Clithero. Our scheme was, for the most part, a patriarchal one. Each farmer was surrounded by his sons and kinsmen. This was an exception to the rule. Clithero was a stranger, whose adventures and character, previously to his coming hither, were unknown to us. The Elm was surrounded by his master's domains. An actor there must be, and no one was equally questionable.   (14)

Clithero, the unattached Irish immigrant, is the natural scapegoat, the itinerant other who does not fit the national, patriarchal scheme. The image of the cabin in the woods, of the homestead on which the nation was reared, reappears later in the center of Norwalk, as Queen Mab's rustic dwelling. It is a complicated parody of the patriarchal ideal. On the one hand, and gender aside, Queen Mab, or Old Deb, is the last surviving elder of the tribe whose lands these were, a matriarch who has stayed on, stubbornly, in order to maintain her nation's land claim (208–209). Edgar repeats the patronizing attitude of the community, which finds amusement in Old Deb's pretensions to maintain the native laws of the place. On the other hand, she is Queen Mab, Mercutio's diminutive sprite, who flies up the noses of men and women while they sleep, inducing dreams of wish fulfillment, fit emblem for a sleepwalker such as Edgar and another hint from Brown that we should not overly invest ourselves in the literal truth of Edgar's story. And then, later, Clithero himself comes to take Queen Mab's place, in her shack, after Old Deb's arrest for her role in the uprising. As a topography, Norwalk is overlaid with first nations' tribal lore, customs, and law; with iconic imagery of the republic; and with European folklore and the literary traditions of England.

Old Deb's place, then—like the Selby homestead that initially appears to be the abode of "rural innocence" but turns out to harbor a viciously abusive paternal figure (226–230)—is a kind of parodic counterpoint to the image of the American homestead, the cornerstone of the nation. All that has been abjected in the process of forming the ideal coalesces, in a layered fashion, in Queen Mab's hut: the question of the indigenous inhabitants; land claims and rights; the European as the nonnative itinerant; the inescapability of the European literary tradition in even trying to imagine this complexity—all this comes together in Norwalk, Brown's brilliant rendition of the American unconscious, which, in its layers, is also inescapably European. Hence, in the first flickering moments of his sleep of reason, Edgar imagines himself a figure in a European Gothic novel—perhaps the man in the iron mask (a popular stage play in London) or Vivaldi awakening in the cells of the Inquisition (from Ann Radcliffe's *The Italian*). Only then does his imagination switch to an American key.

The tendency of history's unfinished business to haunt the present has been a consti-tutive element of the Gothic ever since its first modern exemplar—Horace Walpole's *Castle of Otranto* (1764)—stressed *mortmain*, the dead hand of the past that stretches out to palsy the living. American Gothic, in this respect, is a variation on a theme. Whereas in European Gothic the past that cannot be escaped tends to center on feudal remnants, in the American Gothic the repressed past is linked to the consequences of modernity, to the unavoidably violent nature of nation building in a new land, to the col-lateral damage of national "self-determination." However, for peculiar reasons, Brown's Gothic is not just American but also strangely modern, more so, I think, than either Hawthorne's or Melville's or, perhaps, even Poe's. Brown's Gothic is a world of universal dislocation. Communities fragment into deluded monads; no one is indigenous, not even the natives, as their displacement is already a given; nearly everyone is a migrant, whether Americans leaving their local communities or recent arrivals from Europe; and regardless of origin, many of them, like Sarsefield, Clithero, Carwin, Martinette, or Ormond, seem to have traveled much of the globe. All of Brown's characters seem to be on the move. Internally, few characters are in touch with their own motives. I can think of no other novelist where there is so much introspection and so little self-knowledge. The complex, passive constructions of his narrators' sentences, as they turn the spotlight on either their own actions or those of others, suggest a pervasive dislocation between self, will, and agency, where the act of piecing together cause and effect becomes a laborious process that takes Brown's narrators farther away from, rather than closer to, the truth, as we saw earlier.

Jefferson may offer a clue to Brown's thinking. In his *Notes on the State of Virginia*, Jefferson warns that American principles are being undermined by immigration, which threatens to reduce the population to "a heterogeneous, incoherent, distracted mass" (quoted in Ferguson 37). One way of thinking about the problems facing the new nation was the difficulty inherent in "scaling up" its nascent democratic institutions. The Revolution was built on town-hall meetings and on a system of correspondence that created a "networked" platform, composed of new information "protocols," as William Warner calls them, that linked cells of revolutionary interest. But overall, it was built on an oral culture among known quantities. To be sure, the new system of revolutionary correspondence was based on writing, but it was writing as a medium of speech in which entitled actors communicated intelligence vital to national awakening authorized by their own personal reputation, or brand. As such, it was a levered version of the republic of letters, which was a commonplace on both sides of the Atlantic, as a pillar of what Jürgen Habermas calls the bourgeois public sphere. The American public sphere had not yet succeeded in adapting to the fundamental reality of a modern, "structurally transformed" public sphere, which is distinguished by the consolidation of the transition from a topical to a metatopical space, from a variant of the Athenian agora, where all enfranchised actors met in person to form the opinion that legitimized political authority in the polis, to a series of mediations in which opinion was formed remotely, was "mediated," through the emerging institutions of an advanced print culture.

Michael Davitt Bell helpfully comments that "In the late 1790's, during the very years in which his novels appeared, [Brown] was undergoing an intellectual transformation from radical idealism to pragmatic conservatism—from a belief in absolute sincerity to a recognition of the supremacy or inevitability of circumstance." Like the ideal community of like-minded souls that marks the beginning of *Wieland*, the revolutionary project of creating a new society of emancipated and equal individuals can only succeed if everyone in the community is known, is sincere, and is capable of sincerity. But the actual republic, as Jefferson notes, is composed not of a patriarchal model where democracy rests on town-hall meetings of known individuals but of emerging democratic institutions of a remote, representative, nature and of an itinerant ever-changing community of migrants. Another of Brown's Gothic innovations was to turn to "infection," to disease, as a source of horror, principally in *Arthur Mervyn* and *Ormond*. But by infection, Brown means the contamination not just of the body but also of the mind. "To point up the dangers of private judgment once it is released from institutional restraints, Brown exploits the theme of religious delusion" (Clemit 128). Religious mania is one such form of infected intellect. Pamela Clemit phrases the point well, but I would refine it by arguing that what she says is true if we understand "institutional restraints" to refer to the pre-Revolutionary kind that had obtained for centuries in Europe and that were brought over by the colonists. The post-Revolutionary decades were an interregnum in the nation's history, as old institutions fell away and new ones, capable of remotely mediating the nation's business, developed. This moment of rupture and promise, of hope and melancholy, was also ripe for the dreaming of post-Enlightenment dystopias, much as it was in Spain, which was experiencing its own disturbed, and disturbing, interregnum between revolutionary hope and a repressive aftermath. Brown's possible conversion, then, from idealism to pragmatic conservatism, may be understood as the skepticism that arose from the recognition that the old institutions were gone while new, emerging ones, were not yet capable of filling their place. Without these restraints, the time was truly ripe for the dream of reason.

While Brown frequently echoes Godwin, he departs from him in his pessimism. Brown is far more dystopic in his outlook than Godwin, who, despite everything, clung to his hopeful version of utilitarianism. But the two are alike in their abstract approach to the novel, to a form of the Gothic that may also be called "philosophical romance" (Miles 159–169). Like Godwin, Brown dispenses with the obvious accoutrements of the Gothic—castles, ghosts, *banditti*—in order to focus on its animating principle: how it is that the "Gothic and unintelligible burden of past institutions" (Godwin I: 33) comes to distort the present, passing on the infections of past violence and grief, fracturing society into a dysfunctional collection of isolated monads, where philosophical discourse—reason—as often as not fetters and misleads. But as the inventor of American Gothic, Brown concentrates less on feudal remnants that batten on the present, such as the incubus in Fuseili's *Nightmare*, and more on the "flourishing of new ideas," in a "new context," that go disastrously wrong, divorced, as they are, from the institutional restraints that had previously given them their meaning. For this reason, the moral panic over the alleged Jacobinical conspiracy of the Bavarian Illuminati served Brown's purposes exactly as a dystopic "dream of reason," material he refers to first with Carwin and the backstory with Ludloe and then with Ormond (Wood; Levine 15–59). Allegedly devoted to the betterment of mankind, their philanthropic efforts inevitably miscarry, as the realities of power pervert their generous desires. And so it is with Brown's Gothicism generally: it turns on metaphorical, rather than literal, live burial, on the fettering of reason even in the moments of would-be altruism and insight, when it dreams.

Note

1. http://www.metmuseum.org/toah/works-of-art/18.64.43.

Works Cited

Barnes, Elizabeth. *States of Sympathy: Seduction and Democracy in the American Novel.* New York: Columbia University Press, 1997.

Bell, Michael Davitt. "'The Double-Tongued Deceiver': Sincerity and Duplicity in the Novels of Charles Brockden Brown." *Early American Literature* 9:2 (1974): 143–163.

Ciofalo, John J. "Goya's Enlightenment Protagonist—A Quixotic Dreamer of Reason." *Eighteenth-Century Studies* 30.4 (1997): 421–436.

Clemit, Pamela. *The Godwinian Novel: The Rational Fictions of Godwin, Brockden Brown, and Mary Shelley*. Oxford: Clarendon Press, 1993.

Crow, Charles L. *History of the Gothic: American Gothic*. Cardiff: University of Wales Press, 2009.

Ferguson, Robert A. *The American Enlightenment, 1750–1820*. Cambridge, Mass.: Harvard University Press, 1997.

Gilmore, Michael T. "The Constitution and the Canon." *William and Mary Law Review* 29.1 (1987): 35–40.

Goddu, Teresa A. *Gothic America: Narrative, History, and Nation*. New York: Columbia University Press, 1997.

Godwin, William. *An Enquiry Concerning Political Justice, and Its Influence on General Virtue and Happiness*, 2 vols. Dublin: Luke White, 1793.

Israel, Jonathan. *Democratic Enlightenment: Philosophy, Revolution, and Human Rights 1750–1790*. New York: Oxford University Press, 2013.

Lázaro-Reboll, Antonio. "Counter-rational Reason: Goya's Instrumental Negotiations of Flesh and World." *History of European Ideas* 30.1 (2004): 109–119.

Levine, Robert S. *Conspiracy and Romance: Studies in Brockden Brown, Cooper, Hawthorne, and Melville*. Cambridge: Cambridge University Press, 1989.

Martin, Robert K., and Eric Savoy. *American Gothic: New Interventions in a National Narrative*. Iowa City: University of Iowa Press, 1998.

Miles, Robert. *Romantic Misfits*. Basingstoke, UK: Palgrave Macmillan, 2008.

Monnet, Agnieszka Soltysik. *The Poetics and Politics of the American Gothic: Gender and Slavery in Nineteenth-Century American Literature*. Farnham, UL: Ashgate, 2010.

Nehamas, Alexander. "The Sleep of Reason Produces Monsters." *Representations* 74.1 (Spring 2001): 37–54.

Porter, Roy. "Review of Paul Ilie, *The Age of Minerva. Volume 1: Counter-rational Reason in the Eighteenth Century—Goya and the Paradigm of Unreason in Western Europe*." *British Journal for the History of Science* 30.2 (1997): 236–238.

Ringe, Donald Arthur. *American Gothic: Imagination and Reason in Nineteenth-Century Fiction*. Lexington: University Press of Kentucky, 1982.

Sedgwick, Eve Kosofsky. *The Coherence of Gothic Conventions*. New York and London: Methuen, 1986.

Stewart, Matthew. *Nature's God: The Heretical Origins of the American Republic*. New York: W. W. Norton, 2014.

Warner, William B. *Protocols of Liberty: Communication Innovation and the American Revolution*. Chicago: University of Chicago Press, 2013.

Wood, Gordon S. "Conspiracy and the Paranoid Style: Causality and Deceit in the Eighteenth Century." *William and Mary Quarterly* 39.3 (1982): 402–441.

CHAPTER 27

···

BROWN, SENSIBILITY, AND SENTIMENTALISM

···

MICHELLE BURNHAM

CHARLES Brockden Brown's 1800 "A Lesson on Concealment; or, Memoirs of Mary Selwyn" begins with a letter from Dr. Molesworth to his young apprentice Henry Kirvan that reports the death of the doctor's wife. The doctor admits that just before she fell ill, he covertly witnessed his wife and Kirvan "in secret conference" wherein the two "shared...tears." Believing that Kirvan was privy at that moment to a secret that "she laboured to conceal" (174) from her husband, the doctor pleads with the young man to "tell me, I beseech thee, what is it that has killed my wife" (175). The scene suggests that Mrs. Molesworth (née Mary Selwyn) died from the affective excess caused by the exposure of a terrible secret once concealed, and the doctor accordingly requests what amounts to an emotional autopsy from his pupil.

Henry's "Answer" offers an autobiographical account that begins with his arrival several years earlier in America from Europe. Destitute and alone in New York, he meets a wealthy merchant named Haywood, to whom Henry promptly recounts his family's recent history, beginning with an attempted emigration from England to America. When their ship is captured en route, the family members find themselves imprisoned in France. There they lose their hard-earned property, Henry's sister dies from malnutrition brought about by their sudden poverty, and his father dies shortly thereafter. In response, his mother becomes "frantic and desperate," proceeding to "tear her clothes," engage in "ravings," and lie down on the "hard and tattered bed" from which the corpse of her husband had just been dragged, before she, too, dies (176). Henry narrates this tragic account "with all the sensibility which such recent and horrible disasters could not but produce," and its telling has a correspondingly "powerful effect upon Haywood," who responds to the young man's narrative with tears (his "eyes overflow with compassion") and benevolence (he quickly offers Henry "accommodation in his house" and a job "keeping and arranging his accounts") (176). Already, a mere three pages into the story, Brown suggests that while feeling itself can be deadly (after all, it killed both Henry's mother and the doctor's wife), *stories about* feeling can be as profitable as they are moving. Brown's writing is everywhere marked by the recognition and exploration of these intertwined powers and dangers of feeling.

I begin with Brown's relatively little-known "Lesson on Concealment" rather than with his more widely read novels, however, in an effort to reconfigure the place given to sensibility and sentimentality in Brown's writing by standard literary histories and biographies. Those narratives have often depended on temporal chronologies (which divide his earlier work from his later work), spatial geographies (which position him within or outside a national tradition), political alliances (with more radical or more conservative positions), and literary categories (which separate novels from other writing and Gothic from sentimental forms) that obscure the complex entanglement of affect with issues of gender, economics, and aesthetics throughout Brown's writing and thought. The American nineteenth-century "separate sphere" rubric that segregated a private and feminized domestic sphere of emotions from a public and masculinized market sphere of politics is a poor model for understanding the earlier period within which Brown wrote, and yet it has left a long-lasting and anachronistic imprint on the critical reception of his work.[1] Stephen Shapiro notes this discrepancy between Brown's own historical moment and its scholarly treatment when he observes that "the period's claims for these elements never compartmentalized sentiment and publicity in the ways that recent criticism routinely enacts" (Shapiro 21). Replacing that rubric with a more integrated model that recognizes the complex cross-articulation of emotion with economics, of sentiment with speculation, and of feeling with finance is crucial, I maintain, to understanding the late-eighteenth- and early-nineteenth-century world that Brown's writing depicted and within which it circulated.

I. LITERARY HISTORY AND FEELING

"Lesson on Concealment" may be one of the lesser-known (and even less often studied) of Brown's fictions, but its melodramatic displays of excessive feeling and dramatic reversals of intense sentiment should appear to readers of Brown as consistent with his longer and better-known fiction. Consider, for example, Edgar Huntly, who writes to Mary Waldegrave that she "wilt catch from my story every horror and every sympathy which it paints. Thou wilt shudder with my forboding and dissolve with my tears" (EH 6), and who responds to the stranger Clithero's "mighty anguish and... heart-bursting grief" with "every sentiment" and "sympathy" (11) until "tears found their way spontaneously to my eyes" and "I was prompted to advance nearer and hold his hand" (11). Arthur Mervyn reacts to his own compassionate response with "a passionate effusion of tears. I was ashamed of this useless and child-like sensibility; and attempted to apologize to my companion. The sympathy, however, had proved contagious, and the stranger turned away his face to hide his own tears" (AM 151). Jane Talbot asks her brother's forgiveness when she denies his request for money, but when he "pressed me to his breast while tears stole down his cheek," Jane finds herself "thoroughly subdued," since "the most opposite emotions fill, with equal certainty my eyes" (JT 190). Sympathetic feeling circulates as consistently throughout Brown's fiction as it does between his characters.

Placing such scenes together would seem to confirm Winfried Flück's remark that "sentimental forms and formulas can be found throughout Brown's writing" (101), and in fact, scholars over the years have with some consistency considered Brown's fiction in relation to the culture, politics, and aesthetics of feeling in the decades surrounding the turn into the nineteenth century. But it is also worth historicizing this critical tradition, in part because the developments that have characterized it are revealing of the changing role of Brown within literary history. On the one hand, there has been a consistent acknowledgment that Brown's novels both participate in and interrogate an eighteenth-century culture of sensibility and its tradition of the sentimental novel. Julie Ellison, for instance, identifies Edgar Huntly as a "man of sensibility" (160) and reads Edgar Huntly as a novel of "masculine sensibility" (149). Bruce Burgett locates in Clara Howard a "melodrama of sentimental manhood" (116), Bredahl acknowledges that "sentimental eighteenth-century readers" would have found Wieland deeply satisfying (54), and Sydney Krause identifies Ormond as an instance of the seduction plot popularized by Samuel Richardson's sentimental and Horace Walpole's Gothic traditions. Siân Silyn Roberts reads in Arthur Mervyn a failed Smithian model of sympathy, and Caleb Crain identifies all of Brown's fiction as engaging with the pleasures and problems of sympathy. As brief and partial as it is, this survey indicates the consistency with which Brown's work has been aligned over several decades of criticism with the tradition of the sentimental seduction novel and its central affect of sympathy.[2]

The cultural and aesthetic valuation of this tradition, however, has changed dramatically over the past half century or so, and the reception of Brown's work has tended to rise or fall along with sentiment's own volatile stock. Thus, when Leslie Fiedler in the 1960s found Brown's earlier novels salvageable for a thesis about American masculinity's rejection of the feminized and domestic space of the home, he dismissed and belittled Brown's later novels for portraying "a world of female interests regarded through female eyes, perhaps partly as a bid for the alluring female audience that had already made Mrs. Rowson's fortune" (Fiedler 99). This diagnosis—with its Hawthornean "scribbling women" animus—has left a surprisingly durable imprint on Brown studies, which has yet entirely to recover from the simultaneously gendered, generic, and political division of his novels into an earlier progressive masculine Gothic and a later conservative feminine sentimental.[3] Burdened by this uneven discrimination, earlier treatments of Brown often sought to elevate his novels' engagement with the devalued form of sentiment above their presumably more conventional use by such female American contemporaries as Susanna Rowson or Hannah Webster Foster.[4]

More recent work such as that of Julia Stern, however, has pointed out the impossibility of tearing the sentimental apart from the Gothic in republican-era fiction, in which the emotions of tearful grief and bloody rage are never very far apart and in which "sympathy itself simultaneously depends on and must bury its constitutive relationship to violence" (Stern 78). It is just such interconnection that Ellison recognizes when she simultaneously characterizes Edgar Huntly as a novel of "masculine sensibility" (149) and one of "the paranoid Gothic" (150). Rather than submit, then, to a dichotomized construction of Brown's literary output, we might do better to recognize the ways in which these two sensational subgenres collaborate through the entire body of Brown's fiction. Moreover, greater attention to his nonnovelistic writings—including such pieces as the March 1800 "Lesson on Concealment"—will assist in generating more flexible and integrated alternatives to the now well-worn and discarded assumption that Brown's life, literary style, and political commitments somehow all abruptly changed at some point in the year 1800.[5]

Ongoing literary recovery efforts are both expanding the Brown archive and putting that archive into greater dialogue with an enriched sense of the literary context in which that work circulated—although more remains to be done in this latter regard especially.[6] One is struck, for instance, by the size and diversity of the large literary catalog within which Tremaine McDowell conducted, nearly a century ago, his review of the eighteenth-century American novel of sensibility. He included such now-familiar titles as *Wieland*, *Edgar Huntly*, and *Arthur Mervyn* along with *Charlotte Temple* and *The Power of Sympathy* but also such unfamiliar ones as *The Hapless Orphan*, *Fortune's Foot-Ball*, *The History of Constantia and Pulchera*, and countless others. Indeed, his inventory of emotionally excessive American novels somewhat hilariously (but also revealingly) concludes by including "every novel of the century save *The Oriental Philanthropist* (1800) by Henry Sherburne" (McDowell 399). At the same time, many of Brown's own fictional works have been overlooked because they were only ever published as periodical pieces or because they are considered unfinished. Including for consideration such works as the "Henrietta Letters" and *Memoirs of Stephen Calvert* might usefully reperiodize Brown's fictional output, and such an expanded chronology might, in turn, encourage a rethinking of the role of sensibility and sentimentality in Brown's work.

The bifurcated model that has for so long shaped critical work on Brown, in fact, depends on a whole series of gendered, generic, aesthetic, national, historical, and political divisions. It is likely the reinforced layering of these multiple divisions that has made it so difficult to dislodge that model and its effects. Yet the more scholars undo those divisions, the better we understand Brown and his work. This undoing really began with the important work on the early American novel by Jane Tompkins and Cathy Davidson in the 1980s. Tompkins's *Sensational Designs* and Davidson's *Revolution and the Word* were absolutely critical to the recovery of forgotten early American women novelists such as Rowson and Maria Susanna Cummins, but they were also critical to the recovery of the novels of Brown. Moreover, both scholars' reconsideration of the early American novel hinged on their engagement with discourses of feeling, for their reader-response orientation emphasized sensation's significant political work rather than its insignificant aesthetic value. Since then, the scholarship on sensibility, sympathy, and sentimentality has been so voluminous that it would be hopeless to attempt to review it here in any kind of comprehensive way. My inevitably partial treatment of this scholarly tradition here emphasizes the ways in which this body of work has continued to erode the assumptions underlying earlier models like Fiedler's by developing a more historically and politically complex account of discourses of feeling, which seldom observed the kinds of boundaries by which some critics have sought to contain it.

II. The Vocabulary of Feeling

Sensibility studies (or what has sometimes been called emotion criticism or affect theory) is home to an entire vocabulary of feeling that, despite being consistently reviewed and defined by scholars, still produces as much confusion as it does clarity. What is the distinction, for instance, between sensibility, sentimentality, and sensationalism? What is sympathy, and how does it differ from pity or empathy or passion? What is the relationship between these feelings and such categories as compassion, charity, benevolence, humanitarianism, and reformism? In what ways are such literary and cultural forms as domesticity, melodrama, and seduction related to the sentimental? What is the relationship between Gothic sensations of anger and fear and sentimental ones of sympathy and passion? Some critics have sought to keep sentimentality and sensibility apart, insisting that the former represents a bourgeois, compromised, and consumerist version of the latter's more refined, utopian, and progressive feeling. Jerome McGann, for example, describes an eighteenth-century poetics of sensibility giving way to a nineteenth-century regime of sentimentality, which Sean Gaston has recently characterized as an effort to "keep 'sentiment' away from 'sensibility,' " to distinguish "a refined and discriminating materialization" from "an excessive materialization" (Gaston 130). This distinction may preserve a politically and aesthetically sanitized sensibility from infection by sentimentality's bourgeois commodification, but what complexities and entanglements does such a desire bury? And what does it mean that this separation is also historically and culturally gendered, so that—as Ellison puts it—"sensibility becomes fashionable when men practice it" (4)? This division, as suggested earlier, is furthermore encrusted with a multitude of other distinctions: between British and American literary and cultural traditions, between eighteenth- and nineteenth-century productions, between a rejection of and service to the capitalist market.

Rather than attempt to define and differentiate between the multiple terms and categories that inhabit sensibility studies, I follow the eighteenth-century practice of allowing them to circulate together, while providing some historical and cultural context for their collective status in the late eighteenth century and in the work of Brown. It's not that there are no valid differences between these terms but rather that any attempt to draw such distinctions will inevitably highlight as much their blurring and interpenetration as their idiosyncrasies. Moreover, overdrawing those distinctions might prevent us from seeing their shared participation in complicated efforts at social change. In doing so, I follow the lead of a feminist scholarly tradition on affect, including such scholars as Adela Pinch, who finds that "the many names for emotion travel as freely as emotions themselves" (16); Ellison, who remarks that what such terms as *emotion, feeling, affect, sensibility, sympathy,* and *sentiment* "have in common is much more important than what differentiates them" (4); and June Howard, who describes the term *sentimentality* as "plastic" and who argues that "the link between [nineteenth-century] sentiment and eighteenth-century notions of sympathy and sensibility should be reclaimed" (63). Howard likewise targets the opposition between authentic sensibility and inauthentic sentimentality, suggesting that we ought to "vacate, once and for all, the discourse of judgment that has characterized so much work on sentimentality," and argues for restoring the continuities between "sentiment and eighteenth-century notions of sympathy and sensibility" obscured by some practitioners of American literary history (63). While this refusal to compartmentalize generates a certain kind of messiness, it may well be that it is precisely such messiness that, paradoxically, allows the role of affect in the work of Brown to be more clearly understood and contextualized. Moreover, such messiness may be a more historically accurate depiction of the late eighteenth and early nineteenth centuries, when a word like *sentimental*, as historian Emma Rothschild suggests, was "vague, indefinite, and indeterminate," less a discrete and isolated term than "one of the words which evoke 'clusters of ideas' and 'multitudes of concepts'" (Rothschild 9).[7]

If these terms tended not to observe the borders and boundaries of meaning that critics have since sought to impose on them, they also tended not to observe the geopolitical borders that have sometimes been retroactively imposed on them. While Brown's narratives are consistently marked by emotional intensity and his narrators frequently characterized by their state of heightened emotion, these were features of fiction (and, indeed, of literary and cultural production more generally) on both sides of the Atlantic world in the late eighteenth and early nineteenth centuries. While feminist recoveries of literary history like Tompkins's and Davidson's discarded the gendered aesthetics of a model like Fiedler's that had determined the earlier reception of Brown's texts, they did so largely within the outlines of a national literary tradition that has since then been increasingly redrawn within transnational and transatlantic terms. Therefore, the impulse to separate and differentiate national and/or disciplinary lines of influence from each other might be productively exchanged for a model that seeks instead to understand their cross-circulation and dialogue in the Atlantic world. Ellison has positioned sympathy in an Anglo-American transatlantic context, and more recently, Ashley Hales has suggested in her reading of *Edgar Huntly* that sympathy is transatlantic rather than national and corresponds to a horizontal or "rhizomatic" rather than a vertical or hierarchical arrangement (Hales 138, 140). While recent scholarship more regularly engages with such Anglo-American exchanges, an even wider transcontinental and multilingual context might include German (Johann Wolfgang von Goethe's *Werther*, for instance) and French (Jean-Jacques Rousseau's *Nouvelle Heloise*, for instance) literary and philosophical contributions to the discourse of sensibility within the period.

Adopting such a framework allows us to see Brown's writing as participating simultaneously in multiple cultural and literary traditions, including a residual British common-sense philosophical tradition that developed earlier in the century, the contemporaneous tradition of radicalism represented by Mary Wollstonecraft and William Godwin (a tradition that Philip Barnard and Stephen Shapiro have usefully labeled

Woldwinite), and the emergent tradition of the sentimental novel that would flourish on both sides of the Atlantic during the eighteenth and nineteenth centuries. Each of these traditions depended on an understanding of sensibility as "the receptivity of the senses" which allowed consciousness to be "further sensitized in order to be more acutely responsive to signals from the outside environment and from inside the body" (Barker-Benfield xvii). The vogue of sensational psychology associated with John Locke and Isaac Newton and the interest in sympathy among Scottish moral sense philosophers such as David Hume and political economists such as Adam Smith all contributed to the development and popularity of sentimental fiction, which both enacted and reflected on the possibilities for social change and improvement that such circulations of feeling implied.

If discourses of feeling moved almost indiscriminately across national and disciplinary borders, however, states of feeling themselves are often characterized by the difficulties of translating or transporting them across historical, cultural, or social boundaries. Expressions of popular feeling sometimes seem to have a shelf life akin to that of filmic special effects; a scene that is experienced as genuinely moving, astounding, or terrifying to one generation or community might register as profoundly cheesy, insulting, or downright comical to the next. Such contingency makes it difficult retroactively to judge the historical or local reception of a particular text or the political and historical effects of such affective work. Therefore, while sentiment and sympathy crossed the borders of continents, nations, communities, and persons, their meanings and effects may very well have changed profoundly as they moved. G. J. Barker-Benfield maintains that the culture of sensibility was an international phenomenon that nevertheless took on slightly different forms in such different nations as France, England, and Holland. The recent historical treatment of emotion in pre-Revolutionary Pennsylvania by Nicole Eustace emphasizes the cultural power of affect in relation to colonial politics, while Sarah Knott's study places sensibility's revolutionary possibilities at the very center of colonial and early national politics in North America. Such studies confirm Chris Jones's astute observation that sensibility was in the 1790s a site for the contest between conservative and radical ideas.

Environmental psychology's belief that "human selves were made, not born" (Barker-Benfield xvii) endowed sensibility and the circulation of feeling with the radical potential to generate social and political change. As Ellison remarks, "sensibility in the Anglo-American political tradition started with the efforts of elite men to imagine political opposition and to understand political change" (4). That power proved to be surprisingly transportable while also generating considerable and often swift backlash. The ensuing contest over the politics of feeling was often played out *within* the discourse of feeling itself, a point that demonstrates both the plasticity and the power of sentimental forms. There is perhaps no domain within which this battle was more fierce or complicated than that of feminism. As Barker-Benfield points out, the belief that selves were made through circulating sensations (rather than born into or out of a predetermined status) made it possible for women to claim mental equality, even as such a promise "soon began to be short-circuited by the restoration of a model of innate sexual difference" (xvii).

Despite the ways in which criticism has since feminized feeling and its literary and cultural forms, sensibility and sentimentality were (and are) fields created, consumed, and critiqued by men and women alike. The conservative Edmund Burke could invoke sentimental affect to generate antirevolutionary sympathy for Marie Antoinette, for example, while Wollstonecraft famously responded by warning against the dangers of sensibility. Bryce Traister, building on the work of Philip Gould, reminds us that "American sentimentality was not exclusively or even preponderantly gendered female, as has for some time been believed" (Traister 15), and critics such as Crain, Burgett, and Shapiro have demonstrated the central role of male-male sympathy and "male sentimentalism" within Brown's work and life. Bryan Waterman's recovery of the associational urban networks of men in which Brown participated offers an excellent case study of sentiment's fluid complexity. Intense feelings circulated in relationships of same-sex friendship whose contours emphasized romantic love; at the same time, such intimate associations also facilitated the economic relations of a commercial society and could invoke considerable political dangers, as they did in the case of the anti-Illuminati crusade of the late 1790s (Waterman 32). Brown is consistently consumed by these intersecting networks of ideas, possibilities, and risks—in his later as much as in his earlier work. A more nuanced understanding of sensibility and sentimentality in their historical, cultural, and political contexts should therefore allow students and scholars to look at, say, *Edgar Huntly* and *Jane Talbot* together, to see their plots, styles, and themes as mutually concerned with an ongoing project.

III. Speculation and the Politics of Feeling

Emotional intensity is everywhere in Brown's fiction, and it invariably seems to bring with it a grab bag of threats and promises: contagion and attachment, risk and rescue, deception and affection. But scenes of emotional exchange frequently also operate profitably, as in Henry Kirvan's narrative for the merchant Haywood in "Lesson on Concealment." Similarly, in *Ormond*, when Constantia tells the story of her family's fall into poverty and destitution, it was "calculated deeply to affect a man of Mr. Melbourne's humanity" (O 107), and he responds by offering her the means to make money and a prepayment for the future products of her labor. Weymouth's "mournful tale" (EH 154) of his struggles and poverty likewise leads Edgar Huntly to relinquish the inheritance that would have made it possible for him to wed Mary. And when Jane Talbot's brother responds with emotion to her expression of forgiveness, it not only inspires sympathetic tears in Jane but also leads her to loan him the very money she'd just denied him to invest in a risky financial scheme.

Scenes such as these suggest an awkward intimacy between feeling and money that is at the very heart of sentimentality's ambivalent politics. Indeed, this connection has been a topic of considerable recent scholarship, from Elizabeth Jane Wall Hinds's and Karen Weyler's explorations of such relations in Brown and his American contemporaries to Catherine Ingrassia's and Catherine Gallagher's influential work on the interpenetrations of feeling and finance in the eighteenth-century British novel. Such studies suggest that we ought to include a term like *speculation* in our study of sensation, even at the risk of making the already unwieldy dictionary of emotion even larger. The term *speculation* foregrounds precisely the tensions and connections (rather than the distinctions and oppositions) between feeling and reason, between private and public, between the home and the market, that are at the heart of Brown's work. It therefore has the advantage of foregrounding for the study of Brown and sensibility the cultural and historical complexities that were written over in the course of the nineteenth century and that were subsequently simplified in so much of the foundational literary history and biography about Brown.

Rothschild's study, *Economic Sentiments*, restores to the late eighteenth century the interpenetration of feeling and economics that was drained out by later assumptions that opposed the "cold" calculations of finance to the "warm" feelings of sentiment. Her study of Smith, Hume, Marquis de Condorcet, and others recognizes the indelible presence of sentiment in eighteenth-century thinking about economics but explains that it has since been erased, "as though the two sides in subsequent political philosophy lie strewn...across the entire landscape of the old Europe" (Rothschild 25). Knott likewise highlights the ways in which structures of feeling and finance emerged together during this period, noting that sensibility marked "a groping reaction to the anonymity of the market and to the depersonalizing and cruel effects of finance capital," while at the same time supplying "supple if unctuous instruments among the commercial classes for building trust, facilitating exchange, and getting past snobby forms of social exclusiveness" (Knott 13–14). These studies supplement Barker-Benfield's claim that the culture of sensibility developed in the context of an emerging consumer society made possible by British imperialism: "It was in the interests of commerce that men cultivated politeness and sensibility" (Barker-Benfield xxv), and the "self-indulgence, the 'luxury' of feeling, [that] was at the heart of the culture of sensibility" was also "basic to the consumer psychology the polite and commercial economy required" (xxvi). The culture of sensibility therefore took shape between indulgent consumption on the one hand and moral repugnance for and opposition to such indulgent consumption on the other. But it facilitated both. Shapiro similarly understands sensibility as a mechanism that provided social bonds in the wake of an older hierarchical status system's collapse. As he puts it, "sensibility provides the medium through which an expanded cohort of the bourgeoisie could train themselves to take the risk of trusting each other within the flows of fictional capital—credit and stock speculation—that are the prerequisites for an enlarged price-setting marketplace" (Shapiro 59). Bonds of sympathy and fellow feeling therefore offer an antidote to a world increasingly characterized by risk, uncertainty, and speculation, but they also encourage and sustain precisely such uncertain and speculative risk-taking. Besides, sentimental novels were themselves "stuffed full of stuff, chock-full of cash and other forms of capital" (Knott 13). Feeling served as a bulwark against the commercial self-interest that it also fueled, and efforts to separate private feelings and the public market into two divided spheres only mask this threat of self-cancellation. Sympathy lubricates the wheels of commerce whose destructive effects it seeks to stop. Brown's work seems consistently aware that attempts to run backward on this wheel might not stop its progress so much as propel it faster forward. It is precisely this double bind that Brown's fiction explores and exposes, and we might well take the strange pace of his narratives—which often seem to be speeding nowhere—as evidence of these competing impulses.

I'm not sure one can find a better discussion of this affective package than Ellison's, for whom sensibility and sentiment register a particularly paralytic kind of political investment, in which one benefits from an arrangement that one is unable to change. For Ellison, sentiment is at once "system-serving and system-exposing" (36), a claim echoed in Lauren Berlant's perceptive analysis of sentiment's ability to "register not merely…stuckness but…the conditions of bargaining that allow people to maintain both their critical knowledge and their attachments to what disappoints" (Berlant 22). There is something at once determinedly hopeful and desperately hopeless in what Berlant calls sentimentality's perpetually "unfinished business," where disappointment inescapably partners with fulfillment (13).[8] In "A Lesson on Concealment," the merchant Haywood weeps when he hears of the injustice with which Henry's family has been treated, and he offers a job and a home to Henry as an individualized compensatory response to the inequalities and injustices of the Atlantic world-system over which he has no direct control. This structure of feeling abounds in Brown's work, where it reflects the sense of utopian possibility and its bitter curtailment that characterized transatlantic society as it transitioned out of a revolutionary age.

I end with a very brief consideration of the ways scholarly approaches to a relatively neglected novel like Brown's *Jane Talbot* might be invigorated by such a renewed rubric.[9] The novel's first half, for instance—which foregrounds the familial relationships between Jane, her father, and her brother, Frank—is really about the seductive dangers of financial speculation. Jane is repeatedly torn between her sense of familial duty and the patently irrational schemes in which her brother is investing (and losing) the family money. The novel's second half, on the other hand, emphasizes marital relationships and the dangers of sexual and intellectual speculation. Jane is here torn between loyalty to her foster mother, Mrs. Fielder, and attraction to her lover, Henry Colden, whose adoption of radical Woldwinite ideas makes him an unacceptable candidate for marriage in Mrs. Fielder's eyes. Frank and Henry are both presented as potential seducer figures to Jane but only if we are prepared to think about seduction in relation to money and investment as well as in relation to sex and sensibility. It is ultimately the brother, Frank, who repeatedly dismisses and mocks Jane's ideas and opinions because she is a woman, who is unmasked as the deceiver who manipulates feeling to get what he wants. The suitor, Henry, whose radical ideas about gender equality appear to render him inherently dangerous, on the other hand, is revealed to be unthreatening. No less than *Ormond* or *Arthur Mervyn* or *Wieland*, *Jane Talbot* positions speculation as a site of seduction and seduction as a site of speculation and reveals the private domestic space of individualized feeling to be also a public space of global citizenship.[10] In her book *Statistical Panic*, Kathleen Woodward insists on recognizing "the epistemological edge of emotion that, in a dialectical relation to thought, can serve to disclose the structures of the world in which we are situated" (Woodward 13). Such everyday emotions as panic or boredom, for instance, should be keyed to and seen as symptomatic of the "financialization of everyday life" (10) in contemporary America. We might likewise read in the sensational and affective fictional worlds depicted by Brown a recognition that the financialization of everyday life has been under way since his own time and that the production and consumption of sentimental writing have always been a way of recording, managing, and critiquing its effects.

NOTES

1. Of course, this nineteenth-century model of separate spheres has been strongly challenged even as a particularly helpful account of the nineteenth century, most notably in the "No More Separate Spheres!" issue of *American Literature* edited by Cathy Davidson in 1998 (and published as a book in 2002).
2. See also Hales, who calls *Edgar Huntly* "a project of sympathy" (135), and Boren, who identifies it as "a masculine colonization of the novel of feeling" (165). Many other critics place Brown's novels in the tradition of the sentimental seduction novel; see, for instance, Barnes, who reads *Wieland* as a "seduction novel" (53), and Traister, who identifies *Arthur Mervyn* as an instance of "the libertine-maiden seduction plot" (6).
3. Every repeated reference to Brown's "four major novels" has the unfortunate effect of reinforcing this overdetermined division. Even so recent and careful a reader as Crain divides Brown's fictional output around his "generic shift from Gothic to sentimental fiction and his protagonist's psychological shift from dependence on men to dependence on women" (128)—a shift that is also keyed to a political transformation from "left to right" (129). Such repeated alignments have unarguably generated an uneven scholarly treatment of Brown's work; a quick search of the MLA bibliographic database, for example, returns 148 hits for a search on "Wieland" and "Charles Brockden Brown" versus 8 hits for "Clara Howard" and "Charles Brockden Brown," 97 for "Edgar Huntly" and "Charles Brockden Brown" versus 8 for "Jane Talbot" and "Charles Brockden Brown."
4. Krause, for instance, reads *Ormond* as a superior treatment of seduction and sentiment to those at work in *Charlotte Temple* and *The Power of Sympathy* (574), while Flück suggests that *Jane Talbot* aims (even if it ultimately fails) to move beyond the sentimental form's compromised cultural and aesthetic status. To be fair, Flück does position Rowson's later work as a similar effort to transcend the form's earlier limitations. Ultimately, however, neither Brown nor Rowson reaches the standard that Flück seems to hope for: an American Jane Austen who might have rescued the sentimental novel from the discount racks of American literary history.
5. See Watts for the claim that "on or about April 1800, Charles Brockden Brown changed" (131). Like the "four major novels" tagline, however, this assertion gets repeated far too often and interrogated far too little.
6. See especially the Charles Brockden Brown Electronic Archive and Scholarly Edition, under the editorship of Mark Kamrath and Philip Barnard (www.brockdenbrown.ucf. edu). The recent edition of *Studies in American Fiction* titled "Beyond *Charlotte Temple*" marks an effort to expand our sense of the range and diversity of Rowson's work.

7. Rothschild points out, for instance, that within the first few lines of *Theory of Moral Sentiments*, Adam Smith uses the various terms "emotions, sentiments, senses, sensations, and faculties" (43).

8. Berlant describes sensationalism's "politically powerful suturing device of a bourgeois revolutionary aesthetic" as expressing "a generic wish for an unconflicted world, one wherein structural inequities, not emotions or intimacies, are epiphenomenal" (20, 21). This account suggests that sentimentality's validation of emotion entails turning a blind eye to the "structural inequities" that fuel those emotions, but by describing this process as a "suturing device," it also suggests that those political inequities are never foreclosed, are always only partially hooded beneath the lid of feeling.

9. Burleigh's fascinating reading of equivalence and the law in both *Clara Howard* and *Jane Talbot* is recent evidence that these novels may be receiving renewed attention.

10. Consider, for instance, Ellison's claim that sensibility's apparent interest in interiority is, in fact, "often a highly coded claim to serious world citizenship" (75).

WORKS CITED

Barker-Benfield, G. J. *The Culture of Sensibility: Sex and Society in Eighteenth-Century Britain.* Chicago: University of Chicago Press, 1992.

Barnes, Elizabeth. *States of Sympathy: Seduction and Democracy in the American Novel.* New York: Columbia University Press, 1997.

Berlant, Lauren. *The Female Complaint: The Unfinished Business of Sentimentality in American Culture.* Durham, N.C.: Duke University Press, 2008.

Boren, Mark Edelman. "Abortographism and the Weapon of Sympathy in Charles Brockden Brown's *Edgar Huntly; Or, the Memoirs of a Sleepwalker.*" *Style* 43.2 (2009): 165–193.

Bredahl, A. Carl. "The Two Portraits in *Wieland.*" *Early American Literature* 16.1 (1981): 54–59.

Brown, Charles Brockden. "A Lesson on Concealment; or, Memoirs of Mary Selwyn." MM 2.3 (March 1800): 174–207.

Burgett, Bruce. *Sentimental Bodies: Sex, Gender, and Citizenship in the Early Republic.* Princeton, N.J.: Princeton University Press, 1998.

Burleigh, Erica. "Incommensurate Equivalences: Genre, Representation, and Equity in *Clara Howard* and *Jane Talbot.*" *Early American Studies* 9.3 (2011): 748–780.

Crain, Caleb. *American Sympathy: Men, Friendship, and Literature in the New Nation.* New Haven, Conn.: Yale University Press, 2001.

Davidson, Cathy N. "Preface: No More Separate Spheres!" *American Literature* 70.3 (1998): 443–463.

Davidson, Cathy N. *Revolution and the Word: The Rise of the Novel in America.* New York: Oxford University Press, 1986.

Eustace, Nicole. *Passion is the Gale: Emotion, Power, and the Coming of the American Revolution.* Chapel Hill: University of North Carolina Press, 2008.

Fiedler, Leslie A. *Love and Death in the American Novel,* rev. ed. New York: Dell, 1966.

Flück, Winfried. "Novels of Transition: From Sentimental Novel to Domestic Novel." In Udo J. Hebel, ed., *The Construction and Contestation of American Cultures and Identities in the Early National Period,* 97–117. Heidelberg: Universitätsverlag Winter, 1999.

Gallagher, Catherine. *Nobody's Story: The Vanishing Acts of Women Writers in the Marketplace, 1670–1820.* Berkeley: Univ. of California Press, 1994.

Gaston, Sean. "The Impossibility of Sympathy." *Eighteenth Century: Theory and Interpretation* 51.1–2 (2010): 129–152.

Hales, Ashley. "'Was It Proper to Watch Him at a Distance?': Spectatorship, Sympathy and Atlantic Migration in *Edgar Huntly.*" *Symbiosis* 10.2 (October 2006): 133–146.

Hinds, Elizabeth Jane Wall. *Private Property: Charles Brockden Brown's Gendered Economics of Virtue*. Cranbury, N.J.: Associated University Presses, 1997.

Howard, June. "What Is Sentimentality?" *American Literary History* 11.1 (1999): 63–81.

Ingrassia, Catherine. *Authorship, Commerce, and Gender in Early Eighteenth-Century England: A Culture of Paper Credit*. Cambridge: Cambridge Univ. Press, 1998.

Jones, Chris. *Radical Sensibility: Literature and Ideas in the 1790s*. New York: Routledge, 1993.

Knott, Sarah. *Sensibility and the American Revolution*. Chapel Hill: University of North Carolina Press, 2009.

Krause, Sydney. "*Ormond*: Seduction in a New Key." *Early American Literature* 44.4 (1973): 570–584.

McDowell, Tremaine. "Sensibility in the Eighteenth-Century American Novel." *Studies in Philology* 24.3 (1927): 383–402.

McGann, Jerome. *The Poetics of Sensibility: A Revolution in Literary Style*. Oxford: Oxford University Press, 1996.

Pinch, Adela. *Strange Fits of Passion: Epistemologies of Emotion, Hume to Austen*. Stanford, Calif.: Stanford University Press, 1996.

Rothschild, Emma. *Economic Sentiments: Adam Smith, Condorcet, and the Enlightenment*. Cambridge, Mass.: Harvard Univ. Press, 2001.

Shapiro, Stephen. *The Culture and Commerce of the Early American Novel: Reading the Atlantic World-System*. University Park: Pennsylvania State University Press, 2008.

Silyn Roberts, Siân. "Gothic Enlightenment: Contagion and Community in Charles Brockden Brown's *Arthur Mervyn.*" *Early American Literature* 44.2 (2009): 207–232.

Stern, Julia. *The Plight of Feeling: Sympathy and Dissent in the Early American Novel*. Chicago: University of Chicago Press, 1997.

Tompkins, Jane. *Sensational Designs: The Cultural Work of American Fiction, 1790–1860*. New York: Oxford University Press, 1985.

Traister, Bryce. "Libertinism and Authorship in America's Early Republic." *American Literature* (2000): 1–30.

Waterman, Bryan. *Republic of Intellect: The Friendly Club of New York City and the Making of American Literature*. Baltimore: Johns Hopkins University Press, 2007.

Watts, Steven. *The Romance of Real Life: Charles Brockden Brown and the Origins of American Culture*. Baltimore: Johns Hopkins University Press, 1994.

Weyler, Karen A. *Intricate Relations: Sexual and Economic Desire in American Fiction, 1787–1814*. Iowa City: University of Iowa Press, 2004.

Woodward, Kathleen. *Statistical Panic: Cultural Politics and Poetics of the Emotions*. Durham, N.C.: Duke University Press, 2009.

CHAPTER 28

....

BROWN AND THE NOVEL IN THE ATLANTIC WORLD

....

SIÂN SILYN ROBERTS

ANY discussion of Charles Brockden Brown's relationship to the novel in the late eighteenth century should probably begin by sounding a note of caution, for the simple reason that the category we habitually call "the early American novel" is not as generically or nationalistically stable as it implies.[1] It does not easily encapsulate the heterogeneous array of fictional and nonfictional forms of writing that early American readers understood to be "novels," nor does it manage to capture the complicated, circum-Atlantic relationship that such writing maintained to imported and transplanted anglophone literary conventions. It is a useful shorthand for scholars working on early US fiction, but its implied stable geopolitical and generic taxonomies ("American" and "novel") run the risk of marginalizing works that don't fit neatly into our critical expectations of a national literature. The implicit master category of the "American novel" to which an "early" form exists in subordinate relation invokes a teleological trajectory along which literary history travels, from an originary moment (usually inaugurated by the act of political independence) to the more sophisticated literary culture of the nineteenth century. Unless we're careful, we wind up looking retrospectively for evidence of an incipient "American" tradition, where the qualities of more mature artistic successes are always already present in the moment of that tradition's origins.

From the 1960s to the 1990s, American literary scholarship largely reproduced this line of reasoning by focusing on a small cluster of novels drawn from the critically overprivileged decade of the 1790s that supported a nationalistic rendering of American literary history. These arguments inherited some commonplaces from nineteenth- and early-twentieth-century formal-generic thinking: that a variety of sociological and material factors (poor distribution networks, limited leisure time in a subsistence economy, etc.) stunted the growth of an American novelistic tradition, the United States was culturally immature and preferred imitating British forms, the early American novel's critical value lay primarily in its sociological content, and the incipient indications of a nationalistic tradition were only fully realized in the more artistically successful works that started to appear in the 1830s. Until the last decade of the twentieth century, these assumptions largely shaped our understanding of Brown's relationship to the "early American novel." From the 1950s to the 1980s, Brown was often viewed as something of an outlier, an idiosyncratic genius whose flawed works anticipated the more sophisticated Gothic works of the nineteenth century; and from the 1980s to the late 1990s, an almost exclusively historicist interest in Brown as a novelist meant that we tended to conjugate his Gothic in a negative declension, by the degree to which it encoded the buried erasures, betrayals, persecutions, and national guilts attending revolution and the spirit of republicanism.

In the last several decades, these views have shifted considerably, as critics have turned their attention to the insistently dialectical nature of cultural development in a broader eighteenth-century Atlantic world. In our current moment, we are more likely to recognize the category of the "novel" as a motley literary form that underwent different phases and degrees of regional activity, distribution, and generic alteration in response to globally contested and contingent reconfigurations of statehood, literary production, the politics of popular sovereignty, market relations, colonialism, labor, and slavery. Likewise, Brown is viewed no longer as the paternal forefather of an "American" novelistic tradition but as a prominent node on a dense, multidirectional Atlantic matrix of ideas contoured by shifting flows of material and cultural exchange.

This revised critical perspective invites us to rethink Brown's larger oeuvre in terms of international contact and exchange, but it also makes room in our discussion for those works that have hitherto been deemed too fragmented, derivative, unoriginal, short, or factual to count as "novels." In the United States in particular, the literary marketplace was crowded with different kinds of imaginative narratives that often claimed the appellate of "novel" but bear little resemblance to the sort of thing we associate with the emergent tradition of British domestic realism. To be sure, imported, reprinted, adapted, and translated editions of British and European novels by authors such as Ann Radcliffe, Samuel Richardson, William Godwin, Johann Wolfgang von Goethe, Charlotte Smith, or Carl Grosse—to name just a few—were available up and down the East Coast alongside homegrown adaptations of Gothic, sentimental, and picaresque traditions by Anglo-American authors (a sample list of which include such familiar names as Brown, Hannah Webster Foster, William Hill Brown, Susanna Rowson, or Royall Tyler and less often-taught figures such as Enos Hitchcock, Helena Wells, Sukey Vickery, Caroline Matilda Warren, George Watterson, or Sally Wood). Nonetheless, American readers were just as likely to read more conventional novels alongside a vast array of miscellaneous fiction that appeared in the colonies long before 1776 allegedly ushered in the era of the indigenous novel. This fiction inhabited a multitude of different forms: novelistic fragments, serialized and short fiction printed in journals or magazines, fictionalized retellings of factual events, captivity narratives, pamphlets, satires, anonymous or pseudonymous novels, invented narratives that nonetheless claimed to be "based in fact" or "literally true," travel narratives, orientalist tales, ethnographies, natural and provincial histories, and didactic essays.[2]

This body of imaginative writing requires a more nuanced critical metric than that offered by "the early American novel." Such a metric would need to account for early novelistic literature's often ephemeral nature (much of this writing circulated widely in magazines and periodicals but enjoyed a relatively brief life span), its great capacity for redundancy (in the sentimental and Gothic traditions in particular, stock characters, didactic exhortations, and conventional plot elements are recycled time and again), its indebtedness to colonial historiographic traditions (many works present themselves as factual accounts), and its nonnationalistic coordinates (few novels written before James Fenimore Cooper confine their plots to North American geopolitical boundaries). Arguably, to card out these different literary-historical strands, it would be historically more accurate to do away with the category of "the early American novel" altogether and replace it with something along the lines of "a series of generically motley, transatlantic displacements in novelistic convention, circulating throughout the Atlantic world."

Until we can come up with a less cumbersome formulation, however, I've gone a more expedient route, substituting "Brown and the early American novel" with "Brown and the novel in the Atlantic World."[3] Doing so allows us to get around the issue of unwieldy taxonomic categorization by shifting our attention to Brown's engagement with the various generic, aesthetic, and geopolitical variations on this heterogeneous eighteenth-century form. At the risk of obfuscation, I use a more elastic vocabulary ("imaginative," "fictional," or "novelistic" writings, etc.) in an effort to distinguish between commonsensical definitions of the novel and the generically variable array of fiction that emerged before 1830. It pays to remember that Brown was not primarily a novelist but worked tirelessly as a translator, essayist, historian, reviewer, and editor over the course of his career. That is to say, he was immersed in the culture of literary miscellany that proliferated alongside the comparatively exclusive form of the conventional novel. It therefore makes sense to read his major novels for the way they theorize their relationship to the generically variable nature of early American literary production more generally—not only in terms of their indebtedness to the novelistic discourses of the picaresque, sentiment, and the Gothic but also to the fragmentation and cacophony that characterized early American print more broadly at the end of the eighteenth century. What follows does not give a complete picture of such a task, but I do hope to sketch out a few related ways in which we might assess Brown's contributions to this larger culture of novelistic writing in early America.

I. HISTORIOGRAPHY AND THE NOVEL IN EARLY AMERICA

Let me begin by suggesting that imaginative writing in late colonial and post-Revolutionary America took root by grafting itself onto two established literary traditions: the colonial tradition of historiographic and ethnographic writing and the transplanted Enlightenment cultural logics such as self-sovereign individualism, sentimental contractualism, and sympathy, which were transmitted to colonial North America by way of the English and European novel. By adapting the conventions of captivity, ethnography, provincial histories, exploration, and travel on the one hand and English modes of sentimentalism, the Gothic, and the picaresque on the other, American fiction sought to formulate in literary terms a series of responses to the contingencies and vagaries of life in the New World. In fictionalized captivity narratives such as "The Panther Captivity" (1787) or Shepard Kollock's "A True Narrative of the Sufferings of Mary Kinnan" (1795), for example, romance conventions populate the imagined Gothic space of the American wilderness with anti-individualistic phenomena—say, a giant, a cruel father, or the "ferocious, cruel, and obdurate" (Kollock 112) Delaware Indians— only to banish such elements and leave the world inhabited by characters whose desires and motivations arise solely within themselves. To much the same purpose, the language of sentimentalism attests to the protagonists' cultural purity, provides an imagined cultural home to which they may return by virtue of the quality of their feelings, and rhetorically excludes any atavistic or barbaric energies that cannot be incorporated into a community thus constituted. Such innovative generic-historical hybrids illuminate the "double resonance," as Michael Drexler and Ed White call it, of early American *literary history*, where "literature" and "history" exist in a mutually constitutive relationship. Early imaginative fiction, in other words, is often "an attempt to extend or develop history in an imaginative fashion" (Drexler and White 148).[4] Thus, any attempt to go looking for commonsensical definitions of the novel in the Revolutionary era—that is, the kind of "continuous" prose narrative (Frye 303) that favors the "harmonious" (Watt 296) resolution of difference as telos—is bound to come up short against a prolific literary culture of quasi-fictional, often fragmented generic experimentation.

The persistently historiographic dimensions of early American imaginative literature help explain why so much novelistic writing in the post-Revolutionary era compulsively reviews its own fictionality. Both at a paratextual level (in prefaces, addresses to the reader, dedications, etc.) and in interpolated scenes that reflect on the acts of reading, writing, literary circulation, criticism, or signification more generally, early fiction is acutely aware of itself *as* fiction. It is a well-established fact of early American literary history that writers felt compelled to respond to contemporary debates over the moral and didactic value of reading novels by making such metacritical observations, but the novel's rootedness in early colonial historiography also suggests a preoccupation with theorizing the intersection of history and literature.[5] Like many of her contemporaries, for instance, Martha Read claims that *Monima; or, The Beggar Girl* (1802) is both a "novel" and "chiefly founded on fact" (Read v). This commonplace generic ellipsis aims to soothe alarmist fears about the dangers of misrepresentation by reassuring readers that the events contained therein are factually true, but it also imagines the "novel" elaborating on and extending "fact" in a historically aware fashion. Perhaps no other novelist from the period took this principle as seriously as Brown.

Consider, for example, *Edgar Huntly's* (1799) well-known prefatory address "To the Public." Brown claims that historical experience in the New World ("incidents of Indian hostility, and the perils of the western wilderness") demands indigenous literary forms "peculiar to ourselves" (EH 3). It has been generally accepted critical practice to invoke this statement as the rallying cry of American literary nationalism, but Brown's reliance on the received cultural authority of imported literary materials (the British romance, theories of the sublime, the cultural logic of individualism and contractualism, material- ist models of sensory psychology, etc.) tells us that Brown's version of literary nationalism is a peculiar one, where assertions of literary originality and difference "walk hand in hand with the acknowledgment of foreign emulation" (Tawil 4).[6] That is to say, Brown reconciles American historical experience to formal innovation in a somewhat para- doxical way, by imagining the novel as an ongoing appropriation and negotiation of literary practices that originate elsewhere. His promise to depict New World histories in "vivid and faithful colours" carries out the fairly conventional didactic imperative of "calling forth the passions and engaging the sympathy of the reader" (EH 3), but he simultaneously theorizes the New World novel's inescapable historiographic imaginary as a function of its reliance on British conventions.

In the closely allied essays "The Difference between History and Romance" (1800) and "Walstein's School of History" (1799), Brown elaborates his interest in the historio- graphic dimensions of American fiction into a complex narrative theory. Here the difference between an empirically recoverable notion of "history" and the more proba- bilistic realism of the romance is calculated in terms of their respective didactic and emancipatory dimensions.[7] Echoing the sentiments of many of his contemporaries, Brown argues that fiction has a moral imperative to provide, "in an eloquent narration, a model of right conduct" (Walstein 408), but his ideas about how such an end may be attained are developed primarily from British radical-democratic writers such as William Godwin, Mary Wollstonecraft, and Thomas Holcroft. Broadly speaking, these Anglo-Jacobin authors posited that progressive social behavior—not institutions of the old regime—will reform society from the ground up. Arts and manners provide virtuous models worthy of imitation, spreading their influence through local and interpersonal relations. Brown adopts these principles by suggesting that the moral worth of novels lies in their ability to translate complex philosophical ideas into accessible imaginative narratives—a style of writing he calls "fictitious history" (Walstein 409). Unvarnished history, he argues, often fails "to illuminate the understanding, to charm curiosity, and sway the passions" (337) by offering readers a bald recitation of facts and past occur- rences, or what he calls the tedium of "abstract systems, and theoretical reasonings" (338). Fictitious history, on the other hand, animates such information, capturing the reader's attention through "artfully linked" and "vividly depicted" events. The job of the romancer, as Brown sees it, is to assign probable causes (or "motive") to empirically knowable but causally disjointed scenes, transforming fiction into a kind of hypothetical or suppositional test case.[8]

To this end, each of Brown's Gothic and sentimental novels places ordinary people in extraordinary circumstances and forces them to examine, in extremis, the principles and assumptions upon which they construct their ideas about collective histories and speculative futures. As a general rule, Brown's novels are not so much narrative histories as "historiographic trials" (Emerson 126), where past and future events are subject to multiple and contradictory retellings or predictions. Edgar Huntly, for instance, habitually speaks in what might be called the "suppositional mode," where he supplements the limited capacity for empirical knowledge that "nature has imposed upon human faculties" (EH 92) with speculative reasoning about the "probable issue" (113) of events and human actions. He must navigate an ever-shifting phantasmagoric world in which verifiable sensory information competes with unreliable conjecture, where he is overtaken and controlled by emotions that either do not necessarily originate within himself or originate within a part of his mind to which he has only intermittent access. In *Arthur Mervyn* (1799–1800), Brown shifts the mantle of these epistemological difficulties to the reader. In that novel, a realist's logic cannot yield anything resembling a transparent world of objects, because the notoriously ambiguous eponymous protagonist represents different things to different people. We may be tempted to tease out Arthur's "true" character and motives, but Brown reminds us time and again across his writings that "motives are modifications of thought which cannot be subjected to the senses. They cannot be certainly known" (Difference 252). There is no "real" Arthur there, only the realist's desire to produce one.

The ontological opacity of Brown's Gothic worlds testifies to his interest in the invisible operations of causality and historical contingency, or what in chapter 1 of "Annals of Europe and America" (1807) he calls the endless "chain of successive and dependent causes" (Annals 3). This interest arguably manifests in his novels as a habitual refusal to subordinate competing histories to the liberal sovereignty of rational thought. Rather, in the absence of a shared, consensus history, Brown asks us to think in conjectural rather than realist terms, that is, in terms of possibility, scenario, and contingency. By this line of reasoning, the generic or nationalistic distinctiveness of Brown's novels resides not in character, setting, or native "theme" but in their abiding fictionality or the ways in which they theorize and inhabit the rhetorical pose of their own invention. Brown's Gothic conceptualizes different modalities of fiction (verisimilitude, probability, credibility, etc.) to probe the grounds on which we calculate believability or plausibility. Once ascribed in the 1950s and '60s to a lack of technical skill, Brown's habitual uses of gaps, ellipses, disjointed and embedded histories, coincidence, belated exposition, and narrative dead ends are actually evidence of a contingent imaginative world characterized by sudden reversal and unintended detours. The degree to which Brown's characters successfully navigate such a world may be taken as a measure of their success as "American" protagonists.

II. Brown and the Early American Adventure Tale

As it turns out, this characteristic places Brown's novels in dialogue with a large grouping of writings that we might think of as "American adventure tales." The dislocations, digressions, internal instabilities, and vicissitudinous reversals characteristic of Brown's novels and much early American novelistic writing more generally suggest an affinity with the picaresque, a contentious taxonomic category that nonetheless may be usefully recast here for the purpose of grouping such works as stories of adventure. This kind of narrative draws on the conventions of the picaresque to subject its protagonists to dizzying reversals in fortune and abrupt displacements; examples might include *The History of Constantius and Pulchera* (1789 and 1794), *Amelia; or, The Faithless Briton* (1798), *Adventures in a Castle* (1806) by "a Citizen of Philadelphia" who identifies himself as "Julius," and the confessional autobiography *The Memoirs of Stephen Burroughs* (1798), as well as Royall Tyler's *The Algerine Captive*, Isaac Mitchell's *The Asylum* (1804, 1811), and Martha Read's *Margaretta* (1807). What distinguishes these narratives as adventure tales is their tendency to recycle elements of the British and European romance, Barbary and Indian captivity narratives, and the sentimental epistolary novel and mash them up with a series of sensational but familiar tropes: shipwrecks, mutinies, robberies, kidnappings, ferocious beasts, cross-dressing, disguises, threatening forests, lost and recovered fortunes, journeys into unknown lands, separation from and reunion with loved ones, captivity, escape, and thwarted love. More often than not, characters seem to possess only tenuous control over their movements and actions as the fluctuations of immigration, accident, chance, circumstance, and opportunity abruptly reroute the trajectories of plot. In *Constantius and Pulchera*, George Watterston's *Glencarn* (1810) *St. Herbert*, or James Butler's *Fortune's Foot-ball* (1797), for instance, the narratives lurch from crisis to crisis in a variety of sentimental, Gothic, and picaresque registers, often sprawling across the same kind of wide international arena we see in Brown's Gothic and sentimental novels. Abrupt and bizarre transitions at the level of plot abound, and conflicting chronotopes intrude into fragile realist frames. Just as Pulchera is about to be killed and cannibalized in *Constantius and Pulchera*, for example, a bear miraculously appears to save the shipwrecked crew from starvation. In *Glencarn*, the eponymous protagonist seems to defy the laws of physics when he materializes just in time, from far away, to save his endangered fiancée. At times, the episodes making up the novels' action seem to bear only a tangential relationship to one another, with no single event taking priority. These episodic structures are often exciting but also abruptly transitional, oblique, and curiously redundant at the level of both form and plot, drawing on conventional plot devices and even repeating certain action sequences.

To put it mildly, the adventure tale is emphatically *not* the kind of tidy, unified narrative we might expect from a "realist" novel. Rather, it asks to be read as something like a generic "assemblage," less a taxonomic category than a set of discursive relations, stitching together narrative components that may seem unrelated and discordant but whose very heterogeneity dictates how we apprehend their meaning.[9] Unlike the English domestic novel, the adventure tale is far less concerned with cultivating characters distinguished by a unique interiority than with moving people around. Ultimately, how characters adapt to different things, places, and experiences ultimately matters far more than their development of a unique, maturing personality (or what the realist novel invites us to think of as "growth"). But the "episode" and the "fragment" also have a formal role to play: having the same thing happen time and again, or having disjointed or unrelated events pile up, invites a range of aesthetic and epistemological considerations, including pleasure in the text (especially the pleasures of deferral in dilatory or recursive forms, or what David Brooks suggestively calls "the erotics of form" [339]), experiences of absorption and distraction, and chains of determining relation. As Pulchera puts it, "all impossibilities...become practicable" (Anonymous 6) when a narrative is governed by unseen causal links. To explore what's at stake in the adventure tale's grammar of repetition and disjunction, Brown's theories of somnambulism offer a useful test case.

Consider, for example, the sleepwalking interlude that begins in Chapter 6 of *Edgar Huntly*, where Clithero imagines his abrupt change in circumstance as a kind of shipwreck. His "flowing fortunes," he explains, were "destined to ebb with unspeakably greater rapidity, and to leave me, in a moment, stranded and wrecked" (EH 58). That "moment" is the death of Wiatte, Mrs. Lorimer's beloved but evil twin brother, whom Clithero kills in self-defense. The scene in which Clithero defends himself against Wiatte and lapses into a somnambulistic state is therefore framed as the kind of abrupt episodic and experiential shift, rhetorically akin to a shipwreck, that we encounter in a story like *Constantius and Pulchera*, where "without foresight of a previous moment," Clithero undergoes "an entire change" (73). That transformation, which he experiences as sleepwalking, affects the way he links ideas together. Prior to Wiatte's death, he tells Edgar, "I was calm, considerate, and self-collected. I marked the way I was going. Passing objects were observed. If I adverted to the series of my own reflections, my attention was not seized and fastened by them. I could disengage myself at pleasure, and could pass, without difficulty, from attention to the world within, to the contemplation of that without. Now my liberty, in this respect, was at an end. I was fettered, confounded, smitten with an excess of thought, and laid prostrate with wonder!" (74). The ability to create rational chains of cause and effect, to "mark the way" forward spatially and temporally, has been replaced by an "excess of thought" that prompts a compounding series of increasingly illogical associations that have no causal relation to one another. Wiatte's death, Clithero wildly concludes, was intentional and a mark of his own ingratitude toward Mrs. Lorimer. From here, it is a short step to even stranger conclusions: Clithero has signed Mrs. Lorimer's death warrant, because the news of her brother's death will kill her, the only solution to which is to kill his patroness preemptively himself. All impossibilities, it seems, have become practicable. Once Edgar begins to mimic Clithero's somnambulism, he likewise starts thinking in associative rather than causal terms. His delirium in the cave in Chapter 16, for instance, is characterized by "rambling meditations" (162) and the "capricious combinations" (161) of ideas. Rapid changes at the level of plot, made especially visible in the ellipsis between the end of Chapter 15 and the beginning of Chapter 16, become mirrored in the tumult of crowded, unrelated ideas that cascade through his mind.[10]

We might think of these sleepwalking passages, with their "capricious combinations" of ideas and sensations and abrupt transitional ellipses, as a formal expression of the adventure tale's characteristic multiplicity and episodic form presented in psychological terms. Drawing on contemporary theories of determinism and rationality, *Edgar Huntly* transforms the rapid vicissitudes of the adventure tale into its own theory of knowledge.

Indeed, in Brown's hands the tropes of adventure are transformed into a sophisticated vocabulary with which he explores what Richard Brodhead calls "the social relations of literary forms" (11). In *Jane Talbot*, for example, the mutiny that strands Henry Colden "naked" and "forlorn" (JT 423) on the distant shores of Japan allows Brown to reconfigure the language of cosmopolitanism in a way that renders Henry eligible to reenter a contractual system of exchange. Unlike the mercantile relays of exchange found in Manila (in the Spanish colony of the Philippines) or Batavia (present-day Jakarta in Indonesia, the former Dutch East Indies), which allow a trader like Montford to thrive, Japan bears a striking resemblance to the kind of closed community we encounter in the first half of *The Algerine Captive*. There, the entrenched regionalism of the United States puts Underhill's "New England ideas" (Tyler 83) at odds with local customs and manners, making it impossible for him to find "a place of settlement" (62). In much the same way, Henry presents Japan as a world unto itself, a "feudal or territorial" (JT 424) society intolerant of outsiders even as it observes Kantian laws of universal hospitality. Henry finds himself "on the borders of a new world,—a world civilized indeed, and peopled by men, but existing in almost total separation from the other families of mankind; with language, manners, and policy almost incompatible with the existence of a stranger among them" (423). By transposing Japan onto the United States as the "new world" of the East, Brown suggests that the United States must likewise learn to account for "the existence of a stranger" like Henry. It is for this reason, we can assume, that during his time in Japan, Henry only ever acquires "a *smattering* of the language, and *some* insight into the policy and manners" (424, emphasis added). He can tolerate cultural difference, it seems, but, unlike many of Brown's other protagonists, he preserves his cultural purity, in this case by refusing to adapt to Japanese life. The very "restlessness" (426) that makes a Carwin or an Ormond so successful as Gothic protagonists in an international arena makes Henry wholly unsuited to a cosmopolitan world, prompting his return to the United States. This allows Henry to claim for himself the kind of developmental trajectory characteristic of the self-sovereign individual: "the incidents of a long voyage, the vicissitudes through which I have passed…have made *my mind whole*" (427). Thus, the question of whether his conversion at the novel's end is sincere or merely expedient is of secondary importance to the larger point that his marriage to Jane is contingent on contractualism's adaptation to a culture of ontological and cultural opacity, which will invariably include people like Henry, who cannot be submitted to Enlightenment rules of judgment and whose allegiances are not necessarily tied to one place or kinship group.

III. The Political Economy
of Sentimentalism

Early cultural arbiters may have broadly condemned the pre-1820 novel in America as preposterously far-fetched or poorly plotted, a lazy assortment of random coincidences, chance encounters, and stories "encumbered by 'episodes' without organic relation to the plot" (Loshe 6), but we do better to assume that such formal characteristics constitute an act of generic self-exploration at the intersection of narrative form, historical experience, and imaginative possibility. The suppositional and conjectural epistemologies we encounter time and again in Brown's novels arguably present themselves as imaginative solutions to the contingencies of Revolutionary-era existence. In order to present themselves as such, however, Brown's novels and much early fiction in general had to grapple with a disconnection between the transmitted cultural forms of English sentimentalism, Gothicism, and the picaresque and the new social setting in which they took root. In particular, the kind of autogenerative national community imagined by the cultural logic of sentimentalism often found itself at odds with a broader cosmopolitan identity that construed Americanness as the ability to circulate through multiple points of exchange throughout an Atlantic world. That is to say, competing claims of commonality, or the shared appeal of identities construed in ethnic, religious, or economic terms, clashed with the diversity, mobility, and opacity of disparate, mobile populations and the ruptures of almost continual political crisis. Under such conditions, the vision of republican nationalism offered by the sentimental novel—Myra and Worthy in *The Power of Sympathy* (1789), say, or the exemplary Richman family of *The Coquette* (1797)—offered a partial, often exclusionary solution to the exigencies of global catastrophe, an emergent global economy, and cosmopolitanism. To see how Brown and his contemporaries confronted this problem, let us briefly review the operations of sentimental contractualism in the pre-1820 novel.

A good place to start is the generally accepted premise that the eighteenth-century sentimental tradition authorizes and naturalizes the bourgeois subject and the contractual state at the level of the family. That is to say, sentimentalism underwrites the logic of contractual individualism by reproducing the marriage contract as a miniature version of the civil state. The marriage contract operates in a manner analogous to the social contract: two differentiated but compatible parties of equal merit are fully individuated through marriage when each supplements the other with something he or she lacked prior to the exchange. Thus, sentimental works like *The Power of Sympathy* or Brown's *Clara Howard* (1801) seek to reproduce the rights and protections supposedly safeguarded by the British domestic haven by making contractual social relations the basis of civic membership in the new United States.

A problem arises, however, when we recognize that the logic of contractualism construed in such terms places exclusive limits on who may count as a subject. In Judith Butler's terms, "liberal versions of human ontology" have a tendency to think in terms of "bounded beings—distinct, recognizable, delineated subjects" (24). Enlightenment epistemologies of the modern subject restrict civic membership to only those figures of self-sovereign authority who fit the definition of the individual in the first place. Indeed, in an urban, cosmopolitan environment of competing market interests, heterogeneous cultures, and altogether different notions of political and personal authority, the British model of the individual civic subject comes to represent something of an impossible fantasy. This is not to say that the early American sentimental novel somehow "failed" to duplicate the logic of individualism to an American setting; rather, it illustrates how the appealing sense of communal identity generated by the concept of the contractual state is underwritten by exclusionary standards of personal sovereignty that necessarily exclude those who fail to meet those standards.

It is for this reason, I suspect, that early American sentimentalism often construes like-minded sympathetic subjects as little more than replicas of one another. In Hannah Webster Foster's *The Coquette* (1797), for example, the republican Mrs. Richman imagines her ideal male counterpart as nothing less than "a second self" (123). Likewise, the sentimental couple Roswell and Lucretia in *Julia* recognize "their own virtues in each other" (225). The marriage of Jane and Henry at the end of Brown's *Jane Talbot* (1801), a marriage that is strictly contingent on the reformation of Henry's dissenting, Godwinian principles, is allowed to proceed only on the grounds that Henry learn to "partake with [Jane] in every thought, in every emotion, both *here* and *hereafter!*" (JT 430). As Jane informs Henry, their union would be "*very* far from completing my felicity, unless our hopes and opinions, as well as our persons and hearts, were united" (430). As these examples suggest, the sentimental marriage contract demands an extraordinarily prescriptive and exemplary degree of compatibility. It should come as no surprise, then, to find sentimental contractualism running into problems in the new American republic, which includes people whose provenance and intentions are remote, hidden, or otherwise unrecoverable. These are precisely the kinds of beings, as the narrator of Rebecca Rush's *Kelroy* (1812) puts it, "who may be said to spring from nobody knows where; and rise in the world nobody can tell how" (67).

Arguably, many of Brown's Gothic scenarios (and, indeed, those of his nineteenth-century successors) pivot on this problem. In *Edgar Huntly*, for example, the closed "patriarchal" system of Solebury is destabilized by the presence of Clithero, "a stranger, whose adventures and character, previous to his coming hither, were unknown to us" (EH 14). By placing Clithero decisively at odds with the property-based household that structures the domestic (white, settler) community of feeling, Brown makes it clear that the Irish immigrant cannot be incorporated through the kind of intimate, sustained commonality of feeling required of individuals in the sentimental tradition. Small wonder, then, that Edgar's faith in the redemptive power of republican sympathy and contractual social relations fails abysmally as a means of suturing strangers together; the "random efforts" (36) of sympathy, as Clithero damningly puts it, create nothing but a "tissue of destructive errors" (35–36). Indeed, if Carwin, Ormond, Arthur Mervyn, Thomas Welbeck, and Clithero have anything in common, it is their hostility to—and ineligibility as constituents within—sentimental structures of feeling. Carwin's ability to parrot the erudite conventionalities of sentimental discourse may earn him a place in the Wieland community, but his tendency to appropriate the "garb, aspect, and deportment" (W 67) of other cultures and religions distinguishes him as a peculiarly cosmopolitan constituent who can slip in and out of different cultural spheres at will, transforming everything into potentially useful information. He thus embodies a contradiction that cannot be contained within the imaginative limits of the "nation": he is both the object of identification (Clara unexpectedly finds that her "heart overflowed with sympathy" [52] on their first encounter) and an abject outsider whose profound difference is fundamentally at odds with the harmonious circle to which he seeks entry. This contradiction registers as the dissonance between his ability to talk like a "mellifluent" literate subject (52) and his grotesque physical appearance. We often find this kind of representational excess erupting in Brown's Gothic novels at precisely the moment when sentimental contractualism finds itself at odds with constituents who are not cut from individualism's cloth. It is for this reason, we might assume, that Arthur Mervyn has a phobic reaction to his future wife: on the eve of his marriage, he is "possessed," "unhallowed," gripped by "a nameless sort of terror," his mind "lost to itself; bewildered; unhinged; plunged into a drear insanity" (AM 436). That he confronts his impending marriage in Gothic rather than sentimental terms is not to say that Arthur finds his betrothed repugnant; rather, Brown is demonstrating how hard he has to work to make this particular couple fit into a contractual arrangement. To show that these two people are less than human in the Enlightenment sense, Brown inverts their gender roles (Achsa is masculinized, possessing more worldly experience and property than Arthur, who describes himself as "a mere woman" [398], prone to weepiness), and then uses Gothic tropes to describe an alliance that is awkwardly trying to fit into a contractual mold because its constituents do not meet sentimental standards of being.

Taking this argument one step further, we might suggest that Brown's novels are part of an established literary tradition that assaults the cultural institution of the self-contained, autonomous, static household to imagine community in the more dynamic terms of exchange, mobility, adaptation, reiteration, and circulation. Read's *Margaretta* (1807) and Leonora Sansay's *Secret History* (1808), for example, prove relentlessly skeptical about sentimental social relations on the grounds that they fail to take into account vast and heterogeneous groups of people who, dispersed across a wide geographic area, ostensibly lack the requisite qualities of autonomy, self-ownership, and national affiliation that underwrite civil society. In *Secret History*, characters come to us as representatives of mass populations (slaves, rebels, refugees, Creoles, women, children, the elderly, etc.) that have been scattered across the Caribbean. They are vulnerable in their lack of paternal protection and constantly on the move for lack of a home to which they can return. Much like Sansay's beleaguered Clara St. Louis, Read's Margaretta is transferred through multiple points of exchange in a series of erotic transactions that mirror the novel's geographic displacements from the United States to the Caribbean to Britain. In both novels, social relations are defined less in terms of nation, origin, or the household to which their protagonists belong than in those of the cultural information to which people are granted access as they circulate through a massive Atlantic world characterized by displacement, slavery, heterogeneous cultures, and altogether different notions of political subjecthood. Put another way, Sansay and Read put Brown's skepticism about domestic social relations to work in a cosmopolitan, transatlantic context.

Circling back, Brown's Gothic novels likewise imagine early American society as porous and contingent on its constituents' unimpeded movement through different cultural spheres in an international network of exchange. Brown's Gothic protagonists are almost always adaptable and protean: Ormond and Martinette adopt different names and guises at will; Arthur's superficial affability allows him to negotiate and exploit Philadelphia's different social milieus; Carwin appeals to the Wielands through managed social performance; both Carwin and Sarsefield prove particularly adept at religious conversion when expediency demands it; and Edgar incorporates himself somatically and culturally into the Delaware wilderness when he sheds his Quaker pacifism and turns Indian killer. That these protagonists find themselves at the novels' end outside a conventional domestic sphere—whether through death (Ormond), exile (Carwin), a self-imposed refusal to join (Edgar), or marrying a masculinized, racialized woman and thereby neatly inverting the conditions of conventional sentimental marriage (Arthur)—tells us that their constitutive restlessness is at odds with an American identity imagined in terms of stasis, enclosure within a household, or return to a point of origin.

To my mind, Brown's skepticism about the political economy of sentimentalism reverberates across American imaginative writing throughout the long eighteenth century. From Carwin's obliteration of the Wieland household to the collapse of the Usher family to Captain Delano's racist faith in the harmonious relationship between master and slave, our most well-known Gothic set pieces arguably derive from the catastrophic consequences of mistaking others as autonomous, individuated subjects who respect the boundaries of self-ownership and then attempting through the operations of sympathy to incorporate them into a British domestic arrangement to which they prove invariably hostile. The novels of Brown and his contemporaries often confront this problem by rejecting assumptions about the commonality of feeling as misguided at best and downright dangerous at worst. Social relations are instead conceived as the spread of ideas, goods, and people across borders, forming networks of exchange that circulate through a vast, unpredictable geopolitical sphere.

Conventionally, Brown's desertion of the novel form after 1801 has been taken as a kind of conservative retrenchment, where incipient bourgeois respectability and the related demise of his youthful radicalism led him to reject the "terrific materials" and "wild narratives" (Brown 1807, 411–412) of his youth. To be sure, Brown made disparaging remarks about the conventionalities of sentimentalism and the redundancy of the popular costume Gothic: any hack, he jokes in "A Receipt for a Modern Romance," can insert a terrified female into a decrepit castle, fill it with bats, owls, and "ghosts dressed in white" (Brown 1798, 278), and call it a novel.[11] But it is equally possible that such dismissive remarks reflect Brown's increasing dissatisfaction with the possibilities of the novel form. As his career advanced, he continued to investigate the limits and possibilities of consensus history and objectivity by turning his attention to different kinds of historical representation, including plausible or revisionist histories, historical sketches, "found" documents, and reviews of contemporary provincial histories. This suggests that, for Brown at least, historiography surpassed the imaginative potential of the novel, and his preoccupation with producing a national literature made him return to prenovelistic, historiographic forms of writing. If we broadcast this skepticism about the novel form across pre-1820 literary culture more widely, we can see that writers beyond Brown had similar concerns about the viability of the novel and the sorts of stories it was supposed to tell. In making such a claim, it is not my intention to circle back to the formal-generic argument that the novel in the New World was somehow an artistic failure. Far from it. Rather, we need to recalibrate the critical gauges by which we have conventionally measured the success of imaginative writing in the early republic. In doing so, we can see Brown less as a paternal forefather or nationalistic trailblazer and more as a skilled editorial and authorial relay, transmitting and redirecting the multi-variable generic disruptions and fragmentations characteristic of novelistic culture in early America.

Notes

1. Some sections of this chapter are modified from my Broadview Press edition of *Edgar Huntly* (2018). They are reproduced here by permission of Broadview Press.
2. As Lillie Deming Loshe recognized as early as 1907, so much of the writing that appeared in periodicals "is left unsigned, so little scruple is felt at borrowing from foreign sources, or from one American magazine to another, that a formidable tangle of possible authorships awaits any venturesome person who may undertake to investigate the early America short story, or its forerunners" (16). Thankfully, a few venturesome persons are now undertaking just such work; see, for instance, Gardner and also White and Faherty's online project Just Teach One.
3. I am indebted to Matthew Pethers's incisive observation that we need "a more rigorous distinction between 'the novel in America' and 'the American novel' (wherein the former is not just a synonym for the latter)" (794).
4. There is a rich array of fluid novelistic forms from the period that are still excluded from literary histories of the novel because of their so-called factual content (J. Hector St. John de Crèvecoeur's *Letters from an American Farmer* is a case in point). On the relationship between colonial historiography and the novel form, see Drexler and White; Larkin.
5. Koenigs and Lukasik provide helpful overviews of eighteenth-century debates over novel reading. For Brown's own discussions of the moral value of novel reading, see especially "A Student's Diary" (1804).
6. Literary evidence suggests that American readers had no difficulty reconciling calls for a sui generis nationalistic tradition with the transplantation and adaptation of imported cultural forms and an insistently global perspective, as the prefaces to Royall Tyler's *The Algerine Captive* (1797) and Isaac Mitchell's 1811 edition of *The Asylum* suggest. On the relationship between the early novel and Old World forms more generally, see Tennenhouse; Woertendyke; Tawil (2006/2007); Silyn Roberts.
7. On the contemporary debates over the differences between the romance, history, and related narrative forms such as the historical novel, the travel narrative, and the secret history, see especially Woertendyke; Baym.
8. As Shapiro puts it, Brown imagines the romance as "hypothetical ratiocination: a narrative experiment that explores the possible preconditions for historical events" and, as such, seeks to "guide the reader's social interaction and future planning" (220). Along similar lines, Gardner has argued that Brown's preoccupation in novels such as *Jane Talbot* or *Arthur Mervyn* with the difficulties of passing judgment in a world of "necessarily unreliable representation" suggests a more collaborative world of making meaning, where to "refuse *all* judgments, all loading up of the evidence one way or another," reframes the novel form itself "as a collection of fragments" and, therefore, "a truly neutral history" (22). On Brown's historiographic theories, see especially Kamrath.

9. See Dillon.

10. On the intersection of imagination, narrative, and this kind of associative excess, see especially Cahill.

11. It is highly likely, but not definitively established, that "A Receipt for a Modern Romance" was written by Brown. He certainly published it in the *Monthly Magazine* while he was the editor there.

Works Cited

"A Citizen of Philadelphia." *Adventures in a Castle.* Harrisburg, J. Elder, 1806.

"An American Lady." *St. Herbert, a Tale.* Windsor, VT: Thomas M. Pomroy, 1813.

Anonymous, *Amelia: or, the Faithless Briton.* Boston: W. Spotswood and C. P. Wayne, 1798.

Anonymous. *The Story of Constantius and Pulchera; or, Constancy Rewarded.* Salem, Mass.: T. C. Cushing, 1795.

Baym, Nina. *Feminism and American Literary History: Essays.* New Brunswick, N.J.: Rutgers University Press, 1992.

Brodhead, Richard. *Cultures of Letters: Scenes of Reading and Writing in Nineteenth-Century America.* Chicago: University of Chicago Press, 1993.

Brooks, David. "The Idea of a Psychoanalytic Literary Criticism." *Critical Inquiry* 13.2 (1987): 334–348.

Brown, Charles Brockden. *Edgar Huntly; or, Memoirs of a Sleepwalker.* Edited by Siân Silyn Roberts, Broadview Press, 2018.

Brown, Charles Brockden. "For the Literary Magazine: On the Cause of the Popularity of Novels." LM 7.45 (June 1807): 410–412.

Brown, Charles Brockden. "A Receipt for a Modern Romance." WM 2.22 (June 1798): 278.

Brown, Charles Brockden. "A Student's Diary." LM 1.5 (February 1804): 323–328; LM 1.6 (March 1804): 403–408.

Burroughs, Stephen. *Memoirs of the Notorious Stephen Burroughs of New Hampshire.* New York: Dial Press, 1924.

Butler, James. *Fortune's Foot-ball: or, the Adventures of Mercutio.* Harrisburg: John Wyeth, 1797.

Butler, Judith. *Precarious Life: The Powers of Mourning and Violence.* London: Verso, 2006.

Cahill, Ed. *Liberty of the Imagination: Aesthetic Theory, Literary Form, and Politics in the Early United States.* Philadelphia: University of Pennsylvania Press, 2012.

Dillon, Elizabeth Maddock. "Obi, Assemblage, Enchantment." *J19: The Journal of Nineteenth-Century Americanists* 1.1 (2013): 172–178.

Drexler, Michael, and Ed White. "Literary Histories." In Shirley Samuels, ed., *A Companion to American Fiction, 1780–1865,* 147–157. Hoboken, N.J.: Wiley-Blackwell, 2006.

Emerson, Amanda. "The Early American Novel: Charles Brockden Brown's Fictitious Historiography." *Novel: A Forum on Fiction* 40.1/2 (Fall 2006/Spring 2007): 125–150.

Foster, Hannah Webster. *The Coquette* (1797). Carla Mulford, ed. New York: Penguin, 1996.

Frye, Northrop. *Anatomy of Criticism: Four Essays.* Princeton, N.J.: Princeton University Press, 1957.

Gardner, Jared. *The Rise and Fall of Early American Magazine Culture.* Champaign: University of Illinois Press, 2014.

Kamrath, Mark L. *The Historicism of Charles Brockden Brown: Radical History and the Early Republic.* Kent, Ohio: Kent State University Press, 2010.

Koenigs, Tom. "Fictionality Risen: Early America, the Common Core Curriculum, and How We Argue about Fiction Today." *American Literature* 89.2 (2017): 225–253.

Kollock, Shepard. "A True Narrative of the Sufferings of Mary Kinnan." In Kathryn Zabelle Derounian-Stodola, ed., *Women's Indian Captivity Narratives*, 105–116. New York: Penguin, 1998.

Larkin, Ed. "The Cosmopolitan Revolution: Loyalism and the Fiction of an American Nation." *Novel: A Forum on Fiction* 40.1/2 (Fall 2006/Spring 2007): 52–76.

Loshe, Lillie Deming. *The Early American Novel, 1789–1830*. New York: Columbia University Press, 1907.

Lukasik, Christopher. *Discerning Characters: The Culture of Appearance in Early America*. Philadelphia: University of Pennsylvania Press, 2011.

Mitchell, Isaac. *The Asylum*. Poughkeepsie, N.Y.: Joseph Nelson, C.C. Adams & Co., Printers, 1811.

Pethers, Matthew, et al. "21st-Century Studies in the Early American Novel: A Roundtable on the Thirtieth Anniversary of Cathy N. Davidson, *Revolution and the Word: The Rise of the Novel in America* (New York: Oxford University Press, 1986)." *Journal of American Studies* 50 (2016): 779–824.

Read, Martha. *Margaretta; or, the Intricacies of the Human Heart*. Charleston: Edmund Morford, 1807.

Read, Martha. *Monima; or, The Beggar Girl*. New York: Johnson, 1802.

Rush, Rebecca. *Kelroy: A Novel* (1812). Dana D. Nelson, ed. New York: Oxford University Press, 1992.

Sansay, Leonora. *Secret History; Or, the Horrors of St. Domingo*. Ed. Michael Drexler. Ontario: Broadview Press, 2007.

Shapiro, Stephen. *The Culture and Commerce of the Early American Novel: Reading the Atlantic World-System*. University Park: Pennsylvania State University Press, 2008.

Silyn Roberts, Siân. *Gothic Subjects: The Transformation of Individualism in American Fiction 1790–1860*. Philadelphia: University of Pennsylvania Press, 2014.

Tawil, Ezra. "New Forms of Sublimity: *Edgar Huntly* and the European Origins of American Exceptionalism." *Novel: A Forum on Fiction* 40.1/2 (2006/2007): 104–124.

Tawil, Ezra. *Literature, American Style: The Originality of Imitation in the Early Republic*. Philadelphia: University of Pennsylvania Press, 2018.

Tennenhouse, Leonard. *The Importance of Feeling English: American Literature and the British Diaspora 1750–1850*. Princeton, N.J.: Princeton University Press, 2007.

Tyler, Royall. *The Algerine Captive; or, The Life and Adventures of Doctor Updike Underhill* (1797). Toronto: Modern Library, 2002.

Watt, Ian. *The Rise of the Novel*. Berkeley: University of California Press, 1957.

Watterston, George. *Glencarn; or, the Disappointments of Youth*. Alexandria: Cottom and Stewart, 1810. White, Ed, and Duncan Faherty. Just Teach One. January 20, 2017. http://jto. common-place.org/just-teach-one-homepage.

Woertendyke, Gretchen. "Romance to History: A Secret History." *Narrative* 17.3 (2009): 255–273.

Wood, Susan Sayward Barrell Keating. *Julia and the Illuminated Baron. A Novel: Founded on Recent Facts, Which Have Transpired in the Course of the Late Revolution of Moral Principles in France, by A Lady of Massachusetts*. Portsmouth: New Hampshire, Oracle Press, 1800.

CHAPTER 29

....

BROWN AND CLASSICISM

....

OLIVER SCHEIDING

THE legacy of classical antiquity was crucial in shaping the new republic. Not only historians but also literary scholars have recognized the persistence of the classical world that mesmerized American life and thought in post-Revolutionary America (see Reinhold). While some studies discuss early American writers and their familiarity with the works of classical literature, no systematic attempt has ever been made to explore Charles Brockden Brown's intimacy with classicism. Given his education, Brown was quite conversant with the canon of Greek and Latin literature, although he distanced himself from the "pedantic nonsense" of classical learning and the "perpetual allusions" to the muses caused by the new republic's classical craze.[1] Contrary to these "vain pursuits" in pedagogy (Brown, "On Classical Learning," 257), Brown embraced the classical tradition in English literature to a great extent, as can be seen from his many references to Greek and Roman historiographers, poets, and philosophers. Brown had a special interest in ancient characters and events, which he took as examples to study "the mechanism of human society, and the principle of human nature" (Brown, "Classical Learning No Anti-Christian Tendency," 187). Besides, Brown's retelling of ancient events and his portraits of classical figures questioned central maxims in the writing of history which derived from Cicero and had been practiced by the later school of eighteenth-century exemplary historiography. While Brown's classicism has been frequently interpreted along the line of the growing political tensions in the 1790s, his adaptations of classical sources are motivated less by a partisan spirit than by Brown's understanding of himself as a civic commentator and public intellectual. In his tales and essays on ancient events, he scrutinizes "the errors and calamities of mankind" (Brown, "Parallel," 92). Brown's Roman stories and his numerous essays on topics related to classical antiquity have to be seen as an intervention in the formation and enlargement of public opinion in the early national period.

Brown's treatment of classical antiquity derives from a twofold motivation: on the one hand, as a writer of prose who styles himself a "moral painter" (EH 3), he is very much interested in the narrative dimension of classical historiography; on the other hand, as an editor of numerous magazines who converses with the public and molds its opinion, he assumes the role of a mediator governed by reason who thus avoids the extremes of "enthusiasm and popular passions" (Brown, "Joan of Arc," 227). In his magazine essays, such as "A Modern Socrates" (1800) or "On the Merits of Cicero" (1805), Brown promotes such figures as Socrates (469–399 BCE) and Titus Pomponius Atticus (110–32 BCE), rediscovered and celebrated for their nondogmatic character and universal attitude by eighteenth-century Enlightenment thinkers. Brown's portraits of these classical figures offer examples to a people needing guidance in times of an expanding public and the democratization of its opinion and, together with his Roman stories, join the battle over truth and liberty of thinking that dominate the public sphere in the opening years of the nineteenth century (cf. Warner, 152–173).

Brown's preoccupation with classicism is, however, not guided by the neoclassical principle of imitation. He challenges "the idolatrous tendency of classical education" ("Classical Learning No Anti-Christian Tendency," 191) and questions the zeitgeist that aims at "perfect Writing by imitating the engraved Copies" (Franklin 81). In addition, as Gordon Wood aptly puts it, "in the eighteenth century to be enlightened was to be interested in antiquity, and to be interested in antiquity was to be interested in republicanism" (Wood 100). While his contemporaries considered studying the history of the ancient republics as a moral exercise since it provided examples for civic virtue and disinterestedness, Brown subordinates his Roman stories to the world of romance.[2] In opposition to classical modes of explanation, such as a cyclical understanding of the course of history, Brown provokes a new model of representation based on what he calls "filling up the outline sketched by the best historians, amplifying and drawing out the unnoticed parts, charming the attention by minute details, and filling the fancy by luminous displays of actions and motives" ("Joan of Arc," 227). In his readings of ancient history, he is therefore obsessed with the "deficiencies of history" (227). In his historical tales and essays, Brown thus offers his readers alternative views on well-known ancient events and characters. He provides examples of diverse and multiple truths and forces his readers to rely on their private judgment. In general, Brown's writings contribute to the democratization of mind in the early national period. His excursions into the world of classical antiquity ultimately unfold analogies allowing the reader to realize the contingent forces that govern the course of modern history.[3]

I. Brown's Essayistic Writings and Classical Antiquity

Like David Hume, Edward Gibbon, and William Robertson, the eighteenth-century historians he admired most, Brown considers himself a "narrator of great events" ("Parallel," 92). For Brown, the historiography of classical antiquity is a storehouse of tales and characters to be used by the modern writer in order to explain "the progress of society" ("Joan of Arc," 226). Unlike other writers of his age, who follow neoclassical premises and simply copy their exempla from ancient sources, Brown rearranges past events in light of present conditions and develops a particular interest in periods of revolutionary change such as the fall of the Roman republic or the late antiquity. This can be seen in two of the first American historical short stories written by him, "Thessalonica: A Roman Story" (1799) and "Death of Cicero, A Fragment" (1800). Rather than being political allegories that disclose Brown's partisanship for one of the political camps of the time or present him as a "Federalist in making" (Levine 15–75; see Merz), his Roman stories are literary case studies in which he experiments with "fictitious narratives" (Brown, "Joan of Arc," 226) to provoke "moral and political instruction" (227). Brown goes beyond the "propagation of slavish maxims and national delusions" (226) that characterizes the literary market and its epic output. By contrast, in his Roman stories, Brown creates a democratic prose seeking to avoid the "frigid, indirect, and feeble manner" (229) of the epic's limiting and determining world view.

In "A Modern Socrates," Brown hints at one of the central principles that sustain his narratives. It also demonstrates the reason for Brown's forays into the history of classical antiquity. Since Socrates "talked to mankind, and reformed their errors, upon subjects in which all of them, from king to peasant, had an equal concern" (Brown, "Modern Socrates," 326), Brown advocates a history from below that has a strong emphasis on human affairs. Like other eighteenth-century intellectuals before him, Brown heralds Socrates as a human being and martyr of "beneficial truths" ("Joan of Arc," 227). It is of no relevance to him whether pagan history provides false examples that misguide the young republic's citizens, an issue hotly debated among Brown's contemporaries. In his essay "Classical Learning No Anti-Christian Tendency" (1805), he criticizes zealous value judgments and narrow-minded conclusions concerning the utility of classical learning.[4] Brown recognizes the human aspects of Socrates's character and admires his autonomous and liberal thinking that shuns any kind of political and religious orthodoxy. In light of a clamorous partisan press and its alarmist rhetoric of factionalism, Brown uses Socrates to establish his position as an editor choosing a middle ground among the contending political forces that seek to manipulate the public opinion in the early national period. Brown concludes his essay on the following note:

> The success of the *Spectator* is a proof, that in the most factious and corrupt times, a daily paper may widely circulate and be much read, which yet is not a paper of news. As the world then could be brought to listen to one who told them nothing of the price of stocks, the proceedings of parliament, and the events of the campaign; who never suffered tories or whigs, republicans or jacobites, to dispute with him; who never praised or censured Bolingbroke or Marlborough, so at this day, it only wants wit, eloquence and learning, to be joined with benevolence and knowledge of men, to captivate all ears, without mentioning Adams or Jefferson; without inveighing against aristocrats or jacobins; without relating sea-fights in the West Indies, or battles on the Rhine.   ("Modern Socrates," 328)

In the heated climate of partisanship after 1800, Brown's search for a neutral ground becomes obvious in a number of essays on Cicero and Atticus, the intimate friend of the Roman orator. For these essays, Brown borrows from many sources and, in doing so, seeks to participate in a revival of classical writers caused by the establishment of William Poyntell's Classic Press in 1802. While Cicero has been favorably received and ardently praised for his "principles of nature and eternal reason" (Adams 12), which were central to the American Revolutionary rights, Brown abstains himself from all sorts of idealization. Following Plutarch's model of parallel lives, he compares both characters in "On the Merits of Cicero." The idea behind this essay derives from Brown's earlier reading of a British journal in which the editors summarize Johann Heinrich Samuel Formey's *Considerations on the Second Tusculan of Cicero, concerning Pain* (1785; see Anonymous 594–595). There Cicero is presented as a "poor philosopher" (Brown, "On the Merits," 368), an idea that Brown develops further in his essay by drawing the reader's attention to the "pompous" (368) and "extravagant" (369) arguments of the Roman orator. Although Brown copies the critique on Cicero's reflections from the *Monthly Magazine*, his own thoughts on Cicero's "[v]anity" (369) frame the essay. He ends it by sketching Atticus as the "wisest man of Cicero's times," who has been "quite superior to the meretricious charms of power or popularity" (369). His final warning against "the Ciceros and Brutuses of the age" (369) has been frequently read as a sign of Brown's growing conservative mind. However, it is in such statements that Brown positions himself as an editor whose miscellanies stay in the middle ground between political extremes. The nondogmatic character of Atticus is a label Brown uses to claim a distinct nonpartisan profile for *The Literary Magazine, and American Register*, a place for dispassionate public brokerage which distinguishes itself from the "restless patriots" (Brown, "Character," 333) and their divisive political agendas.

In the companion pieces "Ciceronians" (1805) and "The Character of Atticus" (1806), Brown's unbroken effort to function as a mediating voice in forging public opinion becomes obvious. Brown's triple set of Ciceronian essays also shows his embedding technique. The argumentation is twofold. First, it criticizes the "votaries of Cicero" as a bunch of pedantic followers who ardently idealize the works of Cicero and defend "all his opinions, moral, political, and critical, to be infallibly true" ("Ciceronians," 405). This line of thought Brown borrows from reading Isaac Disraeli's *Miscellanies: or, Literary Recreations* (1796), a source he has frequently visited for ideas and reprints. Brown disembeds a footnote he has found in an essay on imitation by Guillaume Colletet (1598–1659) in which the French writer mocks the myopic and doctrinaire scholarship of the Ciceronians in monumentalizing their master. In a second step, Brown rearranges this information by blending it into his own reflections on the doubtful reception of Cicero's work. Brown contends:

> Cicero's good fortune manifested itself not only in the preservation of so many of his own works, but likewise in the total destruction of the works of those who were his rivals while he lived. All the dialogists, letter writers, and orators of the same age have perished, and have thus enabled Cicero to monopolize all the fame which they might have otherwise shared with him.   ("Ciceronians," 405)

The idea of monopolizing the truth through questionable reconstructions of past characters and events is repeated in "The Character of Atticus." The main part contains a reprint of a character sketch Brown had found earlier in an issue of the *Spectator*

(1712; see Budgell 447). The original sketch alludes to the difficulties in obtaining reliable information about Cicero's dialogue partner. Since Atticus's own works are lost, particularly his Roman history, posterity only knows about him by what is filtered through Cicero's letters or found in Cornelius Nepos's biography written while Atticus was still alive. Brown's essay follows the speculative type of essay frequently practiced in the pages of the *Spectator* by adding to the reprint a visionary note on Atticus's "wisdom and sagacity" (333). Brown's commentary encourages readers to adopt a critical and analytical attitude toward classical sources, rather than simply approaching them with reverence. Brown's essays ultimately evoke alternative scenarios that challenge the reader to revision conventional and universally accepted truths and world views.

II. Brown's Historical Sketch on Cicero

Besides this series of thematically related essays, Brown has written the historical tale "Death of Cicero, A Fragment," which shows another programmatic side of his classicism.[5] Brown's Roman story reconstructs the last days of the orator's life. The whole case is presented in a letter to Atticus written by Cicero's former slave Tiro. The story echoes Brown's skepticism about exemplary historiography being the predominant mode of the interpretation of history in the early republic. Interpretations of the past primarily relied on the implication that the formation of civilizations evolves in patterns of development, such as the rise and fall of republics, and that the endless repetition of such patterns allows for a comparison from which essential lessons for the present can be deduced. Brown's "Death of Cicero" challenges the widely accepted reading of the history of the classical republics as models that should be emulated. Furthermore, as an exercise in fictitious history, Brown's historical tale functions as a disclaimer of his essay "Walstein's School of History" (1799), in which he expounds on the idea of exemplary historiography and in which he problematizes its implicit claim of the exemplarity of the past.

While the essays mirror the comparative model of parallel lives, "Death of Cicero" functions as a counterpoise to "Walstein." Brown's Roman story is a testing of the validity of exemplary readings of the past, to which Walstein, the fictitious historian in his essay, had so enthusiastically subscribed. Read in terms of a comparison, the tale can be viewed as a text that challenges the contemporaneous reader's didactic notion of history. In "Walstein," Brown focuses on a fictitious professor of history and head of a school of young historians. This professor employs the theory of exemplary history as a guiding principle for two biographies of famous people that are supposed to serve the contemporaneous reader's moral edification. Walstein "composes" exemplary history and transforms, for instance, Cicero's biography into his exemplary narrative, "[T]he Life of Cicero" (Walstein 336). Walstein echoes the classical idea of exemplary history as it can be found in Plutarch's *Lives* with its paired biographies of illustrious Greeks and Romans. According to Walstein, the utility of exemplary historiography is based on its inductive method, its didactic purpose, and the authority of the classical rhetoricians' and historians' "portraits of human excellence" (337).

Brown's historical tale deals with Cicero, who helped to shape the method of exemplary history. For Cicero, history is the "witness of the past," the "light shed on truth," the "life-giving force to recollection," the "guide to life," and the "herald of ancient days" (Cicero I, book II, ix). It was the orator's duty to commit the truth of history to immortality by giving exemplary lessons for individual and public emulation. According to this definition, history turned into a narrative of instruction primarily because it was founded on truth. Writers insisted on the truth behind the narratives of exemplary lives, thus advocating an attitude that classical antiquity had regarded as the very core of the concept of exemplarity, an attitude that was then carried on in post-Revolutionary America by such representative thinkers and politicians as Alexander Hamilton, James Madison, and John Jay. The authors of *The Federalist Papers* (1788) regarded the models taught by exemplary history as "factual" evidence of the viability of the republican principles on which the future nation should be constructed, and they pointed out that the historical lessons drawn were not merely didactic fabrications founded "in speculation or conjecture" but had to be seen as "illustrations of [history's] truth" (Madison, Hamilton, and Jay 158). As the history of classical antiquity provided a rich quarry of authentic and usable examples, it was considered the empirical basis of the republican concepts that defined the national project in the early republic.

Walstein's "Life of Cicero" reflects the prevalent mode of historical thinking in the early republic. As Walstein wants to use *his* Cicero as a means of making republican virtues plausible to his readers, he seeks to give a "deeper insight into human nature, a more accurate acquaintance with the facts, more correctness of arrangement" (Walstein 337–338). His "Life of Cicero" is addressed to Atticus, the most intimate of Cicero's friends. Atticus actually plays an important role in Cicero's own writing, but in Walstein's "biography" of Cicero, he primarily serves as a reflector figure through which the modern reader's own questions and interests are voiced. Walstein's imitation of the Socratic dialogue between master and pupil underscores the instructive strategy of his own "imaginary history" (337). Walstein tries to fuse the "genuine productions of Cicero" (337) with real and invented facts, which "are either collected from the best antiquarians, or artfully deduced from what is known, or invented with a boldness more easy to admire than to imitate" (338). Walstein's historical narrative claims to tell the "elementary truths of morals and politics" (336); his historian becomes a "moral reasoner" (336) who discovers universal principles. Exemplary history forms a happy union of instruction and entertainment since it paints "[n]ew and striking portraits...of the great actors on the stage. New lights are cast upon the principal occurrences. Every where are marks of profound learning" (337). The historical example serves to highlight the fact that truth can be found in history, and thus, Walstein's "Life of Cicero" adds to the contemporary notion of history as an already authentic collection of examples capable of guiding the citizens' conduct for the public good.

In contrast to Walstein's biographical narrative of Cicero as an exemplary hero, the tale "Death of Cicero" focuses on the highly uncertain events that surround the final stages of the Roman's life, namely, the events that allegedly happened after his flight from Astura until his death as an outcast. Moreover, in the tale, Atticus no longer functions as the official "attestor of [Cicero's] virtue, and his vindicator with posterity" (Walstein 337). Instead, the tale shifts its focus from Atticus to Tiro, a freed slave of Cicero's train who witnesses his master's death. Tiro's "faithful account" ("Death," 4) does not, however, eulogize Cicero's death as a reminder of a virtuous "great man's" commitment to the cause of the res publica and its fight against its enemies. In contrast to Walstein's account of a hero, Tiro rather "calumniate[s] the memory of Cicero" (48) when he seeks to analyze the motivations that led his master to "[throw] himself before the executioner" (46). Brown's historical tale reveals that Tiro is driven by contradictory impulses that, on the one hand, make him give a faithful report of the events and, on the other hand, force him to pay homage to his dead master and portray him as a heroic figure. As an eyewitness who feels obliged to convey "to his Atticus a faithful account of [Cicero's] death" (4) but who cannot even decipher his master's motivation, Tiro finally feels free to interpret his master's death in such a way that it may appear as a heroic deed. Brown's "Death of Cicero" makes the reader aware of the unavoidable partiality of the final interpretation that Tiro imposes on the events in order to make sense of history. Given the problems that Tiro, the eyewitness of Cicero's death, has in giving a faithful account of the events, Brown's historical tale becomes a counterexample that primarily (and somewhat paradoxically) "exemplifies" the very constructedness of historiography and thus subverts the premises on which its exemplarity is based.

Brown's "Death of Cicero" plays with the conflicting narratives of Cicero's assassination offered by the narrator as both initial eyewitness ("a powerless spectator of the deed" [42]) and later historian ("the remembrance of the duties, which his death would leave to be performed by me" [42]). The tale's narrative framework mirrors the juxtaposition of the two narrative approaches to the truth. Subsequently, the promise to relate a "faithful account," which Tiro gives early on in the narrative, and his epitaphlike conclusion reflect contradictory points of view. At the beginning, the eyewitness account relates Tiro's futile attempts at convincing his master to seek help from his loyal supporters in Asia, and in order to evoke an authentic immediacy (on the narrative level of the eyewitness account), the tale introduces several scenes in which the reader directly participates in the dialogue between Cicero and Tiro. Tiro's advice is influenced by his belief in the efficacy of his master's former deeds and his hopes that posterity will judge his master according to the res gestae. As a "powerless spectator," Tiro repeatedly muses on the effects of an overtly "ignominious and detestable" (25) death: "What indignities would not be heaped upon [Cicero's] lifeless remains!... the endless theme of ridicule and mockery?" (35). According to the historical logic to which Tiro adheres, his master will be written off by history.

Tiro eventually succeeds in persuading his master to leave Italy. However, it is too late. Cicero has been betrayed by one of his servants, and he is killed during the final escape. At the end of the tale, Tiro's narrative perspective shifts from the immediacy of an eyewitness account to a mode of retrospective interpretation. Tiro begins to "muse upon the events that led to this disaster" (45). He fulfills the task of a historian whose "duties" are to "remember" the "mutilated figure" (44) of Cicero. To perform his duty of "remembrance" (42) and in order to give a conclusive account of his master's last "deed" (42), he has to explain his master's motivation in a plausible way. By so doing, however, his own subjective perception of the events as eyewitness and his retrospective "duties" as "remembrancer" collide. His narrative performance as eyewitness unfolds his limited understanding of the events and the internal causes that finally "led" to Cicero's death. Although he has been the most intimate companion of Cicero, he is finally unable to solve the enigmatic conduct of his master, who, "perceiving the approach of the tribune, held forth his head, as if to facilitate the assassin's office" (43).

Tiro ultimately feels the need to downplay Cicero's aged cowardice by highlighting his master's exemplary virtue as a public orator and a tragic hero in history. His retrospective musings on the events contradict, however, his initial heroic interpretation of the immediate causes that led to Cicero's death. On the one hand, Tiro still cannot find an answer to the question "Was there cowardice or error in refusing to mingle in the tumults of war?" (48); on the other hand, he offers explanations that are not substantiated by his own narrative. At first, he reasons that it "seemed as if [Cicero's] most flagitious folly, had given birth to this insupportable evil" (45), only to question immediately afterward his master's character as a model of right conduct: "But was not Cicero himself the author of his evil destiny? Irresolute, desponding or perverse, he thwarted or frustrated the measures conducive to his safety" (21). Subsequently, Tiro unfolds an alternative course of events that might have happened had Cicero spoken to the enemy with all his rhetorical ingenuity. Before completely damaging his master's reputation, however, Tiro offers a reconciliatory interpretation of the events. He draws on the notion of Cicero as a tragic hero who is inevitably destined to be "crushed" in the "ruins" of the empire. Tiro stresses the fact that even if Cicero had escaped, he probably would have ended his life "lonely, succourless, in chains and immured in a dungeon" (48).

In the further course of the narrative, Tiro, however, storifies Cicero's death not so much in the fashion of the demise of an individual tragic figure but in terms of the fate of a representative of an entire civilization in a state of rapid decline. His emplotment finally discards all doubts concerning his master's allegedly "folly death" by offering a conclusive interpretation that stresses the fact that the purpose of all of Cicero's deeds "was the benefit of mankind" (48). Tiro constructs a synecdochic analogy between his master's destiny and the decline of the Roman Empire; he interprets the assassination of his master as part of the cyclical movement of the rise and fall of great empires.

But as Tiro's interpretation of Cicero's death seems to be primarily the result of a retrospective endeavor of glorification, which is not at all justified by Tiro's perception of the rather inscrutable events, the very notion that history as such (without the interposition of an interpretative mind) is the teacher of life is contested. Moreover, the title and subtitle of Brown's historical tale contradict Tiro's retrospective interpretation of events in terms of exemplary historiography. The tale's title, "Death of Cicero, A Fragment," can be read as the implied author's self-reflexive comment on and refutation of Tiro's original claim to give a "faithful account" of the events. Tiro narrates the events that "led" to Cicero's assassination in such a way that they finally foreground the "usefulness" (48) of exemplary figures in history. His objective is to tell "Death of Cicero." Contrary to Tiro's intention, the obtuse and "undefined" title, "Death of Cicero, A Fragment," completely undercuts the exemplary endeavor put forward by the narrator of the tale. The indeterminacy and incompleteness of the title implies the impossibility of "re-membering" the "mutilated" events of the past in a conclusive way that allows for an exemplary reading. The subtitle, "A Fragment," questions the authenticity of Tiro's eyewitness account as a sufficient basis for the tale's intended exemplary "usefulness."

III. Brown's Roman Story "Thessalonica"

The companion piece, "Thessalonica: A Roman Story," is another one of Brown's attempts to come to terms with notions of authenticity and "history proper" in reconstructing past events. At the center of the story is a well-known event of late antiquity, the massacre of Thessalonica that occurred in 390. Brown derived the idea for this tale from Edward Gibbon's *The History of the Decline and Fall of the Roman Empire* (1776–1788). Gibbon gives the following story repeating the traditional chronicle of events as it has been handed down by most ecclesiastical historiographies. Butheric,[6] a Roman military com-mander, arrested a popular charioteer for sexual offense. The people of Thessalonica demanded the charioteer's release. Since Butheric refused to succumb to the populace's will, a furious mutiny ensued in which he was killed. As soon as the emperor Theodosius heard of the revolt, he ordered a retaliation which led to the massacre of the city's inhab-itants. Brown's Roman story has frequently been read as an example of human misconduct that mirrors the tensions between the Federalists and Thomas Jefferson's "mobocracy."[7] Contextual readings of Brown's stories and tales overlook, however, the programmatic nature of many of his writings and the fact that Brown experiments with what he calls "approaches to the truth" (Walstein 336) in using a variety of fictitious forms.[8] Brown deviates from Gibbon's factual documentation of the event and reconstructs the massacre from two contradictory points of view, both contained within the narrative offered by the tale's narrator, the prefect Malchus. In doing so, Brown creates a double-voiced and highly disputative narrative discourse. Malchus begins the story by narrating in the third person and anonymously, and the apparently omniscient perspective of historiography frames the action. He starts his reconstructive endeavor with an extended description of the city's importance, based on historical facts. Gradually, however, the narrator reveals his subjective interpretation of past events. He utterly dislikes the "passions of the multitude" (Brown, "Thessalonica," 100) that threaten the "empire of order" (100). Commenting on Butheric's murder, he states: "The mob poured into the passages.... [T]hose who had been leaders in the tumult, conspired to engage them in the same outrages.... [T]he seats of the Senators were filled with a permiscuous crowd,... the fury of the populace it was impossible to foresee.... [T]he temper of the people was revengeful and sanguinary" (101).

Thus, Malchus's historiographic retrospections echo the Federalists' fears of "King Mob." Since they ardently believed in a cyclical progress of history, Jefferson's mob rule foreshadowed the decline of the republic. Likewise, this historiographic perspective ultimately explains the people's revolt and the ensuing massacre as part of a higher law that governs the course of history. Malchus concludes: "The horrors of this scene are only portions of the evil that has overspread the Roman world, which has been inflicted by the cavalry of Scythia, and which will end only in the destruction of the empire, and the return of the human species to their original barbarity" (117).

Brown's double-voiced narrative strategy, however, reveals the limitations of the historian's omniscient perspective. From paragraph 34–90 (104–112), the narrative begins to use the first-person "I" while mixing this voice with the third-person presentation. From paragraph 143 on (116–117), the narrator, using his first-person voice, reveals that he is, in fact, the prefect Julius Malchus who is often referred to in the same narrative in the third person. Thus, the reader is presented with a jarring juxtaposition of third- and first-person narrative perspectives that problematizes the historiographic framing that the story's beginning led the reader to expect. In the middle of the story, in paragraph 56 (106), Malchus states that his task is "to draw up a statement of truth, from such information as I had already received, or should speedily obtain" (106). While the historian believes that he has found "a memorable proof from what slight causes the most disastrous and extensive effect may flow" (108), the first-person Malchus is unable to find a plausible explanation that allows him to render a "statement of truth." While interrogating eye-witnesses in order to detect the cause of Butheric's death, he only receives highly inconsistent pieces of information. By further investigating the case, Malchus finally discovers that it was Butheric himself who had caused the tumult. Thus, the interpretation the reader receives from Malchus's first-person discourse differs from the one that emerges from his more distanced third-person discourse. He concludes: "It would transfer, in some degree, the guilt of the sedition from the people to their own order" (109). Contrary to the historian's attempt to give an accurate account of past events, Malchus's first-person remarks can only offer conjectures that are in "some degree" (109) true. Unlike the historian's totalizing explanations, the prefect fails to deliver "a faithful narrative" to "posterity" (117). Malchus remains a "dealer, not in certainties, but probabilities" (Difference 251).

Brown's Roman story illustrates the ways in which a constructive imagination works. In his essay "The Difference between History and Romance" (1800), Brown summarizes his narrative exercises in producing a historical text. He reasons: "They [useful narratives] must, commonly, consist of events, for a knowledge of which the narrator is indebted to the evidence of others. This evidence, though accompanied with different degrees of probability, can never give birth to certainty" (Difference 253). Likewise, Malchus provides a "disjointed and mutilated tale" ("Thessalonica," 104). His final confession ("my eloquence is too feeble to impart to others the conceptions of my own mind" [117]) reveals the programmatic nature of Brown's Roman stories. He uses fictitious narratives on the subject of ancient events to reflect on the manifold motives of human actions and the varying truths behind them. In doing so, Brown questions the historian's claim to offer the reader "memorable proofs." The didactic potential of classical exempla in providing instructive lessons for the present turns out to be highly ambivalent, since they only exemplify the impossibility of a narration of facts.

IV. CONCLUSION

Given Brown's focus on unreliability in his Roman stories, and given the intentional falsification of biography by means of a narrative in which Cicero, for instance, becomes an exemplary figure, his tales and essays on subjects related to ancient history have to be understood as counterexamples. If they exemplify anything, they demonstrate that history only makes sense because it is made according to preestablished models of world making. These models themselves make sense because they satisfy a culture's specific need for historical explanation. By juxtaposing the seemingly factual eyewitness account with the retrospective interpretation of the events, Brown's historical tales subvert the explanatory effect that historians commonly attempt to achieve in their representations of the past. Brown's use of contradictory narrative perspectives in the stories problematizes the authenticity of historiography. His stories expound on the collision between historical interpretation and the alleged factuality already found in historical data. They also show that this alleged factuality is only made "real" by an act of sense making.

Therefore, especially in light of the didactic purpose of literature at the time, one can see why Brown valued the ability of narratives to captivate and to illuminate the reader's imagination. Brown does not always present a fully developed idea in his essays but uses his writings for free reflection and associative connection. He is fascinated not with synthesis but with the contrasting of opposites, as can be seen in his Roman stories. He knew the limits of his own judgment and preferred that the reader use reflection as a means of insight. His classicism is thus paradoxically modern, as his essays and Roman stories connect the reader with specific ways of knowing the world, and at the same time, they prefigure new themes and techniques in the literary representation of the past, which turns Brown's miscellaneous writings into a productive field for reassessing literature's role in a democratic America.

NOTES

1. Brown entered the Friends Latin School in Philadelphia when he was eleven and was trained by Robert Proud for five years. As Brown never received a college education, most of his reading remains unsystematic; in his essays on classicism, he often echoes contemporary intellectual trends. Nevertheless, he very early formed his own opinion on the limited usefulness of ancient languages. In the 1792 epistolary fiction known as the "Henrietta Letters," Brown's character advises his female interlocutor: "I cannot admit that the knowledge of Ancient languages are otherwise to be esteemed than as they humanise the heart and polish the Understanding, and though I am sincerely of opinion that it does not merit even this

encomium, which indeed I must confess to be extremly high, yet I am willing to bestow it but must ask whether the study of British French or Italian literature is not equally conducive to the same end" (Letters 695).

2. According to the classical model, historical examples function both as an investigation of the historical circumstances of exemplary men and as a description of the particular virtues that one is supposed to imitate in the present. Investigation and description are closely related to the narration of the exemplum as a story that, on the one hand, offers a putative and plausible report of past events, while, on the other hand, it interprets the past in such a way that it gains an instructive appeal; see Scheiding 2003, 40–56.

3. On Brown and historiography, see Kamrath.

4. Besides his private journal and letters, this is one of the few essays in which Brown refers to his own training in ancient languages and literature (189). For the debate on education, see Cody 106–113; Moroney 295–307).

5. The story was originally published as an appendix to the second edition of Brown's novel *Edgar Huntly* (1800). For a detailed interpretation, see Scheiding 1998, 39–50; cf. Barnard and Shapiro ix–xlvi.

6. "Butheric" is the spelling used in modern scholarship; Brown and Gibbon use the spelling "Botheric."

7. See, for instance, Watts 170–177; for a more recent interpretation of the story that "call[s] into question some 'positive' forms of manhood in the early republic," see Slawinski 63; cf. Scheiding 1997, 93–110.

8. Hume's influence can be seen in Brown's essay "Walstein's School of History," in which he states: "Actions and motives cannot be truly reflected. We can only make approaches to the truth" (Walstein 336). Hume holds that "[b]efore knowledge cou'd come to the first historian, it must be convey'd thro' many mouths" (Hume 145); for a comprehensive collection of Brown's tales, see Weber.

WORKS CITED

Adams, John. *Novanglus, and Massachusettensis; or Political Essays, Published in the Years 1772–1775*. Boston: Hew and Gross.

Anonymous. "Speculative Philosophy." *The Monthly Review, or Literary Journal* 81 (July–December 1789): 594–595.

Barnard, Philip, and Stephen Shapiro. "Introduction." In Charles Brockden Brown, *Wieland; or, the Transformation, An American Tale with Related Texts*, ix–xlvi. Indianapolis: Hackett, 2009.

Brown, Charles Brockden. "The Character of Atticus." LM 5.32 (May 1806): 332–333.

Brown, Charles Brockden. "Ciceronians." LM 3.21 (June 1805): 404–405.

Brown, Charles Brockden. "Classical Learning No Anti-Christian Tendency." LM 4.24 (September 1805): 185–191.

Brown, Charles Brockden. "Death of Cicero, A Fragment." In *Edgar Huntly; or, Memoirs of a Sleep-Walker. To Which Is Annexed,* The *Death of Cicero, a Fragment*, 3–48. Philadelphia: Maxwell, 1800.

Brown, Charles Brockden. "[Review of] Joan of Arc: An Epic Poem, by Robert Southey." MM 1.3 (June 1799): 225–229.

Brown, Charles Brockden. "A Modern Socrates: To the Editor of the Monthly Magazine." MM 2.5 (May 1800): 326–328.

Brown, Charles Brockden. "On Classical Learning." LM 3.19 (April 1805): 256–258.

Brown, Charles Brockden. "On the Merits of Cicero." LM 3.20 (May 1805): 368–369.

Brown, Charles Brockden. "Parallel between Hume, Robertson and Gibbon." MM 1.2 (May 1799): 90–94.

Brown, Charles Brockden. "Thessalonica: A Roman Story." MM 1.2 (May 1799): 99–117.

Budgell, Eustace. "No. 385. Thursday, May 22, 1712." In *The Spectator* [1712], 447. London: Isaac Tuckey, 1836.

Cicero, Marcus Tullius. *De Oratore*, 3 vols. E. W. Sutton and H. Rackham, eds. Cambridge, Mass.: Harvard University Press, 1967.

Clark, David Lee. *Charles Brockden Brown: Pioneer Voice of America*. Durham, N.C.: Duke University Press, 1952.

Cody, Michael. *Charles Brockden Brown and the Literary Magazine: Cultural Journalism in the Early Republic*. Jefferson, N.C.: McFarland, 2004.

Franklin, Benjamin. *The Autobiography of Benjamin Franklin*. Leonard W. Labaree, ed. New Haven, Conn.: Yale University Press, 1970.

Gibbon, Edward. *The History of the Decline and Fall of the Roman Empire*. 6 vols. London: I.W. Strahan and T. Cadell, 1776–1788.

Hume, David. *Treatise of Human Nature* (1739–1740). L. A. Selby-Bigge, ed. Oxford: Oxford University Press, 1978.

Kamrath, Mark L. *The Historicism of Charles Brockden Brown: Radical History in the Early Republic*. Kent, Ohio: Kent State University Press, 2010.

Levine, Robert S. *Conspiracy and Romance: Studies in Brockden Brown, Cooper, Hawthorne, and Melville*. Cambridge: Cambridge University Press, 1989.

Madison, James, Alexander Hamilton, and John Jay. *The Federalist Papers* (1788). Isaac Kramnick, ed. Harmondsworth, UK: Penguin, 1987.

Merz, Harald. *Charles Brockden Brown als politischer Schriftsteller*. Frankfurt am Main: Lang, 1994.

Moroney, Siobhan. "Latin, Greek and the American Schoolboy: Ancient Languages and Class Determinism in the Early Republic." *Classical Journal* 96.3 (February–March 2001): 295–307.

Reinhold, Meyer. *Classica Americana: The Greek and Roman Heritage in the United States*. Detroit: Wayne State University Press, 1984.

Scheiding, Oliver. *Geschichte und Fiktion: Zum Funktionswandel des frühen amerikanischen Romans*. Paderborn: Schöningh, 2003.

Scheiding, Oliver. "'Nothing but a Disjointed and Mutilated Tale': Zur narrativen Strategie der Doppelperspektive in Charles Brockden Browns historischer Erzählung 'Thessalonica: A Roman Story." *Literarisches Jahrbuch* 38 (1997): 93–110.

Scheiding, Oliver. "'Plena exemplorum est historia': Rewriting Exemplary History in Charles Brockden Brown's 'Death of Cicero.'" In Bernd Engler and Oliver Scheiding, eds., *Re-Visioning the Past: Historical Self-Reflexivity in American Short Fiction*, 39–50. Trier: Wissenschaftlicher Verlag, 1998.

Slawinski, Scott. *Validating Bachelorhood: Audience, Patriarchy, and Charles Brockden Brown's Editorship of the Monthly Magazine and American Review*. New York and London: Routledge, 2005.

Watts, Steven. *The Romance of Real Life: Charles Brockden Brown and the Origins of American Literature*. Baltimore and London: Johns Hopkins University Press, 1994.

Warner, Michael. *The Letters of the Republic: Publication and the Public Sphere in Eighteenth-Century America*. Cambridge, Mass.: Harvard University Press, 1990.

Weber, Alfred, ed. *Charles Brockden Brown: Somnambulism and Other Stories*. Frankfurt am Main: Peter Lang, 1987.

Wood, Gordon. *The Radicalism of the American Revolution*. New York: Vintage, 1991.

CHAPTER 30

BROWN'S STUDIES IN LITERARY GEOGRAPHY

MARTIN BRÜCKNER

Henri Lefebvre's assertion "that any search for space in literary texts will find it everywhere and in every guise," while intended as a critique, is an immensely productive proposition for readers of Charles Brockden Brown's prose (Lefebvre 15). Brown's texts—from his novels, historical sketches, and magazine essays to his translations and editorial work—explore a panoply of spaces. On the most rudimentary level, Brown's fiction and nonfiction construct literary spaces that are always already "enclosed, described, projected, dreamt of, speculated about" (Lefebvre 15). This applies to his literary spaces set in America, exhibiting the mid-Atlantic countryside and the city space of Philadelphia, urban mansions and country houses, the banks of the Schuylkill and the Delaware Rivers, and the Atlantic coast. And this applies to his stories set abroad, where Brown's settings involve European countries and where gazetteer-like references send characters on quixotic journeys visiting the Mississippi River and Cayenne, French Guiana; Sioux country in the American West and Paris, France; Lausanne, Switzerland, and Barcelona, Spain; and the deserts of Mongolia. In addition, Brown invokes geographical metaspaces, some of which are real, some mythical: the American continent and the nation-state; picturesque landscapes and geological formations; the "western wilderness" and "Indian-country"; the oceanic worlds of the Atlantic, Caribbean, and Pacific; and imaginary settings that include historical sites in ancient Rome, ancestral castles in medieval Great Britain, or a contemporaneous "Eutopia" in the South Pacific.

While many of these spaces reflect a spatial imagination that is representative of late-eighteenth-century literary sensibilities, Brown's writings not only imitate but frequently reimagine the role of literary spaces in startlingly self-conscious and modern ways. Brown does this most effectively by drawing attention to the literary and social function of man-made environments (pastures, gardens, streetscapes), natural environments (wilderness areas, geological formations, climate zones), or a combination of both (frontier housing, early suburbia, disaster zones). That said, Brown also questions the role of literary geographies by scrutinizing the sources of his spatial imagination.

The sources under scrutiny include the human body, its sensory experience of space, and its placement in the physical world; eighteenth-century aesthetic and social theories about land, property, and representation; political doctrines of territoriality and sovereignty; and Enlightenment fantasies of fixed spaces in the age of globalization. One source that is especially being put to the test and one that is crucial to many of Brown's spatial imaginings is the science of geography and its attending methods of creating spatial knowledge in the late eighteenth and early nineteenth centuries, in particular the encyclopedic geography book and the abstract image of the modern map.

Confronting the abundance of references to space, place, and geography, any project seeking to make sense of Brown's literary spaces faces a methodological dilemma. In order to assess Brown's spatial imagination, we have to understand that he wrote and published the bulk of his fiction in a short span of time. Between 1797 and 1801, he worked simultaneously (rather than successively) on six novels, several fictional sketches, and nonfiction essays. Because of this temporally compressed mode of literary production, a survey of Brown's literary use of space cannot readily apply the critical approaches provided by traditional literary history, especially approaches that emphasize progressive or evolutionary models of periodization, literary form, and genre. At the same time, however, scholars have demonstrated that Brown's literary work can be divided into two distinct periods marked by a paradigmatic shift: after 1801, having published the novel *Jane Talbot*, the author turned his literary energies noticeably away from the production of novels to that of magazines, from fiction to nonfiction, from inquiries into imaginative thinking to inquiries into classificatory thinking.[1]

While shifts like these have provided Brown scholarship with a source of argument about the classification of his work (as the father of the American Gothic, as the detached Romantic genius, as the polemicist pushing agendas such as feminism or expansionism), it must be noted that "geography" provided the proverbial bookends defining the author's literary life. Since his early childhood, and thus before producing the bulk of his work, Brown was known to eagerly recite geography lessons to anyone who cared to listen (Dunlap 1815, 7, 12–13). Toward the end of his life, after having completed the bulk of his fictional work, Brown's final project was a two-volume textbook, *A System of General Geography* (Bennett 219; Watts 164). In order, then, to best describe and interpret the spatial world invoked by Brown's writings, this chapter supplements the tools of cultural geography and spatial theory for those of literary analysis. The chapter pursues three goals: first, to provide a thematic survey of Brown's literary spaces; second, to describe key spatial concepts as they inform selected works; and third, to outline major shifts and continuities in Brown's spatial imaginary by tracing the use of geography across a body of work that spans two decades of writing and publishing in the early republic.

A survey of Brown's literary spaces must begin paradoxically with a disclaimer of traditional definitions of geography. Throughout the eighteenth century, theorists defined "geography" as "a description of the Earth" intent on "writing" or "drawing" (from the Greek *grapho*) "the nature, figure, and magnitude of the earth; the situation, extent and appearance of different parts of its surface; its productions and inhabitants" (Morse 24). In practice, the descriptions of spatial phenomena and artifacts were encyclopedic compilations that, always moving from the general to the particular, recorded everything from physical features of a country to cultural institutions of a town. Eighteenth-century literature—including magazines, histories, and travelogues— by and large embraced the encyclopedic model of spatial representation, applying it to descriptions of places, world events, or local customs (Bowen 154–170; Brückner 142–172).

However, readers of Brown's fiction and nonfiction will find it difficult to match up his literary spaces with a geographical universe predicated on authentic places or their empirical delineation. To be sure, Brown's major fiction makes a point of launching its plots and stories in familiar places. Most of his fiction is set in the region of eastern Pennsylvania, before branching out to other locations in the world. His best-known works—*Wieland* (1798), *Ormond* (1799), *Arthur Mervyn* (1799–1800), *Edgar Huntly* (1799), *Clara Howard* (1801), *Jane Talbot* (1801), and *Memoirs of Carwin the Biloquist* (1803–1805)—have characters who inhabit the greater region of Philadelphia, showing them to move freely between the city, suburbs, and countryside. But with the exception of *Arthur Mervyn* and *Ormond*, where specific landmarks and streets are identified, Brown's nominal geographical references are just that, literary spaces in name only, lacking those determinative vectors that allow readers to map Brown's singular settings onto particular geographies (Axelrod xix).

Consider the description of the setting of *Wieland*, the fictional country estate called Mettingen, which with Brown's use of a couple of place names must be imagined as one of the eighteenth-century mansions overlooking the banks of the Schuylkill River:

> At the distance of three hundred yards from his house, on the top of a rock whose sides were steep, rugged, and encumbered with dwarf cedars and stony asperities, he built what to a common eye would have seemed a summer-house. The eastern verge of this precipice was sixty feet above the river which flowed at its foot. The view before it consisted of a transparent current, fluctuating and rippling in a rocky channel, and bounded by a rising scene of cornfields and orchards.   (W 11)

Or let's consider the description of Brown's "rude retreats of Norwalk" in *Edgar Huntly*, an area resembling Pennsylvania's Great Valley region—more specifically, the tract of land acquired by British colonists from the Delaware people during the corrupt transaction of the "Walking Purchase" (Berthold 72–73; Kafer 173–175):

> The basis of all this region is *limestone*; a substance that eminently abounds in rifts and cavities. These, by the gradual decay of their cementing parts, frequently make their appearance in spots where they might have been least expected. My attention has often been excited by the hollow sound which was produced by my casual foot-steps, and which shewed me that I trod upon the roof of caverns. A mountain-cave and the rumbling of an unseen torrent, are appendages of this scene, dear to my youthful imagination. Many of romantic structure were found within the precincts of Norwalk.   (EH 22)

In both examples Brown's descriptions generate literary spaces that are, despite the use of abundant topographical detail, geographically indeterminate. Descriptions of "romantic structure[s]," such as cliffs, rivers, and caves, are literary geographies that render Brown's Pennsylvania indistinguishable from the settings used in Gothic fiction set in Italy or the south of France, as in Horace Walpole's *Castle of Otranto* or Ann Radcliffe's *Mysteries of Udolpho* or in romantic folk tales set in the mountains of central Germany such as Friedrich Schiller's play *Die Räuber (The Robbers)* and Ludwig Tieck's tale "Der Runenberg" ("Rune Mountain"). By contrast, the writing protocols of geography— and these protocols were embraced by the specialist and the reading public consisting of schoolchildren and armchair geographers—demanded descriptions of places that were determinate, empirical in observation, object-driven, and comparative, in short, written with the goal to generate the fullest and most accurate account of particular geographical phenomena (Brückner 1–15; Withers 167–233).

Readers who are invested in understanding Brown's geographies thus have to come to terms with a simple but important realization: if it were not for the use of place names, Brown's descriptive language would not lend itself to connecting his literary spaces to concrete, historically verifiable places. Nor does Brown's choice of language make his literary spaces distinctly "American" in the eighteenth-century sense of geographical writing. Instead, as suggested by his strategic call on "romantic structure," his mode of description anticipates a different kind of geography, one resembling the emerging nomenclature and methods of modern humanist geographers, such as Alexander von Humboldt and Carl Ritter. In their view, geography was a method of description ("Erdbeschreibung") intent on providing a comparative anatomy ("vergleichende Anatomie") of the earth; be it the mountains of Libya or Europe, or rivers such as the Niger and the Danube ("Ister"), discrete geographical features were considered interconnected organs of a universal geography (Ritter 21–22). Similarly, Brown approaches spatial settings like a physiologist and comparatist; he treats them perhaps not as organisms as such but as organic systems that can be assessed in two ways: according to organizational form (rather than specific attributes) and according to the settings' respective functions inside spatial systems. Brown's most recognizable spaces resemble conceptual categories that resonate with the traditional geographer's lexicon establishing spatial hierarchies and subdivisions. The categories are the country, the city, and habitations located somewhere between. But whereas in Enlightenment geographies these spaces tend to be fixed, as if anticipating the work of new humanist geographers, Brown's spaces are flexible; depending on plot or action, they can intersect or overlap, suddenly shift geographic connotations or jump spatial scales.

I. Country, Desert, Wilderness

Brown's fiction uses "country" somewhat loosely to signify the natural environment or rural areas showing signs of human activity; on occasion, the term can also refer to the nation-state ("our country"). Brown's spatial imagination carefully divides country into two distinct literary spaces: "cultivable space" and "desert" (EH 96). Spaces marked as "cultivable" contain the markers of an eighteenth-century agrarian society familiar to European and North American preindustrial audiences. These include shorthand references to "fields" and "orchards," "fences," and "roads" and descriptions of rural "settlements" ranging from rustic frontier houses to "spacious farms" to manorial estates (see Brown, "Somnambulism"; W; EH; AM; JT; Brown, "Trials of Arden"; MC). Brown's "cultivable space" is further defined by labels such as "township" or "district," which denote the political geography of modern land management. Other terms, such as "tract," "land," and "master's domain," point to a historical geography in which land is defined as property and thus as a space subject to legal codes and the laws of the marketplace.

The "desert" is Brown's signature space. "Admit[ting] neither plough nor spade" (EH 96), Brown's "desert" is a space not defined by extreme climate, as geographers would have it. Nor is the lack of human economic activities the central meaning of this space. Rather, elaborate topography is its central feature. Brown develops the literary space of the "desert" in settings called Norwalk in *Edgar Huntly*, Norwood in the short story "Somnambulism: A Fragment," and the nameless variant published in *Memoirs of Carwin*. All three share the following topographical elements: Norwalk is described as "a maze, oblique, circuitous, upward and downward, in a degree which only could take place in a region so remarkably irregular in surface, so abounding with hillocks and steeps, and pits and brooks...[on] the skirts of the wilderness" (EH 23). Norwood is "a desolate tract...a region, rude, sterile, and lonely, bestrewn with rocks, and embarrassed with bushes" ("Somnambulism," 343). And Carwin discovers his skill of ventriloquism in "a tract" of land marked by "abrupt points and gloomy hollows," where narrow passes, river glens, and steep paths turn the country into a "maze" (MC 249). Significantly, as suggested by the passage in *Edgar Huntly*, "wilderness" emerges as the synonym for desert spaces.

For the physical geographer, Brown's "wilderness" formally resembles the geomorphology of a karst landscape; grounded in limestone and susceptible to water erosion, karsts are hollowed-out terrains marked by extensive cave networks and best known for irregular topography and infertile soils. For the literary geographer, however, the physical description of the karst becomes a topos rich with figurative spaces. When describing the attributes of his "wilderness," Brown invokes typological deserts familiar to readers of the Old and New Testaments. "Oblique" form and topographical asymmetry allude to baroque and picturesque landscape theories made popular by the literary and visual arts. Moreover, Brown's juxtaposition of geographical extremes, especially of heights and distances, resembles the sensational (or rather vertiginous) settings used in Gothic fiction. And finally, by introducing the desert space as the "western wilderness" in *Edgar Huntly*, Brown opens the door to historical geographies of North America, ranging from the artificial division of the continent along cardinal lines into colonies or nation-states, to mythical spaces of the frontier, its borderlands, and the American middle ground (Marx 73–144).

II. Cities and Suburbs

If we were to draw Brown's literary spaces along a continuum, the wilderness would be placed opposite to cities, in particular the city space of Philadelphia. Throughout his fiction—including *Ormond, Arthur Mervyn,* "The Trials of Arden," *Jane Talbot,* and *Memoirs of Carwin*—Brown inserts brief urban references, be they in the form of place names mentioned in letterheads or eyewitness accounts, in snippets of polite conversation, or in narrative moments of omniscience. Place names such as New York, Baltimore, Dublin, London, Lausanne, Liege, Barcelona, or Saint-Domingue show Brown's characters to be cosmopolitan, which is true especially for those characters who are uprooted, homeless, or otherwise rendered mobile in the broadest sense of the term *mobility* (geographical, social, and moral). By concentrating on Philadelphia, Brown's most developed literary setting is intentionally modeled on modern metropolitan designs.

Throughout the eighteenth century, Philadelphia was celebrated as a model of urban planning. Designed in 1682, it was one of the first cities in North America to be built using the rectangular survey system (fig. 30.1). Following instructions from the city's designers, William Penn and Thomas Holme, builders plotted out wide streets intersecting at right angles stretching from the Schuylkill River in the west to the Delaware River in the east. Divided into urban blocks and suburban "liberties," the plan included several squares of dedicated parkland. The stated goal for this orderly design was urban self-preservation: open roads and the spacious distribution of housing were to protect people against overcrowding, fire, and disease. Or, as the narrator of *Ormond* describes the benefits of urban life as perceived by a house-hunting Constantia Dudley: "Its situation, near the centre of the city, in a quiet, cleanly, and well-paved alley, was far preferable to that of her present habitation, in the suburbs, scarcely accessible in winter, for pools and gullies, and in a neighbourhood abounding with indigence and profligacy" (O 31).

After the American Revolution, the rectangular survey system evolved from being a design intent on safeguarding a city to one securing the future of a whole nation. The Land Ordinance of 1785 made geographic grid lines the basis for measuring the nation. When coupled with visionary plans, such as Thomas Jefferson's agrarian society spelled out in his *Notes on the State of Virginia* (Query XIX), the grid promised the fair distribution and management of the new republic's most ubiquitous resource: land. In the context of Philadelphia, compared with the palace-oriented radial layouts of eighteenth-century capitals built by absolutist states—such as Paris in France or Karlsruhe in Germany—the equilinear design of the new nation's first capital was viewed by many as a symbolic space: its geometrical organization fulfilled Enlightenment ideas of accessibility and accountability; the grid's use of geographical coordinates promised not only an elegant spatial order but a political tool for organizing the nation into a "democratic space" (Reps 147–324; Feeney; Fisher).

Yet Brown's representation of Philadelphia consistently undercuts its urban ideal. In particular, the novel *Arthur Mervyn* turns the much-vaunted designs upside down: wide avenues give way to narrow alleys; clean spaces are supplanted by muddy paths; the city's

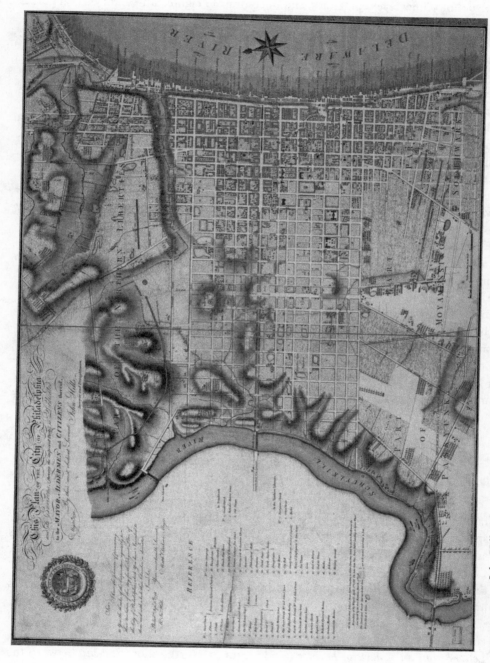

FIGURE 30.1 John Hills, *This Plan of the City of Philadelphia* (Philadelphia, 1797). Courtesy, The Library Company of Philadelphia.

population lives either in soul-crippling isolation or in crowded and often unsanitary conditions; instead of providing protection against disease, Philadelphia is the perennial hotspot of yellow fever epidemics; and in contrast to eighteenth-century travel guides that celebrated Philadelphia's architectural landmarks for their national significance— such as Independence Hall or the nation's first bank—Brown's Philadelphia tends to emphasize less glamorous institutions such as the hospital, insane asylum, and prison.

Brown's detailed descriptions of the city countermand many of the Enlightenment's sensory principles of spatial production. Instead of moving through airy and well-lit parkways, characters repeatedly wander along dimly lit alleyways or grope their way blindly from house to house. In Brown's fictionalized adaptation, the city hinders spatial mobility. After Arthur Mervyn crosses the Schuylkill River, having quickly moved from the western farm country through the western suburbs of Philadelphia to the core of the city's built environment (the area between First and Seventh Street), his progress is repeatedly stymied by unexpected house fronts, walled-in courtyards, and a mazelike warren of townhouse architecture. Brown further impedes Arthur's movements by exploring Philadelphia's urban centrality as a marketplace and port city. Oblique references to spaces containing early American traffic in capital and goods, men and women, cargo and slaves—such as the street, covered markets, taverns, slums, brothels, and so on—turn the city into a multitiered spatial, material, and cultural obstacle course (AM 27–38, 61–67, 110–111, 138–146, 173, 220–221, 315–323).[2] In *Ormond* and *Arthur Mervyn*, Brown's representation of Philadelphia is less an exercise in constructing spatial binaries (inside/outside, upstairs/downstairs, etc.) than it is a documentary of the spatial density and functional diversity of urban geographies. Brown's spatial arrangements generate both order and disorder: the official city plan's promise of equality coexists with the reality of unequal neighborhoods; the gestures of brotherly love and neighborly comity are balanced by criminality and corruption; and the city grid's fixed geometrical units are rendered porous by amorphous spaces.

III. House, Home, Settlement

Located between the country wilderness and the city lies Brown's third cluster of literary spaces, the isolated farmhouse, summer home, and frontier settlement. These settings are prominent features in the fiction of *Wieland, Edgar Huntly, Ormond, Arthur Mervyn, Clara Howard, Jane Talbot, Memoirs of Carwin*, "Somnambulism," "The Trials of Arden," the *Historical Sketches*, and the "Ellendale" fragments. Significantly, these settlements are located inside the confines of Brown's "cultivable space" but outside the "desert/wilderness" and outside the "city/suburb." Thus placed, they are set inside the cultural landscape that J. Hector St. Jean de Crèvecoeur described as the "intermediate space" in *Letters from an American Farmer* (Crèvecoeur 71); furthermore, located between the backwoods and the coastal market towns, they are host to the idealized "mass of cultivators" as imagined in Jefferson's *Notes on the State of Virginia* (Jefferson 217). Occasional references to spatial distance and dimensions invoke other historical settlement patterns: when characters have to walk "three miles" to the nearest neighbor, Brown acknowledges the seventeenth-century settlement system of New England villages; or, when he describes Norwalk as a "six-mile" unit in diameter, he alludes to lot sizes devised by the Land Ordinance (Brückner 198–203).

In these examples, Brown's "middle ground" consists of isolated habitations that are anticommunal; detached from more densely settled areas, they are also removed from the social customs and manners that constitute basic village or semiurban life. That said, Brown's rural places show signs of modern spatiality. Bounded by fences and surrounded by fields or pastures, they are situated inside proprietary "enclosures" that, depending on the social status of the occupants, resemble one particular European settlement type: the country retreat. By the late eighteenth century, this settlement form had become a popular literary space celebrated by genres as different as "country house" poetry and sentimental novels. Associated with the country seat was the pastoral fantasy that it provided characters a place of "retirement," an escape from politics, the marketplace, and technological change. Thus defined, the rural retreat became home to the geographical character type of the "gentleman farmer," who delegated the back-breaking labor involved in running a farm while remodeling farmland into a picturesque landscape that hid the presence of work (Williams 96–107).

Brown's isolated settlements internalize the spatial logic of the country retreat. The Wieland family lives on an architecturally landscaped estate ("summer-house"), while Clara Wieland's house sits inside a fenced-in field. In the epistolary fragment "Ellendale," the eponymous place is marked as an "estate" situated on the banks of the Schuylkill River (Letters 841). In *Ormond*, Constantia Dudley occupies successively a rural summer residence and a deserted farmhouse in "Perth Amboy," New Jersey, just south of New York City. In *Edgar Huntly*, the narrator lives with his uncle's family in a secluded "three-story" farmhouse, and when roaming the wilderness area of Norwalk, he discovers in a lonely cottage a "model of cleanliness and comfort" (EH 226). Arthur Mervyn finds shelter from the yellow fever outbreak at a Quaker farm a day's ride from the city. In *Jane Talbot*, the heroine purposefully removes herself from society by buying a farm "on the Banks of the Delaware" (JT 408). And in "The Trials of Arden," the hero's brother spends the end of a happy life on a "spacious farm . . . in the new settlements in Tenessee" ("Trials," 35).

Although Brown frequently implies that these settlements are safe spaces, or sanctuaries, in the course of his stories, the country retreat emerges as a literary space more dangerous than the desert wilderness or the dark city streets. The Wielands' home becomes the scene of familicide; Clara's home is repeatedly invaded, either by Carwin's voice or by a brother intent on killing her. Burglars ransack Edgar Huntly's uncle's house, and his visit to the model frontier cottage ("cleanliness and comfort") reveals a broken home in which a family endures the abuses of a "debauched husband and father" (EH 228). Arthur Mervyn is driven from his family farm by a hostile stepmother. And in *Ormond*, the shelter provided by the lonely farmhouse in Perth Amboy turns into a libertine's trap, with Constantia Dudley barely escaping being raped.

Brown's retreats are subverted by at least two factors shaping literary spaces and American historical geography. On the one hand, country seats are settings that explore the relationship of landownership and labor, or, rather, the absence of labor; none of the male characters work the land (and if they do, like Carwin in the *Memoirs*, they do it only reluctantly). In those instances where leisure becomes the main form of employment, the characters' lives are quickly set on a path of self-destruction. And if indeed there is "happiness" to be found on a country estate, such as the one in Tennessee, it is implicitly purchased by the work of slaves. On the other hand, the individual fates of the country-house inhabitants dramatize the potentially disastrous outcomes of a new federal land system governed by the Jeffersonian ideal of a homogeneous agrarian society. While the Land Ordinance makes it possible for characters like Jane Talbot to own her farm removed from the ills of urban or suburban society, it also is responsible for establishing a cultural landscape in which the survey system increases the geographical distance between citizens, amplifying the occupants' social isolation (Brückner 193–196).

Each of the three categories discussed so far includes literary spaces that are as densely layered in their formal arrangement as they are complex in their literary function. But when read in combination, Brown's writings generate spatial patterns commonly discussed in theories of cultural geography. For example, his fictional representations of Norwalk or Philadelphia or even Ireland contain references that have his characters inhabit not just a particular setting but an array of social, economic, and otherwise geo-coded spaces. In fact, Brown's metaspaces compare well to modern textbooks teaching cultural geography; a quick look at key geographical concepts shows how Brown's fictional world corresponds with some of the more prominent spatial theories developed over the past two centuries.

IV. CORE-PERIPHERY MODEL

Brown's literary geography of the Philadelphia region resembles the spatial model developed by early-nineteenth-century economist Johann Heinrich von Thünen. Seeking to study the influence of distance between markets and how transportation costs determine the value of agricultural production, Thünen proposed the model of the "isolated state" (Thünen 5–8). This ideal state had no trade connections with the outside world; its only marketplace was located centrally in the state; and its physical attributes, such as soil, climate, and terrain, were uniform throughout. Several of Brown's literary spaces discussed earlier match this model when we assign the role of the "isolated state" to Philadelphia and divide its surrounding areas into ringlike spheres defined by economic activities: garden crops (suburbs), wood/fuel and field crops (farmland), and unprofitable lands (wilderness). Thünen's premise of isolated centers applies particularly well to Brown's solitary country houses, which upon closer inspection also correspond with Thünen's graduated core-periphery model (house at center, surrounded by garden and fenced-in fields, followed by unprofitable wilderness). When evaluated as a metasetting, Brown's city-country pattern even approximates Thünen's economic conclusion. Increased distance from the city forces transportation costs to reach a critical point at which farmers no longer can gain adequate returns for their goods (Thünen 12–18, 56–69). When applied to Brown, increased distance from the city has his characters also occupy a conceptual space of diminished returns; rural retreats cease to generate the kind of gains promised by land speculators or country-house poets.

V. Spatial Systems: From "Picaresque" to "Thirdspace"

As with most modern theories of cultural geography, Brown's writings leave no doubt about the fact that economic action (or inaction) rarely happens in social isolation or in an economic vacuum. New humanist geographers, such as Carl Ritter in Germany and Arnold Guyot in the United States, linked modern geographical thinking to the cultural behaviors of Homo economicus and to the insight that as economic beings, people constantly shape and reshape the space around them, including spaces that are not physically connected to a particular locale. Brown's spatial imagination anticipates aspects of these theories by using the literary convention of the picaresque novel. Much of Brown's fiction chronicles the lives of characters of lower social rank who, marked by high geographical mobility, make their living by wit rather than actual labor. Brown's characters are in constant motion, visiting not only American cities and the surrounding countrysides but a seemingly random assortment of places around the globe. In *Wieland*, Clara's father emigrated from Germany, while Henry Pleyel spent several years in Germany, Spain, and France. In *Arthur Mervyn*, the character Clavering arrives from England, and Achsa Fielding is connected to the cities of Liege, Rouen, and Frankfurt. In *Clara Howard*, an unnamed woman tours France and Sicily. In one of the *Historical Sketches*, "A Specimen of Political Improvement," the lord of the manor, Alexander, spent his youth in France and Italy. And in *Ormond*, a young painter studies in Italy. Indeed, the character Ormond impresses Constantia with "narratives [that] carried her beyond the Mississippi, and into the deserts of Siberia. He had recounted the perils of a Russian war, and painted the manners of the Mongals and Naudowessies [Ojibwa]" (O 205). In contrast to Carwin and other male characters who resemble the unreliable figure of the *picaro*, Constantia—representative of Brown's mobilized female characters— does not lead a life of pranks, nor do her predicaments lend themselves to political satire.

On the surface, Brown's choice of places and character movements resembles the erratic geography created by late-eighteenth-century cartographic board games in which with each roll of the dice, players move haphazardly from city to city (players use figures; numbered positions correspond with geographical entries about the location printed in the map's margins; see fig. 30.2). A closer look, however, suggests that Brown's use of spatial mobility is a function of cultural geography. The novels' spatial allusions and erratic travels are anything but random; rather, they assert the interconnectedness of local cultural spaces and global spatial systems. Here are three examples:

(a) *Religious geography.* In *Wieland*, the personal history of Wieland the elder alludes to spatial patterns studied today by the geography of religion, which transposes travel into pilgrimage, geographical mobility into forced emigration, settlement into religious community, colonial habitations into sacred architecture.

(b) *Political geography of nation-states.* In *Edgar Huntly*, the imaginary township of Solebury and the desert of Norwalk represent competing political geographies in North America, pitting Native American land claims against those made by residual British colonial geography and the new American geography marked by national sovereignty and western colonization (see also the "Ellendale" fragment). The novel's allusion to the Land Ordinance, the "militia," and institutions such as the "confinement for lunatics" are further keywords signaling a nascent political landscape resembling the imaginings of a national community (Anderson 30; Lefebvre 68–115).

(c) *Hemispheric systems and empire.* In *Edgar Huntly*, the ownership of a "Bengal" rifle (EH 187) by the novel's peripatetic cosmopolitan character, Sarsefield, abruptly forces the novel's plots and actions away from America and into the global context of British imperialism and its attending spread of military power and capitalism (Said; Harvey). In *Arthur Mervyn*, several characters emphasize the flow of international capital to and through the United States, be it in the form of monetized landed property imported from Europe or profits derived from the sale of Caribbean plantations and slave labor.

Brown's fiction establishes world-systemic spaces that are both networks and enclaves, or what postmodern geographer Edward Soja calls the "Thirdspace," a metasetting containing the spatial tension between the "liberties" and the "carceral." These spaces rarely exist in sui generis. Rather, they are collaborative spaces that chart the uneven development of global capitalism along axes that, while they combine the local with the global, are motivated by patterns of spatial expansion: for example, in *Memoirs of Carwin*, the protagonist leaves the rustic Philadelphia farm, naively embarking on a grand tour of Europe (as propagated by the early proponent of English nationalism, Francis Bacon), only to end up in Ireland (a part of the British Empire), where he discovers a map figuratively and literally representing the plot of imperial and capitalist power in the form of a utopian settlement scheme in the South Pacific. Or, in *Edgar Huntly*, the working-class character Clithero grows up in Ireland inhabiting what to historical geographers signifies the typical English gentleman's estate, that is, a visibly bounded and fully mapped piece of land, replete with the centrally located manor house surrounded by the cottages of dependent tenant farmers. After emigrating to America, the homeless Clithero brings these spatial expectations to the uncharted territory of Norwalk, a space contested by the actions of colonialism, modern capitalism, the bureaucratic nation-state, and indigenous land claims.[3]

FIGURE 30.2 Thomas Jefferys, *Royal Geographical Pastime* (London, 1770). Courtesy, The Williamsburg Foundation. Museum Purchase.

Throughout his fiction and the *Historical Sketches*, Brown's characters occupy spatial systems predicated on fluid spaces that are porous and never fixed. In *Edgar Huntly*, the desert space of Norwalk expands or contracts to connote the local township, the nation-state, and the North American continent. In *Arthur Mervyn*, urban characters are set adrift or swept away by the economic tides of the oceanic worlds of the Atlantic and the Caribbean. In pamphlets such as *An Address to the Government of the United States on the Cession of Louisiana to the French*, etc. (1803), the integrity of the nation-state is imagined to dissolve at the slightest hint of territorial encroachment. In *Memoirs of Carwin*, the story pivots around an antipodal axis, linking the Atlantic world of northern Europe to South Pacific islands. Indeed, as much as Brown's spatial tropes hinge on the rhetoric of spatial isolation, his writings consistently construct spaces in which the rhetoric of "isolationism," that is, the call for absolute sovereignty of both individuals and communities, becomes deconstructed by spatial systems, such as commerce, that have "the wonderful power of annihilating...even space itself" (Annals 3).

VI. Experiential Spaces

As Brown's characters inhabit lofty metaspaces, they are frequently shown to negotiate places close to the ground. In their responses to physical geography, Brown engages with a mode of geographical analysis that includes psychoanalytical accounts of spatial descriptions and ecocritical responses to human action; in short, they include the human geographer's inquiries into "topophilia," or the affective understanding of geography (Tuan 1–12). This kind of geography is inherently anthropocentric, and as Brown's writings show, it is exclusively concerned with individual subjectivity, with the human body, its sensory perception, and its cognitive placement inside physical, cultural, or otherwise imaginary spaces.

Edgar Huntly offers some of the best examples illustrating Brown's use of sensory geographies, but they can also be found in "Somnambulism," *Wieland*, "A Jaunt to Rockaway," and *Memoirs of Carwin*. Seeking to navigate his way out of the wilderness space of Norwalk, Edgar is distracted by "the vexatious obstacles which encumbered our way."

> The ground was concealed by the bushes, and we were perplexed and fatigued by a continual succession of hollows and prominences. At one moment we were nearly thrown headlong into a pit. At another we struck our feet against the angles of stones. The branches of the oak rebounded in our faces or entangled our legs, and the unseen thorns inflicted on us a thousand wounds.   (EH 182)

Brown conveys the geography of the land through sensory observations, in particular those generated by vision ("concealed," "unseen"), touch ("struck"), fear ("nearly thrown headlong"), and pain ("thousand wounds"). By privileging the visceral over the visual, Brown forces his subject to engage with geography not as a form of detached knowledge predicated on the act of seeing, mapping, and reading; rather, his sensory geography consists of the agentic experience of space in which the particularity of the place assumes power usually reserved for human actors ("we were nearly thrown," "the branches of the oak rebounded"). Sense-driven settings are not reserved for natural environments; they are operative in Brown's descriptions of the interior architecture of houses, as in *Wieland*, *Ormond*, and *Arthur Mervyn* in particular. Brown's detailed delineation of the sensory experience enacts one of the core techniques that cultural geographers tend to use for identifying "lived places," that is, places where the entanglement of the human body with the natural environment provides the first step toward establishing affective bonds between people and their settings (Tuan 113–149).

Working with picturesque landscape descriptions in particular, Brown develops a sensory geography that, while it is predicated on the visual, examines the relationship of affect and the spatial emplacement of characters. As many studies have shown, these descriptions are grounded in conventions established by the aesthetic of picturesque symmetry, the sensationalism of Gothic fiction, and the Romantic concept of the beautiful and sublime.[4] It has often been noted that Brown applies William Gilpin's treatise on the picturesque, in particular his *Three Essays: On Picturesque Beauty; On Picturesque Travel; and On Sketching Landscape* (1792) and *Remarks on Forest Scenery* (1791). Brown's short story "The Rhapsodist" links his sensory approach to the picturesque by imagining geography as a visual contemplation experienced from the vantage point of a body floating down a river perfectly isolated and immobilized; accordingly, the ideal condition for spatial imaginings is corporeal self-dissociation tethered to visual omniscience (and thus anticipating a subject position similar to Ralph Waldo Emerson's "transparent eyeball"). In *Edgar Huntly*, Brown imitates Gilpin's geographic formula for describing rural landscapes, especially in narrative episodes where Edgar is positioned successively on summits from which the world "was subjected, at one view, to the eye." There the view extends from "extensive scenes" of "fertile lawns and vales" to a "winding course of the river," creating a "delight[ful] . . . contrast" between "lightsome and serene" elements and the "glooms" of Norwalk's wilderness (EH 101–102). Panoramic surveys like this offer Brown's characters the cartographic experience of gaining ocular control over space; at the same time, by assuming the cartographer's bird's-eye view, the experience turns topophilic, offering a sense of peace and a psychological groundedness that usually escape Brown's characters (Brown frequently mixes claustrophobic with agoraphobic anxiety).

However, the panoramic element of Brown's picturesque geography is predictably upended by its failure to see "at one view" the landscape hidden in the "glooms." "Concealed landscapes," especially visually concealed spaces, are a hallmark of Brown's sensory geographies (Toles 134). Be they the mazelike caves of Norwalk or the bedrooms of country houses and Philadelphia residences or the desks, chests, and closets containing letters, maps, and books, these spatial settings deny visual perception proper, escape ocular surveillance, and are causes of sensory deprivation and psychological disorientation. In these places, characters from Clara Wieland to Arthur Mervyn, Constantia Dudley to Carwin, experience physical and psychological stress paired with the sense of fear, alienation, and abjection. As a result of both limited sensory perception and limited spatial horizons, Brown's concealed spaces reinscribe discrete physical places with the conceptual space of a nascent modern interiority. In combination, the dimly lit landscapes, tunnel-like caves, and dark bedrooms anticipate modern representations of individual consciousness.

Brown's sensory geographies thus invite more specialized modes of spatial analysis. From the psychoanalytical point of view, Brown's literary spaces and their nested Chinese-box effects become settings that are evocative of traumas ranging from birth to rape to genocide.[5] Similarly, the spatial play of hide-and-seek that quickly escalates into more serious hunter–prey relationships between characters invites comparison with Foucauldian spaces of discipline or Jay Appleton's habitat theory of the predatory gaze (Appleton 70–74). Furthermore, the use of concealed natural landscapes occupied by landless characters resonates with old and new Marxist critiques of the picturesque in which landscapes are thinly disguised representations of class conflict and political alienation (see Hinds; White). Looking at the critical literature addressing Brown's work over the past decades, it becomes clear that Brown's literary spaces are captivating in the double sense of the word precisely because they are not just "imagined spaces" in addition to being not "real" in the conventional geographical sense but because they are "emoted spaces"—places structured by affective orders (or disorders), heterotopic plateaus of variable scales where action and reaction can be gauged by a calculus of spatial feeling (Hsu 3–8).

VII. The Geographical Turn: Facts, Maps, and Textbooks

But when all is told, Brown's literary spaces are produced in dialogue with the scientific discipline and study of geography.[6] This dialogue begins tentatively in magazine essays, such as the *Weekly Magazine's* "The Schemer" (1798), in which Brown's narrator considers geographical accounts to be more useful than fiction. The dialogue intensifies after *Jane Talbot*. Having recently taken on the editorship of the *Literary Magazine*, Brown included the sketch "A Jaunt to Rockaway, in Long Island" (1803), in which, true to his earlier fictional characters, the narrator rails against his fellow passengers (or implied readers), whose noses are glued to windows making empirical observations or are stuck in books reading maps. Dismissive of conventional geographers, the narrator exclaims, "An accurate history of the thoughts and feelings of any man, for one hour, is more valuable to some minds than an entire system of geography" (12). But while here Brown's fictional narrator dismisses the science of geography, his personal letters reveal him to be the empirical geographer he had mocked. After being asked by the Reverend Samuel Miller to review the latter's book, *A Brief Retrospect of the Eighteenth Century* (1803), Brown explains his comments, stating that "geography was the only subject in which I was at all qualified to correct any mistakes you have committed, and, on this I have not been sparing, as you will find" (Bennett 218).

This is the less-known Brown, the pedantic geographer and future author of the ultimate literature of space, the geography book. American readers had glimpses of this change in authorship in Brown's translation of C. F. Volney's natural history, *A View of the Soil and Climate of the United States of America* (1804). Throughout the volume, Brown offers extensive notes, many of which resemble geographical textbook entries. Over the next few years, Brown, who in his fiction relegates maps to the status of useless paper constructs (EH; MC), went on to publish rather technical articles on geography, such as the "Improvement of Geography" (1805), teaching readers about the technique of isomorphic mapping. At the same time, he also offered a critique of the literary application of geography in "Literary Blunders" (1805). Writing, editing, and compiling geographic information were central to Brown's last employment. Working as the editor of the *American Register* (1807–1810), he devoted much energy to the tabulation, classification, and interpretation of scientific news, in particular reports on the nation's geography.

During the last years before his death, the editorial discussion of geography had become Brown's literary obsession. While working as magazine editor, Brown prepared a substantial manuscript (allegedly a thousand pages long), which was advertised in 1809 as *A System of General Geography*. According to the "Prospectus" (the manuscript is lost), Brown's geography was intended to join the existing canon of encyclopedic geographies and schoolbooks. In contrast to his fiction, Brown embraces the normative conventions of geographical writing, the classification and organization of spaces according to continental divisions and a prescriptive lexicon. At the scripted moment, in keeping with the tradition of textbook authors who define "Geography" rather plainly as "a description of the earth," Brown offers his definition of the discipline:

> In like manner, if we describe the various ranks of organized beings, from man to moss, we describe the earth, and therefore be considered as geographers. If we view the surface of the earth, as divided horizontally into land and water, and vertically into hill, valley, and plain…we are geographers. If we consider man in his social, political, or physical condition, and the surface and products of the earth in relation to the works and subsistence of men; as divided among nations; as checkered by cities, villages, and fields; as ploughed, or pastured, or resigned to the reign of nature, we are still geographers. (*System*, 4)

In this assessment, geographic writing not only encompasses fields that today are identified as geology, botany, natural history, anthropology, political science, sociology, agricultural science, and many other disciplines, but it is conceived as a form of literature totalizing knowledge and universalizing human experiences.

In the "Prospectus," Brown purposefully omits the arts. Overtly limiting the representation of space to scientific writing, he repudiates fiction as a source of spatial production. Yet the authorial persona of the "Prospectus," and thus Brown's final self-description as an author, manages to give the proposed geography book the air of a literary manifesto. Through the voice of the geographer, Brown maintains his fictional persona of the solitary author who through his writing continues to perform acts of spatial work. Although the authorial figure of the disciplined geographer situates Brown's last literary effort somewhere between bookish science and comparative geography, Brown allows the discourse of geography to have the last word: "Geographical systems are, in general, collections of miscellaneous knowledge, in which that particular branch of information will predominate, in which the writer is most conversant, or to which he is most addicted" (*System* 2). Writing this at the end of his life, Brown confesses that geography was his own literary addiction and the lasting passion informing his literary career as a novelist, editor, and professional writer.

Notes

1. For critical discussions using a historically periodized perspective, see Seelye 168–186; Watts 71–130. On Brown's shift in literary production, see Bennett 212–223; Gilmore 659–660.
2. On the urban geography of Philadelphia, see Smith 7–39; Nash 79–143.
3. Brown's fascination with the interconnectedness of local cultural spaces and global spatial systems informs his *Historical Sketches*, pamphlets, and "Annals." For an example, see "Preface," AR 1 (1807): v–vi.
4. Critical studies examining Brown's landscapes address eighteenth-century aesthetics (Berthold), literary history (Lawson-Peebles), and philosophy (Tawil).
5. Brown's serially nested spaces resemble the architectural psychology delineated by Gaston Bachelard in his *Poetics of Space*. Shirley Samuels and Jared Gardner discuss the way these spaces witness sexual transgressions and racial violence.
6. For an extended analysis of this dialogue in Brown's work and early American literature and culture more broadly, see Brückner 184–203.

Works Cited

Anderson, Benedict. *Imagined Communities*. London: Verso, 1991.

Appleton, Jay. *The Experience of Landscape*. New York: Wiley, 1975.

Axelrod, Alan. *Charles Brockden Brown, an American Tale*. Austin: University of Texas Press, 1983.

Bachelard, Gaston. *The Poetics of Space* (1958). Maria Jolas, trans. Boston: Beacon Press, 1994.

Bennett, Charles E. "Charles Brockden Brown: Man of Letters." In Bernard Rosenthal, ed., *Critical Essays of Charles Brockden Brown*, 212–223. Boston: G. K. Hall, 1981.

Berthold, Dennis. "Charles Brockden Brown, Edgar Huntly, and the Origins of the American Picturesque." *William and Mary Quarterly* 41.1 (1984): 62–84.

Bowen, Margarita. *Empiricism and Geographical Thought: From Francis Bacon to Alexander von Humboldt*. Cambridge: Cambridge University Press, 1981.

Brown, Charles Brockden. "Improvement of Geography." LM 3.17 (1805): 99–101.

Brown, Charles Brockden. "A Jaunt to Rockaway, in Long Island." LM 1.1 (October 1803): 10–16.

Brown, Charles Brockden. "Literary Blunders." LM 3.18 (March 1805): 188.

Brown, Charles Brockden. "The Schemer—No. XI." WM 2.17 (May 26, 1798): 99–100.

Brown, Charles Brockden. "Somnambulism: A Fragment." LM 3.20 (May 1805): 335–347.

Brown, Charles Brockden. *A System of General Geography* [Prospectus]. Philadelphia, 1809.

Brown, Charles Brockden. "The Trials of Arden." MM 3.1 (July 1800): 19–36.

Brückner, Martin. *The Geographic Revolution in Early America*. Chapel Hill: University of North Carolina Press, 2006.

Crèvecoeur, J. Hector St. Jean de. *Letters from an American Farmer*. New York: Penguin Classics, 1981.

Feeney, Joseph J. "Modernized by 1800: The Portrait of Urban America, Especially Philadelphia, in the Novels of Charles Brockden Brown." *American Studies* 23.2 (Fall 1982): 25–38.

Fisher, Philip. "Democratic Social Space." *Representations* 24 (Fall 1988): 60–101.

Gardner, Jared. *Master Plots: Race and the Founding of an American Literature, 1787–1845*. Baltimore: Johns Hopkins University Press, 1998.

Gilmore, Michael T. "Charles Brockden Brown." In Sacvan Bercovitch, ed., *The Cambridge History of American Literature*, Vol. 1, 644–660. New York: Cambridge University Press, 1994.

Harvey, David. *Justice, Nature, and the Geography of Difference*. Cambridge: Blackwell, 1996.

Hinds, Jane Wall. "Charles Brockden Brown's Revenge Tragedy: *Edgar Huntly* and the Uses of Property." *Early American Literature* 30.1 (1995): 51–70.

Hsu, Hsuan. *Geography and the Production of Space in Nineteenth-Century American Literature*. Cambridge: Cambridge University Press, 2010.

Jefferson, Thomas. "Notes on the State of Virginia." In Merrill D. Peterson, ed., *The Portable Thomas Jefferson*. 223–232. New York: Penguin Books, 1977.

Kafer, Peter. *Charles Brockden Brown's Revolution and the Birth of American Gothic*. Philadelphia: University of Pennsylvania Press, 2004.

Lawson-Peebles, Robert. *Landscape and Written Expression in Revolutionary America*. Cambridge: Cambridge University Press, 1988.

Lefebvre, Henri. *The Production of Space* (1974). Donald Nicholson-Smith, trans. London: Blackwell, 1992.

Marx, Leo. *The Machine in the Garden*. London: Oxford University Press, 1964.

Morse, Jedidiah. *American Universal Geography*. Boston: Isaiah Thomas and Ebenezer T. Andrews, 1793.

Nash, Gary B. *First City: Philadelphia and the Forging of Historical Memory*. Philadelphia: University of Pennsylvania Press, 2002.

Reps, John. *The Making of Urban America*. Princeton, N.J.: Princeton University Press, 1965.

Ritter, Carl. *Die Erdkunde* (1817). Berlin: Reimer, 1822.

Said, Edward W. *Culture and Imperialism*. New York: Vintage, 1993.

Samuels, Shirley. *Romances of the Republic: Women, the Family, and Violence in the Literature of the Early American Nation*. New York: Oxford University Press, 1996.

Seelye, John. "Charles Brockden Brown and Early American Fiction." In Emory Elliott, ed., *Columbia Literary History of the United* States, 168–186. New York: Columbia University Press, 1988.

Smith, Billy G. *The "Lower Sort": Philadelphia's Laboring People, 1750–1800*. Ithaca, N.Y.: Cornell University Press, 1990.

Soja, Edward. *Thirdspace*. Cambridge: Blackwell, 1996.

[Thünen, Johann v.] *Von Thünen's Isolated State* (1826). Carla M. Wartenberg, trans. Oxford: Pergamon Press, 1966.

Tawil, Ezra. "'New Forms of Sublimity': *Edgar Huntly* and the European Origins of American Exceptionalism." *Novel* 40.1–2 (2006/2007): 104–124.

Toles, George. "Charting the Hidden Landscape." *Early American Literature* 16.2 (1981): 133–153.

Tuan, Yi-Fu. *Topophilia*. Boston: Prentice-Hall, 1974.

Watts, Steven. *The Romance of Real Life: Charles Brockden Brown and the Origins of American Culture*. Baltimore: Johns Hopkins University Press, 1994.

White, Ed. *The Backcountry and the City: Colonization and Conflict in Early America*. Minneapolis: University of Minnesota Press, 2005.

Williams, Raymond. *The Country and the City*. New York: Oxford University Press, 1973.

Withers, Charles W. J. *Placing the Enlightenment: Thinking Geographically about the Age of Reason*. Chicago: University of Chicago Press, 2007.

CHAPTER 31

BROWN, THE VISUAL ARTS, AND ARCHITECTURE

SARAH BOYD

Where'er his lucid colours glow,
Manners and Life the portrait know;
And through the canvass, fiction deem'd
Reality's bold features beam'd.
Nor only his the skill to scan
The outward acts of varied man;
But his was Nature's clue, to wind
Through mazes of the heart and mind.
The moral painter well portray'd,
The cause of each effect survey'd;
And breath'd upon the lifeless page
The informing soul, the "noble rage."

—Anonymous, "Stanzas, Commemorative
of the late Charles Brockden Brown"

THIS early poetic portrait of Charles Brockden Brown as the "painter" of modern life highlights the visual and graphic dimensions of not just his writing but also his philosophy of fiction. Its painterly tropes echo Brown's own description of his work in the well-known preface to *Edgar Huntly* (1799), which evokes the "new views" America has "opened . . . to the naturalist and the politician" as well as the figure of the "moral painter" who represents them in "vivid and faithful colours" (EH 3). This characterization of the romancer's work in turn echoes distinctions that Brown articulates in key essays, most notably "The Difference between History and Romance" (April 1800), concerning the work of the fiction writer as conjectural historian. On Brown's account of romance writing, there is a crucial difference between "romance" or fiction and history, though the two remain intimately connected. While history documents events, romance probes their possible causes and consequences and delineates, in the words of the above elegy, the "mazes of the heart and mind."

Within this approach to fictional method, moreover, the verbal and the visual have a similar interrelation. More than merely a metaphor for writing, the identification of fiction with moral painting argues the importance of vision, perception, and artistic represen- tation for Brown and his audience. Art objects speak to the cultural work of perception, the process of representation, the power of forms, and the complexities of memory, in the sense that artistic representations do not simply see and record what is but interpret and reflect on the significance of what is seen. Brown's uses of and commentaries on the visual arts dramatize problems of vision and representation for a new nation that has yet to discern a clear image of itself, that has yet to write its own history, and that is still struggling with the social and political implications of unequal representation.

Brown's engagement with the visual arts is a large question with several subdivisions, but it has received relatively little commentary over the course of his reception history. By way of introduction, then, this chapter will address three important subtopics: Brown's adaptations of contemporary aesthetic categories, as he encounters them in the transition between neoclassicism and early-Romantic tendencies; his career-long fascination with architecture on a number of levels, from architectural drawings to theoretical and fictional discussions; and the ways in which the fiction presents visual art, in this case the role of miniature portraiture in *Ormond* and *Arthur Mervyn*.

I. VISUAL AESTHETICS

Before Brown became a moral painter, he crafted the fictional persona of "The Rhapsodist" in a four-part periodical essay published in the Philadelphia *Columbian Magazine* (1789). In these essays, the Rhapsodist explains that he aspires to sincerity, both of and for representation. He hopes to find it not as a "spectator" or "retailer"—whose ends and means devolve into gossip and inaccuracy—but as a solitary artist-as-rhapsodist, who, in withdrawing from conversation and society, can better describe and delineate people and events spontaneously, "as they have really passed before the eyes of the describer" (Rhapsodist 467). For the naive and initially overoptimistic Rhapsodist, problems of truthful representation can be resolved through disinterested perception, best achieved through appropriate poetic or artistic modes of representation, requiring imagination, aesthetic distance, time, and a "sublime and elevated devotion" (539). In short order, how- ever, the Rhapsodist reveals an inability to put theory into practice, and the series ends in comical awkwardness when the narrator withdraws his aesthetically adventurous voice before a hostile editorial correspondent who condemns his "delirium of fancy" (665).

Thus, from his earliest writings, Brown is engaged with topical discussions of aes- thetics, and he displays a keen interest in emerging theories of aesthetic experience that develop now-familiar categories such as the sublime, the beautiful, and the picturesque, all associated with competing aesthetic tendencies in the era's neoclassical and Gothic or early-Romantic shifts. Indeed, Brown cribbed and copied from a number of contemporary landmarks in late-Enlightenment aesthetic theory, including Richard Payne Knight's *An Analytical Inquiry into the Principles of Taste* (London 1805) and William Gilpin's *Observations on the River Wye, and Several Parts of South Wales* (1782), which introduced the concept of picturesque beauty, as well as Gilpin's *Three Essays on Picturesque Beauty* (1792).[1]

In 1800, apparently fascinated by the alternative sentiment that Gilpin's picturesque offers to the then-well-established dialectic between the soft, relaxing ease of beauty and the terror of sublimity that was introduced by Edmund Burke in *A Philosophical Enquiry into the Origin of Our Ideas of the Sublime and Beautiful* (1757), Brown ventured his own comments on the picturesque. Writing in the persona of an intellectually curious "Looker-On" conversing with a learned companion, Brown published the dialogue sketch "On a Taste for the Picturesque" in his *Monthly Magazine* (July 1800), later republishing the piece in the *Literary Magazine* for June 1804. Looker-On's companion reasons that "[t]o examine with a picturesque-discerning and a cause-enquiring eye, every scene that really occurs; to ponder in like manner on the landscapes of painters and picturesque travelers, many of whom delineate and describe at the same time, seems to be the best mode of opening, in your breast, this source of high and beneficial pleasure" (Brown, "On a Taste," 13). Here the aesthetic gaze, with its "picturesque-discerning" and "cause-enquiring eye" evokes the same "cause-enquiring" activity authorized in Brown's theory of romance as conjectural history. Punctuated by activity, curiosity, and bodily movement, the picturesque is an elevated mode of perception, allowing the imaginative viewer to see and experience more than its beautiful or sublime counterparts.

When it came to cultivating such aesthetic modes of perception, audiences in the early republic were often self-conscious in their perceived provinciality or secondariness in relation to the prestige of European models. Early US periodicals are filled with responses to European claims that Americans have little taste, literature, art, or manners. Brown's interest in cultivating such aesthetic vision, then, may in part respond to this collective anxiety. In "American Prospects" (February 1805), for example, writing against claims that "America contained nothing of the picturesque," Brown constructs a rebuttal that casts the local landscape as intensely and inherently picturesque despite the lack of its Euro-centric forms: "That part of the picturesque which arises from the elaborate arrangements of art, and especially from the architectural monuments of ancient times, it is true, we do not possess. No crumbling walls are scattered over our vallies; no ivy clad tower reposes on the brow of our hills" (97). After countering this perceived cultural lack, Brown turns to positive claims that the picturesque inheres in every American "valley, precipice and stream," backing this assertion by quoting a brief passage from Alexander Mackenzie's travels (Brown, "American Prospects," 97). Just as picturesque vision provides an important mode of perception for a local cultivation of the "cause-enquiring eye," the picturesque views offered in American landscapes are the perfect stage for honing this aesthetic, perceptive gaze.

These discursive cultivations of American landscapes are part of an emerging picturesque tourism, a species of early American boosterism designed to match and invigorate the period's expanding geographic boundaries and market economy. Brown participated in this trend, for example, when he traveled in the summer of 1801 up the Hudson River and into Massachusetts and Connecticut. Brown's account of the trip delineates scenes in a decidedly picturesque manner: the traveler delights in the voyage and its withdrawal from urban environs, "the receding city and the glimmering lights; first of quays and avenues, and afterwards of farms and village" (Dunlap 1815, 51). In Connecticut, he notes the "view of wooded slopes, rocky promontories and waving summits" from his cabin situated in the highlands of the mountainous North River District and fixes his attention on the Revolutionary War ruins of Fort Putnam at Stony Point: "It is a rocky and rugged mass advancing into the river, the sides of which are covered with dwarf cedars, and the summit conspicuous still with some remains of fortification, a general solitude and vacancy around it, and a white cow grazing within the ruinous walls, produce a pleasing effect on my imagination. A craggy eminence, crowned with the ruins of a fortress, is an interesting spectacle every where, but a very rare one in America" (51). As in this example, the Gilpinesque urge to see picturesquely led viewers to gaze upon real landscapes as would-be painted landscapes, often with the aid of a "Claude glass," a tinted looking device designed for this purpose.[2]

Following the precedent of only slightly earlier Gothic novelists from Matthew Lewis to Ann Radcliffe, Brown's novels likewise incorporate the picturesque aesthetic imaginary. If, as commentators often note, a novel like *Edgar Huntly* constructs a landscape that is thoroughly symbolic or allegorical, it does so by adapting the new vocabularies of the Gothic and picturesque to the tensions of its settler-colonial spaces. Brown, as Dennis Berthold notes, "recognized that the descriptive conventions and emotional associations of picturesque travel provided visual analogues to the romantic hero's psychological state; in this way, picturesque aesthetics mediated between nature and the ego, the 'eye' of vision and the 'I' of selfhood, and so helped balance the conflicting claims of wildness and disorder, on the one hand, with those of civilization and order on the other" (Berthold 63). Thus, "Edgar's picturesque vision," Berthold maintains, "tames the wilds of Norwalk and helps him dominate physically what he comprehends aesthetically," allowing him to remain a detached observer and "an appreciative tourist who moves freely and safely between wilderness and civilization" (77). Beth Lueck similarly argues that the novel creates an appropriately distanced picturesque tourism as Romantic quest. In Huntly's final wilderness journey, Lueck writes, "Brown reveals that, in order to become whole and to live realistically in the American wilderness, Huntly must resolve these twin concerns: he must recognize and accept the dark half of himself, and he must acknowledge and learn to live with the dark side of the wilderness" (Lueck 35). In other words, Lueck contends, Huntly must "resolve the disjunction of his inner and outer worlds" (35). Here Lueck and Berthold propose different readings, as, for Berthold, Brown foils (rather than reconciles) Edgar's measured aesthetic appreciation with his dark double, Clithero, in order to illustrate "what happens to those untrained in the picturesque" (Berthold 77). Because Clithero "lacks the discriminating picturesque eye," Berthold concludes, he "cannot maintain a detached perspective" and thus "succumbs to its savagery" (77–78).

Whether readers concur with Lueck or Berthold or draw their own conclusions regarding Brown's novelistic deployment of the picturesque, his interest in adapting contemporary aesthetic languages for cultivating proper American taste clearly suggests his abiding interest in the utility of these theories for new cultural work on the American landscape. Ultimately, Brown's recurring concern with aesthetic response and perception revolves around his interest in the power of the visual arts to arrest, deceive, delight, and control their audiences by different means and toward different ends. Aesthetic distance is key here and remains important for Brown from his first rhapsody to the end of his writerly career.

II. Architecture, Institutions, and Power

Along with his engagement with contemporary aesthetic theory, a second major aspect of Brown's interest in visual arts concerns architecture. Throughout his career, he remains fascinated with architecture as a discipline, with its cultural history, and with a complex set of themes and questions that revolve around architecture's relation to social institutions and power. Architecture materializes historical relations, shapes and in certain respects dictates behavior, demarcates public from private spaces, and helps define social roles. Its appearance in Brown's novels and other writings consistently registers these social and cultural effects.

The aesthetic project of Gothicizing nature was, of course, not new when Brown undertook it in *Edgar Huntly*, and from the start, it linked architecture with print culture and visual art.[3] Edgar's vexed aesthetic responses to the wild and civilized spaces he inhabits, for example, also register the ways the built environment reflects complex legacies of (il)legitimate ownership in the settler-colonial landscape. As Duncan Faherty observes, as Edgar journeys from wilderness to civilization, he "must navigate between ruins and the legacies manifest in abandoned structures and multiple layers of architectural inscription" (Faherty 60). In effect, "[b]y marking Huntly's journey from wilderness to civilization architecturally, Brown accentuates how houses register environmental and cultural histories" (61). Timothy Sweet likewise comments on Edgar's journey, remarking that it maps the three stages of frontier development (with the goal of western expansion) outlined by Benjamin Rush in his collected *Essays* published just one year before Brown's *Huntly* (Sweet 117). For Sweet, Edgar's course through this symbolic architectural landscape is a satirical take on Rush's optimistic narrative of frontier development, from Old Deb's rough, "unhewn" log cabin, formerly occupied by a Scottish émigré, to the "small and low" but hospitable habitation of an impoverished farm family, and finally to the deceptively civilized Selby residence, which, though appearing to be a "model of cleanliness and comfort" and classically "embellished with mouldings and a pediment," offers no safe retreat for Edgar, having been twice plundered by raiding Indians and, even worse, corrupted by Selby's own patriarchal abuse (EH 226). Instead of offering a "stadial narrative of agrarian virtue," Brown's three "stages" seem to chart a disturbing devolution to counter Rush's optimistic narrative of frontier development (Sweet 117).

Other commentators have frequently noted Brown's architectural imagination as it recurs throughout his career. In his early review of Dunlap's 1815 biography, Gulian C. Verplanck contends that this architectural imagination was a basic component of Brown's work in fiction, pointing to his unusual ability to describe an abandoned house (Verplanck 74). More recently, Norman S. Grabo points to Brown's "cultivated architectural sense" (182), while Robert Lawson-Peebles observes the unique "spatial nature" of Brown's imagination (236). Faherty contends that Brown's minute meditations over empty architectural spaces foreground his "pointed ability to describe how the residential history of a house lingers long after particular tenants have abandoned it, evincing the depth of Brown's absorption with houses as registers of the ways in which the past continues to inform the present" (49–50). Indeed, one subtext of all Brown's novels and miscellaneous fiction pertains to how architecture frames and shapes behavior. Faherty's analysis of *Wieland* (1798), in particular, points out how Brown uses architecture to meditate on the interdependence of the past and the future, the problems that individuals and families encounter when they attempt to inhabit spaces designed and constructed by previous generations, and the troubling consequences of the younger Wielands' attempts to simply remodel and therefore disown their family legacy by remaking their father's temple of worship into a retreat for rational enlightenment (51–52). Thus, Brown repeatedly reflects on how "structures emblematic of one set of cultural values cannot easily be remade to serve another purpose, and moreover, no space can be safely occupied without addressing its history" (Faherty 56). In a related manner, Philip Barnard has remarked on how Brown explores the intersection of architecture, history, and power over the longue durée, over multiple generations, in the 1805–1806 *Historical Sketches*.

Although they have remained little known to all but the most specialized scholars up to the present, a set of early architectural drawings from Brown's own hand, apparently dating from 1792–1793 and now housed at the Harry Ransom Center at the University of Texas at Austin, demonstrate that his fascination with architecture was joined to narrative projects from a very early point in his career. In the 1815 biography, Dunlap recounts that as a boy, Brown "would for hours be absorbed in architectural studies, measuring proportions with his compasses, and drawing plans of Grecian temples or Gothic cathedrals, monasteries, or castles" (Dunlap 1815, 89). The once-bound notebook containing thirty-eight surviving drawings features a variety of Gothic and Palladian-neoclassical elevations, floor plans, and architectural embellishments, as well as calculations, syllabics for translations, notes for an unidentified work or works of fiction, and what appears to be a plan for a campus of some undetermined educational or monastic variety.

Fifteen of the thirty-eight pages feature elevations and floor plans with neoclassical elements, making the neoclassical the dominant generic category in the drawings, as it is in the period. Fueled by the late-Enlightenment vogue for Andrea Palladio's *I quattro libri dell'architettura* (1570), a revival of Vitruvius's *De architectura*, and the lavish illustrations of volumes such as Robert Wood's *The Ruins of Palmyra, otherwise Tedmor in the Desart* [sic] (1753), Continental and anglophone architects and builders—Thomas Jefferson, John Trumbull, and Benjamin Henry Latrobe, to cite only the best known—enthusiastically embraced neoclassical theories and precedents in their own designs.

Brown likewise bases his drawings on this classical revival, visually quoting from Wood, Palladio, or Giovanni Battista Piranesi in his amateur efforts.[4] Two of the fifteen neoclassical drawings feature multistory Georgian-style elevations complete with pedimented doors and lintel- or flat-arch-style windows more closely resembling the architecture of Brown's Philadelphia and Elfreth's Alley in particular.[5] Most of the structures, however, project the imagined temples, monasteries, Gothic cathedrals, neoclassical theaters, and other enormous domed structures that Dunlap recalls Brown constructing.

Alan Axelrod's initial reading of the drawings connects them to Brown's *Historical Sketches* due to the strong resemblances between the drawings and fanciful structures described in that work (Axelrod 101). He observes that the drawings are collected with other manuscripts dated to 1793, that they often represent educational institutions, that they offer an unusual admixture of neoclassical and Gothic designs, and, finally, that because neoclassical style takes precedence, they may reflect the "official" culture of the early republic. Axelrod, however, remarks that linking the drawings to the historical fictions is nevertheless problematic, insofar as the dimensions given in the *Sketches* and those scribbled on Brown's drawings simply do not match up (101). Subsequent work on the drawings suggests that they were executed in 1792–1793 and thus well before the *Sketches*, confirming Axelrod's suspicions (Letters 840, 853).

Certainly one of the more striking elements of the drawings is their sense of scale. Several of the floor and dome plans delineate structures of colossal proportions. One drawing, for example, outlines an immense two-domed floor plan, the design of which was possibly influenced by the competition of 1792–1793 for a capitol building and president's house.[6] The dimensions for the entire structure—464 by 920 feet for the main building and 800 by 1240 feet for the entire structure—add up to 426,880 square feet, or more than twice the size of the current US Capitol building (751 by 350 feet, or roughly 175,170 square feet). Moreover, the dimensions Brown imagines for each dome (380 feet or 115 meters) would make them the largest of their kind at this time and more than twice the size of the Pantheon (142 feet or 43 meters), a comparison that Brown likely considered, as that Roman temple was iconic and often admired by contemporaries from Piranesi and Hubert Robert to Thomas Jefferson.

Such fantastic dimensions align Brown intriguingly with the period's French visionary architecture movement, represented in the designs and theories of Claude Nicolas Ledoux (1736–1806), Etienne-Louis Boullée (1728–1799), Charles de Wailly (1730–1798), and Jean-Jacques Lequeu (1757–1826). Ledoux, Boullée, and Wailly formulated related theories of utopian architecture, in which architectural forms expressed or symbolized their social functions and in which scale formed new relations between subjects and objects.[7] In the 1780s, Boullée, in particular, began to defy convention with unprecedented designs for public buildings and monuments. Emphasizing enormous geometric forms and bare surfaces, Boullée's projects evoke a utopian order in which vast dimensions and inflated symbolism subordinate individuals to the immensity of the state, the cosmos, death, or whatever function the colossal structure represents, constructing a homogeneous community of equals disciplined by the overwhelming power of collective oversight. While there is no direct evidence that Brown was aware of Boullée, he did, however, encounter

Wailly's and Lequeu's designs in Denis Diderot's *Encyclopédie, ou dictionnaire raisonné des sciences, des arts et des métiers* (1751–1772). By 1792–1793, Brown and his Belles Lettres Society circle were familiar with this landmark text and discussed translating the introduction and other articles during the same period as the drawings (Letters 122, 124; the *Encyclopédie* features similarly in the "Henrietta Letters," Letters 692, 704). In these drawings, as in the later *Sketches*, Brown imagines and describes monumental built environments with the power to shape an imagined citizenry.

III. ALIENATED PORTRAITS

Unlike Continental and British aficianados, who variously acquired landscapes, history paintings, genre scenes, or still lifes and other genres, consumers of painting in the early republic primarily purchased portraits (Lovell 8). Although this preference might appear idiosyncratic at first glance, Margaretta Lovell argues that portraiture answered specific social needs (8). Because portraits function generically to present a performed or ideal self to one's immediate social circle, they speak to or reflect the dynamics of those circles. At stake in the growing consumer market for the genre in post-Revolutionary America, then, is a new concern not just for personalized identity but also for family status in the midst of a consumer revolution that made portraits a manifestation of inheritable wealth and social mobility among merchant and gentry classes, thereby fueling demand for individual and family portraits to bolster newly acquired status (9–10). As a reinvented genre evoking the prestige of tradition in this period, portraits document "the vestiges of a semifeudal sense of the family" while also participating in "the modern economy of the eighteenth century with as much energy and power as the newer revolutionary consumer products such as ceramic tablewares" (11). As a costly yet negative investment (roughly nine weeks' wages for a skilled journeyman artisan) with virtually no resale or return value, a portrait's exchange value of "was as non-financial as that of a tombstone" and served somewhat the same purpose (9).

Brown's knowing use of this visual genre in his fiction registers its complicated aesthetic, social, and economic valorization in the early republic. Portraits recur in his narratives, are intimately attached to concerns about identities performed and real, and clearly play on the genre's concern, in this context and moment, with family and hereditary wealth, along with the social and economic leverage they supply. But rather than circulating within these traditionally inscribed boundaries, the aberrant portraits in Brown's narratives typically circulate outside the family, alienated from their conventionally ascribed functions. Brown orchestrates two rather extraordinary episodes surrounding the loss and recovery of miniature portraits in *Ormond* (1799) and *Arthur Mervyn* (1799–1800). In both texts, alienated portraits register anxieties surrounding the fluidity and instability of individual identity and family fortune and inscribe a second level of visual reference alongside the imaginative architectural or built spaces described in the novels.

In *Ormond's* Chapter 8, long before the novel's narrator and potential "secret witness," Sophia Courtland, inserts herself into the narrative as an active character in Chapter 23, she curiously inserts her likeness into the text in the form of a miniature portrait that miraculously comes to Constantia Dudley's aid in a financial crisis. As a last resort and means of raising collateral to avoid eviction and starvation, Constantia offers her miniature portrait of Sophia to the relentless landlord M'Crea as a sort of promissory note, valued not for its aesthetic or sentimental qualities, which are worthless to a stranger, but for its gold casing. As the narrator, Sophia, emphasizes, the socially and emotionally isolated Constantia treasures the portrait as "a precious though imperfect substitute for sympathy and intercourse with the original" (O 75). Constantia's longing for companionship and sociability, which verges on "a species of idolatry," significantly contrasts with M'Crea's purely economic valuation of the portrait; she consigns the idol into his "rapacious hands," doubting "the promises of this man, that he would keep it safely till she was able to redeem it" (75).

As Sophia's commentary suggests, portraits of this kind were important tokens meant to promote sympathy between friends, if present, and, if absent, to bridge temporal and geographic distance or death. Susan Stabile's assessment of an intergenerational literary women's salon in the Delaware Valley from 1760 to 1840, for example, uncovers the social significance of the commissioning and exchange of objects—commonplace books of poetry, miniature shell collections, and miniature portraiture—in eighteenth-century America. The miniature as a mnemonic object held specific value as a token of friendship when exchanged between women, its complex subjectivity typifying the "collaboration of collective reminiscence" (Stabile 170). In such collaborative reminiscence, eighteenth-century women collected and saved the images of friends and associates rather than of themselves, thus relying "not only on collective narratives during their bittersweet daydreams but also on the familiar rendition of another woman's face" (170). For Constantia, Sophia's portrait becomes both a mnemonic and a metonymic device, allowing her to recall and delight in the "sympathy and intercourse" she currently lacks in her forlorn situation.

In the context of Brown's narrative, Sophia's miniature functions as more than a complicated device that saves our heroine from eviction and later reunites two friends, the narrator and her heroine; the episodes surrounding the lost and found miniature are really about establishing Sophia's narrative authority, her position as a family intimate, and her own social and class position. Brown's readers would know that only the merchant and gentry classes purchased such portraits. As Sophia later divulges, her only claim to middle-class respectability stems from her time with the Dudley family; she lived with the Dudleys after her mother, a prostitute and confidence woman, abandoned her as an infant and until she and Constantia were age seventeen, when the mother removed Sophia from the security of the Dudley household during a brief period of penance and reform. In Chapter 25, Sophia explains that the miniature portrait was commissioned as one of a matching pair just prior to this extended separation; Constantia was represented "with the cincture of Venus" and Sophia "with the crescent of Dian" (O 243). Representing a greater enthusiasm for romantic and familial bonds, miniature portraits of this kind betoken a marked growth in American romanticism. For the commission, Constantia and Sophia seek out "a Saxon painter, by name Eckstein" (243), whose name refers to a recently emigrated miniaturist, Johann Eckstein (or possibly his son, also a portraitist mentioned by Brown in other texts), one of the many portrait painters who entered the early US market hoping to profit from the increased demand for miniatures.[8]

Within the context of shifting codes concerning romantic and familial bonds, portraits are still essentially family matters and often commissioned in pairs, though more commonly for husbands and wives than for close friends. Thus, in form, this portrait pair establishes Constantia and Sophia's close pseudo-familial kinship, despite their lack of blood ties. In content, they likewise suggest the complicated aesthetic tension between radical sensuality and conservative restraint that Brown develops elsewhere in the novel. Depiction of clothing was crucial in miniature painting, as much as if not more so than that of the sitter's face, so these charged allegorical attributes—quite common in this period—bear significance. Constantia's portrait seems the more provocative of the two. The cincture of Venus is a girdle commonly depicted in her iconography, usually encircling the waist of the nude or partially clad goddess, sometimes securing a bow or arrow. The crescent of Diana is a moon typically depicted on her headdress. As a pair, the miniatures depict the range of female sexual experience from chastity to sensuality, although either image may evoke the erotic, since it was common for women, especially when rendered allegorically in miniatures, to hazard risqué depictions of themselves, sometimes by revealing a bare breast or breasts but more often by wearing gauzy, translucent drapery that suggests the mere outline of breasts and areola.[9] Playing with tensions between innocence and experience, intimacy and restraint, and framed within the safety of allegorized classical references, the girls could indulge in pseudo-sexual play without the fear of derision or censure.

The veiled hint of unsavory sexual exchange embedded in M'Crea's "rapacious" grasp, then, would not be lost on Brown's readers, since the commission and exchange of portraits, miniatures in particular, often marked important moments in the sitter's life: coming of age, betrothal or marriage, and death. The exchange of such likenesses would be between intimates—family, friends, or lovers—further inscribing the art object within a sphere of intimacy and secrecy. Such a characterization of the trade between impoverished tenant and greedy landlord, moreover, forecasts the potentially sexually compromising position in which Sophia finds herself when the portrait, in Chapter 25, inexplicably appears on the breast of Mr. Martynne, an English émigré attempting to titillate and impress a Miss Ridgeley, who is, coincidentally, cousin to Constantia. Essentially nonthreatening, Martynne is less a seducer of women than of "opinion," as Jay Fliegelman posits, but his decision to flash the image in front of Miss Ridgeley nevertheless represents a social transgression (Fliegelman 38). For, in using the miniature as a public commodity rather than a private souvenir, he turns the image and reverses its intended concealed use (which would have inward, facing the breast, and thus available only for private viewing, commemoration, and contemplation), turning the image outward, toward personal gain and social leverage. In short, Sophia's sexual and public image is now not entirely in her own hands.

Julia Stern sees these transgressive moments involving the fetishization of portraiture as perversions of fellow feeling and representation, articulating anxieties about identity, "apprehension over the validity of national origin and the legitimacy of republican political processes unleashed in the aftermath of the post-Revolutionary settlement" (Stern 154). These episodes of loss and recovery, moreover, underscore the idea that, at least in *Ormond*, "identifications are made and identity is established through acts of reflective vision extending beyond the purview of embodied relations," suggesting that "in a culture whose own origins remain inchoate, fragile, and insecure, even two-dimensional images that cannot return their bearer's gaze wield the power to constitute and authorize a certain form of selfhood" (185). The power to constitute or authorize selfhood in this manner, however, remains tenuous for all of Brown's fictional characters, particularly those who, like Martynne or Arthur Mervyn, are more tenuously situated within the social landscape. While such miniature portraits serve to establish (in Sophia's case) or try to establish (in Martynne's) a certain form of selfhood, the real power to constitute personhood resides less in the artifact itself than in its perception by others. Indeed, the miniature itself held little interest for Miss Ridgeley beyond its acute likeness to Sophia, just as the jeweler who sells Mr. Martynne the miniature in the first place assumes his interest in the portrait stems from his acquaintance with its original (O 242–244). At work in these moments of perception and reception of artifacts is a concern for the tensions between originals and copies and, by extension, sincerity and imposture and the acts of perception that enabled proper discernment between the two.

Early American anxieties about identity, particularly as they pertain to acts of perception, were, of course, not Brown's alone. In examining spaces of visuality and display, especially those spaces in which the "representational equivocations of illusion" were called forth for public scrutiny, Wendy Bellion argues that popular pictorial and optical illusions, from trompe l'oeil paintings to phantasmagorias, became important pedagogical cultural tools that enabled citizens to learn how to discern and participate in the public sphere. Both addressing and exploiting anxieties about identity and perception, such illusions provided citizens a platform for practicing good or proper perception, encouraging them to look closely, to refine their visual senses in order to understand how appearances can be deceiving or easily manipulated to fool the careless looker-on (Bellion 16). In many ways, the early republic's interest in honing proper perception matches the "picturesque-discerning" and "cause-enquiring eye" that Brown encouraged his fellow Americans to cultivate in his periodical writings. *Ormond*'s portraits, along with the many disguises and aliases adopted by the novel's major characters, speak to this fascination with political, social, and economic illusion and dissimulation and to contested boundaries between public and private identities, all resonating in the crisis atmosphere of the late 1790s.

Arthur Mervyn, as many have noted, is likewise preoccupied with imposture, masquerade, forgery, and other modes of dissimulation. Significantly, Brown's impossibly sincere protagonist shares a similar idolatrous obsession with a "miniature portrait" (AM 82, 250). The self-portrait was drawn by a sickly young man named Clavering who sought shelter with the Mervyn family for a brief period during Arthur's youth. Perceiving a strong likeness between the visage of this stranger and that of her own darling, Arthur's mother takes the deranged youth into her care (29–30). In Clavering, Arthur appears to have forged a bond of sympathy and companionship similar to that of Constantia and Sophia's youthful intercourse. Their sympathetic ties are short-lived, however, as Clavering dies from a lingering illness not long after he arrives. Arthur explains, "I love him, for whatever reason, with an ardour unusual at my age, and which this portrait had contributed to prolong and to cherish" (30). Arthur's prized portrait is likewise lost and recovered, in connection with the machinations of Welbeck, associating Arthur with several fraudulent schemes concerning other people's goods, money, and commercial prospects.

Arthur first loses the portrait upon his arrival in Philadelphia. Naive in the ways of city life, he stops to rest at a market stall, leaving his small bundle of possessions on the ground. Though he quickly returns to the stall, the bundle containing his meager possessions is already gone. His rediscovery of the portrait is singular. He encounters it at the mansion of the wealthy Mrs. Wentworth, one of Welbeck's recent marks: "I scanned the walls, the furniture, the pictures. Over the fire-place was a portrait in oil of a female. She was elderly and matron-like. Perhaps she was the mistress of this habitation, and the person to whom I should immediately be introduced. Was it a casual suggestion, or was there an actual resemblance between the strokes of the pencil which executed this portrait and that of Clavering? However that be, the sight of this picture revived the memory of my friend and called up a fugitive suspicion that this was the production of his skill" (64). Arthur's fugitive suspicion proves correct when he discovers "the well-known pacquet… which enclosed the portrait of Clavering!" (65), a discovery that only serves to deepen his involvement in Welbeck's fraudulent schemes.

Significantly, forgery is a crime of resemblance, and resemblance is a crime of which Arthur is accused repeatedly. The young man is assumed to look like Clavering, the wealthy aristocrat who dies mysteriously at his provincial home with his self-portrait, and he is also accused of looking like Clemenza Lodi's deceased brother Vincentio. Upon finding "a miniature portrait" of Vincentio in Clemenza's abandoned chamber, Arthur is, in fact, hard-pressed not to believe that it was not drawn in his own image (82). In many ways, portraits produce their own types of illusion concerning the values attributed to their likeness to an original. These episodes refer to contemporary practices of portraiture in order to explore anxieties in the early republic about art's relation to in imposture and illusion in all their forms.

IV. Aesthetics and Politics

While portraiture offers Brown a useful platform for commenting on problems of vision and discernment, his incorporation of specific artists and minute descriptions of art and architecture enable him to convey the ideological valences of different aesthetic modes in his novels and *Historical Sketches*. *Ormond* furnishes a dramatic example of this treatment of the contemporary politics of art. In it, Brown portrays his only formally trained artist protagonist in the character of Stephen Dudley. Brown apparently modeled aspects of this character on his close friend William Dunlap, who was formally trained in London under Benjamin West and would go on to establish the field of American art history with his *History of the Rise and Progress of the Arts of Design in the United States* (1834). By his own admission, Dunlap squandered his early opportunity, lounging around London with other young men and frequenting the theater but rarely appearing in West's studio. However tenuous, these studies were cut short when his ailing father called him home to assist in running the family shop, Samuel Dunlap & Son. On his father's death in 1791, Dunlap was forced to manage the store on his own until 1796, when he took on partners so he could devote himself entirely to the theater. Dunlap eventually returned to painting after going bankrupt as a theater manager in New York in 1805, and for a time he became an itinerate portrait painter in order to support his family.

In *Ormond*, Constantia Dudley's father shares a similar academic trajectory. Like Dunlap, he was sent abroad by his merchant father to study under two masters affiliated with the Royal Academy—engraver Francesco Bartolozzi (1725–1815)[10] and painter Henry Fuseli (1741–1825)—in order to became a landscape painter, a genre that, oddly, neither artist practiced and which had yet to gain real popularity in the United States.[11] Fuseli produced history and literary genre paintings, while Bartolozzi gained renown with his engravings of paintings by others, notably Angelica Kauffman's figural allegorical studies. In giving Dudley such a remarkable and in many ways conflicted pedigree, Brown lays the groundwork for what may be read as a pointed commentary on the cultural associations of competing visual and aesthetic references in the early republic.

The Swiss-born Fuseli was alternately associated with the classical revival in his early years, particularly with his translation of Johann Winckelmann's *Reflections on the Painting and Sculpture of the Greeks* (1765), and the Romantic and Gothic movements when he turned to darker subjects later in his career. The troubling subject matter and attenuated stylization of his best-known painting, *The Nightmare* (1781), which Brown later used as a frontispiece for Volume IV of his *Literary Magazine*, illustrates this turn. Given the wide circulation of its engraving, it was an image closely associated with Fuseli's reputation and one Brown probably had in mind when writing *Ormond*. Italian-born Bartolozzi, on the other hand, known to Brown and his circle for his illustrations of a 1796 translation of Gottfried Bürger's "Lenore," made his reputation with a novel method of stipple engraving. Though more efficient than traditional line engraving, Bartolozzi's method was considered a less meticulous and more feminized style, appropriate only for classical and feminine subjects because of the soft tonal effects it could produce.

Through their association with the Royal Academy, both Fuseli and Bartolozzi were leading figures in elite and progressive London art and literary circles in the 1780s and 1790s, and both were closely associated with influential female intellectuals and artists (Fuseli with Mary Wollstonecraft and Bartolozzi with Kauffman). Both held "outsider" status to one degree or another, Bartolozzi for his work as an engraver (considered a technical rather than a fine art) and his method of stipple engraving, Fuseli for his radical take on traditional subjects. Though welcomed into the academy as an invigorating force, Fuseli was equally applauded and criticized for his work. He became a brand name, the

Fusilesque, identified with supernatural and horrific subjects as well as with obscure and sublime scenes from literature. He combines the often dialectical oppositions of the appetite and intellect, defined by his fusion or confusion of the ideal and the popular. Joshua Reynolds's and Fuseli's rival *The Death of Dido* paintings are often-cited examples of his departure from convention.[12] Both paintings were presented at the Exhibition of the Royal Academy in 1781. Reynolds's is horizontal and conventional, portraying a supine Dido in the visual language of the seventeenth-century baroque, whereas Fuseli's vertical canvas refers to classical forms but perverts and transforms them.

Fuseli's problematic or troubled classicism—illustrated, for example, in *The Artist in Despair over the Magnitude of Antique Fragments* (1778–1780)—in many ways parallels or prefigures Brown's own, particularly as it appears in the tension between the neoclassical and Gothic styles in the early architectural drawings and in the more complex tension between sober neoclassicism and sensual Gothic or Italianate styles that is developed in *Ormond*.[13] The competing influences of the neoclassical and the Gothic in Brown's architectural designs may point to competing ideologies, in Enlightened rationalism and its Gothic twin, that he later delineates in Dudley's conflicted artistic training and throughout the 1799 novel. In Brown's early compass-and-ink drawings, the Gothic is not entirely in competition with the neoclassical, but his attempts to rework the Gothic into the neoclassical may represent an uncertain attempt at a fusion of the two at the turning of the tide. Likewise, in selecting Fuseli and Bartolozzi as the sources of Dudley's artistic tutelage, Brown presents a conflicted aesthetic legacy to which Constantia must reconcile herself: both artists exemplify period tensions between, on the one hand, a classical-Augustan aesthetic of balance, regularity, order, geometry, harmony, and idealization of precedents and preexisting order and, on the other, a Gothic, pre-Romantic aesthetic that prioritizes expression over its regulation, irregularity, sensuality (through bodily and emotional intensities), and modernizing departure from convention. Brown implicitly politicizes these opposing aesthetic modes throughout the novel, juxtaposing the novel's many contrasts between the (neo)classical and its aesthetic others with more directly ideological contrasts such as that between the novel's reactionary narrator, Sophia, and the revolutionary Amazon Martinette de Beauvais, both of whom compete for the affection of the protagonist, Constantia. Ultimately, in staging tensions between juxtaposed aesthetic and sociopolitical worldviews, whether in drawings, periodical writings, or fictions, Brown links aesthetic debates to wider cultural and political struggles over the shape of the new republic.

NOTES

1. Brown excerpted long passages from London reviews of Knight's *Analytic Inquiry* for several 1806 articles in his *Literary Magazine*. See, for example, "Connoisseurship and Its Pleasures," LM 5.32 (May 1806): 365–366.
2. Employed by artists, tourists, and connoisseurs, the Claude glass was a small convex mirror, typically tinted black or a dark rose color. It was named after Claude Lorraine, the creator of the landscape genre, whose name became synonymous with the picturesque aesthetic in

the eighteenth century. To use the device, the viewer turns his or her back to the scene and views the landscape through this tinted mirror, framing the scene and abstracting its tonal values to lend it a painterly quality.

3. According to Kenney and Workman, "the adaption of the neoclassical concept of nature to include the Gothic, took place with the extension to architecture of two ideas from the sizable literature on landscape gardening: first, quite early in the century, the idea that the Gothic in architecture was a direct imitation of nature—carrying the garden, as it were, indoors—and, second, the principle of irregularity, which was developed in 1757 in Edmund Burke's essay, *The Sublime and the Beautiful*" (Kenney and Workman 133).

4. Brown refers to Palmyra in the early "Henrietta Letters" (c. 1789–1792 and thus roughly contemporaneous with these drawings) and his longest poem, "Devotion" (1794); see Letters. In Henrietta Letter XIV, the "CBB" persona contrasts his modest hut to the grandeur of Tedmor: "I am not less delighted or benefited in gazing at the loosened cement and stragling bricks than in Contemplating the broken shafts and shattered intablatures of Tedmor and Persepolis" (Letters 724). In "Devotion," Brown styles himself the "Child of Vetruvian, and Paladian Art" (Letters 276).

5. "The buildings there [in Elfreth's Alley] represent the modest—though ambitious—achievements of the artisan families who bought and constructed their houses and shops in this urban center during several building peaks in the mid- and late-eighteenth century" (Herman and Guillery 208). As a representation of middling aspirations, Elfreth's Alley reflects a democratic market culture that promised upward mobility without pretension.

6. Wells Bennett and Fiske Kimball collaborated on a six-part series of articles examining various contributions to this design competition, with a particular emphasis on the drawings of William Thornton and Stephan Hallet.

7. This visionary style was also called "architecture parlante," or speaking architecture, because its designs plainly speak to or explain their functions.

8. Eckstein father or son appears in Philadelphia directories of 1796–1797, as well as in 1805–1806 and 1811–1812 as a portrait painter and modeler in clay and is known to have engraved in the stippling manner after Francesco Bartolozzi. Brown visited his gallery, "John Eckstein & Sons," with three female friends, Deborah Ferris, Ruth Paxson, and Mary Attmore, in April 1795. He later mentions the Ecksteins in "On Painting as a Female Accomplishment" PF, (October 12, 1802).

9. An example of the titillation that such portraiture might provide is Sarah Goodridge's *Beauty Revealed* (1823). Painted on a $2\frac{5}{8}$-by-$3\frac{1}{8}$-inch sliver of ivory, the popular miniature artist depicted only her bare breasts for this salacious self-portrait. The miniature was a gift to her friend, client, and frequent correspondent, Daniel Webster.

10. Bartolozzi was the first engraver invited to join the Royal Academy.

11. The landscape comes to prominence in America in the antebellum years with the rise of Thomas Cole and the Hudson River School.

12. Myrone 84–86.

13. For a discussion of this tension between neoclassical style and its Romantic or Gothic others and this tension's role in the larger formal issues at play in *Ormond*, see Barnard and Shapiro xviii–xix.

Works Cited

Anonymous. "Stanzas, Commemorative of the late Charles Brockden Brown, of Philadelphia, author of *Wieland, Ormond, Arthur Mervyn*, &c." PF 4.3 (September 1810): 287.

Axelrod, Alan. *Charles Brockden Brown, an American Tale.* Austin: University of Texas Press, 1983.

Barnard, Philip. "Culture and Authority in Brown's *Historical Sketches.*" In Philip Barnard, Mark L. Kamrath, and Stephen Shapiro, eds., *Revising Charles Brockden Brown: Culture, Politics, and Sexuality in the Early Republic,* 310–331. Knoxville: University of Tennessee Press, 2004.

Barnard, Philip, and Stephen Shapiro. "Introduction." In Charles Brockden Brown, *Ormond; or, The Secret Witness, with Related Texts,* ix–lii. Cambridge, Mass.: Hackett, 2009.

Bellion, Wendy. *Citizen Spectator: Art, Illusion, and Discernment in Early National Philadelphia.* Chapel Hill: University of North Carolina Press, 2011.

Bennett, Wells, and Fiske Kimball. "The Competition for the Federal Buildings, 1792–1793." *Journal of the American Institute of Architects* (1919): 7.1: 8–12; 7.3: 98–102; 7.5: 202–210; 7.8: 355–361; 7.12: 521–528; 8.3: 117–124.

Berthold, Dennis. "Charles Brockden Brown, *Edgar Huntly,* and the Origins of the American Picturesque." *William and Mary Quarterly* 41.1 (1984): 62–84.

Brown, Charles Brockden. "American Prospects." LM 3.17 (February 1805): 97.

Brown, Charles Brockden. "Connoisseurship and Its Pleasures," LM 5.32. (May 1806): 365–366.

Brown, Charles Brockden. "On a Taste for the Picturesque." MM 3.1 (July 1800): 11–13.

Brown, Charles Brockden. "On Painting as a Female Accomplishment." PF (October 12, 1802).

Burke, Edmund. *A Philosophyical Enquiry into the Origins of Our Ideas of the Sublime and Beautiful.* 1757. London: Printed for J. Dodsley in Pall-mall, 1767.

Diderot, Denis. *Encyclopédie, ou dictionnaire raisoné des sciences, des arts et des métiers.* Vol. 1–17. Paris: Briasson, David, Le Breton, Durand, 1751–1765.

Dunlap, William. *History of the Rise and Progress of the Arts of Design in the United States.* New York: G.P. Scott and Co., 1834.

Faherty, Duncan. *Remodeling the Nation: The Architecture of American Identity, 1776–1858.* Lebanon: University of New Hampshire Press, 2007.

Fliegelman, Jay. *Prodigals and Pilgrims.* New York: Cambridge University Press, 1982.

Gilpin, William. *Observations on the River Wye, and Several Parts of South Wales.* London: Printed for R. Blamire, 1782.

Gilpin, William. *Three Essays on Picturesque Beauty.* London: Printed for R. Blamire, 1792.

Grabo, Norman S. *The Coincidental Art of Charles Brockden Brown.* Chapel Hill: University of North Carolina Press, 1981.

Guillery, Peter and Bernard Herman. "Negotiating Classicism in eighteenth-century Deptford and Philadelphia." *Articulating British Classicism: New Approaches to Eighteenth-Century Architecture.* Ed. Barbara Arciszewska and Elizabeth McKellar. Burlington, VT: Ashgate, 2004. 187–225.

Kenney, Alice P., and Leslie J. Workman. "Ruins, Romance, and Reality: Medievalism in Anglo-American Imagination and Taste, 1750–1840." *Winterthur Portfolio* 10 (1975): 131–163.

Knight, Richard Payne. *An Analytical Inquiry into the Principles of Taste.* London: Printed for T. Payne, Mews Gate; and J. White, Fleet-Street, 1805.

Lawson-Peebles, Robert. *Landscape and Written Expression in Revolutionary America.* New York: Cambridge University Press, 1988.

Lovell, Margaretta M. *Art in a Season of Revolution: Painters, Artisans, and Patrons in Early America.* Philadelphia: University of Pennsylvania Press, 2005.

Lueck, Beth L. "Charles Brockden Brown's *Edgar Huntly*: The Picturesque Traveler as Sleepwalker." *Studies in American Fiction* 15.1 (Spring 1987): 25–42.

Mackenzie, Alexander. *Voyages from Montreal, on the River St. Lawrence, through the Continent of North America to the Frozen and Pacific Oceans in the Years 1789 and 1793.* London: T. Cadell Jr. and W. Davies, 1801.

Myrone, Martin. "The Sublime as Spectacle: The Transformation of Ideal Art at Somerset House." In David H. Solkin, ed., *Art on the Line: The Royal Academy Exhibitions at Somerset House 1780–1836,* 77–91. New Haven, Conn.: Yale University Press, 2001.

Rush, Benjamin. *Essays, Literary, Moral, and Philosophical.* Philadelphia, Thomas and William Bradford, 1798.

Stabile, Susan. *Memory's Daughters: The Material Culture of Remembrance in Eighteenth-Century America.* Ithaca, N.Y.: Cornell University Press, 2004.

Stern, Julia. *The Plight of Sympathy.* Chicago: University of Chicago Press, 1997.

Sweet, Timothy. *American Georgics: Economy and Environment in American Literature, 1580–1864.* Philadelphia: University of Pennsylvania Press, 2001.

Verplanck, Gulian C. [Review] "Art. V. *The Life of Charles Brockden Brown.*" *North American Review* 9 (June 1819): 58–77.

West, Benjamin. *History of the Rise and Progress of the Arts of Design in the United States.* 1834.

Winckelman, Johann. *Reflections on the Painting and Sculpture of the Greeks.* Tran. Henry Fuseli. London: Printed for the Translator and sold by A. Millar, 1765.

Wood, Robert. *The Ruins of Palmyra, otherwise Tedmor in the Desart.* London: 1753.

PART VIII

....

RECEPTION

....

CHAPTER 32

··

BROWN'S LITERARY
AFTERLIFE

··

EZRA TAWIL

IF one takes the long view of Charles Brockden Brown's reception over the two centuries since his death from tuberculosis in 1810, the graph of his literary prestige looks something like an inverted bell curve: from early heights, caving into a long obscurity, then swooping upward to a new critical prominence and scholarly attention.[1] While he was not exactly a literary star during his lifetime, Brown's posthumous reputation and influence among elite anglophone writers during the Romantic era, which is the focus of this chapter, were rather significant on both sides of the Atlantic and remained so until the end of the 1850s. That status would erode in the last few decades of the century, though the reasons had less to do with a reassessment of Brown specifically than with a more general shift in dominant literary modes—one that brought realism and naturalism to the cultural fore, while Gothicism and sentimentalism became increasingly associated with a primitive or otherwise abjected literary past. Brown never fell entirely off the cultural radar during that period, but by 1900 or so, he had become a passing figure of obligatory mention rather than a compelling object of substantial critical treatment. The recent renaissance in Brown criticism, then, represents less the critical discovery of a heretofore unappreciated literary figure and more the restoration of a stature that he had already largely possessed in the eyes of (now canonical) writers in Great Britain, Europe, and the United States during roughly the first half of the nineteenth century.

Moreover, the nineteenth-century phase of Brown's reception is marked by an interesting if peculiar feature, namely, that his posthumous reputation was initially far more robust in Europe than it was in America. Granted, this state of affairs is only paradoxical if we are inclined to assume that Brown's reception was always shaped by the blunt cultural politics of literary nationalism or that it must necessarily be viewed predominantly through that lens. This has been a particularly difficult presumption to leave behind, since for much of the twentieth century, critics in the United States worked so hard to turn Brown into a literary founding father. By the time of Leslie Fiedler's landmark 1960 chapter on Brown, "Charles Brockden Brown and the Invention of the

American Gothic," this was already a common critical reflex; after Fiedler's treatment, it became, for a time, nearly inescapable.[2] Yet if we want to understand the Brown of the nineteenth century, the trick is to recover his reputation as it first unfolded, rather than retrojecting twentieth- and twenty-first-century critical presumptions onto it. The transatlantic divergence in his reception, for example, has complex causes and forms an interesting episode in reception history. And for reasons that will soon become clear, the story can best be told by moving back and forth across the Atlantic in an effort to reimagine the circulation of ideas, influences, and aesthetic norms that first framed Brown's work and gave it meaning and value for a transatlantic readership.

Brown's major novels saw several reissues in England before 1820, during which time they drew the fascination and praise of literati such as William Hazlitt, Thomas Love Peacock, Mary and Percy Bysshe Shelley, William Godwin, John Keats, and Walter Scott.[3] Brown's were also the first US novels to be translated into European languages—*Ormond* in German in 1803 and *Wieland* in French in 1808. From the 1820s on, European publishers often published his works in combined editions with those of Mary Shelley and Friedrich Schiller. Though it is hard to generalize about what the entire range of European readers and critics saw in Brown during this period, he was most often described as a Gothic "romancer," the most prominent American working in the mode of an Anne Radcliffe or a Matthew "Monk" Lewis. For others, particularly in the British context, he was the "American Godwin," a node in the network of British radicals emanating from William Godwin and Mary Wollstonecraft and a practitioner of what critics would later identify as the "Godwinian novel."[4]

At the same time, Brown's work was only scantily republished in his own country in the first decades after his death; the first full second American edition of his novels would wait until S. G. Goodrich's 1827 *Collected Edition*. For a certain mainstream strain of American critical reception, Brown tended at first to be treated with a peculiar combination of respect and condescension—a posture whose origins can be traced to William Dunlap's biography of Brown.[5] First published in 1815, this literary biography stamped Brown criticism at its very outset with what would become an infinitely reproducible trope: Brown as brilliant but limited literary progenitor, a fertile yet flawed precursor whose untamed, even wild genius had later to be disciplined by others in a simultaneous act of fulfillment and overcoming.[6] According to this common conception, Brown possessed a vigorous intellect but also an unregulated one; his literary output evidences an imaginative faculty and a prose style that need to be defended for their excesses even as they were celebrated for their sublimity. "[T]he ardor with which he speaks," Dunlap wrote, "unless the peculiarity of his character is known—unless his warm and sublimated fancy—his intense feelings—are taken into consideration, will need an apology."[7]

Read in the context of the period's prevailing aesthetic assumptions, however, there is somewhat more to this kind of double-edged critical treatment than meets the eye. Though undercutting in an obvious sense, it also draws on the notion of "original genius" as it had developed in British poetic criticism over the course of the long eighteenth century.[8] As critics began to emphasize early in that century, the faculty of poetic genius was marked, first and foremost, by "enthusiastic passion" rather than technical skill or polish; the great poets are thus characterized less by "correctness" than by imaginative heat or vitality.[9] Consequently, they can often be found wanting or even "defective in some points that relate to external embellishments."[10] By the latter half of the eighteenth century, this counterintuitive notion served as the basis of a recognizably pre-Romantic cult of poetic genius. In a 1767 treatise, for example, Scottish critic William Duff described this model of the poet, who, by virtue of his enthusiastic passion, is most recognizable by irregular greatness: "Sometimes indeed he will be happy enough to paint his very thought, and to excite in others the very sentiments which he himself feels: he will not always however succeed so well, but, on the contrary, will often labour in a fruitless attempt; whence it should seem, that his composition will upon certain occasions be distinguished by an irregular and unequal greatness."[11] In eighteenth-century British criticism, this kind of aesthetic vitality was most strongly associated not with contemporary poets such as John Milton but with the ancient bards. The poets of Europe's antiquity, the logic goes, were capable of reaching such sublime heights precisely because no regular forms had yet arisen to constrain their untutored imaginations; their very lack of perfection is thus the paradoxical sign of their authenticity. Hugh Blair's celebration of the work of Ossian, for example, tellingly employed this trope of the blessed defect; Blair actually proceeded by focusing on the poetic *faults* of "our rude Celtic bard" in contrast to the more polished and skillful Homer.[12] Ossian's writing is marred by "a few improprieties"; he is at times "uncouth and abrupt"; and he no doubt lacks "the extensive knowledge, the regular dignity of narration, the fullness and accuracy of description, which we find in Homer and Virgil."[13] Yet by virtue of these same features, Ossian's poetry is "sublime...in an eminent degree."[14]

Though this critical discourse was focused, of course, on poetic enthusiasm in particular, it does lie to some extent in the background of some early critical assessments of Brown's own impassioned prose stylistics among American critics. This is important to bear in mind, as the history of Brown's critical reception is littered with otherwise unaccountable ambivalence, backhanded compliments, and oxymoronic evaluations. Aside from Dunlap's literary biography, one early critical treatment of Brown that helped establish this pattern was Richard Henry Dana, Sr.'s essay on "The Novels of Charles Brockden Brown," which appeared in *The United States Review and Literary Gazette* for August 1827. "Brown's genius not only wanted variety," Dana writes; "it seemed to be without even pliability."[15] Yet "even the want of variety, and the defects of style in Brown have in some measure helped to the impression of the truth of his stories."[16] The aesthetic argument on which Dana draws here is not simply that genius is erratic because it eschews formal niceties. The key move is the reversal by which artistic genius exists *in* certain stylistic flaws, not just despite them. For Dana, Brown's "defects of style" actually deepen the "impression of...truth" in the minds of his readers. Moreover, there is an important national dimension to this application of topoi which British criticism had associated strongly with the cult of the ancient bards. For in this way, Anglo-American critics could retool these aesthetic concepts as a way of grappling with the problem, endemic in the early republic, of defining US literary culture in the face of its obvious youth and underdevelopment. Indeed, decades before Walt Whitman sounded his "barbaric yawp" as a point of literary-nationalist pride, some critics used this kind of uncultivated aesthetic to celebrate the "splendid barbarism" of American writing—to invoke that remarkable phrase from Edward Tyrell Channing's 1816 essay, "On Models in Literature."[17]

Meanwhile, Brown was being talked about rather differently during this period by British critics, who could view him without the tint of literary nationalism. Two early landmark years in his British reception were 1821 and 1822, when most of Brown's major prose works were issued in new editions by A. K. Newman and Henry Colburn, along with the latter's carefully synchronized British reprint of Dunlap's 1815 biography in an abridged form, opening the way for a transatlantic reception that would profoundly shape Brown's stature abroad. These republications, and the British market's favorable receipt thereof, may seem remarkable given the infamous quip of Sydney Smith in the *Edinburgh Review* just two years before: "In the four quarters of the globe, who reads an American book?"[18] US literary historiography commonly points to Washington Irving and James Fenimore Cooper as the triumphant, if slightly belated, responses to Smith's rhetorical question, but as S. W. Reid has suggested, Brown's earlier prominence suggests that for many British readers, he had already begun to answer it—and not just in spite of his Americanness but, in part, precisely because of it.[19] For though we are accustomed to the traditional national battle lines in the Anglo-American "paper war"—in which British writers represented America only as the barren site of philistinish anticulture, and American writers strove only to prove them mistaken—we must also remember that for many British Romantics around the turn of the nineteenth century, "America" represented a place of extravagant aesthetic possibility and the promise of cultural renewal. Samuel Taylor Coleridge and Robert Southey, for example, fantasized their mid-1790s utopian emigration scheme of "Pantisocracy" as taking place in America, where they and "a small company of chosen individuals" formed the idea of "trying the experiment of human Perfectibility."[20] The specific site upon which they settled for this plan (never actually executed) was Charles Brockden Brown's own figurative backyard in Pennsylvania, "on the banks of the Susquehanna River," as they usually put it—though their source for this particular geographical fantasy was not, of course, Brown's Pennsylvania-set fictions (published a few years later) but the earlier regional narratives of J. Hector St. Jean de Crèvecoeur and John Bartram, on which Brown himself partly drew.

In the case of some British Romantics, the Brown connection and the dynamics of his influence can be documented rather clearly. Peacock famously detailed Percy Shelley's fascination with Brown and the imprint left on the young poet's formative imagination by Brown's romances: "He was especially fond of the novels of Brown—Charles Brockden Brown, the American, who died at the age of thirty-nine," wrote Peacock in his *Memoirs of Shelley*. Singling out four of Brown's works (*Wieland, Ormond, Edgar Huntly,* and *Arthur Mervyn*) for their particular impact on Shelley, Peacock explains:

> These four tales were unquestionably works of great genius, and were remarkable for the way in which natural causes were made to produce the semblance of supernatural

effects. The superstitious terror of romance could scarcely be more strongly excited than by the perusal of Wieland. Brown's four novels, Schiller's Robbers, and Goethe's Faust, were, of all the works with which he was familiar, those which took the deepest root in his mind, and had the strongest influence in the formation of his character.... He devotedly admired Wordsworth and Coleridge, and in a minor degree Southey: these had great influence on his style, and Coleridge especially on his imagination; but admiration is one thing and assimilation is another; and nothing so blended itself with the structure of his interior mind as the creations of Brown. Nothing stood so clearly before his thoughts as a perfect combination of the purely ideal and possibly real, as Constantia Dudley.[21]

Peacock gave little detail about the particular period of Shelley's "assimilation" of Brown, but later scholars have attempted to fill in the blanks and also to follow suit by attributing specific aspects of Shelley's aesthetic practice—from his youthful experiments with the Gothic romance to certain thematic and stylistic aspects of his mature poetry—to his encounter with the American "romancer."[22]

Another transatlantic line of influence having to do with Brown's experiments with prose "romance"—one with particular importance also to Brown's cisatlantic influence, as we shall see—runs to Scott. The full historical record on Scott's opinion of Brown, it must be said, is somewhat more ambivalent than that of other British Romantics. According to a later anecdote, Scott spoke somewhat dismissively of Brown at a dinner party in 1824. "Brown had wonderful powers," he reportedly said, "...but I think he was led astray by falling under the influence of bad examples, prevalent at his time. Had he written his own thoughts, he would have been, perhaps, immortal: in writing those of others, his fame was of course ephemeral."[23] Nevertheless, there is much to suggest that he regarded Brown's literary corpus as significant. Scott's library included both early (c. 1803) reissues of Brown's fiction and later (c. 1820) reprints; Scott initially planned to include novels by Brown as he compiled *Ballantyne's Novelist's Library* in the early 1820s. More significantly still, Scott's own novel *Guy Mannering, or the Astrologer* (1815) paid explicit homage to Brown by including a character named Arthur Mervyn connected to one of the plot's minor intrigues. (The protagonist's old friend Mervyn is the one responsible for protecting Mannering's daughter from the overtures of a young man named Brown.)[24] Beyond that allusion, moreover, critics have noted the resonances of Brown's *Edgar Huntly* in some of the turns of Scott's plot. As Fiona Robertson observes, this line of influence raises the intriguing possibility that "works generally accepted as precursors of American romance could also be creative recollections *of* American romance."[25] If we take this suggestion seriously, the standard literary-historical questions about the emergence of the American romance appear in a new light; in particular, we get a more complex picture of the movement from Brown's fiction to Cooper's frontier novels, with Scott serving as a kind of transatlantic way station.

American literary history has not traditionally drawn very specific lines of influence from Brown to Cooper, tending instead to render the latter in more general terms as a more successful and more realized incarnation of Brown's more tentative project of forging a bona fide national tradition a few decades earlier.[26] The most obvious formal sources for Cooper's most celebrated fictions, which is to say, the ones in the "frontier romance" mode, were Scott's historical romances. But even as Cooper clearly adopted Scott's form, he also adapted it in important ways; Cooper would not have been Cooper had he not infused that literary mode with hyperbolically regional materials of setting, character, and theme. But this was also Brown's precise stated goal in the preface to *Edgar Huntly*: to use "native" themes and environments such as the "incidents of Indian hostility, and the perils of the Western wilderness" (EH 3) to generate the literary materials on which a new national tradition might be built. And on the face of it, Brown's experiment with setting and theme in that novel almost provided a template for the frontier form on which Cooper famously built his literary reputation. Indeed, reading Cooper's wilderness settings with Brown in mind, it becomes almost impossible *not* to think of the landscapes of Brown's fictional Pennsylvania. Take, for example, the extravagantly sublime backdrop of the Glens Falls episode in *The Last of the Mohicans*.[27] Cooper in that passage hits all the marks in Brown's description of Norwalk in *Edgar Huntly*: precipitous heights, craggy cliffs, secluded recesses, obscure woods, roaring cataracts, and, conceptually uniting them all, the "appalling" fascination of the sublime American wilderness. Cooper was certainly aware of Brown's novel and of its distinctive use of setting specifically, as evidenced by the reference he had made, in the preface to *The Spy* (1821), to the "cave scene in *Edgar Huntly*."[28] Yet if we also consider Robertson's argument that Scott himself also in some fashion absorbed Brown's American experiments with comparable modes, we are faced with the possibility that Brown's influence on Cooper may have flowed in two ways: directly, via his own readings of his American predecessor, and indirectly, via his study of Scott. This kind of tangled transatlantic movement bears mention here because it enables a richer understanding of the dynamics of Brown's nineteenth-century reputation, not to speak of the literary culture of the period more generally. We begin to be able to see literary "influence," that is, not as a unidirectional vector from, say, Old World sources to New World emulations but as a more complex circulation and recirculation of cultural materials.

Perhaps the most historically significant axis of this kind began with the contacts between members of Brown's New York circle and the group of British radicals around Godwin and Wollstonecraft, inaugurating a transatlantic interchange of ideas that is taken up in a wider sense by Abigail Smith Stocker in chapter 17 of this volume. From the perspective of Brown's reception, the most consequential event was Godwin's encounter with Brown's writing. Godwin read Brown's *Alcuin* in the summer of 1798, as soon as it was available in London, thus completing the circle that opened when Brown first read Godwin's *Enquiry Concerning Critical Justice*—a book the young Brown referred to as his "oracle." Brown criticism has traditionally been focused on Brown's intellectual debt to Godwin and, by extension, on how the posthumous attention of the Woldwinites (as the Godwin-Wollstonecraft group has recently been designated)[29] gave Brown immediate currency among writers interested in that particular literary lineage. Certainly, the whole encounter did shape Brown's reception among British writers such as Mary Wollstonecraft Shelley, Percy Shelley, Peacock, and others. At the same time, as more recent work has begun to explore, the influence may have been no less consequential in the other direction. In 1816, for example, Godwin returned to Brown's writing, "devour[ing] five of Brown's works in one five-week glut."[30] There is reason to think that this reencounter partly inspired Godwin's return to fiction with *Mandeville: A Tale of the Seventeenth Century in England*, which appeared the following year.[31] Not least, we have Godwin's direct acknowledgment of his debt in his opening to that novel:

> The impression, that first led me to look with an eye of favour upon the subject here treated, was derived from a story-book, called Wieland, written by a person, certainly of distinguished genius, who I believe was born and died in the province of Pennsylvania in the United States of North America, and who calls himself C. B. Brown.[32]

As one literary historian has it: "Whatever influence Godwin had transmitted to Brown had made the return trip."[33]

Nor, to push the matter still further, do the transatlantic crossings end there. For this image of Brown on the far side of the Atlantic was then reflected back across the ocean once again, as Brown passed through a European lens to catch the eye of American writers. That is, by drawing on early European Romantic thought, Brown in effect made his own work available for absorption by the emerging generation of Romantics, who in turn served as models and sources of inspiration for the next generation of US literary producers, and so on. Thus, for example, the lines of connection between Brown and Scott and, via Scott, between Brown and Cooper, illustrate this kind of tangled transatlantic movement. So, too, with the process by which Brown's influence moved through the Woldwinites to American writers such as Edgar Allan Poe and, via Poe, to mid-century American writers George Lippard, Nathaniel Hawthorne, and Margaret Fuller.

Interestingly, when Poe referred to Brown as an early shaping force in American literature, he actually did so in a discussion of Cooper. In a review of Cooper's *Wyandotté* in 1843, Poe placed Brown reverentially at the head of a list of "American writers of the less generally circulated, but more worthy and more artistical fictions."[34] This gesture, of course, also raises the question of Poe's own relation to Brown. Poe's contemporaries noted some form of a connection between the two; Rufus Griswold averred in 1845 that "Mr. Poe resembles Brockden Brown in his intimacy with mental pathology, but surpasses that author in delineation."[35] Later scholarship traces the lines of artistic influence from Brown to Poe in terms as general as a shared "morbidity" of imagination and as specific as Brown's incipient explorations of crime and detection as fictional themes and epistemological problems—Brown as an early forerunner of the "city mystery" or "urban Gothic" modes of the later nineteenth century.[36] One of the most productive of these critical avenues is the recent argument that Godwin and Brown together enabled the emergence of nineteenth-century sensationalism in the hands of such authors as Lippard.[37]

Indeed, no nineteenth-century writer was more explicit about his debts to Brown as a literary ancestor than Lippard, a fellow Philadelphian. Lippard's 1845 novel *The Quaker City; or, The Monks of Monk Hall* began with the words "Inscribed to the memory of Charles Brockden Brown."[38] Stylistically, thematically, in terms of setting, and in many other ways, *The Quaker City* carried distinct and clear echoes of Brown's fictions a half-century earlier. In one sense, Lippard's "record of human weakness, wretchedness, and crime"[39] would seem particularly indebted to Brown's *Wieland* and *Edgar Huntly*. From another perspective, Lippard's novel—subtitled *A Romance of Philadelphia Life, Mystery, and Crime*—had as its more direct antecedents those works by Brown with more predominant use of city settings, *Arthur Mervyn* and *Ormond*.

Meanwhile, other writers of the period, perhaps less amenable to sensationalism, seemingly had trouble figuring out how to register the importance of a writer like Brown, whose literary significance seemed to them undeniable but whose themes seemed in some ways extravagant, perhaps even amoral. In a fascinating article titled "Fanaticism," John Greenleaf Whittier leads into his discussion of Brown by referring to a recent real-life crime: "There are occasionally deeds committed almost too horrible and revolting for publication. The tongue falters in giving them utterance; the pen trembles that records them."[40] After this rather Brownian narratorial throat-clearing, Whittier narrates "the ghastly horror of a late tragedy in Edgecomb, in the State of Maine," where a formerly "respectable and thriving citizen and his wife" formed a murder-suicide pact. Addled by a deranged religious enthusiasm born of years "engaged in brooding over the mysteries of the Apocalypse," they "came to an agreement that the husband should first kill his wife and their four children and then put an end to his own existence. This was literally executed, the miserable man striking off the heads of his wife and children with his axe, and then cutting his own throat."[41] From here, Whittier turns to "Charles Brockden Brown, a writer whose merits have not yet been sufficiently acknowledged."[42] In *Wieland*, his "strange and solemn romance," Brown has given us an "analysis" of what Whittier calls "diseased conscientiousness," such as that which tragically misrecognizes "the mad suggestions of a disordered brain as the injunctions of Divinity."[43] Throughout the piece, Whittier tellingly oscillates between a focus on the novel's aesthetic effects and its moral or philosophical contributions. At one point, for example, Whittier praises Brown's narration of the same type of ghastly scene Whittier himself tremblingly recorded at the beginning of his essay, namely, the scene in which Wieland, in a fit of enthusiastic madness, "sacrifices" his family in what he believes to be the fulfillment of divine will:

> In the entire range of English literature there is no more thrilling passage than that which describes the execution of this baleful suggestion. The coloring of the picture is an intermingling of the lights of heaven and hell,—soft shades of tenderest pity and warm tints of unextinguishable love contrasting with the terrible outlines of an insane and cruel purpose, traced with the blood of murder. The masters of the old Greek tragedy have scarcely exceeded the sublime horror of this scene from the American novelist... described with an intensity which almost stops the heart of the reader.[44]

The concept of "sublimity" here perhaps helps Whittier to navigate his apparent ambivalence about the coincidence of "thrilling" aesthetics and bloody thematics—for what would it say about him that he experiences the heights of pleasure in reading of such violence? Later in the piece, he flatly declares that "*Wieland* is not a pleasant book."[45] Whittier then tellingly compares it to a contemporary work that seemed to many to suffer from the same unsavory emphasis on the anatomy of terrible cruelty: "In one respect [*Wieland*] resembles the modern tale of *Wuthering Heights*: it has great strength and power, but no beauty." Yet unlike Emily Brontë's novel, Whittier clarifies, Brown's possesses "an important and salutary moral."[46] In this way, as well, he recuperates Brown, whose novel seems not to be guided by a morbid fascination with violence but, rather, to offer "a powerful and philosophical analysis of [a] morbid state of mind."[47]

This image of Brown, not just as a dispenser of fictional pleasures but as an analyst of complicated and sometimes dark philosophical and psychological themes, was somewhat prevalent in the mid-nineteenth century. Fuller's expansive assessments in the late 1840s are a particularly compelling case in point. In two essays published in 1846, "Charles Brockden Brown" and "American Literature: Its Position in the Present Time and Prospects for the Future," Fuller celebrated Brown as "a novelist by far our first in point of genius and instruction as to the soul of things."[48] Significantly, she turns his lack of current popularity, and even his constant danger of falling out of print, into a mark of terminally underrated genius: "It is their dark, deep gloom that prevents their being popular, for their very beauties are grave and sad."[49] On the one hand, this insistence on gloominess tends to draw Brown toward the nineteenth-century type of the poète maudit, an aesthetic outsider who can never really find a proper home in society, or a proper literary audience, precisely because he is "against" sociality itself. On the other hand, Fuller insists that Brown and his contemporary, Godwin, were "Hegelians" with "the highest idea of the dignity, power, and beauty of which human nature is capable." In this sense, she also positioned Brown's "precious revelations" as early stirrings of the transcendental spirit emerging in her own time.[50] In both ways, Fuller's Brown was— and here she inaugurated another trope that would come to be a staple of Brown criticism— a man ahead of his time. In relation to gender, for example, she once again finds him historically precocious, perhaps too much so, for the sake of his own reception: "a prophet in this respect of a better era, he has usually placed this thinking royal mind in the body of a woman. This personage... is always feminine, both in her character and circumstances, but a conclusive proof that the term feminine is not a synonym for weak"[51] Fuller cites Brown's Constantia Dudley and Clara Wieland as two characters who "have loving hearts, graceful and plastic natures, but they have also noble thinking minds, full of resource, constancy, courage."[52] In this way, for Fuller, Brown in some ways surpassed her transcendentalist contemporaries in his more universal rendering of what Emerson had termed "Man Thinking."[53]

No doubt, the most fascinating reference to Brown by a "classic" American author is his appearance in Hawthorne's 1846 tale, "P's Correspondence," a peculiar experiment in alternative history in which a "partially disordered" British narrator, writing in London in 1845, indulges in mental wanderings and encounters Romantic authors long since dead. Given the explicitly delusional frame of the narration and the epistolary form— exactly as in *Edgar Huntly*, the bulk of Hawthorne's tale is a letter detailing P's "misty excursions beyond the limits of sanity"[54]—it is not surprising that Brown himself is one of a very few American authors given prominent mention, in the letter's postscript: "P.S. Pray present my most respectful regards to our venerable and revered friend, Mr. Brockden Brown. It gratifies me to learn that a complete edition of his works, in a double-columned octavo volume, is shortly to issue from the press, at Philadelphia. Tell him that no American writer enjoys a more classic reputation on this side of the water."[55] Effectively fictionalizing, embellishing, and extending Brown's literary production and transatlantic reception beyond death, Hawthorne symbolically transforms Brown, not just into a literary forebear but into a fantasy alter ego.

It is not a stretch to suggest that Hawthorne's homage speaks also to a deep literary indebtedness. In the most general terms, we might identify Brown as a source of Hawthorne's signature aesthetic of ambiguity; both authors certainly experimented with undecidability and narrational disorientation as techniques for producing sublime literary effects. More particularly, we can spot Brown's footprints in the Gothic turns of Hawthorne's major "Romances" of the early 1850s—the description of Holgrave's spell over Phoebe in Chapter 14 of *The House of the Seven Gables*, for example, recalls the psychic boundary violations perpetrated by Brown's Carwin.[56] Shades of Carwin's "invisible power," too, are seen in Chillingworth's diabolical imposition on the mind of Dimmesdale in *The Scarlet Letter*: "A revelation, he could almost say, had been granted to him.... The victim was for ever on the rack; it needed only to know the spring that controlled the engine;—and the physician knew it well!"[57] The mechanistic metaphorics of "springs" and "engines" as figures for the workings of the mind seem almost lifted from Brown's pages. So, too, does the account of the effects of the physician's machinations on the poor minister, who sleepwalks compulsively to a scene of past violence in the precise manner of Edgar Huntly: "Walking in the shadow of a dream, as it were, and perhaps under the influence of a species of somnambulism, Mr. Dimmesdale reached the spot where, now so long since, Hester Prynne had lived through her first hour of public ignominy."[58]

If this mid-nineteenth-century moment in some ways represents the high-water mark of narratives of Brown's literary influence, a period when his importance was etched into our narratives of literary development, it may also paradoxically explain why Brown subsequently receded from critical view for a time. On the one hand, thanks in part to the explicit testimony of some of the authors themselves, Brown was routinely hailed as an early and indispensable precursor to the best prose practitioners of the day, many of them canonical authors of nineteenth-century romanticism and Transcendentalism. On the other hand, these same authors came to overshadow him in the standard literary-historical narratives of development. One cause of this dynamic lies in the concept of literary influence itself. In Brown's case, at least, being "influential" has always been a double-edged sword, for grounding his literary reputation in that way has the unintended consequence of locating his literary worth in sites essentially external to his own oeuvre. To herald Brown as "seminal," that is, is also implicitly to assert the greater maturity of the later growths over the generative origin. This chapter has attempted to avoid such narratives of development, and the ahistorical perspectives they often smuggle into literary history, by moving beyond linear narratives of "influence" to recover a more panoramic view of Brown's place in nineteenth-century literary culture.

NOTES

1. For a treatment of Brown's early reception, with a focus on mainstream reception in the United States, see Michael Cody's chapter 33 in this volume. On the later (twentieth- and twenty-first-century reception of Brown, from the rise of American studies in the interwar period to the present, see Janie Hinds's chapter 34. For a cogent overview of the phases of Brown's posthumous critical reputation, see also Barnard, Kamrath, and Shapiro.

2. Fiedler gave Brown pride of place in his critical genealogy of an "anti-bourgeois" (Fiedler 105) literary tradition that finally succeeded in creating a national literature distinct from its European models. Fiedler's ability to rattle off genealogical lineages beginning with Brown—referring with glib but powerful imprecision to "our best fictionists from Charles Brockden Brown to Edgar Allan Poe to Hawthorne and Melville" (93), or to the theme of "alienation" marching down through American fiction "from Brockden Brown through George Lippard to Paul Bowles and Carson McCullers" (142–143)—suggests that Brown had enormous utility for Fiedler as a literary-cultural power station. The current renaissance in Brown criticism might share nothing of substance with Fiedler's myth-critical cultural nationalism, but it is safe to say that from Fiedler forward, Brown's seriousness could never again be underestimated.

3. See Reid.

4. See Clemit.

5. The content and composition history of Dunlap's biography is treated in careful detail by Cody in chapter 33 of this volume.

6. Kazanjian observes that Brown is often made to function just this way for later literary-nationalist criticism (175).

7. Dunlap 69.

8. I discuss this critical aesthetic, which was an essential piece of an emergent Romantic or proto-Romantic aesthetic theory, in *Literature, American Style*. As I argue at length there, the emergence of this aesthetic in British criticism also cleared a discursive path for Anglo-American critics who wished to identify their own "rude bards" and hence elevate them over the modern poets of hypercivilized Europe, pitting them imaginatively against metropolitan artifice, polish, and inauthenticity. See Tawil 11–12, 113–120.

9. Dennis 35.

10. Blackmore 42.

11. Duff 175.

12. Blair 74.

13. Ibid.

14. Ibid.

15. Dana 52.

16. Dana 54.

17. Channing 206.

18. Smith 79.

19. Of the 1822 republication of Brown's novels, Reid speculates, "the fact that they were American might have been an additional selling point" (189).
20. Coleridge 431.
21. Peacock, 193–194. (Peacock's "memoirs" of Shelley were first published serially in *Frasier's Magazine* between 1858 and 1862.)
22. For three classic critical treatments of the Shelley–Brown connection, see Solve; Sickels; Power. On Shelley's "Gothic" prose, see Halliburton.
23. Robertson 113.
24. On the connections between Brown's writing and Scott's *Guy Mannering*, see Robertson 8–11. For a brief discussion of a suite of references to *Arthur Mervyn* through the nineteenth century in British novels and poems, including the possibility that the "Mervyn" character in Comte de Lautréamont's satire of urban potboiler fiction also refers back to Brown via these other nineteenth-century urban Gothic fictions, see Barnard and Shapiro xxix n. 31.
25. Robertson 113.
26. "[N]o one approached the height [Brown] rested on," wrote Dana, "till the author of the 'Pioneers' and 'Pilot' appeared" (48).
27. "The river was confined between high and cragged rocks, one of which impended above the spot where the canoe rested. As these, again, were surmounted by tall trees, which appeared to totter on the brows of the precipice, it gave the stream the appearance of running through a deep and narrow dell. All beneath the fantastic limbs and ragged tree tops, which were, here and there, dimly painted against the starry zenith, lay alike in shadowed obscurity. Behind them, the curvature of the banks soon bounded the view by the same dark and wooded outline; but in front, and apparently at no great distance, the water seemed piled against the heavens, whence it tumbled into caverns, out of which issued those sullen sounds that had loaded the evening atmosphere. It seemed, in truth, to be a spot devoted to seclusion, and the sisters imbibed a soothing impression of security, as they gazed upon its Romantic though not unappalling beauties" (Cooper, *Last of the Mohicans*, 48–49).
28. Cooper, "Preface," v.
29. See Barnard and Shapiro xv, 11 n. See also Stocker's chapter 17 in this volume.
30. Apap 31.
31. Ibid. 31, 38. See also St. Clair 380.
32. Godwin ix.
33. Apap 31.
34. Poe 4.
35. Griswold, *The Prose Writers*, 24. Griswold's book also includes a full essay on Brown (107–111). The comment about the resemblance between Brown and Poe first appeared in Griswold, "Tale Writers."
36. One classic treatment is Carter. For a fuller recent discussion, see Luciano.
37. See Apap 36–37; Luciano.
38. Lippard 3.
39. Ibid. 491.
40. Whittier 391.
41. Ibid.
42. Ibid. 392.
43. Ibid.
44. Ibid. 393.

45. Ibid. 395.
46. Ibid.
47. Ibid. 392.
48. Fuller, quoted in Rosenthal 62.
49. Ibid.
50. Ibid. 63.
51. Ibid.
52. Ibid. David S. Reynolds takes this connection between Brown and Fuller a bit further, crediting Brown with having given American fiction the first incarnation of a literary type he calls "the adventure feminist" and attributing Fuller's admiration in part to this fact. In *Ormond*'s Martinette, who has "slain men in two Revolutions and holds distinctly progressive ideas about politics and sex roles," Reynolds finds a fictional fore-echo of Fuller's famous line about women, "Let them be sea-captains, if you will." See Reynolds 345.
53. Emerson 57.
54. Hawthorne, "P's Correspondence," 139.
55. Ibid. 161.
56. Jay Fliegelman points out that Brown's description of Carwin's "biloquism" represents it as an "invisible power" that exerts an "almost mesmeric influence" over Clara. See Fliegelman 238–239.
57. Hawthorne, *Scarlet Letter*, 140.
58. Ibid. 147.

WORKS CITED

Apap, Christopher. "Irresponsible Acts: The Transatlantic Dialogue of William Godwin and CBB." In Jennifer Phegley et al., eds., *Transatlantic Sensations*, 23–40. London: Routledge, 2012.

Barnard, Philip, Mark L. Kamrath, and Stephen Shapiro. "Charles Brockden Brown and the Novel in the 1790s." In Theresa Gaul et al., eds., *Blackwell Companion to American Literature*, Vol. 1. Forthcoming.

Barnard, Philip and Stephen Shapiro. "Introduction." In Charles Brockden Brown, *Arthur Mervyn; or, Memoirs of the Year 1793, with Related Texts*, ix–xliv. Indianapolis: Hackett, 2008.

Blackmore, Sir Richard. "An Essay on the Nature and Constitution of Epic Poetry." In Andrew Ashfield and Peter de Bolla, eds. *The Sublime: A Reader in British Eighteenth-Century Aesthetic Theory*, 40–42. Cambridge: Cambridge University Press, 1996.

Blair, Hugh. *A Critical Dissertation on the Poems of Ossian*. London: T. Becket and P. A. De Hondt, 1763.

Carter, Boyd. "Poe's Debt to Charles Brockden Brown." *Prairie Schooner* 27 (1953): 190–196.

Channing, Edward Tyrell. "On Models in Literature," *North American Review* 3.7 (July 1816): 206.

Clemit, Pamela. *The Godwinian Novel: The Rational Fictions of Godwin, Brockden Brown, and Mary Shelley*. Oxford: Clarendon Press, 1993.

Coleridge, Samuel Taylor. *The Works of Samuel Taylor Coleridge: Prose and Verse*. Philadelphia: Crissy and Markley, 1852.

Cooper, James Fenimore. *The Last of the Mohicans*. Richard Slotkin, ed. New York: Penguin, 1986.

Cooper, James Fenimore. "Preface." In *The Spy*, Vol. 1, XX–XX. New York: Wiley and Halstead, 1821.

Dana, Sr., Richard Henry. "The Novels Of Charles Brockden Brown." In Bernard Rosenthal, *Critical Essays on Charles Brockden Brown*, 48–58. Boston: G. K. Hall, 1981.

Dennis, John. "The Grounds of Criticism in Poetry." In Andrew Ashfield and Peter de Bolla, eds. *The Sublime: A Reader in British Eighteenth-Century Aesthetic Theory*, 35–39. Cambridge: Cambridge University Press, 1996.

Duff, William. "An Essay in Original Genius." In Andrew Ashfield and Peter de Bolla, eds. *The Sublime: A Reader in British Eighteenth-Century Aesthetic Theory*, 173–177. Cambridge: Cambridge University Press, 1996.

Dunlap, William. *Memoirs of Charles Brockden Brown, the American Novelist*. London: Henry Colburn, 1822.

Emerson, Ralph Waldo. "The American Scholar." In Joel Porte and Saundra Morris, eds., *Emerson's Prose and Poetry: Authoritative Texts, Contexts, Criticism*, XXX–XXX. New York: W. W. Norton, 2001.

Fiedler, Leslie. "Charles Brockden Brown and the Invention of the American Gothic." In Leslie Fiedler, *Love and Death in the American Novel*, 126–161. New York: Criterion Books, 1960. Quotations from this text are from the Dalkey Archive Edition of 1997.

Fliegelman, Jay. *Prodigals and Pilgrims: The American Revolution against Patriarchal Authority 1750–1800*. Cambridge: Cambridge University Press, 1982.

Fuller, Margaret. "American Literature: Its Position in the Present Time and Prospects for the Future." In Perry Miller, ed., *Margaret Fuller, American Romantic: A Selection from Her Writings and Correspondence*, 249–250. Ithaca, N.Y.: Cornell University Press, 1963.

Fuller, Margaret. "Charles Brockden Brown." In Perry Miller, ed., *Margaret Fuller, American Romantic: A Selection from Her Writings and Correspondence*, 223–226. Ithaca, N.Y.: Cornell University Press, 1963.

Godwin, William. *Mandeville: A Tale of the Seventeenth Century in England*. London: Longman, Hurst, Rees, Orme, and Brown, 1817.

Griswold, Rufus. *The Prose Writers of America*. Philadelphia: Carey and Hart, 1847.

Griswold, Rufus. "Tale Writers." *Daily National Intelligencer*, August 30, 1845.

Halliburton, David G. "Shelley's 'Gothic' Novels." *Keats-Shelley Journal* 16 (Winter 1967), 39–49.

Hawthorne, Nathaniel. *The House of the Seven Gables*. Boston: Ticknor and Fields, 1851.

Hawthorne, Nathaniel. "P's Correspondence." In *Mosses from an Old Manse*, Vol. 2. New York: Wiley and Putnam, 1846.

Hawthorne, Nathaniel. *The Scarlet Letter: A Romance*. Columbus: Ohio State University Press, 1962.

Kazanjian, David. *The Colonizing Trick: National Culture and Imperial Citizenship in Early America*. Minneapolis: University of Minnesota Press, 2003.

Lippard, George. *The Quaker City; or, The Monks of Monk Hall*. Philadelphia: George Lippard, 1847.

Luciano, Dana. "The Gothic Meets Sensation: Charles Brockden Brown, Edgar Allan Poe, Lippard, George and E. D. E. N. Southworth." In Shirley Samuels, ed., *A Companion to American Fiction, 1780–1865*, 314–329. Oxford: Wiley-Blackwell, 2004.

Peacock, Thomas Love. *Memoirs of Shelley, with Shelley's Letters to Peacock*. H. F. B. Brett-Smith, ed. London: Frowde, 1909.

Poe, Edgar Allan. "Cooper's *Wyandotte*" [1843] in *The Works of Edgar Allan Poe*, Vol. 7, 3–18. New York and Pittsburg: Colonial Company, 1903.

Power, Julia. *Shelley in America in the Nineteenth Century: His Relation to American Critical Thought and His Influence* (1940). New York: Haskell House, 1964.

Reid, S. W. "Brockden Brown in England: Notes on Henry Colburn's 1822 Editions of His Novels." *Early American Literature* 9.2 (Fall 1974): 188–195.

Reynolds, David S. *Beneath the American Renaissance: The Subversive Imagination in the Age of Emerson and Melville*. New York: Knopf, 1989.

Robertson, Fiona. "Walter Scott and the American Historical Novel." In J. Gerald Kennedy and Leland Person, eds., *Oxford History of the Novel in English*, Vol. 5, *The American Novel to 1870*, 107–123. New York: Oxford University Press, 2014.

Rosenthal, Bernard. *Critical Essays on Charles Brockden Brown*. Boston: G. K. Hall, 1981.

Sickels, Eleanor. "Shelley and Charles Brockden Brown." *Publications of the Modern Language Association* 45.4 (December 1930): 1116–1128.

Smith, Sydney. "Review of Seybert's Annals of the United States." *Edinburgh Review* (January 1820): 69–80.

Solve, Melvin T. "Shelley and the Novels of Brown." In *Fred Newton Scott Anniversary Papers*, 141–156. Chicago: University of Chicago Press, 1929.

St. Clair, William. *The Godwins and the Shelleys: A Biography of a Family*. Baltimore: Johns Hopkins University Press, 1991.

Tawil, Ezra. *Literature, American Style: The Originality of Imitation in the Early Republic*. Philadelphia: University of Pennsylvania Press, 2018.

Whitman, Walt. *Leaves of Grass and Other Writings*. Michael Moon, ed. New York: Norton, 2002.

Whittier, John Greenleaf. "Fanaticism." In *The Works of John Greenleaf Whittier*, Vol. 7, 391–395. Cambridge, Mass: Riverside, 1866.

CHAPTER 33

BROWN'S EARLY
BIOGRAPHERS AND
RECEPTION, 1815–1940S

MICHAEL A. CODY

CHARLES Brockden Brown's reception history begins with *The Life of Charles Brockden Brown*, a biographical miscellany that was initially drafted by Paul Allen before being extended to two volumes and brought to publication in 1815 by Brown's close friend and associate William Dunlap. Any consideration of the reception history necessarily begins with this volume's complex history, the ambiguous and incomplete view of Brown's writings that it provides, and the long shadow that it cast over subsequent Brown reception well into the twentieth century.

I. THE ALLEN/DUNLAP *LIFE*

In the June 1814 issue of Philadelphia's *Port Folio*, an anonymous correspondent complained that Brown's legacy had been neglected during the four years since the author's death on February 22, 1810. "Of his private life I know nothing," the correspondent writes, "but of his writings it is saying little to repeat that they show an improved mind, a powerful but sometimes irregular imagination, and often a transcendent command of language" (Anonymous, "Inquiries," 572). After a favorable comparison of Brown with William Godwin and a positive appraisal of *Arthur Mervyn* as an example of his achievement, the correspondent asks what has happened to the "account of his life and writings" that was "to be published for the benefit of his family" (573). Here the writer refers to a work announced three summers earlier, in the July 1811 issue of the *Port Folio*. At that time, in response to a correspondent's essay titled "Critique on the Writings of Charles B. Brown," then *Port Folio* editor Nicholas Biddle added this note:

A biography of Charles B. Brown, and a selection from his manuscripts, are about to be published. The profits of the work will be exclusively applied to the family of the deceased. The work will be comprised in two volumes. We have not the smallest doubt that the pen of a writer, whose works are deemed worthy of a publication in England, will receive a liberal patronage in his native country.   (Anonymous, "Critique," 35)

The biography in question was Paul Allen's *The Life of Charles Brockden Brown*. The author's executors, widow Elizabeth Linn Brown and younger brother Elijah, Jr., had signed a contract with Allen that commissioned him to complete Brown's *System of General Geography* as well as a life-and-letters biography, intended to generate income for the young family Brown left behind at his death.

Sometime early in 1814, three years after his commission, Allen submitted a first volume of *Life* to printer Samuel Merritt for typesetting. Merritt printed at least one copy, which Allen delivered to the Browns for approval. Brown's executors rejected Allen's submission and withdrew their commission, partly because Allen had accomplished too little in three years. Of the volume's 383 pages, Allen's original material makes up roughly 10 percent, and the biographical portion deals mostly with Brown's youth. The remaining pages offer excerpts from unpublished writings. The inclusion of selections from an author's works was typical for biographies of the period, but the paltry portion of biographical details was not. One section of Allen's original material in *Life* rationalizes the volume's meager chronicle of Brown's maturity by asserting that for a "literary man" biographical details are ultimately less significant than a writer's productions: "The *incidents* in the life of an author, are his ideas, and those who look for more than these in the history of an author, must expect to find what they deserve—disappointment" (Allen 68, 69).

More important, Allen proposes a surprisingly dismissive perspective on Brown as author that is presumably out of keeping with the biography's goals. Although a broadside proposal distributed in 1811 suggests that Brown's "merits as a writer require no comment" (quoted in Bennett ix), Allen offers a largely negative view of the author's output. Whereas correspondents and editors in periodicals such as the *Port Folio* characterized Brown as a significant if "irregular" talent with considerable intellectual scope, Allen closes his *Life* with the suggestion that the novelist lacked the focus and will to become a truly accomplished writer. Claiming that most of what Brown wrote, even the published work, was left "in an unfinished state" (387), Allen prefaces a few paragraphs of sharply critical analysis of *Ormond* and *Wieland* with the suggestion that their author

considered all his fanciful works as mere matters of recreation and amusement. As long as his imagination was prolific in blossoms, he scattered them with the same prodigal profusion. When this light employment was accomplished, he patiently waited for the seasons of blooms to return without endeavouring to arrange those which he had already collected into a beautiful bouquet.... If he had thought more seriously on such subjects, and taken time to weave the various threads of the narrative into one consistent web, no question can remain of his capacity to excel in this department of letters. His novels are therefore evidences of what he *might* have done, not of what he has accomplished. It was the excess of his genius that prevented him from excelling.   (388–389)

Seemingly aware that this evaluation would diminish Brown's reputation, the executors suppressed Allen's *Life* and handed the project over to Brown's longtime friend Dunlap. When Allen learned that Dunlap had been selected to complete the book, he wrote the newly commissioned biographer from Baltimore on July 8, 1814, giving up "all right to interfere" and affirming that all the materials in his first volume were "entirely at your service" (quoted in Bennett xii).

Dunlap—portrait painter, playwright, theater owner, biographer, and historian—took Allen at his word, beginning his own two-volume *The Life of Charles Brockden Brown* (1815) by retaining much of Allen's first forty pages, portions of it word for word. Likewise, throughout the volume, possibly constrained by the exigencies of typesetting, he included many of Allen's original passages and selections in an attempt to minimize printing costs. The constraint of working with a preexisting text clearly caused difficulties, and Dunlap provided more than one disclaimer to explain the shape of the first volume. Introducing "Sketches of a History of Carsol," for example, Dunlap writes: "I would not have presented these Sketches until later in the work, but that I find them already selected and printed for this part of the first volume, because they were undoubtedly written by Mr. Brown, at a period subsequent to that of which I am now treating, and after he had become an author by profession" (1: 169). Furthermore, although Allen might have met his subject at some point, Dunlap and Brown had a close and long-standing friendship after they were introduced by Elihu Hubbard Smith in 1793–1794. "For several years," Dunlap writes, "it was my good fortune to have him as an inmate with my family, . . . sometimes at New York, and sometimes at Perth Amboy" (1: 56). Yet Dunlap's rich personal knowledge of Brown and his access to Brown's manuscripts and surviving family seem to have provided him with little more understanding than Allen had of that work—the novels—for which Brown was best known.

That Dunlap gave a platform to Allen's dismissal of Brown's fiction may suggest that he, too, had little patience for Brown as self-proclaimed rhapsodist or as novelist. The assumption of the "character of the rhapsodist" in the youthful Brown's 1789 series for the *Columbian Magazine* was, according to Dunlap, a mistake that Brown recognized even in the text of the series itself but could not undo: "That Charles thus early saw the error of indulging in this romancing vein, and perceived that it unfitted him for the conversation and duties of real life is . . . evident; but that he had at this time or even much later in life, corrected the evil, was not true" (1: 17). In a related argument, Dunlap identifies Brown's rejection of a career in law as another grave error, especially as it was founded upon the error of "indulging in this romancing vein." Useful work as a lawyer could have "led to competence, honour, and self-approbation," but the rhapsodist, the romancer, in Brown led him so far astray from these accomplishments that the anxiety of traveling an erroneous path "undermined his health" and, by extension, led to his early death (1: 41). Yet Dunlap seems reluctant to discount altogether Brown's talent and sincerity as a writer of fiction. When later in the first volume of *Life*, he continues in the same dismissive vein, he concludes a few paragraphs meant to bridge the texts of Brown's unfinished *Historical Sketches* with the following: "Before writing the 'Sketches of a History of Carsol,' and 'Sketches of a History of the Carrils and Ormes,' Mr. Brown had seen the inconveniences and mischief arising from his first mode, and I doubt not but he would have given in these works [the *Sketches*], if he had lived to finish and fill up his plans, volumes which would have delighted, instructed and satisfied the reader" (1: 261). A more mature Brown could have written better and more useful fiction.

The second volume of Dunlap's *Life* begins with Brown's yellow fever experiences, introducing the topic with reference to the Philadelphia epidemic of 1793 that figures in *Ormond* and *Arthur Mervyn* and focusing on the New York epidemic of 1798. Letter excerpts and Dunlap's personal knowledge reveal Brown's experience of the 1798 epidemic, which he barely survived, but Brown seems a secondary character in a narrative segment that focuses on Smith and his death. Brown fled New York after Smith died and took up residence with Dunlap in Perth Amboy. After a brief transition from the events of September 1798 to Brown's return to New York the following December, Dunlap provides extensive description and limited analysis of the novels and the later political pamphlets. The final five pages of the fewer than ninety that make up the biographical portion of the second volume are devoted to Brown's death, while the remaining 373 pages feature additional selections from the writings.

The reviews of Dunlap's achievement in the *Life* were not as kind as contemporary reception of Brown seems to have been. One reviewer for the *Portico* in 1816 claims to "have ever possessed a high respect" for Brown's "genius" and to "have always estimated, to the full extent of their intrinsick excellence," his "productions" (Anonymous, "Rev. of *The Life*," 381). But the reviewer suggests that "Mr. Dunlap was either unfit for the station he assumes, or too indolent to gather the necessary information, for a biography; which, in every sense, is tantamount to incapacity" (382). In a related manner, the *North American Review* in 1819 takes Dunlap to task for the idea—carried over into his biography from Allen's original text—that the life of an author is intellectual in nature and largely without "incident":

> The usual complaint is that the life of a man of letters is almost necessarily wanting in incident, and when the writer has made this general apology for a meagre narrative, he too often feels at liberty to be as deficient at every thing as may suit his ignorance, indolence, or want of discrimination.... It is hardly possible that a faithful, judicious history of a literary man should not be full of amusement and important instruction; but it cannot be made so by relating only what is common to him and every one else, or what would be equally interesting if told of another.
> (Anonymous, "Art. V," 58)

This reviewer takes the inadequate biographical information Dunlap offered, combines it with close readings of Brown's work, particularly the letters, and then proposes, by way of implied example, a more nuanced and adequate analysis. Of Brown as intellect and author, he writes, "He wanted something from without to draw his attention from himself, and make him a sober, practical thinker; he needed regular employments that always tended to something, and produced some visible effect; he had yet to learn what man was made of and why he was placed here, and that the same world that offended the sensitiveness of the weak, was a fine school for character and might be a nursery for the tenderest feeling" (61). This review and others like it condemn Dunlap for laziness and incompetence as a biographer. The charge should be brought against both Allen and Dunlap, but the latter may indeed be the guiltier. Given his long association with Brown and access to the circles around him, Dunlap was in a position to provide a richer narrative of Brown's life and character but did not do so. The subject seems to elude the biographer in some fundamental way, as Dunlap remarks, channeling Allen, that Brown's letters were curiously devoid of personal information: "in his own letters he sedulously avoided the mention of himself, on the ground that he had nothing personally to communicate" (1: 54).

Some reviewers of Dunlap's *Life* predicted that his attempt at biography would be an embarrassment for the new nation's literary ambitions, even as Brown's fiction, flawed though it might be, was applauded and republished abroad. In spite of dire predictions, however, Dunlap's work—reduced to one volume composed of a memoir and selections from Brown's writings—was republished as *Memoirs of Charles Brockden Brown* for English readers in 1822 by Henry Colburn, who had for some years been publishing London editions of Brown's novels. Apparently ignoring—or ignorant of—the disdain American reviewers held for *Life*, Dunlap provided Colburn with the same basic biographical text used in the two-volume work, with portions of the prose still from Allen's pen, deleting much of the juvenilia and removing the bulk of its selections. Or perhaps Colburn himself, having taken to heart reviews such as one that suggested that Dunlap's two-volume *Life* was "only an apology…for republishing" selected pieces that had already appeared in print, and "certainly a very poor one" at that (Anonymous, "Art. V," 60), attempted to change the perception of the book by transforming it from biography to memoir and creating a more reasonable balance between the biographical material and the selections. An English reviewer reprinted in the *Atheneum* appreciated the attempt, at least to some extent; the brief review of *Memoirs* begins, "We never heard of this work till a few days ago. But, having read it, we begin to believe, that we spoke, the other day, somewhat more sharply than we should, of American apathy, concerning the genius of Brown" (Anonymous, "Late American Books," 238). Admiration for Brown seems apparent in this introduction, but afterward, the English reviewer's language becomes slippery. Dunlap's efforts to analyze Brown's work, the reviewer suggests, are "bad enough"; the selections are judged as "*chrononhotonthology*—with a tedious good-for-nothing essay or two—and a few letters not worth reading." In spite of this, "the book is a pretty good sort of a book: that is—of the whole 337 page octavo, about eighty or a hundred—small duodecimo—would be worth reading,—and yet, we are not sorry for having waded over the whole. It has been of great use to *ourself;* it has enabled us to correct several errors, of time or fact, or both, into which we have been led of late, while inquiring about poor Brown" (238). In all likelihood, the "eighty or a hundred" useful pages make up the biographical material, because the remainder of the review that follows is simply a litany of biographical details that might contribute to correcting the "errors, of time or fact, or both": "By this LIFE, we perceive that he was born Jan. 17, 1771; that he died (we know not where by the book; but we suppose, in Philadelphia)— Feb. 22, 1810; that he was educated for the bar (like most of the chief writers, and all the chief statesmen of North America)—that beside the books, . . . he was the author of two political pamphlets, of great value," and so on (238). The tongue-in-cheek, sarcastic tone makes the reviewer's opinion somewhat difficult to pin down. But the biographical list is long and rather pointless, suggesting that the account of Brown's life and works is little more than a series of details, lacking analytical qualities that would make it more informative and insightful.

Between the British publication of Dunlap's *Memoirs* in 1822 and Harry R. Warfel's *Charles Brockden Brown: American Gothic Novelist* in 1949, almost all biographical notices of Brown appear as articles in periodicals, encyclopedic works and histories, or passing discussions in books on various American and literary topics. Dunlap's 1815 *Life* provided most of the scant catalog of biographical details that would be drawn on again and again for more than a century. In *Poems and Prose Writings* (1850), in a chapter titled "The Novels of Charles Brockden Brown," Richard Henry Dana, Sr., registered his regrets about this: "In 1815, Mr. Dunlap gave us a Life of him; an ill-arranged and bulky work, yet too meagre where it should be particular and full. To this, however, we are indebted for all we know of his life; and we owe to it also an article on Brown, which appeared in the North American Review for 1819, an article which, we fear, has left us little to say" (326).[1] Dana refers to the *North American Review* article already cited, which takes the "meagre" details Dunlap's biography provides and develops a picture of Brown's character that Dunlap seems unwilling or unable to present clearly. Dana suggests that Dunlap's *Life* was, in a sense, completed by the *North American Review* article, since it is the latter and not the former that "has left us little to say."

While Dana participated in the early nineteenth century's scholarly-critical conversation about Brown in the period's journalism, as a minor Romantic poet, he also reveals a literary interest that mirrors enthusiastic responses to Brown from many canonical writers throughout the Romantic era—from Godwin, Mary and Percy Shelley, Walter Scott, and François-René de Chateaubriand in Europe, to Nathaniel Hawthorne, John Greenleaf Whittier, Edgar Allan Poe, and Margaret Fuller in the United States. Brown's novels were translated into German (1802), French (1808), and Spanish (1818), making him the first American novelist to appear in European languages and speaking to his widespread reception in the Atlantic world. European audiences perceived Brown as part of a generational wave that included Friedrich Schiller, the Shelleys, and others, and his novels appeared repackaged with Mary Shelley's *Frankenstein*, Schiller's *The Ghost-Seer*, and Robert Southey's *The Curse of Kehama*. Thus, numerous reprints, translations, and repackagings suggest why the *Atheneum*'s anonymous reviewer was so interested in Brown in 1825 and sustained Brown's wider reputation while the scholarly-critical reception progressed slowly and unevenly.[2]

II. The 1827 "Memoir"

As periodical notices of Brown's life and work appeared sporadically throughout the remainder of the nineteenth century and the early decades of the twentieth, and as their authors drew repeatedly from a stagnating pool of biographical details, what changes is the way the authors of these notices reinterpret Brown and his work according to the cultural moments in which they write. This ability to adapt to or even transcend cultural shifts might be a reason Brown's work—and, by extension, Brown himself—still inhabits our literary imagination when so much of the writing and so many of the writers from his time do not. The author of the 1819 *North American Review* article writes, "There is no call, as far as we know, for a second edition of any of his works" (Anonymous, "Art. V," 63–64). Yet in 1827, only eight years later, S. G. Goodrich in Boston published new editions of all of Brown's novels. Introducing the first volume, *Wieland*, Goodrich included an anonymous biographical essay, "Memoir of Charles Brockden Brown." Daniel Edwards Kennedy argues that the author of this memoir was Brown's widow, Elizabeth Linn Brown, and describes it as "the most important memoir of Brown ever published" (66A). Part of Kennedy's reasoning for attributing this work, dated "Philadelphia, March 3d, 1827," to Elizabeth (whose life dates are 1775–1834 and who thus would have written the "Memoir" at age fifty-two) has to do with the text's language and word choices. In the first paragraph of the memoir, addressing Brown's claims to "distinction," the author writes, "It is no less the duty than the pleasure of friendship, to fortify and sustain these claims. The impartiality of criticism cannot but confirm the anticipations of affection" (Anonymous, "Memoir," iii). Kennedy reasons that "the pleasure of friendship" and "anticipations of affection" suggest a close relationship. The language throughout the memoir is certainly different from Dunlap's in the *Life*, although many of its details and points of analysis follow Dunlap closely. In a brief reference to this memoir in his review of Goodrich's publication of Brown's novels, Dana complains that the "notice of him, at the beginning, gives not a single new fact, or peculiarity in his character, that we recollect" (326). Kennedy begs to differ but does so in a vague passage: "Dana's recollection was at fault. She did give new facts, but she must be read carefully to see them for she has a clever wile of packing a lot of meaning in a few words and at times introduces an artful tarrot [sic] more than half ironical when she writes a general comment. Taken for what it only pretends to be, it is the most important memoir of Brown ever published" (66A).

The 1827 "Memoir" begins with a rehearsal of what had already, after Dunlap, become a standard account of Brown's youth: his "delicate and frail" physical condition (iv), his precocious devotion to literature and intellectual pursuits, his classical education in Robert Proud's school, the effect of study on his health and the beginnings of "excursions into the country" for his health (vi), his professional education in Alexander Wilcocks's law office, his final rejection of a law career, and his early literary efforts culminating in those "essays which he published, under the title of the 'Rhapsodist'" (viii). The memoirist, following Dunlap, briefly describes Brown's life in the six years between the end of the legal apprenticeship and "his becoming professedly an author, in the year 1798" (ix). The reader learns that the toll of rejecting his family's and friends' desire that he become a lawyer led to depression and physical decline but that Brown found his spirits—and to some degree, regained his health—in an atmosphere more congenial to his character, when he encountered Elihu Hubbard Smith and the members of the Friendly Club, including Dunlap, in New York. If the memoirist is indeed Elizabeth Linn Brown, then the author's widow proves surprisingly censorious, writing, for example, of *Alcuin*, "It is an eloquent and ingenious speculation, of which, though we may praise the eloquence of the language, the originality of the style, and the subtlety of the argument, we cannot but condemn the unsoundness of the doctrine" (xi).

Brown's novels receive the same mixed response: the lost novel "Sky-Walk," which followed *Alcuin*, "was indeed a prelude to a series, which he now in rapid succession produced, of the most original, powerful, and masterly, though faulty, and in some respects, imperfect and objectionable, works of fiction, of which American literature could then, or perhaps can now, boast" (xii). Oddly, since virtually all interest in Brown in this period is focused on his novels and "Memoir" is printed as an introduction to a new set of the novels, it devotes only three paragraphs, barely a page, to these key works. More than half of "Memoir" is devoted to Brown's writing career after 1801, in other words to the postnovelistic years when the author married and settled into family life in Philadelphia. A suggestive description of changes in the author's character after the novelistic period introduces his return to Philadelphia at the end of 1800: "Riper years, and more extensive communion with his fellow-men, during his residence in New York, corrected without weakening his moral enthusiasm and romantic sensibilities. The realities of experience were gradually and imperceptibly substituted for the visions of a glowing and luxurious imagination, and his moral progress was eminently beneficial and salutary" (iv). For the memoirist, Brown's three political pamphlets weigh more heavily than the novels, and more space is devoted to these works than to the novels. Likewise, a brief discussion of Brown's *Literary Magazine, and American Register* focuses exclusively on those passages in the October 1803 "Editors' Address to the Public," in which past works and possible indiscretions appear to be rejected for a new solidity and in which the editor proclaims himself "the ardent friend and the willing champion of the Christian Religion" (xvii). After a brief mention of Brown's marriage, a full paragraph devoted to his biographical memoir of his brother-in-law John Blair Linn, and high praise of the solid worth of his final magazine, the *American Register*, the memoirist concludes with the same account of Brown's final days that concluded Dunlap's *Life*: a passage composed by Elizabeth Linn Brown. What Kennedy saw as new and important in this "Memoir of Charles Brockden Brown" seems questionable, but the text is undoubtedly influential. Republished with new editions of Brown's novels in 1827, 1857, and 1887, this text introduced new readers to Brown through much of the nineteenth century, thereby shaping the reception of his work more than eighty years after his death.

III. Prescott, Barrett, and Lippard, 1834–1849

Among the first works that attempted to create a history of the United States through the biographies of notable individuals was *The Library of American Biography*, edited by Jared Sparks. The first volume appeared in 1834 and included four extensive biographical articles, the second of which was William H. Prescott's "Life of Charles Brockden Brown." Early in his discussion, Prescott acknowledges Dunlap but criticizes the latter's *Life* for not including "more copious extracts...from [Brown's] journal and correspondence, which, doubtless,...must afford the most interesting, as well as authentic materials for biography" (Prescott 121). That a better biography from Dunlap would have satisfied seems unlikely, however, as the staunchly conservative Prescott clearly finds Brown's Enlightenment and Godwinian tendencies distasteful. He bemoans Brown's "turn from the honorable fame" his legal studies might have won him: "His prospects, but lately so brilliant, seemed now overcast with a deep gloom.... Instead of the careful discipline, to which [his mind] had been lately subjected, it was now left to rove at large wherever caprice should dictate, and waste itself on those romantic reveries and speculations, to which he was naturally too much addicted" (128). The discussions of Brown's novels that make up a significant portion of Prescott's biography follow and extend the opinions of Brown's original biographers, Allen and Dunlap. Prescott agrees, for example, that the occurrences of spontaneous combustion and the agency of ventriloquism in *Wieland* fall far outside the experience of most readers, making these plot devices less believable even than supernatural events, with which, real or not, Brown's readers were more conversant. While Dunlap attempts to soften such criticism, Prescott sharply condemns Brown for trickery: "The reader, who has been gorged with this feast of horrors, is tempted to throw away the book in disgust, at finding himself the dupe of such paltry jugglery" (142). The biography continues with somewhat less disparaging discussions of Brown's other novels but provides a decidedly negative overall appraisal, determined to present its subject as at best wrongheaded and at worst a failure. Once Brown is dead, Prescott belittles his style—its "elaborate, factitious air" and its "verbal blemishes" (177, 179)—and then closes with a weak attempt not "to part, with any thing like a tone of disparagement lingering on our lips" (180). It is too little too late.

Through the first half of the nineteenth century, many US commentators followed Prescott in accepting, to one degree or another, the censorious perspective on Brown's fiction that was first intimated in Allen and Dunlap. But in the revolutionary year 1848, fourteen years after Prescott's "Life," a younger and less conservative generation of readers produced two responses that inflect Brown's reception in new directions. More positive about Brown's fiction than perhaps any writer before him, Joseph Hartwell Barrett, in the *American Review* for March 1848, rejected the typical rehearsal of biographical details, appealing instead "to the only sure index and representative—his *work*—in order to gain any correct knowledge, or to form any true judgment" of "the real man" (262). Barrett proposes a substantial discussion of *Wieland* and, in a rare example of engagement between early commentators, chides Prescott for his animus against Brown: "We cannot forbear stating...our regret, that a man of such celebrity and authority in the republic of letters as Mr. Prescott has since become should have undertaken the biography of one for whom he could claim no higher consideration, and in the increase of whose reputation he could feel no more interest" (270). From this point, Barrett's text becomes a rejection of Prescott's pejorative evaluation. In affirming Brown, Barrett appeals to a richer sense of literary history and practice than Prescott. He suggests that Prescott's reading of *Wieland*, with its focus on Carwin's ventriloquism, is shallow and misses the novel's point concerning religious fanaticism: "Viewed in its true light, the...whole destiny of the Wielands is made to rest upon the character of Wieland himself. All the calamities that follow, unspeakable as they are, the author very plainly attempted to attach entirely to the uneducated and ungoverned religious passion of the main actor in these events; and he has, beyond question, succeeded" (271). Barrett is intent on improving Brown's reputation and simply rejects Prescott's evaluation. "How many," he asks, "will be caught reading a book of which they have received such intimations?" (269). Barrett offers qualified praise on a multitude of fronts, writing that the novelist observed society closely, although "mainly confined within the limits of a particular circle, in his native city" (271), and suggesting that longer experience might have made him the young nation's greatest writer: "Could Brown have lived to become a complete master of himself, to reduce all his faculties under perfect control; had the long discipline of years and of severe experiences wrought out a way whereby the genial impulses that visited his spirit could find full and free access to the minds of his fellows; envy itself must have done him reverence" (274).

Also in 1848, Philadelphia novelist George Lippard published one of the century's most striking pieces on Brown in the miscellany *The Nineteenth Century*. Akin to graveyard poetry from the eighteenth century, "The Heart-Broken" is a melodramatic dialogue between two people lingering near Brown's grave, one who remembers the author and one who knows nothing of him. The piece provides some customary biographical details but in a melodramatic and sentimental style. Affirming a strong kinship with his subject, Lippard celebrates Brown's talent and worth without reservation or qualification:

beneath that clump of sod, a strong Heart, throbbing with impulses that were breathed into its veins by Almighty God, mouldered into dust. Yes, beneath this rank grass and hard clay, dig only five feet, and you will find a skull that once flashed with divine fire from the eyes, and worked immortal Thoughts within its brain. Dig five feet down, and you will find the skeleton which once was an Embodied Soul, and, mark you, a Great Soul, worthy to stand in solemn dignity among the mightiest names of earth. (20)

As a fellow novelist, writing at the height of American romanticism, Lippard empathizes with Brown's plight. "Yes, he sat himself down in the prime of his young manhood," he writes, "to make his bread by his pen. At that time the cow with seven horns, or the calf with two heads and five legs, exhibited in some mountebank's show, was not half so rare a curiosity as an—*American Author*" (21). If Lippard's voice in the dialogue empathizes with and celebrates Brown, then the responding voice is that of mainstream society, willing to dismiss Brown as a writer of "idle fictions" and "a miserable fool, to forsake the Bar for the Pen" (22). In the end, Lippard calls for "the Authors of America" to "bear the bones of Brockden Brown" to a more appropriate burial site and erect there "a solitary column of white marble" to "record the neglect, and wo, and glory of the Author's life" (27). Like the 1827 "Memoir" that introduced Goodrich's edition, Lippard's article had a long life, reappearing in 1865 and 1894.

Standard notices from the mid- and late nineteenth century, such as those appearing in Rufus W. Griswold's *The Prose Writers of America* (1849), the Evert and George Duyckinck's *Cyclopaedia of American Literature* (1855), or that of Carl Van Doren in *The Cambridge History of American Literature* (1917), added no new details to Brown's biography. While each focuses on different biographical details, these appreciations primarily serve to reinforce a consensus reading according to which Brown was a perhaps fascinating but ultimately minor figure in American literary history. Griswold joined Barrett, probably unaware that he was doing so, in defending Brown against Prescott's earlier attack. The Duyckincks include Thomas Sully's anecdote about seeing Brown at work in his window and John Neal's account of Brown's dwelling. Van Doren, with his longer view of literary history, reports that Brown is not forgotten, despite his relegation to minor status. "In his native country," Van Doren writes, "Brown has stood, with occasional flickering of interest, firmly fixed as a literary ancestor" (292).

IV. Smith and Woodberry to Kennedy, 1878–1920s

Writing in England for the *Fortnightly Review* in 1878, George Barnett Smith was one nineteenth-century scholar who feared that readers of his time had forgotten Brown. This was surprising, he suggests, given that as early as 1819, the reviewer of Dunlap's *Life* wrote, "He is rarely spoken of but by those who have an habitual curiosity about every thing literary, and a becoming pride in all good writing which appears amongst ourselves" (Anonymous, "Art. V," 64; quoted in Smith 399). Smith prefaces the usual biographical details drawn from Dunlap with one of the more insightful observations in all of the early biographical notices: "To a daring imagination—the most singular and flexible, perhaps, yet witnessed amongst American writers—Charles Brockden Brown united a placid temperament and a contemplative intellect. Such a combination of seemingly discordant, and yet sharply defined qualities, is almost unique" (399). Following earlier commentators such as Barrett and Lippard, Smith argues against detractors who interpret his subject's "singular reservation and self-repression" as the behavior of a "mere misanthrope": "What seemed misanthropy was reserve, whose barriers could not be broken down—a reserve due in the first instance to his sensitive temperament, but deepened by regret over decisions precipitately acted upon, and his extreme shrinking from wounding the susceptibility of others" (403). Smith provides an extended analysis of the novels but makes no mention of the magazines or pamphlets. His major focus is *Wieland*, but he touches on the other novels as well before raising questions about why Brown "has never enjoyed the distinction of a popular writer." He reasons that Brown's apparent lack of humor may be a factor in his neglect but adds "that the link between his creations and humanity in general is missing." Smith concludes by drawing an analogy between Brown and the young country in which he lived: "Like the great nation of which he formed a part, he was struggling with a youth of noble potentialities....He was the intellectual product of a people as yet in its nonage, and which stepped forth amidst the nations of the world with all the hope and elasticity of youth, yet lacking the stronger fibre of manhood" (421).

In the early twentieth century, as in the late nineteenth, discussions of Brown appeared primarily in the form of brief notices published in journals or as parts of larger works on American literature or biography. Biographical materials doggedly remain the same, but the tenor of Brown's reception continues to change with the reader and the times. Annie Russell Marble, for example, contributed a brief "Centenary of America's First Novelist" in a 1910 issue of *The Dial*. Whereas biographical notices in the nineteenth century mentioned *Alcuin* only to dismiss it, Marble, acknowledging that Brown's "personality is still veiled in shadow," lingers with the early dialogue: "Brown's first book, 'Alcuin,' was a dialogue-essay on the then novel subject of Equal Suffrage.... This argument on a subject of current discussion is interesting to-day, in spite of its diffuse and extravagant phrasing; it reveals the progressive ideas and broad mental outlook which characterized Brown's later editorials and political pamphlets" (109–110).

In an 1888 essay brought forward for reprinting in 1921's *Literary Memoirs of the Nineteenth Century*, George Edward Woodberry adopts the negative appraisals that first appeared in Allen/Dunlap and extends them to dismiss Brown altogether, as "not remarkable" (276). For Woodberry, Brown's novels hold little more interest to a twentieth-century reader than his biography: "The truth is, these novels are as much gone by as the Algerian pirates, with whom they were contemporary; even Mrs. Radcliffe and Monk Lewis have kept better pace with the modern reader than has Brown" (278). Brown's only interest for this reader is in his transatlantic connection with Godwin and Shelley, and Woodberry's final judgment is damning: "He was a romancer of the old kind, although he made efforts in the direction of realism; he has no art; he is awkward, long-winded, and melodramatic, interested almost wholly in adventure, and save for the accident of coming first and being a Philadelphian would be without note" (282).

At the same time that Woodberry was rehearsing an earlier phase of the reception history for perhaps the last time, the early-twentieth-century emergence of American literary studies produced a new and more scholarly wave of interest. As of the 1920s, antiquarian and enthusiast Kennedy, like English professor David Lee Clark, made Brown an object of archival and scholarly research, producing new information and perspectives that continue to resonate today. Just as the story of early Brown reception begins with an unpublished but highly influential biographical work, Allen's *Life*, it ends with Kennedy's never-completed and never-published "Charles Brockden Brown: His Life and Writings." As the last commentator to emerge from the nineteenth-century culture of gentlemanly amateur erudition, Kennedy might justifiably be said to have been obsessed with Brown. Although by no means a professional scholar, in the sense of a specialist trained in disciplinary methods, he devoted much of his life from the 1920s to the 1940s to compiling information about Brown and archival resources concerning his life and writings. His draft of a biographical study, acquired in 1966 by the Kent State Institute for Bibliography and Editing as part of its work on the 1977–1987 Bicentennial Edition of Brown's novels and related works, is a massive project. Running to more than two thousand pages, part annotated and corrected typescript, part manuscript, Kennedy's research provided large amounts of previously unknown information concerning Brown's life and career, as well as a great deal of eccentric commentary. "Mr. Kennedy," he writes of himself, "is peculiarly endowed and fitted for a work of this kind. His interests from boyhood have been of the character to give him a sympathetic and intelligent understanding of an unusual number of Brown's characteristics.... With the exception of those who are keeping their material for their own literary use there has been no side of Brown's life or work left uninvestigated. Practically nothing of importance has been left for any future investigator" (1, 4). Imbued with such endearing swagger, Kennedy's manuscript, as Robert Hemenway describes it, "should be acknowledged as an essential source for any future study of Brockden Brown. Over 635,000 words long,... the manuscript is an impressive monument to [Kennedy's] skill as a scholar and bibliographer... [and] may eventually inspire the writing of a new biography of Brown" (17).

Although Clark's *Charles Brockden Brown: Pioneer Voice of America* was not published until 1952, he produced new commentary on Brown in the context of the emerging American Studies movement of the 1920s. In 1923, he published an extended abstract of his Columbia dissertation titled "Charles Brockden Brown: A Critical Biography." Clark uses archival research to correct long-standing errors concerning Brown's biography and marshals emerging literary-critical methods to recover Brown as a significant early American writer. While most earlier biographies, including Dunlap's, asserted that Brown's family arrived on the same ship with William Penn, for example, Clark writes, "the fact is that the Browns did not come over with William Penn... but preceded him by some years" (1923, 7). Besides updating biographical narratives that had been in place since the earliest phase of reception, Clark provides new perspectives on other long-standing themes such as the traditional complaint about the disjointed nature of Brown's fiction: "It may be affirmed with confidence... that Brockden Brown, with a turn of mind essentially collegiate, would have profited much by the systematizing influence of a good college education" (17). As one contributor to a new wave of literary-critical scholarship that would culminate in two new biographies published at mid-century, Clark continued to publish articles on Brown over the next thirty years, pursuing research that established a new critical groundwork for the increasingly specialized considerations that followed.

NOTES

1. This chapter in Dana's book is basically a reprint of his review of S. G. Goodrich's multi-volume *Novels of Charles Brockden Brown*. The review originally appeared in *United States Review* 2 (August 1827): 321–333.
2. For more on the cultural elite's reception of Brown see chapter 32 in this volume.

WORKS CITED

Anonymous. "Art. V.—Rev. of *The Life of Charles Brockden Brown*, by William Dunlap." *North American Review and Miscellaneous Journal* 9 (June 1819): 58–77.

Anonymous. "Critique on the Writings of Charles B. Brown." PF 6.1 (July 1811): 30–35.

Anonymous. "Inquiries respecting Dennie and Brown." PF 3.6 (June 1814): 570–573.

Anonymous. "Late American Books." *The Atheneum; or, Spirit of the English Magazines* 15 (December 1825): 238–243.

Anonymous. "Memoir of Charles Brockden Brown." In Charles Brockden Brown, *Wieland; or, The Transformation*. Vol. 1 of *The Novels of Charles Brockden Brown*, iii–xxiv. Boston: Goodrich, 1827.

Anonymous. "Original Sketches. Notices of Distinguished Characters. Charles Brockden Brown." *New-York Mirror: A Weekly Gazette of Literature and the Fine Arts* 4 (February 1823): 241.

Anonymous. "Rev. of *The Life of Charles Brockden Brown*, by William Dunlap." *The Portico, a Repository of Science and Literature* 1 (May 1816): 380–383.

Barrett, Joseph Hartwell. "Charles Brockden Brown." *American Review: A Whig Journal* n.s. 1 (March 1848): 260–274.

Bennett, Charles E. "Introduction." In Allen v–xxiv.

Clark, David Lee. "Charles Brockden Brown: A Critical Biography." Ph.D. dissertation, Columbia University, 1923.

Dana, Richard Henry. *Poems and Prose Writings*, Vol. 2. New York: Baker and Scribner, 1850.

Duyckinck, Evert A., and George L. Duyckinck. *Cyclopaedia of American Literature, etc.*, Vol. 2. New York: Scribner, 1855.

Griswold, Rufus Wilmot. *The Prose Writers of America, with a Survey of the Intellectual History, Condition, and Prospects of the Country*, 3rd rev. ed. Philadelphia: Carey and Hart, 1849.

Hemenway, Robert. "Daniel Edwards Kennedy: A Forgotten Collector of Charles Brockden Brown and Early American Literature." *Serif* 3–4 (December 1966): 16–18.

Kennedy, Daniel Edwards. "Charles Brockden Brown: A Biography" (c. 1923–1945). Typescript with manuscript additions. Charles Brockden Brown Bicentennial Edition Records (bulk 1917–1995). Special Collections and Archives, Kent State Libraries, Kent, Ohio.

Lippard, George. "The Heart-Broken." *The Nineteenth Century: A Quarterly Miscellany* 1 (1848): 19–27.

Marble, Annie Russell. "The Centenary of America's First Novelist." *Dial* 48 (1910): 109–110.

Prescott, William H. "Life of Charles Brockden Brown." In Jared Sparks, ed., *The Library of American Biography*, Vol. 1, 117–180. Boston: Hilliard, Gray, 1834.

Smith, George Barnett. "Brockden Brown." *Fortnightly Review* n.s. 24 (September 1878): 399–421.

Sparks, Jared. "Advertisement." In Jared Sparks, ed., *The Library of American Biography*, Vol. 1, iii–iv. Boston: Hilliard, Gray, 1834.

Tuckerman, Henry T. *Mental Portraits; or, Studies of Character*. London: Richard Bentley, 1853.

Van Doren, Carl. "Fiction I: Brown, Cooper." In William Peterfield Trent et al., eds., *The Cambridge History of American Literature*, Vol. 1, 284–306. New York: Putnam, 1917.

Woodberry, George Edward. *Literary Memoirs of the Nineteenth Century*. New York: Harcourt, 1921.

CHAPTER 34

··

BROWN'S LATER
BIOGRAPHERS AND
RECEPTION, 1949–2000S

··

ELIZABETH JANE WALL HINDS

Two biographies and two dissertations in the mid-twentieth century steered the direction of reading Charles Brockden Brown for a long generation. Concerned with securing Brown's place in an American Cold War–era literary canon, scholars from 1949 until the mid-1980s emphasized nationalism as a primary interpretative and evaluative criterion, claiming a specifically "American" character for Brown's writing and highlighting his position as a "first"—the first US citizen to try to make a living at writing, the first American Gothic novelist—in the immediate post-Revolutionary age. These readings focused on issues to do with all things American: the American landscape, the American psyche, and the American political situation. Relatedly, they were interested in the history of ideas, so Brown studies during this era read his work—primarily the first four novels—as embodiment of various sources, such as Enlightenment thought and its critique; political and gender radicalism inherited from writers such as Jean-Jacques Rousseau, William Godwin, and Mary Wollstonecraft; and a nascent romanticism teleologically pointed toward later American writers such as Edgar Allan Poe. This generation typically leaned toward allegorical reading; the novels were either allegories of the post-Revolutionary political situation or allegories of the mental workings of the author.

Beginning in the mid-1980s, Brown studies proliferated in several directions. Less psychobiographical, more recent scholarship and biography position Brown within a shifting environment of cultural, intellectual, and social phenomena. Increasing attention to the nonnovelistic writing, particularly Brown's writing after 1800, saw Brown increasingly responding and contributing not just to national culture but also to issues and material realities of the Atlantic world-system. Across both generations, however, important recovery projects appeared steadily, grounding studies of Brown in a progressively updated understanding of his canon.

I. LITERARY NATIONALISM, 1949–1985

This era of Brown readership was marked by the aim of canonizing Brown's writing against the prevailing formalist aesthetics of the New Criticism, which had valued formal "unity" and a more elliptical style than Brown's. Defenders registered surprise that some of their contemporaries, when they read Brown at all, thought of him as a bad writer of melodrama and "turgid prose" (Powell). This generation sought to raise Brown's status by shifting the discussion away from aesthetics and toward cultural and political readings, their historicism positioning Brown as both reflector of and contributor to a specifically "American" literature and culture. Thus, though biographers such as Harry Warfel and David Lee Clark prioritized Brown's fiction, they began a long, multigenerational shift toward serious study of his journalism and other nonfiction to support their form of historicism.

Warfel's 1949 *Charles Brockden Brown: American Gothic Novelist* and David Lee Clark's 1952 *Charles Brockden Brown: Pioneer Voice of America* formulated a Brown that was first and foremost an American. Both literary scholars, these biographers were interested in Brown's traditionally "literary" output, with an eye toward reviving interest in Brown that had flagged since the mid-nineteenth century. Both sought to canonize Brown, if only for some "minor fictional classics" (Warfel 10). In the wake of World War II, they touted what Clark calls "the significant work that he did in fostering American literary independence" (Clark 1950, 365). Yet, despite nationalist objectives, these readers undervalued Brown's nonnovelistic writings—work that addressed more directly the position of the United States in the Atlantic world-system—to focus almost exclusively on the first four novels, read overwhelmingly as Gothic. Warfel's point of view can be summarized in this evaluation of Brown's career: "After writing four excellent novels and numerous fragments, all in the tradition of the terror novel as modified by a concern with ideas, Brown let himself be maneuvered into editorial and hack work" (164). For this era of readers, it was as a reinventor, an Americanizer, of British and European literary genres that Brown was seen to have made his greatest contributions; even his last two novels, the epistolary and sentimental *Clara Howard* and *Jane Talbot*, were barely studied, novels though they were, perhaps because mid-twentieth-century readers considered the sentimental novel to be derivative of British fiction and—possibly worse—"female" in its concerns. Warfel's view of the shape of Brown's career, in fact, influenced reception of Brown's work through much of the twentieth century. Readers largely studied, in the first novels, a handful of topoi, literary and cultural, to make a case for Brown as a unique writer, whether good or bad. R. W. B. Lewis's *The American Adam: Innocence, Tragedy, and Tradition in the Nineteenth Century* (1955); Richard Chase's, *The American Novel and Its Tradition* (1957); and James Justus's "Arthur Mervyn, American" (1970) are characteristic of the period's construction of Brown as a nationalist writer, representing uniquely American themes.

Partly because they studied primarily the first four novels, these students of Brown had ample evidence for such nationalistic claims. Brown began his novel-publishing career with a clear assertion of American difference; the preface to *Edgar Huntly* declares:

That new springs of action, and new motives to curiosity should operate; that
the field of investigation, opened to us by our own country, should differ essentially
from those which exist in Europe, may be readily conceived....It is the purpose of
this work...to exhibit a series of adventures, growing out of the condition of our
country.   (EH 3)

And one of *Wieland*'s subtitles was, of course, *An American Tale*. The isolated social and
geographical positions of characters in *Wieland* and *Edgar Huntly* and the historical
backdrop of yellow fever in *Ormond* and *Arthur Mervyn* and its effect on moral behavior
were favorite subjects in fixing Brown's position in the nationalist canon (see Ferguson).
A small but influential group of studies found Brown's Gothic novels to express or comment on the paranoia surrounding immigration that grew through the 1790s, particularly during the Reign of Terror in France; in these readings, Brown's city novels *participate*
in the spread of paranoia, for example, with his shadowy French characters, or these
novels *critique* such paranoia, though the latter reading appears more often later. As
late as 1982, Alan Axelrod's *Charles Brockden Brown: An American Tale* positions these
novels as fundamentally American in that they—*Edgar Huntly* literally, the others
figuratively—embody mental "wilderness," confusion, and corruption, all enabled by
and released, if not created, by the New World.

In short, many of this generation read Brown's fiction as allegories of Enlightenment
thought as it eventuated in the American republic, tested by the irrational impulses
of individuals. The novels were read as allegories of democracy, of the wilderness, of
"savagery," of Federalist or Republican governments; the "city" novels *Ormond* and
Arthur Mervyn were read as representing or providing "a portrait of urban America"
(Feeney). The weakness of these allegorical readings is their assumption of a unified,
coherent early national culture. Clark's *Pioneer Voice of America*, however, despite its title,
rides the nationalist argument less hard than many others of this era. Where Warfel had
lauded Brown's Gothicism, Clark proposed a figure both more "rational" and more
proto-Romantic than in Warfel. Warfel's interest in the Gothic, like that of many other
scholars, more or less limited him to the study of the early Gothic novels. Clark, on the
other hand, either published in full or analyzed at length "The Man at Home," excerpts
from the *Literary Magazine* and *American Register*, and Brown's late political writings.
And significantly, he spent as much time in analysis of *Clara Howard* and *Jane Talbot* as
he did on the first four novels. As a result, his Brown appears as a more varied writer *and*
subject; Clark's Brown, for example, changes over time, whereas Warfel's does not.

Warfel did, however, include some previously unpublished and little-known writings
of Brown, such as some of the "Henrietta Letters." Clark extended this work exponentially.
The great contribution of his volume is, in fact, the mass of newly published
manuscripts, available there for the first time, as Clark repeatedly points out. In addition to the "Henrietta Letters," he includes several complete letters from Brown to
friends such as William Wood Wilkins and Joseph Bringhurst, and family members
such as Brown's brothers Armitt and James. Until the publication of Brown's complete
letters in 2013, Clark's biography was for a good half-century extremely useful to
Brown scholars.

Pioneer Voice included most of the "Henrietta Letters" in a modernized transcription, where Clark treats them much as he does the other previously unpublished Brown texts in his biography: as psychobiography. Clark read Brown, therefore, as literally a Romantic, suffering young man opening his soul, for example, to an actual love interest, Henrietta, when most other readers realize the letters were fictional epistolary texts. Analyses of the "Henrietta Letters," Brown's letters, his journalism, and even the novels consist, often, of sorting through Brown's literary and historical influences: Rousseau and Godwin especially shore up the young-Romantic thesis. Perhaps to support Clark's "pioneer voice" depiction, his Brown appears more alone and more penurious than Brown's other biographers allow.

Working from the Warfel and Clark biographies, produced in the five years before his own study, Warner Berthoff in his massive 1954 Harvard dissertation, "The Literary Career of Charles Brockden Brown," expands both the allegory-of-America theme—Brown's writing was "an index to American thought and culture in the early years of the republic" (2)—and the Brown-as-young-Romantic portrait: "mid-way between the Revolution and the era of Emerson, Poe," Brown shared in "that 'revolt against maxims,' and against the rule of unfeeling rationality, which distinguished the Romantic generation" (1, 3).

However, both here and in published essays on Brown's *Historical Sketches* and other "political" writings, Berthoff extended his analysis to the relationships between Brown's fiction and his political writings, to the effect that Brown becomes, in this interpretation, much more than a Gothic novelist. Looking at Brown's later writing, Berthoff provided a much-needed reshaping of Brown's career, both in ideas and in genres. The earlier studies (and some later ones, as we will see) read Brown's turn from Gothicism to other types of fiction and journalism as signaling a conservative turn; Berthoff saw more nuance and less psychobiography in these changes of genre. For instance, in this reading, Brown's view of political justice, introduced to him by Godwin, shifted from an uncritical advocate, proto-Romantic, in idealistically imagining that everyone everywhere could be brought to rational and therefore just actions if only brought to similar cultural and philosophical practices; to a novelist invested in *testing* blind belief in rationalism, with results that began to cast doubt on the universality of human "capacity" and therefore justice; and finally to one with a noncynical but disinterested view of humanity as bending rationalism to its own, nationalistic ends. But, Berthoff argues, in the end, Brown came to predict that under the banner of international capitalism, all nations will be leveled and the need for war will be over, a view that completes a circuit back to the early idealism of political justice. The through line is Brown's interest in political justice, which he steadily tested and revised throughout his short lifetime. Despite the fact that it was never published, Berthoff's dissertation marked a new level in the interpretation of Brown's overall body of writings and had great influence among scholars. The dissertation and later published articles drawn from it were among the first thorough attempts to explore Brown's larger corpus of writings beyond the novels.

In addition to its primary emphasis on US nationalism, scholarship during the Cold War emphasized psychology as a major category for interpreting and exploring Brown's writings, whether from the perspectives of the author's mind (pyschobiography) or a presumed national psyche (psychosymbolism). This tendency was fostered by this generation's concentration on the first four novels, which combined paranormal activities with explicit violence—standard fare for the Gothic and fodder for depth-psychology-type readings. Through the Gothic focus of mid-twentieth-century readings, biographers positioned Brown as himself Romantic and morbidly sensitive, and since studies of the psychology of madness were part of the Gothic mode, *Wieland*, by some accounts the study of a madman, and *Edgar Huntly*, an exploration of the irrational state of sleepwalk-ing, were especially of interest. Issues related to questioning Enlightenment rationality as dramatized in aberrant psychology make up the focus of much work through this period; delusion, deception, immorality, secrecy, and even conspiracy all appear with regularity in the scholarship.

In many ways, the psychosymbolic treatment of Brown's novels peaked in 1960 with Leslie Fiedler's *Love and Death in the American Novel*, which drew from Jungian arche-typal psychology. Like many of his generation, Fiedler took the novels as surreal out-croppings of Brown's own experience and mental state. Typical of this class of reader, Fiedler romanticized Brown at the same time as he took literally Brown's Romantic rep-resentations of himself to his friends in letters. Brown was, Fiedler wrote, "the victim of American philistinism," and so he died "wracked by poverty and disease" (146). Fiedler's summary of Brown's life and writing, in prose purple enough to shore up any Romantic reading, captures the main threads of the depth-psychology interpretations of Brown's life and writing, so it merits quotation at length:

> If Brown deserved no other credit, he should be remembered at least as the inventor of the American writer.... That he tried the impossible and that he failed; that he had disavowed his own art before his untimely death of tuberculosis at the age of thirty-nine; that he hardened from a wild disciple of the Enlightenment, a flagrant Godwinian...into a pious conservative; that he drew his inspiration from loneliness and male companionship, and that he ceased to be a creative writer when he married; that over his whole frantic, doomed career, the blight of melancholy presides.   (145)

Like that of Warfel, Clark, and Berthoff before him, Fiedler's Brown is a "first," for which he deserves canonization in the American pantheon. Also typical of this generation, Fiedler looks almost exclusively at the novels and declares them flawed, despite which they embody, this argument goes, a rough-and-ready "truth" of American male psychology, which substitutes terror and anarchy for sex and, as a result, is punished socially (with "loneliness") and as an author ("he failed"). That he dies young and unfulfilled after a turn toward conservatism is a mark of this generation's reading. Only by overvaluing the first four novels and dismissing Brown's later writing is it possible to come to these conclusions.

At the end of the Vietnam era came Richard Slotkin's *Regeneration through Violence: The Mythology of the American Frontier* (1973), a study of the ideology of (masculinist) violence in US narratives of the colonial and Revolutionary eras in the "American" male—and in American society. A study that combines claims for Brown's "Americanness" and interest in the violence of the Gothic novels, Slotkin's influential work was tinged with the teleology of mid-century Brown studies, as the violent and land-hungry psychic energy of the American pioneer is fashioned here to point straight to American involvement in Vietnam during the book's creation. Norman Grabo continued the psychosymbolic reading of Brown with *The Coincidental Art of Charles Brockden Brown* (1981), which combines many themes of the Cold War generation: a formalist approach, a nationalist agenda, and a claim for aesthetic greatness. Grabo's interest in doubling and paradox hints that Brown's novelistic coincidences are purposeful, that they go beyond trope to form a stronger infrastructure than these novels had been granted previously, hints at the poststructuralist readings to come throughout the 1980s. Yet *Coincidental Art* concludes that Brown's coincidences mark an allegorical mode of writing revealing the doubleness of all things, particularly of character. While Grabo's reading isn't one of American allegory or even psychobiographical allegory, that it reads characters as allegorical at all suggests the same tendencies found in other mid-century readings: it reaches past Brown's very rich surface to validate his place in the canon on formalist, particularly structuralist interpretative grounds.

Another contribution this generation produced in its bid to canonize Brown was the important work of location and recovery, of getting into print Brown's unpublished or unedited writing. In mid-century, Warfel's biography included some previously unpublished work, such as some of the "Henrietta Letters," while he had published "The Rhapsodist" and other lesser-known texts such as "The Man at Home" ten years earlier. Clark, of course, printed great masses of Brown's unpublished manuscripts in his biography. Twenty years later, Charles Bennett's dissertation, "The Charles Brockden Brown Canon" (1974) made important inroads in broadening critical attention beyond the novels to include Brown's poetry, other fiction, and journalism. His "The Letters of Charles Brockden Brown: An Annotated Census" appeared two years later; this work tracked down all of the then-known letters, housed in libraries around the United States.

Bernard Rosenthal's *Critical Essays on Charles Brockden Brown* (1981) provides a cumulative view of this generation of readings. Almost all of its chapters focus on the first four novels, with only a nod toward Brown's larger corpus, and most of the critical essays study Gothic and nationalist themes. This volume republished early critical responses such as William Dunlap's biography and reviews contemporary with Brown, along with its original readings. It also included Charles A. Carpenter's "Selective Bibliography of Writings about Charles Brockden Brown," thus contributing to the small but steady stream of bibliographic studies that had helped guide Brown studies throughout this generation.

Lulu Rumsey Wiley's *The Sources and Influences of Charles Brockden Brown's Novels* (1950) listed, despite the title, primary texts by Brown other than the novels, together with sources about Brown's writing and other texts deemed influential on his work. Sydney Krause, in "A Census of the Works of Charles Brockden Brown" (1966), includes Brown's writings held in libraries, not merely those included in print bibliographies. Paul Witherington's 1974 "Charles Brockden Brown: A Bibliographical Essay" has been important in updating studies of Brown's works, with bibliographies of both primary and secondary texts. As Brown studies proliferated through the latter half of the twentieth century, it was important to keep track of these secondary sources as well, and a few scholars stepped up to that task.

Possibly the most important work on Brown during the Cold War era were the Kent State editions of *The Novels and Related Works of Charles Brockden Brown*, in six volumes between 1977 and 1987, edited by Sydney Krause and S. W. Reid. All six of Brown's novels, plus *Alcuin*, were edited to the highest standards of the time, earning the Modern Language Association Center for Scholarly Editions seal, and for the first time, *Clara Howard* and *Jane Talbot* merited attention equal to that of the first four novels. Each volume included, in addition to textual essays explaining the editorial choices, a historical essay, each written by a different high-profile Brown scholar and summarizing the historical context, relevant biographical information, and representative interpretations based on scholarship to date. These historical essays amounted to short monographs in themselves, representing the most complete work on Brown of their era.

II. Inclusive Views of Charles Brockden Brown, 1985–Present

While largely escaping the anachronisms of earlier, proto-Romanticist analyses of Brown, readers since the 1980s increasingly frame his work within more postmodern, global, and inclusive terms. This work has significantly expanded our understanding of both Brown and his cultural situation. Critical and historical readings of Brown's nonnovelistic writing; the continued canonization of Brown, including the teaching of his work; and notable projects in recovery and publication of unpublished work have all populated the landscape of early American and cultural studies in numbers far surpassing the earlier years of reception. The publication of two full-length biographies by historians and a handful of shorter biographical interventions between 1994 and the present are indexes of a vibrant and growing commitment to Brown studies. The creation of the Charles Brockden Brown Society in 2000, at the midway point of this era, gave voice to all of these trends. Unlike most single-author "societies," the CBBS encourages work on Brown *and* his contemporaries, which is to say, on Brown and his historical, cultural landscape, inclusively. In biennial meetings since 2000, presentations have been on subjects as diverse as Brown and postcolonialism, race and the yellow fever epidemic of 1793, and Islam and on Brown's relationship to places, such as the Mediterranean, New Orleans, and Germany. The CBBS also encourages work on Brown's nonnovelistic writing, without discouraging work on the novels.

The period of biography and reception from 1985 to the present is divided here into two equal periods of time, primarily for convenience rather than to taxonomize them as remarkably different periods. There is a great deal of overlap in scholarly and critical readings and methodology, though over the thirty years covered, some distinct changes can be seen. The New Historicist methods of the first subperiod were concerned with the early American republic, for example, while the second, most recent period, increasingly views Brown's writing within a larger world-system.

(i) Expanding the Brown Canon, 1985–2000

Readers during this period worked to crack open the interpretative window of Brown studies, looking at his writing with an eye to sex, gender, and class issues and thus to a Brown profoundly embedded in culture rather than the "outsider" of earlier analyses. Seldom during this period did scholars or biographers overtly defend the canonization of Brown's work, since Brown has become firmly canonized through early American course syllabi and scholarship. Important recoveries of Brown's out-of-print work during this period, Alfred Weber's 1987 publication of *Somnambulism and Other Stories* and Alfred Weber and Wolfgang Schafer's 1992 *Charles Brockden Brown: Literary Essays and Reviews*, contributed to Brown's now-secure position in the canon.

Scholarship after the Cold War positioned Brown as an alembic in which political, economic, and social aspects of his era combined, intersected, and reconstituted. Whereas Cold War–era scholarship was interested in psychobiography and Revolutionary-era national politics, supported by possessive individualism and progressive US ideologies, this late-twentieth-century period expanded both the canon and the critical perspectives from which to read Brown; interested in material culture and the constructedness of ideology, these readers studied Brown more inclusively, incorporating his journalism, political writing, and other nonnovelistic writing as circulating written products in anglophone culture. Largely concentrating on the US context, with a particular interest in the early republican era, this scholarship looked more intently at the cultural dialogue Brown participated in and less at an interiorized, Romantic Brown. This period studied issues as varied as print culture, Jacobinism and extremist countercultures of the 1790s, geography, sentiment, the history of the body, race and racialism, and gender and sexuality.

American literary and cultural studies in the mid-1980s worked to expand the canon overall, with profound long-term implications for the study of Brown. This period began with two studies of the novel that had far-reaching consequences for the definition, study, and canonization of nonnovelistic genres. Cathy L. Davidson's *Revolution and the Word: The Rise of the Novel in America* (1986) examines the material conditions of novels in and as culture—buying, selling, and advertising, for instance—to argue that the early American novel was antipatriarchal in supplanting traditional, male sources of instruction. Davidson's study of sentimental novels, among which she includes *Arthur Mervyn*, their popularity, their didacticism, and their picaresque form, supports historicist, not formalist, methods. The following year, Jane Tompkins's *Sensational Designs* helped to produce a sea change in interpretative strategies, not only for the study of Brown, on whom she has two chapters, but also for American literary study generally. Her subtitle points to this new direction: *The Cultural Work of American Fiction, 1790–1860*. Tompkins's revolutionary argument, to be read alongside Davidson's, was that, contra formalist readings, in their own historical context, American novels between the Revolution and the Civil War were designed episodically, with stereotypical characters, to speak to the tastes of their readers and thus to serve the purpose of morally educating the public. Scholarly conclusions prior to Tompkins, she explains, erroneously found Brown's work "flawed" because they measured his novels against modernist aesthetic criteria.

Sensational Designs began a years-long upending of critical assumptions about early American writing, demonstrating that early texts such as Brown's had distinctly moral and political purposes—*uses*—and thus were not *designed*, generically speaking, to meet modern expectations about, for example, the novel. Of *Arthur Mervyn*, Tompkins writes, "Plot...has no place in this narrative," just as "character, in the sense of individual identity, is nonexistent," since repetition of types of "rescuers" was the moral point of this novel (67). *Wieland* exemplifies the inability of isolated individuals to govern themselves (Chapter II) and does so by making the "Wielands' miniature society" (53) the family that is, as the novel itself mentions, "a model from which to sketch the condition of a nation" (W 30). Many readers since Tompkins have not only taken this kind of New Historicist approach to Brown's novels but also, as a logical consequence of this methodology, have more and more centrally studied Brown's work other than the novels.

Steven Watts's biography, *The Romance of Real Life: Charles Brockden Brown and the Origins of American Culture* (1994), is the first modern cultural biography following this new paradigm. It examines late-eighteenth-century to early-nineteenth-century economic expansion, growing market capitalism, and concurrent attempts at nation building that created not only a marketplace of ideas but also a fragmented and fragmenting cultural "psychology." This volatile period allowed liberty for chameleonic impersonation, Watts argues, an extreme version of the self-made man. Like Tompkins but with a greater emphasis on economic forces, Watts sees growing out of these mercurial forces an anxiety-driven brooding on the problem of individual volition and a renewed US concern with choice over both moral and economic destiny.

Watts contextualizes a broad range of Brown's written work, for instance, *Alcuin*, the "Ellendale" fragment, "Walstein's School of History," "The Man at Home," Brown's letters to fiancée Elizabeth Linn, the late *Historical Sketches*, and even Brown's architectural drawings. Watts devotes three full chapters to all six novels; even in this period of great interest in Brown's nonnovelistic writings, the novels do continue to anchor many studies. Like Davidson and Tompkins, Watts looks at the cultural uses of writing. The novel, Watts argues, worked culturally to simultaneously liberate and constrain; as "agents of class formation," novels in the new nation functioned morally, economically, and psychologically (19).

For all of his forward-looking contributions to the study of Brown, Watts replicates some of the distortions of earlier psychobiographical criticism. He pictures Brown, for example, as a fragmented, chameleonic personality resulting from his mercurial culture. Watts's Brown is as extreme a radical in youth as he is a near saber-rattling hawk in his thirties; he notoriously states at the beginning of his sixth chapter, "On or about April 1800 Charles Brockden Brown changed" (132). Since he identifies several consistencies over Brown's lifetime—his utopianism, his fascination with gender and sex, and the importance of property in his understanding of human character—this assertion of an abrupt shift in Brown's values, and on the extremity of Brown's ideological positions before and after the shift, is not supported by the evidence.

Michael Warner's *Letters of the Republic: Publication and the Public Sphere in Eighteenth-Century America* (1990) works from a similar methodology, using Jürgen Habermas's analysis of the bourgeois public sphere to analyze the centrality of writing—print—to the consolidation of a public, civic domain of self-governance in the United States. Thus, authors in the early republic sought less individual expression than support for public "virtues" such as benevolence and industry; democracy necessitates a public sphere wherein citizens can govern themselves. Novels in the early republic have been misread, Warner says, following Tompkins and Davidson, through modern aesthetic lenses. Instead, it makes more sense to read novels like Brown's *Arthur Mervyn* as part of the creation of the public sphere. In this, Warner overtly rejects the practice of psychobiography in its focus on interiority; instead, we should look at the public uses of print in the consolidation of democracy and citizenship. Participating in the public sphere, Brown's didacticism, *Arthur Mervyn's* episodic structure, and what some critics regard as excessive "intellection" on the part of Brown's characters—all of these were qualities of public discourse designed to communicate broadly and popularly. *Arthur Mervyn* thus both represents the practice of virtue in the character of Arthur and *performs,* in writing, an exercise of benevolence toward a virtuous democratic population. Christopher Looby's *Voicing America: Language, Literary Form, and the Origins of the United States* (1996) similarly argues that novels, including Brown's, offer a counter to emerging liberal ideology around 1800.

Robert Levine's *Conspiracy and Romance* (1989) balances readings of the new republic as optimistic, Jeffersonian future-building freedom with an unearthing of some of the fears of anarchy that followed the Revolution. To demonstrate the paranoia of some early American "romances," Levine studies, among other things, ministers's sermons on the dangers of libertine, atheistical potentialities inherent in the new liberty. Europe was especially suspect as the seat of the French Revolution and the Reign of Terror but also of clandestine, power-seeking groups such as the Illuminati. The public rhetoric of paranoia—murky backdrops, superintelligent villains hailing from some "alien" land, warnings about trust in strangers—in short, the rhetoric of the Gothic, supported cultural anxieties regarding foreigners and, as Levine demonstrates persuasively, insidiously connected these fictional foreigners to social and moral "infection." For a novel like Brown' *Ormond*, set during the yellow fever epidemic of 1793, it was not a far leap from the one idea to the other.

Julia Stern's *The Plight of Feeling: Sympathy and Dissent in the Early American Novel* (1997) makes the important argument that novelists of the early republic, Brown among them, were engaged in exploring the value of sympathy and its inadequacies, consequent on post-Revolutionary civic and psychic trauma. Steeped in readings of Adam Smith, Jean-Jacques Rousseau, and Edmund Burke, these writers tested the ability of sympathy—imaginative connectedness among individuals and across the public sphere—to bind a newly liberated population together toward successful independence. Much as Watts's biography did, Stern makes the case that writers like Brown, experiencing a cultural postwar "melancholy," were aware of the decade's encroaching unfettered liberal capitalism as a condemnation of market capitalism. Stern investigates, for example, *Ormond's* attention to the absence of rights, in such a society, of "those 'others' who do not count as citizens," such as African Americans and women (153).

Cynthia Jordan's chapter on *Wieland* in *Second Stories: The Politics of Language, Form, and Gender in Early American Fictions* (1989) historicizes the role of language in the new forms of authority in the early republic, to examine the patriarchal investment in these new forms despite the presence, also, of "second" or suppressed stories of the disempowered. Elizabeth Jane Wall Hinds's *Private Property: Charles Brockden Brown's Gendered Economics of Discourse* (1997), which encompasses class and gender concerns in 1790s American culture, is also informed by Habermas and studies the Lockean and Adam Smithian implications of sympathy. Mary Chapman's introduction to *Ormond* (1999) historicizes class and gender issues, while Bruce Burgett's *Sentimental Bodies: Sex, Gender, and Citizenship in the Early Republic* (1998) parses the male body with respect to sentiment, particularly in readings of *Clara Howard* and *Jane Talbot*.

Historicist and other approaches expanded readings of Brown's novels in addition to those interested in gender. Sydney Krause's influential "Historical Essay" in the Kent State edition of *Edgar Huntly* (1984) and Bill Christophersen's *Apparition in the Glass: Charles Brockden Brown's American Gothic* (1993), for example, examine, among other things, historical practices around race and ethnicity. Teresa Goddu's chapter on Brown in her *Gothic America: Narrative, History, and Nation* (1997) positions the Gothic counternarrative to Enlightenment progress as "disease," particularly the disease of language. Like a few others expanding the Brown canon, John Holmes published articles in 1990 and 1995 on Brown's letters; Steven Frye brought out an article on *The Monthly Magazine, and American Review* in 1998; and William Scheick published on "Somnambulism" in 1999, all contributing to rehistoricizing Brown.

(ii) Global Perspectives, 2000–Present

Readings of Brown since the turn of the millennium extend 1990s historicist and material culture methodologies but possess some key differences from previous eras. This Brown is embedded in culture, no longer positioned as an outsider; resisting psychobiographical readings, this period's readings result in a Brown of more consistent—and more consistently radical and critical—politics and writing practices over the course of his life. This era also positions Brown in a geographically global or world-system. Relatedly, there is an expanding interest in Brown's writing beyond the novels and beyond the period of his novel writing.

Stephen Shapiro's 2008 *The Culture and Commerce of the Early American Novel: Reading the Atlantic World-System* best articulates this generation's major concerns and methodologies, as it brings forward the historicism of the previous period to synthesize the study of material, social, and intellectual culture at the end of the long eighteenth century. Looking at a variety of Brown texts, before, during, and after the novel era, Shapiro persuasively makes the case that Brown and other cultural contributors of the 1790–1820 period did not view the United States as the center of global politics, that despite some claims from Brown and others for an "American" literature (e.g., in Brown's preface to *Edgar Huntly*), the United States was understood within what Shapiro calls, borrowing from Immanuel Wallerstein, a "world-system of capitalist trade" (Shapiro 2). Under this system, nations are profoundly affected by far distant but globally central actions; Brown stated plainly, for example, in his late history "Annals of Europe and America," that the key players affecting the Atlantic world were Spain, France, and England because of their belletristic control of trade and, therefore, their effect on imports and exports, including the importing of slaves to America. Both Brown's novels and his nonfiction were experiments, then, in countering the "insurgent liberalism" of the nineteenth century with reformulations of sensibility and sentiment. His long fictions "ought to be read as critiques of the social violence immanent" in new forms of consensus building, "laden with power designs and willing to enact actual violence on subaltern groups when their members seek the equality that these public institutions advertise as available to all" (44).

This period of scholarship produced, along these lines, a Brown more aware of social, cultural, and economic changes than previously, a Brown more observant and critical of culture than a carrier of it. Readings such as Karen Weyler's 2004 *Intricate Relations: Sexual and Economic Desire in American Fiction, 1789–1814* and Elizabeth Maddock Dillon's chapter on marriage in *The Gender of Freedom: Fictions of Liberalism and the Literary Public Sphere* (2004) continue this progressive work on Brown and gender. Postcolonial studies in the same vein likewise appear with some regularity now. To take just one example of advancing scholarship around a single topic, studies of geography and postcoloniality as performed and represented in *Edgar Huntly* can be traced directly from Sydney Krause's groundbreaking 1994 *American Literature* article, "Penn's Elm and Edgar Huntly: Dark 'Instruction to the Heart'" and Jared Gardner's "Alien Nation: Edgar Huntly's Savage Awakening" in the same issue, to the more detailed readings of *Huntly* and the postcolonial in Hinds's "Deb's Dogs: Animals, Indians, and Postcolonial Desire in *Edgar Huntly*" in 2004 and Chad Luck's "Re-Walking the Purchase: *Edgar Huntly*, David Hume, and the Origins of Ownership" in 2009.

Readings since 2000 have also examined a much broader array of Brown's writing over his lifetime. For example, Mark Kamrath's *The Historicism of Charles Brockden Brown: Radical History and the Early Republic* (2010) studies an extensive selection of historical writings and writing about historicism from Brown, to demonstrate his postmodernity in the sense that Brown, like postmodern ("new") historicists, did not pretend to or believe in objective reporting on historical "truth"; rather, he viewed history as an always coordinated relationship between the past and the present, with no objective position from which to view history (a historical relativity theory). Brown's inclusion of subaltern points of view in historical writing also anticipates postmodern historiography. Fiction is a kind of "domestic history," Kamrath stresses. He looks in detail at the *Historical Sketches*, Brown's magazine essays, the "Annals," and, of course "The Difference between History and Romance," among other writing, and from this comprehensive view concludes against previous generations' assertions of Brown's turn to conservatism in midlife.

A partial overview of nonnovelistic writings studied in this period would include "Thessalonica: A Roman Story"; a growing number of *Alcuin* studies; *Clara Howard* and *Jane Talbot*; "The Rhapsodist"; "Somnambulism"; the *Historical Sketches*; "The Scribbler"; dissertations on the *Monthly Magazine, and American Review*; and chapters in collections or monographs from Ed Cahill on aesthetics and politics, Michael Cody on Brown's journalism, Andy Doolen on American imperialism, Bryan Waterman on the Friendly Club, and Jared Gardner on early American magazine culture and studies of Brown's letters by Elizabeth Hewitt and Marc Amfreville.

The first Brown biographer after 2000, Peter Kafer, historicizes Brown according to his family's Quaker experience. Earlier biographers did neglect this aspect of Brown's life, and Kafer's *Charles Brockden Brown's Revolution and the Birth of American Gothic* (2004), much more historically specific, adds a good deal of productive archival research into Quaker history and Brown's cultural context. His sources are as wide-ranging as Brown family histories and letters, diaries of Quakers such as Elizabeth Drinker and Sarah Fisher, tax lists and the *Philadelphia Directory*, and various holdings of the Quaker Collection at Haverford College. This magisterial work amasses study of extended family connections among immigrant Quakers from 1650 to 1800, the associations among neighbors in and around Vine Street in Philadelphia throughout those years, and the doctrinal and experiential implications of Quaker doctrine and Quakers' predisposition against Scots-Irish Presbyterians.

Kafer represents a biographical shift back to a Gothic Brown and, as such, is more the heir of Warfel than of Clark or Dunlap in the earlier generations. If Kafer's historical evidence is broad, his reading of Brown's writing can be somewhat narrow: primarily the four earliest novels and a few of Brown's shorter fictional pieces, read as allegories of Brown's trauma, as a child, during the arrest and incarceration of his father for refusing to sign the Patriots' Oath of Allegiance. Kafer does, however, align post-Revolutionary political culture with Brown's Gothicism, a connection not made earlier. "Where was extremity, *intensity* in middling, Quaker Philadelphia?" (xv). What, in other words, could possibly be "Gothic" about ordinary America? The Quakers' inner light is his answer. Their obligation to try to know, "objectively" and "inwardly," the direct revelation of God appropriates the language of the senses, making it ready-made for Gothic writing.

As with other Gothic-Brown advocates, Kafer subscribes to the idea that Brown changed drastically in mid-career: after the first four novels, Brown "ceas[ed] to be an artist" (194). In 1800, Brown "positively chose to become a generic American, and he only deepened that identity in 1804 when he married the Presbyterian Elizabeth Linn" (194). In this respect, Kafer's theoretical framing of Brown's life belongs to an earlier period, though his archival work makes invaluable contributions to the current study of Brown.

Caleb Crain and Fredrika Teute have made important biographical contributions to the new framing of Brown's life based on close attention to Brown's writing over his full lifetime. Teute's "A 'Republic of Intellect': Conversation and Criticism among the Sexes in 1790s New York," in Barnard, Kamrath, and Shapiro's *Revising Charles Brockden Brown*, and the chapter called "The Decomposition of Charles Brockden Brown: Sympathy in Brown's Letters," in Crain's *American Sympathy: Men, Friendship, and Literature in the New Nation* (2001), both use meticulous archival research to situate Brown within a broader, more diverse circle of friends and correspondents than biographers have previously appreciated. Looking at heterosocial circles of conversation, formal and informal, in the 1790s, Teute demonstrates mutual influence and education among men and women associated with the New York Friendly Club. Brown's conversation circles demonstrate a kind of theory of dialogue: conversation could educate and broaden the mind beyond mere personal opinion, Brown believed. It could also level social hierarchy and thus, according to Teute, offered an alternative, for the twenty-something New York generation of the 1790s, to the elite salon culture of the then capital city. Young republicans of this era, like Brown and his circle, were suspicious of any "American aristocracy" (154) and formed groups like the Friendly Club—with members including Erasmus Darwin, Samuel Latham Mitchill, Anthony Bleecker, William Johnson, William Dunlap, and, of course, Elihu Hubbard Smith—as the new nation's burgeoning "republic of intellect" (155).

Situated within this cosmopolitan, shifting circle, the dailiness of Brown's life appears more concretely than ever. Crain's chapter on Brown's letters similarly rounds out a social Brown, though Crain's portrait shares with some earlier biographers a psychobiographical tendency. Crain may not have read more letters than other Brown scholars, but his "Sympathy in Brown's Letters" chapter constructs from them a more useful and coherent picture of Brown than those of many previous biographers. This Brown puts friendship at the center of his life, a fact evident in the sheer number of letters amassed here and in Brown's frequent commentary *about* friendship. Crain revises the standard partitioning of Brown's life—the pre- and post-1800, republican and Federalist chapters—into a three-phase division linking Brown's writing to subtler nuances of his friendships. These two short biographical studies of Brown's social circles, along with Kafer's and Watts's, indicate a recent and current newer-historicist trend toward study of Brown and material culture. They open up many possibilities for new studies in the future and, like Brown's own work with and among his friends, are best read as pieces of a larger, ongoing cultural project.

Like the Cold War era, this later period produced a very useful collection of essays on Brown. Philip Barnard, Mark Kamrath, and Stephen Shapiro's *Revising Charles Brockden Brown: Culture, Politics, and Sexuality in the Early Republic* (2004) foregrounds the "cultural work" of Brown's writing over psychosymbolic readings of texts (xiii). This collection asserts, with good reason, that Brown is no longer considered a "minor" writer; the Brown of these essays "emerges less as a 'single author' than as a viable and productive matrix for the investigation of numerous issues in early American studies and scholarship" (xvi) and, as such, can be seen as central to the study of the early republic. These readers foreground a complex Brown within the cultural dialectic of a liberalism that was growing throughout his adult life and the republicanism, promised by the Revolution, that stressed public virtue. Looking closely at Brown's writing over his full lifetime, this collection, like several projects in recent years, offers a corrective to the critical commonplace that Brown's politics changed around 1800, just at the time he stopped writing Gothic novels and turned to other genres and types of novels. Instead, Brown progressed from "cultural and political issues on the micro-level"—"the subjective, individualized experience of novelistic protagonists, for example... to the larger, regional, national, and global levels that, in a systems sense, create the effects that the novels earlier dramatized on the personal scale" (Barnard, Kamrath, and Shapiro 258).

A 2009 issue of *Early American Literature* amounts to another, albeit small, collection of essays. Here five articles on Brown were collected not because a call for papers had been made for a Brown issue but because the journal had received so many quality submissions on Brown. That this issue could come about so organically prompts Waterman to introduce the articles with the incontrovertible claim that "Brown's canonicity becomes ever more secure" ("Introduction," 236). The appearance in 2011 of Jeffrey Andrew Weinstock's *Charles Brockden Brown* in the University of Wales Gothic Authors: Critical Revisions series, I would add, is but one piece of evidence for this secure canonicity. Waterman notes, as did Kamrath in his 1999 review essay, the historicist methodology of much recent Brown scholarship, but he also makes clearer than ever that the historical scholarship tends to occupy two camps: those who read Brown in his culture "sympto-matically," seeing in Brown evidence of his culture's ideologies, and those who read him as a "diagnostician of his culture," as consciously commenting on the major threads of late-eighteenth- and early-nineteenth-century cultures. Articles in this quite original collection fall into both camps (slightly leaning toward the diagnostician camp), deeply considering Brown's use of eighteenth-century medical discourse to analyze sleep-walking as a disease; his analysis of "republican fantasy," as opposed to symptomatically representing republican fantasy; his critical diagnosis of Adam Smith's *Theory of Moral Sentiments* and the practice of sympathy at large; his foundational and ultimate criticism of the history of Anglo-America's negotiating with Native Americans for territory via the Walking Treaty as it haunts the dark geography of *Edgar Huntly*; and his interest in local and transnational culture in "The Trials of Arden."

This period has also produced a healthy number of new editions and more recovery and publication projects than any previous generation of scholarship. Barnard and Shapiro's Hackett classroom editions of the four Gothic novels, published between 2006 and 2009, include a helpful assortment of related texts, including important theoretical statements from Brown on the novel and history, and additional texts such as Brown's commentary on Cicero for the *Wieland* edition. Waterman's 2010 Norton Critical Edition of *Wieland* and *Memoirs of Carwin* has the most complete apparatus to date, including texts regarding social and intellectual backgrounds, criticism contemporary to Brown, and a strong showing of recent scholarship on *Wieland* and *Carwin*.

This generation's attention to Brown's nonnovelistic writing has generated an exponentially larger number of recovery projects than in the history of Brown criticism. Bucknell University Press is publishing what might be seen as the completion of the Kent State editions of the novels; under the general editorship of Philip Barnard, Elizabeth Hewitt, and Mark Kamrath, a scholarly edition all of the nonnovelistic writings is being published in seven volumes. The first volume, *Letters and Epistolary Writings*, appeared in 2013 and, working from years of editorial work by John Holmes, comprehensively collects all known letters and Brown's early epistolary fictions, such as the "Henrietta Letters," together with historical and textual essays, biographies of correspondents, and other contextualizing work that, when complete, will bring balance across Brown's writing life to the available print literature.

The Charles Brockden Brown Electronic Archive and Scholarly Edition is of major importance to current study of Brown. Fully searchable, the archive currently makes available all of Brown's writing and is moving toward inclusion of several thousand secondary texts on Brown. It is the electronic companion to the Bucknell scholarly editions. Under the direction of Mark Kamrath, with Philip Barnard serving as textual editor, this project stands to reach more scholars and graduate and undergraduate students than any other single collection of Brown's work and work on Brown. With this massive and growing collection, Brown studies has fully entered not only the twenty-first century but also the era of digital humanities.

Works Cited

Amfreville, Marc. "Sang d'encre: Les 'Henrietta Letters" de Charles Brockden Brown." In Ada Savin and Paule Lévy, eds., *Mémoires d'Amérique: Correspondances, journaux intimes, récits autobiographiques*, 42–52. Paris: Michel Houdiard, 2008.

Axelrod, Alan *Charles Brockden Brown: An American Tale*. Austin: University of Texas Press, 1983.

Barnard, Philip, Elizabeth Hewitt, and Mark L. Kamrath, eds. *Letters and Early Epistolary Writings. Collected Writings of Charles Brockden Brown*, Vol. 1. Lewisburg, Pa.: Bucknell University Press, 2013.

Barnard, Philip, Mark L. Kamrath, and Stephen Shapiro. *Revising Charles Brockden Brown: Culture, Politics, and Sexuality in the Early Republic*. Knoxville: University of Tennessee Press, 2004.

Barnard, Philip, and Stephen Shapiro, eds. *Arthur Mervyn; or, Memoirs of the Year 1793, with Related Texts*. Indianapolis: Hackett, 2008.

Barnard, Philip, and Stephen Shapiro, eds. *Edgar Huntly; or, Memoirs of a Sleep-Walker, with Related Texts*. Indianapolis: Hackett, 2006.

Barnard, Philip, and Stephen Shapiro, eds. *Ormond; or, The Secret Witness, with Related Texts*. Cambridge: Hackett, 2009.

Barnard, Philip, and Stephen Shapiro, eds. *Wieland; or, The Transformation, with Related Texts*. Cambridge: Hackett, 2009.

Bennett, Charles. "The Charles Brockden Brown Canon." Ph.D. dissertation, University of North Carolina, Chapel Hill, 1974.

Bennett, Charles. "The Letters of Charles Brockden Brown: An Annotated Census." *Resources for American Literary Study* 6.2 (Autumn 1976): 164–190.

Berthoff, Warner. "The Literary Career of Charles Brockden Brown." Ph.D. dissertation, Harvard University, 1954.

Brown, Charles Brockden. *The Novels and Related Works of Charles Brockden Brown*. Ed. Sydney J. Krause and S. W. Reid. 6 vols. Kent, Ohio: Kent State University Press, 1976–1984.

Burgett, Bruce. *Sentimental Bodies: Sex, Gender, and Citizenship in the Early Republic*. Princeton, N.J.: Princeton University Press, 1998.

Cahill, Edward. "An Adventurous and Lawless Fancy: Charles Brockden Brown's Aesthetic State." *Early American Literature* 36.1 (2001): 31–70.

Carpenter, Charles A. "Selective Bibliography of Writings about Charles Brockden Brown." In Bernard Rosenthal, ed., *Critical Essays on Charles Brockden Brown*, 224–239. Boston: G. K. Hall, 1981.

Chapman, Mary. "Introduction." In Charles Brockden Brown, *Ormond: or, The Secret Witness*. Ed. Mary Chapman, 9–31. Peterborough, Ont.: Broadview, 1999.

Chase, Richard. *The American Novel and Its Tradition*. New York: Doubleday, 1957.

Christophersen, Bill. *Apparition in the Glass: Charles Brockden Brown's American Gothic*. Athens: University of Georgia Press, 1993.

Clark, David Lee. *Charles Brockden Brown: Pioneer Voice of America*. Durham, N.C.: Duke University Press, 1952.

Clark, David Lee. "Review of *Charles Brockden Brown: American Gothic Novelist*, by Harry R. Warfel." *American Literature* 22 (1950): 365–367.

Cody, Michael. *Charles Brockden Brown and the Literary Magazine: Cultural Journalism in the Early American Republic*. Jefferson, N.C., and London: McFarland, 2004.

Crain, Caleb. *American Sympathy: Men, Friendship, and Literature in the New Nation*. New Haven, Conn.: Yale University Press, 2001.

Davidson, Cathy L. *Revolution and the Word: The Rise of the Novel in America*. New York: Oxford University Press, 1986; expanded ed., 2004.

Dillon, Elizabeth Maddock. "Contracting Marriage in the New Republic." In Elizabeth Maddock Dillon, *The Gender of Freedom: Fictions of Liberalism and the Literary Public Sphere*, 161–83. Stanford, Calif.: Stanford University Press, 2004.

Doolen, Andy. *Fugitive Empire: Locating Early American Imperialism*. Minneapolis: University of Minnesota Press, 2005.

Feeney, Joseph. "Modernized by 1800: The Portrait of Urban America, Especially Philadelphia, in the Novels of Charles Brockden Brown." *American Studies* 23.2 (Fall 1982): 25–28.

Ferguson, Robert A. "Yellow Fever and Charles Brockden Brown: Context of the Emerging Novelist." *Early American Literature* 14.3 (1979): 293–305.

Fiedler, Leslie. *Love and Death in the American Novel*. New York: Criterion Books, 1960.

Frye, Steven. "Constructing Indigeneity: Postcolonial Dynamics in Charles Brockden Brown's *Monthly Magazine and American Review*." *American Studies* 39 (1998): 69–88.

Gardner, Jared. "Alien Nation: Edgar Huntly's Savage Awakening." *American Literature* 66 (1994): 429–461.

Gardner, Jared. "The Literary Museum and the Unsettling of the Early American Novel." *ELH* 67.3 (2000): 743–771.

Goddu, Teresa. *Gothic America: Narrative, History, and Nation*. New York: Columbia University Press, 1997.

Grabo, Norman. *The Coincidental Art of Charles Brockden Brown*. Chapel Hill: University of North Carolina Press, 1981.

Hewitt, Elizabeth. "The Authentic Fictional Letters of Charles Brockden Brown." In Elizabeth Hewitt, *Letters and Cultural Transformations in the United States, 1760–1860*, 79–98. Farnham, UK: Ashgate, 2009.

Hinds, Elizabeth Jane Wall. "Deb's Dogs: Animals, Indians, and Postcolonial Desire in *Edgar Huntly*." *Early American Literature* 39.2 (2004): 323–354.

Hinds, Elizabeth Jane Wall. *Private Property: Charles Brockden Brown's Gendered Economics of Discourse*. Newark: University of Delaware Press, 1997.

Holmes, John R. "Charles Brockden Brown's Earliest Letter." *Early American Literature* 30 (1995): 71–77.

Holmes, John R., and Edward Saeger. "Charles Brockden Brown and the 'Laura-Petrarch' Letters." *Early American Literature* 25 (1990): 183–188.

Jordan, Cynthia. *Second Stories: The Politics of Language, Form, and Gender in Early American Fictions*. Chapel Hill: University of North Carolina Press, 1989.

Justus, James. "Arthur Mervyn, American." *American Literature* 42 (1970): 304–324.

Kafer, Peter. *Charles Brockden Brown's Revolution and the Birth of American Gothic.* Philadelphia: University of Pennsylvania Press, 2004.

Kamrath, Mark L. "Charles Brockden Brown and Contemporary Theory: A Review of Recent Critical Trends in Brown Scholarship." *Profils américains: Charles Brockden Brown* 3.11 (1999): 213–277.

Kamrath, Mark L. *The Historicism of Charles Brockden Brown: Radical History and the Early Republic.* Kent, Ohio: Kent State University Press, 2010.

Krause, Sydney. "A Census of the Works of Charles Brockden Brown." *Serif* 3 (1966): 27–55.

Krause, Sydney. "Historical Essay." *Edgar Huntly; or, Memoirs of a Sleep-Walker.* In Sydney J. Krause and S. W. Reid, eds., *The Novels and Related Works of Charles Brockden Brown*, Vol. 4, 295–400. Kent, Ohio: Kent State University Press, 1984.

Krause, Sydney. "Penn's Elm and *Edgar Huntly*: Dark 'Instruction to the Heart.'" *American Literature* 66 (1994): 463–484.

Levine, Robert. *Conspiracy and Romance: Studies in Brockden Brown, Cooper, Hawthorne, and Melville.* Cambridge: Cambridge University Press, 1989.

Lewis, R. W. B. *The American Adam: Innocence, Tragedy, and Tradition in the Nineteenth Century.* Chicago: University of Chicago Press, 1955.

Looby, Christopher. *Voicing America: Language, Literary Form, and the Origins of the United States.* Chicago: University of Chicago Press, 1996.

Luck, Chad. "Re-Walking the Purchase: *Edgar Huntly*, David Hume, and the Origins of Ownership." *Early American Literature* 44.2 (2009): 271–306.

Powell, J. H. *Bring Out Your Dead: The Great Plague of Yellow Fever in Philadelphia in 1793.* Philadelphia: University of Pennsylvania Press, 1949.

Rosenthal, Bernard, ed. *Critical Essays on Charles Brockden Brown.* Boston: G. K. Hall, 1981.

Scheick, William J. "'Assassin in Artful Disguise': The De-Signed Designs of Charles Brockden Brown's 'Somnambulism.'" In Marc Amfreville and Francoise Charras, eds., *Profils américains: Charles Brockden Brown*, 27–46. Montpellier: Presses de l'Imprimerie de l'Universite Paul-Valery, 1999.

Shapiro, Stephen. *The Culture and Commerce of the Early American Novel: Reading the Atlantic World-System.* University Park: Pennsylvania State University Press, 2008.

Slotkin, Richard. *Regeneration through Violence: The Mythology of the American Frontier, 1600–1860.* Middletown, Conn.: Wesleyan University Press, 1973.

Stern, Julia. *The Plight of Feeling: Sympathy and Dissent in the Early American Novel.* Chicago: University of Chicago Press, 1998.

Teute, Fredrika. "A 'Republic of Intellect': Conversation and Criticism among the Sexes in 1790s New York." In Philip Barnard, Mark L. Kamrath, and Stephen Shapiro, eds., *Revising Charles Brockden Brown: Culture, Politics, and Sexuality in the Early Republic*, 149–181. Knoxville: University of Tennessee Press, 2004.

Tompkins, Jane. *Sensational Designs: The Cultural Work of American Fiction, 1790–1860.* New York: Oxford University Press, 1985.

Warfel, Harry. *Charles Brockden Brown: American Gothic Novelist.* Gainesville: University of Florida Press, 1949.

Warner, Michael. *Letters of the Republic: Publication and the Public Sphere in Eighteenth-Century America.* Cambridge, Mass.: Harvard University Press, 1990.

Waterman, Bryan. "The Friendly Club of New York City: Industries of Knowledge in the Early Republic." Ph.D. dissertation, Boston University, 2000.

Waterman, Bryan. "Introduction: Reading Early America with Charles Brockden Brown." *Early American Literature* 44.2 (2009): 235–242.

Waterman, Bryan, ed. *Wieland and Memoirs of Carwin the Biloquist: A Norton Critical Edition.* New York: W. W. Norton, 2010.

Watts, Steven. *The Romance of Real Life: Charles Brockden Brown and the Origins of American Culture.* Baltimore: Johns Hopkins University Press, 1994.

Weber, Alfred. *Somnambulism and Other Stories.* Frankfurt am Main: Peter Lang, 1987.

Weber, Alfred, and Wolfgang Schäfer, eds. *Charles Brockden Brown: Literary Essays and Reviews.* Frankfurt am Main: Peter Lang, 1992.

Weinstock, Jeffrey Andrew. *Charles Brockden Brown.* Cardiff: University of Wales Press, 2011.

Weyler, Karen. *Intricate Relations: Sexual and Economic Desire in American Fiction, 1789–1814.* Iowa City: University of Iowa Press, 2004.

Wiley, Lulu Rumsey. *The Sources and Influences of Charles Brockden Brown's Novels.* New York: Vantage Press, 1950.

Witherington, Paul "Charles Brockden Brown: A Bibliographical Essay." *Early American Literature* 9.2 (1974): 164–187.

CHAPTER 35

··

BROWN STUDIES NOW
AND IN TRANSITION

··

HANNAH LAUREN MURRAY

IN the introduction to his 2011 critical biography of Charles Brockden Brown, Jeffrey Weinstock wryly notes that Brown is "the most important American author no one has ever heard of" (Weinstock 4). While Brown does not have the same hold on the wider public imagination as later writers Edgar Allan Poe, Nathaniel Hawthorne, or Herman Melville, his work remains a cornerstone of early national literary studies and American Gothic studies in the twenty-first century. Furthermore, Brown regularly features in studies of American literature from the colonial period onward that employ a multiplicity of approaches and contexts, which cements Brown's legacy as the leading cultural commentator of the early republic.

Furthering historicist and cultural work of the 1980s and 1990s, scholarship in the twenty-first century debates to what extent Brown is a reactionary or progressive voice in early republican cultural, social, and political spheres along lines of gender, sexuality, race, class, and nationality. Philip Barnard, Mark Kamrath, and Stephen Shapiro's edited collection *Revising Charles Brockden Brown: Culture, Politics, and Sexuality in the Early Republic* (2004) exemplifies the approach of understanding early national culture through readings of "the role of politics, race, class, and sex-gender" in Brown (Barnard, Kamrath, and Shapiro xii). Rather than viewing these identities as discrete categories, these inquiries intersect with the interests of the wider American literary studies field since 2000: the transnational turn, the juncture between medicine and literature, and the interaction between finance, the literary marketplace, and fiction. At the same time, recent work sees a return to questions of form and aesthetics through reinvigorating discussions of genre, the role of fiction, and the reading experience. This chapter takes a thematic approach to covering the recent and emergent trends in Brown scholarship since 2000 in four categories: geographies, medical humanities, economies, and aesthetics. Across these themes, the four Gothic novels remain central, but growing attention to Brown's minor fiction and nonfiction writing addresses these texts as stand-alone works rather than supplementary or subordinate pieces.

I. Geographies: Mapping Brown

(i) Transatlantic, Imperial, and Postcolonial Brown

Scholarship has long focused on the transatlantic characters and plots in Brown, in particular his depiction of Irish radicalism and the French Revolution as perceived or real threats to the new nation. Since 2000, these readings continue to investigate the presence of Europe in Brown's works, from Sydney Krause's historical research on German immigration in *Wieland* in "Charles Brockden Brown and the Philadelphia Germans" (2004), to María DeGuzmán on Spanish threats in *Wieland* in *Spain's Long Shadow: The Black Legend, Off-Whiteness, and Anglo-American Empire* (2005), to Leonard Tennenhouse on the failure of the British man of feeling in *Clara Howard* in *The Importance of Feeling English: American Literature and the British Diaspora, 1750–1850* (2007), to Juliet Shields's discussion of Gothic Irish uncanniness in *Edgar Huntly* in *Nation and Migration: The Making of British Atlantic Literature, 1765–1835* (2016). Two monographs widen this transatlantic lens into a circum-Atlantic one: Sean Goudie's *Creole America: The West Indies and the Formation of Literature and Culture in the New Republic* (2006) and Stephen Shapiro's *The Culture and Commerce of the Early American Novel: Reading the Atlantic World-System* (2008). Considering the influence of the Caribbean on early national literature, Goudie reads *Arthur Mervyn* as structured through entangled encounters between the United States and the West Indies, which underscores "uneasy affinities" between a virtuous America and the "degenerate empires of Europe and their creole" (177). Similarly, Shapiro reads Brown's America as one enmeshed in a "world-system of capitalist trade" shaped by the flows of capital, namely the slave trade between Europe, the West Indies and the United States (2). In *Arthur Mervyn*, Brown challenges the social violence of the slave trade corrupting Philadelphia through a radical proposal of "egalitarian miscegenation . . . as the best vehicle for overcoming racism in a postslavery society" (265). Offering the perspective of a much more progressive Brown, Shapiro responds to criticism of the 1980s and 1990s that positions Brown as a reactionary writer seeking protection for America from immigrants and nonwhite figures.

Both Goudie and Shapiro contribute to an ongoing project of expanding the geopolitical horizons of Brown scholarship, including reading the early republic as an imperial power and America as a postcolonial space. With two chapters on the *Monthly Magazine* and *Arthur Mervyn*, Andy Doolen's *Fugitive Empire: Locating Early American Imperialism* (2005) reads Brown as an imperialist figure. The *Monthly Magazine* is "a cultural archive of U.S. imperialism" that urges readers to support Federalist authority through printing national narratives, poems and speeches tied to a white American dominance (xxv). On *Arthur Mervyn*, Doolen argues that a fear of immigrants transforms into a nativist backlash against African Americans, whom Brown depicts as resistant fugitives in white America. In *Dislocating Race and Nation: Episodes in Nineteenth-Century American Literary Nationalism* (2008), Robert Levine takes a "Federalist-nationalist post-Revolutionary perspective" on the 1803 Louisiana pamphlets but, in contrast to Doolen, reads Brown's imperialism as encouraging "respect for peoples of color, particularly the black rebels of Saint Domingue" (26). Against Steven Watts's claim that "On or about April 1800 Charles Brockden Brown changed" (Watts 131), Levine, like Shapiro, cautions against reading a pre/post-1800 political divide into Brown's writings. Instead, these projects take a holistic view of Brown's fictional and political writings.

Since 2000, this imperial frame has extended to readings of *Wieland* and *Memoirs of Carwin*. While Laura Doyle contends that the novel is not "fully naming its colonial investments," works by David Kazanjian and Hsuan L. Hsu attend to the indigenous presence in the text and its prequel through Carwin's "Mohock savage" cry (Doyle 231; MC 250). Rejecting readings of a spectral or repressed native presence in *Wieland*, Stefan Schöberlein argues that a 1798 audience would recognize the text's indigenous references, which are a deliberate "authorial and political strategy of Brown aimed at fundamentally *unsettling* the colonial mindset of his protagonists" (537). Among growing scholarship on *Edgar Huntly* as a postcolonial text is Eric Goldman's reading of America as a colonial space in relation to the expanding British Empire in India. While attempting to articulate American exceptionalism in contrast to British imperialism, Goldman contends that "the novel expresses America's struggle with its prospective imperial identity in an international global context of European imperialism" (558). Like Goldman, Paul Giles in *Antipodean America: Australasia and the Constitution of the U.S. Literature* (2013) orients scholarship toward global colonial readings of Brown. Australia acts as a point of comparison for Brown to "reconceptualize the United States within larger epistemological perspectives" (99). Across Brown's writing, colonial Australia acts as a "doppelganger of an American republic" that reflects both the utopian opportunity of migration and the philosophical and political tensions of a newly independent nation incorporated in "concentric geospatial orbits" (114). Giles's work opens up avenues for planetary readings of Brown and comparisons with writers and contexts beyond the Atlantic.

(ii) Environs

Turning from political to physical geographies, recent criticism has focused on the depiction of the natural world and the role of natural science as a discipline in Brown's writing. Martin Brückner's *The Geographic Revolution in Early America: Maps, Literacy and National Identity* (2006) traces the development in Brown's geographical writing, at times "properly classified and organized according to conventional divisions and taxonomies" but at other times "expansive, totalizing and even chaotic" (187). For Brückner, geographical study in *Jane Talbot* seduces Jane and isolates her from social relations. Geography shapes the genre of the text: Brown replaces the sentimental European novel with the "(American) geography book" as empathic connections between characters are supplanted by Jane's pleasurable solitary acts of demographic memorization (191). On *Edgar Huntly*, Brückner argues that Brown initially creates a "geographical sensorium" for a reader familiar with the cartographic and agricultural nomenclature of the early republic (198). Brown writes later sections of the novel as an "antigeographical exercise" that resists organization and reflects the Romantic vision of nature (198). This destabilized geographic order threatens the subjectivity of the white citizen and the white reader, lost in the wilderness. Most recently, Christopher Sloman concurs that *Edgar Huntly*'s confused environment shows Brown torn between Romantic European and utilitarian American thinking on the natural world. Bridget Bennett brings together landscape and architecture in order to redress the critical silence around the hut in *Wieland*. Drawing on architectural history, she demonstrates that eighteenth-century garden-design strategies, whereby both neoclassical temples and humble huts were naturalized as part of the landscape, played an integral part in reconciling republican values of reason and liberty with the enslaved labor on which the leisured communities of Montpelier, Monticello, and the fictional Mettingen depended. She argues that the text of *Wieland*, written as it is in Clara's voice, performs a similar elision of the voices of those who labor. The oral account of the Wieland family's demise offered by the hut dwellers at the end of the novel is written over by the elite and authoritative voices of Clara, Mr. Conway, and Mrs. Baynton demonstrating that the "voices from the hut" and the enslaved subjects "they symbolically represent, can [n]ever be given proper acknowledgment in early American texts" (394).

Katy Chiles's *Transformable Race: Surprising Metamorphoses in the Literature of Early America* (2014) reinforces Brückner's claims of Brown as a well-informed reader of natural history who intervenes in debates over the environmental causes of racial difference and transformation. On *Edgar Huntly*, Chiles's work unsettles Jared Gardner's idea in "Alien Nation: Edgar Huntly's Savage Awakening" (1994) that Brown exorcises the Indian to bolster American whiteness. Rather, Chiles utilizes environmentalist thinking to contend that "Edgar is always already becoming" the native because both figures are shaped by the same frontier (Chiles 130). As a result, Brown "offers his readers anything but a definitive and thus reassuring answer" on the future and stability of whiteness in America (130). Likewise, Christopher Stampone problematizes early national whiteness in *Edgar Huntly*'s Irish figures. Reading Clithero as "an Irish savage in his home country *before* he comes to America," Stampone reorients racial thinking in the novel to show white figures as inherently savage, rather than symbols of European degeneration in America or Native American primitivism (415). Employing a critical whiteness lens, Stampone demonstrates that whiteness in Brown and the early national period is contingent on moral and social actions and values, rather than superficial physical markers. In attending to the boundaries of whiteness, these recent works further discussions of race in Brown beyond the representation of nonwhite marginal figures.

II. Medical Humanities: Mind and the Body in Brown

Recent biographical research from Caleb Crain and Bryan Waterman has restated the professional and personal networks Brown maintained with early national physicians Elihu Hubbard Smith and Samuel Latham Mitchill. Detailed readings of Brown's fiction show the extent to which he was well versed in contemporary medical science discussions, particularly in the work of Benjamin Rush, the early republic's leading physician and nascent psychiatrist. Justine S. Murison and Emily Ogden both employ Rush's work on the mind to set out a relationship between citizenship and cognitive science in *Edgar Huntly*. In "The Tyranny of Sleep: Somnambulism, Moral Citizenship, and Charles Brockden Brown's 'Edgar Huntly'" (2009), Murison argues that Rush creates a psychological model for the citizen, one that requires control of mental faculties and memory. The alternative cognitive state of sleepwalking "allows Brown to explore the consequences of the tendency in 1790s America to make citizenship—and national identity more broadly—a state of mind" (244). Brown's writing demonstrates the intertwined relationship between treatises on physical and mental health and discussions of what qualities made a good citizen. Readings of early national psychological and medical discourses extend to *Wieland*, with Gale Temple on ventriloquism as symbolic of the polluting masturbatory body ("Carwin the Onanist?" 2009) and Eric Vallee on suicide prevention ("'A Fatal Sympathy': Suicide and the Republic of Abjection in the Writings of Benjamin Rush and Charles Brockden Brown," 2017).

The 1793 Philadelphia yellow fever outbreak remains central to criticism on *Arthur Mervyn*. The rise of medical humanities in American literary studies has led to less symptomatic readings of the contagion as symbolic and greater attention to the plague in itself, and the relationship between medicine and fiction. Ellen Ledoux, Nicholas Miller, Sari Altschuler and Stacey Margolis consider the civic implications of the disease. Ledoux contends that Brown criticizes failing institutional healthcare in the novel, instead offering possibilities where "suffering can be mitigated by altruistic acts shared between civic brethren" (21). Debates over immunization influence what Miller calls "immunological citizenship" in *Arthur Mervyn* and *Ormond*, in which citizenship is redefined "as both a political and biological category" cutting across lines of race and class and determined by communities' resistance to the fever (145, 147). Altschuler argues that Brown intervenes in debates over the civic function of literature during an epidemic. Rather than disseminating health advice, Brown uses Gothic fiction as a form of "narrative inoculation" to expose readers to disease and force them to confront and overcome difficult public-health questions (69). Margolis attends to the transmission of the plague, arguing that the randomness of the contagion in *Arthur Mervyn* is a "stark, dramatic way of visualizing the city's reordering of social connection" (23). Margolis's work brings Brown into the new field of network studies that investigates the connections between individuals and the transmission of information, material goods, and printed works across social and economic networks.

III. ECONOMIES: FINANCE, THE LITERARY MARKETPLACE, AND FORM

Criticism since 2000 has returned Brown to the financial world of the early republic and its literary marketplace. A chapter in Jennifer Baker's *Securing the Commonwealth: Debt, Speculation, and Writing in the Making of Early America* (2005) reads the corruption and financial precarity in *Arthur Mervyn* as a potential for "communal union," since economic and therefore sympathetic bonds form between characters and readers (120). On *Ormond*, Scott Ellis contends that Brown criticizes a marketplace that does not distinguish between artistic and material goods. The novel, Ellis states, "allows us to view alternative modules of property exchange in which works of art circulate beyond the dictates of the marketplace," which asks how authors can sit both within and alongside a financial market (3). Scott Slawinski, Michael Cody, and Jared Gardner focus on the literary marketplace in their studies of Brown's magazine fiction in the *Monthly Magazine*, the *Literary Magazine*, the *American Register*, and the *Port Folio*. Not only do these studies add to the discussion of the cultural work Brown's short fiction performs, but they emphasize the extent to which the early national literary marketplace was organized through and directed by periodical publication, rather than novels. Indeed, in *The Rise and Fall of Early American Magazine Culture* (2012), Gardner boldly suggests that "it is perhaps time to start marginalizing *Edgar Huntly*—and the novel form in general" in favor of the substantial periodical material written throughout Brown's career (4).

Economic and marketplace discussions of Brown are often tied to questions of form, particularly in relation to *Arthur Mervyn* and *Ormond*. Liam Corley reads *Arthur Mervyn*'s palimpsest form as a textual evasion of the culpability for Philadelphia's hidden economic system, the slave trade. On the novel's partial periodical publication, Kristina Garvin argues that its seriality is a form of risk that creates a "contract between readers and writers ... unfolding over a period of time and without a preordained ending" (738). The deferral inherent to the serial mode reflects the "pro-longed and open-ended" financial system of the novel, in which Arthur is a "corporate, aggregate person" having to negotiate the marketplace, rather than "a clearly defined economic individual" (739). In *Against Self-Reliance: The Arts of Dependence in the Early United States* (2015), William Huntting Howell argues that *Ormond* presents a contrasting view of character. *Ormond* challenges the tradition of replication, copying, and imitation in print culture, which results in character "as a material, imitative, and iterable textual effect" (20). Instead, "structured by forgery, mimicry, contagion, and endless repetition—the poisoned doubles of imitation, emulation, and the other arts of dependence," *Ormond* critiques these reproductive self-making practices to usher in nineteenth-century economic and civic individualism (160).

Extending these formal investigations to representations of class, Matthew Pethers considers *Ormond* and *Jane Talbot* as part of a group of "parabolic social mobility narra-tives," in which abandoned or orphaned heroines suffer an economic downfall, only to be rescued by a final act of sudden fortune (708). This formal plot device soothes early national anxieties over failed social mobility and widening economic inequality—"a form of imaginary compensation for these frustrated ambitions" (713). Most recently, in *The Illiberal Imagination: Class and the Rise of the U.S. Novel* (2017), Joe Shapiro focuses on how Brown represents poverty in *Arthur Mervyn* and *Ormond*. Arguing for readings that attend to Arthur as a laborer, Shapiro claims that *Arthur Mervyn* is less about "an emergent capitalist ethos of acquisitive individualism" than it is "largely a story about being poor in a massively unequal society" (36). However, differing from Pethers, Shapiro contends that Brown depicts poverty as an improving force through rewriting the

Bildungsroman genre. In his urban fiction, fictive poverty offers financially comfortable Brown the means to create "captivating stories" of young men and women navigating deprivation (39). Precarity is "an ideal of subject formation" because it offers freedom from the bourgeois restrictions of marriage and landownership (54). Pethers's and Shapiro's insights offer opportunities for further discussion of class as an underacknowledged territory for scholars of Brown and other writers at the turn of the nineteenth century.

IV. Aesthetics: Reading Brown

As the works on economics demonstrate, the field of Brown studies has seen a return to questions of form to consider generic and aesthetic devices as integral to social, cultural, and political concerns. In part, this move is a response (if sometimes not acknowledged) to the larger field's turn away from or questioning of historicism, exemplified in Rita Felski's *The Uses of Literature* (2008), Stephen Best and Sharon Marcus's "Surface Reading: An Introduction" (2009), and Christopher Looby and Cindy Weinstein's edited collection *American Literature's Aesthetic Dimensions* (2012). These works exhibit a weariness or frustration with historicist critique that can rely on symptomatic or suspicious reading of texts and instead call for an aesthetic turn that employs close reading, surface reading, and description to recognize literature as a unique textual form.

In their introduction to a 2016 special issue of *Early American Literature* on aesthetics, Edward Cahill and Edward Larkin sum up the state of historicist early American scholarship through the example of *Wieland*:

> Thus, today, for example, work on Charles Brockden Brown's novel *Wieland* is much less interested in questions of narrative or novelistic form than in cultural histories of feminism, religious radicalism, mental illness, law, and incarceration. In privileging historical proximity, however, we tend to lose not only a sense of the particularity of the literary but also an understanding of the ways that form can make visible relationships across genres, cultures, and historical periods.   (241)

Cahill and Larkin are correct that the majority of *Wieland* criticism—and, by extension, Brown criticism—focuses on cultural questions through a historicist lens. However, the most recent work on the novel does attend to the "particularity of the literary" in investigating the reading experience itself (241). Both Thomas Koenigs and Christine Hedlin consider the novel to be a critique of didacticism found in the eighteenth-century novel. Koenigs claims that Brown encourages participatory reading, rather than teaching through example, while Hedlin states that the novel "ironize[s] the self-assuredness of eighteenth-century didactic novels" in the advent of a secular age that casts doubt on the certitude of religious explanations for strange phenomena (Hedlin 735). Likewise, David Zimmerman reads *Wieland* as participatory, suggesting that Brown's novels take synoptic views of ensembles of characters in order to "explore accountability relationships" and encourage the reader to determine who is complicit in acts of corruption and violence (668). Nancy Armstrong and Leonard Tennenhouse also discuss how Brown "overstocks his narrative with minor characters" (25). In *Novels in the Time of Democratic Writing: The American Example* (2018), they argue that *Arthur Mervyn*'s arrangements of characters afford "access to a process that connects one stranger to another" rather than centering a single protagonist (27). In contrast to his British peer Jane Austen, Brown employs "a distinctively American vernacular English" to demonstrate new democratic formulations of social relation (29). Returning to the tradition of criticism before the 1980s, which understands Brown as a nationalist writer, Armstrong and Tennenhouse see Brown forming a specifically American literature through these formal choices in character and speech. Unlike Armstrong and Tennenhouse, Paul Gilmore reassesses historicist and political readings as explanatory practices. Placing Brown in conversation with David Hume, Gilmore argues that "Brown in his romances deploys something akin to Hume's skepticism in undermining the ability of characters and readers to discern or reconstruct the causes behind human actions with certitude" (119). Therefore, Brown's Gothic fictions "explicitly work against reducing characters or plot devices to evidence for political or scientific theories and laws," which in turn problematizes reductive historicist interpretation of his work (119).

These debates over historicist and cultural readings of Brown extend to the studies of Brown as a Gothicist. Peter Kafer's and Jeffrey Weinstock's monographs on Brown center him as the inventor of American Gothic, channeling pressing national and personal questions into a new genre. Kafer's *Charles Brockden Brown's Revolution and the Birth of American Gothic* (2004) draws on meticulous research into Brown's Quaker upbringing to offer a psychobiographical reading of his fiction as processing his childhood trauma. In *Charles Brockden Brown* (2011), Weinstock organizes Brown's fiction into four overlapping subgenres—the frontier Gothic, the urban Gothic, the psychological Gothic, and the female Gothic—to cover the four major novels, along with short sections on *Alcuin, Clara Howard, Jane Talbot,* and "Somnambulism." As an accessible student-friendly work for the University of Wales Gothic Authors: Critical Revisions series, Weinstock's volume synthesizes broadly historicist twentieth-century criticism on Brown to cement his position as a foundational American author and a pioneer of the Gothic genre. In his genre-led reading, Weinstock firmly places Brown as the founding father in a genealogy of American Gothic, making connections to later nineteenth- and twentieth-century Gothic writing and visual culture from Poe to *Buffy the Vampire Slayer*.

With two chapters on Brown, in *Gothic Subjects: The Transformation of Individualism in American Fiction, 1790–1861* (2015), Siân Silyn Roberts examines why the Gothic genre significantly changes when crossing the Atlantic at the end of the eighteenth century. However, unlike previous American Gothic critics, most notably Leslie Fiedler's *Love and Death in the American Novel* (1960), she emphatically turns away from the "guilt thesis" tradition that claims American Gothic as a site of repression of national sins, namely, slavery and indigenous genocide (Silyn Roberts 21). Instead, she "regard[s] the American gothic as a transformation in the cultural logic of British individualism that produces a complex and wholly distinct theory of the political subject in a diasporic setting" (6). Rather than directly comment on historical, political, or cultural events, Brown's Gothic fiction contributes to how Americans thought of the self, individualism, subjectivity, community, and citizenship in response to Enlightenment thought. On *Arthur Mervyn*, the first chapter argues that the trope of contagion characterizes the American subject as "porous, fluid, and projected beyond the metaphysical boundaries of the body," able to circulate between and across communities (41). The second chapter, on *Edgar Huntly*, interprets the novel's frontier landscape as a rhizomatic environment where "going native" in the wilderness encourages the individual to subsume into a much larger collective mass (61). Silyn Roberts's work refreshes and extends understandings of the Gothic as a "versatile rhetorical mode" rather than a set of plots, characters, and motifs (142). Other recent examinations of genre beyond the Gothic include Mark Kamrath on Brown's radical historical short fiction, Christopher Lukasik on *Ormond* as a critique of the seduction novel, and Erica Burleigh on the interpersonal and political possibilities of the sentimental genre and epistolary form in *Clara Howard* and *Jane Talbot*.

V. Looking Ahead in Brown Studies

This survey has emphasized the health of Brown studies, as recent scholars are able to take multiple approaches in interpreting Brown, and they can consult and utilize a wide range of cultural and social contexts and archives. There is emergent work in the strands discussed that suggests new directions and fields of enquiry. For example, Margolis's and Silyn Roberts's work on formulations of community and the individual open up generative readings of Brown that engage with new materialism studies. This approach enables scholars to examine the heterogeneous human, nonhuman, biological, inanimate, and invisible actors that populate Brown's texts, in order to understand the forming of attachment between characters and with the environment. A new materialist reading decenters the Enlightenment ideal of the individual and unsettles hierarchical social relationships, which is particularly vital for Brown's America grappling with the enforced racial hierarchies of indigenous oppression and slavery that run through his fiction. In the same vein, ecological readings of Brown's texts, as seen in Brückner's work, could extend beyond the frontier and the centrality of *Edgar Huntly* to consider the city as its own environs in Brown's urban fiction.

Another potential direction comes from the less symptomatic readings of race and the application of critical race theory to Brown's works. In particular, Chiles's work on racial transformation and Stampone's essay on savage Irishness show scholars thinking critically about whiteness and white citizenship. This is an approach that encourages reading beyond *Edgar Huntly* in order to consider characters on the borders of belonging in early national society, whose civic status is precarious. For example, when reading "Somnambulism," the text is often viewed as an early draft of *Edgar Huntly*, with the monstrous feral figure of Nick Handyside seen as a stand-in for the novel's Lenni Lenape. However, a critical whiteness lens inverts this reading to instead question why Brown would choose to frame a white man as a nonwhite noncitizen, rather than creating native characters, and to ask what is at stake in crossing these racial boundaries. Reading Nick as a representative of liminal or marginal whiteness, rather than a symbol of the Native American, turns away from the "guilt thesis" that reads Brown's fiction conveying the repression and return of native genocide (Silyn Roberts 21). The figure of Nick, a cognitively impaired young man excluded from society (a roaming "idiot" with a "misshaped head"), is cloaked in indigenous references: animalism, insensibility, irrationality ("Somnambulism" 343). Unable to participate in civic life due to his disability, Nick becomes less than white. His position on the physical and metaphorical peripheries of white society illuminates a concern in early national literature that the privileges whiteness accrued could be lost due to an inability to demonstrate civic qualities that became increasingly inseparable from whiteness itself, such as rationality, respectability, autonomy, and industry. The white unemployed, disabled, immigrant, insane, and itinerant all existed on a sliding scale of states below full social, legal, and political citizenship. Through Nick, Brown asks to whom citizenship is to be extended if these qualities are assumed to be absent. Reading Brown in a critical whiteness framework reinforces our understanding of race as a constructed and shifting category that exists beyond physical markers. Reorienting the fragment as a text about racialized discourses of disability and citizenship enriches our understanding of how Brown attends to the place of young Americans within a nexus of gender, class, race, and ability that determined their position within or on the margins of society.

With the ongoing publication of the Bucknell University Press *Collected Writings of Charles Brockden Brown*, it's certain that in the next decade, further attention will be given to the limited, but varied, collection of Brown's tales and verse. In particular, the seventh volume, *Poems*, will support studying Brown's underacknowledged poetry and enrich our understanding of his position as a writer in the early republic. Assisted by the launch of the Charles Brockden Brown Electronic Archive and Scholarly Edition, which digitizes the works and includes a comprehensive secondary bibliography, Brown's archive becomes a living, accessible body of work inviting further study.

Growing attention to the minor novels, periodical work, and pamphlets, as discussed here, encourages future scholars to consider Brown beyond the usual narrow scope of 1798–1801. But as the growth in New Formalism indicates, we might also think about Brown beyond the parameters of his own historical period. Gilmore's work on Brown's romance calls for "a renewed emphasis on the role of curiosity and imagination into the production of all narrative, including our critical ones," which invites Brown scholars to become reenchanted with his work, an enchantment that cuts across historical periods (139). What does reading Brown bring to our understanding of the twenty-first century? What might be the connections between Brown's world and our own? We can turn to Melville's works as an example of how nineteenth-century American literature is felt in the contemporary moment. As Russ Castronovo details in "Occupy Bartleby" (2014), Melville's demurring scrivener, a striking worker who disrupts the workplace, resonates for the Occupy Movement critiquing and opting out of the capitalist status quo in 2011. Likewise, Carolyn Karcher discusses how *Moby-Dick*'s readers today are "experiencing the novel anew in the light of the war on terror" to recognize post-9/11 threats of demagoguery, white supremacy, and American imperialism aboard the *Pequod* (306). Rather than show Melville as a prophet of the twenty-first century, this renewed attention to antebellum-contemporary connections evinces that his works are catalysts to consider how one might protest against and dismantle long-standing systems of inequality.

Americans are still living in Brown's world of social, economic, and political corruption and uncertainty. Often read as a microcosm of the nation, the Wieland family is tricked by disembodied voices from a mysterious interlocutor. Brown shows the family-as-nation so disturbed that the very foundation of its Enlightenment identity—empirical reasoning, rooted in the senses—is shown to be fallible in the presence of an unclassifiable chameleon such as Carwin. In 2019, Mettingen would be threatened not by thrown ventriloquial voices but by the misdirection of fake news and the dissemblance of Russian bots. Reading *Wieland* after the 2016 US presidential election is to receive a warning against the civic failure to correctly judge and protect against misinformation and deception. Just as the Wieland-Pleyels "gradually withdrew ourselves from the society of others" (W 21) and shut out dissenting skeptical voices, the online echo chamber today does not protect citizens but amplifies irrational desires and assumptions. If we read the novel as a political cautionary tale, *Wieland* tells us that democratic citizenship must be collaborative and participatory, instead of isolated and passive. These interrogations of civic responsibilities are as alive in the twenty-first century as they were for Brown in the eighteenth. To bring Brown and the contemporary together does not mean reading his works as necessarily ahead of his time or out of his time but, rather, as Hilary Emmett writes, "insisting instead that we as scholars and lovers of literature have never left his" (206). By seeing Brown's America in the twenty-first century, Brown studies can succeed in bringing the author to today's public.

WORKS CITED

Altschuler, Sari. *The Medical Imagination: Literature and Health in the Early United States.* Philadelphia: University of Pennsylvania Press, 2018.

Armstrong, Nancy, and Leonard Tennenhouse. *Novels in the Time of Democratic Writing: The American Example.* Philadelphia: University of Pennsylvania Press, 2018.

Baker, Jennifer J. *Securing the Commonwealth: Debt, Speculation, and Writing in the Making of Early America.* Baltimore: Johns Hopkins University Press, 2005.

Barnard, Philip, Mark L. Kamrath, and Stephen Shapiro. "Introduction." In Philip Barnard, Mark L. Kamrath, and Stephen Shapiro, eds., *Revising Charles Brockden Brown: Culture, Politics, and Sexuality in the Early Republic,* ix–xxi. Knoxville: University of Tennessee Press, 2004.

Bennett, Bridget. "'The Silence Surrounding the Hut': Architecture and Absence in *Wieland.*" *Early American Literature* 53.2 (August 2018): 369–404.

Best, Stephen, and Sharon Marcus. "Surface Reading: An Introduction." *Representations* 108 (Fall 2009): 1–21.

Brown, Charles Brockden. "Somnambulism: A Fragment." LM 3.20 (May 1805): 335–347.

Brückner, Martin. *The Geographic Revolution in Early America: Maps, Literary and National Identity.* Chapel Hill: University of North Carolina Press, 2006.

Burleigh, Erica. *Intimacy and Family in Early American Writing*. New York: Palgrave, 2014.

Cahill, Edward, and Edward Larkin. "Aesthetics, Feeling, and Form in Early American Literary Studies." *Early American Literature* 51.2 (August 2016): 235–254.

Castronovo, Russ. "Occupy Bartleby." *J19: The Journal of Nineteenth-Century Americanists* 2.2 (October 2014): 253–272.

Chiles, Katy L. *Transformable Race: Surprising Metamorphoses in the Literature of Early America*. Oxford: Oxford University Press, 2014.

Cody, Michael. *Charles Brockden Brown and the Literary Magazine: Cultural Journalism in the Early American Republic*. Jefferson, N.C.: McFarland, 2004.

Corley, Liam. "The Middle Passages of *Arthur Mervyn*." In Darby Lewes, ed., *Double Vision: Literary Palimpsests of the Eighteenth and Nineteenth Centuries*, 207–225. Lanham, Md.: Lexington Books, 2007.

Crain, Caleb. *American Sympathy: Men, Friendship, and Literature in the New Nation*. New Haven, Conn.: Yale University Press, 2001.

DeGuzmán, María. *Spain's Long Shadow: The Black Legend, Off-Whiteness, and Anglo-American Empire*. Minneapolis: University of Minnesota Press, 2005.

Doolen, Andy. *Fugitive Empire: Locating Early American Imperialism*. Minneapolis: University of Minnesota Press, 2005.

Doyle, Laura. *Freedom's Empire: Race and the Rise of the Novel in Atlantic Modernity, 1640–1940*. Durham, N.C.: Duke University Press, 2008.

Ellis, Scott. "Charles Brockden Brown's *Ormond*: Property Exchange and the Literary Marketplace in the Early American Republic." *Studies in the Novel* 37.1 (Spring 2005): 1–19.

Emmett, Hilary. "Brownian Motion: Directions in Charles Brockden Brown Scholarship." *Early American Literature* 50.1 (March 2015): 205–221.

Felski, Rita. *The Uses of Literature*. Malden, Mass.: Blackwell, 2008.

Fiedler, Leslie A. *Love and Death in the American Novel*. New York: Stein and Day, 1960.

Gardner, Jared. "Alien Nation: Edgar Huntly's Savage Awakening." *American Literature* 66.3 (September 1994): 429–461.

Gardner, Jared. *The Rise and Fall of Early American Magazine Culture*. Champaign: University of Illinois Press, 2012.

Garvin, Kristina. "Corporate Ties: *Arthur Mervyn*'s Serial Encounters." *Early American Literature* 50.3 (November 2015): 737–761.

Giles, Paul. *Antipodean America: Australasia and the Constitution of U.S. Literature*. Oxford: Oxford University Press, 2013.

Gilmore, Paul. "Charles Brockden Brown's Romance and the Limits of Science and History." *English Literary History* 84.1 (Spring 2017): 117–142.

Goldman, Eric. "The 'Black Hole of Calcutta' in Charles Brockden Brown's America: American Exceptionalism and India in *Edgar Huntly*." *Early American Literature* 43.3 (November 2008): 557–579.

Goudie, Sean X. *Creole America: The West Indies and the Formation of Literature and Culture in the New Republic*. Philadelphia: University of Pennsylvania Press, 2006.

Hedlin, Christine. "'Was There Not Reason to Doubt?' *Wieland* and Its Secular Age." *Journal of American Studies* 48.3 (August 2014): 735–756.

Howell, William Huntting. *Against Self-Reliance: The Arts of Dependence in the Early United States*. Philadelphia: University of Pennsylvania Press, 2015.

Hsu, Hsuan L. "Democratic Expansionism in 'Memoirs of Carwin.'" *Early American Literature* 35.2 (August 2000): 137–156.

Kafer, Peter. *Charles Brockden Brown's Revolution and the Birth of American Gothic*. Philadelphia: University of Pennsylvania Press, 2004.

Kamrath, Mark. *The Historicism of Charles Brockden Brown: Radical History and the Early Republic*. Kent, Ohio: The Kent State University Press, 2010.

Karcher, Carolyn L. "*Moby-Dick* and the War on Terror." In Jill Barnum, Wyn Kelley, and Christopher Stern, eds., "*Whole Oceans Away*": *Melville and the Pacific*, 305–315. Kent, Ohio: The Kent State University Press, 2007.

Kazanjian, David. "Charles Brockden Brown's Biloquial Nation: National Culture and White Settler Colonialism in *Memoirs of Carwin the Biloquist*." *American Literature* 73.3 (September 2001): 459–496.

Koenigs, Thomas. "'Whatever May Be the Merit of My Book as a Fiction': *Wieland's* Instructional Fictionality." *English Literary History* 79.1 (Fall 2012): 715–745.

Krause, Sydney J. "Charles Brockden Brown and the Philadelphia Germans." *Early American Literature* 39.1 (March 2004): 85–119.

Ledoux, Ellen Melenas. *Social Reform in Gothic Writing: Fantastic Forms of Change, 1764–1834*. Basingstoke, UK: Palgrave Macmillan, 2013.

Levine, Robert S. *Dislocating Race and Nation: Episodes in Nineteenth-Century American Literary Nationalism*. Chapel Hill: University of North Carolina Press, 2008.

Looby, Christopher, and Cindy Weinstein, eds. *American Literature's Aesthetic Dimensions*. New York: Columbia University Press, 2012.

Lukasik, Christopher J. *Discerning Characters: The Culture of Appearance in Early America*. Philadelphia: University of Pennsylvania Press, 2011.

Margolis, Stacey. *Fictions of Mass Democracy in Nineteenth-Century America*. Cambridge: Cambridge University Press, 2015.

Miller, Nicholas E. "'In Utter Fearlessness of the Reigning Disease': Imagined Immunities and the Outbreak Narratives of Charles Brockden Brown." *Literature and Medicine* 35.1 (Spring 2017): 144–166.

Murison, Justine S. "The Tyranny of Sleep: Somnambulism, Moral Citizenship, and Charles Brockden Brown's *Edgar Huntly*." *Early American Literature* 44.2 (August 2009): 243–270.

Ogden, Emily. "*Edgar Huntly* and the Regulation of the Senses." *American Literature* 85.3 (November 2013): 419–445.

Pethers, Matthew. "Poverty, Providence, and the State of Welfare: Plotting Parabolic Social Mobility in the Early Nineteenth-Century American Novel." *Early American Literature* 49.3 (November 2014): 707–740.

Schöberlein, Stefan. "Speaking in Tongues, Speaking without Tongues: Transplanted Voices in Charles Brockden Brown's *Wieland*." *Journal of American Studies* 51.2 (May 2017): 535–552.

Shapiro, Joe. *The Illiberal Imagination: Class and the Rise of the U.S. Novel*. Charlottesville: University of Virginia Press, 2017.

Shapiro, Stephen. *The Culture and Commerce of the Early American Novel: Reading the Atlantic World-System*. University Park: Pennsylvania State University Press, 2008.

Shields, Juliet. *Nation and Migration: The Making of British Atlantic Literature, 1765–1835*. Oxford: Oxford University Press, 2016.

Silyn Roberts, Siân. *Gothic Subjects: The Transformation of Individualism in American Fiction, 1790–1861*. Philadelphia: University of Pennsylvania Press, 2014.

Slawinski, Scott. *Validating Bachelorhood: Audience, Patriarchy, and Charles Brockden Brown's Editorship of the Monthly Magazine and American Review*. New York: Routledge, 2005.

Sloman, Christopher. "Navigating the Interior: *Edgar Huntly* and the Mapping of Early America." In Steven Petersheim and Madison P. Jones IV, eds., *Writing the Environment in*

Nineteenth-Century American Literature: The Ecological Awareness of Early Scribes of Nature, 1–14. Lanham, Md.: Lexington Books, 2015.

Stampone, Christopher. "A 'Spirit of Mistaken Benevolence': Civilizing the Savage in Charles Brockden Brown's *Edgar Huntly*." *Early American Literature* 50.2 (August 2015): 415–448.

Temple, Gale. "Carwin the Onanist?" *Arizona Quarterly: A Journal of American Literature, Culture, and Theory* 65.1 (Spring 2009): 1–32.

Tennenhouse, Leonard. *The Importance of Feeling English: American Literature and the British Diaspora, 1750–1850*. Princeton, N.J.: Princeton University Press, 2007.

Vallee, Eric. "'A Fatal Sympathy': Suicide and the Republic of Abjection in the Writings of Benjamin Rush and Charles Brockden Brown." *Early American Studies: An Interdisciplinary Journal* 15.2 (Spring 2017): 332–351.

Waterman, Bryan. *Republic of Intellect: The Friendly Club of New York City and the Making of American Literature*. Baltimore: Johns Hopkins University Press, 2007.

Watts, Steven. *The Romance of Real Life: Charles Brockden Brown and the Origins of American Culture*. Baltimore: Johns Hopkins University Press, 1994.

Weinstock, Jeffrey Andrew. *Charles Brockden Brown*. Cardiff: University of Wales Press, 2011.

Zimmerman, David. "Charles Brockden Brown and the Conundrum of Complicity." *American Literature* 88.4 (December 2016): 665–693.

INDEX